Lecture Notes in Computer Science   7759

Commenced Publication in 1973
Founding and Former Series Editors:
Gerhard Goos, Juris Hartmanis, and Jan van Leeuwen

W0036323

Services Science

Subline of Lectures Notes in Computer Science

Aditya Ghose   Huibiao Zhu   Qi Yu
Alex Delis   Quang Z. Sheng   Olivier Perrin
Jianmin Wang   Yan Wang (Eds.)

Service-Oriented Computing - ICSOC 2012 Workshops

ICSOC 2012 International Workshops: ASC, DISA,
PAASC, SCEB, SeMaPS, WESOA, and Satellite Events
Shanghai, China, November 12-15, 2012
Revised Selected Papers

 Springer

Volume Editors

Aditya Ghose, University of Wollongong, NSW, Australia
E-mail: aditya@uow.edu.au

Huibiao Zhu, Eastern China Normal University, Shanghai, China
E-mail: hbzhu@sei.ecnu.edu.cn

Qi Yu, Rochester Institute of Technology, NY, USA
E-mail: qi.yu@rit.edu

Alex Delis, University of Athens, Greece
E-mail: ad@di.uoa.gr

Quang Z. Sheng, Adelaide University, SA, Australia
E-mail: qsheng@cs.adelaide.edu.au

Olivier Perrin, Nancy 2 University, Vandoeuvre lès Nancy, France
E-mail: olivier.perrin@loria.fr

Jianmin Wang, Tsinghua University, China
E-mail: jimwang@tsinghua.edu.cn

Yan Wang, Macquarie University, NSW, Australia
E-mail: yan.wang@mq.edu.au

ISSN 0302-9743   e-ISSN 1611-3349
ISBN 978-3-642-37803-4   e-ISBN 978-3-642-37804-1
DOI 10.1007/978-3-642-37804-1
Springer Heidelberg Dordrecht London New York

Library of Congress Control Number: 2013935326

CR Subject Classification (1998): H.3.4-5, D.2.1, D.2.5, D.2.11-13, H.4.1-3, C.2.4,
J.1, H.5.3, K.6.3-5, H.2.8

LNCS Sublibrary: SL 2 – Programming and Software Engineering

Typesetting: Camera-ready by author, data conversion by Scientific Publishing Services, Chennai, India

Printed on acid-free paper

Springer is part of Springer Science+Business Media (www.springer.com)

Preface

This volume contains the proceedings of the scientific satellite events that were held in conjunction with the 2012 International Conference on Service-Oriented Computing, which took place in Shanghai, China, November 12–15, 2012. The satellite events provide venues for specialist groups to meet, to generate focused discussions on specific sub-areas within service-oriented computing, and to engage in community-building activities. These events helped significantly enrich the main conference by both expanding the scope of research topics and attracting participants from a wider community. The selected scientific satellite events were organized around three main tracks, including a workshop track, a PhD symposium track, and a demonstration track:

- **Workshop Track**: The ICSOC 2012 workshop track consisted of six workshops on a wide range of topics that fall into the general area of service computing:

- ASC 2012: First International Workshop on Analytics Services on the Cloud

- DISA 2012: First International Workshop on Data Intensive Services-Based Application

- PAASC 2012: Second International Workshop on Performance Assessment and Auditing in Service Computing 2012

- SCEB 2012: First Workshop on Service Clouds in the Enterprise and Beyond

- SeMaPS 2012: First International Workshop on Self-Managing Pervasive Service Systems

- WESOA 2012: 8th International Workshop on Engineering Service-Oriented Applications

- **PhD Symposium Track:** The ICSOC PhD Symposium is an international forum for PhD students to present, share, and discuss their research in a constructive and critical atmosphere. It also provides students with fruitful feedback and advice on their research approach and thesis.

- **Demonstration Track**: The ICSOC Demonstration Track offers an exciting and highly interactive way to show research prototypes/work in service oriented computing (SOC) and related areas.

A special thanks goes to the workshop, PhD symposium, and demonstration authors, keynote speakers, and panelists, who together contributed to this important aspect of the conference. It is our great pleasure and privilege to present these proceedings. We hope that these proceedings will serve as a valuable reference for researchers and practitioners working in the service-oriented computing domain and its emerging applications.

January 2013

Huibiao Zhu
Aditya Ghose
Qi Yu
Olivier Perrin
Jianmin Wang
Yan Wang
Alex Delis
Quang Z. Sheng

Organization

Honorary Chair

Junliang Chen   Beijing Post and Communication University, China

General Chairs

Jian Yang   Macquarie University, Australia
Liang Zhang   Fudan University, China

Advisory Committee

Jifeng He   Eastern China Normal University, China
Jian Lv   Nanjing University, China
Baile Shi   Fudan University, China
Zhaohui Wu   Zhejiang University, China

Program Chairs

Chengfei Liu   Swinburne University, Australia
Heiko Ludwig   IBM Almaden Research Center, USA
Farouk Toumani   Université Blaise Pascal, France

Workshop Chairs

Aditya Ghose   University of Wollongong, Australia
Huibiao Zhu   Eastern China Normal University, China

Industry Chairs

Yanbo Han   Chinese Academy of Sciences
Nanjangud C. Narendra   IBM India Software Lab, Bangalore, India
Surya Nepal   ICT CSIRO, Australia

Demonstration Chairs

Alex Delis   University of Athens, Greece
Quang Z. Sheng   Adelaide University, Australia

Panel Chairs

Cesare Pautasso   University of Lugano, Switzerland
Thomas Sandholm   HP Labs, USA

PHD Symposium Chairs

Olivier Perrin   Nancy 2 University, France
Jianmin Wang   Tsinghua University, China
Yan Wang   Macquarie University, Australia

Publicity Chairs

Florian Daniel   University of Trento, Italy
Yunzhan Gong   Beijing Post and Communication University,
                              China
Zaki Malik   Wayne State University, USA

Local Organization Chairs

Jian Cao   Shanghai Jiaotong University, China
Zhenying He   Fudan University, China
Guohua Liu   Donghua Univesity, China
Budan Wu   Beijing Post and Communication University,
                              China

Corporate Sponsor Chairs

Genxing Yang   Shanghai Software Industry Association, China
Shiyong Zhang   Fudan University, China
Yingsheng Li   Fudan University, China

Financial Chair

Weiwei Sun   Fudan University, China

Publication Chair

Qi Yu   Rochester Institute of Technology, USA

Web Chair

Xiang Fu   Hofstra University, USA

ASC Workshop Organization Co-chairs

Yu Deng   IBM T.J. Watson Research Center, USA
Liangzhao Zeng   IBM T.J. Watson Research Center, USA

DISA Workshop Organization Co-chairs

Ying Li   Zhejiang University, China
Shiyong Lv   Wayne State University, USA
Shuiguang Deng   Zhejiang University, China

PAASC Workshop Organization Chair

Claudia-Melania Chituc   University of Porto, Portugal

SCEB Workshop Organization Co-chairs

Hua Liu   Xerox Research Center at Webster, USA
Lam-Son Le   University of Wollongong, Australia
Alex Norta   University of Oulu, Finland

SeMaPS Workshop Organization Co-chairs

Weishan Zhang   China University of Petroleum, China
Klaus Marius Hansen   University of Copenhagen, Denmark
Paolo Bellavista   Università di Bologna, Italy

WESOA Workshop Organization Co-chairs

George Feuerlicht   HCTD, University of Technology, Sydney,
                          Australia
Winfried Lamersdorf   University of Hamburg, Germany
Guadalupe Ortiz   University of Cádiz, Spain
Christian Zirpins   Seeburger AG, Germany

Table of Contents

Workshop Track

ASC 2012

DISA 2012

PAASC 2012

SCEB 2012

SeMaps

WESOA 2012

Phd Symposium Track

Demo Track

The 1st International Workshop on Analytics Services on the Cloud (ASC 2012)

This proceeding contains all the papers that were selected for presentation at the First International Workshop on Analytics Services on the Cloud (ASC 2012), which was held in Shanghai, China, November 12, 2012.

Every day, quintillions of bytes of data are created in different domains, including Internet, healthcare, retail and so on. The term "big data" is used to describe such data, which has three major characteristics: large volume, high speed of data flow and heterogeneous data types. Studies have shown that leveraging knowledge from big data via analytics will generate tremendous business impact. In the foreseeable future, the use of big data will become a key basis of competition for enterprises.

With the needs of analytics growing at ever increasing speeds, it becomes clear that traditional data processing techniques are in no way able to meet the demands. The use of big data has raised tremendous challenges on analysis techniques, e.g., data integration and linkage, data storage, pattern mining, IT infrastructure to support massive and scalable data processing, and visualization of the analysis results. Therefore, Cloud Computing becomes a perfect candidate for delivering big data analytics. However, the emerging Cloud Computing technology adds another interesting dimension in this complex area since Cloud technology enables a new service model when delivering analytics to end users.

To provide a balanced coverage and an equal emphasis across all aspects of analytics services on the cloud, ASC 2012's topic were divided in to three major areas: performance, service infrastructure and applications. We solicited 15 high quality submissions. Only 7 papers were accepted for the program. The paper "Kachako: a Hybrid-Cloud Unstructured Information Platform for Full Automation of Service Composition, Scalable Deployment and Evaluation", written by Yoshinobu Kano, was selected for the best paper award sponsored by IBM Research.

This outstanding workshop program was a testament to the efforts of many dedicated individuals who were committed to the success of ASC 2012. This success would not have been possible without the enthusiastic support from the Program Committee, the efficient organizational efforts from the ICSOC 2012 workshop organizers and the significant contributions from the authors who submitted their work to ASC 2012. They all deserve our deep gratitude for the efforts they have made.

Yu Deng, Liangzhao Zeng
IBM T.J. Watson Research Center
P.O. Box 704
Yorktown Heights, NY 10598 USA
dengy@us.ibm.com, lzeng@us.ibm.com

A. Ghose et al. (Eds.): ICSOC 2012, LNCS 7759, pp. 1–2, 2013.

Organization

Workshop Officers

General Chair

- Yu Deng, IBM Research - Watson Lab, USA
- Liangzhao Zeng, IBM Research - Watson Lab, USA

Presentation Chair

- Minkyong Kim, IBM Research - Watson Lab, USA

Program Committee

- Han Chen, IBM Research - Watson Lab, USA
- Shiping Chen, CSIRO ICT Centre, Australia
- Liana Fong, IBM Research - Watson Lab, USA
- Lipyeow Lim, University of Hawaii at Manoa, USA
- Marco Aurelio Stelmar Netto, IBM Research - Brazil Lab, Brazil
- Vugranam Sreedhar, IBM Research - Watson Lab, USA
- Timothy Wood, George Washington University, USA
- Xifeng Yan, University of California at Santa Barbara, USA
- Wlodek Zadrozny, IBM Research - Watson Lab, USA
- Sai Zeng, IBM Research - Watson Lab, USA
- Youhui Zhang, Tsinghua University, China
- Shuigeng Zhou, Fudan University, China

A Performance Evaluation of Public Cloud Using TPC-C

Jinhui Yao[1,3], Alex Ng[2], Shiping Chen[1,3], Dongxi Liu[3],
Carsten Friedrich[3], and Surya Nepal[3]

[1] School of Electrical and Information Engineering, University of Sydney, Australia
jin.yao@sydney.edu.au
[2] The University of Ballarat, Australia
alexckng@ieee.org
[3] Information Engineering Laboratory, CSIRO ICT Centre, Australia
{firstname.familyname}@csiro.au

Abstract. Cloud is becoming the next-generation computing paradigm for enterprises to deploy services and run business. While most Cloud service providers promise some Quality of Service (QoS) through a Service Level Agreement (SLA), it is very hard for Cloud clients to know what impacts these QoS have on their businesses. In this paper, we study this issue by conducting a simple performance evaluation of two public Clouds. We selected TPC-C to benchmark three types of instances (Small, Medium and Large) provided by the Cloud providers in order to find out how the typical online transaction process systems perform on the cloud nodes. Our testing results show that the different Cloud environments deliver very different performance landscapes with different Cloud instances. Our work demonstrates the importance and opportunity to choose the appropriate Cloud instance in achieving an optimal cost-performance ratio for a class of cloud applications.

Keywords: Cloud Computing, Public Cloud, QoS, Service Level Agreement, Performance, TPC-C Benchmarking.

1   Introduction

Cloud is becoming the next-generation computing paradigm for enterprises to deploy services and run business. According to IDC, Cloud Computing will generate 14 million jobs [11] and $72.9 billion revenues [15] by 2015. Cloud Computing enables IT organisations to become more agile and cost effective with less emphasis on the efforts in maintaining traditional in-house software and hardware. Cloud Computing offers three major delivery models: Infrastructure-as-a-Service (IaaS, for compute, memory, storage, and network resources), Platform-as-a-Service (PaaS, for application development tools and runtime services) and Software-as-a-Service (SaaS, for applications delivered as a service). The primary deployment models include on-premise (private Cloud), off-premise (public Cloud), or a mix of both (hybrid Cloud). Cloud Computing promises to deliver a range of benefits, including avoiding the significant start-up IT investment, reducing operational costs, and enabling greater

A. Ghose et al. (Eds.): ICSOC 2012, LNCS 7759, pp. 3–13, 2013.
© Springer-Verlag Berlin Heidelberg 2013

agility. By adopting Cloud Computing, business organisations can be more focused on their core business so they can offer better services and innovations to stay competitive in the market.

Service Level Agreement (SLA) is a formal binding contract stating the Quality-of-Service guarantees offered by the Cloud provider (typically including maximum response time, throughput and error rate). Other non-functional QoS such as timeliness, scalability, and availability may also be included. While most Cloud service providers can promise some QoS through the SLA, it is very hard for Cloud clients to know the impacts of these QoS on their businesses. For instance, a Cloud service provider may guarantee that the remote virtual machine the client is hiring has the computing power equivalent to a 1000GHz Intel CPU, however, this statement tells little about how many transactions per minute that virtual machine is able to handle. Furthermore, considering the various virtualization techniques available [2], and the issues with resource sharing among different virtual instances [8] it is quite possible that, while Cloud providers are trying to save money by utilizing resources optimally. Cloud customers (including PaaS and SaaS) are concerned with the runtime performance of their platform and applications. Therefore, it is important and valuable to understand how different Cloud services perform in specific commercial environments for a specific class of applications and how their performance outcomes are related to their claimed SLAs.

In this paper, we conducted a simple performance evaluation of two public Clouds to clarify the above concerns. We selected TPC-C to benchmark three types of instances (Small, Medium and Large) provided by the two public Cloud providers respectively in order to find out the performance of typical online transaction process systems deployed on these different computing instances. We provided our testing results with our observations and analysis in this paper. Since the core of this paper is to study the cloud performance behaviors of different clouds rather than head-to-head comparison, we intend to provide only relative data of cloud instance specifications and prices to preserve the identity of the Cloud vendors.

The rest of this paper is organised as follows: a brief discussion of the Cloud Services versus QoS and SLAs is given in Section 2. Section 3 explains the rationales of our choice of the TPC-C benchmarking technique in performance evaluation of our target Cloud providers. Section 4 provides details of our setup parameters in the Cloud environments and the TPC-C benchmark settings. Section 5 provides the results of our analysis of the data collected in our measurements. Section 6 discusses related work and our conclusions are presented in section 7.

2   Cloud Services vs QoS/SLA

Nowadays, the term 'Cloud' has many different definitions. But in its essence, 'Cloud' always refers to the computing resources that are to be provided to the clients. Different kinds of resources are provided as different services on a pay-as-you-go basis to extend one's computing capacity. Amazon S3, for example, is a storage service that allows clients to store and fetch data; another example is Amazon EC2, which provides computing instances (virtual machines) to let clients deploy and run whatever programs they want.

Coming along with those services, are the QoS guarantees that the service provider offers. QoS guarantees are stated in the form of SLAs which specify the details about the commitment; and (usually) the compensation strategy that will be applied should any violations occur. For example, Amazon offers an SLA about Amazon S3 which states that, if the uptime of the service is less than 99%, the client is entitled to apply for a refund of 25% of his charges incurred in the same billing cycle[1]. It is apparent that the SLAs about storage services are relatively easier to verify and understand than other QoS guarantees about different types the service, which can be unambiguously defined, such as upload speed, download speed, uptime, consistency, etc. However, as we have briefly discussed in the introduction, certain types of the QoS of the computing instances the Cloud is providing is difficult to evaluate. In the practise, what concerns the clients is not how fast the CPU can conduct arithmetic computation; rather, it is the efficiency of whatever program that is running in the instance.

It is the ambiguous link between the SLA, and the true QoS that the client experiences that motivated our research. We are interested to testify the consistency between the claimed and the actual computing capacity of the computing instances offered by Cloud service providers. While it may be infeasible to estimate the true performance of the computing instance based on the performance of a given program; alternatively, we can evaluate the performance of the same program on different computing instances, which are offered by different service providers with the same or similar claimed computing capacity. Significant differences among the results indicate inconsistency in one or more service providers, i.e. the service provider(s) is either over-claiming, or under-claiming.

3   Why TPC-C?

We used Hammerora[2] - an open source load test tool to conduct TPC-C [1] (industry standard benchmark for on-line database processing) to evaluate the performance of two public Clouds. The TPC-C benchmark provides a standard mechanism for performance evaluation of the two different Clouds using the same database architectures and operating systems.

TPC-C is one of the industry-standard benchmark for online transaction processing. TPC-C simulates a complete on-line transaction environment where a population of users executes transactions against a database. The benchmark is built upon a set of principal activities (transactions) of an order-entry environment. These transactions include entering and delivering orders, recording payments, checking the status of orders, and monitoring the level of stock at the warehouses. TPC-C is established since 1992 and has been widely used by the database community for many years and it continues to evolve in order to remain as representative of the current

---

[1] The complete and formal SLA can be found at http://aws.amazon.com/ec2-sla/

[2] Hammerora http://hammerora.sourceforge.net/

practice as possible. Both the database and software architecture communities can readily understand the performance figures produced from this exercise.

As shown in Table 1, TPC-C involves a profile of five concurrent transactions of different types and degrees of complexity. The database is comprised of nine types of tables with a wide range of records and population sizes.

Table 1. Summary of TPC-C Transaction Profiles

Transaction	Query Weighing	Database Access	Frequency of Execution	Response Time Requirements
New-Order	Moderate	Read and Write	High	Stringent response time requirement to satisfy on-line users
Payment	Light	Read and Write	High	Stringent response time requirement to satisfy on-line users
Order-Status	Moderate	Read Only	Low	Low response time requirement
Delivery	Light	Read and Write	Low (with deferred execution)	Must complete within a relaxed response time requirement
Stock-Level	Heavy	Read Only	Low	Relaxed response time requirement

Although there are other benchmark standards (e.g. TPC-E & TPC-H) available, we choose TPC-C due to the distributed nature of TPC-C which fits nicely in the distributed requirements of this evaluation exercise. Further, TPC-C sample test codes are readily available from existing software libraries which can shorten the development effort for this exercise and minimize the effect of newly written programs instability issues. Finally, TPC-C is mature and widely recognized as a standard benchmark for database, OS and whole online transaction processing systems.

4   Benchmark Setting

We selected two public Cloud providers (we shall refer to them as Cloud-A & Cloud-B in this paper) to benchmark their Small, Medium and Large Instances respectively. In an effort not to disclose any hint that can be used to identify these two providers, certain ambiguities are introduced in this paper when elaborating the details about the benchmarking processes and results.

All types of instances are running the same operating system. CPU and memory specifications of the instances of the same type provided by the two providers are slightly different. Their differences are listed in the following table.

Table 2. Differences of Cloud-A and Cloud-B Processing Environments

	CPU power	**Memory**
Small instance	25%	3%
Medium instance	25%	7%
Large instance	25%	13%

Please note that the performance results to be shown in the next section does not necessarily correlated to the differences listed (i.e. the computing instance with less claimed CPU power may outperform the one with more).

MySQL 5.1 is installed in each of the subject instances, along with Hammerora 2.10. In every set of load testing, we create different amount of virtual users in Hammerora who will conduct the testing on the local MySQL server by sending requests at a constant rate, then we record the maximum NOPM. The more virtual users created the more concurrent transactions the local MySQL server will undertake. Our presumption for maximum NOPM is that, initially, increasing the number of users will result an increase of NOPM, however, at a certain point, an increase in the number of virtual users will no longer result a higher NOPM, as it has reached the limit of the computing power of the instance, and this is the maximum NOPM the subject instance is able to achieve.

5   Experimental Results and Analysis

We are going to discuss in this section the performance metrics used in our experiments and the analysis of the results observed.

5.1   Performance Metrics Used

TPC-C is measured in transactions per minute (tpm). In our experiments, we measured the Number of TPC-C Opeartion Per Minute (NOPM). We increased the numbers of concurrent Virtual Users gradually from 8 to 256. We then measured the maximum NOPM as experienced by each Virtual User.

The second metric we use is the Peak-to-Saturation-Bottom (PTSB) ratio to determine how stable the Cloud environments are. We calculate the ratio between the Peak NOPM value and the Lowest/Bottom NOPM value (as the instance went into saturation mode) offered by a particular instance for a particular Cloud environment. The ratio between these two values will give a good idea how well the Cloud environment can offer a stable processing environment to meet the increase in demand. Therefore, the closer this ratio is to 1 the better.

The third metric we use is the Total NOPM (TNOPM) which calculates the total NOPM offered by a particular instance. It is the total sum of all individual NOPMs. This metric will give a good idea how well the instance will cope with all the transactions working within a particular instance.

The fourth metric is the Cents-Per-Million-NOPM (CPMNOPM), it looks at the cost required to deliver One Million NOPM for each instance of Cloud-A and Cloud-B. It is a ratio of the costs of acquiring each instance and the total number of NOPM supported by each instance. This metric will inform us the actual cost of supporting the application.

5.2 Cloud-A Analysis

Figure 1 shows the maximum NOPM experienced by different of number of concurrent virtual users for Cloud-A using the Small, Medium and Large Instances of Cloud-A.

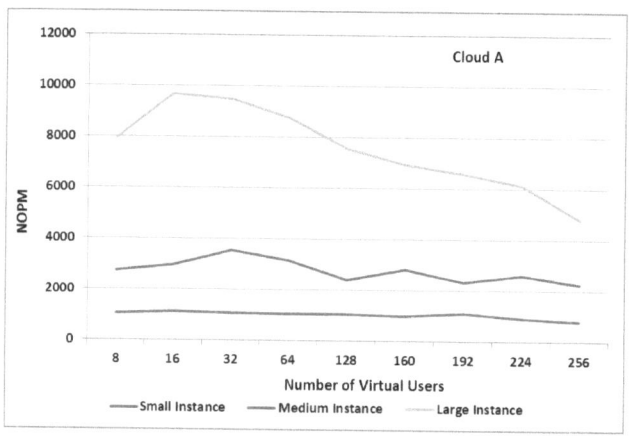

Fig. 1. Cloud-A Number of Operation Per Minute

We observed that Cloud-A with Small Instance is able to deliver a fairly steady NOPM for different number of virtual users with peak 1100 NOPM at 192 virtual users and bottom 795 NOPM at 256 virtual users. Cloud-A with Medium Instance provides peak performance of 3554 NOPM at 32 virtual users and then decreases gradually to 2246 NOPM when the number of virtual users increases to 256. As for Large Instance in Cloud-A, the peak 9691 NOPM occurs at 16 virtual users and then decreases steeply to 4807 NOPM at 256 virtual users. This analysis of NOPM for Cloud-A shows the following:

1. The NOPM jumps from 1015 NOPM for Small Instance to 2758 NOPM for Medium Instance and 7542 NOPM for Large Instance. We found that Medium Instance offers 170% increase in NOPM to Small Instance and Large Instance also offers 170% increase in NOPM to Medium Instance.

2. We use the Peak-to-Saturation-Bottom (PTSB) ratio to determine how stable (close to 1 is stable) the Cloud environment offers. It seems the Small Instance of Cloud-A provides a more stable operating environment (PTSB ratio of 1.38) than the Medium Instance (PTSB ratio is 1.58) and the Medium Instance is more stable than the Large Instance (PTSB ratio is 2.01) of Cloud-A.

At this point, we would like to assert that the larger the resource instance for Cloud-A, the slower, or more time is required to compensate for the increase in the demand for more resources. Our explanation is that it is a logical behaviour because the larger the instance, the more effort and time are required to acquire the extra resources to meet the increase in demand. Hence, this is an important research area for Cloud providers in identifying better algorithms in dealing with this situation.

The PTSB ratio of NOPM only gives us an idea how well different instances are able to provide a stable and consistent environment when the workload is varied from small to large number of concurrent virtual users. This shows the perspective of NOPM as seen at each Virtual User only and may not reveal the overall elasticity nature of the Cloud. We calculate the Total NOPM (TNOPM) for different number of Virtual Users to find out the total volume handled by each instance. The results are summarised in the following Figure 2.

We can see that the TNOPM for Cloud-A Small, Medium and Large Instances all increase in a linear fashion until the maximum values occur at 224 Virtual Users, with 203616 TNOPM for Small Instance, 583520 TNOPM for Medium Instance, and

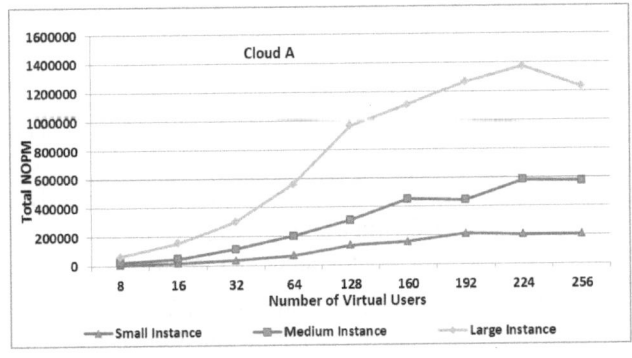

Fig. 2. Cloud-A Total Number of Operation Per Minute

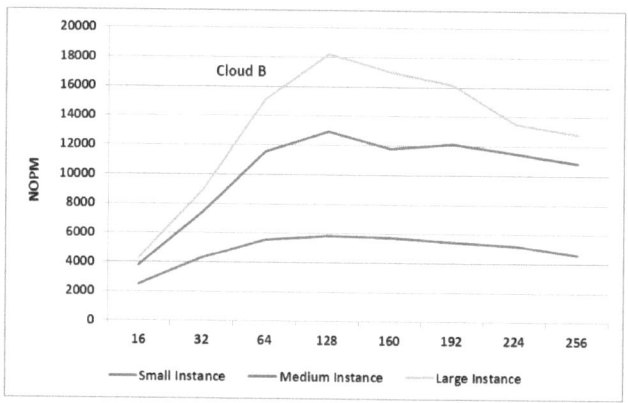

Fig. 3. Cloud-B Number of Operation Per Minute

1371328 TNOPM for Large Instance. At 256 Virtual Users, all three instances either maintained at similar level or start to show decrease in TNOPM. This shows that Cloud-A is able to scale linearly, or elastic, up to a certain threshold point, in this case 224 Virtual Users. Hence, we consider that Cloud-A is able to demonstrate good elasticity nature from 8 to 224 Virtual Users.

5.3   Cloud-B Analysis

We observed that Cloud-B with Small Instance delivers a steady NOPM for different number of virtual users with peak 5831 NOPM at 128 virtual users and decrease gradually to 4619 NOPM at 256 Virtual Users. Cloud-B with Medium Instance provides peak performance of 12942 NOPM at 128 virtual users and then decreases slightly to 10811 NOPM when the number of Virtual Users increases to 256. As for Large Instance in Cloud-B, the peak 19214 NOPM occurs at 128 Virtual Users and then decreases steeply to 12790 NOPM at 256 Virtual Users. This analysis of NOPM for Cloud-B shows the following:

1. The NOPM for Small Instance is 4909, Medium Instance is 10245 and Large Instance is 13248. Medium Instance offers 108% increase in NOPM to Small Instance and Large Instance offers only 29% increase in NOPM to Medium Instance.
2. Cloud-B seems offer more stable operating environment than Cloud-A as we observed the PTSB ratio for Small Instance is 1.26, Medium Instance is 1.19 and Large Instance is 1.42, all offers lower value than the corresponding Cloud-A environment. That means Cloud-B seems able to react quicker than Cloud-A in acquiring extra resources to meet the increase in demand from the increasing number of Virtual Users.

The TNOPM figures for Cloud-B (Figure 4) show that all three instances were able to scale linearly with no sign of saturation even up to 256 Virtual Users. There was a dip in the Large Instance from 192 Virtual Users to 224 Virtual Users but the upward

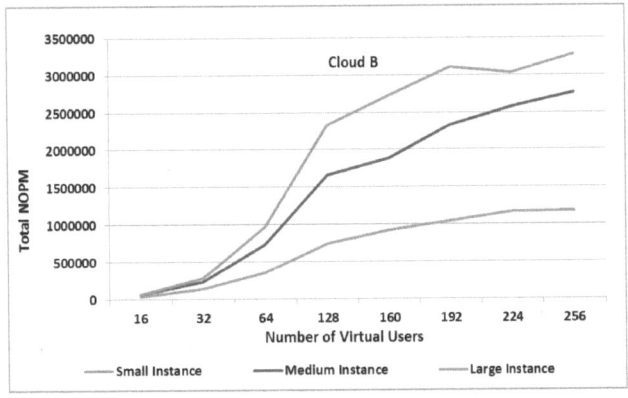

Fig. 4. Cloud-B Total Number of Operation Per Minute

trend continued at 256 Virtual Users. The maximum values are 1182464 TNOPM for Small Instance, 2767616 TNOPM for Medium Instance and 3274240 TNOPM for Large Instance. From this TNOPM analysis, we observed that Cloud-B outperforms Cloud-A in the elasticity aspect of a Cloud environment because Cloud-A reached its saturation point at 224 Virtual Users for all three instances while Cloud-B did not saturate even at 256 Virtual Users.

5.4   Cost Analysis

The next aspect we are interested in the performance of a Cloud environment is the cost effectiveness. Since the costs of acquiring each instance are readily available from the Cloud vendors, we use the metric Cents-Per-Million-NOPM (CPMNOPM) to look at the cost required to deliver One Million of NOPM for each different instances of Cloud-A and Cloud-B. The results are summarised in the following table (only the ranges are provided to preserve the identity of the Cloud vendors):

Table 3. Cents Per Million NOPM for Cloud-A & Cloud-B

	Cloud-A	**Cloud-B**
Small Instance	High – 18.2	High – 4.98
	Low – 0.72	Low – 0.17
Medium Instance	High – 13.9	High – 6.63
	Low – 0.52	Low – 0.14
Large Instance	High – 9.62	High – 11.7
	Low – 0.44	Low – 0.24

We can see that for Small and Medium instances, Cloud-A is more expensive (over 100%) than Cloud-B to support one million NOPM. When it comes to Large Instance, the landscape is a little bit different, because in the case of small number of Virtual Users a low volume level of NOPM is achieved, then Cloud-B appears to be more expensive than Cloud-A to support one million NOPM. This is because the entry cost to acquire Cloud-B Large Instance is more expensive than Cloud-A. With low transaction volume level, it does not fully utilise the resources available at Cloud-B so that it becomes more expensive than Cloud-A. However, at high level of transaction volume, Cloud-B becomes more cost effective than Cloud-A to run because Could-B is able to deliver much higher number of NOPM than Cloud-A.

This is an interesting but logical finding which shows that when investing into acquiring a Cloud environment to support an application, a proper capacity estimation should be performed to avoid over investment.

6   Related Work

SLA between consumers and Cloud providers is one of the key research topics in dealing with the dynamic natures of the Cloud environment which requires continuous monitoring on various QoS attributes as well as considering many other factors such as delegation and trust. The research in Cloud QoS is progressing [3]. Different mechanisms were proposed to monitor QoS attributes in the Cloud, for example, the Web Service Level Agreement (WSLA) framework [12] for Cloud Web Services; SLA-aware management framework [6, 7]; and using business service management reservoir approach in governing the SLAs for individual application's non-functional characteristics [13].

Bautista et al. [4] integrated software quality concepts from ISO 25010 to measure seven different Cloud quality concepts (Maturity, Fault Tolerance, Availability, Recoverability, Time Behaviour, Resource Utilisation, and Capacity). We found these quality concepts lack clearly measurable metrics.   The evaluation methodology used in this work is simpler and can produce more meaningful results.

We found only a few analysis on Cloud performance were available either with focus on the Amazon's EC2 Cloud environment [5] or Cloud for scientific computing [9, 14]. CloudCmp [10] uses a matrix of measures in the elastic computing, persistent storage, and networking services offered by a cloud to act as a comparator of the performance and cost of cloud providers. We consider CloudCmp to be too complicated for the general public.

7   Conclusion

Very little studies are available on the benchmarking of the characteristics of different commercial Cloud platforms. In this paper, we have presented our understanding on the performance of 2 public Cloud environments on supporting typical commercial applications.

We have used the TPC-C benchmarking technique to study the NOPM, PTSB, TNOPM and CPMNOPM characteristics of the 2 Clouds. Our findings are: (1) both Clouds are able to provide stable and elastic processing environments to meet the demand of increase in load; (2) the NOPM analysis, Cloud-B with higher CPU processing power is able to deliver higher NOPM than Cloud-A; (3) the PTSB analysis, Cloud-B is able to react quicker than Cloud-A in acquiring extra resources; and (4) the CPMNOPM analysis reveals that the cheaper cloud environment does not necessary provide the more cost-effective processing environment. It is very important to understand the cost-effectiveness aspect in acquiring the appropriate Cloud Instances so as to avoid over investment.

Our studies present only the first step in understanding the performance characteristics of the public Clouds. There are more cloud aspects needed to evaluate including the characteristics of Transparency, Trust, Portability, Interoperability, and Continuity in public Clouds.

References

[1] TPC-C Home Page, http://www.tpc.org/tpcc/default.asp (accessed April 26, 2012)

[2] Understanding Full Virtualization, Paravirtualization, and Hardware Assist, VMWare (2007)

[3] Armstrong, D., Djemame, K.: Towards Quality of Service in the Cloud. In: Proceedings of the 25th UK Performance Engineering Workshop, Leeds, UK (2009)

[4] Bautista, L., Abran, A., April, A.: Design of a Performance Measurement Framework for Cloud Computing. Journal of Software Engineering and Applications 5(2), 69–75 (2012)

[5] Dejun, J., Pierre, G., Chi, C.-H.: EC2 Performance Analysis for Resource Provisioning of Service-Oriented Applications. In: Dan, A., Gittler, F., Toumani, F. (eds.) ICSOC/ServiceWave 2009. LNCS, vol. 6275, pp. 197–207. Springer, Heidelberg (2010)

[6] Ferretti, S., Ghini, V., Panzieri, F., et al.: QoS-Aware Clouds. In: Proceedings of the IEEE 3rd International Conference on Cloud Computing (2010)

[7] Fito, J.O., Goiri, I., Guitart, J.: SLA-driven Elastic Cloud Hosting Provider. In: Proceedings of the 18th Euromicro Conference on Parallel, Distributed and Network-based Processing (2010)

[8] Gupta, D., Cherkasova, L., Gardner, R., Vahdat, A.: Enforcing Performance Isolation Across Virtual Machines in Xen. In: van Steen, M., Henning, M. (eds.) Middleware 2006. LNCS, vol. 4290, pp. 342–362. Springer, Heidelberg (2006)

[9] Iosup, A., Ostermann, S., Yigitbasi, M.N., et al.: Performance Analysis of Cloud Computing Services for Many-Tasks Scientific Computing. IEEE Transactions on Parallel and Distributed Systems 22(6), 931–945 (2011)

[10] Li, A., Yang, X., Kandula, S., et al.: CloudCmp: comparing public cloud providers. In: Proceedings of the 10th Annual Conference on Internet Measurement (IMC 2010), Melbourne, Australia, pp. 1–14 (2010)

[11] McKendrick, J.: Cloud Will Generate 14 Million Jobs By 2015: That's A Good Start (March 5, 2012), http://www.forbes.com/sites/joemckendrick/2012/03/05/cloud-will-generate-14-million-jobs-by-2015-thats-a-good-start/ (accessed April 16, 2012)

[12] Patel, P., Ranabahu, A., Sheth, A.: Service Level Agreement in Cloud Computing. In: Proceedings of the Cloud Workshop at OOPSLA (2009)

[13] Rochwerger, B., Breitgand, D., Levy, E., et al.: The Reservoir model and architecture for open federated cloud computing. IBM Journal of Research and Development 53(4) (2009)

[14] Wang, G., Ng, T.S.E.: The Impact of Virtualization on Network Performance of Amazon EC2 Data Center. In: Proceedings of the INFOCOM 2010 (2010)

[15] http://www.idc.com/prodserv/idc_cloud.jsp

An Efficient Data Maintenance Strategy for Data Service Mashup Based on Materialized View Selection

Peng Zhang[1,2], Yanbo Han[2], and Guiling Wang[2]

[1] North China University of Technology, 100041, Beijing, China
[2] Institute of Information Engineering, Chinese Academy of Sciences,
100093, Beijing, China
{zhangpeng,wangguiling}@software.ict.ac.cn, yhan@ict.ac.cn

Abstract. While end-users enjoy the full-fledged data service mashup with high convenience and flexibility, such issues as the response efficiency and the maintenance cost have popped up as the major concerns. In this paper, an efficient data maintenance strategy for the data service mashup is proposed. The strategy proposes a data maintenance model to measure the response cost and update cost of a group of data service mashups in terms of the request frequency and update frequency. Based on the model, a materialized view selection for data service mashup is proposed. Experiments show that our strategy can effectively reduce the maintenance cost of a lot of hosted data service mashups.

Keywords: Data Mashup, Data Service, Data Maintenance, Materialized View Selection.

1   Introduction

Data service mashup has become so popular over the last few years. It is a special class of mashup application that combines information on the fly from multiple data sources. Its applications vary from addressing transient business needs in modern enterprises to conducting scientific research in e-science communities [1]. The data sources are provided through Web Services, also known as DaaS (Data-as-a-Service) or Data Service [2, 3]. While providing enhanced immediacy and personalization to explore, aggregate and enrich data from various heterogeneous sources, data service mashups also pose distinct data maintenance challenges. In general, the mashup results are often cached in order to enhance the performance of responding to end-users' request. However, when the primitive data sources are updated, the cache should be updated to ensure their consistency with the underlying data sources, which brings the high maintenance cost. For a mashup platform which hosted a lot of mashup applications, some cached results may be shared and reused by other mashups. So it will be more efficient to materialize certain "shared" mashup results to achieve the best performance with minimum consistency maintenance cost. In this paper, we call this problem as the data maintenance problem. The challenges to solve this problem are analyzed from the following three aspects:

A. Ghose et al. (Eds.): ICSOC 2012, LNCS 7759, pp. 14–23, 2013.

Firstly, most of the mashup platforms allow all kinds of users to develop their own mashups, so there are often a large number of data service mashups hosted on the mashup platforms, which implies that the data maintenance cost for mashup platforms is much higher.

Secondly, data service mashups are often designed by non-technical-savvy end-users, and hence they are not necessarily optimized from the point of view of data maintenance.

Thirdly, the data sources often have various non-functional characteristics such as update frequency, data volume and so on but the data service mashups lack of their description. So they can not optimize the data maintenance utilizing these characteristics.

All these reasons make it quite necessary to consider the data maintenance of a lot of hosted data service mashups. Unfortunately, the efficiency aspects of mashup platforms have not received enough attention from the research community. Only a few works give some preliminary research results [4, 5]. In this paper, we present an efficient data maintenance strategy for data service mashup, which has the following special features.

- We establish the maintenance cost model for the data service mashup, and propose the materialized view selection strategy based on the maintenance cost model.
- We evaluate the performance of our proposed strategy through standard datasets from TPC-H and demonstrate that our strategy achieves significant improvements.

The paper is organized as follows: Section 2 gives an example to formulate the problem. Section 3 introduces the maintenance cost model and materialized view selection strategy. A detailed example is introduced. Section 4 is experiment and discussion. Section 5 introduces related works. Section 6 sums up with several concluding remarks.

2   Problem Description

Consider an example data service mashup. Firstly, it invokes data service M_1 and M_2, fetches the popular movies from mtime.com and movie.hao123.com (two famous movie guide portal in China). Secondly, the output of M_1 and M_2 are combined as $M_1 \cup M_2$. Thirdly, it invokes the movie review API from douban.com (the most popular book & movie reviews portal in China). The result is a complete popular movie list with reviews as $(M_1 \cup M_2) \triangleright_{Ri} R$. The mashup steps are shown in Figure 1, where the data services from the two popular movie websites are abbreviated as M_1 and M_2, and the data service from the movie review website is abbreviated as R.

In fact, in order to get the same results, different users may use different mashup scheme. The right side of Figure 1 shows the other mashup scheme. In this scheme, at first, the movie lists from mtime.com and movie.hao123.com are each used as the input to invoke the API from douban.com. Then both the outputs are combined. The outputs of both mashups are the same.

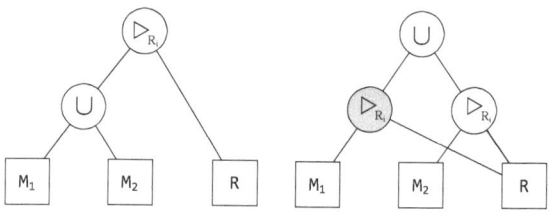

Fig. 1. An example data service mashup

According to the interaction between user and the data mashup, we can make a distinction of the execution mode of mashup between active and passive as shown in Table 1. At the active mode, when some data sources are updated, the platform actively sends the update to users. At this mode, we design a "materialized data view" to cache the results on the client side. As such, the maintenance cost of a mashup in active mode is equal to the cost of responding to the update of the data sources.

While for those mashups in passive mode, they send the results to users only when there comes in a user request. At this mode, there is no materialized data view for the mashup. The mashup gets results by re-computing the underlying data sources from bottom to top. Compared with the "materialized data view" to cache the results, it can be called the "virtual data view". In order to make it more efficient, the mashup can reuse some materialized results. As such the maintenance cost of a mashup in passive mode is equal to the cost of responding to request.

Table 1. The maintenance cost category

Execution Mode	View Mode	Maintenance Cost
Active	Materialized	update cost of the data sources
Passive	Virtual	response cost of the user's request

Therefore, given a group of mashups, the data maintenance cost is composed of two parts: one part is the response cost of all virtual data views, and the other part is the updating cost of all materialized data views, where some virtual data views can reuse some materialized execution results of the materialized data views.

When the outputs of several mashups are the same, their execution costs may not be the same from the following analysis. For example, as shown in the right part of Figure 1, if $M_1 \rhd_{Ri} R$ is executed in active mode, and $(M_1 \rhd_{Ri} R) \cup (M_2 \rhd_{Ri} R)$ is executed in passive mode, then $(M_1 \rhd_{Ri} R) \cup (M_2 \rhd_{Ri} R)$ can reuse the materialized execution result of $M_1 \rhd_{Ri} R$ to reduce response cost, so that the data maintenance cost is reduced. However, because there are no common part between the mashup shown in the left part of Figure 1 $(M_1 \cup M_2) \rhd_{Ri} R$ and $M_1 \rhd_{Ri} R$, so the $(M_1 \cup M_2) \rhd_{Ri} R$ can not reuse the materialized execution result of the mashup $M_1 \rhd_{Ri} R$, and maybe generate higher data maintenance cost. So in Figure 1, though $(M_1 \rhd_{Ri} R) \cup (M_2 \rhd_{Ri} R)$ has the same results as the $(M_1 \cup M_2) \rhd_{Ri} R$, the data maintenance costs are different.

In addition, for single mashup, the mashup schema also has an impact on the data maintenance cost. For instance, one schema first filters the popular movie list from "mtime.com" according to the category, and then sorts the list by their score. The other schema sorts the list ahead of filtering. The former one's data maintenance cost is lower than the latter one even if they have the same results. This is because when data sources are updated, filtering generally makes the intermediate results for computation reduced.

Based on above analysis, we can get such a conclusion that given that different mashup schemas and execution modes, even if the mashups output the same results, their data maintenance cost may be different, so our goal can be defined as follows: Given a group of mashups, how to select the mashup schema and execution mode, in order to get the minimum data maintenance cost.

3   Materialized View Selection

The mashup operators include *count, filter, union, unique, join, sort, projection, truncate, tail, rename*, which are similar to the operators in the relational algebra, and we use Σ, σ, $\cup$, μ, $\rhd_j$, s, π, t, τ, r respectively to represent them, so the mashup can represented by tree that could be transformed into equivalent results according to the equivalent tranformation rules [6]. In order to select mashup schema and execution mode for each mashup to get the minimum data maintenance cost, our solution includes two steps: the first step is to establish the maintenance cost model for the mashups; the second step is to solve the model to get the optimization results. Here, we still take the two mashups $(M_1 \cup M_2) \rhd_{Ri} R$ and $M_1 \rhd_{Ri} R$ for example to firstly introduce their data maintenance cost model.

3.1   Maintenance Cost Model

For simplicity, we neglect the join attribute in this example, and use the upper case letter to represent the name of set or function, and use the lower case letter to represent the element of the set, where the length of set indicates the number of elements. For example, $V=\{(M_1 \cup M_2) \rhd_{Ri} R, M_1 \rhd_{Ri} R\}=\{v_1, v_2\}$, represents a set of mashups, and their maintenance cost model as shown in formula 1:

$$c_V = \min\nolimits_{P \cup A = V' \wedge V' \in E(V)} (c_P + c_A) \tag{1}$$

Where P represents the set of mashups with the passtive mode, A represents the set of mashups with the active mode, c_V represents the data maintenance cost of the mashups, c_P represents the response cost of the mashups with the passive mode and will be introduced in following section, c_A represents the update cost of the mashups with the active mode and will be introduced in following section, and V' is an equivalent set of V. In order to calculate them, we first have to obtain the following three matrices EV, BE, AB. At the same time, some symbols, such as logic negative "¬", logic and "∧", dot product "⊗", matrix multiplication "×", matrix or vector transpose "T", and the function L changing any non-zero to zero are introduced.

$E(v_i)$ is the set of the mashups which are equivalent to the mashup v_i. $E(v_i)$ can be obtained by equivalence transformation rules. E represents all mashups which are equivalent to any element in the set V, and we call any element of E equivalent mashup. In this example, $E(v_1)=\{(M_1 \cup M_2) \ \triangleright\ _{Ri}R, \ (M_2 \cup M_1) \ \triangleright\ _{Ri}R, (M_1 \ \triangleright\ _{Ri}R) \cup (M_2 \ \triangleright\ _{Ri}R), (M_2 \ \triangleright\ _{Ri}R) \cup (M_1 \ \triangleright\ _{Ri}R)\} = \{e_1, e_2, e_3, e_4\}, E(v_2) = \{M_1 \ \triangleright\ _{Ri} R\} = \{e_5\}, E = \{e_1, e_2, e_3, e_4, e_5\}$. EV is a 0-1 Boolean matrix with $|V| \times |E|$, and if and only if $E(v_i)=e_j$, $EV(i, j)=1$, else $EV(i, j)=0$. In this example,

$$EV = \begin{bmatrix} 1 & 1 & 1 & 1 & 0 \\ 0 & 0 & 0 & 0 & 1 \end{bmatrix}$$

$B(e_i)$ is the set of all intermediate results of the equivalent mashup e_i. B represents the set of all intermediate results of all equivalent mashups in E, and we call any element of B intermediate result. In this paper, we only consider the re-computing cost of the intermediate results. In fact, there is also communication cost, but it has no impact on our model. In this example, $B = \{M_1 \cup M_2, M_2 \cup M_1, M_1 \triangleright\ _{Ri}R, M_2 \triangleright\ _{Ri}R, (M_1 \cup M_2) \triangleright\ _{Ri}R, (M_2 \cup M_1) \triangleright\ _{Ri}R, (M_1 \triangleright\ _{Ri}R) \cup (M_2 \triangleright\ _{Ri}R), (M_2 \triangleright\ _{Ri}R) \cup (M_1 \triangleright\ _{Ri}R)\}$. BE is a 0-1 Boolean matrix with $|E| \times |B|$, if and only if $B(e_j)=b_i$, $BE(i, j)=1$, otherwise $BE(i, j)=0$. In this example,

$$BE = \begin{bmatrix} 1 & 0 & 0 & 0 & 1 & 0 & 0 & 0 \\ 0 & 1 & 0 & 0 & 0 & 1 & 0 & 0 \\ 0 & 0 & 1 & 1 & 0 & 0 & 1 & 0 \\ 0 & 0 & 1 & 1 & 0 & 0 & 0 & 1 \\ 0 & 0 & 1 & 0 & 0 & 0 & 0 & 0 \end{bmatrix}^T$$

$A(b_i)$ is the set of all atomic data services related with the intermediate result b_i, and we call any element of A atomic data service. In this example, $A=\{M_1, M_2, R\}$. AB is a 0-1 Boolean matrix with $|B| \times |A|$, and if and only if $A(b_j)=a_i$, $AB(i, j)=1$, otherwise $AB(i, j)=0$. In this example,

$$AB = \begin{bmatrix} 1 & 1 & 1 & 0 & 1 & 1 & 1 & 1 \\ 1 & 1 & 0 & 1 & 1 & 1 & 1 & 1 \\ 0 & 0 & 1 & 1 & 1 & 1 & 1 & 1 \end{bmatrix}^T$$

p^V is a 0-1 Boolean vector representing the execution modes of the mashups, where 1 represents the mashup is executed in active mode, and 0 represents the mashup is executed in passive mode. r^V and u^A are the request frequency vector of the mashups and the update frequency vector of atomic data services respectively. They can be obtained from monitoring and service interface description. In order to facilitate the computation of the data maintenance cost, in this example, we assume that $r^V=[1,1]$, and $u^A=[1,1,1]$. c^B is the cost vector of the single-step-computing of intermediate results. For example, the cost of the single-step-computing of the $(M_1 \cup M_2) \triangleright\ _{Ri}R$ is the cost of join operation between $M_1 \cup M_2$ and R. The c^B can be obtained by testing. In this example, we suppose that $c^B=[1,1,2,2,3,3,1,1]$. The cost of the single-step-computing of $(M_1 \cup M_2) \triangleright_{\text{Ri}} R$ is set to 3, which is lower than the sum of $M_1 \triangleright_{\text{Ri}} R$ (set to 2) and $M_2 \triangleright_{\text{Ri}} R$ (set to 2), and higher than any of them. The above information is all input to establish the data maintenance cost model of the mashups. Next, we will explain how to compute the c_P and c_A in our example.

$c_P=((((r^V \times EV) \otimes x^E) \times BE) \otimes c^B) \times (L(x^E \times BE) \wedge \neg x^{BP})^T$ is the total cost of the single-step-computing of the intermediate results, where x^E is a 0-1 vector, 0 indicates that the equivalent mashup is not selected and 1 indicates the equivalent mashup is selected. The $(r^V \times EV) \otimes x^E$ is the request frequency vector of the selected equivalent mashups, and the $((r^V \times EV) \otimes x^E) \times BE$ indicates the number of the single-step-computing of the intermediate results of the selected equivalent mashups. After the $((r^V \times EV) \otimes x^E) \times BE$ is multiplied by c^B, we can get the total cost of the single-step-computing of the intermediate results without taking into account reusing the materialized results. The total cost is multiplied by the transpose of $L(x^E \times BE) \wedge \neg x^{BP}$ to eliminate the cost of the single-step-computing of materialized results, where the $x^{BP}=L((p^V \wedge x^E) \times BE)$ represents the materialized results of all selected equivalent mashups.

$c_A=((x^{BP} \otimes c^B) \times AB) \times (u^A)^T$ is the total cost of the single-step-computing of the intermediate results related with the atomic data services when the atomic data services are updated. Firstly, we multiply c^B and x^{BP} to get the total cost of all single-step-computing of intermediate results. AB represents the relationships between atomic data services and intermediate results, which is multiplied by $x^{BP} \otimes c^B$ to get the total cost of the all single-step-computing of intermediate results when all atomic data services are updated. The total cost further is multiplied by the transpose of u^A to get the final total update cost, where u^A is the update frequency vector of all atomic data services. In this example, we use a genetic algorithm as shown in [3] to solve the 0-1 programming to get the approximate optimal solution, and the solution is as follows: $p^V=[0,1]$ and $x^E=[0,0,1,0,1]$, namely the $(M_1 \cup M_2) \triangleright_{\text{Ri}} R$ and $M_1 \triangleright_{\text{Ri}} R$ is passive mode and active mode respectively, and the script of $(M_1 \cup M_2) \triangleright_{\text{Ri}} R$ is replaced with the script of $(M_1 \triangleright_{\text{Ri}} R) \cup (M_2 \triangleright_{\text{Ri}} R)$.

4   Experiment and Discussion

Our experimental setup is based on our data service mashup platform-DSM [7]. We simulate a group of data services spread out on the Internet based on TPC-H[1]. TPC-H describes a multi-part production and sales scenario, involving eight data tables. The tables are encapsulated into a group of Internet accessible data services. Since the experiment only considers the number of mashups, the request frequency of mashups, and the update frequency of the atomic data services, the data size of the output of the atomic data services is kept unchanged. We configure the default value to be 100 KB. In the future, we will consider the dynamic data size of data services.

---

[1] http://www.tpc.org/tpch/

In the following experiments, we build 10 mashups. To simulate the real data service mashups, the average number of operators in one data service mashup is limited less than 8, which is similar to those mashups on Yahoo! Pipes [8]. To simulate the real large-scale mashup platform scenario, we duplicate 80 mashups according to the Zipfian distribution with α=0.9 based on the statistical observation from syndic8, which has been studied in paper [4].

We use JMeter[2] to simulate the stress testing on a single machine with 2GB memory and 2.26GHz CPU. In following experiments, we quantify the performance benefits of the materialized selection strategy. The materialized selection strategy is compared with two other strategies: "All Materialized" and "No Materialized", the former means all results are materialized and the latter means no result is materialized. These three strategies are compared with respect to the total cost incurred by the mashup platform in serving the end-user requests. For an individual mashup, the cost is quantified as the associated computational latency at the mashup platform. In Figure 2, we randomly select mashups, and compare the data maintenance cost of three strategies as the number of the mashups increases from 4 to 80. The mean of the request frequencies is set to 50, and the mean of the update frequencies is set to 5. As the results indicate, the data maintenance cost incurred by DSM is lower than the other two strategies throughout the simulated range. The most important thing is DSM's curve shows log tendency rather than linear tendency, and the reason is that the probability of reuse increases as the number of the mashups increases.

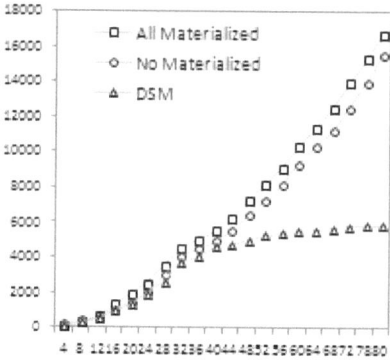

Fig. 2. The maintenance cost comparison

In Figure 3(a), we compare the three strategies as the mean of the request frequencies of all the one thousand mashups varies from 10 requests per unit time to 100 requests per unit time. The mean of the update frequencies of the data services is set to 5. The system is assumed to have enough storage to materialize the results of all mashups. Figure 3(a) shows the data maintenance cost per unit time for the results of the experiments. As the results indicate, the data maintenance cost incurred by DSM's

---

[2] http://jmeter.apache.org/

materialized selection is lower than the other two strategies throughout the simulated request frequency range. The data maintenance cost incurred by the "All Materialized" strategy is essentially constant as the requests are served using materialized results without additional computations. For this "All Materialized" strategy, the data maintenance cost is mainly due to re-computing of the materialized results when the associated atomic data services used in the mashups are updated. At very low request rates, the data maintenance cost of "No Materialized" strategy is comparable to those of the DSM. However, with the request frequency increases, the data maintenance cost of "No Materialized" strategy raises quickly. It is to be noted here that although the data maintenance cost of the DSM strategy increases with the increasing request frequency, its curve becomes flat once upon reaching the "All Materialized" cost levels. In Figure 3(b), we study the effect of update frequencies of data services on the data maintenance cost of the three strategies. The setup is very similar to that of the previous one except that the mean request frequency is fixed at 50 requests per unit time whereas the update frequency of all data services is varied from 1 to 10 per unit time. Again, we see that the DSM has the best performance than the other two strategies. However, in this experiment, the data maintenance cost of the "No Materialized" remains constant. This is because there are no materialized results that need to be recomputed when the data services are updated.

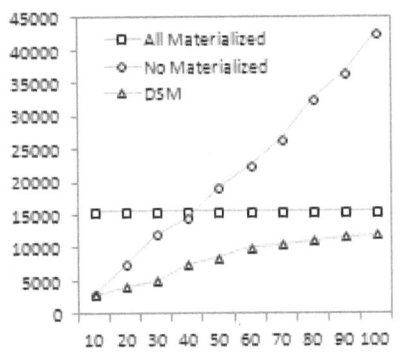
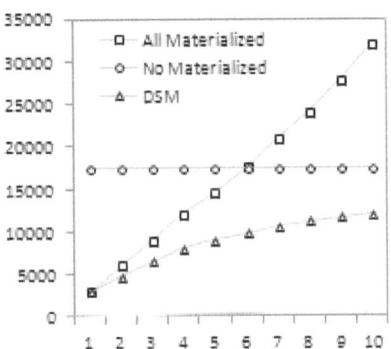

(a) Maintenance Cost When Request Frequency is Variable   (b) Maintenance Cost When Update Frequency is Variable

Fig. 3. The maintenance cost comparison

We thus conclude that the maintenance cost reduction of the DSM system is achieved when there are higher request frequencies, update frequencies and the number of mashups.

5   Related Works

Since Harinarayan published the first paper about materialized view selection [9], the materialized view selection had been gradually warmed up in the database research, and attracted a growing number of researchers. Many research results continue to emerge, including the static selection [10], the dynamic selection [11] and the hybrid approach [12], but all of them focus on traditional data integration on the data warehouse. On the contrary, this paper focuses on the popular data integration on the Web called data mashup. So although our maintenance cost model is similar to the MVPP framework for materialized view design [10], we consider the interaction between user and the mashup (the execution mode of mashup) which is different from MVPP.

In recent years, Web 2.0 technologies have been widely developed. There have been many tools and platforms to support just-in-time data mashup for non-professional users, however, seldom works have focused on the performance combined with maintenance. Hassan has presented a dynamic caching framework MACE [4] to improve the performance of data mashups. MACE continuously observes the execution of mashups, and collects statistics such as request frequencies, update frequencies and cost and output size values at various nodes of mashups. It then performs cost-benefit analysis of caching at different nodes of mashups, and chooses a set of nodes that are estimated to yield the best benefit-cost ratios. For each new mashup, MACE platform analyzes whether any of the cached results can be substituted for part of the mashup workflow. If so, the mashup is modified so that the cached data can be re-used. To a great extent, MACE enhances the performance of mashups, but MACE does not consider the reuse possibility through the mashup equivalence transformation. In addition, the paper [5] provides AMMORE platform to support mashups construction. AMMORE represents mashups as strings, and then it detects the longest common components across mashups, and merges mashups with other mashups by common components to minimize the total number of operators that the mashup platform has to execute. The longest common components can be used by multiple mashups. In this way, the maintenance cost of mashup platforms is reduced, but AMMORE does not establish their maintenance cost model. In fact, the DSM merges mashups based on the mainteance cost model, and also can minimize the number of maintenanced mashups.

On the mashup maintenance, the paper [13] presents techniques that help mashup developers to maintain applications by identifying when and how the original applications' UIs change, but the techniques are mainly used to search best matched widgets. Our prior work [2] introduces the maintenance cost model for the data service mashup, but the introduction is simple.

6   Conclusions and Future Works

Data service mashup is a special class of mashup application that combines information on the fly from multiple data sources. A challenging problem is how to achieve the best performance with the minimum maintenance cost.

This paper presents an efficient strategy, based on materialized view selection. The strategy use the data maintenance model to measure the response cost and update cost of a group of data service mashups in terms of the request frequency and update frequency. Based on the model, a materialized view selection for data service mashup is proposed. Experiments show that our strategy can effectively reduce the maintenance cost of a lot of hosted data service mashups.

Acknowledgements. The research work is supported by the National Natural Science Foundation of China under Grant No.61033006.

References

1. Barhamgi, M., Ghedira, C., Benslimane, D., et al.: Optimizing DaaS Web Service based Data mashup. In: SCC 2011, pp. 464–471 (2011)
2. Zhang, P., Wang, G.L., Ji, G., Han, Y.B.: An Efficient Data Maintenance Model for Data Service Mashup. In: IEEE International Conference on Services Computing (SCC 2012), pp. 699–700 (2012)
3. Zhang, P., Wang, G.L., Ji, G., Liu, C.: Optimization Update for Data Composition View Based on Data Service. Chinese Journal of Computers 34(12), 2344–2354 (2011)
4. Hassan, O.A., Ramaswarny, L., Miller, J.A.: The MACE Approach for Caching Mashups. International Journal of Web Services Research 7(4), 64–88 (2010)
5. Hassan, O.A., Ramaswamy, L., Miller, J.A.: Enhancing Scalability and Performance of Mashups Through Merging and Operator Reordering. In: Proceedings of the IEEE International Conference on Web Services, pp. 171–178 (2010)
6. Lin, H.L., Zhang, C., Zhang, P.: An Optimization Strategy for Mashups Performance Based on Relational Algebra. In: Sheng, Q.Z., Wang, G., Jensen, C.S., Xu, G. (eds.) APWeb 2012. LNCS, vol. 7235, pp. 366–375. Springer, Heidelberg (2012)
7. Han, Y., Wang, G., Ji, G., Zhang, P.: Situational data integration with data services and nested table. In: Service Oriented Computing and Application, pp. 1–22 (2012)
8. Yahoo! Pipes: Rewire the web (2011), `http://pipes.yahoo.com/`
9. Harinarayan, V., Rajaraman, A., Ullman, J.D.: Implementing data cubes efficiently. ACM SIGMOD Record 25(2), 205–216 (1996)
10. Yang, J., Karlapalem, K., Li, Q.: Algorithm for materialized view design in data warehousing environment. In: Jarke, M., Carey, M.J., Dittrich, K.R. (eds.) Proc. of the 23rd Int'l Conf. on Very Large Data Bases (VLDB 1997), pp. 136–145. Morgan Kaufmann Publishers, Athens (1997)
11. Kotidis, Y., Roussopoulos, N.: A case for dynamic view management. ACM Trans. on Database Systems 26(4), 388–423 (2001)
12. Shah, B., Ramachandran, K., Raghavan, V., Gupta, H.: A hybrid approach for data warehouse view selection. Journal of Data Warehousing and Mining 2(2), 1–37 (2006)
13. Maxim, S., Spiros, M.: On the maintenance of UI-integrated Mashup Appliactions. In: International Conference on Software Maintenance (ICSM 2011), pp. 203–212 (2011)

Homomorphic-Encryption-Based Separation Approach for Outsourced Data Management[*]

Yang Zhang and Jun-Liang Chen

State Key Laboratory of Networking and Switching Technology,
Beijing University of Posts & Telecommunications,
Beijing 100876, China
YangZhang@bupt.edu.cn

Abstract. With the rapid application of cloud computing technologies, service and data outsourcing has become a practical and useful paradigm. In order to manage sensitive information in this outsourcing scenario, combined use of access control technologies and cryptography was proposed by many researchers. However, the rigid combination in existing approaches has difficulty in satisfying the flexible data management for diverse applications. In this paper, we advocate a separation methodology where an authorization policy is not required to be embedded into ciphertexts or keys during encrypting data, and can be linked to the ciphertexts at any time. Authorization is independently carried out as usually without involving encryption, and encryption plays a foundational mechanism without considering authorization. We propose a separation approach based on homomorphic encryption to realize outsourced data management, where an encryption procedure is separated from authorization, and dynamically integrated with authorization policy according to subjects' attributes at any time.

Keywords: Outsourced Data Service, Access Management, Homomorphic Encryption.

1 Introduction

1.1 Motivation

When cloud services become popular on the Internet, users are more and more resorting to service providers for publishing resources shared with others. Service providers are requested to realize data and service outsourcing architecture on a wide scale. For example, YouTube and MySpace are such service providers. Their basic assumption that service providers have complete access to the stored resources is not applicable for all actual scenarios such as outsourcing sensitive data. Current solutions adopt

---

[*] Supported by Project of New Generation Broadband Wireless Network under(Grant No.2010ZX03004-001, 2011ZX03002-002-01, 2012ZX03005008-001).

A. Ghose et al. (Eds.): ICSOC 2012, LNCS 7759, pp. 24–34, 2013.

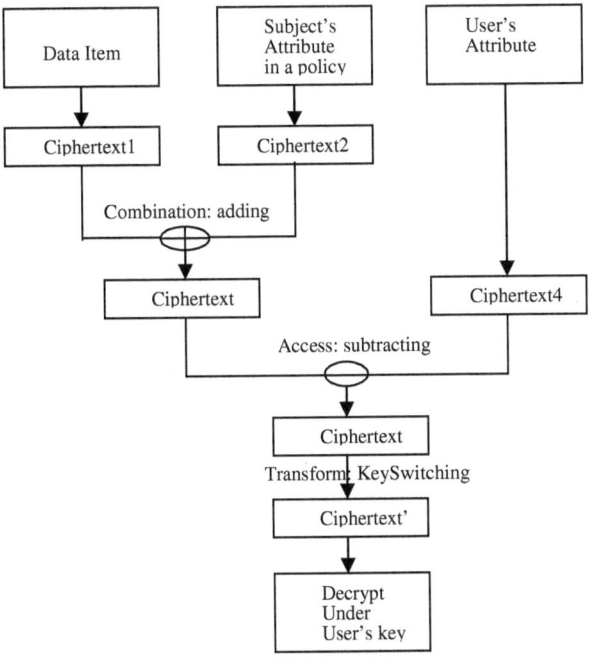

Fig. 1. Separation based on encryption homomorphism

encryption techniques instead of the legal protection offered by contracts when enforcing access control, i.e. the data owner encrypts data, sends ciphertexts to the service providers for storage, and distributes the corresponding key to authorized users [1], [2], [3], [4], [5].

In particular, since neither the data owner nor the service providers can solely assume the access control task for either efficiency or security reasons, realizing access control via the stored data themselves appears more applicable. As an example, the selective encryption technique was adopted to encrypt different data with different keys, which guarantees that legal users can retrieve the key to decrypt the encrypted resource [6], [7], [8], [9], [4], [12], [13]. However, those approaches need user to derive all the keys of authorized data items according to a public catalog of tokens, or assume that users' attributes are a set without inner structures. The complexity of authorization policies is passed to cryptographic operations, and end users directly face with it. This also results in static data management without supporting practical attribute structure, and policies are hard to be updated. Therefore, we advocate a relative separation methodology, where authorization and cryptographic operations both independently carried out, and are transparently combined for users.

In this paper, according to the separation methodology, the authorization policies are independently made and data is independently encrypted. When a policy should be applied to a data item which could have become a ciphertext, the data owner translates the policy into another ciphertext and uses a homomorphic function to get the sum of the two ciphertexts (add ciphertexts), i.e. combining the policy with the data item. The outsourcer has the ciphertext of a user's attribute, and subtracts this ciphertext from the sum. If the user's attribute is equal to the subject's attribute in the authorization rule, the sum is transformed into the ciphertext of the data item. This cloud data management idea is illustrated in the below figure 1.

From the figure 1, we can know the owner does combination, i.e. adding ciphertexts, the outsource does subtracting and transforming, and the user transparently decrypts ciphertexts under her or his private key. If she or he has the proper attribute, the user gets a correct ciphertext, i.e. the value of *Ciphertext3 – Ciphertext4* being equal to *Ciphertext1*. The key points are designing homomorphic function and preventing homomorphic attacks. The homomorphism brings designers great power. It also provides adversaries a homomorphic attack method. The scheme designers should try to limit the capacity of adversaries.

1.2   Contributions

Contributions of our paper are as follows:

1. A separation methodology is adopted to get a flexible data management framework for cloud data services.
2. Based on the homomorphic key-switching scheme, a cloud data management solution is proposed. The data owner can authorize before, during, or after doing encryption. The complex subject attribute relationship is supported.

2   Preliminaries

2.1   Attribute-Based Authorization Policy

We adopt the attribute-based access control model.

Definition 1. Attribute Tuple. *The attribute of a subject* S *is denoted by* $s_k = (s\_attr_k, op_k, value_k)$ *and the attribute of an object* O *as* $o_n = (o\_attr_n, op_n, value_n)$, *where* s_attr *and* o_attr *are attribute names, value is the attribute value, and* op *is some attribute operator such as* $op \in \{=,<,>,\leq,\geq,in\}$. *The action attribute can be one of object's attribute. The attribute tuple is* $< s_1, s_2, \cdots, s_K >$ *or* $< o_1, o_2, \cdots, o_N >$, *where the relationship among the attributes is conjunction. S can be represented by the set of attribute tuples* $\{< s_1, s_2, \cdots, s_K >\}$, *and* O *by* $\{< o_1, o_2, \cdots, o_N >\}$.

In our paper, the op is simplified as $\{=\}$ by describing digital attributes with careful intervals.

Definition   2.   Authorization   Rule. *An   attribute-based   rule   is* $rule = (< s_1, s_2, \cdots, s_k >, < o_1, o_2, \cdots, o_n >) = (SA, OA)$. *The   j−th   subject attribute is written as   rule.s$_j$. The   j−th   object attribute is written as   rule.o$_j$.*

An   access   control   policy AP_i can   be   defined   as $AP_i = \bigcup_{j=1}^{L} rule_{i,j}$.   Then,

$$AP_i.SA = \bigcup_{j=1}^{L} rule_{1,j}.SA, \quad AP_i.OA = \bigcup_{j=1}^{L} rule_{i,j}.OA.$$

2.2   Access Expression

Let Γ be an access expression representing the subject attributes required to access some data, which uses logic operators to associate the attributes. According to the authorization policy $AP.SA = rule_1.SA \cup \cdots \cup rule_l.SA$, the access expression Γ could be   represented   as $\Gamma = (w_{1,1} \wedge \cdots \wedge w_{1,n_1}) \vee \cdots \vee (w_{l,1} \wedge \cdots \wedge w_{l,n_l})$,   where $w_{i,j} ::= "s\_attr_{i,j} = value_{i,j}"$, $1 \le i \le l$, $1 \le j \le n_l$.

Definition 3 (Satisfying an access expression Γ). *If a subject attribute expression* $\gamma = (w_{1,1} \wedge \cdots \wedge w_{1,n_1'}) \vee \cdots \vee (w_{l',1} \wedge \cdots \wedge w_{l,n_{l'}'})$ *satisfies Γ, we denote it by $\Gamma(\gamma) = 1$, else* $\Gamma(\gamma) = 0$. *We compute $\Gamma(\gamma) = 1$ as follows:*

For $(w_{i,1} \wedge \cdots \wedge w_{i,n_i})$, $1 \le i \le l$ in Γ, there is a $(w_{j,1} \wedge \cdots \wedge w_{1,n_j'})$, $1 \le j \le l'$ in γ satisfying:

For each $w_{i,x}$, $1 \le x \le n_i$ in $(w_{i,1} \wedge \cdots \wedge w_{i,n_i})$, there is a $w_{j,x'}$, $1 \le x \le n_j'$ satisfying $w_{j,x'} = w_{i,x}$.

We add such $(w_{i,1} \wedge \cdots \wedge w_{i,n_i})$ into the set Δ which is filled with all such rules (sub-expression).

We denote Δ as $\Gamma \cap \gamma$, i.e., $\Gamma \cap \gamma = \Delta$. If Δ is not empty, we think that γ and Γ are matching, i.e. $\Gamma(\gamma) = 1$.

In a word, the access expression Γ for a data item represents the subject attributes in authorization rules of the data owner, and the subject attribute expression γ represents a user's attributes. These attributes have inner structures, i.e. attribute conjunction and disjunction.

3   Separate Data Management Framework

The Figure 2 demonstrates our core idea to realize separate data management for cloud services. During authorization, the data owner chooses a random value as an

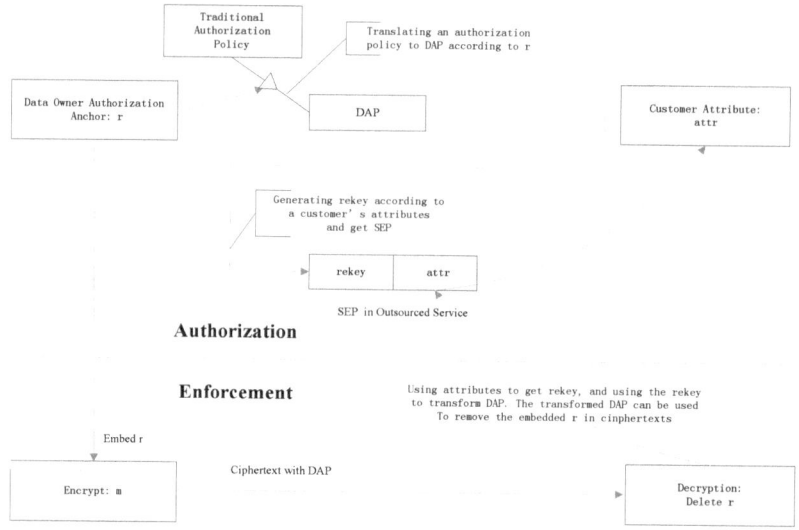

Fig. 2. Data Management Framework

authorization anchor *r* and translates authorization policies into data access polices (DAP) according to the anchor *r* . DAP can be informally considered as the ciphertexts for the subject attributes in authorization rules. The anchor *r* is used to randomize DAP such that even if the same authorization rule is applied to different data items, there are different DAPs which are not interchangeable. DAP can be generated before operating data encryption because it is linked to a random *r* . Subject encryption policies (SEP) are generated according to customers' attributes *attr* at any time, and can also be considered as the ciphertexts for *attr* . At the same time, re-encryption keys are given to the outsourced data service who uses them to keyswitch ciphertxts, i.e. translating one ciphertext under the data owner's public key into another ciphertext under a user's public key. In our framework, each participant has only one public/private key pair to identify herself. During runtime, the encryption scheme allows for embedding the anchor *r* in the ciphertext. The outsourced data service makes matching between SEP and DAP, and gets one matched DAP if the requesting user has been granted the privilege. The matched DAP is keyswitched. The keyswitched DAP includes the anchor *r* . The keyswitched DAP can be used to remove the anchor *r* in the data ciphertext. The user recovers the data by her or his private key.

There are two difficulties. One is how to embed and remove the anchor, where the anchor is secret. The other is how to decrypt the ciphertext under the data owner's key, where we do not hope to carry out complex key distribution schemes to issue a series of keys to the customer. In this paper, we adopt a homomorphic encryption scheme to address the first issue. We design a switching key approach to address the second issue. That is to say, a ciphertext under the data owner's keys can be switched into a ciphertext under customers' keys. Our solution has the following characteristics:

1) The attributes of a subject can have inner structures, that is to say, there are logic 'AND' and 'OR' relations among them.
2) The authorization policies can be generated or modified after the ciphertexts have been computed. It can also be generated before the ciphertexts are produced.

4   Fundamental Encryption Scheme

We adopt the fully homomorphic encryption scheme in [10] which is CPA-secure based on the RLWE (Ring Learning with Errors) assumption. We rewrite the scheme in our words (some details can be found in [10]). According to the encryption scheme, we modify a little the key switching scheme, where the customer's private key need not be disclosed to the data owner during generating switching keys. If a reader is familiar with the encryption scheme in [10], she or he could skip this section.

4.1   Homomorphic Encryption

The following homomorphic encryption scheme only supports multiplication one time, which is a simplified version of the one in [10]. A prime $t < q$ defines the message space $R_t = Z_t[X]/f(x)$, the ring of integer polynomials modulo $f(x)$ and t. We can adopt the message encoding algorithm used in [11] to optimize performance.

— *FHE.Setup*(1^λ) : It takes as input the security parameter λ. It chooses appropriately the dimension d, which is a power of 2, the modulus q which is a prime such that $q = 1(mod\ 2d)$ and $R = Z_q[X]/(x^d + 1)$, a prime t which defines the message space, an error distribution χ over R which depends sub-logarithmically on q ($d = \Omega(\lambda \cdot log(q/B))$), to ensure that the scheme is based on a RLWE instance that achieves 2^λ security against known attacks.   Let $N = log\ q$ and let $params = (q, d, \chi)$.

— *FHE.SecretKeyGen*$(params)$: It draws $s' \leftarrow \chi$. Set $sk = s \leftarrow (1, s') \in R^2$.

— *FHE.PublicKeyGen*$(params, sk)$: It takes as input a secret key $sk = s \leftarrow (1, s')$, which $s[0] = 1$ and $s' \in R$ and the parameters $params$. It generates matrix $A' \leftarrow R^{N \times 1}$ where a vector $e \leftarrow \chi^N$ and set $b \leftarrow A's' + te$. Sets A to be 2-column matrix consisting of b followed by the columns of $-A'$. (Obs erve: $A \cdot s = te$). Set the public key $pk = A$.

— *FHE.Enc(params, pk, m)* : To encrypt a message $m \in R_t$, it sets $\bar{m} = (m,0) \in R^2$,

  samples $r \leftarrow R_t^N$ and outputs the ciphertext $c \leftarrow \bar{m} + A^T r \in R^2$.

— *FHE.Dec(params ,sk ,c)* : It outputs $m \leftarrow [[<c,s>]_q]_t$ or $m \leftarrow [[<c,s\otimes s>]_q]_t$ if

  the length of c is longer than N , where $<,>$ means the dot product of two
  vectors, and $[]_q$ means *mod q*.

— *FHE.Add(params ,pk ,c_1 ,c_2)* : It takes two ciphertexts encrypted under the same

  key. It sets $c_3 = c_1 + c_2$.

— *FHE.Mult(params ,pk ,c_1 ,c_2)* : It takes two ciphertexts encrypted under the same

  key. The new ciphertext, under the secret key $\bar{s} = s \otimes s$, is the coefficient vector

  c_3 of the linear equation $L_{c_1,c_2}^{long}(x \otimes x)$ where $L_{c_1,c_2}^{long}(x \otimes x) = <c_1, x> \cdot <c_1, x>$, $x \otimes x$

  is the tensoring of x with itself. $c_3 = (c_1[0]c_2[0], c_1[0]c_2[1] + c_1[1]c_2[0], c_1[1]c_2[1])$.

Decryption works correctly because:

$$[[<c,s>]_q]_t = [[(\bar{m}^T + r^T A) \cdot s]_q]_t$$

$$= [[m + t \cdot r^T e]_q]_t$$

$$= [m + tr^T e]_t$$

$$= m$$

The ciphertexts produced by *FHE.Enc* contains two ring elements. Homomorphic
addition is done by simple component-wise addition of two ciphertexts. For
homomorphic multiplication, letting each ciphertext being the coefficients of the
polynomial of symbolic variable, we can symbolically (treating the symbolic variable
as an unknown one) open the parenthesis in $L_{c_1,c_2}^{long}(x \otimes x)$ to compute the product. The
ciphertext product is decrypted under the key $\bar{s} = s \otimes s$, i.e. $m_1 \times m_2 \leftarrow [[<c_3, s \otimes s>]_q]_t$.

4.2   Proxy Key Switching Scheme

Key switching consists of two procedures: first, a procedure takes as input a customer's
public key and a data owner's private key, and outputs some switching keys that
enables the switching; and second, a procedure takes the switching keys and a

ciphertext encrypted under the data owner's public key, and outputs a new ciphertext that encrypts the same message under the customer's public key. Although it is inspired by the key switching algorithm in [10], our key switching scheme does not require the customer to provide its private key, such that ours can be used in outsourcing scenarios. When the data owner gets the customer's public key, it chooses a secret random matrix B_j which is used to blind the public key of customers. The customer cannot recover the B_j even if it gets the blinded public key. The data owner then embeds its private key in the blinded key. When the embedded public key is used to re-encrypt a ciphertext, the decryption under the embedded private key and encryption under the customer's public key take place at the same time. According to the *FHE .PublicKeyG en* algorithm, the random matrix does not impair the customer's decryption capability. The tensor of data owner's private key can be used when switching the product of ciphertexts, where no modulus switching implies that the ciphertext multiplication is supported only once.

The following two functions were introduced in [10].

(1) *BitDecomp(x):* $x \in R^n$. $x = \sum_{j \in [0,\cdots,\log q]} 2^j \mu_j$, $\mu_j \in R_2^n$. Let $L = n\log q$, output

$(\mu_1,\cdots,\mu_{\log q}) \in R_2^L$

(2) *Powersof 2(x):* $x \in R^n$.   Output $(x, 2x, \cdots, 2^{\log q} x) \in R_q^L$

If it is known a priori that x has coefficients in $[0,B]$ for $B << q$, then *BitDecomp* can be optimized in the obvious way to output a shorter bit-decomposition in $R_2^{\log B}$.

Observe that *BitDecomp* and *Powersof 2* do not affect the dot product, in the following sense (Referring to [10]):

For vectors c and s of equal length, we have

$$< BitDecomp(\quad c), Powersof2(\quad s) >=< c, s > m \ odq$$

The proxy key switching scheme is as follows:

Proxy.KeyGen(i, j) : i generates key (sk_i, pk_i) , j generates key (sk_i, pk_i) ,

$pk_j = (b_j, -A'_j) \in R^{N \times 2}$.

Proxy.ReKeyGen(sk_i, pk_j)   : i randomly   chooses $e' \leftarrow \chi^{3N}$,

$B_j \in R_2^{3N \times N}$,   computes $pk'_j = (b'_j, A''_j) = (B_j \cdot b_j, B_j \cdot (-A'_j))$,

$rekey_{i \rightarrow j} = (b'_j + Powersof 2(sk_i \otimes sk_i) + t \cdot e', A''_j)$

Proxy.Enc(pk_i, m) : $c = FHE.Enc(pk_i, m)$.

Proxy .SwitchKey (rekey ,c) : $c' = BitDecomp(c) \cdot rekey_{i \rightarrow j}$.

Proxy.Dec(sk_j, c') : $m = FHE.Dec(sk_j, c')$.

The key switching procedure preserves the correctness of decryption under the new key because

$$< c', sk_j >= BitDecomp\ (c)^T \cdot rekey_{i \to j} \cdot s_j$$

$$= BitDecomp\ (c)^T \cdot ((B_j \cdot e + e')t + Powersof\ 2(s_i \otimes s_i))$$

$$= t \cdot < BitDecomp\ (c),((B_j \cdot e + e')> + < BitDecomp\ (c)\ ,Powers\ of\ 2(s_i \otimes s_i)>$$

$$= t \cdot < BitDecomp\ (c),((B_j \cdot e + e')> + < c, s_i \otimes s_i >$$

$$= t \cdot < BitDecomp\ (c),((B_j \cdot e + e')> + < c, s_i >.$$

5   Separation Construction

In our construction, each participant has one public/private key pair to identify herself. We adopt an anchor-embedding approach to translate the data owner i's authorization polices into DAPs.

All attributes in one conjunction of the access expression are bound together through the hash function and a random, where the random assures that even if two conjunctions are equal, their DAPs are different. If a user's attributes are the same as the subject's attributes in the authorization rules (access expression), the user can remove the embedded attributes, the random, and the anchor from the data ciphertext to recover data. Each attribute of the user is independently translated into SEP such that SEPs can compose as needed. The binding function through hash (such as ho_x) is used to prevent homomorhic attacks. For example, faking a attribute ciphertxet through homomorhic adding and multiplication of attribute ciphertexts is hard. We then define the detail construction.

The attacks to the construction include (1) the outsourced data service uses its stored re-encryption keys, DAPs and all users' SEPs to recover the secret data; (2) users use attributes and their key-pairs to access to unauthorized data; (3) the corrupted data service and users collude to disclose secret data. The homomorphic attack is the primary threat.

For the first kind of attack, the data service can use stored re-encryption keys to switch any DAP to the ciphertext under any user's public key, and does subtraction to remove the authorization anchor and embedded attributes from the data ciphertext. Because the data service does not have users' private keys, it cannot remove the binder ho_x. The binder ho_x is computed by the one-way function (hash function) on attributes and the random r_x. If the random r_x is unknown, the probability to correctly guess ho_x is negligible. The ciphertext for ho_x and the attribute conjunction cannot be faked by homomorphic attacks because ho_x is one-way. Thus, the data service cannot get the correct ciphertext for the data item. This also prevents the curious behavior of the data service from leaking secrets, that is to say, the data service is not corrupted, but it does some unscheduled actions such as sending any ciphertext to any user.

For the second kind of attack, the DAPs are ciphertexts encrypted under the data owner's public key and the SEPs are ciphertexts encrypted under users' public key such that the homomorphic function cannot operate on them. Users have not re-encryption keys to switch the key of DAPs. Because ϖ_i is secret, $\varpi_i w_{y,x}$ cannot be computed. Users' attributes cannot be interwoven either, i.e. inserting one attribute in one conjunction into another conjunction for binding each attribute in one conjunction. Users only by themselves cannot disclose the data included in ciphertexts.

For the third kind of attack, we cannot prevent. So we assume the outsourced data service is half honest. That is to say, the data service does not collude with users, but it may try to get some secret by itself or send any ciphertext to any user.

6   Conclusions

In this paper, we address the problem of how to realize separate cloud data management in this outsourcing scenarios to manage the sensitive data of owners. The homomorphic encryption scheme is adopted as a foundation for our framework, and the homomorphic attack is also discussed. Based on the former, the relative separation could be achieved with combining encryption and authorization. The solution also realizes simple key management and the capacity to compose attributes with inner structure. How to prevent the collusion of the data service and users is left open, which is also our future research target. Therefore, our solution will provide strong building blocks for the design and implementation of manage the sensitive information in cloud computing.

References

1. Ceselli, A., Damiani, E., De Capitani di Vimercati, S., Jajodia, S., Paraboschi, S., Samarati, P.: Modeling and assessing inference exposure in encrypted databases. ACM Trans. on Information and System Security 8(1), 119–152 (2005)
2. Hacigumus, H., Iyer, B., Mehrotra, S.: Providing database as a service. In: Proc. of ICDE 2002, pp. 29–39. IEEE Computer Society, Washington (2002)
3. Hacigumus, H., Iyer, B., Mehrotra, S., Li, C.: Executing SQL over encrypted data in the database-service-provider model. In: Proc. of ACM SIGMOD 2002, pp. 216–227. ACM, New York (2002)
4. De Capitani di Vimercati, S., Foresti, S., Jajodia, S.: Preserving Confidentiality of Security Policies in Data Outsourcing. In: Proceedings of the 7th ACM Workshop on Privacy in the Electronic Society, pp. 75–84 (2008)
5. Samarati, P., de Capitani di Vimercati, S.: Access Control: Policies, Models, and Mechanisms. In: Focardi, R., Gorrieri, R. (eds.) FOSAD 2000. LNCS, vol. 2171, pp. 137–196. Springer, Heidelberg (2001)
6. Damiani, E., De Capitani di Vimercati, S., Foresti, S., Jajodia, S., Paraboschi, S., Samarati, P.: Selective Data Encryption in Outsourced Dynamic Environments. Electronic Notes in Theoretical Computer Science, 127–142 (2007)

7. Damiani, E., De Capitani di Vimercati, S., Foresti, S., Jajodia, S., Paraboschi, S., Samarati, P.: Metadata Management in Outsourced Encrypted Databases. In: Jonker, W., Petković, M. (eds.) SDM 2005. LNCS, vol. 3674, pp. 16–32. Springer, Heidelberg (2005)
8. De Capitani di Vimercati, S., Foresti, S., Jajodia, S., Paraboschi, S., Samarati, P.: Over-encryption: management of access control evolution on outsourced data. In: Proc. of the 33rd VLDB Conference, Vienna, Austria, pp. 123–134 (September 2007)
9. De Capitani di Vimercati, S., Foresti, S., Jajodia, S., Paraboschi, S., Samarati, P.: A data outsourcing architecture combining cryptography and access control. In: Proc. of the 1st Computer Security Architecture Workshop, Fairfax, VA, pp. 63–69 (November 2007)
10. Gentry, C.: Fully Homomorphic Encryption without Bootstrapping (2011), http://eprint.iacr.org
11. Lauter, K., Naehrig, M., Vaikuntanathan, V.: Can Homomorphic Encryption be Practical, http://eprint.iacr.org/2011/133.pdf
12. De Capitani di Vimercati, S., Foresti, S., Jajodia, S., Paraboschi, S., Samarati, P.: Encryption Policies for Regulating Access to Outsourced Data. ACM Transactions on Database Systems, 1–45 (2010)
13. Yu, S.C., Wang, C., Ren, K., Lou, W.J.: Achieving secure, scalable, and fine-grained data access control in cloud computing. In: IEEE INFOCOM (2010)

Protecting Software as a Service
in the Clouds by Validation

Tien-Dung Cao and Kevin Chiew

School of Engineering - Tan Tao University,
Long An province, Vietnam
{dung.cao,kevin.chiew}@ttu.edu.vn

Abstract. The cloud computing has provided customers with various services at its SaaS layer though, few work has been done on the security checking of messages exchanged between a customer and a service provider at SaaS so as to protect SaaS. In this paper we propose a validation model to investigate the SaaS security issue. Rather than installing a set of probes as we have done for the testing web services, in this model we introduce a validation service that plays the role of a firewall and protects our SaaS by verifying the correctness of messages with respect to a set of predefined security rules and forwarding them to their real destinations if they pass the verification or rejecting them otherwise. We develop a prototype model based on the tool known as RV4WS which was developed in our early study on web service runtime verification, as well as a checking engine RVEngine to verify our checking algorithm for the model. A survey on how to use this model for the services deployed on Google App Engine, Window Azure and Oracle Java Cloud Service is also presented.

Keywords: SaaS, Cloud Computing, Security Checking, Rule Specification.

1 Introduction

The cloud computing [1] has been witnessed to grow tremendously in recent years as driven by the ubiquitous availability of high capacity networks, low cost computers and storage devices, as well as the widespread adoption of service-oriented architecture and utility computing. Cloud computing is the delivery of computing as a service rather than a product. The current cloud computing architecture provides clients with three layers of services [2] for them to interact with the clouds:

- IaaS (Infrastructure as a Service) is the fundamental layer providing services for deploying, running and managing virtual machines, networks and storage.
- PaaS (Platform as a Service) is the layer above IaaS by delivering the services for programming and execution, like deploying, monitoring, testing, security, analyzing, etc.

A. Ghose et al. (Eds.): ICSOC 2012, LNCS 7759, pp. 35–46, 2013.

– SaaS (Software as a Service) is the top layer that is the URI software applications providing customers with the shared services.

Given the above layered model, our SaaS (a.k.a, service) is built using the existing PaaS and IaaS such as Google App Engine [3], Window Azure [4], Oracle Java Cloud Service [5], and Amazon S3 [6], due to security and reliability of PaaS and IaaS. In a cloud, however, the services may play the roles of consumers and providers. Therefore, without an adequate protection mechanism our service may breakdown due to customer's and/or provider's unpredictable behaviors. For example, during the communication between a customer and its provider, the messages from the customer/provider may contain untrusted data like virus links which may harm the service, or the customer/provider sends/responds the same message several times within a short duration or accesses a cloud service from different devices (e.g., mobile phones and PCs) at the same time which may bring with unexpected results to the service. Moreover, an untrusted service existing in a composite of services may harm all composition.

To protect the services, an important step is to go through a solid security testing and verification of the software at runtime. The security testing of a software implementation is usually executed via runtime verification. Presently the approaches to runtime verification of software are usually carried out by collecting the messages exchanged and verifying them against a set of constraints [7],[8], in which message collecting is generally practiced by installing a set of points of observation (a.k.a., a set of probes). However, these approaches are not applicable to a cloud environment due to two reasons: (1) SaaS in a cloud uses a dynamic and virtual infrastructure, and it does not function well to install a set of points of observation because of some limitations, for example, only Servlet is supported in Google App Engine, and (2) the points of observation do not allow us to make several decisions like reject, modify or ignore the unexpected messages (from both directions) which are necessary to protect the services.

Given the above situation, in this paper we firstly survey on several clouds and propose the corresponding validation model for security checking of services in these clouds. A validation module which plays the role of a firewall, is actually performing as a kind of intermediary between the customer side and the provider side, serving as the probes to collect messages, and verifying them with respect to a set of predefined security constrains. Secondly, our prototype model is developed with a tool known as RV4WS (Runtime Verification for Web Services) which was developed in our early study on automated runtime verification for web services [9]. Besides, we survey on how to use this prototype for the service composition that are deployed on two popular clouds, namely Google App Engine and Microsoft Window Azure.

The remaining sections of the paper are organized as follows. In Section 2, we review related work on testing of SaaS, and present our security model in Section 3 which includes a validation architecture, rule model and an algorithm to check the correctness of a sequence of messages with respect to a set of security rules, followed by showing our implementation details of prototype development with open discussions in Section 4 before concluding the paper in Section 5.

2   Related Work on Testing of SaaS in the Clouds

There is few published work focusing on either active or passive testing and verification of a cloud application though, some approaches have been proposed to deal with the testing of web services and can be considered as a cloud application if they are applied to a cloud environment.

To protect a web service, Gruschka and Luttenberger [10] proposed a mechanism by validating the SOAP (Simple Object Access Protocol) messages, aiming to filter out the SOAP messages by detecting the malicious ones so as to improve the availability web services. They set up a web service firewall that can validate all incoming and outgoing SOAP messages against the schema, and forward valid messages or reject invalid messages.

Salva *et al.* [11] proposed a security testing method for stated web services. In this work, the security rules defined by the Nomad language are used to construct the test purposes. This security rule set expresses the different properties such as the web service availability, authorization and authentication by means of malicious requests. Using these test purposes, the test cases are then generated from the symbolic specification of web services to test against the service implementation.

The approaches proposed in [8] and [12] focus on invariant satisfiability. These invariants are constructed from the specification and are later on checked based on the collected traces. These approaches use a sniffer-based module which may not be easy to set up on a cloud environment to collect the traces.

Chan *et al.* [13] presented a graph-theoretic model of computing clouds together with a family of model-based testing criteria for testing cloud applications. Their approach is proposed particularly for clouds-in-the-small to predicate the behaviors of applications though, it may not be viable to our study scenario which focuses on protecting SaaS via security testing.

A recent model-based testing process proposed by Endo and Simao [14] suggested using finite state machines to model and support the test case generation for the verification of service-oriented applications. This process focuses on the functional verification of SaaS rather than the security checking.

In [15], Salva defined a proxy-tester as a product between the specification and its canonical tester, which is an intermediary between the client and its implementation. Whenever the proxy-tester receives a message either from the client or from the implementation, it will analyze this message by means of *ioco* for passive testing to detect faults.

Our motivation of this study is based on the idea presented in [10] and the features of clouds. Since a cloud environment is dynamic, virtual and limitation of supported technologies, making it difficult to install a sniffer-based [8] [12] module, we build a firewall, which is either installed totally outside the Clouds or a part depending on the concrete cloud environment, to verify all communicating messages before forwarding them to their destinations so as to protect our services. However, unlike the work in [10] that checks the correctness of messages by comparing the structure of those messages against the schema defined in WSDLs file, we focus on the security issue to protect our service from the

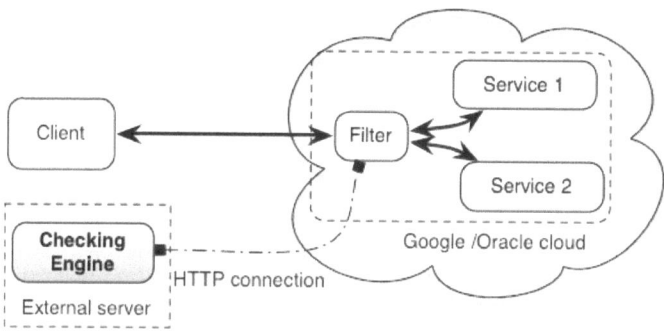

Fig. 1. Testbed architecture using Servlet Filter

untrusted customers or the mistake of partners. For example, the partner responses a message two time, the second one will be rejected. We firstly predefine a set of security rules by giving its syntax, and then verify all messages based on the set of rules defined by this syntax. Amongst these rules, some aspects are considered as time constraint (i.e., future and past time), data correlation, message filtering out by its content, and service behavior.

3   Security Model of SaaS in a Cloud

3.1   A Survey on the Existing Clouds

In this section, we conduct a survey on how the validation model can deploy on the popular PaaS such as Google App Engine (GAE), Window Azure, Oracle Java Cloud Service. Google App Engine [3] supports Java technologies with restrictions at the moment for developing and deploying the services, only Servlet and Rest Web Services are supported. Window Azure [4] supports more standards and it also allows us to configure an application on this environment to call the other one though an HTTP Proxy which is installed outside of the cloud. It allows a service to call to the other one outside the cloud by using the Service Bus or Window Azure Connect [16]. Oracle Java Cloud Service [5] supports full standards of Java EE which allows to call other applications though an HTTP Proxy. However, a little modification of source code is required.

With the services (also service composition) that are developed using Servlet of Java EE, using a Filter[1] as a transparent proxy module, we can capture all communicating message among consumers and providers. This module communicate with Checking Engine that is installed outside the cloud via HTTP Protocol to validate these messages before forwarding them to corresponding Servlet. The Filter is a specialized Servlet which can intercept and transform any requests and responses, therefore it can deploy on the same environment

---

[1] http://www.oracle.com/technetwork/java/filters-137243.html

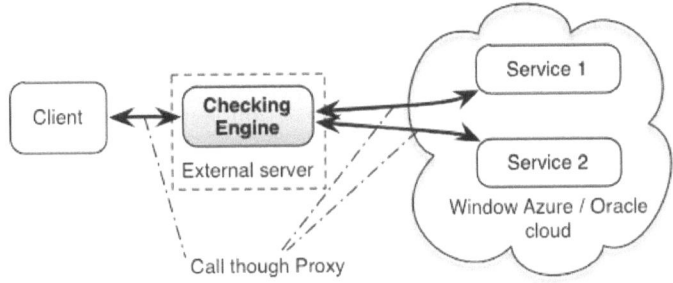

Fig. 2. Testbed architecture though Proxy

with the services. With this architecture, any kind of messages exchanged between a consumer and a provider can be observed without modifying any source code, whereas we do not need to install the checking engine inside the cloud. We can also configure a filter to capture the messages between partners of a service composition. Figure 1 shows the testbed architecture using Servlet Filter. However, an environment, such as Window Azure or Oracle Java Cloud Service, allows the applications to configure to use an HTTP Proxy to call other applications. The checking engine can be integrated into a proxy as shown in Figure 2. However, the consumer is required to call the service though this proxy.

3.2   Security Checking

There have been approaches [8,12] proposed for web services and security checking, which only focus on the behavior of the applications and ignore the data part (i.e., the contents of messages exchanged between a customer and a service provider). However, the security of a service oriented application needs to consider the following aspects, namely (1) *Data Constraints*, i.e. limitations on the structures and contents of the messages sent to the service, (2) *Control-Flow Constraints*, and (3) *Data-aware Control Flow Constraints*, i.e. the authorized sequence of messages depends on relationships between values of multiple messages. To support our model for security checking, in this section we present a checking algorithm that can verify the correctness of a timed trace with respect to a set of constraints. For this purpose, in what follows, we give some formal definitions as preliminaries to the checking algorithm. Our rule definitions and checking algorithm inherit from our previous study [9] on runtime verification of web services.

Rule Definition. The rule definitions include two parts, namely syntax and semantics.

For the syntax part, we consider each message as an atomic action, and use one or several messages to define a formula as a boolean expression. We also use the operation NOT to indicate that a message is prohibited to appear in the trace within a duration. During the formula definition, the constraint on the values of message parameters may be considered. Finally, from these formulas, the rule is defined in two parts, namely supposition (or condition) and context. A set of data correlations are included as an option.

Definition 1. *(Atomic action).* An atomic action is either an input message or an output message, formally denoted as

$$A := Event(Const)|\neg A$$

where

- *Event* represents an input/output message name;
- *Const* := $P \approx V|Const \wedge Const|Const \vee Const$ where
  - P are the parameters. These parameters represent the relevant fields in the message;
  - V are the possible parameters values;
  - $\approx \in \{=, \neq, <, >, \leq, \geq\}$;
- $\neg A$ means $not(A)$.

Definition 2. *(Formula).* A formula is recursively defined as

$$F := start(A) \mid done(A) \mid F \wedge F \mid F \vee F \mid O^{d \in [m,n]}F$$

where

- A is the atomic action;
- $start(A)$: A is being started;
- $done(A)$: A has been finished;
- $O^{d \in [m,n]}F$: F was *true* in d units of time ago if $m > n$, and F will be *true* in the next d units of time if $m < n$ where m and n are natural numbers.

Definition 3. *(Data correlation).* A data correlation is a set of parameters that have the same data type where each different parameter represents a relevant field in a different message, for which the operator = (equal) is used to compare the equality amongst parameters. A data correlation is considered as a property on data.

By putting the time constraints into an interval, we support two types of rules, namely *obligation* and *prohibition*. Obligation means that all traces must satisfy the constraints; whereas prohibition is the negation of an obligation constraint.

Definition 4. *(Rule with data correlation).* Let α and β be formulas, and CS be a set of data correlations based on α and β (CS is defined based on the messages of α and β). A rule with data correlation is defined as $\mathcal{R}(\alpha|\beta)/CS^2$ where $\mathcal{R} \in \{\mathcal{O}$: Obligation; $\mathcal{F}$: Prohibition;$\}$. The constraint $\mathcal{O}(\alpha|\beta)$ or $\mathcal{F}(\alpha|\beta)$ (where $\mathcal{F}(\alpha|\beta) = \mathcal{O}(NOT\ \alpha|\beta)$) respectively means that it is obligated or prohibited to have α *true* when context β holds within the conditions of CS.

Example 1. If we have such a constraint that we do not allow to submit the same login request twice within a period of time, say 3 seconds, then we can use *userId* to distinguish among requests with the following formula:

---

[2] CS is an optional part.

$$\mathcal{F}(start(loginRequest)|O^{d\in[0,3]S}\,done(loginRequest))\,/$$
$$\{\{loginRequest.userId,\,loginRequest.userId\}\}$$

Example 2. We also define a rule to control the client behavior. For example, if a client wants to send a confirmation request to a service provider, then the client must firstly receive a response from the previous operation within maximum 5 minutes where the content of this response is accepted.

$$\mathcal{O}(start(confirmRequest)|O^{d\in[5,0]M}\,done(xxxResponse(resp="accept")))$$

For the semantics part, we have the following definition for a rule model.

Definition 5. *(Rule model).* A model of rules corresponds to a pair $r = (P_r, C_r)$ where

- P_r is a total function that associates every integer x with a propositional formula.
- C_r is a total function that associates every integer x with a pair (α, d) where α is a formula and d a positive integer.

Intuitively, $\forall x$, $p \in P_r(x)$ means that proposition p is *true* at time x; while $(\alpha, d) \in C_r(x)$ means that context of formula α holds (is evaluated *true*) at time t where

- $t \in [x, x + d]$ if we focus on future time.
- $t \in [x - d, x]$ if we focus on past time.

Checking Algorithm. Given the above rule definitions, in what follows we present our algorithm to check a message's security property with respect to a set of constraints. Our algorithm will deal with two cases of rules, namely rules with future time and rules with past time, in which we use two global variables, namely *currlist* and *rulelist*, in which *currlist* is a list of enabled rules that have been activated and *rulelist* is the list of defined rules that are used to verify the system. The full verification algorithm is presented in [9] and it is summarized as follows.

a) Rules with Future Time
Given that each rule has two parts (i.e., the supposition and context parts), a rule will be evaluated as either *true* or *false* or *undefined* if its supposition has been enabled and the current message belongs to its context. At any occurrence time t of message *msg*, our algorithm checks the correctness of a rule by two steps.

- Step 1. Examine the list of enabled rules *currlist* to evaluate their context if the time constraints are valid. If the context of a rule is evaluated to be *true/false*, then it will be removed from the enabled list *currlist* and the corresponding verdict is returned. Otherwise (i.e., the context is *undefined*, meaning incomplete context), we wait for the arrival of the next message and return *true* to the verdict.

Algorithm 1. Checking algorithm for future time rules

    Input   : timed event: (msg, t)
    Output: $true/false$
1 $verdict \longleftarrow true$
    1. For each $r \in currlist$
        – IF the time constraints of r at t are validation
            • IF msg belongs to the context of r
                ∗ Update context of r by msg
                ∗ IF the evaluation of the context of r is $true/false$
                    · Remove r from $currlist$
                    · $verdict \longleftarrow verdict \wedge true/false$
        – ELSE: $verdict \longleftarrow false$
    2. For each $r \in rulelist$
        – IF msg belongs to the supposition of r
            • Update the activated time for r by t
            • Add r into $currlist$ (activated)

– Step 2. Examine the list of rules $rulelist$ to activate[3] them if their supposition contains the current message msg.

Algorithm 1 shows how to check the correctness of a message with a set of future time rules, in which we assume that the rules are *Obligation* (the *Prohibition* rules are the negation of the verdict of the *Obligation* rules), and do not consider data correlation.

b) Rules with Past Time

For a rule with past time, the context part will happen before its supposition, meaning that the context part must be evaluated to be $true/false$ whenever its supposition handles the current message. Upon the arrival of any timed event (msg, t), our algorithm checks correctness of a rule with past time by two steps.

– Step 1. Examine the list of enabled rules $currlist$ to check the correctness of current message msg. If t satisfies their time constraints and msg belongs to their supposition, then remove them from list $currlist$. At the same time, if their context is evaluated to be $false/undefined$, then a $false$ verdict will be assigned; otherwise, a $true$ verdict is admitted. On the other hand, if msg does not belong to their supposition and msg is found in their context, then we update their context by msg and wait the next message to evaluate these rules.
– Step 2. Examine the list of rules $rulelist$ and activate them if their context contains the current message msg.

Algorithm 2 shows how to check the correctness of a message with a set of past time rules under the assumption that the rules are *Obligation*.

---

[3] If a rule exists in the current enable rule list, it will still be activated.

Algorithm 2. Checking algorithm for past time rules

Input : timed event: (msg, t)
Output: $true/false$

1 $verdict \longleftarrow true$

  1. For each $r \in currlist$
     - IF the time constraints of r at t are validation
       - IF msg belongs to the supposition of r
         * Remove r from $currlist$
         * IF the evaluation of the context of r is $false/undefined$
           · $verdict \longleftarrow verdict \wedge false$
       - ELSE IF the context of r contains msg
         * Update the context of r by msg
     - ELSE: $verdict \longleftarrow false$
  2. For each $r \in rulelist$
     - IF msg belongs to the context of r
       - Update the activated time for r by t
       - Add r into $currlist$ (activated)

---

4   Implementation and Discussion

With the above rule definitions and checking algorithm, in what follows we present the implementation of our prototype, as well as applying to a simple example of service composition which can well demonstrate the effectiveness of our security model and method.

To support our security checking method, in the context of WebMov[4] project, we developed a tool known as RV4WS [17][18] (Runtime Verification for Web Services) that checks a timed trace with respect to a set of security rules predefined by the syntax as introduced in Section 3.2. In this tool, a checking engine [19] (i.e., RVEngine) is developed independently in Java language and used as a library of the tool. To support several types of systems, this engine defines an interface known as IParseData which allows us to parse the different structure of messages by implementing it. This interface provides two operations, namely (1) *getMessageName()* which returns the message name by analyzing the structure or content of a message, and (2) *queryData()* which allows us to query a data value from a specific field of a message. The query path of the latter operation depends on the structure of messages. For example, it is an XPath in the case of SOAP message of web services.

To demonstrate the effectiveness of our prototype, we developed a simple service composition where 4 services (i.e., Shopping, Login, Stock and Cart) are developed using Servlet and deployed in Google App Engine [3]. In this composition, Shopping service proposes an interface that allows a client to search a book from Stock service by sending an ISBN (International Standard Book Number). If a book is found, the client can add it into a temporary cart

---

[4] `http://webmov.lri.fr`

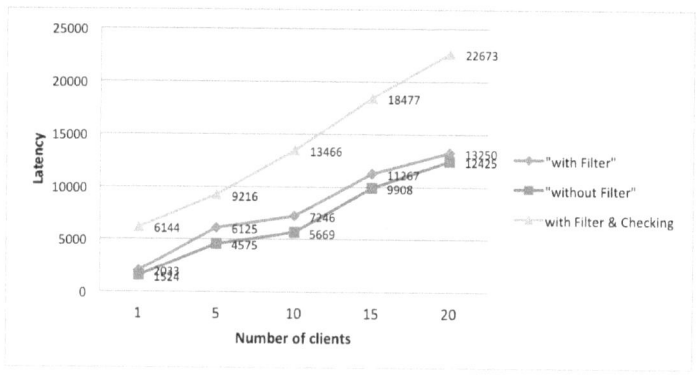

Fig. 3. Latency measurements of composition on GAE Cloud

(i.e., Cart service) and search the other ones. Finally, when one or several books were added into the cart, the client can checkout. However, to use these services, the client is required firstly to access to the Login service to get a ticket. And then, every time when the client is accessing Shopping service, the ticket is required and Shopping service will contact to Login service to validate this ticket. A Filter is also configured to collect all communicating messages from 4 services and the client. These messages will be sent to Checking Engine which is installed on a local machine to validate. We implemented our prototype with 20 instances of mocked client written in Java, which simulate real client applications. They run in a loop and perform the following actions, namely call to Login Service to get a ticket and use this ticket to search a book, add the found book into a temporary cart and check out the cart. In this paper we ignore the correctness of RVEngine because it is proved in [9], but we are interested in the latency of messages while applying our prototype to protect the services. The latency measurement is important since it may lead to an issue if it is equal to or longer than the time set for a connection. Figure 3 shows the obtained latency measurement with GAE. This is the average of total time to complete the sequence of actions with 1, 5, 10, 15 and 20 clients running in parallel. We observe that the difference of time execution between non validation and validation of one instance is 4620 ms (6144-1524) while 18^5 messages were passed to the checking engine. It means that each message is delayed 256 ms for capturing of filter, sending/receiving to checking engine and checking time. However, if many instances are executed in parallel, then the latency can be reduced. For example, with 10 instances, the difference of time is $13466 - 5669 = 7797$ ms for all 180 messages. However, all these latencies depend on the network between our local machine and the Google cloud at different moment.

---

[5] $loginReq \rightarrow loginResp \rightarrow bookReq \rightarrow verifyReq \rightarrow verifyResp \rightarrow stockReq \rightarrow stockResp \rightarrow bookResp \rightarrow addCartReq \rightarrow verifyReq \rightarrow verifyResp \rightarrow cartAddReq \rightarrow cartAddResp \rightarrow addCartResp \rightarrow checkReq \rightarrow checkCartReq \rightarrow checkCartResp \rightarrow checkResp.$

This validation model provides us with some other choices than those described in this paper. We discuss several choices of our validation model in the following.

- *Integrate with a Passive Testing.* All communicating messages of service are passed to it before forwarding to the final destination. Beside the security checking, it also collects the traces. Therefore, a passive testing method can also apply to this step to verify the behavior of the service with respect to a formal specification using these input/output messages. Both on-line [15] or off-line [20] [12] methods can be integrated in this service however, the data correlation must be considered in the case when traces are mixed by many sessions.
- *Integrate with an Analytical Method.* With the model given in Figures 1 and 2 where all communicating messages are collected, an analytical method can be used at the checking engine part for the purpose of understanding and optimizing service usage. Either *off-site* analytical methods such as the measurement of a service's potential audience (opportunity), share of voice (visibility), or buzz (comments) that is happening on the service or *on-site* analytical methods such as service analytics measuring a client's journey can use our model.
- Using this model with a String Solver such as [21] [22], we can apply it to the problem of finding client-side code injection vulnerabilities of the web applications.

5   Conclusion

In this paper, we have proposed a proxy-tester model to protect the security of SaaS. Our contributions are multi-fold. First, we have proposed a firewall model as a validation service for the security checking of SaaS. Second, we have presented an algorithm to check the correctness of messages for both past time and future time cases. Third, we have developed a tool and a checking engine for our model. Fourth, we have conducted a survey on how to use our tool to validate the services that are deployed on several available PaaS. We have also conducted experiments on a simple of service composition which is deployed in GAE and verified the effectiveness of our model. In the future, we plan to investigate our prototype for the real applications and also on Window Azure clouds.

Acknowledgement. Part of the work contributed by K. Chiew was conducted during his visit in Zhejiang University from April to August 2012, which was partly supported by the Chinese Ministry of Science and Technology under Planned-supported Project No. 2011BAD21B0202 and the Natural Science Foundation of China (NSFC) under grant No. 60970081.

References

1. Introduction to cloud computing architecture. White Paper, Sun Microsystems, 1st edn. (June 2009)

2. Lenk, A., Klems, M., Nimis, J., Tai, S., Sandholm, T.: What's inside the cloud? an architectural map of the cloud landscape. In: ICSE Workshop on Software Engineering Challenges of Cloud Computing, pp. 23–31 (2009)
3. Google app engine, http://code.google.com/appengine/
4. Window azure, http://www.windowsazure.com/en-us/
5. Oracle java cloud service,
   https://cloud.oracle.com/mycloud/f?p=service:java:0
6. Amazon s3, http://aws.amazon.com/s3/
7. Leucker, M., Schallhart, C.: A brief account of runtime verification. The Journal of Logic and Algebraic Programming 78(5), 193–303 (2009)
8. Cavalli, A., Benameur, A., Mallouli, W., Li, K.: A passive testing approach for security checking and its pratical usage for web services monitoring. In: NOTERE 2009, Montreal, Canada (2009)
9. Cao, T.D., Castanet, R., Felix, P., Chiew, K.: An approach to automated runtime verification for timed systems: Applications to web services. Journal of Software 7(6), 1338–1350 (2012)
10. Gruschka, N., Luttenberger, N.: Protecting Web Services from DoS Attacks by SOAP Message Validation. In: Fischer-Hubner, S., Rannenberg, K., Yngstrom, L., Lindskog, S. (eds.) Security and Privacy in Dynamic Environments. IFIP, vol. 201, pp. 171–182. Springer, Boston (2006)
11. Salva, S., Laurencot, P., Rabhi, I.: An approach dedicated for web service security testing. In: 5th International Conference on Software Engineering Advances, Nice, France, August 22-27, pp. 494–500 (2010)
12. Morales, G., Maag, S., Cavalli, A., Mallouli, W., de Oca, E., Wehbi, B.: Timed extended invariants for the passive testing of web services. In: IEEE International Conference on Web Service, Miami, Florida, USA, pp. 592–599 (2010)
13. Chan, W., Mei, L., Zhang, Z.: Modeling and testing of cloud applications. In: IEEE Asia-Pacific Services Computing Conference, Singapore, December 7-11, pp. 111–118 (2009)
14. Endo, A.T., Simao, A.: Model-based testing of service-oriented applications via state models. In: IEEE International Conference on Services Computing, pp. 432–439 (2011)
15. Salva, S.: Passive testing with proxy tester. International Journal of Software Engineering and Its Applications 5(4), 1–16 (2011)
16. Using windows azure connect to integrate on-premises web services, http://msdn.microsoft.com/en-us/library/windowsazure/hh697512.aspx
17. Cao, T.D., Castanet, R., Felix, P., Morales, G.: Testing of web services: Tools and experiments. In: IEEE Asia-Pacific Services Computing Conference, Jeju, Korea, pp. 78–85 (December 2011)
18. Cao, T.D., Phan-Quang, T.T., Felix, P., Castanet, R.: Automated runtime verification for web services. In: IEEE International Conference on Web Services, Miami, Florida, USA, July 5-10, pp. 76–82 (2010)
19. Nguyen, K.D.: The development of a testing framework for web services. Master's thesis, Poles Universitaire Française in Ho Chi Minh City (December 2010)
20. Cavalli, A., Gervy, C., Prokopenko, S.: New approaches for passive testing using an extended finite state machine specification. Information and Software Technology 45, 837–852 (2003)
21. Hampi: A solver for string constraints,
    http://people.csail.mit.edu/akiezun/hampi/index.html
22. Kaluza string solver, http://webblaze.cs.berkeley.edu/2010/kaluza/

Identifying Fake Feedback for Effective Trust Management in Cloud Environments

Talal H. Noor[1], Quan Z. Sheng[1], Abdullah Alfazi[1],
Jeriel Law[1], and Anne H.H. Ngu[2]

[1] School of Computer Science, The University of Adelaide, SA 5005, Australia
{talal,qsheng}@cs.adelaide.edu.au
[2] Department of Computer Science, Texas State University, TX 78666-4616, USA
angu@txstate.edu

Abstract. Managing trust in cloud environments is emerging as an important issue in recent years. The highly dynamic, distributed, and non-transparent nature of cloud services makes the trust management of these services difficult. Malicious users may collude to give multiple misleading trust feedback to disadvantage a cloud service, or create several accounts and then leave misleading trust feedback to trick users into trusting cloud services that are not actually trustworthy. In this paper, we propose techniques enabling the identification of fake trust feedbacks and thus provide significant improvement on trust management in cloud environments. In particular, we introduce a credibility model that not only identifies credible trust feedbacks from fake ones, but also preserves the privacy of cloud service consumers. The techniques have been validated by a prototype system implementation and experimental studies.

Keywords: Trust management, cloud computing, credentials, credibility, reputation, security, privacy.

1 Introduction

In recent years, cloud computing has been receiving much attention as a new computing paradigm for providing flexible and on-demand infrastructures, platforms and software as services. Unfortunately, trust management is still considered as one of the key challenges in the adoption of cloud computing. According to the researchers at UC Berkeley [2], trust management and security are ranked one of the top 10 obstacles for cloud computing. The highly dynamic, distributed, and non-transparent nature of cloud services makes the trust management in cloud environments even more challenging [2,10,14,15].

Several researchers have recognized the significance of trust management and proposed solutions to assess and manage trust based on feedbacks collected from participants [5,12,6,14]. In reality, it is not unusual that a trust management system experiences malicious behaviors (i.e., attacks) from its users. For instance, auction systems such as eBay, experience fake trust feedback problem where attackers create several accounts and quickly leave multiple trust feedbacks to

A. Ghose et al. (Eds.): ICSOC 2012, LNCS 7759, pp. 47–58, 2013.

boost their trust results at a glance [1]. Attackers trick users into trusting untrustworthy cloud services through creating several accounts, producing numerous transactions (e.g., creating multiple virtual machines for a short period of time), and leaving fake trust feedbacks.This paper focuses on improving trust management in cloud environments by proposing novel ways to identify fake feedbacks. In particular, we distinguish several key issues including i) *Feedback Collusion* where dynamic interactions of cloud services make the identification of credible trust feedbacks a difficult problem because new cloud service consumers join while others might leave around the clock, ii) *Multiplicity of Identities* where malicious cloud service consumers can use multiple identities [9] to give fake or misleading trust feedbacksor to be able to wipe off their negative historical trust records, and iii) *Cloud Service Consumers' Privacy* where interactions between the cloud service consumers and the trust management service usually involve sensitive information. The cloud service consumers might face sensitive information disclosure while dealing with the trust management service. For example, the accidental leaking of the trust participant's sensitive information such as user name, password, and postal address. is not possible.

In this paper, we overview the design and the implementation of a credibility model. Our model exploits techniques for fake feedback identification and thus provides significant improvement on trust management in cloud environments. In a nutshell, the salient features of our model are as follows:

- *Zero-Knowledge Credibility Proof Protocol.* To avoid the privacy breach problem when managing trust in cloud environments, we introduce the *Zero-Knowledge Credibility Proof Protocol* that not only preserves the cloud service consumers' privacy, but also enables the trust management service to prove the credibility of a particular cloud service consumer's feedbacks.
- *Feedback Density.* We propose this technique to tackle the feedback collusion issue by identifying credible trust feedbacks from fake ones (i.e., trust results manipulation by giving multiple trust feedbacks to a certain cloud service in a short period of time).
- *Multi-Identity Recognition.* We introduce this technique that addresses the multiplicity of identities challenge. This technique identifies fake trust feedbacks from malicious cloud service consumers who use multiple identities to manipulate trust results

The remainder of the paper is organized as follows. The design of the Zero-Knowledge Credibility Proof Protocol, assumptions and attack models are described in Section 2. Section 3 describes the details of our credibility model. Section 4 reports the trust management service implementation and several experimental evaluations for the proposed techniques. Finally, Section 5 overviews the related work and provides some concluding remarks.

2   Zero-Knowledge Credibility Proof Protocol (ZKC2P)

Since there is a strong relation between trust and identification as emphasized in [7], we propose that the *Identity Management Service* (IdM) can help the

Trust Management Service (TMS) in measuring the credibility of a cloud service consumer's feedback. However, processing IdM's information can breach the privacy of cloud service consumers. One way to preserve privacy is to use cryptographic encryption techniques but there is no efficient ways to process encrypted data [15]. Another way is to use anonymization techniques to process IdM's information without breaching the privacy of cloud service consumers. Thus, we propose a *Zero-Knowledge Credibility Proof Protocol* (ZKC2P) to allow TMS to process IdM's information (i.e., credentials) using the *Multi-Identity Recognition* factor (explained in detail in Section 3). TMS processes the credentials without including the sensitive information. Instead, anonymized information is used via consistent hashing (e.g., sha-256). The anonymization process covers all the credentials' attributes except the *Timestamps* attribute.

Identity Management Service (IdM). The cloud service consumers typically have to establish their identity for the first time they attempt to use TMS through registering their credentials at the *Trust Identity Registry*. These credentials typically involve sensitive information. The *Trust Identity Registry* stores an identity record denoted as $\mathcal{I}$ for each cloud service consumer. The identity record $\mathcal{I}$ is represented in a tuple that consists of the cloud service consumer's primary identity $\mathcal{C}$ (e.g., user name), the credentials' attributes (e.g., passwords, postal address, IP address) denoted by $\mathcal{C}_a$ and the timestamps $\mathcal{T}$ which is the cloud service consumer's registration time in TMS. The identity record is thus a tuple $\mathcal{I} = (\mathcal{C}, \mathcal{C}_a, \mathcal{T})$.

Trust Management Service (TMS). The trust behavior of a cloud service is represented by a collection of invocation history records denoted as $\mathcal{H}$. Each cloud service consumer c holds her point of view regarding the trustworthiness of a specific cloud service s in the invocation history record which is managed by TMS. Each invocation history record is represented in a tuple that consists of the cloud service consumer's primary identity $\mathcal{C}$, the cloud service's identity $\mathcal{S}$, a set of trust feedbacks $\mathcal{F}$ and the aggregated trust feedbacks weighted by the credibility $\mathcal{F}_c$ (i.e., $\mathcal{H} = (\mathcal{C}, \mathcal{S}, \mathcal{F}, \mathcal{F}_c)$). Each trust feedback in $\mathcal{F}$ is represented in numerical form with the range of $[0, 1]$, where 0, 1, and 0.5 means *negative feedback*, *positive feedback*, and *neutral* respectively. Consequently, the trustworthiness of a certain cloud service s, the trust result, denoted as $\mathcal{T}_r(s)$, is calculated as follows:

$$\mathcal{T}_r(s) = \frac{\sum_{c=1}^{|\mathcal{V}(s)|} \mathcal{F}_c(c, s)}{|\mathcal{V}(s)|} \tag{1}$$

where $\mathcal{V}(s)$ denotes the trust feedbacks given to the cloud service s and $|\mathcal{V}(s)|$ represents the length of $\mathcal{V}(s)$ (i.e., the total number of trust feedbacks given to the cloud service s). $\mathcal{F}_c(c, s)$ are trust feedbacks from the cth cloud service consumer weighted by the credibility. TMS distinguishes between credible trust feedbacks and malicious ones through assigning the credibility aggregated weights $\mathcal{C}_r(c, s)$ to trust feedbacks $\mathcal{F}(c, s)$ as shown in Equation 2, where the result $\mathcal{F}_c(c, s)$ is held in the invocation history record h and updated in TMS. The details on how to calculate $\mathcal{C}_r(c, s)$ is described in Section 3.

$$\mathcal{F}_c(c, s) = \mathcal{F}(c, s) * \mathcal{C}_r(c, s) \tag{2}$$

In our credibility model, we assume that communications are secure since securing communications is not the focus of this paper. The attack such as *Man-in-the-Middle* (MITM) is therefore beyond the scope of this work. We also assume that IdM is managed by a trusted third party. The attacks that we consider are as follows:

- *Self-promoting Attack.* This attack arises when the malicious cloud service consumers attempt to increase their trust results [8] or their allies. This type of attack can occur either as an *Non-collusive Malicious Behavior* (i.e., when a malicious cloud service user gives numerous fake feedbacks to increase her trust results) or as a *Collusive Malicious Behavior* (i.e., when several users collaborate to give numerous fake feedbacks) also called *Feedback Collusion*.
- *Slandering Attack.* This attack is considered as the opposite of the *Self-promoting* attack that happens when malicious users try to decrease the trust results of certain cloud service [3] due to e.g., jealousy from its competitors. This type of attack can also happen either through *Non-collusive Malicious Behavior* or *Collusive Malicious Behavior*.
- *Sybil Attack.* This attack arises when malicious cloud service consumers use multiple identities [9,8] to give numerous misleading trust feedbacks to increase their allies' trust results or to decrease their competitors' trust results.
- *Whitewashing Attack.* This attack is similar to the *Sybil* attack in the use of multiple identities but differs in the purpose. The *Whitewashing* attack occurs when the malicious cloud service consumers seek new identities to clean their negative historical trust records [11].

3   The Credibility Model

Since the trust behavior of a cloud service is represented by a collection of invocation history records that contain cloud service consumers' trust feedbacks, there is a considerable possibility of TMS receiving *fake* trust feedbacks from vicious cloud service consumers. To overcome these issues, we propose a *credibility model*, which considers several factors including the *Feedback Density* and the *Multi-Identity Recognition*.

Feedback Density. Some malicious cloud service consumers may give numerous fake trust feedbacks to manipulate trust results for cloud services (i.e.,*Self-promoting* and *Slandering* attacks). Several online reputation-based systems such as eBay[1] have used the number of trusted feedbacks to help their consumers to overcome such attacks. The number of trusted feedbacks gives the evaluator a

---

[1] http://www.ebay.com/

hint in determining the feedback credibility [16]. However, the number of trust feedbacks is not enough in determining the credibility of trust feedbacks because a *Self-promoting* attack might have been performed on cloud services.

In order to overcome this problem, we introduce the concept of *Feedback Density* to support the determination of credible trust feedbacks. Specifically, we consider the total number of cloud service consumers who gave trust feedbacks to a particular cloud service as the *Feedback Mass*, the total number of trust feedbacks given to the cloud service as the *Feedback Volume*. The feedback volume is influenced by the *Feedback Volume Collusion* factor which is controlled by a specified volume collusion threshold. This factor regulates the multiple trust feedbacks extent that could collude the overall trust feedback volume. For instance, if the volume collusion threshold is set to 5 feedbacks, any cloud service consumer c who gives more than 5 feedbacks is considered to be suspicious of involving in a feedback volume collusion. The feedback density of a certain cloud service s, $\mathcal{D}(s)$, is calculated as follows:

$$\mathcal{D}(s) = \frac{\mathcal{M}(s)}{|\mathcal{V}(s)| * \mathcal{L}(s)} \tag{3}$$

where $\mathcal{M}(s)$ denotes the total number of cloud service consumers who gave trust feedbacks to the cloud service s (i.e., the *Feedback Mass*). $|\mathcal{V}(s)|$ represents the total number of trust feedbacks given to the cloud service s (i.e., the *Feedback Volume*). $\mathcal{L}(s)$ represents the *Feedback Volume Collusion* factor, calculated as follows:

$$\mathcal{L}(s) = 1 + \left(\frac{\sum_{h \in \mathcal{V}(s)} \left(\sum_{c=1}^{|\mathcal{V}_c(c,s)|} \left(\sum_{|\mathcal{V}_c(c,s)| > e_v(s)} |\mathcal{V}_c(c,s)| \right) \right)}{|\mathcal{V}(s)|} \right) \tag{4}$$

This factor is calculated as the ratio of the number of trust feedbacks given by cloud service consumers $|\mathcal{V}_c(c,s)|$ who give feedbacks more than the specified volume collusion threshold $e_v(s)$ over the total number of trust feedbacks received by the cloud service $|\mathcal{V}(s)|$. The idea is to reduce the value of the multiple trust feedbacks which are given diversely from the same cloud service consumer.

For instance, suppose there are two different cloud services x and y. Both cloud services have the same total number of trust feedbacks (i.e., $|\mathcal{V}(x)| = 150$ and $|\mathcal{V}(y)| = 150$) and very close aggregated feedbacks (e.g., x has 89% positive feedbacks and y has 92% positive feedbacks). However, the *Feedback Mass* of the cloud service x is higher than the cloud service y (i.e., $\mathcal{M}(x) = 20$ and $\mathcal{M}(y) = 5$). If the volume collusion threshold e_v is set to 10 feedbacks per cloud service consumer. Only 4 cloud service consumers gave more than 10 feedbacks to the cloud service x where the total number of their trust feedbacks $|\mathcal{V}_c(c,x)| = 60$ feedbacks; while 2 cloud service consumers gave more than 10 feedbacks to the cloud service y where the total number of their trust feedbacks $|\mathcal{V}_c(c,y)| == 136$ feedbacks. According to Equation 3, the *Feedback Density* of the cloud service x is higher than cloud service y (i.e., $\mathcal{D}(x) = 0.0953$ and $\mathcal{D}(y) = 0.0175$).

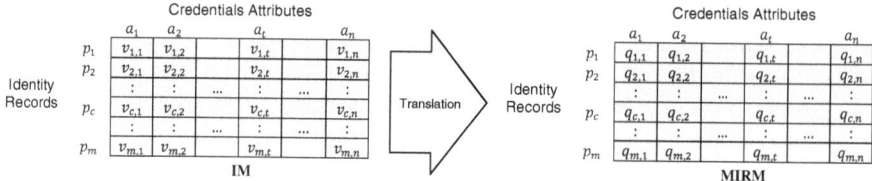

Fig. 1. IM Translation to MIRM

In other words, the higher the *Feedback Density*, the more credible the aggregated feedbacks are (i.e.,the higher possibility of collusion if vice versa).

Multi-Identity Recognition. Since the cloud service consumers have to register their credentials at the *Trust Identity Registry*, we believe that there is a possibility of a *Multi-Identity Recognition* by comparing the cloud service consumers' credentials attributes values from the identity records $\mathcal{I}$. The main goal in the multi-identity recognition factor is to protect TMS from malicious cloud service consumers who use multiple identities (i.e., *Whitewashing* and *Sybil* attacks) to manipulate the trust results. In a typical *Trust Identity Registry*, the entire identity records $\mathcal{I}$ are represented as a list of m cloud service consumers' primary identities $\mathcal{C}_p = \{p_1, p_2, ..., p_m\}$ (e.g., user name) and a list of n credentials' attributes $\mathcal{C}_a = \{a_1, a_2, ..., a_n\}$ (e.g., passwords, postal address, IP address, computer name, etc.). In other words, the entire $\mathcal{C}_p \times \mathcal{C}_a$ (Cloud Service Consumer's Primary Identity-Credentials' Attributes) Matrix, denoted as IM, covers all cloud service consumers who registered their credentials in TMS. The credential attribute value for a particular cloud service consumer $v_{c,t}$ is stored in TMS without including credentials with sensitive information using ZKC2P as mentioned earlier in Section 2.

We believe that TMS can identify patterns in cloud service consumers' anonymous credentials. There is a high possibility that malicious cloud service consumers use similar credentials in different identity records $\mathcal{I}$. Thus, we translate IM to the *Multi-Identity Recognition Matrix*, denoted as $MIRM$, which similarly covers the entire identity records $\mathcal{I}$ represented as the entire $\mathcal{C}_p \times \mathcal{C}_a$. However, the value for a particular cloud service consumer $q_{c,t}$ in the new matrix represents the frequency of the credential attribute value for the same particular cloud service consumer $v_{c,t}$ in the same credential attribute as shown in Figure 1.

The frequency $q_{c,t}$ of a particular credential attribute value $v_{c,t}$ is calculated as the times of appearance $\mathcal{A}_p$ that the credential value appears in the tth credential attribute normalized by the total number of identity records (i.e., the length of a_t) as follows:

$$q_{c,t} = \frac{\sum_{c=1}^{c=m} (\mathcal{A}_p(v_{c,t}))}{|a_t|} \qquad (5)$$

Then, the *Multi-Identity Recognition* factor $\mathcal{M}_{id}$ is calculated as the sum of frequencies of each credential attribute value for a particular cloud service consumer normalized by the total number of identity record as follows:

$$\mathcal{M}_{id}(c) = 1 - \left(\sum_{t=1}^{t=n} q_{c,t}\right) \tag{6}$$

where the sum of $q_{c,t}$ represents the similar credentials distributed over different identity records $\mathcal{I}$ and $\mathcal{M}_{id}(c)$ represents the opposite (i.e., at least that the cloud service consumer has fairly unique credentials).

Based on the specified trust feedback credibility factors (i.e., feedback density and multi-identity recognition), TMS distinguishes between credible trust feedbacks and fake ones through assigning the credibility aggregated weights $\mathcal{C}_r(c, s)$ to each trust feedback as shown in Equation 2. $\mathcal{C}_r(c, s)$ is calculated as follows:

$$\mathcal{C}_r(c, s) = \frac{\rho * \mathcal{D}(s) + \Omega * \mathcal{M}_{id}(c)}{\lambda} \tag{7}$$

where ρ and $\mathcal{D}(s)$ denote the *Feedback Density* factor's normalized weight (i.e., parameter) and the factor's value respectively. The second part of the equation represents the *Multi-Identity Recognition* factor where Ω denotes the factor's normalized weight and $\mathcal{M}_{id}(c)$ denotes the factor's value. λ represents the number of factors used to calculate $\mathcal{C}_r(c, s)$. For example, if we only consider feedback density, λ will be 1; if we consider both the feedback density and the multi-identity recognition, λ will be 2.

4   Implementation and Experimental Evaluation

In this section, we report the *Trust Management Service's* architecture and implementation. The trust management service's architecture evolved from our previous efforts in the *Trust as a Service* (TaaS) framework [14]. Figure 2 depicts the main components of the architecture. The *Providers* component represent the cloud service providers who provide cloud services such as Infrastructure as a Service (IaaS), Platform as a Service (PaaS) and Software as a Service (SaaS). The *Consumers* component represent the cloud service consumers who rent cloud services. The *Registry Service* component allows cloud service providers to advertise their services through the service registry and allows both the trust management service and cloud service consumers to access the service registry to discover cloud services. The *Identity Management Service* component manages cloud service consumers' identity records. The *Trust Management Service* component consists of four layers. The *Trust Data Provisioning* layer discovers the cloud services ID through the *Cloud Services ID Discoverer* module, collects cloud service consumers' trust feedbacks using the *Trust Feedbacks Collector* module and request cloud service consumers' credentials using the *Zero-Knowledge Credibility Proof Protocol* (ZKC2P) module. The *Trust Assessment Function* layer requests and translates anonymized credentials and recognizes multiple identities using the

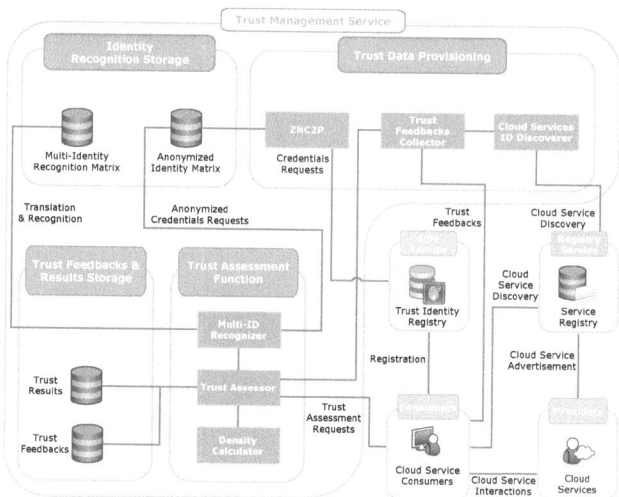

Fig. 2. System Architecture

Multi-ID Recognizer module, calculates the feedback density using the *Density Calculator* module and handle trust queries from cloud service consumers and assesses the trustworthiness of a particular cloud service using the *Trust Assessor* module. The *Identity Recognition Storage* layer stores the anonymized identity matrix and the Multi-Identity recognition matrix. The *Trust Feedbacks and Results Storage* layer stores trust feedbacks from cloud service consumers and trust results for cloud services.

Since it is hard to find some publicly available real-life trust data sets and user credentials, in our experiments, we used Epinions[2] rating data set which was collected by Massa and Avesani [13] and augmented a set of credentials for each corresponding user in Epinions rating data set. The data set has 49,290 users, 139,738 items and 664,824 trust feedbacks. We choose Epinions data set because it is similar in data structure (i.e., consumers' opinions on specific products and services) with our cloud service consumer trust feedbacks. In particular, we considered user_id in Epinions as the cloud service consumer's primary identity $\mathcal{C}$, item_id as the cloud service's identity $\mathcal{S}$ and we normalized the rating_value as the cloud service consumers' trust feedbacks $\mathcal{F}$ to scale $[0, 1]$.

To validate the applicability of our approach, we have imported the Epinions data set for a set of randomly selected cloud services that we are intending to analyze and the number of cloud service consumers is set to one hundred. We evaluate the trust robustness of our credibility model against malicious behaviors of the cloud service consumers. In particular, we conducted experiments under two settings of malicious behaviors namely: the *Feedback Collusion Behavior* and the *Multiplicity of Identities Behavior*. In the *Feedback Collusion Behavior* setting, we aggregate trust results for the cloud services for 10 rounds by varying

---

[2] http://www.trustlet.org/wiki/Downloaded_Epinions_dataset

Table 1. Experiment Factors and Parameters Setup

Experiment Design	ρ	Ω	λ	$Cr(c,s)$
With Credibility factors	1	1	2	
Without Credibility factors				1
Feedback Density factor	1	0	1	
Multi-Identity Recognition factor	0	1	1	

the number of feedbacks by 10% of each round (i.e., *Malicious Behavior Rate*) in which cloud service consumers act dishonestly to manipulate the trust result of the selected cloud services (i.e., the *Self-promoting* attack and the *Slandering* attack). Similarly, in the *Multiplicity of Identities Behavior* setting, we aggregate trust results for the cloud services for 10 rounds by varying the number of cloud service consumers by 10% of each round (i.e., *Multiplicity of Identities Behavior Rate*) in which cloud service consumers act dishonestly by using multiple identities to manipulate trust results of the selected cloud services (i.e., the *Whitewashing* attack and the *Sybil* attack).

To evaluate the trust robustness of our credibility model (i.e., with respect to *Malicious Behavior Rate* and *Multiplicity of Identities Behavior*), we use two experimental designs namely: i) measuring the trust result robustness for each factor in our credibility model including the *Feedback Density* and the *Multi-Identity Recognition*, and ii) measuring the trust result robustness with credibility factors and without the credibility factors (i.e., turning $\mathcal{C}_r(c,s)$ to 1 for all trust feedbacks). The parameters setup for each corresponding experiment factor is depicted in Table 1.

Feedback Collusion Behavior. Figure 3(a) shows the trust result robustness for each factor in our credibility model including the *Feedback Density* and the *Multi-Identity Recognition*. We can observe that the higher the feedback collusion behavior rate, the lower the trust results when considering to calculate the trust based on the feedback density factor only. On the other hand, the trust results show nearly no change to the feedback collusion behavior rate when considering to calculate the trust based on the multi-identity recognition factor. This is true because the malicious cloud service consumers manipulate trust results only through giving multiple fake trust feedbacks. Figure 3(b) depicts the trust result robustness with our proposed credibility factors and without the credibility factors. We note that the higher the feedback collusion behavior rate the lower trust results are when considering to calculate the trust with all credibility factors. We also note that trust results do not differ much when obtained without considering the credibility factors. This indicates that cloud service consumers may make bad decisions by choosing untrustworthy cloud services instead of trustworthy ones when not taking the credibility factors into account. As a result, our credibility model is robust and more sensitive in detecting the feedback collusion behaviors because of the feedback density factor.

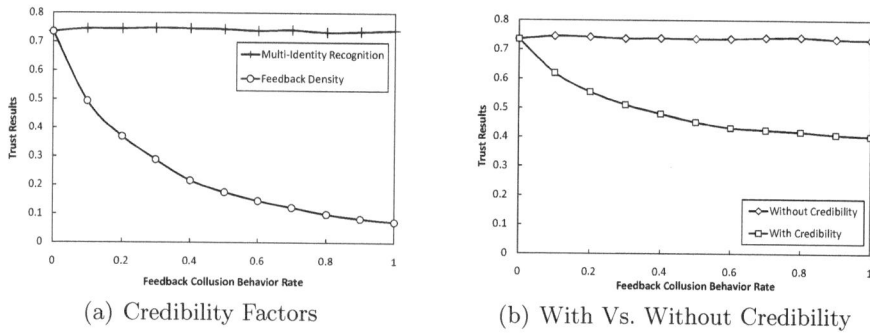

(a) Credibility Factors   (b) With Vs. Without Credibility

Fig. 3. Feedback Collusion Behavior

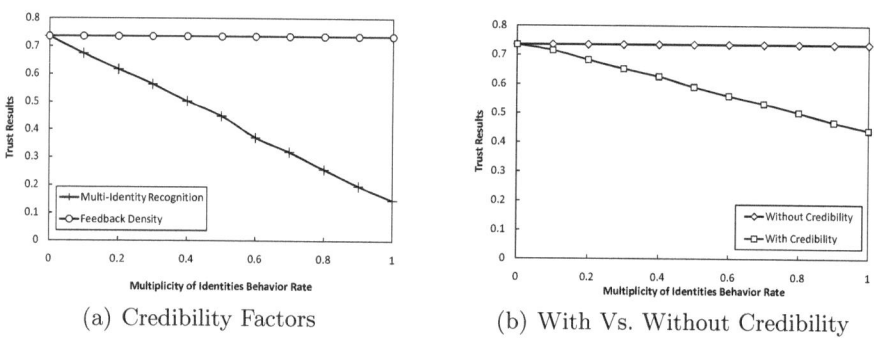

(a) Credibility Factors   (b) With Vs. Without Credibility

Fig. 4. Multiplicity of Identities Behavior

Multiplicity of Identities Behavior. Figure 4(a) shows the trust result robustness for each factor in our credibility model including the *Feedback Density* and the *Multi-Identity Recognition*. We can see that trust results are not affected by the multiplicity of identities behavior rate when calculated based on the feedback density factor only. However, the trust results are very sensitive to the multiplicity of identities behavior rate and drops almost linearly when calculated based on the multi-identity recognition factor only. This is because the malicious cloud service consumers manipulate trust results only through using multiple identities. Figure 4(b) depicts the trust result robustness with credibility factors and without the credibility factors. We can observe that trust results response effectively to the multiplicity of identities behavior rate when calculating the trust using the proposed credibility factors, which are not the case when the proposed credibility factors are not considered. This means that without using our proposed credibility factors, a trust management system can be easily fooled by malicious cloud service consumers who create multiple accounts and quickly leave fake trust feedbacks. As a result, based on the experimental results, we can see that our proposed credibility model can effectively detect multiplicity of identities behaviors.

5   Discussions and Conclusion

Trust management is considered as one of the important issues in cloud computing and is becoming a very active research area in recent years. Several research works have proposed trust management techniques such as policy-based trust management. Brandic et al. [5] proposed a compliant management approach to help cloud service consumers to choose trustworthy cloud services. The approach is developed using a centralized architecture to establish trust between cloud service consumers and cloud service providers. Hwang et al. [10] proposed a security aware cloud architecture that assess the trust for both the cloud service provider and the cloud service consumers. To assess the trustworthiness of cloud service providers, they developed a trust negotiation and data coloring (integration) approach using fuzzy logic techniques. To assess the trustworthiness of cloud service consumers, they exploited the Distributed-Hash-Table (DHT)-based trust-overlay networks among several data centers to deploy a reputation-based trust management technique. Unlike previous works which did not consider the problem of fake trust feedbacks or require extensive computations and the trust participants' collaboration by rating trust feedbacks, we present a credibility model that include several metrics namely the *Feedback Density* and the *Multi-Identity Recognition* that assess cloud services' trustworthiness and identify credible trust feedbacks from fake ones.

Other research works have proposed trust management techniques such as reputation-based trust management. Malik and Bouguettaya [12] proposed several reputation metrics to assess the credibility of the rater such as personal experience for credibility evaluation, majority rating, past rating history, etc. The authors also proposed reputation assessment techniques for Web services based on the existing quality of service (QoS) parameters. Conner et al. [6] focused on assessing the trustworthiness of service requesters by proposing a trust management framework for the service-oriented architecture (SOA). This framework has a decentralized architecture that offers multiple trust evaluation metrics, allowing service providers to have customized evaluations. Unlike previous works, we were inspired by Xiong and Liu who differentiate between the credibility of a peer and the credibility of a feedback [16]. However, their approach is not applicable in cloud environments because peers supply and consume services and they are evaluated on that base. Our work was also inspired by Bertino et al. [4] in developing ZKC2P and the use of zero knowledge proofs but instead of using it for verification purposes, ZKC2P is used to measure the feedback credibility.

In the future, we plan to deal with more challenging problems in trust management such as occasional and periodic attacks detection. We also plan to identify new patterns in cloud service consumers' behaviors that can potentially help identify credible trust feedbacks from the fake ones. The performance optimization of the trust management service is another focus of our future work.

Acknowledgments. Talal H. Noor and Abdullah Alfazi work has been supported by King Abdullah's Postgraduate Scholarships, the Ministry of Higher Education: Kingdom of Saudi Arabia.

References

1. Akwagyiram, A.: How Do You Catch Online Auction Cheats? The British Broadcasting Corporation News (BBC) (July 2010),
   http://www.bbc.co.uk/news/10494724 (accessed May 16, 2012)
2. Armbrust, M., Fox, A., Griffith, R., Joseph, A., Katz, R., Konwinski, A., Lee, G., Patterson, D., Rabkin, A., Stoica, I., Zaharia, M.: A View of Cloud Computing. Communications of the ACM 53(4), 50–58 (2010)
3. Ba, S., Pavlou, P.: Evidence of the Effect of Trust Building Technology in Electronic Markets: Price Premiums and Buyer Behavior. MIS Quarterly 26(3), 243–268 (2002)
4. Bertino, E., Paci, F., Ferrini, R., Shang, N.: Privacy-preserving Digital Identity Management for Cloud Computing. IEEE Data Eng. Bull. 32(1), 21–27 (2009)
5. Brandic, I., Dustdar, S., Anstett, T., Schumm, D., Leymann, F., Konrad, R.: Compliant Cloud Computing (C3): Architecture and Language Support for User-Driven Compliance Management in Clouds. In: Proc. of CLOUD 2010, Miami, Florida, USA (July 2010)
6. Conner, W., Iyengar, A., Mikalsen, T., Rouvellou, I., Nahrstedt, K.: A Trust Management Framework for Service-Oriented Environments. In: Proc. of WWW 2009, Madrid, Spain (April 2009)
7. David, O., Jaquet, C.: Trust and Identification in the Light of Virtual Persons (June 2009),
   http://www.fidis.net/resources/deliverables/identity-of-identity/ (accessed May 10, 2012)
8. Douceur, J.R.: The Sybil Attack. In: Druschel, P., Kaashoek, M.F., Rowstron, A. (eds.) IPTPS 2002. LNCS, vol. 2429, pp. 251–260. Springer, Heidelberg (2002)
9. Friedman, E., Resnick, P., Sami, R.: Manipulation-Resistant Reputation Systems. In: Algorithmic Game Theory, pp. 677–697. Cambridge University Press, New York, USA (2007)
10. Hwang, K., Li, D.: Trusted Cloud Computing with Secure Resources and Data Coloring. IEEE Internet Computing 14(5), 14–22 (2010)
11. Lai, K., Feldman, M., Stoica, I., Chuang, J.: Incentives for Cooperation in Peer-to-Peer Networks. In: Proc. of the 1st Workshop on Economics of Peer-to-Peer Systems, Berkeley, CA, USA (June 2003)
12. Malik, Z., Bouguettaya, A.: RATEWeb: Reputation Assessment for Trust Establishment Among Web Services. The VLDB Journal 18(4), 885–911 (2009)
13. Massa, P., Avesani, P.: Trust Metrics in Recommender Systems. In: Computing with Social Trust. Human-Computer Interaction Series. Springer
14. Noor, T.H., Sheng, Q.Z.: Trust as a Service: A Framework for Trust Management in Cloud Environments. In: Bouguettaya, A., Hauswirth, M., Liu, L. (eds.) WISE 2011. LNCS, vol. 6997, pp. 314–321. Springer, Heidelberg (2011)
15. Pearson, S., Benameur, A.: Privacy, Security and Trust Issues Arising From Cloud Computing. In: Proc. of CloudCom 2010, Indianapolis, Indiana, USA (November-December 2010)
16. Xiong, L., Liu, L.: Peertrust: Supporting Reputation-based Trust for Peer-to-Peer Electronic Communities. IEEE TKDE 16(7), 843–857 (2004)

Sonata: A Workflow Model
for Interactive Mobile Cloud Applications

Verdi March, Yan Gu, and Bu Sung Lee

Cloud Intelligence Lab, Hewlett-Packard Laboratories Singapore
{verdi.march,chloe.yan.gu,francis.lee}@hp.com

Abstract. Workflow is a well-established approach to visually compose large and complex applications out of components. However, existing workflow models do not provide high-level abstractions of two recurring user-interaction patterns in mobile cloud applications, namely backtracking and interactive controls. In this paper, we propose *Sonata*, a workflow model that provides high-level abstractions for implicit and structured backtracking, and interactive controls. We prototype a workflow engine for Android devices and another for a RESTful cloud service platform, each of which orchestrates the execution of mobile components and cloud services, respectively. Choreography between the mobile orchestrator and cloud orchestrator is implemented on top of HTTP using REST-style invocations. An example application workflow incorporating all our proposed constructs is further elaborated.

Keywords: implicit backtracking, structured workflow, interactive control, orchestration, choreography.

1 Introduction

The convergence of mobile and cloud leads to the emergence of mobile cloud applications [6]. A mobile cloud application is composed of cloud services and tasks running on end-point devices (e.g., smartphones, tablets, laptops, and future smart devices). As the number of features in applications increase, the complexity of application development needs to be managed. At present, the industries largely adopt the workflow paradigm to simplify the design, configuration, customization, management, and maintenance of complex applications such as in SOA (service-oriented architecture) [9,8] and big data processing [3,1,5,4]. In this paradigm, an application is viewed as a composition of independent components with a pre-defined execution flow among the components. A component is a self-contained building blocks of an application which, depending on the domain, can range from fine-grained objects (e.g., Java beans and Microsoft COM) to loosely-coupled services (e.g., web or cloud services).

To simplify the application development, high-level abstractions should be provided for two interaction patterns which are commonly found in mobile cloud applications, namely *backtracking* and *interactive control*. Backtracking, supported in all generations of mobile devices, enables the user of an application to

A. Ghose et al. (Eds.): ICSOC 2012, LNCS 7759, pp. 59–71, 2013.

instruct the application to go from one component to another. Interactive control enables the user to directly instruct which component to execute. As an illustration, consider an application for uploading an image to a social-networking website. This application consists of a *gallery* component, a *site selector* component, and a number of *image uploader* components. When the application is invoked, the *gallery* component displays a list of images stored on the phone. The user interacts with the application by selecting an image. This selection triggers a transition to the *site selector* component, which displays the selected image and the list of available social-networking websites. At this point, the user can press the back button of her device to backtrack to the *gallery* component. Alternatively, the user selects the website to publish the selected image (i.e., the interactive control pattern), which further trigger the execution of the appropriate *image uploader* component.

To the best of our knowledge, existing workflow models do not provide high-level abstractions for the above mentioned interactive patterns. *Forward-only models* such as MapReduce [3], Hadoop [1], and Dryad [5] do not support backtracking. *Explicit models* such as BPMN [9] and SPL [4] require the patterns to be implemented explicitly using low-level constructs such as backward edges and gateway nodes. Although Sarasvati supports *arbitrary backtracking* whereby any component can backtrack to any ancestor [2], it may lead to an ambiguous execution state (see Section 4), let alone interactive controls.

This paper proposes *Sonata*, our proposed approach to model the backtracking and interactive control in mobile cloud applications. It is motivated by a simple premise whereby the probability for composition error can be decreased by reducing the number of explicit constructs. Thus, instead of backward edges and gateway nodes, Sonata indicates backtracking by assigning tags to components. We also propose a structure of mobile cloud applications that are free from arbitrary backtracking to guarantee that workflow execution does not enter an ambiguous state. Lastly, Sonata proposes two specific interactive controls, namely *chooser* and *iterator*. We demonstrate the feasibility of Sonata by composing a face recognition application using Android components and RESTful cloud services. Our prototype runtime platform consists of a workflow engine for Android (written in Python) to orchestrate mobile components, a server-side workflow engine (written in Java and MySQL) to orchestrate cloud services, and a REST-based scheme to choreograph these two engines.

The remainder of this paper is organized as follows. Firstly, we compare Sonata with existing workflow models (Section 2). We then describe the interaction patterns in mobile cloud applications(Section 3), followed by our proposed work (Section 4). Afterwards, we describe our prototype (Section 5) and an application use case (Section 6). Lastly, we conclude this paper (Section 7).

2 Related Work

In terms of backtracking, existing workflow models can be classified as forward-only models, explicit models, and arbitrary models.

By design, forward-only models such as MapReduce [3], Hadoop [1], and Dryad [5] do not support backtracking. Hence, they are not suitable for mobile cloud applications in which users may request the application to transition from the current GUI state to a preceding GUI state.

Explicit models such as BPMN [9] and SPL [4] require backtracking to be explicitly specified for every pair of nodes where backtracking may occur. Hence, design scalability is a significant issue since the number of backward edges and gateway nodes (see Section 3.1) increases with the number of components in a workflow. Because the semantic of workflow is left to workflow designers, it is possible to inadvertently create a syntactically correct workflow yet semantically incorrect (see Section 4 for the detail discussion).

Arbitrary models such as Sarasvati [2] do not guarantee that workflow execution remains unambiguous. Sarasvati is programming toolkit to develop Java-based workflow [2]. It does not come with a model to visually compose a new workflow. Sarasvati supports only unstructured backtracking whereby any node can backtrack to an arbitrary ancestor. Therefore, it is prone to the time-travel paradox which is discussed in detail in Section 3.2. Lastly, Sarasvati does not support interactive controls which are an integral part of mobile cloud applications.

Existing workflow models target batch executions, whereby the next component to execute in a conditional execution is automatically triggered based on messages or events generated. No human intervention is required. Hence, conditional executions are implemented using programming-like constructs such as if-else, loop, scoping and fork-and-join. Scripting is typically involved, e.g., to specify the conditional logic of if-else or loop. However, mobile cloud applications are interactive. As such, they include use cases where the next component to execute is solely determined by users, rather being automatically inferred. Hence, implementing the inherently high-level user interactions is unnecessarily complicated. For example, interactive iteration is modeled using a combination of backward edges, explicit marker of the scope of iteration, and filtering rules scripted by application designer in the design time, so that during runtime, applications can automatically decide when to an iteration completes. In contrast to these existing approach, Sonata simply represents an interactive control as a single component, thereby, simplifying the resulted workflow.

3 Design Objectives

Mobile cloud applications are interactive: they wait for input from users, and then perform action based on the input. We identify two common patterns of interactions between users and mobile devices, namely backtracking and interactive controls. A desirable property of high-level abstraction is to minimize the number of explicit constructs to implement the patterns, since this reduces the probability of composition errors. In the followings, we discuss this subject in details.

Fig. 1. Backtracking Interface in Mobile Devices

3.1   Backtracking

Backtracking is inherent in interactive mobile applications, as evident throughout device generations (Figure 1). Backtracking enables applications to go back from one GUI-enabled state to a previous GUI-enabled state. A high-level abstraction of backtracking should address the following issues.

Firstly, it should minimize the number of mandatory constructs required to represent a backtracking step. In explicit models, every backtracking from c to c' (Figure 2a) requires one explicit backward edges and a gateway node (Figure 2b). The gateway node represents the step whereby devices wait for user input. Hence, the number of backward edges and gateway nodes increase as the number of components where backtracking is possible grow.

Secondly, the high-level abstraction must enforce valid backtracking whereby backtracking occurs only between interactive nodes which wait for user input (Figure 3). A backtracking from c to c' can be triggered only if c waits for users to press the back button. Hence, c must be interactive which implies that c has a GUI. When c' is visited, the application displays the state pertaining to c' and waits for user input. This also implies that c' must also be interactive. Should c' is non-interactive, e.g., a cloud service or a logic-only mobile component, then users will perceive that the back button is ignored as c' will execute and immediately the application state returns to c. A low-level abstraction may produce workflows that are syntactically correct but semantically incorrect (i.e., the three invalid

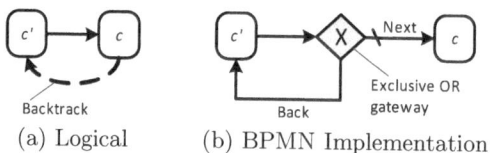

(a) Logical   (b) BPMN Implementation

Fig. 2. Backtracking and its Explicit Implementation

Fig. 3. Valid versus Invalid Backtracking (with GUI Symbols Added for Clarity

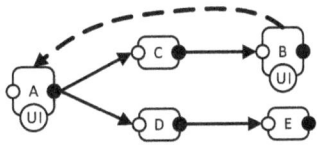

Fig. 4. Time Travel Paradox

backtracking illustrated in Figure 3. It is desirable that such workflows can be prevented by using a high-level abstraction.

Lastly, the high-level abstraction must prevent *time-travel paradox*. This paradox occurs when backtracking causes only a subset of a node's parents to be re-executed. Figure 4 shows a workflow which generates the time-travel paradox. Assume that a backtracking path is defined from B to A. The sequence of workflow execution that leads to the paradox is as follows:

1. Node A completes its execution.
2. Node C and D start their execution.
3. Suppose that before node D completes, node C already finished its execution and node B starts to execute.
4. Node B receives a backtracking command from user. Thus, we backtrack to node A. All the while, node D is still executing.
5. Node A is re-executed. After its completion, node C and D should be re-executed. However, recall that node D is still executing (i.e., from the previous iteration/wave). At this point, time-travel paradox occurs on node D.

To solve the paradox, either:

1. node D cancels its execution from the previous iteration, or
2. after node D completes its execution from previous iteration, node E is executed. Then, node D is re-executed again (i.e., the current/new iteration), which implies that later node E will also be re-executed.

However, the appropriate solution depends on the context of the applications, and explicit notations increases the workflow complexity. Hence, a simpler solution based on preventive strategy is required(Section 4).

3.2   Interactive Controls

Interactive control enables application users to control the execution path of applications. Two types of interactive controls are identified in mobile applications (Figure 5). Firstly, when a workflow forks into multiple disjoint execution paths, users may want to select only one particular path. This is illustrated by the example in (Figure 5a). To other interactive control is iteration (Figure 5b). Iteration enables a list of data items of the same type to be consumed by a node designed to process only one item at a time. When a producer outputs outputs a list of data items, a mobile device will request its users to select a particular data

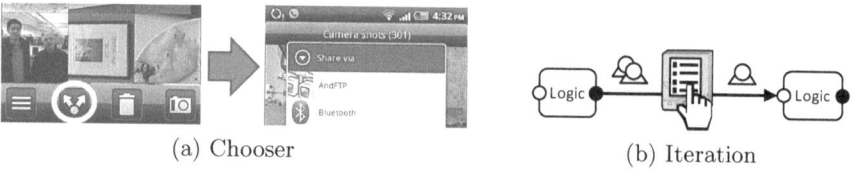

(a) Chooser   (b) Iteration

Fig. 5. Interactive Control in Mobile Applications

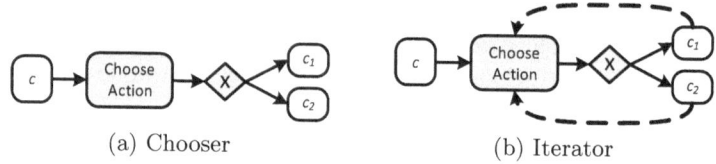

(a) Chooser   (b) Iterator

Fig. 6. Modeling Interactive Controls with BPMN

item from the list. Then, the selected data item is forwarded to the consumer which is designed to accept only one data item per invocation.

The motivation for a high-level abstraction is similar as in the case of backtracking. Firstly, we aim to minimizes the number of edges and gateway nodes (Figure 6). Secondly, we aim to prevent workflows that are syntactically correct but semantically incorrect. For examples, the exlusive OR gateway may be inadvertently replaced with a parallel fork/join, or when the backward edges are removed from an iterator such that it degenerates to a chooser.

4   Proposed Workflow Model

We propose Sonata, a workflow model for interactive mobile cloud applications which are composed of cloud services and tasks running on mobile devices. A workflow is modeled as a directed graph where each node represents a cloud service or a task on a mobile device, and each directed edge represents control and data flow between nodes. The key novelties of Sonata are: (i) implicit backtracking based on node types, (ii) structured workflow to prevent the time-travel paradox, and (iii) interactive control nodes.

Sonata infers backability from the types of nodes (Figure 7); thus, obviating the need for backward directed edges and additional gateway nodes (see Figure 2). Nodes are classified along two dimensions: (i) *interactive* versus *non-interactive*, and (ii) *backtrackable* versus *non-backtrackable*. Interactive components provides a GUI to allow user interaction during execution. On the contrary, non-interactive components do not allow user interaction during their execution. Only mobile components are interactive because users directly interact with mobile devices (i.e., the client-side). On the other hand, cloud services, by definition, are server-side components accessed programmatically by mobile components. Only backtrackable nodes can be re-visited by its interactive successor. Backtrackable are further sub-classed into *backable* and *bookmarked*. A backable node

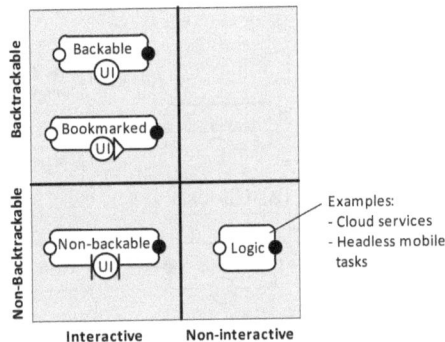

Fig. 7. Taxonomy and visual notation of nodes

can be re-visited only by its *immediate* interactive successor. Backable is the default type for interactive nodes. However, this behavior can be overriden by tagging an interactive node as a bookmarked node so that it can be re-visited by any of its interactive descendants. The bookmark sub-type is intended for larger-screen devices (e.g., tablets, notebooks and desktops) as additional navigation index can be displayed without obscuring the GUI content of a component. With our proposed approach, mobile cloud application workflows remain succinct and elegant, and are clean from redundant backward edges. Notice that in using our classification, the location of a component (i.e., mobile or cloud) is optional so that we do not need to explicitly mark whether a component is mobile or cloud.

To address the time-travel paradox, Sonata adopts a prevention strategy to prevent such an ambiguity to occur. The time-travel paradox occurs due to the structure of a directed graph is arbitrary. Hence, to prevent the paradox, Sonata enforces a *structure* whereby a Sonata workflow is structured as a critical path consisting of a sequence of interactive nodes and region of logic nodes (Figure 8). Each interactive node has at most one interactive successor (see the left-side workflow in Figure 8). Logic nodes between consecutive interactive nodes are grouped in a region, and synchronization barriers are imposed at the entrance and exit of each region (see the right-hand-side workflow in Figure 8). Sonata structure is reasonable for mobile cloud applications. The critical path denotes that interactive nodes must be executed in sequence. This makes sense in mobile devices since concurrent interactive nodes will compete for the device screen to display their GUI, and yet device screen is relatively limited for sophisticated UI mash-up.

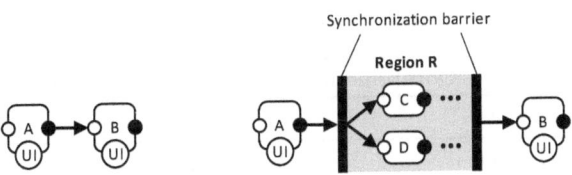

Fig. 8. Structure of Sonata Workflow

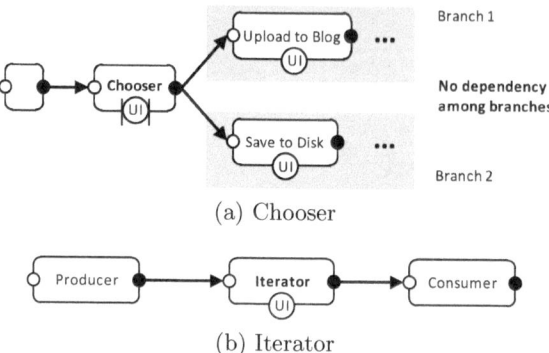

(a) Chooser

(b) Iterator

Fig. 9. Interactive Control Nodes

Sonata defines two interactive control structures, namely chooser (Figure 9a) and iterator (Figure 9b). Both accept user inputs from GUI during runtime, thereby, completely obviate the need for scripting and scoping in design time. Chooser is non-backable and equivalent to the XOR boolean operator. Chooser restricts users to select exactly one and only one execution path out of many during runtime to preserve the critical-path structure. Iterator enables a collection of data items of the same type to be processed by a node designed to process only one item at a time. As illustrated in Figure 9b, when face detection outputs a list of detected faces, the iterator will request users to select a particular face from the list. Then, the selected face is forwarded to face recognition which is designed to recognize one face at a time.

5   Preliminary Prototype

A workflow graph, implemented as a JSON object, is partitioned into a mobile partition and a cloud partition which contains Android-based mobile components and Java-based cloud components, respectively. Barriers and interactive controls within a workflow graph are implemented as built-in components (Table 1). The mobile partition and cloud partition is then executed by a mobile orchestrator and a cloud orchestrator, respectively (Figure 10). Choreography between these engines are implemented using RESTful invocations over HTTP. Within an orchestrator domain, component execution follows the master-and-slave paradigm whereby the orchestrator invokes one component after another,

Table 1. Built-in Components

Built-in Component	Type	Location
Barrier	Logic	Mobile
Chooser	Non-backable	Mobile
Iterator	Backable	Mobile

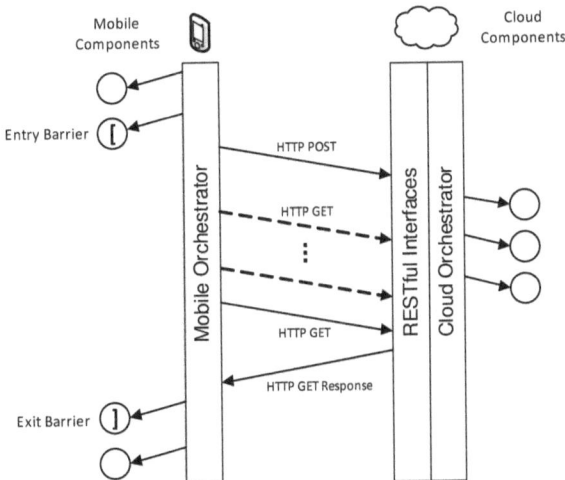

Fig. 10. Choreography between Mobile Orchestrator and Cloud Orchestrator

and data from one component must go through the orchestrator to the next component. The cloud orchestrator is implemented in Java and supports the execution of Java components. Intra-cloud invocations and data forwarding are implemented as native Java method invocations. The mobile orchestrator is implemented in Python using the SL4A[1] (Scripting Languages For Android) environment. Intra-device invocations and data forwarding are implemented via the Android's intent mechanism.

Each component specifies zero or more input and output parameters using `get(key)` and `set(key, value)` operation, respectively. The skeleton of a component is shown in Figure 11. The specific implementations of cloud components and mobile components are as follows:

- *Cloud Components* — We have developed a Java-based SDK to ease the development of cloud components. The SDK provides a framework for component life cycle and input/output APIs, and guarantees that components are re-entrant. A new cloud component is implemented by sub-classing the

```
Component c
    String i₁ = get("i₁");
    String i₂ = get("i₂");
    String o₁ = do_something(i₁, i₂);
    put("o₁");
    put("o₂");
```

Fig. 11. Skeleton of Component with Input $\{i_1, i_2\}$ and Output $\{o_1, o_2\}$

---

[1] http://code.google.com/p/android-scripting

Table 2. RESTful Interfaces of Cloud Component c with Workflow w

Method	URL	Description
POST	/w	Request a new session. Mandatory prior to executing w. Return handle **s**.
POST	/w/s	Start or resume the execution of cloud-portion of w.
POST	/w/s/c	Execute workflow w, starting from component c.
GET	/w/s/c/k	Retrieve output **k** emitted by component c. If the output is a blob object, returns a URL to the object to facilitate subsequent downloads.

CloudComponent class, and then overriding its activate() method with the specific functionality to be provided. Presently, keys are *strings*, whereas values can be *strings* or *blobs*. String values are transient and thus, they can be garbage collected when no longer referred to by any component. On the other hand, blob values are persisted as a file stored in a cloud storage. Components are transparently decorated with RESTful interface to ease their development (Table 2).

– *Mobile Components* — A mobile component is implemented as a native Android application (i.e., an apk package). Each mobile component is a subclass of Activity. Component input and output is implemented using the *Intents* mechanism[2]. In particular, the *get* and *set* operations are achieved using the intent's *extra* APIs in the Android application framework.

To handle state transitions from a mobile device to cloud and vice versa, we adopt the choreography approach whereby interactions between the orchestrator follow a peer-to-peer model (Figure 10), rather than being governed by a centralized entity. The transition from a mobile orchestrator to a cloud orchestrator is encapsulated in a multi-part/form-data HTTP POST request [7] /w/s or /w/s/c shown in Table 2. On the other hand, the transition from a cloud orchestrator to a mobile orchestrator is currently implemented using a pull mechanism. In this scheme, the mobile orchestrator periodically polls whether the cloud orchestrator has completed its execution. Once the cloud execution completes, the mobile orchestrator pulls the necessary data by sending an HTTP GET request /w/s/c/k (see Table 2) to the cloud orchestrator. In response, the cloud orchestrator serializes the data into JSON objects, then serves the serialized data to the mobile orchestrator. The mobile orchestrator then de-serializes the JSON objects before injecting the data to the appropriate mobile components. Polling the cloud orchestrator may be simpler to implement, but may increase the number of round trips. Thus, at the moment, a push-based mechanism is being considered. However, the issue of polling-vs-not is just a non-functional aspect of our implementation which does not affect the functionality the Sonata model.

---
[2] http://developer.android.com/guide/topics/intents/intents-filters.html

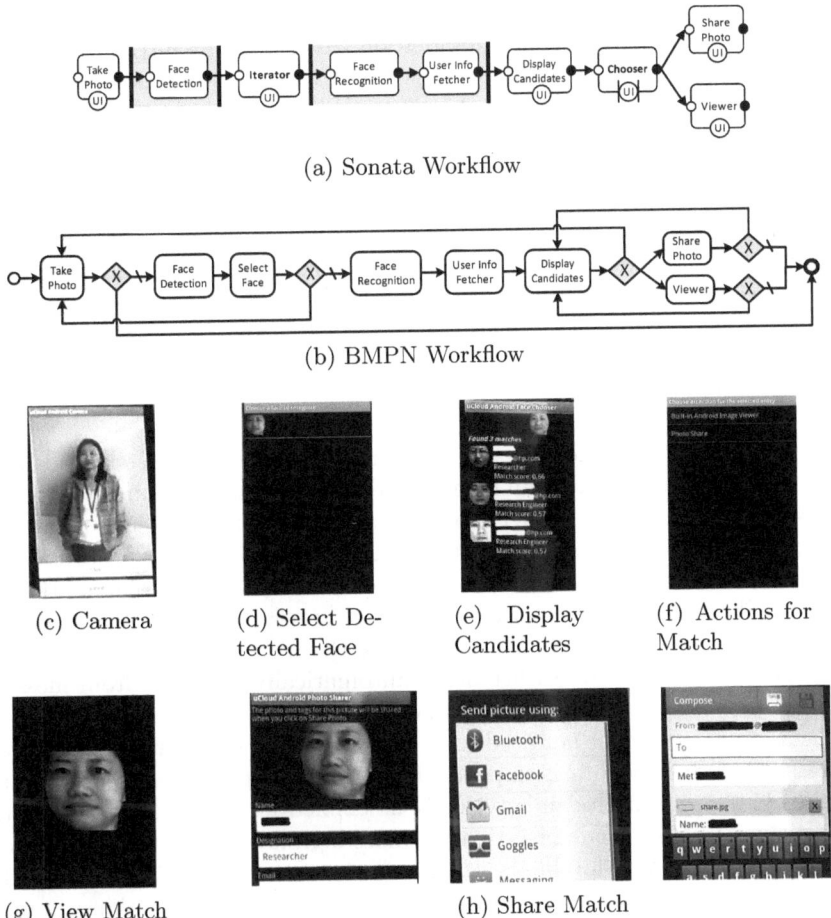

(a) Sonata Workflow

(b) BMPN Workflow

(c) Camera   (d) Select De-   (e)   Display   (f) Actions for
                  tected Face   Candidates   Match

(g) View Match   (h) Share Match

Fig. 12. Face Recognition Application

6   Use Case

Face Recognition enables a user to automatically retrieve the profile of a face
taken with an Android device. As can be seen in Figure 12a–12b, the Sonata
workflow is simpler than the BPMN one. The *Photo Snapper* snaps a photo by
engaging the embedded camera on the mobile phone (Figure 12c). The captured
photo will be sent to and processed by the *Face Detection* cloud service. This
cloud service detects faces in a photo based on the face detection algorithm
proposed by Tong et. al. [10]. The list of detected face images is forwarded to
the mobile device, and then displayed by the *Iterator* component Figure 12d.
Once a user selects the face image, the face image is forwarded to the *Face
Recognition* component. The *Face Recognition* component compares the face
image to available images in a database based on the face clustering algorithms in

Tong et al. [10]. It returns three images with the highest match scores, and their corresponding profile (i.e., name, designation, and email) are further retrieved by *User Info Fetcher*. The face image and profile of the three candidates (i.e., image faces and their profile) is forwarded to the mobile device to be displayed by the *Display* component (Figure 12e). Once a user select a candidate, the *Chooser* component displays two possible actions corresponding to the two successors of *Chooser*, namely *Share* and *Viewer* (Figure 12f. If the user chooses to view, then the *Viewer* component displays the selected candidate image in full-screen mode Figure 12g. Alternatively, if the user chooses to share, then the *Share* component will be invoked to (Figure 12h).

7   Conclusion

Our proposed workflow model is based on the simple premise whereby the probability for composition errors can be decreased by reducing the number of explicit constructs. Our workflow model supports implicit backtracking and interactive controls, which are two recurrent interactive patterns in mobile devices. Our workflow model imposes structured backtracking to prevent workflows that are syntactically correct but semantically incorrect. Interactive controls (i.e., chooser and iterator) are targeted at use cases where the next component to execute is solely determine by users, rather being automatically triggered from messages or events generated by a workflow engine. Therefore, during the design time, the application designer does not need to write the filtering rules with programmatic expressions. When Sonata is implemented into a workflow designer GUI, then mobile cloud application can be visually assembled in a drag-and-drop fashion. Our ongoing works include investigating more high-level constructs into Sonata, including abstractions for life-cycle management and streaming (i.e., tightly-coupled) operations between components. In addition, we are working on quantitative analysis of design scalability and workflow's runtime performance.

References

1. Apache Hadoop, `http://hadoop.apache.org`
2. Sarasvati, `http://code.google.com/p/sarasvati/`
3. Dean, J., Ghemawat, S.: MapReduce: Simplified data processing on large clusters. In: Proc. of OSDI (December 2004)
4. Hirzel, M., Andrade, H., Gedik, B., Kumar, V., Losa, G., Nasgaard, M.M.H., Soule, R., Wu, K.-L.: SPL stream processing language specification. Technical Report RC24897 (W0907-066), IBM Research Division (November 2009)
5. Isard, M., Budiu, M., Yu, Y., Birrell, A., Fetterly, D.: Dryad: Distributed data-parallel programs from sequential building blocks. In: Proc. of EuroSys (March 2007)
6. March, V., Gu, Y., Leonardi, E., Goh, G., Kirchberg, M., Lee, B.S.: μCloud: Towards a new paradigm of rich mobile applications. In: Proc. of MobiWIS (September 2011)

7. Nebel, E., Masinter, L.: RFC1867: Form-based file upload in HTML, http://www.ietf.org/rfc/rfc1867.txt

8. OASIS Standard Committee. Web Services Business Process Execution Language version 2.0 (2007),
http://docs.oasis-open.org/wsbpel/2.0/wsbpel-v2.0.html

9. Object Management Group. Business Process Model and Notation (BPMN) version 2.0 (January 2011), http://www.omg.org/spec/BPMN/2.0/PDF

10. Zhang, T., Xiao, J., Wen, D., Ding, X.: Face based image navigation and search. In: Proc. of the 17th ACM Intl. Conf. on Multimedia (MM), pp. 597–600 (March 2009)

Kachako: A Hybrid-Cloud Unstructured Information Platform for Full Automation of Service Composition, Scalable Deployment and Evaluation

Natural Language Processing as an Example

Yoshinobu Kano

PRESTO, Japan Science and Technology Agency (JST), Japan
kano@kachako.org

Abstract. Automation is the key concept when designing a service platform, because automation could reduce human's work. Focusing on unstructured information such as text, image and audio, we implemented our service platform "Kachako" in a hybrid-cloud way where services themselves are transferred on demand. We suggest making each service specified by its input and output types, and executable of the service portable, compatible and interoperable. Assuming such services, Kachako thoroughly automates everything that users need. Kachako provides graphical user interfaces allowing end users to complete their tasks within Kachako without programming. Kachako is designed in a modular way by complying with well-known frameworks such as UIMA, Hadoop and Maven, allowing partial reuse or customization. We showed that Kachako is practically useful by integrating our natural language processing (NLP) services. Kachako is the world first full automation system for NLP freely available.

Keywords: Automation, Unstructured Information, Service Composition, Scalability, Natural Language Processing.

1 Introduction

One of the primary motivations providing services would be to save users' labor, i.e. *automation*. However, do current services sufficiently provide automation features? If we could thoroughly automate users' service related tasks, what remains as human's task? What do we need to achieve such automation?

Our answer is that the minimum user operations include only two steps: prepare a user account in machines, and specify a service that the user wishes to run. The rest of everything could be automated if we provide an ideal service platform. That said, unfortunately, existing service platforms tend to ask users too many manual tasks that could be potentially automated.

An advantage of web services would be the easiness of using services. However, web services, from users' point of view, have more or less fixed configurations both as software and hardware; services are under control of service providers, so

A. Ghose et al. (Eds.): ICSOC 2012, LNCS 7759, pp. 72–84, 2013.

customization of already deployed services is limited; physical servers of services cannot be changed, which prevents service scalability and availability.

We could provide users the scalability and the availability by making the entire service deployment under control of users themselves. Such a control can be practically available if users could transfer the services themselves, but not the data to be processed, to arbitrary servers that users wish to use. We call this style as hybrid-cloud, because we take benefits of both cloud and local deployments. This is possible due to the recent growth of open source projects, including software from state-of-the-art research tools to enterprise middleware implementations. We exploit such freely available software, together with the decreasing cost of computational resources e.g. the so-called cloud servers, to make such portable services available.

In addition to the portability, services need to be compatible and interoperable to allow automatic service composition. We focus on unstructured information processing where we could assume relatively simpler input and output dependencies.

Assuming such services, a fully automated platform could be available. Kachako, our platform, is just such a full automation system. Kachako is publicly available under open source license[1]. Kachako is designed to thoroughly automate any procedure in using services for unstructured information processing: selection, composition, (parallel distributed) deployment, result visualization, and evaluation of services.

We would like to emphasize here that users of Kachako do not need to know any detail described in this paper, as these details are obscured due to the automation features. Even when users wish to customize our system, users simply have to learn a specific standardized interface which users are interested in.

In this paper, we first describe background and related works of this research in Section 2. Then we discuss ideal form of services from an automation point of view in Section 3. We describe our Kachako system architecture which automates total use of services in Section 4, details discussed in subsections. In Section 5, we describe our domain specific service implementation in natural language processing, showing that the architecture is practically available and useful integrating all of features described in this paper. Section 6 describes limitations of our architecture. We conclude this paper in Section 7, discussing possible future works.

2   Background and Related Works

We adopted Java Standard Edition 7 as the main programming language of our implementation, as Java is suitable to achieve portability over different environments.

Kachako is compliant with Apache UIMA [1]. UIMA, Unstructured Information Management Architecture, is a framework which provides metadata schemes and processing architecture [2]. We selected UIMA not just because we focus on unstructured information processing, but also UIMA is currently the most suitable open framework for the automation features we need; UIMA's block-wise architecture concept potentially offers easier service composition and scalability, although simply

---

[1] The Kachako system will be available from http://kachako.org/

using UIMA is not sufficient. UIMA's processing unit is called a UIMA component. We call a UIMA component as a service in this paper because we make any service into a UIMA component in Kachako. A UIMA workflow consists of a (nested) list of components. A parent component may have a programmable flow controller that decides the processing order of its child components. A collection reader is a special UIMA component which retrieves input data; a collection reader is normally located at the start of a workflow. UIMA-AS (asynchronous UIMA) is a set of UIMA's next generation architectures including UIMA-AS workflow, UIMA-AS web service, etc. UIMA's data structure is called CAS (Common Analysis Structure), which is represented as a Java object at runtime and normally stored as XMI (XML Metadata Interchange) format in the disk. A CAS consists of raw data part and annotations part. The raw data part is normally kept unchanged once stored, holds raw data of e.g. text, audio, image, etc. The annotations part holds directed graphs of feature structures, where some of the feature structures are linked with the raw data by data offset positions. This representation style is called a stand-off annotation style. Any feature structure should be typed by a user defined data type. Types are defined hierarchically in a type system XML file. UIMA-AS uses Apache ActiveMQ [3] (a reference implementation of JMS, Java Messaging Service) as a web server.

We also adopt other open source standards in Kachako. Regarding scalability middleware, we use Apache Hadoop [4] with HDFS. Hadoop is now very widely used and stable enough. Our service repository is based on Apache Ivy [5], which provides remote file fetching system with dependency descriptions either in its original format or in an Apache Maven [6] format.

There are many UIMA related works, while most of them only provide UIMA service components. The IBM's Watson Question-Answer (QA) system [7] is UIMA compliant, but Watson is specific to the QA (and answering the Jeopardy quiz) domain; Watson is commercial software and not publicly available. There are several UIMA compliant resources available [8][9] [10] but they are services not a platform.

There are also a couple of previous studies of workflow oriented systems, but previous discussions remained partial when seen from the automation point of view. U-Compare [11][12][13], our previous product, is a UIMA compliant platform but automation and scalability were insufficient. Taverna [14] is a workflow system widely used in the Bioinformatics domain. In Taverna users can connect web services in a graphical way but service compatibility and interoperability is not sufficiently considered, users need to understand each service behavior in detail and in most cases required to write a script to match their I/O formats. Galaxy [15] is another workflow based system. Galaxy's service I/O is simply files, so preferred by shell-based programmers. However, this easiness rather requires extra human works when connecting different services because each service may have different formats. Langrid [16] is a collection of NLP web services where a service administration system is provided. Langrid uses BPEL to describe workflows, assuming programming work to customize the workflows. GATE [17] is a total text mining programming environment like Eclipse, but is not intended to provide an automation platform like Kachako.

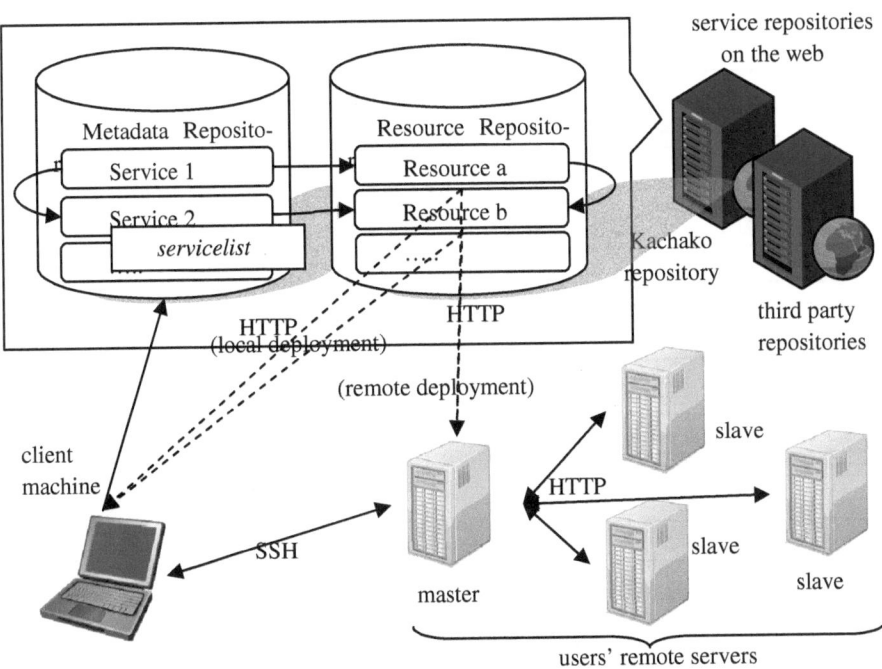

Fig. 1. A conceptual figure of Kachako's physical configuration. This figure illustrates a typical configuration, e.g. there may be no remote server used depending on users' configurations.

3   Forming Services for Automation

Users are often required expert knowledge in order to determine whether a pair of services can be composed or not. Such an interoperability issue depends not only on surficial format definition e.g. XML, but on deeper semantic compatibility. In a worse case, users need to re-implement the original service implementation for the services to be able to be combined. We certainly need automation here, as users are not necessarily programmers or experts. Furthermore, this is not an essential task for users.

Such service compatibility and interoperability problem includes several issues: data format, data type, service metadata, and form of services. As we adopted UIMA as the basic framework, so data format and service metadata description format are guaranteed to be compatible. We discuss the rest of theoretical issues in this section.

While standardization of metadata and data format syntax is often discussed, it tends to be missed in what shape a service should be formed. Some of the existing services are provided as APIs, while others are a large integrated application. From our point of view, reusability is the critical issue for the service users. If a service is smaller, there is more possibility to reuse the service; a smaller service could be more generic than a large application service, which would assume a more specific use case. However, this discussion of service granularity is not sufficient. While APIs (functions of programing languages) could be the smallest service we can provide,

LEGEND | User Operation | | User Operation (optional) | | Automatic System Operation |

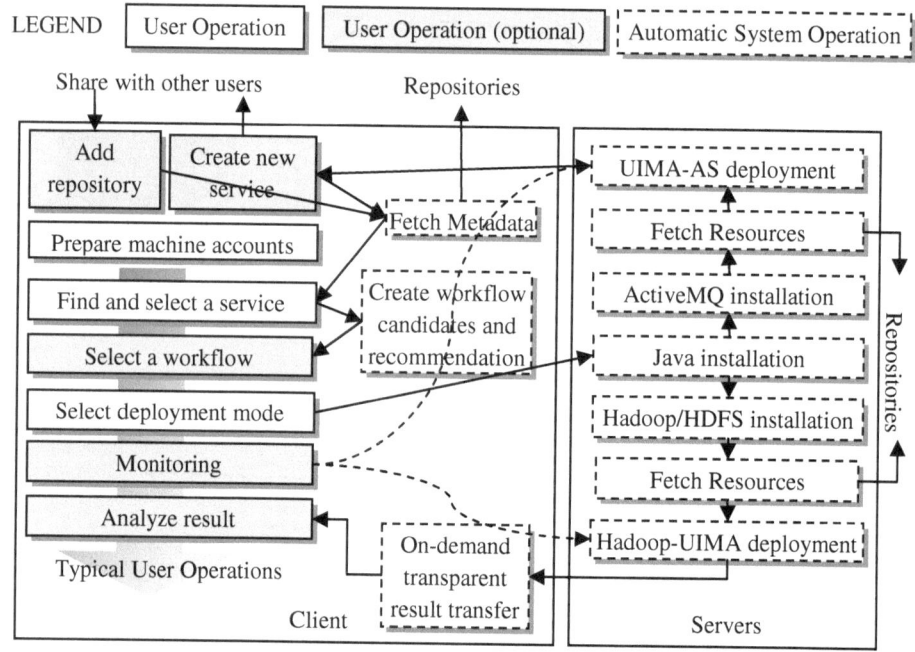

Fig. 2. A conceptual system flow diagram of Kachako's remote deployment

simply providing APIs do not achieve sufficient reusability. APIs are normally described by input data types and output data types. However, an API does not return meaningful result if we just combine arbitrary two API functions whose I/O data types formally match. This is because most of APIs have implicit conditions which are described in machine unreadable documentations, or often not described at all.

In order to allow automatic composition, we suggest that a service metadata should be specified by a list of I/O data types without any other implicit information. This obscures the implicit API conditions, so users and developers do not need to understand inside the service implementations. A service should be as small as possible at the same time, to be more reusable as discussed above. We can create such a service because tasks are composite in nature in case of unstructured information processing.

Scalability is another critical issue that we have to consider together with the reusability. If a service can process a block of input data without referring to another input block, then we can parallelize the service process by dividing the input into independent blocks. This parallelization can scale the entire process out without overheads of distributed communication cost. This is an ideal parallelization from the automation point of view because the original service can be reused without modification. Such block division can be decided by semantic relations in the original input data. For example, a document is normally independent in a collection of documents, while they are sometimes merged into a single file. The number of possible parallelization is decided by the number of blocks. Therefore, the input retrieval service, a collection reader in case of UIMA, should retrieve input by splitting the original data into smallest but semantically independent blocks. If the input is split so, developers can implement a service without aware of such a scalability issue. In case a service needs to collect information over blocks, e.g. search engine indexing, the service should be specially implemented in a scalable way though this is limited to a couple of special purposes. We describe our ready-to-use services of NLP in Section 5.

4   Service Platform for Full Automation

Roughly speaking, Kachako physically consists of three parts: a *client* module including GUIs (Graphical User Interfaces), a *server* module, and repositories on the web. These modules can be used either in an integrated way or in a partial way; using the client only for lightweight tasks, using both client and server for automatic large-scale processing, using the server only to integrate with other existing systems, etc. We also provide modules in smaller granularity for the reusability.

Kachako's *client* runs in a machine where users can configure everything by GUIs. We only require Java 7 to be installed, so machines of any modern OS (Windows, Mac, Linux) are available. Most machines have Java pre-installed nowadays. Installation of Kachako's *client* is automatic. By running our small Java launcher program, all of required binaries and resources are downloaded, cached, and updated if there is any update. Kachako's *client* provides GUIs to configure workflows in an automated way, as described in the later sections. Kachako also provides a command-line mode, where users can run a specified workflow without the GUIs.

Fig. 1 illustrates architecture of the entire Kachako system conceptually. Fig. 2 shows a conceptual flow diagram of the system from the user's point of view.

4.1   Repository Architecture for Finding Services and Resolving Dependencies

Our goal in designing service repository architecture is that files can be shared efficiently, while dependencies between files could be automatically resolved.

For our dependency description, we adopt the Apache Ivy [5] format including Maven. Because Ivy allows specifying multiple repositories, it is possible to configure a cloned backup repository. Any resource is cached in the user's local disk. This mechanism allows efficient and dynamic resource distribution.

We separate our service repository into metadata and actual resources (executable binaries, external data etc.) for efficient data transfer. When users search and configure services into a workflow, they just need the metadata repository. After creating a workflow, the Kachako system can collect required resources assuming resource dependencies are defined properly. Fig. 1 illustrates this architecture conceptually.

Third party service providers can distribute their services by building their own repository. In addition to our default service repository, users can add such a third party repository by simply specifying a repository location URL as described below. Then Kachako seeks for available services and resolves any required dependencies automatically.

4.2   Workflow Oriented Automatic Service Composition

When services are formed as described in the previous section, all of possible combinations of services can be theoretically calculated from services' I/O conditions. Kachako considers data type hierarchy which makes this calculation a bit complex. The entire combinations of services form a directed graph structure in general.

The number of the combinations may become too large for humans to grasp, so a proper filtering feature would be helpful. Because users' goal is usually linked with the final output, Kachako asks users to specify which service they wish to run as the final output service. Kachako also asks users to specify which collection reader to retrieve as workflow input. These are the only decisions of users, which a system cannot automatically determine. Given these input and output services, Kachako's automatic workflow composition GUI shows possible service combinations. Users can further filter workflows by specifying intermediate services, while hasty users can immediately run a suggested workflow.

Kachako provides another workflow creation GUI. Users can specify components one by one manually in a dragging-and-dropping manner, where any UIMA workflow can be created even ignoring the I/O conditions.

Kachako further provides other automatic service composition GUI for comparison and evaluation as described in Section 4.4.

4.3   Automatic Service Deployment, Execution and Monitoring

Kachako provides three service deployment modes: *local*, *batch*, and *listener* deployment mode. Most of users' requirements can be satisfied by using one of, or a combination of these modes. Details are described in subsections.

4.3.1   Local Deployment: Automatic Service Deployment in Local Machine

The local deployment would be suitable for running lightweight tasks immediately. We assume that service metadata and resources are properly configured as described in Section 3. By tracing the dependency information for each service in a workflow,

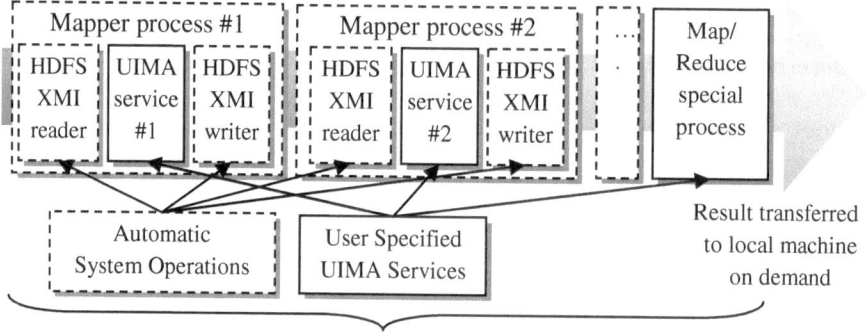

Fig. 3. A diagram of Hadoop-UIMA processing

	Covered Text	begin	end	surface
☑ : Predicate				
☐ : EventNoun	崩壊	722	724	崩壊
	し	724	725	し
☑ : Equal		725	726	、
	世界	726	728	世界
☐ : Morpheme	が	728	729	が
	新	729	730	新
	秩序	730	732	秩序
☐ : NAIST NamedEntity	を	732	733	を
	求め	733	735	求め
☐ : CabochaSegment	て	735	736	て
	いる	736	738	いる
	時期	738	740	時期

Fig. 4. An example of NLP information visualizing co-reference and predicate relations (left) and showing details as a table (right)

Kachako can obtain all of required resources. Each service is assigned a separate Java class loader to avoid version conflicts of libraries, which often occur and difficult to resolve. This is common with other deployment modes. Kachako deploys a specified workflow as a UIMA-AS service locally and saves its result in UIMA's XMI format.

4.3.2 Automatic Server Configuration for Batch and Listener Modes

For the other two modes, remote server configuration is required. We aim to avoid any permission of root authority that becomes a bottleneck in the setup tasks. Kachako's only requirement is that a user should prepare Linux based machines where the user has his/her user account, accessible via SSH and connected to the Internet via HTTP. Once the account is registered, Kachako sets up everything automatically. If a machine configuration is provided by administrator using our importable configuration format, users can skip this registration step.

Kachako uses user's home directory or the OS's temporary directory as its root directory for saving any file. In case of the temporary directory, Kachako prevents the OS to delete the saved files. Kachako automatically installs Java 7 if not installed yet.

4.3.3 Batch Deployment: Remote Batch Scalable Processing with Hadoop

The batch deployment uses Apache Hadoop [4] as a low level API. We assume that a workflow, which a user wishes to run, is given as described in the previous sections.

Installation and deployment of Hadoop are not so easy task for end users. Kachako automatically installs and deploys Hadoop/HDFS. Recent multi-core servers are not efficiently used because required parallelization works arc not essential for the users; users just want to scale out. Kachako's automatic scalable deployment would increase the efficiency. Users can customize configurations when they need specific tuning.

Kachako's server configuration GUI allows users to create a Hadoop/HDFS cluster setting from the registered servers. This setting includes Hadoop's JobTracker, TaskTracker(s), NameNode, and DataNode(s). Using our modules described earlier, Kachako automatically installs Java and Hadoop by creating relevant configuration files for each server in accordance with the user's server setting.

Assumed Gold Standard		Comparison Components		Total (All Documents)					
☑ (.Sentence) ☑ (.Sentence) .Token	☑ (.Sentence)	☑ (.Sentence) .Token	☑ G	☑ T	☑ M	☑ F1	☑ PR	☑ RC
☑ UIMA	☑ UIMA	☑ UIMA	☑ OpenNLP	97	81	71	79.78	87.65	73.20
☑ UIMA	☑ UIMA	☑ UIMA	☑ Genia_with_Tokenization	97	89	86	92.47	96.63	88.66
☑ UIMA	☑ OpenNLP	☑ UIMA	☑ UIMA	81	97	71	79.78	73.20	87.65
☑ UIMA	☑ OpenNLP	☑ UIMA	☑ Genia_with_Tokenization	81	89	74	87.06	83.15	91.36
☑ UIMA	☑ Genia_with_Tokenization	☑ UIMA	☑ UIMA	89	97	86	92.47	88.66	96.63
☑ UIMA	☑ Genia_with_Tokenization	☑ UIMA	☑ OpenNLP	89	81	74	87.06	91.36	83.15

Fig. 5. An example of evaluation statistics comparing three different tokenizers. Left hand columns show service names, right hand numerical value columns show standard evaluation statistics in NLP (F1, precision and recall scores).

Then Kachako will deploy the given UIMA workflow. If there is any required resource created locally, Kachako archives these resources, creates a local Ivy repository, and transfers them over SSH. A collection reader will run first to retrieve input data into HDFS in the XMI format. For each service in the rest of the top level services in the workflow, Kachako runs a Hadoop's Mapper without Reducer. As illustrated in Fig. 4, our special XMI reader and writer transfers XMI files from and to the HDFS file system. These allow mostly any UIMA service to be deployed in Hadoop/HDFS without modifying the original service implementation. Some special services, such as search engine indexing, would need Map/Reduce implementation.

Finally, Kachako provides on-demand result transfer feature. After finishing the workflow in Hadoop, Kachako transfers an index and statistics of result files to the client. When users need the content of the result e.g. for visualization, Kachako transfers relevant files from remote HDFS to the client in an on-demand way.

A monitoring feature is important for users, especially because large scale processing could take very long time, sometimes fails due to unpredictable reasons. Kachako shows Hadoop job's progress status in the GUI, as users' primary concern would be how much the job has progressed, and whether they are dead or alive. Further monitoring information can be shown simply by clicking a button in our GUI.

4.3.4　Listener Deployment: Scalable Remote Deployment with UIMA-AS

The listener deployment mode satisfies broad range of use cases. Firstly, although we assume freely available software, there would be certain requests not to provide source codes but services only. Secondly, some services may take very long time to initialize, or require special environment to run e.g. very large amount of disk space, difficult to setup for end users, etc. We can avoid such problems by deploying specific services as web services using our listener deployment mode.

By the UIMA-AS web service, we can deploy any local UIMA component as a web service. Kachako installs ActiveMQ in a specified remote server first. Then Kachako deploys specified services as UIMA-AS services. Required resources are transferred as same as the Hadoop mode above.

Simply deploying as a UIMA-AS web service does not scale. We provide a load balancer which distributes requests over UIMA-AS service nodes, pretending as a scalable single UIMA-AS service as a whole. Users can deploy such a scalable

UIMA-AS cluster by specifying a load-balancer server and slave servers for the UIMA-AS services. Users can deploy, undeploy, and monitor services via the GUI.

4.4   Automatic Service Evaluation by Combinatorial Workflow Composition

Because there are many similar but different services available, comparison and evaluation of services are critical issues. Services are more or less black-boxed, and behave differently depending on their input. Thus it is impossible to predict the best combination of services for a specific goal without actually running services.

As we discussed in Section 4.2, possible combinations of services can be calculated. Because such combinations tend to share partial graph, we can efficiently run combinations of services rather than separately running each of combinations as independent workflows. The basic concept is similar to our previous work [11], but in the previous work we assumed manual configurations which were difficult for users to configure. In contrast, Kachako automates everything by a new architecture as below.

Firstly, Kachako calculates a possible service combination graph as described in Section 4.2. Then, for each edge of the graph, CAS content is filtered by the input type(s), copied to a new CAS and passed to the next service. After processing the next service, output of the service is internally grouped and stored back into the CAS. This architecture allows an efficient automatic execution of combinatorial workflows, while the original services do not need to be modified.

By plugging comparison metric services, users can obtain statistical values for each pair of comparable service graphs. If a pair includes the so-called gold standard data, i.e. the correct answer, then the comparison becomes an evaluation. Fig. 5 shows an example comparison result for an NLP task, tokenization.

The above discussion raises an issue, in what way data types should be defined. Our automatic service composition is based on the I/O metadata descriptions of services, which are described in terms of data types. Therefore, data types should include, at least, types which are used to describe the I/O metadata. In addition, data types should include concepts which are used to compare and evaluate services as discussed in this section. Actual data type definition is a domain specific issue.

5   Ready-to-Use Implementation for Natural Language Processing as System Evaluation

The Kachako platform architecture we discussed so far is generic. However, we claim that an ideal system should help users by automation as much as possible. It is absolutely required to provide actual implementation for a specific target domain; else the system would be just useless as it is too abstract. We show and evaluate our system's usefulness by implementing domain specific parts of the system, for the NLP domain of text processing.

Domain specific issues include data visualization, data type definition, and actual services. Our system assumes a trial-and-error style use case, in order for users to obtain the most suitable workflow. Thus error analysis, especially the visualization

Table 1. Result of performance test in the batch mode. Input is the BioMedCentral's full text corpus. # of input is the documents processed, # of mappers is parallel process counts, actual time is elapsed time for the processes, total CPU time is sum of CPU time over mappers.

# of Input	20	20	100	100	1000	1000
# of Mappers	5	10	5	10	5	10
Actual Time (s)	130	61	584	379	5684	3666
Total CPU Time (ms)	508,720	68,870	2,442,520	2,483,580	23,963,340	23,959,530

feature, is very important. We have developed a generic visualizer for text which can show annotations and relations of annotations graphically (Fig. 6).

Developing services and defining data types are not a separate issue. We have been developing compatible NLP services from basic linguistic tools to applied text mining tools in different languages. We also provide utilities to help developers wrap existing tools into compatible UIMA services. Everything is integrated into the Kachako system, allowing users to find an NLP service, create and run a workflow, and analyze its result in an ultimately automated way. The number of our services is currently around one hundred, which can generate thousands of possible workflows theoretically.

We have performed a scalability test by using the NLP services. As a realistic scenario, we used the BioMedCentral's full text corpus [18] as input and performed a protein mention extraction task by ABNER [19] in our batch processing mode. Table 1 is the statistics of the testing. Some overhead was observed as expected, but it scaled out as a whole when increasing the number of mappers.

6   Limitation

One of the limitations is authentication. There would be certain needs for user authentication. Our listener deployment could provide authentication of services. The component repository could also limit users. However, these are not supported currently.

Another limitation is the way forming services. Unfortunately, not all the services can be ideally formed like we discussed. For example, dictionaries are often used as external resources in NLP tools. Although it is ideal for such external resources to be compatible, we currently simply specify locations of resources. Such resources are read in the initialization time but not read during the process time, and so it is unnatural and difficult to put the resource into the CAS.

The other type of limitations is stability and compatibility of the data type definitions. We have been implicitly assuming that data types are static. However, if an incompatible type system is used, previously created services and their results become incompatible. A solution would be to develop a type system converter. But it is not a trivial task as there could be many incompatible type systems by different developers.

7   Conclusion and Future Work

In this paper, we proposed architecture to ultimately automate tasks using services, and showed its implementation is practically useful, in the NLP domain as an example. This system, Kachako, is the world first system providing such thorough automation features in a scalable and reusable way; select a service and specify servers to run, that's all. Board range of standards and technologies were harmonized for these automation features to be reusable. Increasing the number of available services, including Map/Reduce services, is the future work. Enhancement of the Kachako system to support other domains would be a future work as well.

Acknowledgements. This work was partially supported by JST PRESTO and KAKENHI 21500130 (MEXT, Japan).

References

1. Apache UIMA, http://uima.apache.org/
2. Ferrucci, D., Lally, A., Gruhl, D., Epstein, E., Schor, M., Murdock, J.W., Frenkiel, A., Brown, E.W., Hampp, T., Doganata, Y., Welty, C., Amini, L., Kofman, G., Kozakov, L., Mass, Y.: Towards an Interoperability Standard for Text and Multi-Modal Analytics. IBM Research Report, RC24122 (2006)
3. Apache ActiveMQ, http://activemq.apache.org/
4. Apache Hadoop, http://hadoop.apache.org/
5. Apache Ivy, http://ant.apache.org/ivy/
6. Apache Maven, http://maven.apache.org/
7. Ferrucci, D.A.: Introduction to This is Watson. IBM Journal of Research and Development 56, 1:1–1:15 (2012)
8. Hahn, U., Buyko, E., Landefeld, R., Mühlhausen, M., Poprat, M., Tomanek, K., Wermter, J.: An Overview of JCoRe, the JULIE Lab UIMA Component Repository. In: LREC 2008 Workshop, Towards Enhanced Interoperability for Large HLT Systems: UIMA for NLP, Marrakech, Morocco, pp. 1–8 (2008)
9. Hernandez, N., Poulard, F., Vernier, M., Rocheteau, J.: Building a French-speaking community around UIMA, gathering research, education and industrial partners, mainly in Natural Language Processing and Speech Recognizing domains. In: LREC 2010 Workshop of New Challenges for NLP Frameworks, Valletta, Malta (2010)
10. Ogren, P.V., Wetzler, P.G., Bethard, S.: ClearTK: A UIMA Toolkit for Statistical Natural Language Processing. In: LREC 2008 Workshop 'Towards Enhanced Interoperability for Large HLT Systems: UIMA for NLP', Marrakech, Morocco, pp. 32–38 (2008)
11. Kano, Y., Miwa, M., Cohen, K., Hunter, L., Ananiadou, S., Tsujii, J.: U-Compare: a modular NLP workflow construction and evaluation system. IBM Journal of Research and Development 55, 11:1–11:10 (2011)
12. Kano, Y., Dorado, R., McCrohon, L., Ananiadou, S., Tsujii, J.: U-Compare: An Integrated Language Resource Evaluation Platform Including a Comprehensive UIMA Resource Library. In: 7th International Conference on Language Resources and Evaluation (LREC 2010), Valletta, Malta, pp. 428–434 (2010)

13. Kano, Y., Baumgartner, W.A., McCrohon, L., Ananiadou, S., Cohen, K.B., Hunter, L., Tsujii, J.: U-Compare: share and compare text mining tools with UIMA. Bioinformatics 25, 1997–1998 (2009)

14. Hull, D., Wolstencroft, K., Stevens, R., Goble, C., Pocock, M.R., Li, P., Oinn, T.: Taverna: a tool for building and running workflows of services. Nucleic Acids Res. 34, W729–W732 (2006)

15. Blankenberg, D., Von Kuster, G., Coraor, N., Ananda, G., Lazarus, R., Mangan, M., Nekrutenko, A., Taylor, J.: Galaxy: a web-based genome analysis tool for experimentalists. Curr. Protoc. Mol. Biol. ch. 19, Unit 19.10.1–19.10.21 (2010)

16. Ishida, T.: Language Grid: An Infrastructure for Intercultural Collaboration. In: Proceedings of the International Symposium on Applications on Internet, pp. 96–100. IEEE Computer Society (2006)

17. Cunningham, H., Maynard, D., Bontcheva, K., Tablan, V.: GATE: A framework and graphical development environment for robust NLP tools and applications. In: 40th Anniversary Meeting of the Association for Computational Linguistics, Philadelphia, USA, pp. 168–175 (2002)

18. BioMed Central's open access full-text corpus, http://www.biomedcentral.com/about/datamining

19. Settles, B.: ABNER: an open source tool for automatically tagging genes, proteins and other entity names in text. Bioinformatics 21, 3191–3192 (2005)

2012 International Workshop on Data Intensive Services Based Application (DISA2012)

Ying Li[1], Shuiguang Deng[1], Guoray Cai[2], and Yuyu Yin[3]

[1] College of Computer Science and Technology, Zhejiang University
Hangzhou China
{cnliying,dengsg}@gmail.com
[2] College of Information Sciences and Technology Penn State University, USA
cai@ist.psu.edu
[3] College of Computer, Hangzhou Dianzi University
Hangzhou China
Yyy718@gmail.com

1   Introduction

On behalf of the Organizing Committee, we welcome you to the 2012 International Workshop on Data Intensive Services based Application (DISA 2012) and to Shanghai, China.

There is no doubt in the industry and research community that the importance of data intensive computing has been raising and will continue to be the foremost fields of research. The data intensive services based applications will become an important one of the applications in SOA. Also, it has become a hot issue in the academia and industry. Potentially, this could have a significant impact on the on-going researches for services and data intensive computing. DISA 2012 focuses on the challenges imposed by data-intensive services based applications, and on the different state-of-the-art solutions proposed to overcome these challenges. The aim of DISA 2012 is to encourage academic researchers and industry practitioners to present and discuss all methods and technologies related to research and experiences in a broad spectrum of data-intensive services based applications. We have a clear mission to develop DISA into a top-class international conference in the near future.

The sessions included presentations by Sida Xue on An End-User Oriented Approach for Business Process Personalization from Multiple Sources, Menmen Wu on A Combination Approach for QoS Prediction of Web Service, Jiawei Yan on Effective and Efficient Web Reviews Extraction Based on Hadoop, Xiaoming Zhang on Intelligent Information Management of Tourist Attractions Based on Semantic Sensor Web, and Zhou Xiangbing on An optimal QoS-based WSMO Web service composition approach using Genetic algorithm.

2   Workshop Co-organizers

- Prof. Ying Li, Zhejiang University, China
- Prof. Shuiguang Deng, Zhejiang University, China

A. Ghose et al. (Eds.): ICSOC 2012, LNCS 7759, pp. 85–86, 2013.

- Prof. Guoray Cai, Penn State University, USA(Invited Honorary Chair)
- Dr. Yuyu Yin, Hangzhou Dianzi University, China

3   Program Committee

Brian Vinter ,Copenhagen University	Thomas E. Potok, Oak Ridge National Laboratory
Dan Grigoras ,University College Cork	Uwe Glässer, Simon Fraser University
Guoray Cai ,Pennsylvania State University	Walter Binder, University of Lugano
Hong-Linh Truong, Vienna University of Technology	SUM Chin Sean, National Institute of Information and Communication Technology
Jiannong Cao, Hong Kong Polytechnic University	Wei Wang, Institute of Communications and Navigation
Jianwei Yin , Zhejiang University	Mea Wang, University of Calgary
Klaus-Dieter Schewe, Information Science Research Centre	Chengzhong Xu, Wayne State University
Lai Xu, Bournemouth University	Zhou Su, Waseda University
Lei Liu, Karlsruhe Institute of Technology	Stephen Wang, Toshiba Telecommunications Research Laboratory Europe
Rodrigo Fernandes de Mello, University of Sao Paulo	Peng Di, University of New South Wales
R.K. Shyamasundar, Tata Institute of Fundamental Research	Robert Lagerstrom, KTH - Royal Institute of Technology
Kumiko Tadano, NEC	Jian Zhao, Institute for Infocomm Research
Amit Dvir, Budapest University of Technology and Economics	Jian Wan, Hangzhou Dianzi University
Xiaofei Zhang, Hong Kong University of Science and Technology	Jiangchuan Liu, Simon Fraser University
Jilin Zhang, Hangzhou Dianzi University	Honghao Gao, Shanghai University

Acknowledgements. We would like to thank program committee members for their hard and excellent work on outstanding reviewing process to select high-quality papers from a large number of submissions. Our special thanks also go to General Chair of ICSOC 2012, Prof. Jian Yang, Workshop Chairs, Prof. Aditya Ghose and Prof. Huibiao Zhu, for their help to hold the workshop. We appreciate all of authors who submitted their high-quality papers to DISA 2012.

An End-User Oriented Approach for Business Process Personalization from Multiple Sources

Sida Xue, Budan Wu, and Junliang Chen

State Key Laboratory of Networking and Switching,
Beijing University of Posts and Telecommunications, Beijing, 100876, China
{xuesida,wubudan,chenjl}@bupt.edu.cn

Abstract. Current service oriented enterprise business process modeling and development technology is conducted by professional IT department, which cannot fulfill the growing requirements of personalized business application by end users. Recent research works about enterprise mashups enable end users to create own business application by assembling and composing widgets, which emphasizes the front-end interface rather than the logical process of business activities. In this paper, we propose an approach for end users to create personalized business process from multiple sources. An integrated framework for modeling, monitoring personalized business process and automated execution is designed. Internal business processes, external web APIs and communication services are all wrapped into this framework for end users to select and compose in a lightweight event-driven fashion. We also design a wizard-based development workspace helping end users without programming skills to build lightweight business application. In addition, an actual business project case is presented to show how our approach is used practically in an enterprise environment.

Keywords: business processes, personalization, lightweight service composition, end-user development.

1 Introduction

Nowadays, most of the enterprise business process management systems adopt Service-Oriented Architecture (SOA). SOA paradigm facilitates business process modeling and development by composing heterogeneous services including classical web service based on SOAP and WSDL, and also including Web APIs (also known as RESTful web service [1]) driven by the Web 2.0 technology [2]. In this context, the business needs are evolving rapidly and becoming more situational and spontaneous, especially for the non-technical business end users, who have interactions with the business processes and applications directly [3].

Existing specifications such as BPMN [4] and WS-BPEL [5] providing graphical tools for both business analysts and technical developer, mainly aim at standardizing the design and implementation of a fixed business process. However, without end users participation, they cannot fully satisfy the dynamic and evolved business needs.

A. Ghose et al. (Eds.): ICSOC 2012, LNCS 7759, pp. 87–98, 2013.

Many research works are making efforts to enable business end users to create business applications in their preferred fashion [6 and 7]. Enterprise mashup [8] concept widely used in these works provides user with an intuitive composition method based on widget technology in a WYSIWYG (what you see is what you get) way. Compared with the "heavy" specifications mentioned above, mashup is a comparative "lightweight" approach, which emphasizes rich user interfaces, process personalization, faster development and content creation [9].

In enterprise mashup environment, end users pay more attention at the front-end presentation, and only simple logical relationship between the widgets, such as input and output match, is supported. Considering this, more mashup styles are figured out for composing services in a logical workflow manner, such as business process mashups [10]. Apparently, more complex mashup styles lead to more difficult learning for end users. The balance between business application complexity and easy-to-use service composition tool is a challenge for all end-user development tools [11].

As a tradeoff, in this paper, we do not consider complex business process which is better to be modeled and developed in "heavy" approaches by professional IT departments in enterprise. Our research focus on the business processes composing multiple service sources, involving end-user interactions, and performing in a lightweight event-driven way.

Lightweight event-driven method is popular on the Internet for ordinary users to compose various Web APIs. In recent years, both industry product, such as ifttt [12], and research works, such as SECE [13], emerge and work in this way. Nevertheless, these works can only compose personal and private services on the Internet, and cannot satisfy those event-driven style requirements which are common in the enterprise business processes.

Our approach is designed for enterprise end users to create personalized business process in this lightweight event-drive way. This work includes two major parts: an integrated framework, including business process modeling, execution and monitoring, and a wizard-based end-user development workspace. In the framework, all services from multiple sources are wrapped into resources with descriptions in a standard format. These descriptions only expose their logical function to end users and hide the complexity of heterogeneous services. There are four types of services described as resources in our work: time and date service, enterprise internal services and processes, external Web APIs and communication services. And the wizard-based workspace will guide the users to select these resources and compose them in the lightweight event-driven way by setting trigger event and corresponding action. Neither in drag-and-drop style nor likes professional programming IDE, the wizard works like a tutorial, which is proved to be necessary when designing end-user development tool [11]. Different from widget based mashup, our approach does not work in the WYSIWYG manner. The end users compose the resources in a logical sequence, which can be described as a lightweight event-driven model. And this composition model is monitored and automated executed in our framework on behalf of the end users.

The remainder of this paper is organized as follows: Section 2 presents an actual business scenario to explain our motivation; Section 3, the major part of this paper, elaborates the framework design, the wizard-based end-user development method and the detailed back-end mechanism; And in Section 4, we conduct a case study to show how our approach is actually used in an enterprise and the technical implementation details are also introduced. Finally, we conclude this paper in Section 5.

2   A Motivating Business Scenario

In this section, an actual business scenario is presented to explain why business process personalization is necessary and how the personalization is from multiple sources.

JF is a company responsible for heating system sales, provision and maintenance for a large number of residential buildings. It possesses a website, a supporting back-end workflow system and also a mail system for customer service. On the website, the users can report heating system failure for repair and the company employers also can handle the request and manage the repair work. Figure 1 shows the process of asking for maintenance by customer in JF.

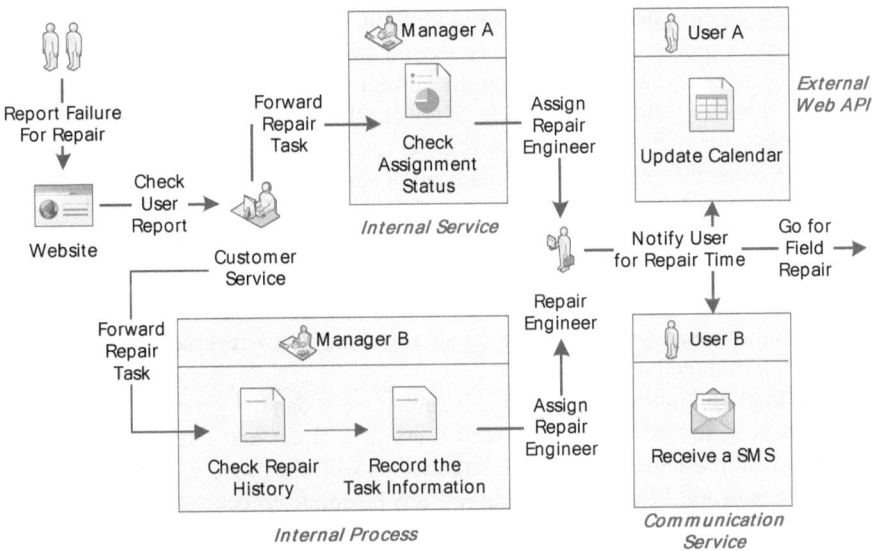

Fig. 1. Customer Service Process for Heating System in JF Company

All users visit the website to fill out a form about heating system failure. The website generates a report according to the form, and the mail system will send a notification mail to the customer service staff. Then the customer service staff will check the report, which includes the detailed description of system failure, the purchase time of the system, the user contact information and so on, to determine whether it needs to assign a repair engineer out for field repair. If it is necessary, the website will generate a repair task and forward it to the manager on duty, who is responsible for personnel scheduling. In a typical situation, the manager will assign the task to a free repair engineer. However, different managers have different considerations when make decisions. For example, as depicted in Figure 1, Manager A is used to check the assignment status. Maybe an engineer has been out for repair at a place near to the task building and Manager A will assign this task to him. Differently, Manager B may need to check repair history, if this building has been repaired for several times, which indicates that the system has long-term problem. Manager B will firstly record the task information by sending a mail to own inbox and then select an experienced engineer to perform this repair work.   After assignment, the repair engineer needs to determine a time for repair, and then notify users of the time. Although User A and User B both report the failure on the website, they may need different notification methods. User A wants to add the repair event in calendar service, such as Google Calendar [14]. User B prefers to receive a notification short message on phone. In the end, the repair engineer will go for field repair at the scheduled time.

Apparently, either the managers or the users in this scenario cannot follow a fixed business process to satisfy their personalized requirements. More importantly, these kinds of requirements for personalization have three prominent characteristics:

- These business requirements are from multiple sources. As shown in Figure 1, in the example process, the part can be personalized may be enterprise internal services (Manager A needs to look up the current status of engineer assignment), internal processes (Manager B usually firstly checks the repair history and then keeps information in own mailbox), external services (User A want to add the repair event in calendar service) or communication services (User B needs a notification short message on the phone).
- These requirements are all in an event-driven like style. For example, according to managers, their personalized part in the process will be triggered every time the customer service staff forwards a repair task to them. The same to users, once a repair engineer has determined the repair time, they will receive a notification in their preferred method.
- These kinds of lightweight event-driven and personalized process from multiple sources need to be developed by end users in a direct and intuitive way. In this scenario, all participants who have interactions with the process, such as managers, repair engineers, heating system users, are business process end users and only themselves knows when and how to make the process work in their preferred way.

3   Approach Overview and Design

Based on the discussion above, we propose an approach for end users to create personalized business process from multiple sources in a lightweight event-driven way. Two main works in our approach, the integrated framework which can be deployed in an enterprise and the wizard based event-driven service composition method for end-user development, will be detailed in subsection 3.1 and 3.2. In addition, a major challenge to realize such a framework and the wizard-based method is how to organize various kinds of services and events and provide them to end users. Thus the mechanism to realize this work in the framework will be introduced in subsection 3.3.

This subsection also describes the complete interaction procedure of the components when personalized business process is created and executed.

3.1 Framework Design

The architecture of the proposed framework is shown in Figure 2. In our approach, this framework should be used in an enterprise environment, hence all the components in Figure 2 is designed to support enterprise business process personalization.

The left part of Figure 2 is a web based workspace for end users to create, load, edit, start and stop their personalized business process. The right part of Figure 2 is the back-end system maintained by the IT department in the enterprise, which is not exposed to end users. These two parts are introduced in turn below.

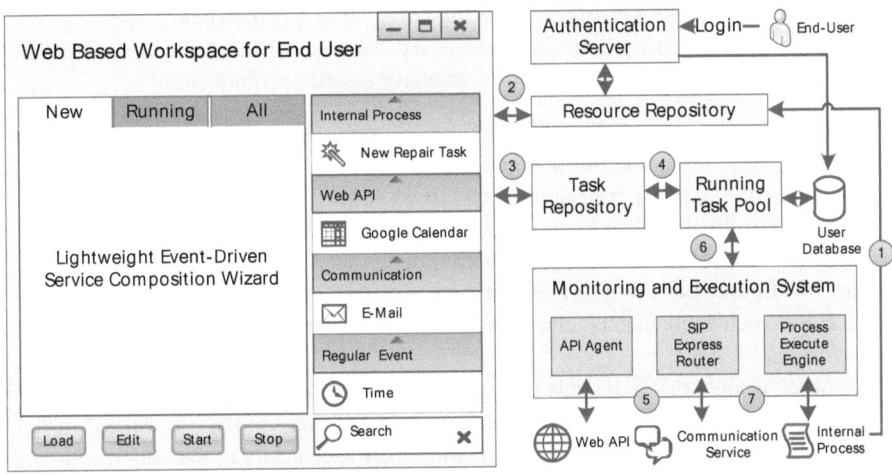

Fig. 2. Components View of the Integrated Framework

A. Web Based Workspace for End-User Development

The account information of end users is needed to be authenticated before visit the workspace. In general cases, the IT department who is responsible for maintain this framework should assign accounts to all staff in the enterprise. Other end users who are not employees, such as the customer in the scenario illustrated in section 2, can register account on the website. It should be noted that the registration should verify the customer information such as product or warranty ID, which ensures that the system is not opened for all Internet users.

After login through the web browser, end users will see the workspace depicted in Figure 2. The center of the workspace is the lightweight event-driven service composition wizard which will be detailed in next subsection. It is neither a canvas for drag-and-drop similar to Mashup, nor a coding area like professional programming IDE. It is an interactive interface to guide user to set the trigger event first, and then the action, and also can edit corresponding parameters. On the right side of the workspace is a palette from which users can search and select available trigger events and actions.

As shown in Figure 2, on the palette, items are categorized by their resource type. As introduced above, in our work, there are four types of services described as resources in our work: time and date service, enterprise internal services and processes, external Web APIs and communication services. Categorized by functionality, some resources can only be used as trigger event, such as time, and also some resources can only be used as action such as some internal process. Particularly, some resources can be used both as trigger event and action, such as e-mail. Therefore the items displayed on the palette are different when user sets trigger event or action.

When end users finish the wizard, they have created a task which can be started and stopped anytime by the creator. All running tasks are monitored and executed automatically by the back-end system. End users can also check all existing tasks, all running tasks, which can be edited, started and stopped in the workspace.

B. Back-End System Architecture of the Integrated Framework

To support the workspace described above and execute all the tasks created by end users, the back-end system of the framework have several components:

- Authentication Server (AS). AS has two major functions. The first one is to per-form authentication when user login. The second one, which is more important, is to manage the access permission of end users to the service repository. Reviewing the scenario illustrated in Section 2, Manager A needs to look up the engineer as-signment status, which is obviously cannot be seen by a customer. Considering this, our framework allows IT department to assign different end users with differ-ent roles, such as managers, engineers, and customer and so on. This assign work is performed by AS.
- Resource Repository (RR). RR is responsible for managing and organizing various kinds of services and events. The description of resource in RR has a fixed format, which indicates the necessary information when user needs to use this resource as trigger event or action. Furthermore, the resource visit permission will be assign to role. When a user logins, the resource repository will connect AS to check the role of the user and provides all resources the role can access to the end user. In addi-tion, it is noted that the mechanism of adding new resource in our approach is not automatic, and it needs to described in our designed format and added manually to RR by the IT department of the enterprise.
- Task Repository (TR). It stores all the tasks created by end users in the workspace. The task is also described in a fixed format, which includes the trigger event needs to be monitored and the action needs to be executed correspondingly.
- Running Task Pool (RTP). When a user starts a task, RTP loads it from TR. Only tasks in RTP will be monitored and executed.
- Monitoring and Execution System (MES). MES monitors all events of running tasks and executes the actions on behalf of end users. To monitor events of differ-ent types, MES embeds several agents to communicate with external services; a telecom gateway server to handle incoming and outgoing communication messag-es; a process execution engine to handle internal process execution.

3.2   Design of Lightweight Event-Driven Service Composition Wizard

As introduced above, we design a wizard guiding user to generate an event-driven task. When user chooses to create a new task in the workspace, the wizard will begin. The wizard has five steps, and at each step the wizard show different content according to different resource types.

Step.1 Select Trigger Event
In this step, the wizard will notify user to select a trigger event from the resource palette on the right side of workspace. There are two types of trigger events in our design. The first one is the event occurrence, and the second one is to perform one action. For example, when an e-mail is arrived, an action can be triggered. And when the user sends an e-mail, an action can also be triggered. Therefore, when user selects one resource on the palette, the wizard will list possible usage and a short description of this resource as trigger events. If it can be used in both two types as introduced above, the wizard will notify user to select one type.

Step.2 Set Trigger Condition Parameter
In this step, the wizard will guide the user to specify the condition of the selected trigger event. The condition parameters can be specified will be shown in the wizard and users can select and edit one or more of them to filter the event they need to be captured. Our approach supports only simple data format when specify the condition parameter. Take the e-mail as example again, we allow users to specify the incoming mail title, sender or sending time, which can be edited in a simple text box or a time select box in the wizard.

Step.3 Select Action
In this step, end users only need to select an action from the palette. Unlike trigger events, if a resource can be used as an action, it usually can only perform a single function.

Step.4 Set Action Content
This step guides end users to specify how to perform the action. Two types of action content are allowed in our approach. One is manually input by end users, and another one is to use the content generated by the corresponding trigger event. The wizard will guide user to choose the type and then give more content for input or selection.

Step.5 (Optional) Set next action
This step is not necessary for all task creation. The action execution result sometimes can be used as a trigger of another action. In this case, the wizard will firstly check whether the action can return an execution result. If it can, the wizard will ask end users whether need to add another action at the end of Step.4. If users choose to add, the wizard will list the parameter for users to specify just like Step.2. Moreover, this step can be repeated to add more actions to generate a sequence of actions.

3.3   Resource Organization and Task Execution Mechanism

It should be firstly clarified that all the description information about the resource is done by IT department manually. Our approach does not contain any automatic discovery and description method for internal or external services. Thus except the description of the resource, its corresponding server or agent needs to be added to MES (This operation is labeled 1 in Figure.2 and only the number in brackets indicates the same meaning below). For example, when an external Google service is added to RR, the IT department should first embed the Google web service agent such as Gmap or Gmail agent to MES. And then the incoming and outgoing request of this kind of resource will be handled by MES.

As introduced above, all resources will be described in a fixed format and the format of resource description is given in Table.1.

Table 1. Resource and Task Description in XML Format

Resource	Task
<id>*value*</id> <name>*value*</name> <icon>*value*</icon> <class>*value*</class> <trigger> 　<condition> 　　<name>*value*</name> 　　<type>*value*</type> 　　<option>*optional*</option> 　</condition> </trigger> <action> 　<content > 　　<name>*value*</name> 　　<type>*value*</type> 　　<option>*optional*</option> 　</content > 　<feedback> 　　<name>*value*</name> 　　<type>*value*</type> 　</feedback> </action> <role>value</role>	<id>*value*</id> <user_id>*value*</user_id> <trigger> 　<trigger_id>*value*</trigger_id> 　<condition> 　　<type>*value*<type> 　　<value>*value*</value> 　</condition> </trigger> <action> 　<action_id>*value*</action_id> 　<content> 　　<type>*value*<type> 　　<value>*value*<value> 　</content> 　<feedback> 　　<type>*value*<type> 　　<value>*value*<value> 　　<action> … <action> 　</feedback> </action>

When the end user successfully login, the workspace will load all available resources from RR according to the account role (2). The workspace only stores the ID of all resources. Data field *name*, *icon* and *class* specify how the resource is displayed and categorized in the workspace. *Role* field indicates which end-user groups have access permission to this resource.

If this resource can be used as trigger event or action, its description will have the *'trigger'* or *'action'* label. After the end user selects a resource as trigger event or action, the wizard needs to load the condition parameter or the action content of resources. The *type* contained in *condition* and *content* label is the data type allow user to input, such as string, number value, time value, date value, and so on. The wizard provides different input UI component according to the data type. And as presented in Step.4 of the wizard, when the actions want to use the data related of the trigger, the wizard match these two data types in condition and content field. If they are of same type, the wizard will notify user to select whether use the trigger event data as the action parameter.

After creation of task, the task will be stored in TR with also a unified description (3). Its format is also given in Table.1. Every task is assigned an identifier, which is used to be monitored and looked up in MES. When a task is started, its description file is loaded to RTP (4). Our mechanism to monitor trigger events is to check RTP when every event occurs. Once an incoming request arrives or an action has performed by the end user, the resource id of these events is captured (5) and MES looks up RTS to check whether there is a running task with the same event type (6). If there is, MES will read the task *condition* data field, and fetch the corresponding data through embedded engine or agent for comparison with the condition. If the condition is satisfied, the *action_id* and *content* data field which indicates which action to perform and how the action should execute will be loaded by MES to perform the action. After execution of the action (7), if there is *feedback* data field exists in the task description, the feedback or response the MES received will be matched to this field. And if the match is successful, MES will then perform the action embedded in this *feedback* label.

Last but not least, how to communicate with agents and servers embedded in MES is not indicated in the description file. The related information, such as the server address, the API URL and so on, is hard-coded partly in RR and partly in MES. When the event is triggered, the MES will look up RR for the corresponding action and at the same time get the server information and then communicates with the server.

4   Case Study and Implementation

The motivating scenario illustrated in Section 2 is an actual business process in a heating system company JF. Our approach designed for JF is under development and will be used in this enterprise. Therefore, we conduct a case study to show how our approach is used in JF, a real enterprise environment.

The existing workflow system used in JF is based on jBPM technology [15]. To realize our framework in JF, we update this existing workflow system and embed it with the mailing system together in our MES. The major modification to the existing system is all jBPM workflow activities messages are passing through MES.

In technical perspective, we are developing this project using Java. The MES including four parts: jBPM workflow engine, mail server, a SIP server based on reSI-Procate SIP stack [16] handling incoming and outgoing communications, and several

Google Web Service Agent including Gmaps, Gcal and Gmail. The regular events including time and date are also supported in our implementation. The time is monitored every fifteen minutes and the date is checked at the start of a new day. To develop web-based workspace, we use Apache web server and MySQL database. And we use ExtJS [17] JavaScript framework to build the workspace with rich UI.

Now we illustrate how to create such a process in our framework using our proposed wizard. Figure.3 shows five steps wizard to create a personalized process by Manager B discussed in Section 2.

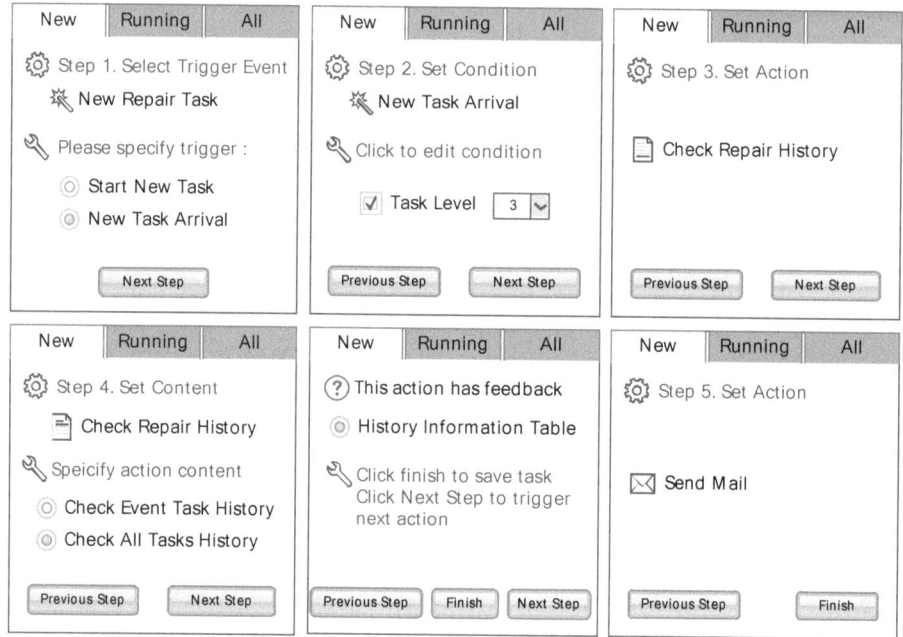

Fig. 3. Wizard Design Example Used in JF Company

Manager B firstly selects the resource "new repair task" as the trigger event. This is a jBPM process wrapped as a resource can be used by end users. In this resource description created by IT department of JF, there are two *trigger* fields. The first one is "start new task", which is triggered every time the end user starts a new repair task. And the second one is "new task arrival", which is triggered when a new repair task arrives to the end user. By loading the *trigger* field in resource description file, the workspace notifies user to select one trigger from these two. If Manager B selects the second, the wizard will refresh and load the *condition* field. There is one condition field with the *name* field as "task level" and *type* field as "integer". Only if Manager B selects the condition displayed and then can edit the parameter. To offer choices for end users to select, several *option* fields are included in description and the wizard will display them in a drop-down box. After set the trigger event, the wizard comes to Step.3. The action Manager B selects is "check repair history" and it can be executed by opening an existing web page displaying repair tasks history. This action offers two options to check repair history information. And the *type* field of action content is "select" which have several options displayed in radio buttons. At last, there is a *feedback* field in the description which indicates the history information can be used as the content of another action. The *type* filed of the feedback is text, which can be used for invoke short message service, mail service and so on. Therefore the Step.5 guides Manager B to select an action from the palette to tackle the text of history information. Finally the wizard prompts Manager B to finish the creation and stores the task into RTP automatically.

The actual result of this personalized business action is as follows. Every time a repair task has larger level than three comes to Manage B, instead of the web page for assigning engineer (which is used in a standard process), but all tasks history information is displayed in a web page. After check the information, Manager B will proceed to assign engineer and the information he checked will be sent to Manager B by mail. This complete procedure is in accordance with the predefined business process developed by Manager B without any IT department participation.

5   Conclusion and Future Work

The growing demand for personalized business process has attracted many researchers making efforts towards enabling end users to create their own business applications. As a tradeoff between the "heavy" approaches such as WS-BPEL and "lightweight" technology such as enterprise mashup, this paper presents a novel approach for business end users to create personalized business process. The approach makes end users concentrate on logical event-driven relationship of resources from multiple sources rather than the front-end interface composition.

The main contribution of this approach has two parts:

- An integrated framework to develop, monitor and execute personalized business process in a lightweight event-driven fashion.
- A wizard-based workspace accessed from Web browser which guides user to select and compose services from internal business process, external Web APIs and communication services. The wizard is a tutorial designed for end users without technical knowledge.

In addition, there are also some open issues for our approach. Firstly, the current resources opened for end users to select are listed in the workspace and only allow end users to search by the name of the resources. We are further designing a complete description and category mechanism of the resources, which enabled user to find the desired resources directly and rapidly. Secondly, since the resources used in JF is not too complex and the event-driven model we use is lightweight, our approach does not contain any validation of the event-driven model. However, if there are a large number of actions having feedback, when end users use the feedback of actions to compose an action sequence, there still some validation needs to be performed. Finally, we are interested in cloud computing and considering how to extend this framework in the cloud environment. We hope to share this framework between different enterprises, which involves security issues and the execution environment based on virtualized machines.

Acknowledgement. This research is supported by the National Natural Science Foundation of China (Grant No. 61003067), National 973 Programs (Grant No. 2011CB302704), and Key Project of National Natural Science Foundation of China (Grant No. 61132001).

References

1. Fielding, R.: Architectural Styles and the Design of Network-based Software Architectures. PhD thesis, University of California, Irvine (2000)
2. Schroth, C., Janner, T.: Web 2.0 and SOA: Converging Concepts Enabling the Internet of Services. IT Professional 9(3), 36–41 (2007)
3. Cherbakov, L., Bravery, A., Goodman, B.D., Pandya, A., Baggett, J.: Changing the corporate IT development model: Tapping the power of grassroots computing. IBM Systems Journal 46(4), 743 (2007)
4. OMG, Business Process Model and Notation (2011),
   http://www.omg.org/spec/BPMN/2.0/
5. OASIS, Web Services Business Process Execution Language Version 2.0 (2007),
   http://docs.oasis-open.org/wsbpel/2.0/wsbpel-v2.0.html
6. Nestler, T., Dannecker, L., Pursche, A.: User-Centric Composition of Service Front-Ends at the Presentation Layer. In: Dan, A., Gittler, F., Toumani, F. (eds.) ICSOC/ServiceWave 2009. LNCS, vol. 6275, pp. 520–529. Springer, Heidelberg (2010)
7. Laga, N., Bertin, E., Crespi, N.: Business Process Personalization through Web Widgets. In: Proceedings of IEEE International Conference on Web Services (ICWS) (2010)
8. Hoyer, V., Stanoesvka-Slabeva, K., Janner, T., Schroth, C.: Enterprise Mashups: Design Principles towards the Long Tail of User Needs. In: Proceedings of the IEEE International Conference on Services Computing (SCC) (2008)
9. Roychowdhury, P., Dasgupta, D.: Take advantage of Web 2.0 for next-generation BPM 2.0 (2008), http://www.ibm.com/developerworks/webservices/library/ws-web2bpm2/index.html
10. de Vrieze, P., Xua, L., Bouguettaya, A., Yang, J., Chen, J.: Building enterprise mashups. Future Generation Computer Systems 27, 637–642 (2011)
11. Namoun, A., Wajid, U., Mehandjiev, N.: A Comparative Study: Service-Based Application Development by Ordinary End Users and IT Professionals. In: Di Nitto, E., Yahyapour, R. (eds.) ServiceWave 2010. LNCS, vol. 6481, pp. 163–174. Springer, Heidelberg (2010)
12. Ifttt (if this then that) (2011), http://www.ifttt.com
13. Boyaci, O., Martinez, V.B., Schulzrinne, H.: Bridging Communications and the Physical World. IEEE Internet Computing, 35–43 (March/April 2012)
14. Google Calendar application (2006), https://www.google.com/calendar
15. jBPM open-source business process management suite,
    http://www.jboss.org/jbpm
16. reSIProcate SIP stack, http://www.resiprocate.org
17. ExtJS JavaScript Framework, http://www.sencha.com/products/extjs

A Combination Approach to QoS Prediction of Web Services

Dongjin Yu, Mengmeng Wu, and Yuyu Yin

College of Computer, Hangzhou Dianzi University
Hangzhou China
{yudj,yinyuyu}@hdu.edu.cn, hdu409meng@126.com

Abstract. With a growing number of alternative Web services that provide the same functionality but differ in quality properties, the problem of selecting the best performing candidate service is becoming more and more important. However, users can hardly have invoked all services, meaning that the QoS values of some services are missing. In this paper, we propose a combination approach used to predict such missing QoS values. It employs an adjusted user-based algorithm using Pearson Correlation Coefficient to predict the QoS values of ordinary services. For services with constantly poor performance, however, it employs the average QoS values observed by different service users instead. An extensive performance study based on a real public dataset is finally reported to verify its effectiveness.

Keywords: Quality of Services, Prediction, Service Selection, Web Services.

1 Introduction

With a growing number of alternative Web services that provide the same functionality but differ in quality properties, the problem of selecting the best performing candidate service is becoming more and more important. Due to some inevitable reasons, e.g., location and network environment, the QoS of the same service to different users may be different. For example, the response time for an USA user u_a to invoke web service located in Spain is 5626ms, while that for a Japan user u_b to invoke the same one is 687ms. A user can hardly have invoked all services, meaning that the QoS values of some services that the user has not invoked are missing. Hence, some effective approaches are urgently needed to provide accurate prediction of the QoS values of different Web services for each user without requiring real Web service invocations.

In recent years, researchers have proposed a number of QoS prediction approaches [1-3]. Inspired by the application of Collaborative Filtering (CF) [4] in product recommendation, CF has been extensively employed to predict QoS values using Web service QoS evaluations from different users. It is often classified as memory-based or model-based. For the memory-based ones, all training data are stored in memory. In the prediction phase, similar objects (users or items) are sorted based on their similarities with the active object. Pearson Correlation Coefficient (PCC) is a widely used method to compute the similarities between objects. Based on the data from similar

A. Ghose et al. (Eds.): ICSOC 2012, LNCS 7759, pp. 99–106, 2013.

users or items, a prediction result can be generated. The most analyzed examples of memory-based methods include user-based methods [4-6], item-based methods [7, 8] and fusion methods [9]. For the model-based ones, on the other hand, training data are used to generate a predicting model that is able to predict the missing data. The most analyzed model-based examples include decision tree [4], aspect models [10] and latent semantic models [11, 12].

Many works have been done to predict the missing QoS values. Shao et al. propose a user-based CF algorithm to make similarity mining and predict the QoS of Web services from consumers' experiences [1]. Zheng et al. present a hybrid approach which combines user-based and item-based approach together to predict the QoS of Web services [2]. Chen et al. discover the great influence of a user's location to the accuracy of prediction and propose a region-based hybrid CF algorithm to predict the QoS of services [3]. However, the prediction accuracies of those methods are far from satisfactory.

To improve the prediction accuracy, we propose a combination approach. The basic idea is that we use different methods to predict the QoS values of different services. Considering unstable network environments, we first classify the services into the poor ones with constantly poor performance, and ordinary ones. The final QoS is estimated by different methods based on the category which the target service belongs to. For ordinary target services, it employs an adjusted user-based algorithm using Pearson Correlation Coefficient, or adjusted UPCC, to predict the QoS values. For services with constantly poor performance, however, it employs IMEAN, i.e., uses the average QoS values observed by different service users, instead.

The contributions of this work are as follows. (1) We propose a combination approach to predict missing QoS values. (2) We evaluate the proposed approach experimentally by employing a real-world Web service QoS dataset.

The rest of this paper is organized as follows: Section 2 presents our QoS value prediction approach in detail. Section 3 describes our experiments. Section 4 concludes the paper.

2   Prediction Approach

In real world, QoS of service not only relies on the executing environment of services, but also heavily depends on unstable network environment. As a result, some services with constantly poor performance (named as poor services for ease of presentation) may be published on the Internet. Our prediction approach is based on the following assumption: poor services should low the prediction accuracy. The approach has three major steps.

1)   Find the top N poor services using IMEAN;
2)   If the prediction service is one of the top N poor services, IMEAN is used to predict its QoS performance;
3)   If the prediction service is not one of the top N poor services, adjusted UPCC is used to predict its QoS performance.

2.1   Classification of Services

To find poor services, we first list the services in descending order from their IMEAN values. Then we classify the top N services and the others into poor services category and ordinary services category respectively. The formula used to calculate IMEAN values is as follows:

$$P_{u,s} = \frac{\sum_{u_1 \in U_s} r_{u_1,s}}{|U_s|}, \tag{1}$$

where $r_{u_1,s}$ is the vector of QoS values of service s invoked by user u_1, U_s is the set of users have invoked s, and $|U_s|$ is number of users have invoked s.

Obviously, the number N of poor services is the key for our approach. Through some tests, we find the most accurate prediction results using our approach could be acquired   when N equals to 5. These tests will be shown in Section 3.

2.2   Prediction of QoS Values

Because we use different predicting methods for services form different categories, we must judge which category the target service belongs to before the calculation of missing value. If the target service belongs to the poor services category, IMEAN is used. Otherwise, adjusted UPCC is used. Due to IMEAN having been introduced in Section 2.1, we present adjusted UPCC method here.

PCC has been introduced in a number of recommender systems for similarity computation, since it can be easily implemented and achieves high accuracy. The similarity between two users u_1 and u_2 based on the PCC is computed using the following equation:

$$\phi_{u_1,u_2} = \frac{\sum_{s \in S}(r_{u_1,s} - \bar{r}_{u_1})((r_{u_2,s} - \bar{r}_{u_2})}{\sqrt{\sum_{s \in S}(r_{u_1,s} - \bar{r}_{u_1})^2}\sqrt{\sum_{s \in S}(r_{u_2,s} - \bar{r}_{u_2})^2}}, \tag{2}$$

where $S = S_{u_1} \cap S_{u_2}$ is the subset of Web service items which user u_1 and user u_2 invoked together, and $\bar{r}_{u_1}$ represents the vector of average QoS values of the user u_1.

Although PCC can provide accurate similarity computation, it will overestimate the similarities of service users who are actually not similar but happen to have similar QoS experience on a few co-invoked Web services. To address this problem, we employ an adjusted formula to reduce the influence of a small number of similar co-invoked items. An adjusted PCC formula for the similarity computation between different service users is defined as:

$$\phi'_{u_1,u_2} = \frac{2 \times |S|}{|S_{u_1}| + |S_{u_2}|} \phi_{u_1,u_2}, \tag{3}$$

After calculating the similarities between different users, a set of similar neighbors can be identified. The selection of similar neighbors is an important step for making accurate missing value prediction, since dissimilar neighbors will decrease the prediction accuracy. Traditional Top-K algorithms rank the neighbors based on their PCC similarities and select the top K most similar neighbors. In practice, some entries in the user-item matrix have limited similar neighbors or even do not have any neighbors. Traditional Top-K algorithms ignore this problem and still include dissimilar neighbors to predict the missing value, which will greatly reduce the prediction accuracy. To solve this problem, we propose an enhanced Top-K algorithm, where neighbors with PCC similarities smaller or equal to ξ will be excluded. A set of target user u' similar neighbors can be found by the following equation:

$$L(u) = \{u_a | u_a \epsilon T(u), \phi'_{u_1,u_2} > \xi, u_a \neq u\}, \tag{4}$$

where $T(u)$ is a set of top K similar users to the user u, and ξ a similarity threshold.

The final prediction method employs the data of similar users to predict the missing value of target service s to target user u as follows:

$$P_{u,s} = \bar{u} + \frac{\sum_{u_1 \in L_u} \phi'_{u,u_1} \times (r_{u_1,s} - \bar{u}_1)}{\sum_{u_1 \in L_u} \phi'_{u,u_1}}, \tag{5}$$

where L_u are a set of user u's similar users, and $\bar{u}$ is a vector of average QoS values of different Web services observed by the active user u.

3   Experiments

3.1   Experimental Setup

We have conducted our experiments using a public real-world Web service QoS dataset, which is collected by Zibin Zheng et.al [2]. It contains the records of 1,974,675 Web service invocations executed by 339 distributed service users on 5825 Web services. The record of each invocation contains 2 parameters: Response Time and Throughput. More details about this dataset can be found in [13]. In this paper, we randomly extract 150 users, 100 Web services and use the invocation records between them as the experimental data.

Our experiments are implemented with Matlab 7.0 and MySQL 5.0. They are conducted on a Dell Inspire R13 machine with a 2.27 GHz Intel Core I5 CPU and 2GB RAM, running Windows 7 OS.

3.2   Evaluation Metric

In our experiments, *NMAE* is used to evaluate the accuracy of prediction. Mean Absolute Error (*MAE*) is as follows:

$$MAE = \frac{\sum_{U,S} |r_{u,s} - \hat{r}_{u,s}|}{N} \tag{6}$$

where $r_{u,s}$ represents the predicted QoS value of service s observed by user u, $\hat{r}_{u,s}$ stands for the expected or real QoS value and N is the total number of predictions. As we know, services QoS value range may differ tremendously. As an adjustment, NMAE normalizes the differences range of *MAE* by computing:

$$NMAE = \frac{MAE}{\sum_{U,S} \frac{r_{u,s}}{N}} \tag{7}$$

Here, the smaller NMAE means the more accurate QoS prediction.

3.3   Performance Comparison

We compare the proposed approach with five typical prediction methods: User Mean(UMEAN), Item Mean(IMEAN), User-based algorithm using PCC (UPCC), Item-based algorithm using PCC (IPCC), and WSRec. UMEAN uses the average QoS of the service user on other Web services to predict the QoS of other Web services, while IMEAN uses the average QoS of the Web service observed by other service users to predict the QoS for the current user. UPCC uses similar users for QoS prediction, while IPCC uses similar services for QoS prediction. WSRec uses a linear combination of the UPCC and IPCC results together. To the best of our knowledge, WSRec is the best one for QoS prediction currently. In the experiment, we set $K=10$ and $\xi = 0.3$. Each experiment is run for 50 times and the average NMAE values are reported.

Table 1 shows the NMAE results of different prediction methods on Response Time and Throughput using 10 and 20 percent densities of the training matrix respectively.   For the users in testing matrix, we vary the number of invoked services (given number) as 10 and 20 by randomly removing entries (named as $g10$, $g20$, and $g30$, in Table 1). In addition, the number of training users is varied as 100 and 140.

From Table 1, under all experimental settings, our method obtains smaller NMAE values in all cases, which demonstrates better prediction accuracy. The prediction results when Training users=140 is more accurate than the results when Training users=100. Meanwhile, the increase of the density of a training matrix enhances the prediction accuracy. The reason is that higher density means more training data for the prediction. In addition, the increase of the number of invoked services ($g10$, $g20$, and $g30$) also improves the prediction accuracy. It indicates that the prediction accuracy can be enhanced by providing more QoS values.

3.4   Evaluation of the Top N

In our paper, parameter N denotes the number of the poorest services. To study the impact of the parameter N on the efficiency of our prediction approach, we vary the value of N from 0 to 10 with a step value of 1. Figure 1 (a) and (c) show the accuracy of prediction, with given number of 20 (g20), with 10, 20, and 30 percent density of training matrix of Response Time and Throughput, respectively. Figure 1 (b) and (d) show the accuracy of 20 percent density with given number 10, 20, and 30 of Response Time and Throughput, respectively.

Table 1. NMAE Comparison with Different Prediction Approaches

Density	Methods	T=100					
		Response Time			Throughput		
		g10	g20	g30	g10	g20	g30
10%	UMEAN	0.9809	0.972	0.9448	1.1335	1.083	1.0812
	IMEAN	0.5368	0.5124	0.5154	0.6182	0.614	0.6258
	UPCC	0.5443	0.4587	0.4272	0.8277	0.7168	0.7018
	IPCC	0.437	0.4127	0.3981	0.7466	0.6906	0.6886
	WSRec	0.4362	0.4107	0.3958	0.7463	0.6896	0.6871
	Our Method	0.3972	0.358	0.3407	0.6913	0.6456	0.6322
20%	UMEAN	0.9861	0.9771	0.9827	1.1152	1.0676	1.055
	IMEAN	0.5173	0.5047	0.4911	0.5916	0.6204	0.6031
	UPCC	0.5012	0.4358	0.4043	0.7521	0.6717	0.626
	IPCC	0.3714	0.3585	0.3409	0.6562	0.6347	0.6154
	WSRec	0.3702	0.3568	0.3394	0.6547	0.6317	0.6115
	Our Method	0.3596	0.3279	0.306	0.6378	0.6055	0.5769
Density	Methods	T=140					
		Response Time			Throughput		
		g10	g20	g30	g10	g20	g30
10%	UMEAN	1.0597	0.94	0.9059	1.1128	1.0793	1.0159
	IMEAN	0.4792	0.493	0.4668	0.6151	0.6106	0.6007
	UPCC	0.5409	0.4347	0.3718	0.7981	0.735	0.6608
	IPCC	0.397	0.3744	0.3555	0.7075	0.6985	0.6445
	WSRec	0.395	0.3727	0.3534	0.7061	0.6963	0.6425
	Our Method	0.373	0.3296	0.2875	0.6722	0.6321	0.59
20%	UMEAN	1.0208	0.9285	0.8551	1.189	1.0811	1.026
	IMEAN	0.4737	0.4571	0.4759	0.5914	0.568	0.5601
	UPCC	0.4886	0.3867	0.3476	0.8243	0.6503	0.5849
	IPCC	0.3386	0.3291	0.3059	0.7062	0.604	0.5725
	WSRec	0.3376	0.3272	0.3039	0.7052	0.6006	0.5689
	Our Method	0.3303	0.3097	0.2877	0.6605	0.5688	0.553

Observing from Figure1, we can draw the conclusion that the value of N impacts the predicted results significantly. In addition, when $N=5$, the most accurate results are provided for both Response Time and Throughput.

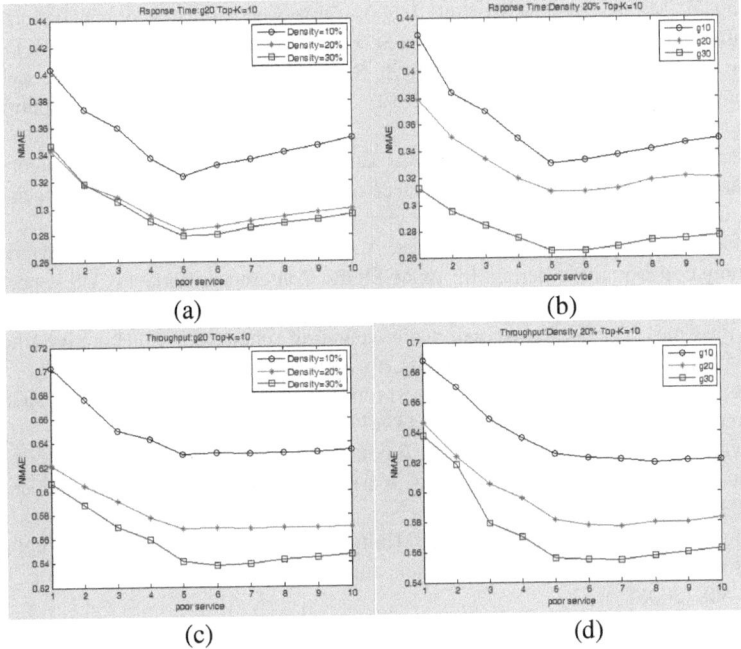

Fig. 1. Impact of the top N

4   Conclusion

In this paper, we present a combination approach to predict the missing QoS values. Different from the previous methods, considering unstable network environment, we classify the services into poor services category and ordinary service category, and use different predicting methods based on the category which the target service belongs to. The experiments based on a public dataset prove that our prediction approach outperforms the existing methods.

In the future, we will explore the service selection framework. Furthermore, we will also collect more QoS data of Web services to improve the scale of our experiments.

Acknowledgments. This research was partially supported by the National Natural Science Foundation of China with grant number of 61100043 and the Natural Science Foundation of Zhejiang with grand number of LY12F02003. The authors would also like to thank anonymous reviewers who gave valuable suggestion to improve the quality of the paper.

References

1. Shao, L., Zhang, J., Wei, Y., Zhao, J., Xie, B., Mei, H.: Personalized QoS prediction for web services via collaborative filtering. In: IEEE International Conference on Web Services, Salt Lake City, USA, pp. 439–446 (2007)

2. Zheng, Z., Ma, H., Lyu, M.R., King, I.: Qos-aware web service recommendation by collaborative filtering. IEEE Transactions on Service Computing 4(2), 140–152 (2011)
3. Chen, X., Zheng, Z., Liu, X., Huang, Z., Sun, H.: Personalized QoS-aware web service recommendation and visualization. IEEE Transactions on Services Computing PP(99) (2011)
4. Breese, J.S., Heckerman, D., Kadie, C.: Empirical analysis of predictive algorithms for collaborative filtering. In: 14th Conference on Uncertainty in Artificial Intelligence, Madison, USA, pp. 43–52 (1998)
5. Herlocker, J.L., Konstan, J.A., Borchers, A., Riedl, J.: An algorithmic framework for performing collaborative filtering. In: ACM SIGIR Conference, Berkeley, USA, pp. 230–237 (1999)
6. Jin, R., Chai, J.Y., Si, L.: An automatic weighting scheme for collaborative filtering. In: ACM SIGIR Conference, Sheffield, UK, pp. 337–344 (2004)
7. Deshpande, M., Karypis, G.: Item-based top-n recommendation algorithms. ACM Transaction on Information System 22(1), 143–177 (2004)
8. Sarwar, B., Karypic, G., Konstan, J., Riedl, J.: Item-based collaborative filtering recommendation algorithms. In: International World Wide Web Conference, Hong Kong, China, pp. 285–295 (2001)
9. Wang, J., Vries, A.P., Reinders, M.J.: Unifying user-based and item-based collaborative filtering approaches by similarity fusion. In: ACM SIGIR Conference, Seattle, USA, pp. 501–508 (2006)
10. Si, L., Jin, R.: Flexible mixture model for collaborative filtering. In: International Conference on Machine Learning, Washington, USA (2003)
11. Hofmann, T.: Collaborative filtering via Gaussian probabilistic latent semantic analysis. In: ACM SIGIR Conference, Toronto, Canada, pp. 259–266 (2003)
12. Hofmann, T.: Latent semantic models for collaborative filtering. ACM Transaction on Information System 22(1), 89–115 (2004)
13. Zheng, Z., Zhang, Y., Lyu, M.R.: Distributed QoS evaluation for real-world web services. In: International Conference on Web Services, Miami, USA, pp. 83–90 (2010)

Effective and Efficient Web Reviews Extraction Based on Hadoop

Jian Wan, Jiawei Yan, Congfeng Jiang, Li Zhou, Zujie Ren, and Yongjian Ren

Hangzhou Dianzi University, School of Computer Science and Technology,
Hangzhou 310018, China
yanjw1988@gmail.com

Abstract. The rapid development of Web 2.0 brings the flourish of web reviews. Traditional web review data extraction methods suffer from poor performance in dealing with massive data. To solve this problem, we propose an effective and efficient approach to extract web reviews based on Hadoop. It overcomes inefficiency when dealing with large-scale data, and enables the accuracy and efficiency in extracting the massive data sets. Our proposed approach consists of two components: a review record extraction algorithm based on node similarity, and a review content extraction algorithm based on the text depth. We design a Hadoop-based web reviews automatic extraction system. At last, we test the extraction system using the massive web reviews page sets. The experimental results show that this extraction system can achieve accuracy of more than 96%, and also can obtain a higher speedup, compared with the traditional web extraction.

Keywords: web reviews, information extraction, massive data, cloud computing, Hadoop.

1   Introduction

Nowadays, hundreds of millions of users can publish various data freely on the Internet, which makes web information data grows rapidly. How we can get valuable information quickly from such a huge-volume data has become a challenging issue.

In the e-Commerce field, a large number of product reviews are emerged, such as commodity reviews, news comments and so on. Mining reviews generated by web users has become an important solution to improve the search quality of goods, which has attracted much attention in the industrial and academic field.

The premise of mining review data is to extract review data. Compared with the general information extraction[1][2][3], review data extraction is much more complex. Review contents of web pages are much diverse and flexible. Web users generally edit the review content with various data types, such as pictures, tables, videos etc. These facts decrease the accuracy and efficiency of review data extraction. With the data volume grows rapidly, traditional information extraction is usually hard to satisfy the performance requirement.

A. Ghose et al. (Eds.): ICSOC 2012, LNCS 7759, pp. 107–118, 2013.

In this paper, we design an effective method for extracting massive review data through Hadoop[4] framework. Nowadays, existing applications of Hadoop mainly focus on the data statistics tasks, and tasks logic is simple and the task is easy to cut. This uses Hadoop framework to implement parallel processing of the web review data extraction. However, due to the complexity of the procedure, design an effective review extraction algorithm and divide review extraction tasks into multiple nodes of Hadoop efficiently become the key problems.

In order to solve these problems, we propose a Hadoop-based web automatic review extraction approach. This paper's mainly contributions as follows:

- We propose a review record extraction algorithm based on the node similarity. This algorithm has effectively improved the accuracy of extraction, by using visual information of a web page and node similarity technology.
- We propose a review content extraction algorithm based on the text depth. According to the different text length of all review record sub-tree nodes, this algorithm uses a method based on text depth to confirm the location of the review content area and generates the corresponding wrapper of review extraction with the same template web pages.
- We design a Hadoop-based web review automatic extraction system. The system can effectively finish extracting review content accurately from web review pages.

The rest of the paper is organized as follows: Section 2 describes the review record and review content extraction algorithm and implementation; Section 3 introduces the Hadoop-based web review automatic extraction system; Section 4 shows the experimental evaluation of this extraction system; Section 5 presents the related work; Section 6 concludes this paper.

2   Web Review Automatic Extraction Approach and Implementation

The Hadoop-based web review automatic extraction approach consists of four modules: 1) Web page parsing; 2) Review record extraction; 3) Review content extraction; 4) Review content storage. Fig 1 shows the overall workflow of the approach.

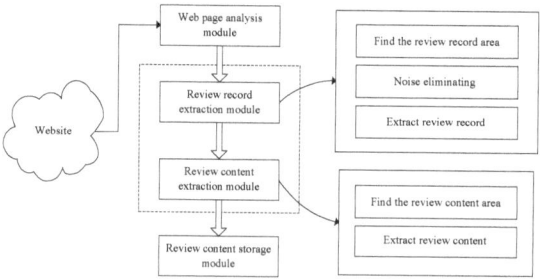

Fig. 1. The procedure of web review automatic extraction approach

2.1   Web Page Parsing

Parsing web page and building the DOM[5] tree is a necessary step in today a number of web information extraction algorithms. In this paper, we mainly study the pure HTML web pages. The HTML file can be transformed into a DOM tree easily, because of HTML tags come in pairs. Each tag pair consists of a start tag (<>) and a closing tag (</>). Each node of the DOM tree is mapped by a pair of tags in the web page file, and the child nodes of this node are mapped by the nested tags.

2.2   Review Record Extraction Algorithm and Implementation

In web review pages using the same template to render, review records are always arranged in the specific location. Based on the observation of a large number of real web review pages, we extract review records according to the following rules:

- *Rule 1*: The review record area contains one or more sub-trees.
- *Rule 2*: Review records with the same template contain the same amount of sub-trees.

The entire review record extraction algorithm contains three parts: 1) Locate the review record area of the web page; 2) Eliminate noisy information in the review record area; 3) Extract the review records, forming as the input of the review content extraction algorithm.

Locate the Review Record Area

As web page tags are lack of semantic information, visual information is used to be merged into the DOM tree. Visual information on the web page has been proved as very effective feature information in the web data extraction algorithm, such as the algorithm in [6]. Based on the feature of the web review page, which there will be published time after web user comment on a product or problem, this paper identifies the review record area.

To facilitate the exposition of these rules, we define some symbols to represent the corresponding component of a DOM tree. Table 1 gives the description of these symbols.

Table 1. Symbols description

Symbols	Content
Root	the root node of web page's DOM tree
Tregion	the minimal sub-tree contains whole review records in DOM tree
Rregion	the root node of *Tregion*
Treview	the tree contains review record in *Tregion*
Tnoise	the tree contains non-review record in *Tregion*
Timenode	the node contains the publish time content in *Tregion*

The algorithm begins to depth-first traverse the DOM tree, and then finds out the nodes with a *Timenode* type child, which often can be *Treview* nodes. And then we find the review records' minimum ancestor node, which is the root node of the review record area *Rregion* according to the *Rule 1*.

Eliminate the Noisy Information

Eliminating the noisy information sub-tree from the review record area is a key step in the review record extraction algorithm. In order to eliminate these noisy information sub-trees, this paper invents a tree similarity algorithm, which calculates the similarity between any two sub-trees of the review record area. For sub-tree X and Y, with root node x and y respectively, the similarity of X and Y is calculated as follows:

$$TS(X,Y) = DS(x,y) + LCS(X,Y) \tag{1}$$

DS (x, y) is the depth similarity of node x or y in the *Tregion*. *LCS (X, Y)* is the similarity of the longest common sequence of sub-tree X and Y.

The formula to calculate *DS (x, y)* is given as follows:

$$DS(x,y) = tan\left(\frac{\pi(depth(x,y) - avgDepth(Tregion))}{2L}\right) \tag{2}$$

Here, *depth (x, y)* is the depth of the node x or y in *Tregion*, *avgDepth (Tregion)* is the average depth of all nodes of *Tregion* in DOM tree and *L* is stand for the difference between maximum and minimum depth of the nodes in *Tregion*. So the value of *DS (x, y)* depends on the *depth (x, y)* and *avgDepth (Tregion)*. We use trigonometric functions to effectively enlarge the depth differences between the nodes, and so that improve accuracy of the following noise eliminating algorithm.

The tree similarity algorithm takes several steps: Firstly, match the root node x and y of the sub-tree X and Y. If not match, terminate the algorithm, *TS (X, Y) = 0*; If match, calculate the value of *DS (x, y)* and *LCS (X, Y)*, and then *TS(X, Y) = DS(x, y) + LCS(X, Y)*. The value of *DS (x, y)* can be calculated according to the formula (2). *LCS (X, Y)* is computed by summing the longest common subsequence's similarity values of the sub-tree X and Y.

The pseudo-code of tree similarity algorithm is illustrated as follows:

Algorithm TS // Tree Similarity.
```
Input: X, Y; //Two subtrees
Output: s; //The similarity between X and Y
Begin
x=the root of X;
y=the root of Y;
if NodeMatching(x,y) is false then
return 0;
return DS(x,y)+LCS(Children(x),Children(y));
End
```

The global similarity of the adjacent two sub-trees is used to describe the variation trend between the review record sub-trees and noise sub-trees. If the noisy information sub-tree exists, the maximum ratio is produced in the first review record sub-tree and the noise sub-tree just before it, and the smallest ratio is produced between the last review record sub-tree and the noise sub-tree after it. Here, global similarity value of a *Tregion* is defined as the maximum value of similarities between each child and its brothers, which are formulized by *gs*.

Base on the above ideas, we propose a noise eliminating algorithm, which can be described as follows:

Firstly, calculate the similarity between any two children sub-trees in the *Tregion* using the tree similarity algorithm. Then, gain the global similarity of each child sub-tree and calculate the ratio of the global similarity between the adjacent child sub-trees. Finally, according to the maximum and minimum value, identify the location of the first review record sub-tree *Start* and the last review record sub-tree *End*.

The pseudo-code of noisy eliminating algorithm is presented as follows:

Algorithm EN // Eliminate Noise.
```
Input: Tregion, n; // Tregion is the tree of review re-
gion, n is the numbers of review trees.
Output: Start, End;   //Start is the first review record
position, End is the last review record position
Begin
T[n]=Children(Tregion);
for i=1 to n do
for j=1 to n do
gs[i]=Max(TS(Ti,Tj));
for i=2 to n do
  Start=Max(gs[i]/gs[i-1]);
End=Min(gs[i]/gs[i-1]);
return Start and End;
End
```

Extract Review Record

Extracting review records from the review record area is the final step of the review record extraction algorithm. Specific ideas described as: use the location information from the noise eliminating algorithm as the output of the Map function directly.

The pseudo-code of extracting the review records is illustrated as follows:

Algorithm RE // Record Extract.
```
Input: URL,Page; //Web review page's URL and content
Output: URL,Treviews;  //Treviews is the review tree
Begin
method Map(URL, Page)
Tregion=Region(Page);
TS(Children(Tregion));
EN(Tregion);
for i=Start to End do
EMIT(URL,Treviews);
End
```

2.3   Review Content Extraction Algorithm and Implementation

In each sub-tree of the review records, the review content corresponds to a complex sub-tree rather than a simple leaf node. Therefore identifying the minimal sub-tree, which contains the whole review content, is the key to the review content extraction algorithm. The review content extraction algorithm consists of two steps: 1) Locate the review content area; 2) Extract the review content from the review content area.

Locate the Review Content Area

In this paper, we define a minimal sub-tree, which contains all the review content in the review record sub-tree, as the review content sub-tree, which is formalized by *Tcontent*. Its root node is formalized by *Rconent*. The semantics are the same among the review content in the review record sub-trees. So we can find out one review record sub-tree's *Rcontent* node, and identify the review content area, which is the location of the review content in the same template pages.

Since of the length of all review text contents in *Tcontent* is most inconsistent, we propose a novel approach of extracting review content based on the text depth of the contents. The detailed approach is described as follows: Firstly, find out the longest length node among the all review record sub-trees. Then, calculate the depth value of this node, and compare to the depth value of this review record sub-tree. If the value is equal, it means that the node is a review content node; If not equal, we recalculated to find the second longest node, and repeat this process. Finally, after finding the review content node, we travel up the review record sub-tree to find the common node of the review content node and the *Timednode*, which are the review record sub-tree's *Rconent*.

Extract Review Content

After identifying the review content area in the sub-tree of the review record, we get the real review content in loop output all text content under the sub-tree of the review record with the same page template. These text contents are the final content of the review extracted, because that the semantics of the order of review records on the same template is consistent with the rules.

The pseudo-code of extracting the review content is given as follows:

```
Algorithm CE // Content Extract.
Input: URL,Treviews;    //Web review page's URL and review
trees
Output: URL,Contents;   // Web review page's URL and re-
view contents
Begin
method Reduce(URL, Treviews)
Ntext=getMaxNode(Treviews);
flag=Compare(Depth(Ntext),Depth(Treview));
if(falg=0)
Rancester=getAncestor(Ntext,getTimeNode(Treviews));
Tcontent=Children(Rancester)
EMIT(URL,getText(Tcontent));
End
```

3   Web Review Automatic Extraction System Design

The input of the Hadoop-based web review automatic extraction system is the web review pages, and outputs are the review text contents, which are extracted from the input pages. The system is able to efficiently extract the review content accurately from the web review pages. The detailed data processing of the system is showed in Fig 2.

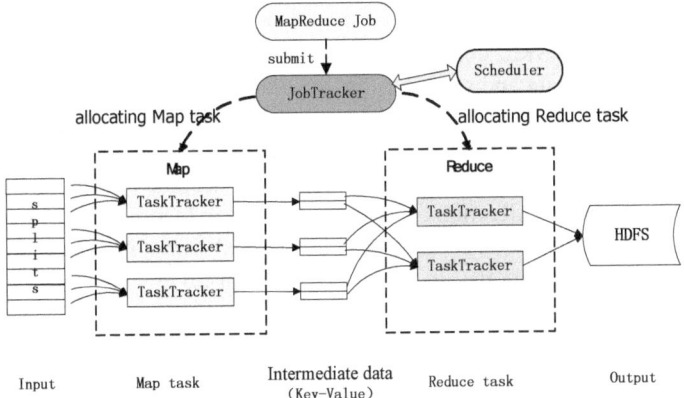

Fig. 2. Data processing in the Hadoop-based Web review automatic extraction system

The workflow of Hadoop-based web review automatic extraction system is described as follows:

1. Each map task is assigned to a part of the input file, which is called a split. In this system, the content of split is the web review page. And the total number of splits determines the number of map tasks.
2. The execution of the map tasks can be divided into two steps: The first step is to read the input splits (web review page), and turn them into the data records (key-value pairs, where as a web page URL - web content). The second step is to apply the map function (implementation of the review record extraction algorithm) to each record.
3. Next is the execution of the reduce task, which is divided into three steps: Firstly, the shuffle phase, gains the intermediate data (review record sub-tree), which are generated by the map task. Each partition of the intermediate data will be transferred to each reduce task. Secondly, in the sort phase, the records with the same key value will be combined together (the same page of review record sub-trees are grouped together). Finally, in the reduce phase, the user-defined reduce function (execute the review content extraction algorithm) will be executed on each record and the corresponding list of values (the review tree in each web page).
4. Finally, the output of the reduce function (review content) will be written to the temporary storage unit of the HDFS. When all the reduce tasks are finished, the output files in the HDFS will be changed the temporary storage unit into the final storage unit automatically.

4   Experiment Evaluation

In this chapter, experiments of web review automatic extraction system based on Hadoop will be conducted to evaluate the overall performance and efficiency of this novel review extraction approach.

4.1   Data Source Collection

The data set of user review content extraction is generated from the Internet. In order to crawl the review data and save it to the local disk, a dedicated crawler is designed. The rules by what the crawler recognizes review pages from web pages are based on regular expressions for distinguishing review page's URL, which is compiled artificially. And the accuracy of the URL recognition accuracy is more than 99.99%. Therefore, the crawler's affection for the experiments is ignored in this paper.

In order to evaluate the extraction results, manual works have been done to count the useful information records. In this paper, the non-review contents are recognized as useless information and are discarded.

4.2   Experiment Platform

In the experiment, 10 PCs are used to form a small Hadoop cluster. Hadoop version is 0.20.2, and the replication of HDFS is set to 1. One PC is as Namenode, and others are as Datanodes. Each PC has Intel Xeon CPU E5150 (2.66 GHz), 4 GB main memory and 75 GB hard disk. The operating system installed on PCs is CentOS 5.6 Final.

In order to evaluate the scalability of extraction system performance, each PC will be installed 5 virtual machines, so there're 50 nodes in all. Then the 50 nodes are used to build the simulated experiment environment.

4.3   Experiment Results and Analysis

In the field of web information extraction, common evaluation criteria are *Precision*, *Recall* and *F-measure*. *Precision* means the ratio between the number of the correct review pages that has been extracted and the whole number of pages that has been extracted as review pages. *Recall* means the ratio between the number of review pages that has been extracted by this system and the number of all review pages in a data source. The formula of *F-measure* is defined as follows:

$$F - measure = 2\, Recall \times Precision\, /\, (Recall + Precision) \qquad (3)$$

These parameters are used to evaluate this novel Hadoop-based web review automatic extraction approach. For each web pages set (the data source), the MDR[7] extraction system is worked in contrast. Fig 3 shows the *Precision* and *Recall* comparison of the two systems.

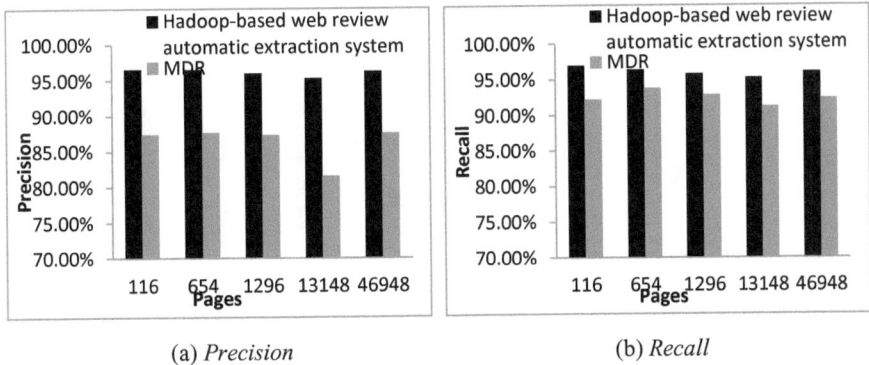

(a) *Precision*   (b) *Recall*

Fig. 3. Experimental extraction results comparison in Hadoop-based web review automatic extraction system and MDR extraction system

According to the formula (3) and Fig 3, we calculate the *F-measure* of Hadoop-based web review automatic extraction system and MDR extraction system. Fig 4 shows the actual *F-measure* of the two systems.

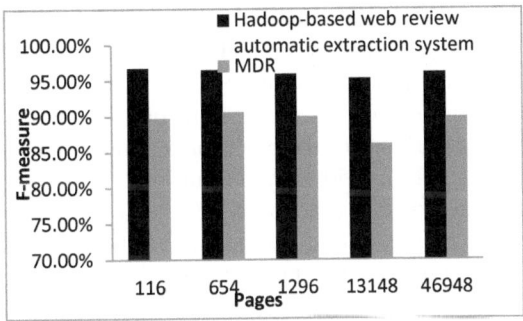

Fig. 4. F-measure of Hadoop-based web review automatic extraction system and MDR extraction system

Through the analysis of experimental results in Fig 3 and Fig 4, we found that the overall accuracy of web review automatic extraction system based on Hadoop is about 7% higher than the web extraction system MDR, and can reach more than 96%. In addition, when increasing the number of web pages, the accuracy of the extraction system will have some minor fluctuations, but overall is relatively stable. The main reasons of the fluctuations can be expressed as: Review record in the DOM tree's structure very differs from the visual information. So it tends to result in extracting the review records by mistake or ignoring as the noise information, affecting the accuracy of the entire experiment. This indicates that the proposed extraction algorithm has basically reached the requirements of practical applications.

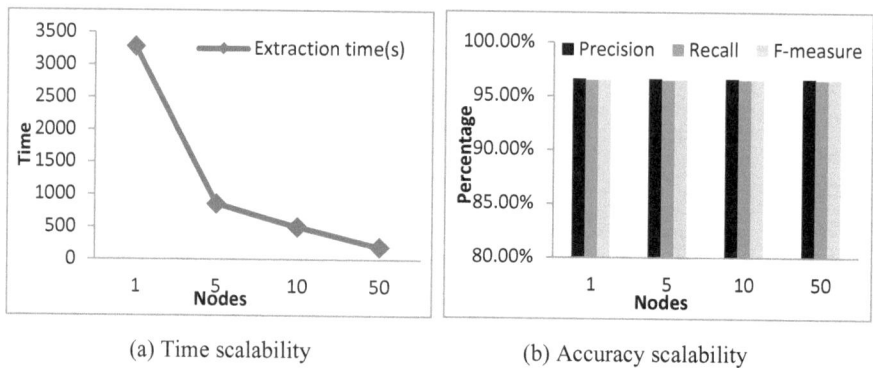

(a) Time scalability   (b) Accuracy scalability

Fig. 5. The scalability of Web review automatic extraction system based on Hadoop

In addition to the need for reliable accuracy, the scalability of Web data extraction approach is also very important. In this experiment, we have conducted a scalability test on the Web review automatic extraction system, which is deployed on different nodes' Hadoop cluster. In order to strengthen the effect of the experimental results and combine with the actual experimental environment, we have done the simulation experiments on the different Hadoop nodes to verify the scalability by using the same web review page data sets. The experimental results are showed in Fig 5.

Fig 5 (a) shows that, with the number of nodes from 1-50 in the expansion process of the extraction system, the time of review content extraction declines significantly. And Fig 5 (b) shows that the accuracy of the extraction system has been maintained above 96%, of which the variance of the precision and recall rate of less than 0.056, when the number of nodes from 1-50 in the expansion process of the extraction system. So the web review automatic extraction system has a very good scalability.

Speedup is the ratio of the time consumption by the same task in the single-processor systems and parallel or distributed processor system, used to measure the performance and effectiveness of the parallelization of parallel or distributed systems or procedures. In this paper, the speedup is the ratio of the time consumption of the extraction system running on one PC and the Hadoop cluster.

By analyzing the experimental results, we find that the speedup of the extraction system is a little small, when the test data size is not large. This case mainly due to: Since in the communication of Hadoop cluster nodes needs to consume a certain amount of time, it's difficult to play Hadoop well to deal with the large-scale mass data, when the size of the test data set is too small. But with the increasing data size, the extraction system will be parallel executed and the speedup of the extraction system becomes bigger.

5   Related Works

Information Extraction is a branch of natural language processing. It refers to extract structured data from resources by analysing the grammar or semantics of the content.

Researchers of IE fields have built many studies and systems of NLP[8], to extract the interested contents from a large number of text materials. However, most of the systems could only be applied in a narrowed domain of the text materials and are difficult to transplant to the new domains.

Web-IE[9] is a branch of IE in the field of Internet application. Web-IE is an extraction and structure from the massive data that has been distributed all over the Internet, which may be structured, half-structured or unrestrained. Typical automatic Web-IE systems are as follows: RoadRunner[10], EXALG[11] and IEPAD[12]. RoadRunner is designed to make a template by comparing similar web pages. Then we can use the template to extract information from massive web pages. RoadRunner treats the web pages as a flow of text and concludes the pattern by various kinds of heuristic algorithms. EXALG uses the similar method with several improvements and has a different algorithm in concluding patterns. While attempting to discover the frequent appearance of continuous marks, IEPAD is able to locate and extract data by constructing a PAT tree. But it could only be used on pages that do not include nested structures.

Hadoop is mainly used in parallel computing and distributed storage of massive data. Nowadays, it is widely used in mass intensive data process.

Rini et al. [13] proposes the GreenHDFS, a self-adaptive, energy-conserving variant of the HDFS. It can cut down on energy consumption of Hadoop cluster and reduce the running cost. The [14] replaces the HDFS of Hadoop by a new BlobSeer data management service based and concurrent optimized data storage layer. It improves the performance of the MapReduce parallel framework immensely. The [15] proposes an EHAD (Elastic Hadoop Auto-Deployer) system. This system is able to create or destroy virtual machine nodes, and also can deploy or distribution the environment configuration of Hadoop in virtual machine nodes. This system greatly improves the flexibility of the Hadoop's configuration.

6   Conclusion

In this paper, we propose a Hadoop-based web review automatic extraction approach, which has better performance on dealing with massive data than traditional web review data extraction methods. This new approach consists of two core algorithms: a review record extraction algorithm based on the node similarity and a review content extraction algorithm based on the text depth. The experiments have proved that our web review extraction approach has been not only reached the accuracy over 96%, but also achieved a high speedup.

References

1. Riloff, E.: Automatically constructing a dictionary for information extraction tasks. In: Proceedings of the Eleventh National Conference on Artificial Intelligence (AAAI), pp. 811–816 (1993)

2. Kim, J., Moldovan, D.: Acquisition of linguistic patterns for knowledge-based information extraction. IEEE Transactions on Knowledge and Data Engineering 7(5), 713–724 (1995)
3. Seymore, K., McCallum, A., Rosenfeld, R.: Learning Hidden Markov Model Structure for Information Extraction. AAAI Technical Report WS, pp. 37–42 (1999)
4. Apache Hadoop, `http://hadoop.apache.org`
5. Document Object Model, `http://www.w3.org/DOM/`
6. Liu, W., Meng, X., Meng, W.: Vision-Based Web data records extraction. In: Zhou, D. (ed.) Proc. of the Int'l Workshop on the Web and Databases (WebDB), pp. 20–25 (2006)
7. Liu, B., Grossman, R.-L., Zhai, Y.: Mining Data Records in Web Pages. In: Proc. of the ACM SIGKDD Intl. Conf. on Knowledge Discovery and Data Mining (KDD), pp. 601–606 (2003)
8. Soderland, S.: Learning information extraction rules for semi-structured and free text. Journal of Machine Learning 34(1-3), 233–272 (1999)
9. Chang, C.H., Kayed, M., Girgis, M.R., Shaalan, K.F.: A survey of Web information extraction systems. IEEE Trans. Knowledge and Data Engineering 18(10), 1411–1428 (2006)
10. Crescenzi, V., Mecca, G., Merialdo, P.: RoadRunner: towards automatic data extraction from large Web sites. In: Proceedings of the 26th International Conference on Very Large Database Systems (VLDB), Rome, Italy, pp. 109–118 (2001)
11. Wang, J., Lochovsky, F.H.: Data extraction and label assignment for Web databases. In: Hencsey, G., White, B. (eds.) Proc. of the Int'l Conf. on World Wide Web (WWW), pp. 187–196. ACM Press, Budapest (2003)
12. Chang, C.-H., Lui, S.-C.: IEPAD: Information extraction based on pattern discovery. In: Proceedings of the Tenth International Conference on World Wide Web (WWW), Hong-Kong, pp. 223–231 (2001)
13. Kaushik, R.T., Bhandarkar, M., Nahrstedt, K.: Evaluation and Analysis of GreenHDFS: A Self-Adaptive, Energy-Conserving Variant of the Hadoop Distributed File System. In: 2010 IEEE Second International Conference on Cloud Computing Technology and Science, pp. 274–287 (2010)
14. Nicolae, B., Moise, D., Antoniu, G., Bouge, L., Dorier, M.: BlobSeer: Bringing high throughput under heavy concurrency to Hadoop Map-Reduce applications. In: 2010 IEEE International Symposium on Parallel & Distributed Processing, pp. 1–11 (2010)
15. Mao, H., Zhang, Z., Zhao, B., Xiao, L., Li, R.: Towards Deploying Elastic Hadoop in the Cloud. In: 2011 International Conference on Cyber-Enabled Distributed Computing and Knowledge Discovery (CyberC), pp. 476–482 (2011)

Intelligent Information Management
of Tourist Attractions Based on Semantic Sensor Web

Xiaoming Zhang[*], Wanzhen Zhou, and Yongqiang Zhang

School of Information Science and Engineering, Hebei University of Science and Technology,
Shijiazhuang, Hebei, China
`{zxm1975,zyqwork}@gmail.com, houwz@hebust.edu.cn`

Abstract. With the development of newly emerging technologies such as sensor network, Internet of Things and Semantic Web, our lifestyles are changing gradually. Sensors deployed in tourist attractions can collect lots of information which can be used to support decision making for tourist attraction managers. However, different sensors have different data format, so it is not easy to let these sensor data work together. Moreover, there is also implicit knowledge hidden in sensor data collected from tourist attractions. This paper proposes an approach for tourist attractions information management based on semantic sensor web. A semantic model for scenery sensor data is designed as an OWL ontology, and based on the semantic model an architecture for intelligent information management of tourist attractions is illustrated. As a case study, an experimental prototype demonstrates the effectiveness of the proposed approach.

Keywords: tourist attraction, semantic web, sensor data, ontology.

1 Introduction

The newly emerging technologies such as sensor network, Internet of Things and Semantic Web are gradually changing our lifestyles. Sensor network makes it possible that people can be aware of the circumstances of the specified places, where sensors are deployed, by collecting the sensor data. Towards the tourism domain, information management of tourist attractions is very important, which includes tourist information, scenery information, culture relic information, environmental information, and the relationships between them. Sensors deployed in tourist attractions can help us collect lots of useful information which can support decision making for tourist attraction managers.

However, different sensors have different data format, so it is not easy to let these sensor data work together. Moreover, there is also implicit knowledge hidden in sensor data collected from tourist attractions. Semantic Web provides a series of technologies to realize the vision of the Web of linked data [1]. The technologies in Semantic Web stack, such as ontology and logic rules, can facilitate the semantic integration of sensor data as well as serve a lot for logic reasoning to implement intelligent informa-

---

[*] Corresponding author.

A. Ghose et al. (Eds.): ICSOC 2012, LNCS 7759, pp. 119–126, 2013.

tion management. Therefore, the research area known as semantic sensor Web [2] is a hot topic being concerned recently.

This paper proposes an approach based on semantic sensor web. A semantic model for tourist attractions sensor data is designed as an OWL ontology, and based on the semantic model an architecture for intelligent information management of tourist attractions is illustrated. As a case study, an experimental prototype demonstrates the effectiveness of our proposed approach.

The reminder of the paper is organized as follows. Section 2 summarizes the related work. Section 3 gives the motivation. In section 4, we propose the semantic model and architecture. Section 5 introduces the experimental prototype. Section 6 concludes the paper.

2   Related Work

Recently, more and more researchers focus on the joint area of Semantic Web and Sensor network. Gray et al. [3] present a service-oriented architecture of a semantic sensor web for environmental decision support systems. In this architecture, a serials of OWL ontologies are used to represent sensor data, schema metadata, web services, features in a specific domain (which is flood emergency planning in this research), etc. Kung et al. [4] propose a food recommendation system for patients. The system uses rule-based reasoning over the sensor data from vital sensors for a specific patient, so as to judge the health status of the patient and give the food recommendations for him/her. Pfisterer et al. [5] argue that the research of semantic sensor web should pay more attention to high-level entities. They describe a vision of Semantic Web of Things, which is toward mapping sensors to high-level semantic entities and connecting sensors and things with the Linked Open Data. SemSOS [6] and the work of Devaraju et al. [7] are the similar researches to use rules-based reasoning over semantic sensor data for detecting Blizzard. The latter research supports the temporal descriptions of a blizzard event.

In tourism domain, SPETA [8] is a social pervasive e-tourism advisor which integrates not only pervasive system and GIS system but also social network and semantics to recommend contextual services to tourists. Grammalidis et al. [9] propose a system that uses optical and infrared cameras as well as wireless sensor networks to realize automatic early warning for the protection of cultural heritage. Garcia et al. [10] present a tourism information representation architecture based on ontology and metadata for both tourists and tourism providers. The motivation of this architecture is to retrieve tourism information more efficiently and precisely. MultimediaN E-Culture project [11] is a Semantic Web application in cultural-heritage domain. By semantic annotation, semantic metadata is harvested for semantic query as well as semantic search. The researches mentioned above focus more on applying either semantic web or sensor network in tourism application, but little on the both (i.e., semantic sensor web).

This paper presents an architecture from the perspective of both semantic web and sensor data to support intelligent information management of tourist attractions.

3   Motivation

The motivation of our work is to design an architecture for integrating sensor data collecting from the specific spots of a tourist attraction, and link these sensor data to provide a view for users to browse and query status information in a semantical way. The main idea of our approach consists of the following three parts:

(1) Building an ontology-based semantic scenery model for tourist attractions to link tourist information, scenery information and sensor information.

(2) Transforming sensor data from raw format to semantic sensor data based on the scenery model.

(3) Developing a web-based application to browse and query sensor data such as tourist location, temperature and humidity of scenery. Furthermore, the system can be used to give warning information by reasoning over the sensor data.

4   Model and Architecture

In order to link sensor data with tourists information and scenery information, we have designed a semantic scenery model as an OWL ontology. As shown in Fig. 1, the main concepts in the semantic scenery model include scenery spot, tourist, sensor, RFID chip, temperature, humidity, wind, etc. Temperature sensor, humidity sensor and wind sensor are three types of sensors used in our information management of tourist attractions. The sensors deployed in a scenery spot will respectively collect environmental data of temperature, humidity and wind in a series of date and time. Each tourist will hold a RFID chip within a e-ticket, and in each culture relic, a RFID chip will also be deployed for safety's sake. Readers will be deployed in scenery spots to collect RFID data. The collected RFID data and sensor data will be sent to the server of the tourist attraction. A warning will be created if the environmental conditions satisfy the logic rule for detecting a specific warning, and the manager of the scenery should be informed of the warning.

For a scenery spot, we should define the maximal number of tourists in it. For every tourist, he/she has a unique ID and the register time will be recorded when he/she enters the gate of the whole tourist attraction. For a sensor, we would like to know the type of the sensor, and the value range of the collected information by the sensor (i.e., the maximal value and the minimal value). An item of collected information such as temperature and humidity will have a specific time and a corresponding value. The main part of the semantic scenery model is shown in Fig. 1.

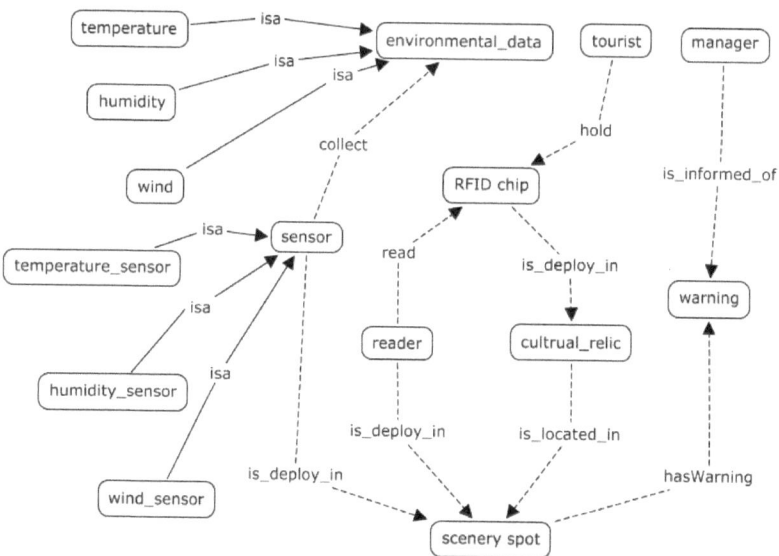

Fig. 1. Semantic scenery model

Based on the model presented above, we designed a four-layer architecture to implement intelligent information management of tourist attractions using Semantic Web technology and sensor data. The architecture is shown in Fig. 2.

The bottom of the architecture is raw data layer. Temperature sensors, humidity sensors and wind sensors are deployed in different scenery spots, and RFID tags are set in e-tickets and cultural relics. These sensors and RFID tags will generate sensor data progressively. However, these sensor data is in their raw formats which are different according to different types of sensors.

Above the raw data layer, it is the layer of semantic sensor wrapper. In this layer, the input is the raw sensor data in different format, and the output is the sensor data in Semantic Web format. Therefore, the semantic sensor wrapper is designed to transform sensor data into RDF (OWL instance) by annotating the received raw sensor data using the semantic scenery model.

The third layer is the layer of knowledge base for semantic sensor data. In this layer, the storage of semantic sensor data in RDF should be considered to improve the query efficiency. On the other hand, to take advantages of the reasoning feature of Semantic Web, we also add some specified logic rules to make the sensor information management more intelligent by reasoning over the semantic sensor data. Furthermore, the semantics in semantic scenery model is limited in a small domain, so we can extend the semantic expressing by linking the semantic scenery model with other domain ontology, and the linking between them can also be expressed by logic rules.

The top layer is the application layer. The three layers below this layer can provide sensor data in a unified view. In the tourist attraction domain, the applications can be divided into two types. One is real-time applications (e.g., dangers warning, tourist location), and the other is data analysis applications (e.g., tourist path tracking, trend analysis).

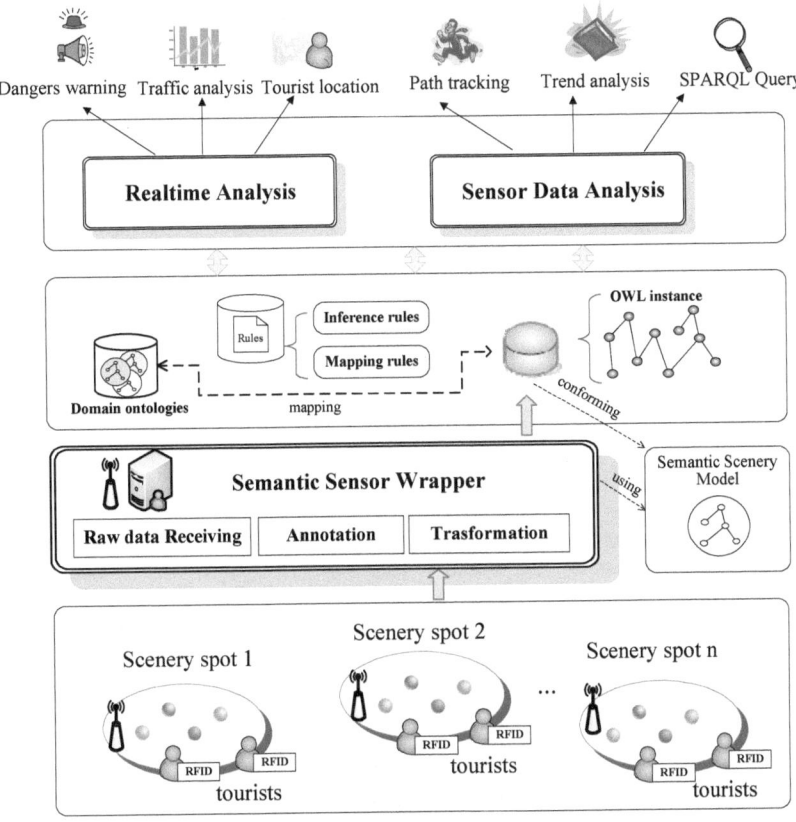

Fig. 2. The proposed architecture

5   Experimental Prototype

In order to evaluate the presented approach, we have developed a Web-based proto-type for intelligent information management of tourist attractions. We use Java Server Faces (JSF) as the main development technology. Primefaces [12] components are used to facilitate the development of the graphic user interface (GUI) of the prototype. We also use Jena [13] API to manipulate the data in Semantic Web format.

As shown in Fig. 3, the main user interface of the prototype is separated in two parts. The left part has two accordion panels. One is to show scenery information such as scenery spots, tourists, and sensors, and the other lists the possible warning types. The right part is a display area where the display content will change according to the select item from the left panel.

For example, if the user selects scenery spot 010 from the left panel, the temperature, humidity and wind information will be shown as line charts on the right area. And the cultural relics in or near the scenery will also be listed for users to navigate.

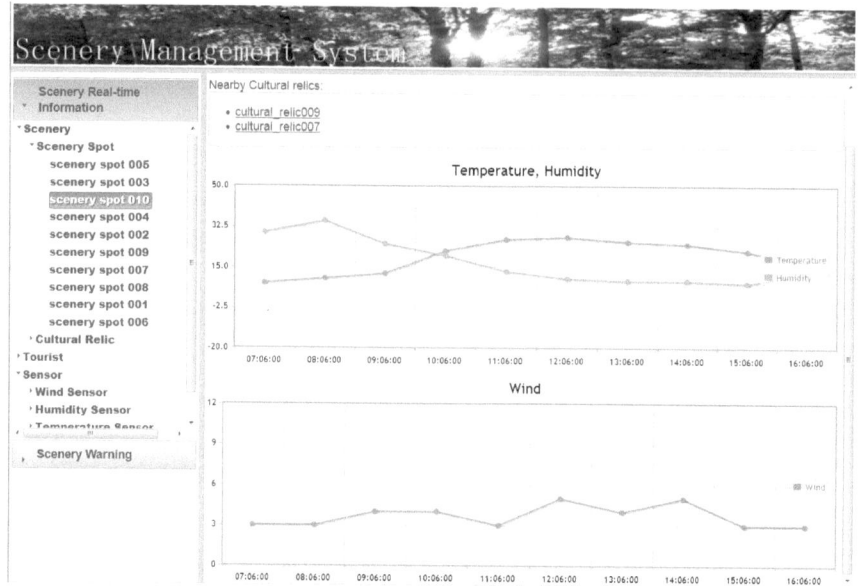

Fig. 3. Scenery information in experimental prototype

As shown in Fig. 4, If the user selects one of the tourist from the tourist list, the tourist's detailed information will show on the right area, and the tourist's touring path can be listed owing to the RFID tag held by the tourist. According the latest scenery spot and visit time, we can infer the approximate location of the tourist.

Fig. 4. Tourist information in experimental prototype

Furthermore, the prototype also can list warnings such as fog warning, ice warning, and crowd warning by reasoning with the logic rules defined in scenery sensor knowledge base.

6   Conclusions

In this paper, we have presented an approach to implement intelligent information management of tourist attractions based on Semantic Web and sensor information. An ontology-based semantic scenery model is designed to describe the relationships between sceneries, tourists and sensors. A four-layer architecture is proposed to support decision making by utilizing sensor information semantically in this domain. An experimental prototype has been developed, and has preliminarily demonstrated the effectiveness of the proposed approach.

Acknowledgments. This work is partially supported by the Research Foundation for the Doctoral Program of Hebei University of Science and Technology under Grant No. QD201036, the Research Foundation of Hebei University of Science and Technology under Grant No. XL201061, and the Research and Development Program of Shijiazhuang under Grant No. 10579405.

References

1. Semantic Web - W3C standards,
   http://www.w3.org/standards/semanticweb
2. Sheth, A., Henson, C., Sahoo, S.: Semantic Sensor Web. IEEE Internet Computing 12, 78–83 (2008)
3. Gray, A.J.G., Sadler, J., Kit, O., Kyzirakos, K., Karpathiotakis, M., Calbimonte, J.P., Page, K., García-Castro, R., Frazer, A., Galpin, I.: A Semantic Sensor Web for Environmental Decision Support Applications. Sensors 11, 8855–8887 (2011)
4. Kung, H.Y., Nguyen, T.M.P., Kuo, T.H., Tsai, C.P., Chen, C.H.: Intelligent Personalized Food Recommendation System Based on a Semantic Sensor Web. In: Chen, R. (ed.) 2011 International Conference in Electrics Proceedings, Communication and Automatic Control. LNEE, vol. 165, pp. 61–68. Springer, New York (2012)
5. Pfisterer, D., Romer, K., Bimschas, D., Kleine, O., Mietz, R., Truong, C., Hasemann, H., Pagel, M., Hauswirth, M., Karnstedt, M.: SPITFIRE: Toward a Semantic Web of Things. IEEE Communications Magazine 49, 40–48 (2011)
6. Henson, C.A., Pschorr, J.K., Sheth, A.P., Thirunarayan, K.: SemSOS: Semantic Sensor Observation Service. In: 2009 International Symposium on Collaborative Technologies and Systems, pp. 44–53. IEEE Computer Society, Washington, DC (2009)
7. Devaraju, A., Kauppinen, T.: Sensors Tell More than They Sense: Modeling and Reasoning about Sensor Observations for Understanding Weather Events. International Journal of Sensors, Wireless Communications and Control. Special Issue on Semantic Sensor Networks 2, 14–26 (2012)
8. García-Crespo, A., Chamizo, J., Rivera, I., Mencke, M., Colomo-Palacios, R., Gómez-Berbís, J.M.: SPETA: Social pervasive e-Tourism advisor. Telematics and Informatics 26, 306–315 (2009)
9. Grammalidis, N., Çetin, E., Dimitropoulos, K., Tsalakanidou, F., Kose, K., Gunay, O., Gouverneur, B., Torri, D., Kuruoglu, E., Tozzi, S.: A Multi-Sensor Network for the Protection of Cultural Heritage. In: 19th European Signal Processing Conference (EUSIPCO 2011), pp. 889–893. EURASIP (2010)

10. Garcia, P.S., Leeraphong, A., Ariyapichai, N.: Applying Ontology and Metadata for Tourism Information. In: 8th International Conference on e-Business (iNCEB 2009), pp. 38–42 (2009)
11. Schreiber, G., Amin, A., Aroyo, L., van Assem, M., de Boer, V., Hardman, L., Hildebrand, M., Omelayenko, B., van Osenbruggen, J., Tordai, A., Wielemaker, J., Wielinga, B.: Semantic annotation and search of cultural-heritage collections: The MultimediaN E-Culture demonstrator. Web Semantics: Science, Services and Agents on the World Wide Web 6, 243–249 (2008)
12. PrimeFaces, http://www.primefaces.org/
13. Apache Jena, http://jena.apache.org/

An Optimal Approach to the QoS-Based WSMO Web Service Composition Using Genetic Algorithm

Zhou Xiangbing[1,2], Ma Hongjiang[1], and Miao Fang[2]

[1] Department of Computer Science, Aba Teachers College, SichuanWenchuan, 623002, China
[2] School of Information Science and Technology, Chengdu University of Technology Chengdu, 610059, China
{3dsmaxmaya,mhj69,mfang}@163.com

Abstract. This paper presents an optimal QoS-based service composition approach to WSMO in helping service requests select services by considering two different contents: reasoning above the matching of semantic linking and GA-based QoS optimization of the WSMO service composition. The experimental results show that the approach being probed in this paper is not only efficient, but also increases availability and reliability of the WSMO service composition.

Keywords: WSMO, Web service, Quality of service, Service composition, Genetic algorithm.

1 Introduction

The semantic Web [1], where the semantic information uses machine-processed languages such as OWL(Web Ontology Language)[2], is considered to provide a number of advantages over the current version of the World Wide Web, which focuses on information automatic processing. Web service is an XML-based application program that enables communication between programs, databases and business functions [3]. The first appearance of the web service on World Wide Web is considered to change Web application schema and structure. As a combination of semantic Web and web service [4], Semantic Web service relies on formal semantic description (such as Description Logic) of web service functionality and interface to enable automated reasoning over web service compositions [5]. Description languages of the semantic web service turn to OWL-S(Ontology Web Language for Services) and WSMO(Web Service Modeling Ontology) for service functions and interfaces description; And the structure for WSMO service composition is derived when combined with VTA(Virtual Travel Agency). In this paper, we'd like to compose the web service by adopting WSMO, and construct a QoS-based WSMO service composition approach by using the GA (genetic algorithm). Our approach is to use both reasoning above the matching of semantic linking and GA-based QoS optimization so that the two perspectives can be included in our probing. The semantic linking matching builds WSMO service matching schema by semantic

A. Ghose et al. (Eds.): ICSOC 2012, LNCS 7759, pp. 127–139, 2013.

reasoning, while the GA-based QoS optimization builds a QoS-based composition model to obtain optimization results, between them is eventually achieved a higher quality service composition for requirements.

The Web service composition synthesizes individual and outsourced web services to turn out a new service; However, this still remains a very complex and challenging issue which defies the present human intelligence. Quality of service (short as QoS) concerns are becoming crucial to the global success in the web service based on computing paradigm [6]. Lots of QoS-based service composition approaches are in every detail discussed and summarized in the [5][6][7][8][12][13]; But most of the discussed approaches haven't made any mention of QoS-based WSMO service composition. Tomas Vitvar et al. [9] proposed WSMO-lite annotations for web services; MatthiasKlusch et al. [10] proposed A hybrid Semantic Web Service Matchmaker; Farshad Hakimpour et al. [11] proposed Semantic Web Service Composition in IRS-III: The Structured Approach , and so on, but the those researchers haven't yet found any good results for the WSMO service composition. In this case, it's of much significance for us to present an optimal approach to the QoS-based WSMO Web service composition by using genetic algorithm.

A WSMO service composition approach is proposed in this paper by considering the following two aspects: (1) an orchestration and a choreography which are called interface. Nevertheless, the interface is described by defining information exchange and matching reasoning methods. According to features of the interface, we have proposed the quantitative formulas for information exchange and matching reasoning; (2) a WSMO QoS model is presented by four aspects like information exchange, time, matching reasoning and price(cost). We define an optimal QoS-based WSMO Web service composition model, then employ genetic algorithm to obtain better results. The rest of the paper is organized as follows: Section 2 introduces our approach; Section 3 presents the experimental results; Section 4 comes to conclusions.

2   Our Approach

Three respects are dissertated and introduced into this section: semantic-based WSMO service composition approach discussed in section 2.1; a quality model of WSMO service presented in section 2.2; GA applied to optimize the quality model which obtains optimum results of composition in section 2.3.

2.1   Description of WSMO Service Composition Methods

The semantic web service is based on ontology, with no exception in WSMO. In other words, the semantic functions of web service can be implemented via WSMO, while these functions are normally described as input and output. Through $\mathcal{DL}\ \mathcal{EL}$ [14], the semantic recognition and conversion of ontology description are accomplished by the $\mathcal{DL}\ \mathcal{EL}$ inference engine [5][10][15]. At present, the main description languages of semantic web service are OWL-S profile and WSMO capability. The contents of WSMO service composition approaches are included in this paper as indicated in the following two aspects:

(1) Semantic linking is used to semantic web service composition;

(2) The quality of service (QoS) is constrained to meet the demands of different consumer(request) services.

Definition 1[5][15]. Give an ontology O which meets $<T, A>$ over $\mathcal{DL}$ $\mathcal{EL}$[14], namely, O: $<T, A>$, and T is a term Box, it is referred to as TBox(intentional knowledge). A is an assertion Box, it is known as ABox(extensional knowledge). TBox, which is usually used to describe different semantics in $\mathcal{DL}$ $\mathcal{EL}$, is recorded as TBox T.

In addition, the TBox in the **Definition 1** is described as **Example 1** with the following information: ***get request, provide offer, receive selection, send confirmation***; ***flight request, hotel request, book flight, book hotel***.

Example 1: A travelers books flight and hotel

$\forall$***get request.(flight request, hotel request***)$\cap\exists$***provide offer.(book flight, book hotel***)$\rightarrow$

$\exists$***get request . flight request*** $\vee$ $\exists$***get request .hotel request***

$\cup\forall$***provide offer. book flight*** $\vee$ $\forall$***provide offer. book hotel*** $\rightarrow$

receive selection.(flight request, hotel request) $\cup$***send confirmation(book flight, book hotel***)

Definition 2. WSMO service interface is described as:

$$WSI=<WS, Voc(In, Out, Share, Contr), \mathcal{E}(Voc), \kappa(\mathcal{E})>.$$

Where,

WS denotes a semantic web service, Voc four models of information exchange: **input, output, sharing and control**, $\mathcal{E}(Voc)$ the message exchange state of ontology example definition, and $\kappa(\mathcal{E})$ state transition structure (which is described as *if*(condition)...*then*(action)...) of layout (or choreography: an interaction between different services) and arrangement (or orchestration: a focus service for realizing the service function) [16]. T is used to describe and meet the requirements of O. At this time, the semantic web service is described as:

$$SWS=<T, O, WSI >$$

If $SWS=\{Sws_1, Sws_2, ..., Sws_i, Sws_j, ..., Sws_N\}$ is a given set, its input parameters and output parameters are described by Tbox T, and semantic linking is engendered through the $\mathcal{DL}$ $\mathcal{EL}$ comments. If each SWS has input(In_s_i) and output(Out_s_j) parameters, then:

$$\text{TBox } T: Sws_i (Out\_s_i \leftarrow WSI_i \rightarrow In\_s_i) \rightarrow$$

$$\text{TBox } T : Sws_j (Out\_s_j \leftarrow WSI_j \rightarrow In\_s_j)$$

In TBox T, SWS matching [5] is realized by using the similarity of various input and output parameters, the service composition is accordingly completed, and finally the satisfactory semantic linking will be accomplished as acquired in this paper.

Definition 3. A semantic linking of WSMO is defined as :

$$sl_{i,j} = < Sws_i, Sim_T (Out\_s_i \leftarrow WSI \rightarrow In\_s_j), Sws_j>$$

If Out_s_i is the immediate successor of SWS, In_s_j is the immediate predecessor of SWS, that is to say, each SWS has input and output parameters, then these parameters are the information exchange foundation of WSI. Namely,

$$\forall_{Sws}, \exists(In\_s_i, Out\_s_i, WSI) \rightarrow Sws$$

And in TBox T, we choose $\pi = (\equiv, \sqsubseteq, \sqsupseteq, \cap, \perp, \sim)$ model to reason for the Sim_T matching calculation method:

Equivalence : $T \models Out\_s_i \xrightarrow{\underset{\equiv}{WSI}} In\_s_j$

Plugin : $T \models Out\_s_i \xrightarrow{\underset{\sqsubseteq}{WSI}} In\_s_j$

Subsume(inverse-plugin) : $T \models Out\_s_i \xrightarrow{\underset{\sqsupseteq}{WSI}} In\_s_j$

Intersection : $T \models Out\_s_i \xrightarrow{\underset{\cap}{WSI}} In\_s_j \sqsubseteq \perp, Out\_s_i \cap in\_s_j \neq \emptyset$

Disjunction : $T \models Out\_s_i \xrightarrow{\underset{\perp}{WSI}} In\_s_j \sqsubseteq \perp, Out\_s_i \cap in\_s_j = \emptyset$

Fuzzy Operation: $T \models Out\_s_i \xrightarrow{\underset{\sim}{WSI}} In\_s_j$

We assess the efficiency of $sl_{i,j}$ in the light of the following formula:

Give a set $|SWS|=N$, we can reason by the Sim_T matching reasoning rules, then the Voc information exchange reasoning efficiency in the WSI is defined as:

$$WSI(Voc_i, Voc_j) = \left\{ I_{(\frac{1}{2},1)} \left\| \left(I_{(\frac{1}{2},1)} \rightarrow Voc_i \right) \prec \left(I_{(\frac{1}{2},1)} \rightarrow Voc_j \right) \right\| \right\} \tag{2.1}$$

In (2.1), $\prec$ denotes the partial order operation of information exchange, | | value of partial order operation. When using WSI to realize information exchange, we choose different operation modes for matching reasoning according to different probabilities (1/2,1) of the WSI information exchange. Since there are four models(**input, output, sharing and control**) for WSI information exchange, its probability can be expressed as $I_{(\frac{1}{2},1)}$.

Where,

when $I=1/2$ is expressed as input and output which are necessary in the Voc, the WSI information exchange state is selected only one from **sharing** and **control**.

When $I=1$ is expressed as input and output which are also necessary in the Voc, the WSI information exchange state select both **sharing** and **control**.

SWS matching reasoning efficiency is defined as:

$$SWS(Out\_s_i, In\_s_j) = \left\{ \begin{array}{l} |(Sws_i, Sws_j)| \\ \|(Out\_s_i \pi Sws_i) \prec (In\_s_j \pi Sws_j)\| \neq \emptyset \end{array} \right\} \tag{2.2}$$

In (2.2), $\prec$ denotes the partial order operation of semantic linking, π is a group of reasoning of semantic linking.

According to (2.1) and (2.2), we can define the semantic linking efficiency, namely the efficiency of $sl_{i,j}$:

$$sl_{i,j}(Out\_s_i, In\_s_j) =$$

$$\frac{\sum_{n \in N} |SWS(Out\_s_i, In\_s_j)|_n}{\sum_{n \in N} |WSI(Voc_j, Voc_j)|_n + \sum_{n \in N} |SWS(Out\_s_i, In\_s_j)|_n} \qquad (2.3)$$

Example 2. Semantic linking efficiency

When $N=10$, (2.1), (2.2) *and* (2.3) *values are computed following*:

$WSI(Voc_i, Voc_j) = \{0.1, 0.3, 0.5, 0.2, 0.4, 0.2\}$

$SWS(Out\_s_i, In\_s_j) = \{2, 4, 3, 2, 5, 1\}$

$$sl_{i,j}(Out\_s_i, In\_s_j) = \frac{2+4+3+2+5+1}{2+4+3+2+5+1+0.1+0.3+0.5+0.2+0.4+0.2} \approx 0.909$$

Definition 4. WSMO service composition

$ASWSC$: $<SWS_N, \max(sl_{i,j}), QoS_E, Tsk>$, the four respectively denote users' demands, maximum semantic web services(N numbers) semantic linking value, service quality evaluation(see Section 2.2) and the executed tasks.

Example 3. WSMO service composition

FWS: Flight web service(WSMO)

HWS: Hotel web service(WSMO)

VAT: Virtual Travel Agency

if FWSrequest then send(FWS, flightRequest)

Start(VTA, FWS)

if getFWSrequest then offerFWS

ComputeFWS(max(sl_{i,j}(Out_s_i, In_s_j)))

if FWSorder then comfirmation

if selection then book(FWS, flightBookingOrder)

Termination(VTA, FWS)

if flightorder then send(HWS, flightRequest)

Start(VTA, HWS)

if getHWSrequest then offerHWS

ComputeHWS(max(sl_{i,j}(Out_s_i, In_s_j)))

if HWSorder then comfirmation

if get(selection, flightBookingConf) then book(HWS, hotelBookingOrder)

Termination(VTA, HWS)

2.2   Quality Model of WSMO Service Composition

Service quality is usually described by response time (including execution time and waiting time), cost, availability, reliability and credibility [3][5][6][7][8][12][17][18]. In this section, WSMO service quality is analyzed by transforming the availability, reliability and credibility into the quality of a *WSI* information exchange and matching reasoning. Then the QoS of WSMO is described as:

$$\text{I: } QoS_E(q) = (Q_{rt(q)}, Q_{Wsi(q)}, Q_{sws(q)}, Q_{p(q)})$$

$$\text{II: } QoS_E(q) \rightarrow AF(\text{Sequence,Switch,Flow,Loop}) \qquad (2.4)$$

Table 1. Aggregation functions per execution path construct of QoS attributes

QoS attribute	Sequence	Switch	Flow	Loop
$Q_{rt(q)}$	$\sum_{i=1}^{n} q_{rt}^{i}$	$\sum_{i=1}^{n} S_{im} \cdot q_{rt}^{i}$	$\max\{(q_{rt}^{i})_{i\in\{1,\cdots,m\}}\}$	$\frac{1}{k} \cdot q_{rt}^{i}$
$Q_{Wsi(q)}$	$\prod_{i=1}^{n} q_{wsi(Vol_i,Vol_j)}^{i}$	$\sum_{i=1}^{n} S_{im} \cdot \log q_{wsi(Vol_i,Vol_j)}^{i}$	$\prod_{i=1}^{m} q_{wsi(Vol_i,Vol_j)}^{i}$	$q_{wsi(Vol_i,Vol_j)}^{\frac{1}{ik}}$
$Q_{sws(q)}$	$\prod_{i=1}^{n} q_{sl_{i,j}(Out\_s_i,In\_s_j)}^{i}$	$\sum_{i=1}^{n}\left(\frac{S_{im} \cdot}{\log q_{sl_{i,j}(Out\_s_i,In\_s_j)}^{i}}\right)$	$\prod_{i=1}^{m} q_{sl_{i,j}(Out\_s_i,In\_s_j)}^{i}$	$q_{sl_{i,j}(Out\_s_i,In\_s_j)}^{\frac{1}{ik}}$
$Q_{p(q)}$	$\sum_{i=1}^{n} q_{p}^{i}$	$\sum_{i=1}^{n} S_{im} \cdot q_{p}^{i}$	$\sum_{i=1}^{m} q_{p}^{i}$	$\frac{1}{k} \cdot q_{p}^{i}$

In (2.4), the each element in the I respectively denote response time, information exchange rate, matching reasoning rate and price, whereas AF in the II describes aggregation functions per epc(execution path construct(Sequence, Switch, Flow, Loop))of QoS attributes [8]. The execution path construct is showed in **Table 1**(k denotes iterations). Different QoS values cannot be calculated and classified effectively, so we have to deal with these values by choosing normalized formula according to different QoS optimization values. So all the values in (2.4) are normalized by using the formula below:

$$q.value = \begin{cases} \dfrac{q.value - q.\min}{q.\max - q.\min} & \text{if} \quad q.\max\text{-}q.\min \neq 0 \\ 1 & \text{if} \quad q.\max\text{-}q.\min = 0 \end{cases} \qquad (2.5)$$

$$Q_{Wsi(q)}, Q_{Asws(q)}, Q_{p(q)}$$

$$q.value = \begin{cases} \dfrac{q.\max - q.value}{q.\max - q.\min} & \text{if} \quad q.\max\text{-}q.\min \neq 0 \\ 1 & \text{if} \quad q.\max\text{-}q.\min = 0 \end{cases} \quad Q_{rt(q)} \qquad (2.6)$$

Given that complete the task j is completed by SWS_N service request i in the service composition, if the choice of a task is made by service request i, we say the value is 1, otherwise 0, descried as follows:

$$S_{ij} = \begin{cases} 1 \\ 0 \end{cases} \qquad (2.7)$$

In Table 1, if a task j is executed by epc(execution path construct) via using service request i, then different execution probability is defined in Table 2.

Table 2. Different execution probability in **Table 1**

QoS attribute	Sequence	Switch	Flow	Loop
$Q_{rt(q)}$	P_{rt}^1	P_{rt}^2	P_{rt}^3	P_{rt}^4
$Q_{Wsi(q)}$	P_{Wsi}^1	P_{Wsi}^2	P_{Wsi}^3	P_{Wsi}^4
$Q_{sws(q)}$	P_{sws}^1	P_{sws}^2	P_{sws}^3	P_{sws}^4
$Q_{p(q)}$	P_p^1	P_p^2	P_p^3	P_p^4

At this time, we get the normalization results of (2.4) according to (2.4)-(2.7) and Table 1 and Table 2:

$$Q_{rt(q)} = P_{rt}^1 \cdot \sum_{i=1}^n q_{rt}^i + P_{rt}^2 \cdot \sum_{i=1}^n S \cdot_{im} q_{rt}^i +$$
$$P_{rt}^3 \cdot \max\{(q_{rt}^i)_{i \in \{1,\cdots m\}}^{n_3}\} + P_{rt}^4 \cdot \left(\frac{1}{k} \cdot q_{rt}^i\right) \tag{2.8}$$

$$Q_{Wsi(q)} = \left(P_{Wsi}^1 \cdot \prod_{i=1}^n q_{wsi(Vol_i, Vol_j)}^i\right)$$
$$\cdot \left(P_{Wsi}^2 \cdot \sum_{i=1}^m S_{im} \cdot \log q_{wsi(Vol_i, Vol_j)}^i\right) \tag{2.9}$$
$$\cdot \left(P_{Wsi}^3 \cdot \prod_{i=1}^n q_{wsi(Vol_i, Vol_j)}^i\right) \cdot \left(P_{Wsi}^4 \cdot \left(q_{wsi(Vol_i, Vol_j)}^{\frac{1}{ik}}\right)\right)$$

$$Q_{sws(q)} = \left(P_{sws}^1 \cdot \prod_{i=1}^n q_{sl_{i,j}(Out\_s_i, In\_s_j)}^i\right)$$
$$\cdot \left(P_{sws}^2 \cdot \sum_{i=1}^m S_{im} \cdot \log q_{sl_{i,j}(Out\_s_i, In\_s_j)}^i\right) \tag{2.10}$$
$$\cdot \left(P_{sws}^3 \cdot \prod_{i=1}^n q_{sl_{i,j}(Out\_s_i, In\_s_j)}^i\right) \cdot \left(P_{sws}^4 \cdot \left(q_{sl_{i,j}(Out\_s_i, In\_s_j)}^{\frac{1}{ik}}\right)\right)$$

$$Q_{rt(q)} = P_p^1 \cdot \sum_{i=1}^n q_p^i + P_p^2 \cdot \sum_{i=1}^n S \cdot_{im} q_p^i +$$
$$P_p^3 \cdot \sum_{i=1}^m q_p^i + P_p^4 \cdot \left(\frac{1}{k} \cdot q_p^i\right) \tag{2.11}$$

In order to make an operation between (2.9),(2.10) and (2.8) ,(2.11), we use logarithm function[6] to convert (2.9) and (2.10) into (2.12), (2.13).

$$
\begin{aligned}
Q_{Wsi(q)} &= \log\left(
\begin{array}{l}
\left(P_{Wsi}^1 \cdot \prod_{i=1}^{n_1} q_{wsi(Vol_i,Vol_j)}^i\right) \\
\cdot\left(P_{Wsi}^2 \cdot \sum_{i=1}^{m} S_{im} \cdot \log q_{wsi(Vol_i,Vol_j)}^i\right) \\
\cdot\left(P_{Wsi}^3 \cdot \prod_{i=1}^{n_3} q_{wsi(Vol_i,Vol_j)}^i\right)\cdot\left(P_{Wsi}^4 \cdot \left(q_{wsi(Vol_i,Vol_j)}^{\frac{1}{ik}}\right)\right)
\end{array}
\right) \\
&= \log\left(\left(P_{Wsi}^1 \cdot \sum_i^n q_{wsi(Vol_i,Vol_j)}^i\right)\right) + \log\left(\left(P_{Wsi}^2 \cdot \sum_{i=1}^m S_{im} \cdot \log q_{wsi(Vol_i,Vol_j)}^i\right)\right) \\
&\quad + \log\left(P_{Wsi}^3 \cdot \sum_i^m q_{wsi(Vol_i,Vol_j)}^i\right) + \frac{1}{k} \cdot \log\left(P_{Wsi}^4 \cdot \left(q_{wsi(Vol_i,Vol_j)}^i\right)\right)
\end{aligned}
\tag{2.12}
$$

$$
\begin{aligned}
Q_{sws(q)} &= \log\left(
\begin{array}{l}
\left(P_{sws}^1 \cdot \prod_{i=1}^{n_1} q_{sl_{i,j}(Out\_s_i,In\_s_j)}^i\right) \\
\cdot\left(P_{sws}^2 \cdot \sum_{i=1}^{m} S_{im} \cdot \log q_{sl_{i,j}(Out\_s_i,In\_s_j)}^i\right) \\
\cdot\left(P_{sws}^3 \cdot \prod_{i=1}^{m} q_{sl_{i,j}(Out\_s_i,In\_s_j)}^i\right) \\
\cdot\left(P_{sws}^4 \cdot \left(q_{sl_{i,j}(Out\_s_i,In\_s_j)}^{\frac{1}{ik}}\right)\right)
\end{array}
\right) \\
&= \log\left(P_{sws}^1 \cdot \sum_{i=1}^n q_{sl_{i,j}(Out\_s_i,In\_s_j)}^i\right) + \log\left(\left(P_{sws}^2 \cdot \sum_{i=1}^m S_{im} \cdot \log q_{sl_{i,j}(Out\_s_i,In\_s_j)}^i\right)\right) \\
&\quad + \log\left(P_{sws}^3 \cdot \sum_{i=1}^m q_{sl_{i,j}(Out\_s_i,In\_s_j)}^i\right) + \frac{1}{k} \cdot \log\left(P_{sws}^4 \cdot \left(q_{sl_{i,j}(Out\_s_i,In\_s_j)}^i\right)\right)
\end{aligned}
\tag{2.13}
$$

At this time, we can get the results of semantic WSMO service composition quality QoS_E according to (2.8),(2.11),(2.12) and (2.13), and set up an optimal model of QoS for WSMO service composition as illustrated in the following.

$$
\max F(S_{11}, \ldots, S_{nm}) = \max\left(\frac{w_{rt}Q_{rt(q)} + w_{Wsi}Q_{Wsi(q)}}{w_{sws}Q_{sws(q)} + w_p Q_{p(q)}} \cdot sl_{i,j}\right)
\tag{2.14}
$$

Where,

$w_l \in [0, 1]$ is the weight assigned to lth quality of WSMO service composition and $\sum_{l \in \{rt,Wsi,sws,p\}} w_l = 1$.

constraints:

Response time: [1, 10000](ms)

Information exchange rate: [0.90, 0.99]

Matching reasoning rate: [0.90, 0.99]

Price: [1, 10000]

These constraints parameters are exploited in some research documents [19][20] where some correlated values are already set. Simulation tests are to be conducted in Section 3, we assume that all WSMO services run within 10000ms, and most of WSMO services are steady enough, then the information exchange rate and matching reasoning rate of WSMO services range from 0.90 to 0.99. Let us assume that it is reasonable for most of WSMO services and that the price is set in [21] on the basis of the access cost of the WSMO services. It can be inferred that all these assumptions go for different applications.

2.3   A GA-Based Optimization for WSMO Service Composition

It is an NP-hard optimization problem [7] to acquire the best set of service for a WSMO composition to optimize a set of constraints. The solution to optimization composition of WSMO services is not functioning well, so we adopt a GA-based approach [5], since this approach supports constraints not only on QoS but also on quality of semantic linking, and requires the set of selected services as a solution to the maximization of a given objective F in the [5].

The optimal solution to GA-based approach is represented by *genotype*. Genotype is determined by simulating the evolution of an *initial population* within lots of generations. This kind of simulation eventually leads up to the survival of the *Fitness* individuals (WSMO service composition) satisfying some *constraints* and selection of WSMO service composition from the previous one.

(1) **Genotype.** The gene is defined by an array of integers. The number of genes in the array is equal to the number of *Tsks* involved in the WSMO service composition. Each gene, in turn, contains an index to an array of candidate services for that *Tsk*, indicating a specific chosen service. Therefore, each composition, as a potential solution, can be encoded using this genotype.

(2) **Initial Population.** According to (1), the initial population consists of an initial set of WSMO service compositions.

(3) **Constraints.** They have to be met by (2) and F.

(4) **Fitness Function.** GA is running, constraints in the (3) have to met F. When constraints in the (3) haven't to met F, Lagrange penalty function is employed to renovate F[5].

$$f(S_{11},...,S_{nm}) = Y - \rho \cdot \frac{g}{mg} \cdot \sum_{k \in \{Q_{n(q)}, Q_{tsl(q)}, Q_{nas(q)}, Q_{p(q)}\}} \left(\frac{\Delta Q_k}{Q_k^{max}(S_{11},...,S_{nm}) - Q_k^{min}(S_{11},...,S_{nm})} \right)^2 \qquad (2.15)$$

$$\Delta Q_k = \begin{cases} Q_k - Q_k^{max} & \text{if } Q_k > Q_k^{max} \\ 0 & \text{if } Q_k^{min} \le Q_k \le Q_k^{max} \\ Q_k^{min} - Q_k & \text{if } Q_k > Q_k^{max} \end{cases} \qquad (2.16)$$

In (2.15), g is current genetic iterations, mg is maximum genetic iterations, $\rho \in [0,1]$ is penalty factor; Q_k^{min} is kth minimum value, Q_k^{max} is kth maximum value.

(5) **Genetic Operations.** They include mutation, crossover and selection. Mutation is random conversion value in an array(Genes), the mutation probability is recorded as $P_{mutation}$; Crossover is exchange of mutation genes and current genes, the crossover probability is recorded as $P_{crossover}$, and is defined as $P_{crossover} > P_{mutation}$; Selection expresses fitness value whether meet constraints, and select a optimized value as a current iterated value.

(6) **Stop Optimization.** When iterated value met constraints, the optimization value stop, and turn to other WSMO service composition.

3   Experimental Results

In this section, we analyze the performances of the approaches mentioned in Section 2 by way of:

(1) Comparison. In section 3.2, the evolution of the matching over the GA generations is considered as the default matching (Only on condition that service type deviations are explicitly granted if the goal derivations are allowed.) in the [10]. And the default matching is a GE (greed exhaustively) method, its generations are the same as GA.

(2) Efficiency. In section 3.3, we employ VTA(http://www.w3.org/Submission /WSMO) to evaluate efficiency(a feasible solution) of the WSMO composition between GA-based and IP-based by varying the number of tasks and candidate WSMO services. And each task is performed by selecting and invoking one or more service.

3.1   Experimental Configuration

We utilize Java programming language to complete these WSMO service composition and quality models and put Java-based programs in VTA and analyze[23] via ISR-III. Our GA extends the GPL library JGAP(http://jgap. sourceforge.net/), and the IP-based optimization problem is solved by running CPLEX[8]. All those experimental programs and tools run on an Inter Pentium (R) G630 2.7GHz 2.7GHz, and 2G RAM, Windows 7 and JDK6.0. , other experimental relation parameters see [5], and test software of VTA run on WSMO environment.

Composition with up to 30 tasks and 40 WSMO candidate services per task is discussed and tested in Sections 3.2 and 3.3, in which convincing results toward quality and feasible solution (Max. Fitness) for WSMO services are derived. The quality of the WSMO service composition is evaluated by means of percentage $(F(S_{11}, ..., S_{nm})$: Max. Fitness$\rightarrow$Generation. Num) of the GA-based solution with respect to the multi-factors global optimum. The latter is procured by running the IP and exhaustive approaches with no time limit.

3.2   Evolution of WSMO Service Matching Efficiency

In this first experiment (showed in Fig.1), we focus on the benefits of WSMO service matching. Toward this end, we study the impact of matching between GA and GE according to [5][8][10].

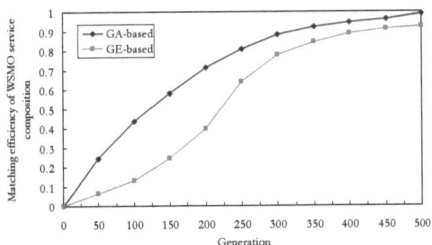

Fig. 1. WSMO service matching efficiency between GA-based and GE-based

To compare the different evolution of WSMO service matching efficiency, we present results between GA-based and GE-based. Results show that GA-based is able to find a good matching which meets the WSMO service composition.

3.3   Evolution of WSMO Service Composition

Fig.2 shows the evolution of the WSMO service composition efficiency (expressed via Fitness Function) over a lot of GA generations, and for different quality factors, we set weight values for assignment of numerous objectives for different number of tasks with 40 WSMO candidate services per task. Here, Fig.3 reports a WSMO service composition of 50 tasks wherein the number of candidate services varies from 1 to 400, and IP-based and GA-based approaches are compared in the Fig.3.

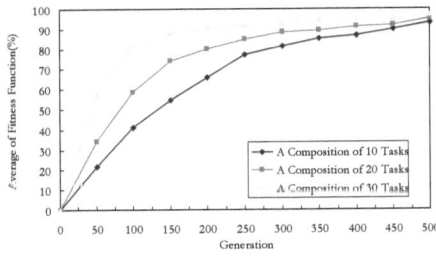

Fig. 2. Evolution of WSMO service composition

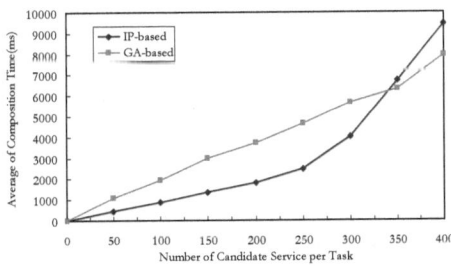

Fig. 3. Number of Candidate Service per Task

4   Conclusions and Future Work

The development of QoS-based and QoS-aware web service composition for subscribers is a popular issue in research since it is often viewed as a foundation of service-oriented computing. In addition, WSMO which is a semantic description method for web services has been applied for service computing. Therefore, we have presented an optimal approach to the WSMO service composition by using the matching model which allows specifying constraints on QoS for subscribers. An optimal QoS-based WSMO Web service composition approach is proposed in the paper in order to obtain higher information exchange rate and matching reasoning rate. The QoS-based WSMO fulfills the functional demands, for it not only helps subscribers to discover more web services, but also it satisfies the QoS constraints. Apart from that, a GA-based optimization is employed to evaluate the system performance of the WSMO service composition. The experimental results show that the QoS-based WSMO service composition approach to which an easy solution can be found is preferable to the IP-based.

In the next step, we plan to complete the framework for a particular application in WSMO domains. We will try to go deep into the QoS-based WSMO service composition like OWL-S-based approach and dynamic service composition, since they are currently beyond the reach of our research.

Acknowledgments. This work is supported by the Natural Sciences of Education and Science Office Bureau of Sichuan Province of China under Grant No. 2010JY0J41,11ZB152.

References

1. Berners-Lee, T., Hendler, J., Lassila, O.: The Semantic Web. Scientific Am. 284(5), 34–43 (2001)
2. Smith, M.K., Welty, C., McGuinness, D.L.: OWL Web Ontology Language Guide. W3C Recommendation, W3C (2004)
3. Ko, J.M., Kim, C.O., Kwon, I.-H.: Quality-of-service oriented web service composition algorithm and planning architecture. Journal of System and Software 81(11), 2079–2090 (2008)
4. McIlraith, S., Son, T.C., Zeng, H.: Semantic Web Services. IEEE Intelligent Systems 16(2), 46–53 (2001)
5. Lecue, F., Mehandjiev, N.: Seeking Quality of Web service composition in a semantic dimension. IEEE Transactions on Knowledge and Data Engineering 23(6), 942–959 (2011)
6. Huang, A.F.M., Lan, C.-W., Yang, S.J.H.: An optimal QoS-based Web service selection scheme. Information Science 179(19), 3309–3322 (2009)
7. Lin, C.-F., Sheu, R.-K., Chang, Y.-S., Yuan, S.-M.: A relaxable service selection algorithm for QoS-based web service composition. Information and Software Technology 53(12), 1370–1381 (2011)
8. Ardagna, D., Pernicl, B.: Adaptive Service Composition in Flexible Processed. IEEE Transactions on Software Engineering 33(6), 369–384 (2007)

9. Vitvar, T., Kopecký, J., Viskova, J., Fensel, D.: WSMO-Lite Annotations for Web Services. In: Bechhofer, S., Hauswirth, M., Hoffmann, J., Koubarakis, M. (eds.) ESWC 2008. LNCS, vol. 5021, pp. 674–689. Springer, Heidelberg (2008)
10. Klusch, M., Kaufer, F.: A hybrid Semantic Web Service Matchmake. Web Intelligence and Agent Systems: An International Journal 5(1-5), 1–20 (2008)
11. Hakimpour, F., Sell, D., Cabral, L., Domingue, J., Motta, E.: Semantic Web Service Composition in IRS-III: The Structured Approach. In: Seventh IEEE International Conference on E-Commerce Technology (CEC 2005), pp. 484–487 (2005)
12. Zeng, L., Benatallah, B., Ngu, A.H.H., Dumas, M., Kalagnanam, J., Chang, H.: Q-aware Middleware for web service composition. IEEE Trans. Software Eng. 30(5), 311–327 (2004)
13. Wang, H.H., Gibbins, N., Payne, T.R., et al.: A formal model of the Semantic Web Service Ontology (WSMO). Information Systems 37(1), 33–60 (2012)
14. Baader, F., Nutt, W.: The Description Logic Handbook: Theory, Implementation and Applications. Cambridge Univ. Press (2003)
15. Meditskos, G., Bassiliades, N.: Structural and Role-Oriented Web Service Discovery with Taxonomies in OWL-S. TEEE Trans. on Knowledge and Data Engineering 22(2), 278–289 (2010)
16. Kelle, U., Lara, R., Lausen, H., Fensel, D.: Semantic Web Services: Theory, Tools and Applications. Jorge Cardoso Press (2007)
17. Canfora, G., Di Penta, M., Esposito, R., et al.: A framework for QoS-aware binding and re-binding of composite web services. Journal of Systems and Software 81(10), 1754–1769 (2008)
18. Tsesmetzis, D., Roussaki, I., Sykas, E.: QoS-aware service evaluation and selection. European Journal of Operational Research 191(3), 1101–1112 (2008)
19. Zheng, Z., Lyu, M.R.: A QoS-aware fault tolerant middleware for dependable serivice composition. In: Proceeding of IEEE/IFIP International Conference on Dependable System & Networks, pp. 239–248 (2009)
20. Pastrana, J.L., Pimentel, E., Katrib, M.: Q-enabled and self-adaptive connectors for Web service composition and coordination. Computer Languages, Systems & Structures 37(1), 2–23 (2011)
21. Alonso, G., Casati, F., Kuno, H., Machiraju, V.: Web service Concepts, Architectures and Application. Springer, Heidelberg (2004)
22. Alrifai, M., Risse, T.: Combining Global Optimization with Local Selection for Efficient QoS-aware Service Composition. In: Proc. Int'l Conf. World Wide Web, pp. 881–890 (2009)
23. Demingue, J., Cabral, L., Galizia, S., et al.: IRS-III: A broker-based approach to semantic Web services. Journal of Web Semantics 6(2), 109–132 (2008)
24. Dang, N.C., Le, D.N., Quan, T.T., Nguyen, M.N.: Semantic Web Service Composition System Supporting Multiple Service Description Languages. In: Nguyen, N.T., Le, M.T., Świątek, J. (eds.) ACIIDS 2010. LNCS (LNAI), vol. 5990, pp. 390–398. Springer, Heidelberg (2010)
25. Vitvar, T., Mocan, A., Zaremba, M.: Formal Model for Semantic-Driven Service Execution. In: Sheth, A.P., Staab, S., Dean, M., Paolucci, M., Maynard, D., Finin, T., Thirunarayan, K. (eds.) ISWC 2008. LNCS, vol. 5318, pp. 567–582. Springer, Heidelberg (2008)
26. Lin, S.-Y., Lin, G.-T., Chao, K.-M., Lo, C.-C.: A Cost-Effective Planning Graph Approach for Large-Scale Web Service Composition. Mathematical Problems in Engineering 2012, Article ID 783476, 21 pages (2012), doi:10.1155/2012/783476

Introduction to the Second International Workshop on Performance Assessment and Auditing in Service Computing (PAASC 2012)

Claudia-Melania Chituc

University of Porto, Faculty of Engineering, Informatics Engineering Department, Portugal
cmchituc@fe.up.pt

Abstract. The main goal of the International Workshop on Performance Assessment and Auditing in Service Computing (PAASC) is to bring together researchers and industry representatives, providing them the opportunity to present and discuss research and development results, lessons learned, and advance new ideas on topics in the area of performance assessment, business modeling and auditing in service computing. Technical papers of high quality have been submitted. Four papers have been accepted and presented at the PAASC 2012 International Workshop.

1 Scope

The PAASC series addresses challenges in the area of auditing, performance assessment and business modeling in SOA. The main goal of the International Workshop on Performance Assessment and Auditing in Service Computing (PAASC) is to bring together researcher, practitioners and industry representatives, providing them the opportunity to present recent research and development results, discuss lessons learned, and advance novel topics in the area of performance assessment, business modeling and auditing in service computing and SOA [1].

Several research questions in this area still remain unanswered, such as: How to quantify the economic benefits of SOA? How to predict performance in SOA? Which are the business models for SOA? Which are the main decision criteria for service selection in services' environments? Which are the most relevant economic theories to support the formal definition and economic performance in SOA? How can SOA be assessed? The PAASC International Workshop aims at addressing such research topics.

Relevant topics for the PAASC 2012 International Workshop included:

- Service computing supporting (economic) performance assessment in different domains (e.g., long term digital preservation domain) or industry sectors (e.g., healthcare, financial).
- Economics of service computing/ SOA (e.g., cost models, cost-benefit analysis)

A. Ghose et al. (Eds.): ICSOC 2012, LNCS 7759, pp. 140–142, 2013.

- Business modeling in SOA (e.g., operational processes and policies, value configuration, technical cost modeling, formal modeling for core aspects on business in SOA)
- Audit in SOA
- Quality of services
- Monitoring and evaluation of services/ SOA
- Audit of services in the cloud
- Strategies and strategic decisions for services (e.g., concerning optimal resource utilization, service selection criteria)
- Analytics of services
- Methods, frameworks and methodologies synthetized for services' performance assessment (e.g., performance indicators, benchmarking methods, frameworks)
- Life-cycle management aspects of service computing
- Self-management aspects for services (e.g., instant management of assigned resources)
- Theories and approaches synthetized for services' representation and formal modeling
- Performance predictability in SOA.

2   Workshop Event

The PAASC 2012 International Workshop comprised four articles, grouped in two sessions.

The first session included the following contributions:

- *Definition of a Framework Supporting High Level Reliability of Services*, Firmino Silva and Claudia-Melania Chituc.
- *A Service-Oriented Approach to Assess the Value of Digital Preservation*, Claudia-Melania Chituc and Petra Ristau.

The second session (MoPoC[1] session) included two contributions:

- *Specification and Deployment of Distributed Monitoring and Adaptation Infrastructure*, Christian Inzinger, Benjamin Satzger, Waldemar Hummer and Schahram Dustdar.
- *Introducing the Vienna Platform for Elastic Processes*, Stefan Schulte, Philipp Hoenisch, Srikumar Venugopal and Schahram Dustdar.

Workshop Chair and Organizer:

Claudia-Melania Chituc, Assistant Professor at the Informatics Engineering Department, Faculty of Engineering, University of Porto, Portugal.

---

[1] The two articles presented in this session have been transferred from the 1st International Workshop on Monitoring and Prediction of Cloud Services (MoPoC).

Acknowledgements . The PAASC 2012 organizer would like to thank all the authors for their contributions to this workshop, and the members of the program committee whose expert input made this workshop possible. A special thank you to the organizers of the MoPoC Workshop – Monitoring and Prediction of Cloud Services (Armin Haller, Philipp Leitner, Rajiv Ranjan, Stefan Tai) who transferred the MoPoC Workshop submissions to the PAASC 2012 Workshop. A special thank you also to the ICSOC Workshop Chairs (Huibiao Zhu and Aditya Ghose) for their direction and guidance.

Reference

1. Chituc, C.-M.: Introduction to the First International Workshop on Performance Assessment and Auditing in Service Computing (PAASC 2010). In: Maximilien, E.M., Rossi, G., Yuan, S.-T., Ludwig, H., Fantinato, M. (eds.) ICSOC 2010 Workshops. LNCS, vol. 6568, pp. 1–3. Springer, Heidelberg (2011)

Towards the Definition of a Framework Supporting High Level Reliability of Services

Firmino Silva[1,2] and Claudia-Melania Chituc[1]

[1] University of Porto, Faculty of Engineering, Informatics Engineering Department, Portugal
[2] Polythechnic Institute of Porto / ISCAP
fsilva@iscap.ipp.pt, cmchituc@fe.up.pt

Abstract. In today's networked economy, an increasing need exists for companies to interact dynamically focusing on optimizing their skills and better serve their joint customers. Service oriented computing provides the means to achieve such objectives. This paper presents an approach towards the definition of a framework supporting a choreography of services built according to customer's requirements. The proposed framework is built on a set of specific metrics that translates the high level reliability of a service, which are calculated at various levels of the choreography, focusing on four main dimensions: technical capacity and performance, product or service purchased, customer satisfaction perspective, and provider's and business partners' choreography. This approach is then illustrated and discussed with a case example from the automotive sector.

1 Introduction

Service Oriented Computing (SOC) provides support to cross-organizational business processes (COBP) build on different applications and crossing heterogeneous computing platforms, based on cooperating services where application components are assembled with little effort into a network of loosely coupled services [1]. These service applications are suitable to run in dynamic business environments and are able to address constantly evolving customers' requirements [2]. Thus, it is important that monitoring approaches (e.g., conceptual frameworks, metrics, tools) are defined so that business partners and managers can have details on process and service assessment and monitoring in order to identify where, how, why and when improvements can be made. Assessment and monitoring of COBP and services are fundamental to understand the real added-value each business partner brought into the choreography and business process. Results obtained from the assessment and monitoring are useful to adapt, correct or adjust the business processes and services and their choreography.

This paper presents partial results of an ongoing research project aiming at developing a conceptual framework and metrics to support high level reliability of services in a business environment. These metrics can be calculated at different levels of a service choreography targeting four dimensions: technology (e.g., technology performance, capacity), process, product or service to be acquired, used or offered (e.g., delivery cost, level of quality), prospect of customer satisfaction (e.g., trust, operability) and the provider (and partners) expectation (e.g., profit, rate of return).

A. Ghose et al. (Eds.): ICSOC 2012, LNCS 7759, pp. 143–154, 2013.

The rest of this paper is organized as follows. The main concepts are presented in the next section. Metrics for high level reliability of services are described in Section 3. The proposed framework and a basic scenario from the automotive industry are introduced in Section 4. Related work is presented in Section 5. The article concludes with a section addressing the need for future research work.

2   Main Concepts

Services are fundamental elements for developing rapid, low-cost, interoperable, evolvable, and massively distributed applications [3][4]. A main goal of SOC is to gather a collection of software services, make them available/accessible via Internet over standardized (XML-based) languages and protocols, which can be implemented via a self-describing interface based on open standards [4]. Their functionalities can be automatically discovered and integrated into applications or composed to form more complex services, and they can perform different functions, e.g., ranging from answering to simple requests, to executing sophisticated business processes requiring peer-to-peer relationships among multiple layers of service consumers and providers. According to [5], SOC based on Web services is currently one of the main drivers for the software industry.

SOC relies on the Service-Oriented Architecture (SOA) to build the service model, where services are autonomous, platform-independent entities that can be self-described, published, discovered, and loosely coupled [3]. They promote a distributed computing infrastructure for both intra and cross-enterprise application integration and collaboration. Service providers supply their service descriptions with related technical and business support, e.g., allowing business partners to discover, select, build and compose services. Service descriptions are used to advertise the service functionalities, interface, behavior, and quality.

As consumers move towards adopting SOA, the quality and reliability of the services become important aspects. The service requirements vary significantly from customer to customer. To balance the customer expectations, a negotiation process must occur and the service must be leveled with the commitment of an agreement: a Service Level Agreement (SLA). The SLA [6] specifies the service level objectives both as expressions of requirements of the service consumer and assurances by the service provider on the availability of resources and quality of service (QoS). In order to guarantee the compliance with the agreed parameters, SLAs typically define the consequences associated with failures or violations.

Web-Service Level agreement (WSLA) has come to constitute an increasingly important instrument of monitoring Web-services environment where enterprises rely on services that may be subscribed dynamically and on demand. The WSLA framework [7] consists of a flexible and extensible language based on XML Schema and a run-time architecture comprising several SLA monitoring services, which is able to handle four different parameter types of metrics: resource metrics, composite metrics, SLA parameters and business metrics.

3   Metrics for High Level Reliability Services

The proposed framework relies on a set of metrics that are defined from: business rules, services, customer requirements, and results of a learning process. These elements are designed to ensure that the service desired by the customer is monitored and assessed and its characteristics are equal to those who represent the highest guarantee to cover all the relevant evaluation aspects of the choreography (agreed in the SLA). These assessments, allowing qualifying and quantifying the performance of services, provide a ranking of the best behaviors enriching the knowledge of the framework. A service evaluation matrix is proposed that stores the assessment results of the services iterations and keeps a ranking (Fig. 1).

High level reliability services refer in this article to the degree to which a choreography is expected to meet the requirements set by the client, allowing the identification of services capable to provide a higher performance considering the client's requirements. This is achieved by calculating the metrics covering the relevant dimensions of analysis for the choreography. The services that are part of the choreography are then selected considering their previous performance, e.g., results evaluations made in previous instantiations. In some cases, the assessment may reveal a value lower than the expected one. As services are ranked based on performance evaluations, choreographies are also evaluated and compared with respect to the performance that was expected to be achieved, and the level of performance actually achieved. This approach is detailed in Section 4.

3.1   Service Evaluation Matrix

According to the business rules for defining the choreography, the functional scope of each service is defined to add each service in the same pool so that they can "compete" in terms of performance within the same type. For each pool of services, a matrix is defined to store the ranking of services. The matrix stores the assessment results for all iterations resulting from their use in choreographies. The weights assigned to the evaluation criteria reflect the clients' requirements and importance assigned to each item. The values of each service evaluation matrix are recalculated taking into account the values characterizing the services in the customer's SLA. However, the scoring algorithm for measuring the rating for each service is always the same though is based on the new values resulting from the distribution of the new weights assigned (e.g.: considering the customer's requirements). Based on these rankings, a choreography of services is selected.

Figure 1 illustrates a simple example. Considering three services: Services A, B and C that perform the same functional context, a weight (w) is assigned by the customer for each service level. Four metrics are represented here by a to d. Each metric has a range of values (e.g.: a[0-3]; b[1-5]; c[2-4]; d[1-6]). The weights allocated to each metric, according to the profile of the service requested by a customer, are listed in each column of the table, e.g.: a[5%]; b[40%]; c[35%]; d[20%]. The calculation of service activity (cAct) is based on the sum of the average (v) of the assessment result of a service, multiplied by the product of the weight (w) of each metric:

			weights						scoring		
			5%	40%	35%	20%					
			metrics								
# in best chor	# iterations	services	a	b	c	d	cAct = Σ v(S).w(M) S∈{A,B,C}; M∈{a,b,c}	+scoring 1	+scoring 2	+scoring 3	ranking
		A									
		B									
		C									

Fig. 1. Evaluation matrix

A scoring algorithm is then used to calculate a rating for each service, based on the information which reflects the behavior of services and the scoring rules. Different rules can be defined for the scoring algorithm, as follows:

— Scoring rule 1: Number of times the service is used in choreographies
— Scoring rule 2: Number of times the service is used in choreographies and its level of performance is above a predefined level
— Scoring rule 3: Ratio between the number of times the service is used by the best choreographies and the total of uses

3.2   Classification of Choreographies

After selecting the service considered the best (e.g., according to the ranking of services made for each functional service scope), the elements of the monitoring system trigger mechanisms to measure the metrics of the activity of each service. The values obtained for each metric are added to tables of iterations of each service and thereafter allow measurements of the degree of excellence of the choreography as it will only be considered an *ideal* choreography if the values of the metrics are above the average value of each one. For example, the framework can point out a suitable (or excellent) choreography if 90% of the obtained values from all the measured metrics from services that integrate the choreography are above their average values. Assuming the example illustrated in Fig. 2, we can state that the average of all the known measured metrics from service "*a*" is 33% which is less than the performance obtained value (42%). The predictable performance expected for the choreography Y was lower (66%) than the executed one (72%) which means that when the choreography was built and run, its performance was higher than it was expected. But this does not mean that this choreography achieves an excellent performance as its performance degree

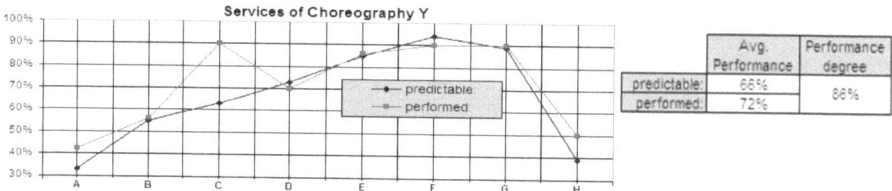

Fig. 2. Predictable vs. executed performance (example)

was 86%, below the conventional value of 90% which guarantees the ideal performed choreographies. If the choreography performance degree exceeds 90%, the participating services (*A* to *H*) would be increased (Scoring rule 2). According to market conditions, the choreography performance degree parameter may be adjusted to configure the appropriate answer to customer needs.

3.3   Metrics

Assessment and monitoring of each service are fundamental to create the perception of real value added to the choreography from each part of the process. Results obtained from the assessment and monitoring are useful to adapt and eventually adjust business processes. Thus, the definition of metrics of a "high level reliability of service" provides the basis for relationships of type win-win. Aspects related to the four following dimensions need to be monitored and assessed. For example, following the approach presented in [20]:

— Technology–related aspects e.g. QoS-related elements, such as: Service availability; Service response; Operation Latency; Time between failures.
— Process and product or service-related aspects, e.g.: Product/service availability; Quantity; Cost of delivery; Delivery time; Service delivery; Form of delivery; Process cycle time;
— Customer-related aspects, e.g. QoE-related elements such as Customer satisfaction, preferences and expectations; Recognizable brand; Product quality; Product variety; Level of trust; Usability; Learnability; Understandability; Operability;
— Supplier (side) of (choreography) customer service and partners-related aspects, QoBiz-related elements such as Quality of Business; QoI - Quality of Information; Cost of choreography; Revenue; Rate of return; Accuracy; Cost of goods; Completeness; Relevancy;

Metrics Definition Approach
The metrics tree definition follows the approaches described in [11][12], Business Activity Monitoring and Key Performance Indicators (KPI) that help an organization define and measure progress toward organizational goals through quantifiable measurements, agreed upon. As illustrated in Fig. 3, KPIs depend on a numerous set of Process Performance Metrics (PPM) [13] and Quality of Service (QoS) metrics [14].

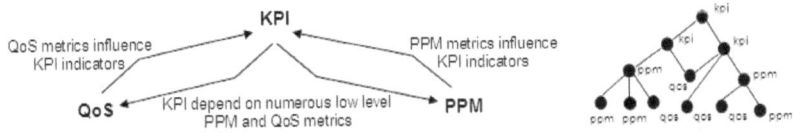

Fig. 3. KPIs, PPMs and QoS metrics(Source: adapted after[11]) and a tree dependency example

PPMs are specified based on process events (e.g. events published by a Business Process Execution Language [15] engine), whereas QoS metrics are measuring technical characteristics of the underlying service infrastructure (such as availability). Due to the correlation between metrics of different layers [16][17], the measurement results of one layer might impact the results of other layer. An example of this dependency is the "Customer Satisfaction" KPI defined on BPM layer, which is influenced by PPM metrics such as "Proposal Delivery Time", which is in turn affected by technical QoS metrics such as the "Availability" of the external services used by the provider for placing the proposal. It is essential to design a tree of dependencies between metrics of different levels to monitor the KPIs within the cross-layer setting based.

4   Proposed Framework

The research work pursued allowed the elaboration of a conceptual framework to support the high reliability of a service.

4.1   Main Elements

The main elements of the proposed framework are presented in Fig. 4 and described in Table 1.

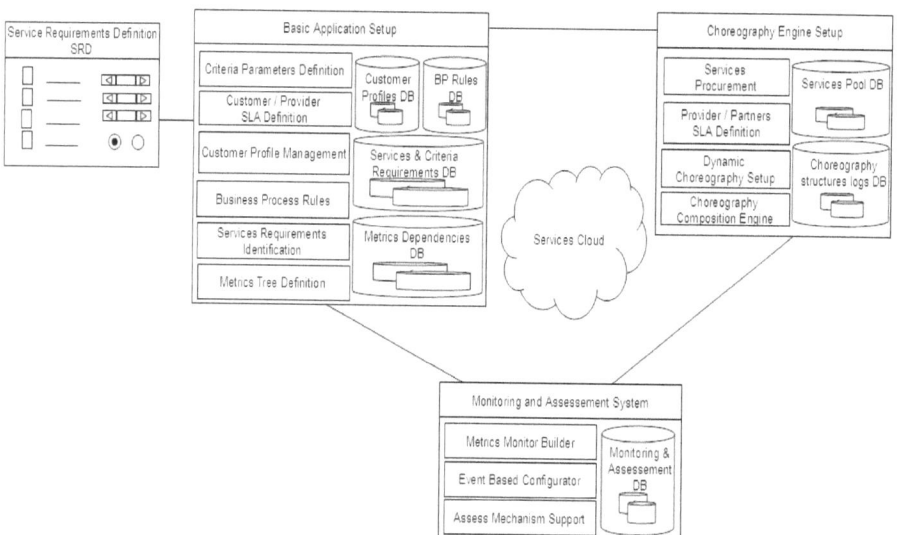

Fig. 4. Framework to support metrics of "high reliability of service"

Table 1. Description of framework elements

Outputs	Functional description	Inputs	Main objectives
	1. Application Support SETUP (Application Basic setup) module		
• Identification of services and their characteristics • SLA parameters and guidelines • Generic metrics	• Criteria Parameters Definition: Service Requirements Definition parsing and transformation into structured criteria parameters. • Provider builds a SLA considering input parameters • Definition of customer profile: if the customer is already known, Customer Profile Management will fulfill the Service Requirements Definition with a purpose based on the customer profile and decisions taken in previous interactions. According to the customer preferences and the level of service chosen, it will help framing and adjusting the system metrics tree to be launched over the choreography. • Business Process Rules: Through the knowledge of business rules and their requirements the required services and their level(s) will be identified. The functional scope of each set of services will receive instructions from the business rule to be organized in pools so that they can "compete" based on their functional behavior. • With the input received from the customer and Business Process Rules, Services Requirements are defined and required generic services and their characteristics are listed. • The generic metrics tree is constructed considering the client's input and metrics dependencies. All criteria and parameters (and their ranges) should be previously defined, e.g., to be able to list a set of metrics for each criteria. A database should provide a relationship between the parameters defined by the customer and the metrics necessary to monitor the service so that it is supplied with the closest approach of excellence of quality.	• Data from customer	• Define the information basic structure, e.g., from customer selected criteria, through the segmentation of customer profile, services aspects identification and metrics definition.
	2. Choreography Engine Setup Module		
• Definition of a SLA between the Provider and each Partner • Definition of the choreography of services	• Services Procurement: - the services with the best performance indicators are selected from the monitoring and assessment database based on the information received from the Services Requirements Identification and customer profile. The scoring algorithm to classify services performances in previous interactions support the service choreography engine to dynamically mount the services better ranked of the database. - in case a particular needed service is not stored in the database or the service last interaction is outdated or its ranking classification is below the required service level, services in the cloud will be procured (e.g., using a benchmarking approach) in order to fulfill the request • Dynamic Choreography Setup: according to rules of the Business Process (from the Basic Application setup) and Services Procurement Application, the choreography of services will be dynamically defined. • Choreography Composition Engine supports the choreography definition and instantiation. The monitoring and assessment system is triggered to activate the measurement of the metrics tree previously defined.	• SLA parameters and guidelines • Services aspects and functions to be accomplished by the procurement application	• Identify and select from the cloud the best scored services and mount the choreography service based
	3. Monitoring and Assessment Module		
• Records data measured from each metric linked to services on database	• Metrics Monitor Builder: based on the definition of the generic metrics tree and definition of services' choreography, the metrics monitor builder defines the monitoring system. • Event Based Configurator: a set of events supports metrics' monitoring that is triggered by the metrics tree and services selected. • Assess Mechanism Support: tool based on the metrics monitor that collects the data by event triggered from each measurement and sends it to the database.	• Generic metrics tree • Definition of services' choreography	• Define a dynamic event based monitoring and assessment engine to assess the metrics tree upon the service acquired by customer.

4.2   Methodology

The proposed approach comprises four main steps:

1. **Pre-Selection:** During the pre-selection step the setup for the whole framework is prepared. Structures of meta-data based on the inter-dependencies between the criteria chosen, the services required to support the business process rules and its requirements, and the ideal set of metrics to optimize the assessment mechanism are "initialized" here. Based on the input data from customer and the definitions stored in the databases, the framework shall support dynamic interaction of components. The setup information built on this step will be used in the following step.
1. **Selection:** During the Selection phase, the instances values from the services cloud or databases are identified and selected in order to fulfill the structures layouts received from the previous step. Aligning the choreography setup with the identification of the services that will be invoked on execution step, and the tree metrics system setup in the previous step will take place.
2. **Execution:** After all the setup tasks are concluded and all inputs are gathered, the Choreography Composition Engine will launch the choreography of the selected services and, at the same time, the Assess Mechanism Support will be triggered to collect values from the metric's tree. The choreography is based on a dynamic environment, e.g., in each interaction with a customer, a different choreography is set. SLAs will be formalized.
3. **Post-Execution:** This step is related to a learning process. It relies on the data collected which is fundamental to enrich the framework for future interactions. A score algorithm will rank the services performance and assigns a value to the choreography behavior, so that it can be used in future, supporting the selection of the best services and suitable choreography at given customer criteria.

4.3   A Simple Scenario Description

A simple scenario from the automotive sector is illustrated in Fig. 5. This sector is currently facing severe difficulties, e.g., due to the global economic crisis. More than ever, it is important to establish and maintain a lasting relationship with the customer, ensuring them that the company is offering the best service available in the market, allowing improved levels of competitiveness. In this scenario, a customer requests a Car Maintenance Operation (CMO) on a Web portal and has to select a set of operational business requirements which may depend on vehicle characteristics, type of mechanical maintenance and customer preferences. It represents a set of customer criteria of how and when the CMO will be performed. The customer has to select also available date and time (e.g., from an agenda, which can be approximate or exact); operation duration (which can be approximate or exact); and type and origin of parts (from the brand, other manufacturers or white brand); hypothetical substitution car and financial loan. A parts list is then identified and their availability is checked. In case of stock rupture, market is queried to provide the necessary services. If the car maintenance takes longer than a certain period of time, the proposal to the client includes an option for vehicle replacement. If the CMO cost exceeds a certain value, the proposal includes a financial loan.

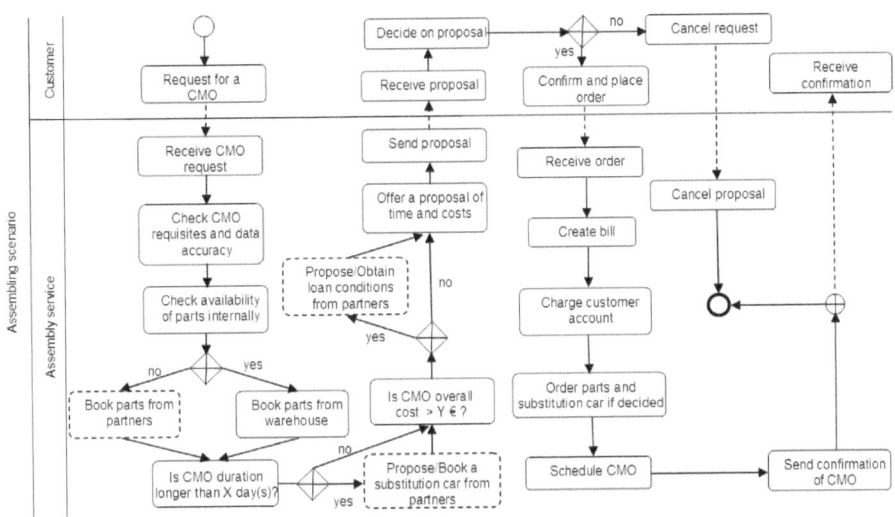

Fig. 5. A simple scenario: Car Maintenance Operation (CMO)

In these cases the market is also queried to provide the necessary services. This set of criteria provides data to the Service Requirements Definition and is needed to identify the customer profile, which in turn will help to decide what type of metrics and services should be proposed. The basic application gathers the customer data and, with support of the Business Process Rules DB, will identify in abstract the needed services to be composed to accomplish the intended level of the customer request. The Metrics Tree definition application, based on the specific business process rules and the service requirements definition, invokes an optimization engine to build the generic metrics tree according to the Metrics dependencies DB.

Based on the knowledge acquired from the learning process, the proposed metrics tree presents the list of interdependent metrics which are characterized to be the most adequate metrics that will measure the whole features of the service ensuring that the choreography is built with the best ranked services. Then, on the Choreography Engine Setup element the generic aspects of services are atomically identified, whether as a result of benchmarking procurement on the cloud of services, or they result as they are best ranked on the pool of services database and are valid for reuse. A monitoring and assessment engine is invoked to monitor and assess the choreography built based on the metrics tree. The results from the metrics measures mechanism will be relevant to assess SLA parameters and will feed the pool of services with a score that ranks the services in the pool. The choreography will also be scored. The results of several executions will always be subject to continuous improvement until it is obtained a stage of full guarantee of high level results.

In order to provide a competitive CMO in the market, several factors need to be considered. Firstly, being a business process built on a choreography of services, involving external business partners, to achieve the objectives of the business proposal one of the characteristics of the choreography refers to the dynamics of its design [8][9][10] so that it can be adjusted to the best service conditions to be proposed to the customer. At a given time, a set of suppliers can provide the best response to a customer request which may be different in other conditions, in particular, according to the characteristics of the vehicle which is involved in the service scheduling, customer preferences and/or market conditions (such as: prices, availability). The choreography should be rebuilt according to customer inputs and composed based on the procurement of services in the cloud or based on the knowledge DB from the framework, following a predefined set of criteria that will support building the choreography with the high level reliability services. The SLA generated should be closely monitored.

5   Related Work

Several approaches for service monitoring and business process monitoring exist, differing mostly in monitoring goals. An approach towards monitoring WS-BPEL processes focusing on runtime validation is presented in [18], focusing on the identification of services that deliver unexpected results (e.g., considering their functional expectation), and not on monitoring process performance metrics. A monitoring approach for WS-BPEL processes that supports run-time checking of assumptions under which a business partner services are expected to participate in a business process and the conditions to be fulfilled is described in [19].

In [20] are analyzed quality characteristics of metrics according to three perspectives: the service itself (without the customer or the business point of view), which is related to QoS - attributes like availability and performance of the service; the QoE that involves metrics which help to measure the customer interactivity (which could reflect subjective results under different occasions or customers), usability and trust; the Quality of Business (QoBiz) which is related to metrics that measure the business activity – e.g., revenue, profit. In [6] are described different quality attributes that are important to Service Based Applications like QoS, QoE and Quality of Information (QoI). Research on automated SLA negotiation between services has produced architectural solutions for negotiation on the fly as in [21].

An integrated framework for run-time monitoring and analysis of the performance of WS-BPEL processes is advanced in [22]. The authors present a dependency analysis, a machine learning based analysis of process performance metrics, and QoS metrics, in order to discover the main factors influencing the process performance (e.g., KPI) which is different from the approach described in this article, where the metrics tree results add values to the knowledge database which feeds the matrices of ranking between services.

A monitoring, predicting and adaptation approach for preventing KPI violations of business process instances is presented in [23]. A decision tree learning to construct classification models (which are then used to predict the KPI value of an instance while it is still running) is also discussed. The monitoring and assessment approach of this article is not focusing on adaptation, but on potential penalties or benefits related to service choreography.

6   Conclusion and Future Work

COBP monitoring and assessment is a challenging task. In this paper, the work pursued towards the development of a conceptual framework and metrics to support high level reliability of services in a business environment that was presented. The proposed framework comprises three elements: Application Support Setup; Choreography Engine Setup; and Monitoring and Assessment module. It is built on a set of specific metrics that translates the high reliability of a service. The metrics supporting service and business process monitoring and assessment are calculated at different levels of the choreography, focusing on four main dimensions: technical capacity and performance, product or service purchased, customer and provider's satisfaction prospect and business partners' choreography. A case example from the automotive sector was also discussed.

Future work will focus on defining new metrics to support COBP monitoring and assessment. Recurring to service composability, a prototype will be implemented to validate this approach. The proposed framework will be formally modeled to be adapted to computer-reading. Future work will also focus on preventing and real-time correction of unexpected behavior of services at run-time.

References

1. Papazoglou, M.P., Traverso, P., Dustdar, S., Leymann, F., Krämer, B.J.: Service-oriented computing: A research roadmap. In: Service Oriented Computing (SOC). Dagstuhl Seminar Proceedings, vol. 05462. IBFI, Schloss Dagstuhl, Germany (2006)
2. Di Nitto, E., Karastoyanova, D., Metzger, A., Parkin, M., Pistore, M., Pohl, K., Silvestri, F., Van den Heuvel, W.-J.: S-Cube: Addressing Multidisciplinary Research Challenges for the Internet of Services. In: Tselentis, G., et al. (eds.) Towards the Future Internet. IOS Press (2009)
3. Papazoglou, M.: Service-Oriented Computing: Concepts, Characteristics and Directions. In: 4th International Conference on Web Information Systems Engineering (WISE 2003) (2003)
4. Papazoglou, M., Traverso, P., Dustdar, S., Leymann, F.: Service-Oriented Computing: State of the Art and Research Challenges. IEEE Computer Society (2007), 0018-9162/07
5. Bichler, M., Lin, K.J.: Service-oriented computing, IT System Perspectives. IEEE Computer 39(3) (2006)
6. S-Cube consortium deliverable, CD-JRA-1.3.3 "Initial Concepts for Specifying End-to-End Quality Characteristics and Negotiating SLAs" (2010), http://www.s-cube-network.eu/ (September 2011)
7. Keller, A., Ludwig, H.: WSLA Framework: Specifying and Monitoring Service Level Agreements for Web Services. Journal of Network and Systems Management (2003)
8. Mukhija, A., Rosenblum, D.S., Foster, H., Uchitel, S.: Runtime Support for Dynamic and Adaptive Service Composition. In: Wirsing, M., Hölzl, M. (eds.) SENSORIA Project. LNCS, vol. 6582, pp. 585–603. Springer, Heidelberg (2011)
9. Schmidt, R.: Web Services Based Architectures to Support Dynamic Inter-organizational Business Processes. In: Jeckle, M., Zhang, L.-J. (eds.) ICWS-Europe 2003. LNCS, vol. 2853, pp. 123–136. Springer, Heidelberg (2003)

10. Di Nitto, E., Ghezzi, C., Metzger, A., Papazoglou, M., Pohl, K.: A journey to highly dynamic, self-adaptive service-based applications. Automated Software Engineering Journal 15(3), 313–341 (2008) ISSN: 0928-8910
11. Wetzstein, B., Leitner, P., Rosenberg, F., Brandic, I., Dustdar, S., Leymann, F.: Monitoring and Analyzing Influential Factors of Business Process Performance. In: Published in EDOC 2009 Proc. of the 2009 IEEE (EDOC 2009) (2009)
12. S-Cube consortium deliverable, PO-JRA-1.3.1 "Survey of Quality Related Aspects Relevant for Service-based" (2008), http://www.s-cube-network.eu/ (September 2011)
13. Wetzstein, B., Strauch, S., Leymann, F.: Measuring Performance Metrics of WS-BPEL Service Compositions. In: The Fifth International Conference on Networking and Services (ICNS 2009), Valencia, Spain, April 20-25. IEEE Computer Society (2009)
14. Menasce, D.A.: QoS issues in Web services. IEEE Internet Computing (2002)
15. Karastoyanova, D., Khalaf, R., Schroth, R., Paluszek, M., Leymann, F.: BPEL Event Model. Technical Report 2006/10. University of Stuttgart (2006)
16. S-Cube consortium deliverable, PO-JRA-1.2.3 "Baseline of Adaptation and Monitoring Principles, Techniques, and Methodologies across Functional SBA Layers" (2009), http://www.s-cube-network.eu/results/deliverables/ (September 2011)
17. Kazhamiakin, R., Pistore, M., Zengin, A.: Cross-Layer Adaptation and Monitoring of Service-Based Applications. In: Dan, A., Gittler, F., Toumani, F. (eds.) ICSOC/ServiceWave 2009. LNCS, vol. 6275, pp. 325–334. Springer, Heidelberg (2010)
18. Baresi, L., Guinea, S.: Towards Dynamic Monitoring of WS-BPEL Processes. In: Benatallah, B., Casati, F., Traverso, P. (eds.) ICSOC 2005. LNCS, vol. 3826, pp. 269–282. Springer, Heidelberg (2005)
19. Barbon, F., Traverso, P., Pistore, M., Trainotti, M.: Run-time monitoring of instances and classes of Web servisse compositions. In: Proc. IEEE Int. Conf. on Web Services (ICWS 2006), pp. 63–71 (2006)
20. van Moorsel, A.: Metrics for the Internet Age: Quality of Experience and Quality of Business. In: Proceedings of the 5th Int'l Workshop on Performability Modeling of Computer and Communication Systems, Erlangen, September 15-16. Arbeitsberichte des Instituts für Informatik, Universität Erlangen-Nürnberg (2001)
21. Chhetri, M., Lin, J., Goh, S., Zhang, J., Kowalczyk, R., Yan, J.: A coordinated architecture for the agentbased service level agreement negotiation of Web service composition. In: Australian Software Engineering Conference (ASWEC 2006), pp. 90–99 (2006)
22. Wetzstein, B., Leitner, P., Rosenberg, F., Brandic, I., Dustdar, S., Leyman, F.: Monitoring and Analyzing Influencial Factors of Business process performance. In: Proc. 2009 IEEE (EDOC), pp. 141–150 (2009)
23. Wetzstein, B., Zengin, A., Kazhamiakin, R., Marconi, A., Pistore, M., Karastoyanova, D., Leymann, F.: Preventing KPI violations in business processes based on decision tree learning and proactive runtime adaptation. Journal of Systems Integration 3(1), 3–18 (2012)

A Service-Oriented Approach to Assess the Value of Digital Preservation

Claudia-Melania Chituc[1] and Petra Ristau[2]

[1] University of Porto, Faculty of Engineering, Informatics Engineering Department, Portugal
cmchituc@fe.up.pt
[2] JRC Capital Management Consultancy & Research GmbH, Germany
pristau@jrconline.com

Abstract. Assessing the economic value of a preservation system that preserves increasing amounts of digital data produced and collected by public and private organizations is a challenging task. The financial sector, in particular the investment business, is characterized by constantly increasing volumes of high frequency market and transaction data which need to be kept for long periods of time (e.g., due to regulatory compliance). Designing and developing appropriate metrics and tools to support the economic performance assessment in the context of long term digital preservation is a complex and difficult process. This article has three main objectives: (1) to present the work pursued towards the elaboration of a set of metrics to support economic performance assessment in the context of long term digital preservation, (2) to exhibit the architecture of the economic performance assessment engine supporting this analysis, (3) to discuss preliminary results of the value assessment of digital preservation for the financial sector obtained by applying the proposed model. This work reflects the R&D activities pursued within the scope of the on-going R&D FP7 project ENSURE – *Enabling kNowledge Sustainability Usability and Recovery for Economic value* (http://ensure-fp7.eu).

Keywords: Service computing, performance assessment, digital preservation, financial sector.

1 Introduction

Assessing the economic value of a preservation system (or preservation solution) that ensures the preservation of increasing amounts of digital data produced and collected by public and private organizations is a complex and difficult task, e.g., due to the lack of awareness for data preservation from industry and the associated added-value. For example, the financial sector, in particular the investment business, produces and collects a big volume of digital data (e.g., market data, transactions data) that needs to be preserved for long term (e.g., for regulatory compliance, research purposes).

Enterprise's decision to adopt a preservation system is a complex process and economic factors (e.g., costs, expected payoffs) influence such a decision. Research on the economics of digital preservation is scarce and is focusing mainly on cost

A. Ghose et al. (Eds.): ICSOC 2012, LNCS 7759, pp. 155–166, 2013.

modeling (e.g.,[1-4]) and currently there are no metrics or tools to support an economic performance assessment analysis in the context of long term digital preservation (LTDP).

Although several advantages of LTDP are claimed (e.g., faster and secure access to preserved e-data compared to manual/traditional preservation or no e-data preservation), formal models, metrics, frameworks or tools to support the quantification of its (expected) economic benefits (e.g., cost-benefit analysis, return on investment in the context of LTDP) are not yet available. Several questions are still unanswered, e.g., What are the specific benefits a particular organization would gain by adopting a preservation system/ preservation solution? How can expected benefits be assessed in the context of LTDP, from an economic perspective? How to predict the economic performance of a preservation system? How to predict the future value of the preserved digital data? These issues are tackled in this article, which reflects the research work pursued within the scope of the on-going R&D FP7 project ENSURE – *Enabling kNowledge Sustainability Usability and Recovery for Economic value[1].*

This article has three main objectives: (1) to present the work pursued towards the elaboration of a set of metrics to support economic performance assessment in the context of LTDP, (2) to exhibit the architecture of the economic performance assessment engine supporting this analysis, developed within the scope of the ENSURE FP7 project, (3) to discuss preliminary results of the value assessment of digital preservation for the financial sector obtained by applying the proposed model.

The rest of this article is organized as follows. The next section briefly introduces the concepts of LTDP and service oriented computing. Section three refers to ways for value assessment in the context of LTDP. Advances towards the development of the Economic Performance Assessment engine are then presented. A case example from the financial sector is discussed in Section five. The article concludes with a section addressing the needs for further research.

2   Digital Preservation and Service Computing: A Brief Overview

2.1   Long Term Digital Preservation: Concept and Challenges

LTDP concerns, in a broad way, the activities related to preserving digital data over long periods of time, ensuring its accessibility and usability [5], allowing the retention of digital data (or digital objects) and its meaning [6]. The Consultative Committee for Space Data Systems [7] defines LTDP as the act of maintaining information, independently understandable by a specific community, supporting its authenticity over the long term.

Technical recommendations establishing a common framework of terms and concepts which make up an Open Archive Information System (OAIS) are presented in the OAIS Reference Model [7-8], which consists of six functional entities (and

---

[1] http://ensure-fp7.eu

related interfaces). Challenges in ensuring long term preservation of digital objects refer to (e.g., [9]): digital (technology) obsolescence, lack of standards and generally accepted methods for preserving information, deterioration (e.g., of digital data recording media), and high data heterogeneity.

Research in this area focused mainly on technical aspects and quality of preserved data. Research on the economics of LTDP is scarce and existing studies concern mainly cost modeling. The work presented in this article aims at advancing research in this area, focusing on economic performance analysis.

2.2   Services and Service Oriented Architecture

Services represent autonomous and platform-independent computational entities, which can be described, published, discovered, and dynamically assembled to deploy distributed interoperable systems (e.g., [10,11]). As emphasized in [12], service-oriented computing promotes the idea of assembling application components in a network of services to create agile applications that cross different geographically distributed computing platforms and organizations. The Service Oriented Architecture (SOA) allows services to communicate and exchange information between distributed systems; it provides means for service providers to offer services, and service users to discover services.

Web services are services that make use of the Internet as communication platform, and open Internet-based standards, such as: Simple Object Access Protocol (SOAP[2]) to exchange data; Web Service Description Language (WSDL[3]) to describe services; Business Process Execution Language for Web Services (BPEL4WS[4]) to specify business processes and interaction protocols [10][13]. Service providers can register their services in a public service registry using the Universal Description Discovery and Integration (UDDI[5]). Web services are currently regarded as the most promising service-oriented computing technology [14]. Web services offer standard-based mechanisms to connect electronically business partners [15].

2.3   Preservation Architecture Approaches

Architectures for data preservation systems need to be designed and specified to support preservation processes. Although there is no generally accepted definition of the data preservation system architecture, several aspects are usually considered as relevant, such as: the fundamental organization of a system, reflected in its components and their relationships to each other and the environment, as well as the principles guiding its design and evolution; the composite of the design architectures for products and their life-cycle processes [16]. Below are referred two examples of preservation architectures:

---

[2] SOAP, http://www.w3.org/TR/soap/

[3] WSDL, http://www.w3.org/TR/wsdl

[4] BPEL4WS, http://www.ibm.com/developerworks/library/specificaion/ws-bpel/

[5] UDDI, http://www.uddi.org and http://www.oasis-open.org/committees/uddi
    -spec

- CASPAR[6] architecture was designed on the following principles: OAIS-compliance, technology-neutrality, loosely-coupled architecture, domain independence, preservation of intelligibility and knowledge dependencies, preservation of authenticity and digital rights.
- SHAMAN[7] reference architecture follows OAIS SOA Reference Model, comprising layered information package, refinement of the information package, pre-Ingest and post-Access activities.

2.4   ENSURE FP7 Project

The on-going R&D ENSURE FP7 project aims at extending the state-of-the art of digital preservation by building a self-configurating software stack addressing the configuration and preservation life-cycle processes in order to create a financially viable solution for specific user requirements [17]. It analyzes the tradeoff between the costs of preservation against the value of the preserved data, tackling quality aspects, focusing on use cases from the health care, clinical trials and financial sector. The ENSURE Reference Architecture[8] for digital preservation follows a SOA approach and was designed to support the OAIS Reference Model.

3   Assessing Value in the Context of LTDP

3.1   Background and Challenges

Few studies on the economics of LTDP exist, referring mainly to cost modeling. A first study on the costs of digital preservation aside storage cost issues is presented in [18], where different data types are identified and a decision model for appropriate preservation methods for the data types is advanced. Although the proposed cost model relies on the cost items identified for seven modules (creation, selection/ evaluation, data management, resource disclosure, data use, data preservation and data use/rights), no quantification of these items is provided. Costs involved in digital preservation were also presented in [19]. A study reflecting the cost of digital preservation and the OAIS Reference Model is presented in [20], where three main aspects determining costs of an archive are identified: content data types and formats, access, and authority and control. A cost model for small scale automated digital preservation archives is presented in [1]. Cost aspects of ingest and normalization compliant to OAIS Reference Model is described in [2]. Challenges on LTDP cost modeling are discussed in [4].

The issue of economic performance assessment in the context of LTDP is of utmost importance for public and private organizations. The Blue Ribbon Task Force [21] concentrated on materials that are of long-term public interest, such as research data, scholarly disclosure, commercially owned cultural content, collectively

---

[6] http://www.casparpreserves.eu

[7] http://shaman-ip.eu/shaman

[8] http://ensure-fp7.eu

produced Web content. As a result, they identified important structural challenges for the economic analysis, i.e., long term horizons, diffused stakeholders, misaligned or weak incentives, and lack of clarity about roles and responsibilities among stakeholders.

Examples of challenges for economic performance assessment analysis are: difficulty to estimate expected value of preserved data, future value of preserved data may increase or decrease in time (e.g., value of market data), change in costs (e.g., cost of information, cost of technology), technology changes (e.g., ICT advances, technology obsolescence), uncertainties related to future policy/ regulations and their impact on the value of preserved data, difficulty of quantify the added value attained by transferring data in paper format to digital format, quantification of the impact of risks on preservation. Private institutions face additional challenges on the economics of LTDP concern, mainly related to data heterogeneity, sector-specific regulations and policies.

An extensive literature survey has been conducted. The most important theories and approaches which can be relevant for the economic performance assessment in the context of LTDP were identified. Game theory and decision theory are only two examples of applicable theories for this analysis, and are briefly described below.

Game Theory. is a branch of applied mathematics that analyzes players who choose different actions in an attempt to maximize their payoffs [22]. A cooperative game allows the formation of coalitions: players join forces based on a binding agreement [23]. Main fields of application are: economic systems [24], biology, philosophy, and computer systems. The modeling approach of game theory is relevant to service computing and LTDP analysis to determine the gains (e.g., ROI) an organization may have by selecting a specific strategy (e.g., adoption of a certain preservation solution/ preservation configuration).

Decision Theory. Given a decision problem, decision theory makes use of probability theory to recommend optimal decisions, or an option that maximizes (expected) utility. Fields of application include economics, economic systems, and artificial intelligence. According to [25], a decision problem presumes: an association of a set of outcomes with each action; a measure U of outcome value which assigns a utility $U(\omega)$ to each outcome $\omega \in \Omega$; a measure of the probability of outcomes conditional on actions $Pr(\omega/a)$ denoting the probability that outcome ω is obtained after action $a \in A$. Based on these elements, the expected utility $EU(a)$ is defined in [25] as the average utility of the outcomes associated with an alternative, weighting the utility of each outcome by the probability that the outcome results from the alternative: $EU(a) = \int_\Omega U(\omega)Pr(\omega/a)d\omega$. Decision theory is relevant for organizations analyzing the

possibility to adopt a preservation system or new preservation solution/ configuration, especially when decision makers need to make forecasts of the expected gains and determine the payback period, for example.

In Table 1 are emphasized the strengths and weaknesses of game theory and decision theory towards economic performance assessment in the context of LTDP. The Expected Utility, for example, could be relevant to estimate the future value of preserved data and added value of a certain preservation solution that will be reflected, for example, in the ROI. Game theory, for example, is relevant to support the estimation of benefits related to the adoption of a preservation solution that is relevant for ROI and payback estimation.

Table 1. Relevant theories

Theory	Definition and basic elements	Pros LTDP	Cons LTDP
Decision Theory[24]	$EU(a) = \int_{\Omega} U(\omega) \Pr(\omega/a) d\omega$	Relevant for forecasting, ROI and payback period modeling.	Often difficult to elaborate reasonable estimates.
Game theory	A game function: $v: 2^N \rightarrow R$ Players, moves or strategies, specifications of benefits for a strategy.	Relevant to model gains and ROI for a specific strategy (e.g., adoption of a preservation solution).	Lack of formal models/metrics to assess or monitor economic parameters.

A precondition for an adequate assessment of preservation systems and preservation solutions is the availability of metrics relevant in the context of LTDP. We can distinguish between measures describing system performance (e.g., preservation system availability, throughput, downtime, response time, and other quality-related attributes), and metrics for assessing the economic performance of a storage solution (e.g., payoffs, ROI, NPV, payback period). Models, metrics, methodologies, frameworks and tools for supporting an economic analysis and assessment in a digital preservation environment are not yet available. However, they would be of utmost importance for managers' decision whether to adopt or not a certain preservation system/ preservation solution.

4   Assessment Approach: Main Activities and Basic Architecture

To support the economic performance analysis in the context of LTDP, research is being pursued towards the development of specific metrics (e.g., return on investment-ROI, return of information, net present value-NPV, payback period). An Economic Performance Assessment (EPA) engine was designed to support the developed metrics. Figure 1 illustrates the main activities of the EPA engine.

The input information for the EPA engine refers to: *user requirements and preferences* (e.g., preservation solution lifetime, initial investment, number of copies, number of storage sites, not accomplish law fee), *results of the Cost Engine* (e.g., annual running cost, total cost associated with a preservation solution/ configuration), and the *global preservation plan* (which is an XML file with relevant information for the EPA analysis, e.g., configuration creation and expiration date) [16][26]. The outputs of the EPA engine will be the values of the metrics supporting economic

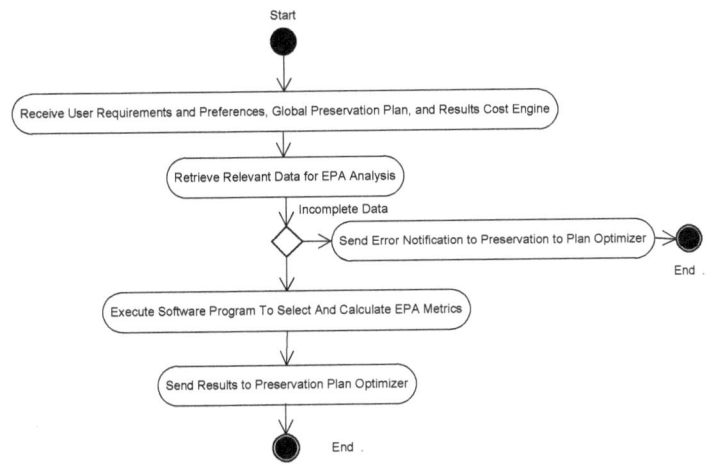

Fig. 1. Simplified flow diagram for the EPA engine

performance assessment, such as: estimated ROI associated to a preservation solution, estimated annual ROI, estimated payback period, estimated NPV.

The basic architecture for the EPA engine (and the environment in which it operates) is portrayed in Figure 2. The EPA Engine is part of the Preservation Plan Optimizer (PPO) component, which is responsible for driving the evaluation and optimization process [16][26]. The Configurator sends parameterized proposed preservation configurations to the PPO, which provides the EPA engine with the following information as input: the ENSURE global preservation plan, user requirements, and results of the Cost Engine [16][26].

A first version of the EPA engine was already implemented at the University of Porto, using Java. A second prototype will be developed. Part of the functionality of the EPA engine is already integrated into the ENSURE preservation stack. Web services are used to transmit the EPA engine results.

5   Case Example from the Financial Sector

5.1   Main Characteristics and Challenges for LTDP

The financial domain, in particular the investment business, is characterized by permanently incoming streams of high frequency market data. The digital data produced and collected by financial institutions (e.g., market data, transactions data) needs to be preserved for long term (e.g., for regulatory compliance, research purposes). In the past, the main focus of R&D was on performance improvement of the IT infrastructure in an attempt to deal with the constantly increasing volumes of data. Today the need of financial institutions for support in compliance to regulations and legal standards takes an increasingly important role [9][27][28].

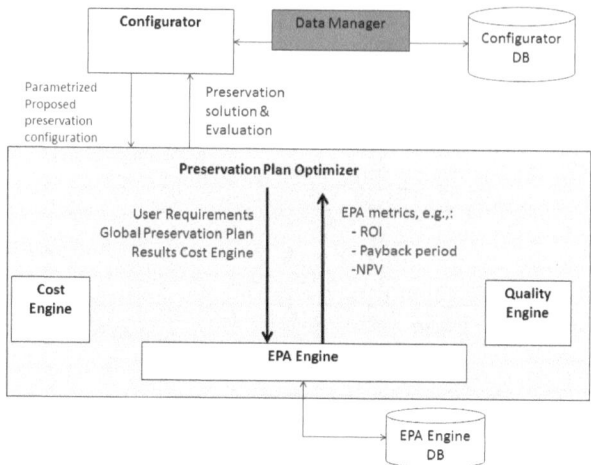

Fig. 2. Basic EPA Engine Architecture

The goals of financial institutions with respect to LTDP are threefold: **1.** to comply with legal and regulatory requirements to fulfill record retention obligations. The period for retention is five years after the termination of the business relationship. The type of documents comprises not only contractual papers and account statements concerning trading activities on behalf of the client, but, in general, every information ever given to the client, including marketing material, e-mails, telephone-protocols, etc. **2.** to protect the commercial value of market data for research purposes. Developing automated trading models requires a rich data base of financial market data, covering a large variety of trading instruments and reaching back over many years, eventually up to ten or twenty years. Tick data, covering every single price change, is expensive to buy and therefore, once purchased, represents a significant business value that has to be preserved. **3.** to ensure traceability of trading decisions even after years. For their own purposes and in order to anticipate eventual future regulatory requirements of transparency, this third goal is to ensure that the actual performance of trading models on historical data can be reconstructed for many years in the past. This requires the interaction of three components: the model, implemented in a proprietary programming language, the execution environment for the model, consisting of a particular version of the used charting and analysis software, and the data, stemming from a particular data source. Any variance in one of these components may lead to significantly large deviations in model performance.

A detailed description of stakeholders for the financial institutions, flows of data between different departments of a typical investment bank and data types that need to be preserved is available in [9]: *Market data* is received from the real time feed and forwarded to the historical database from where it is accessed by the financial engineers located in the R&D department. It is also displayed on the charts on the traders' desktop in the front office as well as fed to the middle office, where it is used for tracking of open positions and risk management. *Client data* (e.g., contracts, account statements, communication) is received from the custodian bank, broker or clearing house. It is the back-office staff that manages this type of data together with any other client related documents and is responsible for the preservation of this type of data. **Trading Models** are developed by the R&D department and installed at the trader's desks. Thus, the financial engineers perform the retention of all models and market data.

Main challenges for LTDP for this sector refer mainly to the heterogeneity of the data that needs to be stored and the retention of the preserved information (e.g., the retention of: client information, proprietary applications due to business purposes, very large amounts of market data stored over time), while meeting regulatory directives and business goals. Thus, a preservation system for this sector needs not only to preserve large amounts of heterogeneous data, but it should also allow conformance to regulatory, contractual and legal requirements, and management of long term authenticity and integrity of intellectual propriety and personal data.

Another characteristic of this scenario is the distribution of stakeholders over two distinct departments. Two different types of users with very different levels of computer literacy will be interacting with the preservation system: basic skilled back-office staff on the one hand, and technically skilled financial engineers on the other. This has consequences on the selection of an appropriate preservation system that can provide for role based access mechanisms, preventing unauthorized data access for the respective group of users, but has also organizational implications that have to be valuated economically. Distributed (and eventually unclear) responsibilities among stakeholders are mentioned by BRTF [21] as one of the main obstacles to the adoption and efficient usage of preservation systems. Hence, additional effort has to be spent on the definition of clear procedures for the preservation in every stage.

5.2   EPA Analysis

The EPA analysis is relevant for managers of financial institutions because it supports decision making (e.g., to adopt a preservation system, to adopt or not a new preservation solution/ configuration). It provides means to perform an economic analysis, e.g., cost-benefit analysis, determine the payback period for a preservation system, and determine the expected return on investment.

A simple example for EPA analysis is illustrated in Table 3. In this example, the results of the analysis reflect negative values of Return on Investment[9] (ROI) (in the case of client data) and positive ROI (in the case of market data). However, the results have to be interpreted with care, e.g., the analyzed preservation configuration might bring positive (high) ROI for a longer lifetime of the analyzed preservation configuration (e.g., more than 10 years).

When performing an economic performance analysis (e.g., to support decision making concerning the adoption of a certain preservation solution), several factors need to be considered, such as: preservation solution lifetime, amount of data to be

---

[9] **Return on Investment (ROI)** is a performance measure commonly used to evaluate the efficiency of an investment or to compare the efficiency of a number of different investments. The benefit (return) of an investment is divided by the cost of the investment. The result is expressed as a percentage or ratio.

preserved, estimated value of the preserved data, estimation of expected payoffs, estimation of operations to be performed (e.g., ingest, access), preservation type (e.g., gold, silver, bronze[10]), costs.

Table 2. A Simple Example

	Market data	Client data
TIME		
Lifetime preservation solution/configuration	2 years	2 years
Preservation period	50 years	50 years
AMOUNT OF DATA		
Annual amount of data to be preserved	10TB	7,5 GB
VALUE OF PRESERVED DATA		
Year 1	50K	invaluable
Year 2	55K	invaluable
POTENTIAL LOSSES (for the preservation period)		
Estimated value	2,5K€	50K€
PAYOFFS		
Potential gains	50K€	
Probability	0,9	
NUMBER OF OPERATIONS (annual)		
Number of *access* operations	30	240
PRESERVATION		
Gold		X
Silver		
Bronze	X	
COSTS		
Initial Investment	5K€	5K€
Cost of cloud (annual)	120€/ year	
Costs related to preservation operations (e.g., ingest, access, retrieval)	1200€/year	
Preservation system administration	1000€/year	
Other costs	180€/year	
RESULTS Economic Performance Assessment (EPA) ENGINE		
RETURN ON INVESTMENT (ROI)		
ROI_{year1}	35%	-0,2%
ROI_{year2}	42%	-0,04%

The metrics need to be correlated with additional information (e.g., uncertainties and associated probabilities) to support decision making (e.g., to adopt a certain preservation solution or not). Figure 2 illustrates a simple example, considering the probability that long-run cost of preservation increases, and policy gets stricter.

6   Conclusions and Future Research Work

Public and private institutions face numerous challenges on identifying and quantifying payoffs to be attained by preserving digital data for future use. Metrics,

---

[10] This is an analogy of 'gold silver bronze service level' used to reduce the number of parameters to be submitted by the user through the GUI, e.g., storage type, validation algorithm, frequency (of ingest).

methodologies and tools to support economic performance assessment in the context of long term digital preservation (LTDP) are not yet available.

Preliminary results of the research work currently being pursued (within the scope of the on-going ENSURE FP7 project) towards the design and development of an economic performance assessment (EPA) engine and metrics to support an economic performance analysis in the context of digital preservation are presented in this article. Part of the functionality of the EPA engine is already integrated into the ENSURE preservation stack. A simple example from the financial sector is also discussed.

Economic performance evaluation results can support decision making about preservation systems in several ways. Depending on the particular goals of preservation, economic considerations can help to choose between alternative preservation solutions or configurations, or to abandon the adoption of preservation technologies at all. Where data is stored for reasons of protection of business values, preservation costs are usually expected to be lower than the values to be protected. In this case, only if the ROI is positive, a decision maker would give green light for the acquisition of a preservation system. On the other hand, where legal obligations dominate the motivation for implementing a preservation system, as in the case of financial client data, considerations about data value are typically helpful for a decision only in the second place. Data value can sometimes be extremely difficult to quantify. Even if we attempt to economically quantify the consequences of data loss, e.g. expressed in fines for breach of record retention obligations, these will typically not consist of a fixed catalogue, but be extremely variable amounts due at the discretion of the regulating authorities. Anyway, if we take into account that the value of preserved data should not be confused with its monetary or financial value *per se*, as emphasized by [21], but consider instead value to be determined by the ways, the data are used after years, the utility measure U from decision theory (Table 1) may point to a way out from this dilemma.

Future research work will focus on the development of new economic performance metrics, relevant in the context of LTDP, and their validation.

Acknowledgements. The research leading to these results has received funding from the European Community's Seventh Programme (FP7/2007-2013) under the grant no. 270000. The authors acknowledge consortium members efforts in the implementation of the different ENSURE components communicating with the EPA engine, and developers of the EPA engine.

References

1. Strodl, S., Rauber, A.: A Cost Model for small Scale Automated Digital Preservation Archives. In: Proc. 8th Int. Conf. on Preservation of Digital Objects, pp. 97–106 (2011)
2. Kejser, U.B., Nielsen, A.B., Thirifays, A.: Cost Aspects of Ingest and Normalization. In: Proceedings 8th Int. Conf. on Preservation of Digital Objects iPRES, pp. 107–115 (2011)
3. Grindley, N.: The Costs and Economics of Preservation. In: Proceedings 8th Int. Conf. on Preservation of Digital Objects iPRES, pp. 116–119 (2011)
4. Xue, P., Shehab, E., Baguley, P., Badawy, M.: Cost modeling for long-term digital preservation: Challenges and issues. In: Proceedings 9th Int. Conf. on Manufacturing Research (ICMR 2011), pp. 187–192. Glasgow Caledonian University, Glasgow (2011)

5. Borghoff, U.M., Rodig, P., Scheffczyk, J., Schmitz, L.: Long-Term Preservation of Digital Documents. Springer, Heidelberg (2003)
6. Lee, K.-O., Stattery, O., Lu, R., Tang, X., McCrary, V.: State of the Art and Practice in Digital Preservation. Journal of Research of the NIST 107, 93–106 (2002)
7. CCDS-The Consultative Committee for Space Data Systems: Reference Model for an Open Archival Information System (OAIS). Draft Recommended Standard, CCSDS 650.0-P-1.1, Pink Book (2009), http://public.ccsds.org/sites/cwe/rids/Lists/CCSDS%206500P11/Attachements/650x0p11.pdf (accessed on February 20, 2012)
8. Giaretta, D.: Advanced Digital Preservation. Springer, Heidelberg (2011)
9. Chituc, C.-M., Ristau, P.: Requirements Elicitation for a Long Term Digital Preservation System: A Case Study from the Financial Sector. In: Proc. 9th Int. Conf. on Preservation of Digital Objects iPRES, Toronto, Canada, October 1-5, pp. 236–243 (2012)
10. Papazoglou, M.P., Traverso, P., Dustdar, S., Leymann, F.: Service-Oriented Computing: State of the Art and Research Challenges. IEEE Computer, 64–70 (June 2007)
11. Papazoglou, M.P., Traverso, P., Dustdar, S., Leymann, F.: Service-Oriented Computing: A Research Roadmap. International Journal of Cooperative Information Systems 17(2), 223–255 (2008)
12. Leymann, F.: Combining Web Services and the Grid: Towards Adaptive Enterprise Applications. In: Proceedings CAiSE 2005 Workshops, vol. 2, pp. 9–21. FEUP Edições (2005)
13. Papazoglou, M.P.: Web Services: Principles and Technology. Prentice Hall (2007)
14. Weerawarana, S., et al.: Web Services Platform Architecture: SOAP, WSDL, WS-Policy, WS-Addressing, WS-BPEL, WS-Reliable Messaging, and More. Prentice Hall (2005)
15. Peltz, C.: Web services orchestration and choreography. IEEE Computer, 46–52 (2003)
16. ENSURE: ENSURE High Level Architecture Specification Deliverable D11.1 (2011), http://ensure-fp7.eu (accessed on July 20, 2012)
17. Edelstein, O., Factor, M., King, R., Risse, T., Salant, E., Taylor, P.: Evolving Domains, Problems and Solutions for Long Term Digital Preservation. In: Proc. of iPRES 2011, Singapore, November 1-4, pp. 194–204 (2011)
18. Hendley, T.: Comparison of methods & costs of digital preservation. British Library Research and Innovation Report 106. British Library Research and Innovation Centers (1998)
19. Ashley, K.: Digital archive costs: facts and fallacies. In: DLM Forum 1999, Brussels, Belgium. European Commission (1999)
20. Granger, S., Russell, K., Weinberger, E.: Cost elements of digital preservation (2000)
21. Blue Ribbon Task Force: Sustainable Economics for a Digital Planet: Ensuring Long-Term Access to Digital Information. Final Report of the Blue Ribbon Task Force on Sustainable Digital Preservation and Access (February 2010), http://brtf.sdsc.edu/biblio/BRTF_Final_Report.pdf (accessed on July 30, 2012)
22. von Neumann, J., Morgenstern, O.: Theory of Games and Economic Behavior (Commemorative Edition). Princeton University Press (2007)
23. Peleg, B., Sudhölter, P.: Introduction to the Theory of Cooperative Games. Springer (2003)
24. Aumann, R.: The Shapley value. Game–theoretic methods in general equilibrium analysis. Kluwer Academic Publishers, Dordrecht (1994)
25. Doyle, J., Thomason, R.H.: Background to Qualitative Decision Theory. AI Magazine 20(2), 55–68 (1999)
26. ENSURE: ENSURE Activity II Deliverable, D20.1a (2011)
27. ENSURE: ENSURE D1.2.1a Requirements Deliverable M4 (2011), http://ensure-fp7.eu
28. ENSURE: ENSURE D1.2.1b Requirements Deliverable M12 (2012)

Specification and Deployment of Distributed Monitoring and Adaptation Infrastructures

Christian Inzinger, Benjamin Satzger, Waldemar Hummer,
and Schahram Dustdar

Distributed Systems Group, Vienna University of Technology
Argentinierstrasse 8/184-1, A-1040 Vienna, Austria
{lastname}@dsg.tuwien.ac.at
http://dsg.tuwien.ac.at

Abstract. This paper presents a new domain-specific language that allows to define integrated monitoring and adaptation functionality for controlling heterogeneous systems. We propose a mechanism for optimal deployment of the defined control operators onto available resources. Deployment is based on solving a quadratic programming problem, and helps to achieve minimized reaction times, low overhead, as well as scalable monitoring and adaptation.

Keywords: Monitoring, Adaptation, Complex Systems, Domain-Specific Language, Deployment, Operator Placement.

1 Introduction

Efficient monitoring and adapation of large-scale heterogeneous systems, integrating a multitude of components, possibly from different vendors, is challenging. Huge amounts of monitoring data and sophisticated adaptation mechanisms in complex systems render centralized processing of control logic impractical. In highly distributed systems it is desirable to keep relevant monitoring and adaptation functionality as local as possible, to reduce traffic and to allow for timely reaction to changes.

In this paper we introduce a domain-specific language (DSL) to easily and succinctly specify system components and their monitoring and adaptation relevant behavior. It allows to define integrated monitoring and adaptation functionality to realize applications based on top of heterogeneous, distributed components. Using the introduced DSL we then outline the process of deploying the integration infrastructure, focusing on the efficient placement of monitoring and adaptation functionality onto available resources.

The remainder of this paper is structured as follows: In Section 2 we outline a motivating scenario that is used throughout the discussion of our contribution. Section 3 introduces a DSL for concise definition of complex service-oriented systems along with their monitoring and adaptation goals, followed by a discussion of the necessary deployment procedure in Section 4. Relevant previous research is presented in Section 5. We conclude the paper in Section 6 and provide an outlook for future research directions.

A. Ghose et al. (Eds.): ICSOC 2012, LNCS 7759, pp. 167–178, 2013.

2 Scenario

In this section we introduce a motivating scenario based on the Indenica[1] FP7 EU project. The project aims at providing methods for describing, deploying and managing disparate platforms based on a virtual service platform (VSP), which integrates and unifies their services. As the focus of this paper is on the deployment and runtime aspects of the developed approach, the reader is referred to the project website for further information.

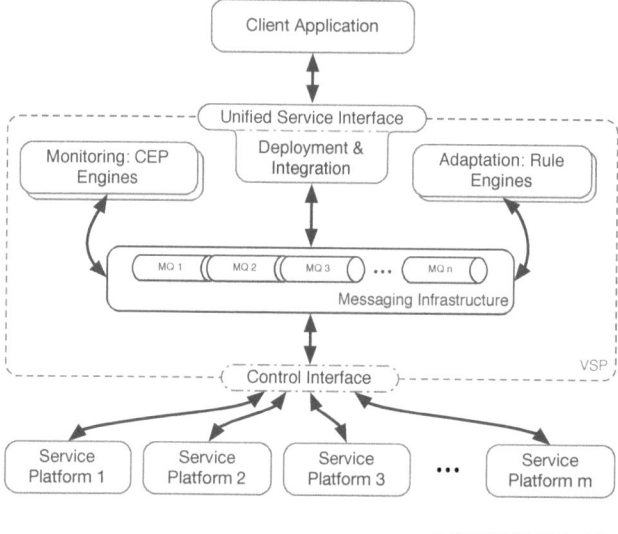

Fig. 1. INDENICA Runtime Architecture

The Indenica runtime architecture is presented in Fig. 1. The VSP provides a unified view on the functionality of the integrated service platforms, which are connected by control interfaces. Monitoring and adaptation are performed by complex event processing (CEP) engines and production rule engines, respectively. The former allows to implement monitoring by aggregating events emitted by service platforms, and the latter supports the definition of complex rules based on the gathered knowledge, which is stored as facts in a knowledge base. The execution of monitoring and adaptation on top of multiple engines allows for scalable control using distributed resources. Communication within the VSP is based on a distributed messaging infrastructure.

In this paper we introduce a novel DSL called MONINA, which allows the user to specify service platform capabilities, monitoring queries, and adaptation rules. In addition to that, we propose an algorithm to deploy the specified functionality onto available resources. Deployment aims at optimal usage of available resources considering locality, minimizing network overhead and taking load distribution into account.

---

[1] http://indenica.eu

3 MONINA Language

In this section we introduce MONINA[2] (Monitoring, Integration, Adaptation), a DSL allowing for concise and reusable specification of platforms integrated into a VSP, along with monitoring and adaptation rules governing their behavior.

```
event RequestFinished {
  request_id : Integer
  processing_time_ms : Integer
}

event AverageProcessingTime {
  processing_time_ms : Integer
}

action DecreaseQuality {
  amount : Double
}

component ApplicationServer {
  emit RequestFinished
  action DecreaseQuality
  host vm1
  cost 32
}

query AggregateResponseTimes {
  from ApplicationServer
```

```
event RequestFinished as e
emit AverageProcessingTime(
  avg(e.processing_time_ms))
window 5 minutes
}

fact {
  from AverageProcessingTime
}

rule DecreaseQualityWhenSlow {
  from AverageProcessingTime
    as f
  when f.processing_time_ms >
    2000
  execute ApplicationServer.
    DecreaseQuality(5)
}

host vm1 { capacity 128 }
host vm2 { capacity 384 }
```

Listing 1. Sample system definition

Listing 1 shows a simple definition for a service platform to be integrated into a VSP. The 'ApplicationServer' component emits 'RequestFinished' events after processing requests and supports a 'DecreaseQuality' action, which can be triggered by adaptation rules. Emitted events are processed by the 'AggregateResponseTimes' query, which aggregates them over five minutes, creating an 'AverageProcessingTime' event. This event is converted to a fact, which might trigger 'DecreaseQualityWhenSlow' adaptation rule. The physical infrastructure consists of hosts 'vm1' and 'vm2'. Runtime elements without defined costs are assigned default values, which are refined at runtime. In the following we will discuss the most important language constructs of MONINA in more detail.

3.1 Event

Indenica follows an event-based approach. Events are emitted by components to signal important information. Furthermore, events can be emitted by monitor-

---

[2] Eclipse plugin available at http://dsgvienna.bitbucket.org/indenica

ing queries as a result of the aggregation or enrichment of one or more source events. Event declarations start with the **event** keyword and an event type identifier. As shown in the figure, an event can contain multiple attributes, defined by specifying name and type separated by a colon. Currently, supported event types are a variety of Java types such as `String`, `Integer`, and `Decimal`, and `Map<?,?>`.

Since listing all available event types for every application would be a tedious and error-prone task, we automatically gather emitted event types from known components to improve reusability and ease of use. This procedure is described in more detail in Section 3.4.

More formally, we assume that E is the set of all event types, T is the set of all data types, and each event type $E' \in E$ is composed of event attribute types $E' = (\alpha_1, \ldots, \alpha_k)$, $\alpha_i \in T \; \forall i \in \{1, \ldots, k\}$. $\mathcal{I}_E$ denotes the set of monitoring event instances (or simply events), and each event $e \in \mathcal{I}_E$ has an event type, denoted $t(e) \in E$. The attribute values contained in event e are represented as a tuple $e = (\pi_{\alpha_1}(e), \ldots, \pi_{\alpha_k}(e))$, where $\pi_{\alpha_x}(e)$ is the projection operator (from relational algebra), which extracts the value of some attribute α_x from the tuple e.

3.2 Action

Complementary to monitoring events described above, adaptation actions are another basic language element of MONINA. Adaptation actions are invoked by adaptation rules and executed by corresponding components to modify their behavior. Action declarations start with the **action** keyword followed by the action type identifier. Furthermore, actions can take parameters, modeled analogously to event attributes.

Similar to events, adaptation actions offered by known components do not need to be specified manually, but are automatically gathered from component specifications, which is further discussed in Section 3.4.

The symbol A denotes the set of all types of adaptation actions, and each type $A' \in A$ contains attribute types: $A' = (\alpha_1, \ldots, \alpha_k)$, $\alpha_i \in T \; \forall i \in \{1, \ldots, k\}$. The set $\mathcal{I}_A$ stores all action instances (or simply actions) that are issued in the system. The values of an action $a \in \mathcal{I}_A$ are evaluated using the projection operator (analogously to event attributes): $a = (\pi_{\alpha_1}(a), \ldots, \pi_{\alpha_k}(a))$.

3.3 Fact

Facts constitute the knowledge base for adaptation rules and are derived from monitoring events. A fact incorporates all attributes of the specified source event for use by adaptation rules. Fact declarations start with the **fact** keyword and an optional fact name. A fact must specify a source event type that is used to derive the fact from. Furthermore, an optional partition key can be supplied. If the fact name is omitted, the fact will be named after its source event.

The partition key construct is used to enable the creation of facts depending on certain event attributes, allowing for the concise declaration of multiple similar facts for different system aspects. For instance, a fact declaration for the event type `ProcessingTimeEvent` that is partitioned by the `component_id` attribute will create appropriate facts for all encountered components, such as `ProcessingTime(Component1), ..., ProcessingTime(ComponentN)`. In contrast, a fact declaration for the `MeanProcessingTimeEvent` without partition key will result in the creation of a single fact representing the system state according to the attribute values of incoming events.

Formally, a fact $f \in F$ is represented as a tuple $f = (\kappa, e)$, for event $e \in \mathcal{I}_E$ and partition key κ. The optional partition key κ allows for the simplified creation of facts concerning specified attributes, to model facts relating to single system components, using $\pi_\kappa(e)$, the projection of attribute κ from event e. Alternatively, the type of event e itself acts as the partition key, aggregating all events of the same type to a single fact.

3.4   Component

A component declaration incorporates all information necessary to integrate third-party platforms into the Indenica infrastructure. Component declarations start with the **component** keyword and a component identifier. A component specifies all monitoring events it will emit with an optional occurrence frequency, supported adaptation actions, as well as a reference to the host the component is deployed to.

As mentioned before, it is usually not necessary to manually specify component, action, and event declarations. The Indenica infrastructure provides for means to automatically gather relevant information from known components through the control interface shown in Fig. 1.

Formally, components $c \in C$ are represented with the signature function[3] $sig : C \to \mathcal{P}(A) \times \mathcal{P}(\{(e_j, \nu_j) | e_j \in E, \nu_j \in \mathbb{R}_0^+\}) \times \mathbb{R}_0^+ \times H$ and the signature for a component c_i is $sig(c_i) \mapsto (I_i^A, \Omega_i^E, \psi_i, h_i)$. The signature function sig extracts relevant information from the according language construct for later use by the deployment infrastructure. Monitoring events emitted by the component are represented by Ω_i^E, and for each emitted event type e_j an according frequency of occurrence ν_j is supplied. Adaptation actions supported by the component are denoted by I_i^A, its processing cost is represented by ψ_i, and h_i identifies the host the component is deployed to.

3.5   Monitoring Query

Monitoring queries allow for the analysis, processing, aggregation and enrichment of monitoring events using CEP techniques. In the context of the Indenica project we provide a simple query language tailored to the needs of the specific solution.

---

[3] For clarity, we use the same symbol *sig* for signatures of components (Section 3.4), monitoring queries (Section 3.5), adaptation rules (3.6), and hosts (Section 3.7).

A query declaration starts with the **query** keyword and a query identifier. Afterwards, an arbitrary number of event sources for the query is specified using the **from** and **event** keywords to specify source components and event types. A query then specifies any number of event emission declarations, denoted by the **emit** keyword followed by the event type and a list of expressions evaluating the attribute assignments of the event to be emitted. For brevity we omit the specification of ⟨*cond-expression*⟩ clause that represents a SQL-style conditional expression. Queries can be furthermore designed to operate on event stream windows using the **window** keyword, specifying either a number of events to create a batch window or a time span to create a time window. Conditions expressed using the **where** keyword are used to limit the query processing to events satisfying certain conditions, using the conditional expression construct mentioned above. Finally, queries can optionally indicate the rate of incoming vs. emitted events, as well as an indication of required processing power. These values are user-defined estimations in the initial setup, and are adjusted continuously during runtime to accommodate changes in the environment. In addition to the query construct presented above, the language infrastructure allows for the integration of other CEP query languages, such as EQL[4] if necessary.

The set of queries $q_i \in Q$ is represented using the signature $sig : Q \to \mathcal{P}(E) \times \mathcal{P}(E) \times \mathbb{R}_0^+ \times \mathbb{R}_0^+$ and the signature for a query q_i is $sig(q_i) \mapsto (I_i^E, O_i^E, \rho_i, \psi_i)$. Input and output event stream types are denoted by I_i^E and O_i^E respectively, while ρ_i represents the ratio of input events processed to output events emitted, and ψ_i represents the processing cost of the query.

3.6   Adaptation Rule

Adaptation rules employ a knowledge base consisting of facts to reason on the current state of the system and modify its behavior when necessary using a production rule system. A rule declaration starts with the **rule** keyword and a rule identifier. After importing all necessary facts using the **from** keyword, a rule contains a number of **when**-statements where the condition evaluates a ⟨*cond-expression*⟩ as described above, referencing imported facts, and the **then** block specifies a number of adaptation action invocations including any necessary parameter assignments. Optionally, a rule can indicate processing requirements, which will be adjusted at runtime.

As with monitoring queries, the adaptation rule module is tailored to the requirements of the Indenica infrastructure but also allows for the usage of different production rule languages, such as the Drools[5] rule language, if more complex language constructs are required.

Formally, the set of rules $r_i \in R$ is represented with the signature function $sig : R \to \mathcal{P}(F) \times \mathcal{P}(A) \times \mathbb{R}_0^+$ and the signature for a rule r_i is $sig(r_i) \mapsto (I_i^F, O_i^A, \psi_i)$. The set of facts from the knowledge base used by the adaptation rule are denoted by I_i^F, while O_i^A representes the adaptation actions performed, and ψ_i represents the processing cost of the rule.

---

[4] http://esper.codehaus.org
[5] http://jboss.org/drools

3.7   Host

Hosts represent the physical infrastructure available for deployment of runtime elements, i.e., components, queries, and rules. A host declaration starts with the **host** keyword and a host name. An address in the form of a fully qualified domain name (FQDN) or an IP address can be supplied. If no address is given, the host name will be used instead. Furthermore, a **capacity** indicator is provided that will be used for deployment decisions.

The set of hosts $h_i \in H$ is represented with the signature function $sig : H \mapsto \mathbb{R}_0^+$ and the signature for a host h_i is $sig(h_i) \mapsto (\psi_i)$ with the capacity of a host represented by ψ_i.

4   Deployment of Monitoring Queries and Adaptation Rules

In this section, we propose a methodology for efficiently deploying runtime elements for monitoring and adaptation, in line with the definitions provided in Section 3. Deployment is based on a MONINA definition. The deployment strategy attempts to find an optimal placement with regard to locality of information producers and consumers, resource usage, network load, and minimum reaction times. Our deployment procedure consists of three main stages. First, an infrastructure graph is generated from the host declarations in the MONINA definition to create a model of the physical infrastructure. Then, a dependency graph is derived from component, query, fact, and rule definitions. Finally, a mathematical optimization problem is formulated based on both graphs, which finds an optimal deployment scheme.

4.1   Infrastructure Graph

The infrastructure graph $G_I = (V_I, E_I)$ is a directed graph which models the available infrastructure. Its nodes (V_I) represent execution environments. We will refer to execution environments as hosts, even though they might not only represent single machines, but more complex execution platforms. The graph's edges $(E_I \subseteq V_I \times V_I)$ represent the network connection between hosts. The node capacity function $c_I : V_I \to \mathbb{R}_0^+$ assigns each host its capacity for hosting runtime elements, e.g., monitoring queries or adaptation rules. A capacity of zero prohibits any runtime elements on the host. Edge weight function $w_I : E_I \to \mathbb{R}_0^+$ models the delay between two hosts. Values close to zero represent good connection. For the sake of convenience we assume that each vertex has a zero weighted edge to itself. Figure 2a shows an exemplary infrastructure graph.

The infrastructure graph is generated based on a MONINA description, i.e., its node set V_I is taken from the description file, which also contains the hosts' physical addresses. The next step is the exploration of the edges based on the *traceroute* utility, which is available for all major operating systems. It allows, amongst others, measuring transit delays. Furthermore, node capacities can be

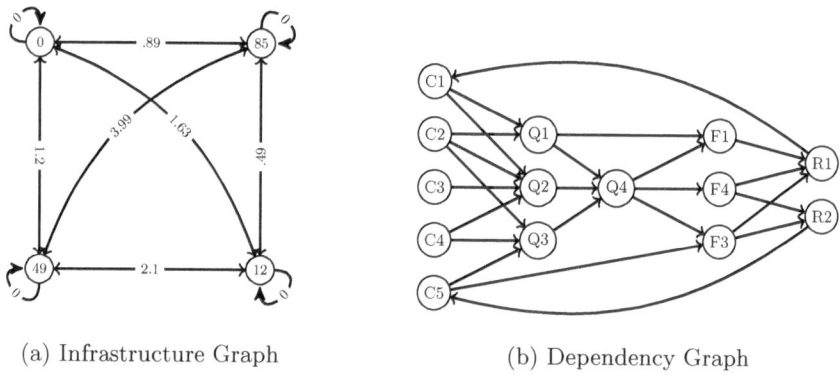

(a) Infrastructure Graph   (b) Dependency Graph

Fig. 2. Graphs generated from a MONINA description

read by operating system tools to complement missing MONINA values. In Unix-based operating systems, for instance, the /proc pseudo-filesystem folder provides information about hardware and its utilization.

4.2   Dependency Graph

Dependency graphs model the dependencies between components, monitoring queries, facts, and adaptation rules. A dependency graph $G_D = (V_D, E_D)$ is a directed, weighted graph, whose node set $V_D = C \cup Q \cup F \cup R$ is composed of pairwise disjoint sets C, Q, F, and R. These represent components, queries, facts, and rules, respectively. Edges represent dependencies between these entities (i.e., exchange of events), and weight function $w_D : E_D \to \mathbb{R}_0^+$ quantifies the event transfer rate along an edge. Another function $e_D : E_D \to E$ maps edges to events they are based on, where E is the set of event types. Components are event emitters, which may be consumed by queries or may be converted into a fact in a knowledge base. Queries consume events from components or other queries producing new events. Knowledge bases convert certain events into facts. Rule engines work upon knowledge bases, and trigger rules if respective conditions become true. Edges link event emitters (components or queries) to respective event consumers (queries or knowledge bases). They also connect knowledge bases to rules relying on facts they are managing. Finally, rules are linked to the components they are adapting, i.e., components in which they trigger adaptation actions. Thus, the edge set is limited to the following subset $E_D \subseteq (C \times Q) \cup (C \times F) \cup (Q \times Q) \cup (Q \times F) \cup (F \times R) \cup (R \times C)$. Figure 2b shows an exemplary dependency graph. Event types and edges weights are omitted for readability.

The generation of a dependency graph is based on a MONINA description. Initially, the dependency graph $G_D = (V_D, E_D)$ is created as a graph without any edges, i.e., $V_D = C \cup Q \cup F \cup R$ and $E_D = \emptyset$, where C, Q, F, R are taken from the MONINA description. Then, edges are added according to the following edge production rules.

Component → Query. An edge $c \xrightarrow{\psi} q$ is added to E_D for every component $c \in C$, query $q \in Q$, and event $e \in (O^E \cap I^E)$, where $sig(c) = ((O^E, \bullet), \bullet, \psi)$ and $sig(q) = (I_i^E, \bullet, \bullet, \bullet)$. In case an edge $c \xrightarrow{\psi_2} q$ is supposed to be added to E_D, but E_D already contains $c \xrightarrow{\psi_1} q$, then the latter is replaced by $c \xrightarrow{\psi_1 + \psi_2} q$. For all following edge production rules we assume that edges that already exist are merged by adding weights, like here.

Component → Fact. An edge $c \xrightarrow{\psi} f$ is added to E_D for every component $c \in C$, fact $f \in F$, and event $e \in O^E$, where $sig(c) = ((O^E, \bullet), \bullet, \psi)$ and $f = (\bullet, e)$.

Query → Query. An edge $q_1 \xrightarrow{\rho} q_2$ is added to E_D for all queries $q_1, q_2 \in Q$ and event $e \in (O^E \cap I^E)$, where $q_1 \neq q_2$, $sig(q_1) = (\bullet, O^E, \rho, \bullet)$ and $sig(q) = (I_i^E, \bullet, \bullet, \bullet)$.

Monitoring Query → Fact. An edge $q \xrightarrow{\rho} f$ is added to E_D for every query $q \in Q$, fact $f \in F$, and event $e \in O^E$, where $sig(q) = (\bullet, O^E, \rho, \bullet)$ and $f = (\bullet, e)$.

Fact → Adaptation Rule. An edge $f \rightarrow r$ is added to E_D for every fact $f \in F$ and adaptation rule $r \in R$, where $f \in I^F$ and $sig(r) = (I^F, \bullet, \bullet)$.

Adaptation Rule → Component. An edge $r \rightarrow c$ is added to E_D for every adaptation rule $r \in R$ and component $c \in C$, where $a \in (O^A \cap I^A)$, $sig(r) = (\bullet, O^A, \bullet)$ and $sig(c) = (I^A, \bullet, \bullet)$.

4.3 Quadratic Programming Problem Formulation

Quadratic programming [2] is a mathematical optimization approach, which allows to minimize/maximize a quadratic function subject to constraints. Assume that $\mathbf{x}, \mathbf{b}, \mathbf{c}, \mathbf{d} \in \mathbb{R}^n$ are column vectors, and $Q \in \mathbb{R}^{n \times n}$ is a symmetric matrix. Then, a quadratic programming problem can be defined as follows.

$$\min_x \; f(\mathbf{x}) = \tfrac{1}{2}\mathbf{x}^T Q \mathbf{x} + \mathbf{c}^T \mathbf{x}$$

Subject to

$$E\mathbf{x} = \mathbf{d} \quad \text{(Equality constraint)}$$
$$A\mathbf{x} \leq \mathbf{b} \quad \text{(Inequality constraint)}$$

We want to achieve an optimal mapping of the dependency graph onto the infrastructure graph. Runtime entities described in the dependency graph that depend on each other should be as close as possible, in the best case running on the same host. This results in fast reactions, timely adaptations, and low network overhead. On the other hand, hosts have capacity restrictions, which have to be considered. Adding more hosts (scaling out) is often the only possibility to cope with growing load. Our mapping approach is able to find the *optimal* tradeoff between the suboptimal strategies (1) putting everything on the same host and (2) evenly/randomly distribute runtime elements among the available hosts.

Since we want to get a mapping from the optimization process, we introduce placement variables p_{v_I,v_D} for each host $v_I \in V_I$ in the infrastructure graph and each runtime element $v_D \in V_D$ in the dependency graph. Each of these variables has a binary domain, i.e., $p_{v_I,v_D} \in \{0,1\}$. The assignment $p_{v_I,v_D} = 1$ decodes that runtime element v_D is hosted on v_I, $p_{v_I,v_D} = 0$ stands for v_D is not running on host v_I. This results in $|V_I| \cdot |V_D|$ binary variables, whose aggregation can be represented as a single vector $\mathbf{p} \in \{0,1\}^{|V_I| \cdot |V_D|}$.

To find out the optimal mapping of the dependency graph onto the infrastructure, we solve the following optimization problem, which can be classified as binary integer quadratic programming problem, based on the form of variable $\mathbf{p}$ and the function to minimize.

$$\min_{\mathbf{p}} \sum_{e_I \in E_I} w_I(e_I) \cdot \sum_{e_D \in E_D} w_D(e_D) \cdot p_{v_I^1,v_D^1} \cdot p_{v_I^2,v_D^2} \tag{1}$$

Subject to

$$\forall c \in C : \ p_{h(c),c} = 1 \tag{2}$$

$$\forall v_D \in V_D : \ \sum_{v_I \in V_I} p_{v_I,v_D} = 1 \tag{3}$$

$$\forall v_I \in V_I : \ \sum_{v_D \in V_D} p_{v_I,v_D} \cdot c_D(v_D) \ \leq c_I(v_I) \tag{4}$$

The function to minimize (1) calculates for each edge $e_I = (v_I^1, v_I^2)$ in the infrastructure graph and each edge $e_D = (v_D^1, v_D^2)$ the weight that incurs if this particular dependency edge is mapped to this particular infrastructure edge. If both runtime elements (v_D^1 and v_D^2) are mapped to the same node no weight is added to the function, because all self-links have weight zero. The first equality constraint (2) fixes the mapping for every component $c \in C \subseteq V_D$ to the hosts they are statically assigned to, as defined in MONINA and represented by $h(c)$, where $sig(c) = (\bullet, \bullet, \bullet, h)$. We assume that components are bound to hosts. If there exist components that can be deployed on any host and do not have an assignment in MONINA, then this can be handled by simply omitting the respective contraint for this component. The second equality constraint (3) defines that each node from the dependency graph is mapped to exactly one node in the infrastructure graph. Finally, the inequality constraint (4) requires that for all hosts the summarized costs of all elements they are hosting is less than the respective capacity. The function $c_D : V_D \to \mathbb{R}_0^+$ represents the costs of executing a runtime element v_D, as defined in the MONINA description.

We use Gurobi [5] for solving the optimization problem as described above. Due to space restrictions we cannot give results of runtime analyses in this paper. For problem sizes typically considered in INDENICA (5-15 hosts, 5-50 runtime elements) the optimization process usually takes less than 10 seconds on a regular laptop computer.

5   Related Work

The query operator placement problem in the context of complex event processing has received considerable attention in the past. To the best of our knowledge, none of these approaches explicitly consider adaptation and the according efficient placement of derived facts and adaptation rules. Also, operator networks usually are either trees or acyclic graphs, in contrast to our dependency graphs.

Some of the previous research is discussed in the following. An approach for minimizing network usage and managing resource consumption in sensor networks by moving query operators is presented in [14]. The work in [1] discusses algorithms for distributed placement of operator trees in wide area networks based on a distributed hash table structure. Another distributed operator placement for wide area networks using an overlay network is presented in [10], focussing on continuous cost optimization by migrating operators. The approach in [13] utilizes a decentralized algorithm based on negotiation between nodes for operator placement in heterogeneous CEP at runtime, minimizing the number of migrations. In [6], dynamic migration of processing elements is used as the basis for optimized multi-query execution in stream processing platforms.

Previous work in monitoring and adaptation of distributed heterogeneous systems deals with various aspects, such as establishing and monitoring SLAs (e.g., [4]), efficient rule generation (e.g., [9]), and adaptations based on QoS-requirements (e.g., [3]). However, there are no approaches that consider the efficient placement of monitoring and adaptation rules themselves, but rely on manual initial placement or human intervention.

Machine learning approaches can be used to automatically generate or improve adaptation rules based on the feedback the system is providing following their execution [8,7]. Adaptation rules based on the condition-action scheme are a popular technique used to control systems. However, for some complex systems the enumeration of all conditions, e.g., all possible types of failures, is often impracticable. Also, the actions to recover the system can become too tedious to be specified manually. Automated planning allows to automatically compute plans on top of a knowledge base following predefined objectives, and helps to enable goal-driven management of computer systems [12,11].

6   Conclusion

In this paper we introduce a domain-specific language that allows to integrate functionality provided by different components and to define monitoring and adaptation functionality. We assume that monitoring is carried out by complex-event processing queries, while adaptation is performed by condition action rules performed on top of a distributed knowledge base. However, our approach can be applied to other forms of control mechanisms with dependencies among functionality blocks. In future work we will present experiments in order to quantify the deployment performance relative to the size of infrastructure and elements to deploy. We also plan to integrate the capability to migrate elements at runtime to adapt according to more precise knowledge and changing environments.

Acknowledgement. The research leading to these results has received funding from the European Commission's Seventh Framework Programme [FP7/2007-2013] under grant agreement 257483 (Indenica).

References

1. Ahmad, Y., Çetintemel, U.: Network-aware query processing for stream-based applications. In: International Conference on Very Large Data Bases (VLDB 2004), pp. 456–467 (2004)
2. Bazaraa, M.S., Sherali, H.D., Shetty, C.M.: Nonlinear Programming: Theory and Algorithms, 2nd edn. Wiley (2006)
3. Cardellini, V., Casalicchio, E., Grassi, V., Lo Presti, F., Mirandola, R.: Qos-driven runtime adaptation of service oriented architectures. In: European Software Engineering Conference (ESEC 2009). ACM (2009)
4. Comuzzi, M., Kotsokalis, C., Spanoudakis, G., Yahyapour, R.: Establishing and Monitoring SLAs in Complex Service Based Systems. In: International Conference on Web Services (ICWS 2009), pp. 783–790. IEEE (2009)
5. Gurobi Optimization, Inc.: Gurobi optimizer reference manual (2012), http://www.gurobi.com
6. Hummer, W., Leitner, P., Satzger, B., Dustdar, S.: Dynamic Migration of Processing Elements for Optimized Query Execution in Event-Based Systems. In: Meersman, R., Dillon, T., Herrero, P., Kumar, A., Reichert, M., Qing, L., Ooi, B.-C., Damiani, E., Schmidt, D.C., White, J., Hauswirth, M., Hitzler, P., Mohania, M. (eds.) OTM 2011, Part II. LNCS, vol. 7045, pp. 451–468. Springer, Heidelberg (2011)
7. Inzinger, C., Hummer, W., Satzger, B., Leitner, P., Dustdar, S.: Towards Identifying Root Causes of Faults in Service Orchestrations. In: International Symposium on Reliable Distributed Systems (SRDS 2012). IEEE (2012)
8. Inzinger, C., Satzger, B., Hummer, W., Leitner, P., Dustdar, S.: Non-Intrusive Policy Optimization for Dependable and Adaptive Service-Oriented Systems. In: Symposium on Applied Computing (SAC 2012), pp. 504–510. ACM (2012)
9. Jung, G., Joshi, K.R., Hiltunen, M.A., Schlichting, R.D., Pu, C.: Generating Adaptation Policies for Multi-tier Applications in Consolidated Server Environments. In: International Conference on Autonomic Computing (ICAC 2008), pp. 23–32 (2008)
10. Pietzuch, P., Ledlie, J., Shneidman, J., Roussopoulos, M., Welsh, M., Seltzer, M.: Network-Aware Operator Placement for Stream-Processing Systems. In: International Conference on Data Engineering (ICDE 2006), p. 49. IEEE (2006)
11. Satzger, B., Kramer, O.: Goal distance estimation for automated planning using neural networks and support vector machines. Natural Computing (2012)
12. Satzger, B., Pietzowski, A., Trumler, W., Ungerer, T.: Using Automated Planning for Trusted Self-organising Organic Computing Systems. In: Rong, C., Jaatun, M.G., Sandnes, F.E., Yang, L.T., Ma, J. (eds.) ATC 2008. LNCS, vol. 5060, pp. 60–72. Springer, Heidelberg (2008)
13. Schilling, B., Koldehofe, B., Rothermel, K.: Efficient and Distributed Rule Placement in Heavy Constraint-Driven Event Systems. In: International Conference on High Performance Computing and Communications (HPCC 2011), pp. 355–364 (2011)
14. Srivastava, U., Munagala, K., Widom, J.: Operator placement for in-network stream query processing. In: Symposium on Principles of Database Systems (PODS 2005), pp. 250–258 (2005)

Introducing the Vienna Platform
for Elastic Processes

Stefan Schulte[1], Philipp Hoenisch[1],
Srikumar Venugopal[2], and Schahram Dustdar[1]

[1] Distributed Systems Group, Vienna University of Technology, Austria
{s.schulte,dustdar}@infosys.tuwien.ac.at
[2] School of Computer Science and Engineering,
The University of New South Wales, Sydney, Australia

Abstract. Resource-intensive tasks are playing an increasing role in business processes. The emergence of Cloud computing has enabled the deployment of such tasks onto resources sourced on-demand from Cloud providers. This has enabled so-called elastic processes that are able to dynamically adjust their resource usage to meet varying workloads.

Traditional Business Process Management Systems (BPMSs) do not consider the needs of elastic processes such as monitoring facilities, tracking the current and future system landscape, reasoning about optimally utilizing resources given Quality of Service constraints, and executing necessary actions (e.g., start/stop servers, move services). This paper introduces ViePEP, a research BPMS capable of handling the aforementioned requirements of elastic processes.

1 Introduction

Business Process Management (BPM) is a multidisciplinary approach, covering organizational, management, and technical aspects, and "includes methods, techniques, and tools to support the design, enactment, management, and analysis of operational business processes" [1]. One particular subtopic of BPM is the automatic execution of modeled processes (process automation), which needs to be supported by concepts, methodologies and frameworks from the field of computer science [18]. The automated part of a business process is also known as a business workflow [17]. Very often, (Web) services are composed to create flexible, dynamic business workflows that may span organizations and computing platforms [20].

Currently, resource-intensive tasks not only are present within scientific workflows (SWFs), but are also becoming more prevalent in business processes. For example, compute and data-intensive analytical processes are found in the finance industry and in managing smart grids in the energy industry. In the latter, data from a very large number of smart grid sensors needs to be automatically gathered, processed, analyzed, and stored in order to offer customers consumption reports or even guarantee grid stability [21,22].

A. Ghose et al. (Eds.): ICSOC 2012, LNCS 7759, pp. 179–190, 2013.

Apart from the functional requirements of resource-intensive tasks, processes comprising them are subject to a number of non-functional requirements (Service Level Objectives – SLOs), especially with regard to the timeliness of the tasks – some of these processes need to be carried out in real-time, while others can be postponed but need to be executed within a particular deadline. As the amount of data, or the number of process instances that need to be concurrently handled, could vary to a very large extent, it is difficult to estimate the ever-changing resource demands of such processes.

Workflows could utilize the *resource elasticity* – to acquire and release resources as and when needed – to scale with shifting workloads [3]. Permanently provisioning IT capacities that are able to handle peak loads is not the best solution for this, as the capacities will not be utilized most of the time, leading to unnecessary high costs. With the advent of Cloud computing, organizations presently have a much more cost-efficient alternative that enables the use of computing resources in an on-demand, utility-like fashion [6]. While resource elasticity is a common way to describe the scalability of single applications as well as workflows, elasticity is not the only constraint that should be taken into account in the context of workflow scalability [8]. Notably, Quality of Service (QoS) in terms of criteria like response time does not necessarily reflect resource elasticity in a linear way, i.e., there may be no proportional relationship between involved resources and QoS. As a result, it is necessary to define *quality elasticity*, which describes the responsiveness of quality regarding changes in resource usage [8]. Last but not least, many Cloud providers make use of dynamic pricing models, which should also be taken into account if Cloud resources are used in order to realize scalable processes. These dynamic pricing models are reflected in *cost elasticity*, i.e., a resource provisioner's responsiveness to changes in costs [8].

To the best of our knowledge, so far, surprisingly little effort has been put into the investigation of methods, algorithms and tools to integrate automatic process execution and Cloud computing in order to realize so-called *elastic processes* under the above-mentioned elasticity constraints. In our experience, there is a lack of a Business Process Management System (BPMS) able to carry out many interdependent service-based workflows in parallel, estimate their current *and* future resource demand under user-specified constraints and preferences, and allocate Cloud resources dynamically to meet them. This needs analysing the process definition to discover which of its steps determine the performance of its execution and prioritising them, reasoning on an optimal resource allocation under the given resource, costs, and quality elasticity constraints, monitoring the actual service execution, and balancing load on the resources.

In this paper, we present selected results from our ongoing research on elastic processes, more precisely the *Vienna Platform for Elastic Processes (ViePEP)*, which is a research-driven, prototypical BPMS capable to execute elastic processes, monitor the current utilization of invoked resources as well as reason about future resource demands, and carry out necessary actions.

The remainder of this paper is organized as follows: After a brief overview of the related work (Section 2), we will present the overall ViePEP architecture and its functionalities (Section 3). Subsequently, we will give some information about our work on reasoning mechanisms (Section 4). Section 5 concludes this paper.

2   Related Work

While little effort has been put into the investigation of elastic processes, there is nevertheless fundamental work in related areas, which needs to be regarded.

First, scalability and cost-effective allocation of single tasks and applications have been studied by many researchers. The earliest research efforts often focused on minimizing Cloud consumer's costs while taking into account maximum allowed execution time [7] while later approaches considered holistic Service Level Agreement (SLA) enforcement [5]. Recently, research efforts have paid special attention to the infrastructure perspective, i.e., the adherence to consumer-defined SLAs under the objective of profit maximization [14] or high resource utilization [9,13,16]. While most of these approaches apply threshold-based fixed rules to identify necessary actions (e.g., stop/start servers, move services), Li and Venugopal [16] make use of a learning-based approach to automatically scale an application up or down based on incoming workload. To the best of our knowledge, existing approaches to scalable Cloud applications and cost-effective allocation lack a process perspective across utilized resources. Instead, allocation is performed based on present service requests, but information about possible future requests derived from the description of elastic processes is not taken into account.

Second, Cloud resources have been used for executing SWFs [2,11,12]. In SWFs, SLAs are typically not as much a concern as they are for business processes; in fact, the most common SLOs regarded in SWFs are the actual costs of a workflow invocation or earliest finishing time of the complete workflow [19]. From an execution point of view, SWFs are dataflow-oriented, i.e., the execution control follows the dataflow. In contrast, in business workflows, the execution control is explicitly modeled, making the integration of some workflow patterns easier but hampering the concurrent processing of data items [17]. In SWFs, (data-related) interdependencies between workflow instances occur very often, while in business workflows, it is quite common that a large number of independent workflow instances are carried out at the same time [17]. In the context of the work at hand, this allows for a higher degree of freedom, as service instances may be carried out on different machines without the need to make a potentially very large amount of data available to a particular machine.

3   Vienna Platform for Elastic Processes

3.1   System Overview

ViePEP aims at supporting the complete process/workflow lifecycle as presented, e.g., by Hallerbach et al. [10]. Common steps of process lifecycles are *Design and*

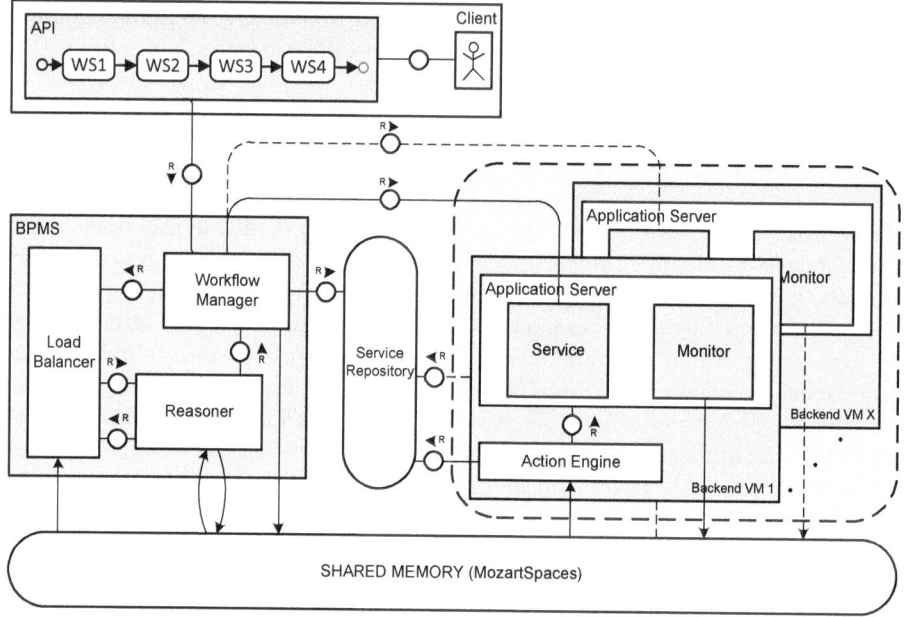

Fig. 1. Workflow Deployment and Cloud Provisioning in ViePEP

Modeling, Instantiation and Selection, Execution and Monitoring, and *Maintenance/Optimization.*

As depicted in Figure 1 (using an FMC Block Diagram), there are five top level entities within ViePEP: First, the *Client* models service-based workflows and defines the necessary SLOs through an Application Programming Interface (API). At the moment, workflows are modeled using an XML-based description template that also defines non-functional constraints and preferences for each step. This description is handed over as a workflow request to the *Workflow Manager* (WfM) of the BPMS in order to instantiate and execute a workflow. A Client may request execution of multiple workflows at the same time. Second, the *BPMS*, performs the central functionalities of controlling the service infrastructure, including the Cloud resources leased from the provider as well as scheduling workflows over service instances. Thus, the BPMS balances the load across the service instances.

Third, a *Backend VM* hosts an instance of a particular service. In a typical ViePEP-based system, many Backend VMs exist at the same time and are controlled by the BPMS. The BPMS and the Backend VM are the central entities in ViePEP and will be discussed in detail in the next section. Fourth, the *Shared Memory* is used to provide data sharing between the BPMS and the different Backend VMs. We chose MozartSpaces[1] for this, as it allows to easily deploy and access a peer-to-peer-based, distributed database. Last but not least, the

---

[1] http://www.mozartspaces.org/

Service Repository hosts service descriptions as well as their implementations as portable archive files, which enables the BPMS to search for services and deploy them on an arbitrary ViePEP Backend VM.

3.2   ViePEP BPMS and Backend VMs

As can be seen in Figure 1, the BPMS features three components: The already mentioned *Workflow Manager*, the *Load Balancer*, and the *Reasoner*. We will introduce these components in the following:

Workflow Manager: The WfM controls and schedules workflow and service executions. It gets the necessary workflow data, i.e., information about the single steps in a workflow and the accompanying SLOs as a *workflow request* from the Client. Afterwards, it looks up services functionally matching the workflow steps in the Service Repository and maps services and workflow steps. This mapping is needed in order to identify already running services instances through the Load Balancer. Based on this information, the WfM is able to issue *service invocation requests* to a particular Backend VM hosting this service and possessing enough resources to serve this invocation under given QoS constraints as defined by the SLOs.

To execute a workflow and its services, a *Workflow Executor* (not depicted in Figure 1) is started. Based on the workflow request and a workflow/service scheduling obtained from the Reasoner (see below), the Executor queries the Load Balancer for the best fitting service instances (Backend VMs) for the workflow steps. Through the executor, the WfM is also able to measure the service response time. This functionality is needed in order to identify deviations from the expected service behavior at an early point of time and avoid breaches of SLAs, which can lead to penalties [15]. Response time includes the service invocation time as well as the network latency. To log service invocations, the response time is stored in the Shared Memory.

In case of a deviation, the WfM may perform replanning for the workflow [4]. Furthermore, the Reasoner needs to take into account this updated information about the current process landscape. Hence, the WfM provides an interface allowing the Reasoner to get information about the number and kind of workflows and services in the queue, the related QoS constraints and preferences, the number of executors, workflows, and services currently running, and how many service instances have to be invoked at what point of time. Furthermore, information about new user issued workflow requests as well as occurring and likely deviations in non-functional service behavior are provided to the Reasoner.

Load Balancer: As the name implies, this component balances the load on the Backend VMs and thus makes sure that the utilization of a Backend VM does not exceed a critical (upper) threshold. Importantly, the Load Balancer is a passive component. On request, it prepares and provides information from the Shared Memory to the WfM and Reasoner, but it does not control the Backend VMs by itself.

The Load Balancer is invoked by the WfM in order to identify the best fitting Backend VM for a service request. For this, it retrieves the actual Backend VM states (in terms of occupied CPU and RAM resources) for the service from the Shared Memory and takes into account scheduling information about current and future service invocations provided by the Reasoner. Based on this information, the Load Balancer links the service request from the WfM to a particular service instance running on a Backend VM.

At the moment, the Load Balancer makes use of a rules-based approach to determine the best fitting Backend VM: Service requests are linked to this VM instance where the degree of utilization is closest to a predefined upper threshold. Thus, the Load Balancer allows the WfM to invoke services until a VM's load reaches this threshold. If the Load Balancer is not able to allocate a service request to a VM, e.g., because all VMs are overloaded or there is currently no VM running this service, it gives this information back to the Workflow Executor, which then may conduct a replanning as mentioned above or trigger a new reasoning.

The Load Balancer is also invoked by the Reasoner in order to determine the best fitting Backend VM for an action. For example, the Reasoner may decide that it is necessary to duplicate a Backend VM, as the service provided by it needs to be invoked too often as if a single VM would be able to handle it in a particular time span. Usually, the VM to be duplicated will be the one with the least load, since the duplication action will produce some additional CPU load. As another example, the Reasoner may decide that a Backend VM is not required anymore as the requests of the hosted service can be handled by another Backend VM. In this case, the Load Balancer will select the VM with the least number of current service invocations; furthermore, it will effectively block further invocations of this service instance, i.e., if a Workflow Executor sends a particular service request to the Load Balancer, the VM to be terminated will not be regarded anymore. As it is a passive component, the actual command to duplicate or terminate a VM will be issued by the Reasoner, not the Load Balancer.

Reasoner: While the WfM controls the execution of single workflows, the Reasoner is responsible for the optimization of the complete process and (Cloud) system landscape. It finds a scheduling for workflows and the included steps (services) under the given cost, resource, and quality constraints and forwards this scheduling to the WfM, which itself will invoke workflows and services based on it. Scheduling is directly related to the control and shaping of the Backend VMs, i.e., the decision to start, terminate, and duplicate Backend VMs, move a service from one VM to another, or exchange the service running on a particular VM. The Reasoner needs to take into account knowledge about the currently and future running workflows and their QoS constraints from the WfM. It also considers deviations from the expected workflow execution behavior in order to find an appropriate countermeasure. The Reasoner gets information about the currently free VM resources (CPU and RAM usage) from the Shared Memory and communicates with the Load Balancer in order to decide whether a particular Backend VM is sufficient to carry out a service, if another VM hosting that service needs to be started (duplication), or if a VM can be terminated due to low load.

At the core of the Reasoner, an elastic reasoning mechanism (ESM) is employed. In our opinion, the investigation of mechanisms which are capable to take into account resource, costs, and quality elasticity and reason about optimal resource allocation is a major research issue for elastic processes. Even though the focus of this paper is not on reasoning, we will present information about possible approaches in Section 4.

While the BPMS controls the process and (Cloud) system landscape, the actual service execution is done on Backend VMs. Each VM provides Software as a Service (SaaS) in terms of a particular Web service, which can be requested and invoked by the WfM. As can be seen in Figure 1, a Backend VM features two major components: The *Application Server* and the *Action Engine*.

Action Engine: The Action Engine is responsible to execute commands to the Application Server. It gets according commands from the Reasoner through the Shared Memory data structure. The most important commands in the context of the work at hand are [16]:

Start a new Backend VM: An empty VM is started by the Reasoner by issuing a corresponding command to the Cloud infrastructure hosting the Backend VMs (in our case: OpenStack; not depicted in Figure 1). When the Backend VM is running, the Action Engine obtains the needed service from the Service Repository and deploys it on the Application Server.

Terminate the Backend VM. Again, the according command is issued by the Reasoner. If the Action Engine receives the command to terminate itself, it first requests information from the Application Server about currently running service invocations. If there are any, the Action Engine regularly polls the Application Server until all service invocations have been finished. The Action Engine unregisters the VM by pushing according status information to the Shared Memory, and finally terminates the VM. Afterwards, the Reasoner and Load Balancer will not take this Backend VM into account anymore.

Duplicate an existing Backend VM. If the Reasoner determines that the resources on the Backend VM hosting a particular service are not sufficient, it can issue an Action Engine the command to duplicate itself. For this, the Action Engine will start a new Backend VM which hosts the same service.

Exchange the hosted service by another service. In some cases, the hosted service is not needed anymore, as there will be no further invocations in the (near) future. However, another service needs to be started. In order to speed up the deployment of a Backend VM running this service, it makes sense to reuse the former Backend VM by exchanging the service running on it. To exchange a service, the Action Engine behaves similarly to the termination of a Backend VM: First, it is checked if the provided service is currently invoked; if this is the case, the Backend VM waits until the invocations have been finished. Second, the current service is replaced by another service from the Service Repository.

Move a running service to another Backend VM: The Action Engine is able to copy the whole system state and move it to another server. Again, running service invocations need to be finished first.

Notably, the delays occurring because a service invocation is still running when terminating a Backend VM or exchanging/moving a service need to be taken into account by the Reasoner. Furthermore, the Load Balancer needs to consider that a service cannot be invoked any further when it is planned to terminate the Backend VM or exchange/move the service instance.

Application Server: In order to host a Web service, a Backend VM needs an Application Server capable to run it. At the moment, we employ Apache Tomcat, but it is possible to switch to any other J2EE application server like Glassfisch or JBoss. The Application Server comprises two components, namely the actual *Service* and a *Monitor*:

Service: As written above, services are stored in the Service Repository. To host a service within the Application Server, the Action Engine retrieves the according *Web application ARchive* (WAR)-file from the repository and deploys it. In the current version we support any RESTful Web service which can be called using an `HTTP GET` request or can be invoked using a remote procedure call.

Monitor: As explained above, the BPMS makes use of information about a Backend VM's resources in terms of CPU and RAM utilization. Hence, ViePEP-enabled Backend VMs feature an Application Server Monitor. Monitoring is conducted on a Platform as a Service (PaaS) level, i.e., the CPU and RAM utilization is measured for the VM, but not the underlying infrastructure. We apply `psi-probe`[2] as server monitoring tool. Monitor data is stored in the Shared Memory.

4   Elastic Reasoning Mechanisms

An ERM is at the heart of a Reasoner and therefore responsible for the scheduling of workflows/services and allocation of (Cloud) resources. As mentioned in our former work [8], an ERM decides how to utilize resources in an optimal way under multi-dimensional constraints. It takes into account dynamic resource, cost, and workflow information and provides not only a scheduling, but also controls Cloud resources by triggering different actions like moving services from one VM to another or starting and terminating servers. In the following, we briefly discuss different concerns that influence the development and success of an ERM:

---

[2] http://code.google.com/p/psi-probe/

Exact vs. Heuristic Reasoning: The usage of linear, mixed or branch-and-bound integer programming, dynamic programming, or multi-constrained optimal path selection is a natural choice for multi-objective optimization and therefore ERMs [26]. As multi-objective optimization is necessarily an NP-hard problem, the so-far mentioned exact approaches may not lead to a solution in polynomial time. Hence, (meta-)heuristic approaches like greedy algorithms, genetic algorithms, or modified integer programming also need to be taken into consideration. While such optimization approaches have also been used in QoS-aware service compositions, as presented, e.g., in [15,23,24,26], these composition algorithms do not take into account resources. Instead, they are based on QoS assurances given by the service providers.

Apart from the mentioned "classic" optimization approaches, it is also possible to apply an approach to find patterns in workflow requests and relate them to resource demand in order to generate rules for resource allocation and workflow/service scheduling. In general, Machine Learning algorithms are capable to generate such rules [27].

Global vs. Local Reasoning: Currently, ViePEP allows ERM through one central reasoner. Such an approach is deemed "global", as it controls the complete system landscape. However, there might be situations where a global optimization is not efficient or not even possible because a central entity is not able to accumulate the data necessary for the global approach. In such cases, it is helpful to make use of a decentralized, local reasoning, which only takes into account the requirements of either a single workflow or a single Cloud resource (Backend VM).

Continuous vs. Interval Reasoning: A continuously operating Reasoner is triggered whenever a change in the ERM input data (workflow requests, monitored service and resource behavior) is assessed to be a significant event, i.e., makes it necessary to perform reasoning under changed constraints. If reasoning is done in predefined time intervals, changes within the system landscape (e.g., new workflow requests or an underperforming Backend VM) are not directly taken into account, but regarded within the next reasoning cycle.

The decision which approach to follow is directly related to the runtime performance of the ERM; if the ERM is relatively slow, it should be invoked in regular intervals; if the ERM is fast enough to produce output before the next significant event appears, a continuous approach is possible. In this context, the possibility to assess if an event is significant or not is crucial.

Hybrid forms of continuous and interval reasoning are also possible. The general workflow scheduling could be done in certain intervals, as its computation usually requires some time. The continuous reasoning could then be used in order to react to the mentioned significant events. In this case, the continuous reasoning would not be done for the complete system landscape but solely be responsible for compensating negative significant events like the aforementioned underperforming Backend VM, thus being some kind of local reasoning. Of course, the local reasoning needs to be taken into account in the next global reasoning cycle.

In the end, all ERM approaches are generally capable to build a model of an ideal future system state with regard to necessary service scheduling and resource allocation actions. It will be a major task of our future work to implement and evaluate according ERMs.

5   Conclusions

Online business processes are faced with varying workloads that require agile deployment of computing resources. One way to reach this goal is the usage of Cloud resources in elastic processes, which take into account resource, cost, and quality elasticity. Within this paper, we have introduced the *Vienna Platform for Elastic Processes* (ViePEP). This platform aims at supporting the complete process lifecycle by allowing consumers to model and request elastic processes, providing a BPMS able to select appropriate services for the single steps of the defined workflows, reason about the optimal scheduling of workflow and service invocations and assignment of resources to the single services, and execute and monitor them.

As ViePEP is a research prototype, not all the functionalities needed for the complete process lifecycle have been thoroughly implemented yet. Most importantly, the provision of feedback about workflow executions to the Client has not been examined in detail. This information could indicate how to optimize process templates with regard to their non-functional requirements (and thus addresses the Maintenance/Optimization steps of a process lifecycle). Nevertheless, the BPMS and Backend VMs as presented are fully functional and have been implemented using the OpenStack IaaS Cloud computing framework. Workflows are executed according to their QoS requirements and Backend VMs hosting service instances are automatically started and terminated based on the non-functional needs of the workflows. Cloud control and scheduling is provided through a first, rather simple reasoning algorithm. A short demo of ViePEP can be found at http://www.infosys.tuwien.ac.at/prototypes/ViePEP/ViePEP_index.html [25].

In the future, we will further extend the functionalities of ViePEP and most importantly work on different reasoning algorithms as indicated in Section 4. In fact, we primarily see ViePEP as a research tool helping us to investigate reasoning mechanisms for elastic processes.

Acknowledgements. This work is partially supported by the Austrian Science Fund (FWF): P23313-N23 and the Commission of the European Union within the SIMPLI-CITY FP7-ICT project (Grant agreement no. 318201).

Part of the implementation has been done during Philipp's stay at the University of New South Wales, which was supported by a scholarship from Vienna University of Technology's International Office. We'd like to thank Han Li for his help with the implementation. ViePEP is partly based on the work presented by Li and Venugopal [16].

References

1. van der Aalst, W.M.P., ter Hofstede, A.H.M., Weske, M.: Business Process Management: A Survey. In: van der Aalst, W.M.P., ter Hofstede, A.H.M., Weske, M. (eds.) BPM 2003. LNCS, vol. 2678, pp. 1–12. Springer, Heidelberg (2003)
2. Abouelhoda, M., Issa, S.A., Ghanem, M.: Tavaxy: Integrating Taverna and Galaxy workflows with cloud computing support. BMC Bioinformatics 13(77) (2012)
3. Armbrust, M., Fox, A., Griffith, R., Joseph, A.D., Katz, R., Konwinski, A., Lee, G., Patterson, D., Rabkin, A., Stoica, I., Zaharia, M.: A View of Cloud Computing. Communications of the ACM 53, 50–58 (2010)
4. Berbner, R., Spahn, M., Repp, N., Heckmann, O., Steinmetz, R.: Dynamic Replanning of Web Service Workflows. In: Inaugural IEEE International Conference on Digital Ecosystems and Technologies (IEEE DEST 2007), pp. 211–216. IEEE Computer Society, Washington, DC (2007)
5. Buyya, R., Ranjan, R., Calheiros, R.N.: InterCloud: Utility-Oriented Federation of Cloud Computing Environments for Scaling of Application Services. In: Hsu, C.-H., Yang, L.T., Park, J.H., Yeo, S.-S. (eds.) ICA3PP 2010, Part I. LNCS, vol. 6081, pp. 13–31. Springer, Heidelberg (2010)
6. Buyya, R., Yeo, C.S., Venugopal, S., Broberg, J., Brandic, I.: Cloud computing and emerging IT platforms: Vision, hype, and reality for delivering computing as the 5th utility. Future Generation Computing Systems 25(6), 599–616 (2009)
7. Cao, Q., Wei, Z.B., Gong, W.M.: An Optimized Algorithm for Task Scheduling Based on Activity Based Costing in Cloud Computing. In: 3rd International Conference on Bioinformatics and Biomedical Engineering (ICBBE 2009), pp. 1–3. IEEE Computer Society, Washington, DC (2009)
8. Dustdar, S., Guo, Y., Satzger, B., Truong, H.L.: Principles of Elastic Processes. IEEE Internet Computing 15(5), 66–71 (2011)
9. Emeakaroha, V.C., Brandic, I., Maurer, M., Breskovic, I.: SLA-Aware Application Deployment and Resource Allocation in Clouds. In: COMPSAC Workshops 2011, pp. 298–303. IEEE Computer Society, Washington, DC (2011)
10. Hallerbach, A., Bauer, T., Reichert, M.: Managing Process Variants in the Process Life Cycle. In: Tenth International Conference on Enterprise Information Systems (ICEIS 2008), vol. ISAS-2, pp. 154–161 (2008)
11. Hoffa, C., Mehta, G., Freeman, T., Deelman, E., Keahey, K., Berriman, B., Good, J.: On the Use of Cloud Computing for Scientific Workflows. In: IEEE Fourth International Conference on e-Science (eScience 2008), pp. 640–645. IEEE Computer Society, Washington, DC (2008)
12. Juve, G., Deelman, E.: Scientific Workflows and Clouds. ACM Crossroads 16(3), 14–18 (2010)
13. Kertesz, A., Kecskemeti, G., Brandic, I.: An Interoperable and Self-adaptive Approach for SLA-based Service Virtualization in Heterogeneous Cloud Environments. Future Generation Computer Systems NN(NN), NN–NN (2013) (forthcoming)
14. Lee, Y.C., Wang, C., Zomaya, A.Y., Zhou, B.B.: Profit-Driven Service Request Scheduling in Clouds. In: 10th IEEE/ACM International Conference on Cluster, Cloud and Grid Computing (CCGrid 2010), pp. 15–24. IEEE Computer Society, Washington, DC (2010)
15. Leitner, P., Hummer, W., Dustdar, S.: Cost-Based Optimization of Service Compositions. IEEE Transactions on Services Computing (2012)
16. Li, H., Venugopal, S.: Using Reinforcement Learning for Controlling an Elastic Web Application Hosting Platform. In: 8th International Conference on Autonomic Computing (ICAC 2011), pp. 205–208. ACM, New York (2011)

17. Ludäscher, B., Weske, M., McPhillips, T., Bowers, S.: Scientific Workflows: Business as Usual? In: Dayal, U., Eder, J., Koehler, J., Reijers, H.A. (eds.) BPM 2009. LNCS, vol. 5701, pp. 31–47. Springer, Heidelberg (2009)
18. Mutschler, B., Reichert, M., Bumiller, J.: Unleashing the Effectiveness of Process-Oriented Information Systems: Problem Analysis, Critical Success Factors, and Implications. IEEE Transactions on Systems, Man, and Cybernetics, Part C 38(3), 280–291 (2008)
19. Pandey, S., Wu, L., Guru, S.M., Buyya, R.: A Particle Swarm Optimization-Based Heuristic for Scheduling Workflow Applications in Cloud Computing Environments. In: 24th IEEE International Conference on Advanced Information Networking and Applications (AINA 2010), pp. 400–407. IEEE Computer Society, Washington, DC (2010)
20. Papazoglou, M.P., Traverso, P., Dustdar, S., Leymann, F., Krämer, B.J.: Service-Oriented Computing Research Roadmap. In: Service Oriented Computing (SOC). Dagstuhl Seminar Proceedings, vol. 05462, pp. 38–45. Internationales Begegnungs-und Forschungszentrum für Informatik (IBFI), Schloss Dagstuhl, Germany (2006)
21. Rohjans, S., Dänekas, C., Uslar, M.: Requirements for Smart Grid ICT Architectures. In: Third IEEE PES Innovative Smart Grid Technologies (ISGT) Europe Conference. IEEE Computer Society, Washington, DC (2012)
22. Rusitschka, S., Eger, K., Gerdes, C.: Smart Grid Data Cloud: A Model for Utilizing Cloud Computing in the Smart Grid Domain. In: 1st IEEE International Conference on Smart Grid Communications (SmartGridComm), pp. 483–488. IEEE Computer Society, Washington, DC (2010)
23. Schuller, D., Lampe, U., Eckert, J., Steinmetz, R., Schulte, S.: Cost-driven Optimization of Complex Service-based Workflows for Stochastic QoS Parameters. In: 19th International Conference on Web Services (ICWS 2012), pp. 66–74. IEEE Computer Society Press, Washington, DC (2012)
24. Schuller, D., Polyvyanyy, A., García-Bañuelos, L., Schulte, S.: Optimization of Complex QoS-Aware Service Compositions. In: Kappel, G., Maamar, Z., Motahari-Nezhad, H.R. (eds.) ICSOC 2011. LNCS, vol. 7084, pp. 452–466. Springer, Heidelberg (2011)
25. Schulte, S., Hoenisch, P., Venugopal, S., Dustdar, S.: Realizing Elastic Processes with ViePEP. In: Zhu, H., Ghose, A., Yu, Q., Perrin, O., Wang, J., Wang, Y., Delis, A., Sheng, Q.Z. (eds.) ICSOC 2012, vol. 7759, pp. 439–442. Springer, Heidelberg (2013)
26. Strunk, A.: QoS-Aware Service Composition: A Survey. In: IEEE 8th European Conference on Web Services (ECOWS), pp. 67–74. IEEE Computer Society, Washington, DC (2010)
27. Witten, I.H., Frank, E.: Data Mining: Practical Machine Learning Tools and Techniques, 2nd edn. Morgan Kaufmann Publishers, San Francisco (2005)

TrustVis: A Trust Visualisation Service for Online Communities

Sanat Kumar Bista, Payam Aghaei Pour, Nathalie Colineau, Surya Nepal, and Cecile Paris

Information Engineering Laboratory
CSIRO ICT Centre, Australia
Firstname.lastname@csiro.au

Abstract. Visualisation of social behaviour of members in online communities is a challenging issue. It provides holistic information on the behaviour of the community to the administrators/moderators and helps individual members in the community to monitor and analyse their own behaviour. This paper presents the design and implementation of a social trust visualisation service, called *TrustVis*, where the social trust is derived from the social behaviour of members in the community. One of the unique features of *TrustVis* is that it supports the faceted browsing and monitoring of members' social behaviour based on activities, contexts, time and roles. *TrustVis* is implemented and deployed in an online community we are currently trialling in collaboration with a government department to deliver support services to welfare recipients during their transition back to work. We describe the look and feel and the working of *TrustVis* in our production environment.

1   Introduction

Recently, the Web has created a space for people to conduct social activities like meeting each other, exchanging ideas, dating potential partners or sharing experiences. The emergence and popularity of many social network sites such as Facebook and LinkedIn have shown a phenomenal success of the Web in creating a social space for everyone. The term *Social Web* was coined by Rheingold to describe websites that support social interactions through web technologies [1]. Social networks can be classified into different categories based on the context of their application and use [2]. With respect to members' participation, social networks can be public (open) or private (by invitation only); with respect to applications, they can be either generic (no specific objective) or be targeted to realise some specific objectives. We have developed a specific member-only online community for a government agency which aims to deliver support services to welfare recipients during their transition back to work [3,4].

Social networks are quite complex. It is thus difficult to have a holistic view of such networks as well as monitor and analyse them to extract meaningful information. Visualisation tools have been widely promoted to monitor social networks [5-8]. The concept of network visualisation is not new. It has been used to monitor and diagnose

A. Ghose et al. (Eds.): ICSOC 2012, LNCS 7759, pp. 191–202, 2013.

computer networks [9-11]. In recent time, similar concepts have been used to analyse and monitor social networks. Examples of such tools include Social Network Visualiser (*SocNetV*)[1], *NetVis*[2] and *Last Forward*[3].

The design of social network visualisation tools can be categorised into two broad groups: analysis-centric design and application-centric design. Analysis-centric designs focus more on identifying degree and density of nodes in the network and are more or less generic in nature (or at least their theoretical models are generic). *Pajek* [12], *Ucinet* [13] and *Tnet* [14] are examples of analysis-centric visualisation tools. These tools offer a way of measuring network properties, such as cohesiveness, degree centrality and friendships. Application-centric designs are driven by the specific needs of the application. The underlying analysis could still be borrowed from standard network analysis theory, but the visualisation is modelled by considering the requirements of the problem scenario. Examples of application-centric designs include Communication and Activity Visualisation for the Enterprise (CAVALIER) [5], student interaction visualisation in online communications [8] and editing behaviour visualisation of Wikipedia editors [15]. From these observations, we come to the following conclusions: visualisation tools are designed to analyse specific properties of the networks. Hence, they are either unsuitable or cannot be used directly to analyse a new property that is not supported (such as social trust); and visualisation tools are designed with a specific application in mind and are not generic enough to be migrated to new applications, as each application brings its own challenge and features (such as an online community for welfare recipients).

We have implemented and deployed an online community to support parents receiving welfare payments so that they can meet parents in similar situation. The purpose of the online community is to provide both emotional and informational support to them during the period of their transition from welfare to work. One of the key research questions we are considering is how to build *social capital* in the community through *social trust*. In our research, the social capital is the density of interactions that benefit the community, and social trust represents the positive interactions between members in the community. Since our application domain has a specific property (i.e., social trust), it has different visualisation needs than those encountered in other online communities. For this reason, we cannot simply adapt an existing visualisation tool and deploy it. Furthermore, none of the existing social network visualisation tools support the visualisation of contextualised social behaviour and social trust. Hence, there is a need to build a visualisation tool.

Visualisation of social trust in our community is complex and multi-dimensional. In addition to aesthetic and layout aspects, the visualisation tool must support a number of different functionalities. First, it has to allow one to visualise the network's interactions in different contexts (e.g., Discussion Forum and Livechat). We define a context as the environment in which an interaction takes place. Second, it has to allow one to visualise the network based on different user activities such as rating,

---

[1] http://socnetv.sourceforge.net/

[2] http://www.netvis.org/index.php

[3] http://lastforward.sourceforge.net/

commenting or inviting others to be friends. Third, it has to support temporal filtering so that one can visualise the network at different time intervals. Fourth, it has to support the exploration of network so that one can find information about nodes and edges including social trust of specific individuals by navigating though the network without much difficulty. Finally, the visualisation should incorporate role-based access to information to preserve privacy and offer different views to people with different roles so that members and administrators can use the same, but have different views of the network. In order to incorporate these requirements, we have developed and implemented a novel social trust visualisation tool, called *TrustVis*. It supports faceted browsing and monitoring of social behaviours of the members in the community and has been implemented as a service.

The rest of the article is organised as follows: Section 2 presents the context of the work in terms of the application and network property in relation to social trust. Application specific requirements are explained in Section 3. Section 4 illustrates the design and implementation of *TrustVis*. Section 5 presents a brief review of related work. The final section presents the concluding remarks and some possible future work.

2   Context

We define the context of our work on *TrustVis* along two dimentions. First, we outline our application scenario, and then, we provide specific information on social trust, a new network property that needs to be supported by *TrustVis*.

2.1   Application

We have built and deployed an online community to deliver government services to citizens as a trial for 12 months [3,4]. In this community, membership is by invitation only, i.e., specific individuals (individuals receiving a specific type of welfare payments and required to look for work) are invited to join the community. This group is in a transition phase, being asked (by legislation) to move from one type of welfare payment to another. The identity of the community members is kept anonymous (i.e., members present themselves with an avatar and a name of their choice). Members have also an individual profile, through which they can choose to disclose what they want to others.

The aim of the community is several fold. First, it is a place for the government to target its information and services when dealing with a specific target group of welfare recipients. Second, it is to bring people with the same concerns together, hoping that they will share experiences, ideas and tips, thus providing social, emotional and moral support to each other. Although they are all strangers to each other, they all share the same situation and concerns. Third, it is a space in which we invite individuals to go on a reflection journey, in order to better prepare them for the transition and their return to work.

2.2   STrust: Social Trust Model

TrustVis is designed to help explore the social behaviour of the community members. It relies on an underlying social trust model, *STrust*[16], that computes trust based on interactions between community members. *STrust* has three unique features. First, it distinguishes three trust types: 1) the popularity trust (*PopTrust*) that captures the trust that an individual member has received from other members in the community; 2) the engagement trust (*EngTrust*), which reflects the trust that an individual member has about other members in the community; and, 3) the social trust (*STrust*), that combines the popularity and engagement trust. The second feature of the *STrust* model is that it considers both active and passive behaviour of members. Active behaviour refers to actions that generate: (a) content for other members in the community to consume (e.g., Contributions to Forum, Livechat, etc.), and (b) actions that require other members to act (e.g., invite somebody to be a friend). Passive behaviour refers to actions that do not generate any content or actions for other members (e.g., visiting the community, reading posts, reading Livechat content, etc.). The third feature of the model is that it considers online communities as two mode social networks, where nodes in the networks can be classified into two types: *active* and *passive*. Active nodes are those that can engage in the community (typically, people), while passive nodes are those that cannot engage in the community (i.e., they do not have engagement trust), such as articles and posts.   Our current implementation of *TrustVis* considers only active nodes. Interactions with passive nodes are treated like active node interactions by removing the intermediate passive node and linking directly the members interacting with the passive node (the activity is then grouped as *Same Interest*).

We now describe the computational aspect of *STrust*. Let M be the total number of members in the online community. Let m_i and m_j represent the members of the community. If a member m_j has a positive interaction with a member m_i, the interaction is represented as "+". Similarly, the negative interaction is represented as "-".   The popularity trust (*PopTrust*) of a member m_i is then defined as:

$$PopTrust(m_i) = \frac{\sum_{j=1, j \neq i}^{M} \frac{| PT_{ij}^{kd+} | + 1}{| PT_{ij}^{kd+} | + | PT_{ij}^{kd-} | + 2}}{M - 1}$$

Where PT_{ij}^{kd+} and PT_{ij}^{kd-} represents the positive and negative popularity interaction a member m_i has with a member m_j with respect to an activity d in the context k. Similarly, the engagement trust (*EngTrust*) of a member m_i is defined as:

$$EngTrust(m_i) = \frac{\sum_{j=1, j \neq i}^{M} \frac{| ET_{ij}^{kd+} | + 1}{| ET_{ij}^{kd+} | + | ET_{ij}^{kd-} | + 2}}{M - 1}$$

with ET_{ij}^{kd+} and ET_{ij}^{kd-} representing the positive and negative engagement interactions between members m_i and m_j respectively.

A member in the community may be involved in a number of activities related to a single context. For example, a member may comment, rate and/or view a post in the forum. Here, the forum represents the *context*, and commenting, rating and viewing are considered as *activities*. It is possible for each activity and context to have different weights. W_d represents the weight for activity d and $\sum w_d = 1$. W_k represents the weight for context k and $\sum w_k = 1$. We need to consider this while evaluating positive and negative engagement and popularity interactions. Thus, the weights for positive and negative popularity and engagement interactions are defined as follows:

$$For \mid PT_{ij}^{kd+} \mid and \mid ET_{ij}^{kd+} \mid \qquad\qquad \mid For \mid PT_{ij}^{kd-} \mid and \mid ET_{ij}^{kd-} \mid$$

$$\sum_{k=1}^{K} w_k \left(\sum_{d=1}^{D} w_d \left(\sum_{x=1}^{X} +1 \right) \right) \qquad\qquad \sum_{k=1}^{K} w_k \left(\sum_{d=1}^{D} w_d \left(\sum_{x=1}^{X} -1 \right) \right)$$

Here, K represents the number of contexts, D the number of activities in each context, and X represents the number of interactions related to the activity and context. The social trust (*STrust*) of an individual member m_i in the community is then given by:

$$SocialTrust(m_i) = \alpha.PopTrust(m_i) + (1 - \alpha).EngTrust(m_i)$$

Where α represents the value of a weight in the range of 0 to 1. If alpha is 1, the social trust of an individual indicates how much other members in the community trust him or her. For further details on trust model, we refer the readers to our earlier work in [17,16].

3   Social Trust Visualisation Requirements

In the introduction, we have listed several unique requirements of our application. In the following, those requirements are explained with a few examples to provide a better understanding of the requirements for *TrustVis*.

Context Filter: A requirement for *TrustVis* is to be able to offer a contextual filter for the community members' social behaviour. A context in our model refers to a setting where specific interactions take place. We have defined a range of contexts. This includes the forum (where members post, rate and comment), the resource section (where members can read and rate information), the activity pages (where members work on some guided tasks such as identifying skills, writing resume, identifying barriers to work and studies, etc), the buddy program (where members socialise with each other sending and accepting invitations), the media page (where members can watch videos and listen to audio resources) and the Livechat room (where members can have live discussions with experts).

Activity Filter: Each of the contexts outlined above can have multiple activities associated to them, such as rating, commenting, viewing, etc. Therefore it is important for *TrustVis* to be able to filter the social behaviours of the members on the basis of such activities.

Temporal Filter: Online communities such as ours evolve over time. Thus, being able to filter social behaviour on the basis of time offers an interesting analysis of the network. By including a temporal filter, *TrustVis* presents the visualisation of selected activities in particular contexts for specific dates or periods of time.

Information: *TrustVis* displays the computations from the social trust model *STrust*. Since *STrust* as well as the context and activity filters are unique to our application, there is a requirement for the visual representation to be able to capture right information and present them at right places. This includes displaying of trust and all other interactions of members at appropriate locations.

Aesthetic and Layouts: An important aspect of any visualisation is aesthetic of the representation of different information. *TrustVis* supports multiple layouts and is easy to use. For example, *TrustVis* offers avatar-based view of members with drag-able nodes supporting multiple layouts. Related information is provided at designated space as well as on mouse over.

Roles: *TrustVis* is required to support role-based views for both community administrators/moderators and individual members. We provide a holistic view of the community (called the *System View*) to the administrators/moderators (referred later as systems users) whereas individual members are only able to access information about their social behaviour (called the *User View*).

Based on these requirements, we designed and implemented the trust visualisation service, *TrustVis*, the details of which are outlined in the following section.

4   Service Design and Implementation

Fig. 1 shows a high level architecture focusing on *TrustVis* components.

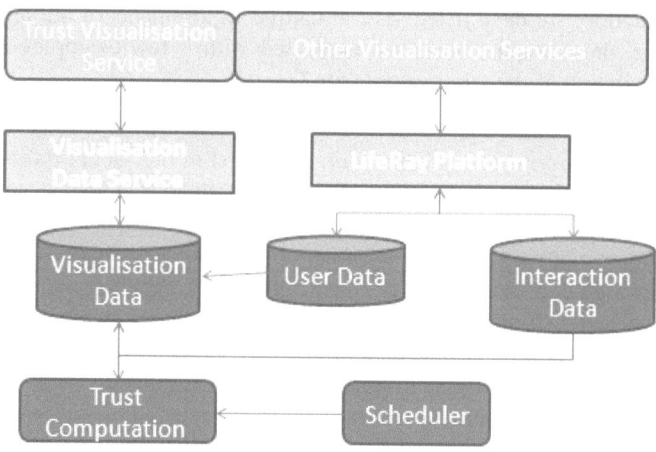

Fig. 1. A High-Level System Architecture Showing the Trust Visualisation Components

User data consist of the data relevant to users (that includes both community members and system users) such as their screen name and profile. This includes user roles. We currently distinguish two user roles: a system user or a community member. As outlined in the requirements, this distinction is necessary as each of these types of users need to see different aspects of the visualisation and can take part in different activities and contexts. Interaction data consist of all active and passive interactions of users. This includes all possible activities in all possible contexts. We extract relevant data from interaction data and user data and create a visualisation data. The trust computation component implements the STrust model described earlier and computes the different types of trust values. The purpose of the scheduler is to schedule the trust computation. In our current implementation, the scheduler computes trust values once a day. This constraint was put to increase the efficiency of the visualisation service. Trust computation is time and resource demanding and this aspects should not limit the visualisation aspect.We plan to improve this aspect in future by optimising the trust algorithms.

TrustVis has been deployed as an applet in the community, and GraphML has been used as a file format for graphs. Users of the system interact with this service to get the visual output to query the system for information. The *Visualisation Data Service,* as an intermediate layer, captures user requests to query required information from the underlying visualisation data (refer Figure 1). In addition to serving the visualisation data, *user data* and *interaction data* also provide necessary information to other elements of the online community, such as the online community user interface. The online community has been developed using the Liferay[4] platform, and TrustVis is developed using JUNG[5].

Fig. 2 presents the user interface of TrustVis for community members. In this view, the display area presents the network representing the member's social behaviour.

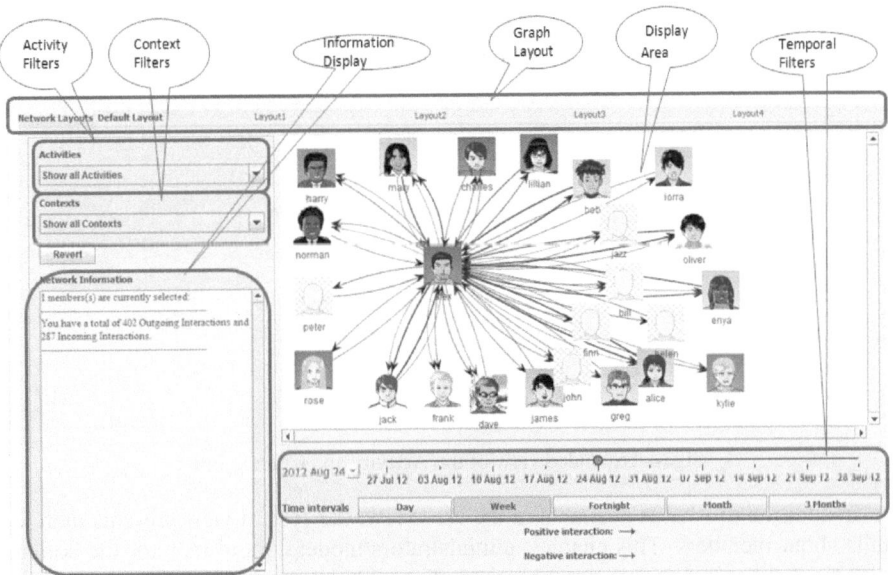

Fig. 2. *TrustVis* User Interface

---

[4] http://www.liferay.com/
[5] http://jung.sourceforge.net/

There are limitations in the amount of information available in this view. Specific trust values are not available to community members. Members are presented with high level information such as their total number of incoming and outgoing interactions with other community members in different contexts. Fig. 3 presents samples of member and link information available to community members. Activity, Context and Temporal filters are enabled in this view.

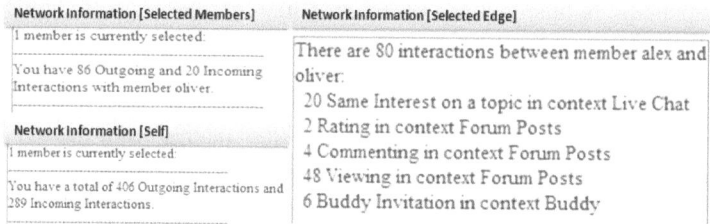

Fig. 3. Network Information in User View

Fig. 4 shows an expanded view of the activity and context filters (there are a total of 8 activities and 8 contexts, and not all activities are applicable to all contexts). Users can   select any of the members or the links between them to see the details of the interactions. Members in the user view are represented by their avatars and the network can be resized by dragging the avatars. Negative interactions such as negative ratings and cancellations of invitations appear as red links while all other positive interactions appear as blue. The thickness of the links is proportional to their values. The greater the value the thicker the link appears in the graph.

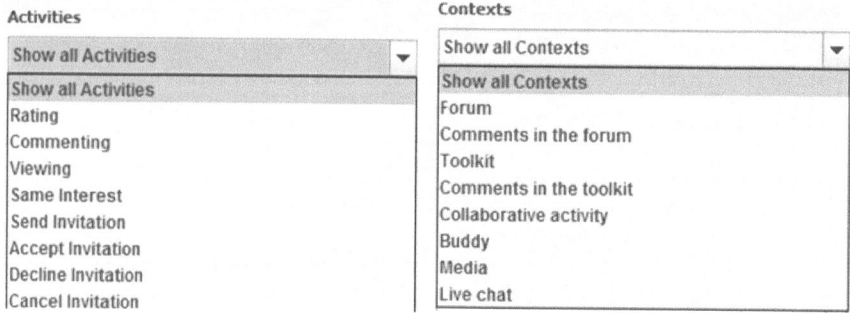

Fig. 4. Expanded view of the Activity and Context Filter

In addition to what is available in the user view, the system view presents more details about members. This enables administrators/moderators to monitor the community more effectively. This view consists of the whole network with the capability to click on individual members and check their exclusive network. Fig. 5 shows a sample network display and the information available on members and their links, including trust values calculated using the STrust model.

System users are also able to select nodes and remove them from the visualisation to see the effect of an individual member on the whole community. In addition, they

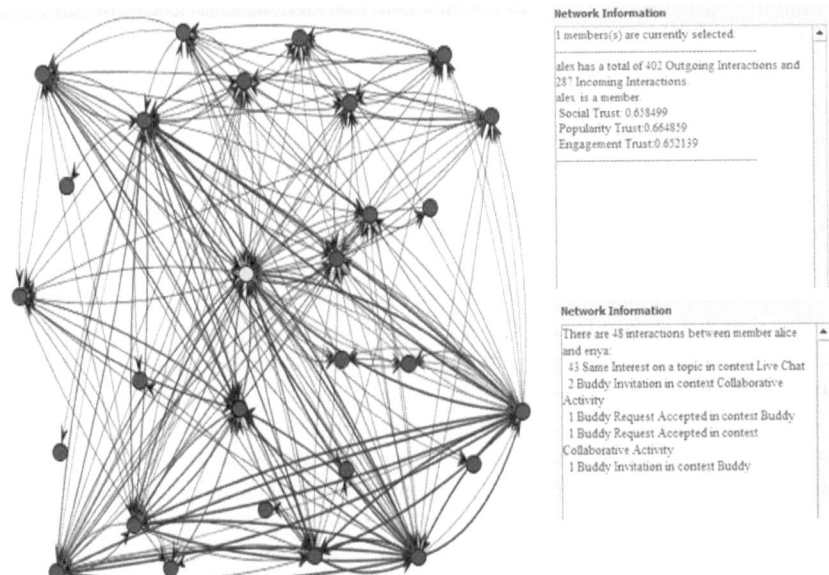

Network Information

1 members(s) are currently selected.

alex has a total of 402 Outgoing Interactions and 287 Incoming Interactions.
alex is a member.
Social Trust: 0.638499
Popularity Trust:0.664859
Engagement Trust:0.652139

Network Information

There are 48 interactions between member alice and enya:
   43 Same Interest on a topic in context Live Chat
   2 Buddy Invitation in context Collaborative Activity
   1 Buddy Request Accepted in context Buddy
   1 Buddy Request Accepted in context Collaborative Activity
   1 Buddy Invitation in context Buddy

Fig. 5. System View of the Network and Related Information

can check the nodes that have not had any interaction with other members in the community yet.

5   Related Work

Visualisation and measurement as central factors to the growth of social network analysis offer investigators new insights of network structure [6]. Node-link (points and lines) and matrix based representations are the two distinct form of display used in visualisation of social networks since the early 1930s [7] [6]. To offer better visualisation and analysis capabilities, hybrid approaches have also been used in recent time. For example, NodeTrix [18] has been developed to use node-link diagrams to show the global network structure, and adjacency matrix to support the analysis of local communities [19]. Analysis of social networks can provide useful information about its actors, roles and positions of actors in the community to name a few [20] [18]. Pajek [12], Ucinet [13] and Tnet [14] support node-link based and adjacency matrix based social network analysis.

Recently, online social networks have gained tremendous popularity leading to an explosive growth in the degree and density of interactions over social networks. While the underlying theory of analysis could still be supported by established principles of network analysis, there is clearly a need to identify better visualisation techniques as required by the context of application. Vizster [7] has been developed over the node-link layout, but with several customisations to better support visual interconnectivity between graphs and with features to automatically identify and visualise community structures. The resulting tool was used to visualise 1.5 million Friendster crawl. Xiong and Donath [21] argue that traditional social network analysis based visualisation, being fairly complex, are more useful to analysts than for an average user who just intends to get a sense of connectedness in the community. They have proposed an interesting visualisation, called *data portrait*, that uses a flower metaphor for individual portraits and garden metaphor for combining the portraits to represent an online interaction environment. Viegas and Donath [22] propose an alternative approach for visualisation of social networks representing the frequency of connections over time (referred to as PostHistory). In contrast to graph visualisations that demonstrate the strength of connections between members in a social network, this visualisation depicts the frequency of connections between the members. Their work underlines that current depictions of social networks have shortcomings and that there is a need to find alternate ways to visualise online social networks.

Visualisation of trust over online communications is also an interesting area of research. O'Donovan et al [23,24] propose a model that extracts negative information from the feedback comments on eBay, computes personalised and feature-based trust and presents this information graphically. The graph shows the trust value and the trust strength calculated based on the number of transactions/comments between two users. In [25], the authors propose a trust-based visualisation of cooperation context between members. Bimrah et al. [26] propose a visualisation language for trust related requirements elicitation.

In line with this body of work, we have also used the traditional node-link representation in TrustVis to visualise the social behaviour of the members in our online community. However, other requirements of TrustVis have originated from the application's needs and the social trust model. These requirements provide us with an opportunity to invent a unique way of visualising social trust and behaviours based on three filters: context, activities and time.

6   Conclusion and Future Works

In this paper, we described the design and implementation of a trust visualisation service, called TrustVis. We deployed TrustVis in an online community that we developed in collaboration with a government agency with the aim of providing informational and emotional support services to welfare recipients transitioning back to work. Due to the inherent requirements of our online community, existing methods of visualisation were either too complex or not sufficient enough to capture the social trust and behaviour requirements we needed. This motivated the development of TrustVis. The key feature of TrustVis is that it enables users to visualise social trust and behaviours using three types of filters: context, activities and time. These three features together offer a unique experience to administrators/moderators and to individual community members. In the future, we intend to extend TrustVis in the following directions: (a) we plan to include both active and passive nodes in TrustVis by providing a functionality to convert a three-mode network to a two-mode network; (b) we plan to provide the provenance of trust by providing the functionality to drill down from the interaction level to the level of activities and contexts; (c) we plan to extend TrustVis to a full-fledged faceted monitoring service including other activities and contexts such as individual activities like login; and (d) we plan to conduct a usability evaluation of TrustVis.

Acknowledgements. This research has been funded under the Human Services Delivery Research Alliance (HSDRA) between the CSIRO and the Australian Government Department of Human Services. We would like to thank Payam Aghaei Pour, Hon Hwang, Brian Jin, Alex Sun and Bo Yan for their contribution to the implementation of this work.

References

1. Rheingold, H.: The Virtual Community: Homesteading on the Electronic Frontier (Revised Edition). MIT Press, USA (2000)
2. Ellison, N.B., Steinfield, C., Lampe, C.: The Benefits of Facebook "Friends:" Social Capital and College Students' Use of Online Social Network Sites. Journal of Computer-Mediated Communication 12(4), 1143–1168 (2007), doi:10.1111/j.1083-6101.2007.00367.x
3. Colineau, N., Paris, C., Dennett, A.: Exploring the Use of an Online Community in Welfare Transition Programs. In: 25th BCS Conference on Human-Computer Interaction, Newcastle-upon-Tyne, United Kingdom, pp. 455–460. British Computer Society (2011)
4. Colineau, N., Paris, C., Dennett, A.: Capitalising on the Potential of Online Communities to Help Welfare Recipients. International Reports on Socio-Informatics (IRSI) 2, 59–65 (2011)
5. Dekker, A.: Visualisation of social networks using CAVALIER. In: Proceedings of the 2001 Asia-Pacific Symposium on Information Visualisation, Sydney, Australia, vol. 9, pp. 49–55. Australian Computer Society, Inc. (2001)
6. Freeman, L.C.: Visualizing Social Networks. Journal of Social Structure 1(1) (2000)
7. Heer, J., Boyd, D.: Vizster: visualizing online social networks. In: IEEE Symposium on Information Visualization, INFOVIS 2005, USA, October 23-25, pp. 32–39 (2005), doi:10.1109/infvis.2005.1532126
8. Jyothi, S., McAvinia, C., Keating, J.: A visualisation tool to aid exploration of students' interactions in asynchronous online communication. Computers & Education 58(1), 30–42 (2012), doi:10.1016/j.compedu.2011.08.026
9. Girardin, L.: An eye on network intruder-administrator shootouts. In: Proceedings of the 1st Workshop on Intrusion Detection and Network Monitoring, Santa Clara, California, vol. 1. USENIX Association (1999)
10. Ball, R., Fink, G.A., North, C.: Home-centric visualization of network traffic for security administration. In: Proceedings of the 2004 ACM Workshop on Visualization and Data Mining for Computer Security, Washington DC, USA, pp. 55–64. ACM (2004), doi:10.1145/1029208.1029217
11. Erbacher, R.F.: Intrusion behavior detection through visualization. In: IEEE Systems, Man and Cybernetics Conference, Cristal City, Virginia, USA, October 5-8, pp. 2507–2513. IEEE (2003), doi:10.1109/icsmc.2003.1244260
12. de Nooy, W., Mrvar, A., Batagelj, V.: Exploratory Social Network Analysis with Pajek. Cambridge University Press, USA (2011)

13. Borgatti, S.P.: Ucinet for Windows: Software for Social Network Analysis. Analytic Technologies, Harvard (2002)
14. Opsahl, T.: Structure and Evolution of Weighted Networks. University of London (Queen Mary College), London (2009)
15. Iba, T., Nemoto, K., Peters, B., Gloor, P.A.: Analyzing the Creative Editing Behavior of Wikipedia Editors: Through Dynamic Social Network Analysis. Procedings of Social and Behavioral Sciences 2(4), 6441–6456 (2010), doi:10.1016/j.sbspro.2010.04.054
16. Nepal, S., Sherchan, W., Paris, C.: Building Trust Communities Using Social Trust. In: Ardissono, L., Kuflik, T. (eds.) UMAP 2011 Workshops. LNCS, vol. 7138, pp. 243–255. Springer, Heidelberg (2012)
17. Nepal, S., Paris, C., Bista, S.K., Sherchan, W.: A Trust Model Based Analysis of Social Networks. International Journal of Trust Management in Computing and Communications (2012) (forthcoming)
18. Henry, N., Fekete, J.D., McGuffin, M.J.: NodeTrix: a Hybrid Visualization of Social Networks. IEEE Transactions on Visualization and Computer Graphics 13(6), 1302–1309 (2007), doi:10.1109/tvcg.2007.70582
19. Henry, N., Fekete, J.D.: MatrixExplorer: a Dual-Representation System to Explore Social Networks. IEEE Transactions on Visualization and Computer Graphics 12(5), 677–684 (2006), doi:10.1109/tvcg.2006.160
20. Scott, J.: Social Network Analysis: A Handbook. Sage Publications, London (1987)
21. Xiong, R., Donath, J.: PeopleGarden: creating data portraits for users. In: Proceedings of the 12th Annual ACM Symposium on User Interface Software and Technology, Asheville, North Carolina, USA, pp. 37–44. ACM (1999), doi:10.1145/320719.322581
22. Viégas, F.B., Donath, J.: Social network visualization: can we go beyond the graph. In: Workshop on Social Networks for Design and Analysis: Using Network Information, Chicago, USA (2004)
23. O'Donovan, J.: Capturing Trust in Social Web Applications Computing with Social Trust. In: Golbeck, J. (ed.) Human–Computer Interaction Series, pp. 213–257. Springer, London (2009), doi:10.1007/978-1-84800-356-9_9
24. O'Donovan, J., Smyth, B., Evrim, V., McLeod, D.: Extracting and visualizing trust relationships from online auction feedback comments. In: Proceedings of the 20th International Joint Conference on Artifical Intelligence, Hyderabad, India, pp. 2826–2831. Morgan Kaufmann Publishers Inc. (2007)
25. Guerriero, A., Kubicki, S., Halin, G.: Trust-Oriented Multi-visualization of Cooperation Context. In: Proceedings of the Second International Conference in Visualisation, pp. 96–101. IEEE Computer Society, Washington, DC (2009), doi:10.1109/viz.2009.48
26. Bimrah, K.K., Mouratidis, H., Preston, D.: Modelling Trust Requirements by Means of a Visualization Language. In: Proceedings of the 2008 Requirements Engineering Visualization, Barcelona, Spain, pp. 26–30. IEEE Computer Society (2008), doi:10.1109/rev.2008.3

Crowd-Sourcing Service Designs: Overview and Research Challenges

Nidhi Rajshree, Bikram Sengupta, and Nirmit V. Desai

IBM Research, Bangalore, India
{nidhi.rajshree,bsengupt,nirmit.desai}@in.ibm.com

Abstract. A service is supposed to embody the needs and interests of its providers as well as its consumers. However, service design has traditionally been the prerogative of service providers, often leading to services that provide unsatisfactory consumer experience. With increasing prevalence of open government initiatives and the advent of social computing in the enterprise, we posit that service design is set to become truly participatory, with the service provider tapping into the wisdom and creativity of the consumer "crowd", and the design of a service resulting from their collective ideation, brainstorming and refinement. This paper seeks to identify the research challenges in crowdsourcing service designs by way of proposing a new high-level framework and describing its application to an elaborate example of driver's license issuance service. The framework is a mix of the richness of crowd participation and the technical rigor afforded by formal analysis of service designs. The framework describes the components and how they come together, thereby leading us to the novel research challenges in realizing the components that should motivate further work on this topic.

1 Introduction

The goal of a service system is to create an experience that generates value for both the consumer and the provider of a service [13]. This suggests that service providers and consumers should collaborate closely to design services that serve their mutual interests. However, service systems have traditionally been designed by providers with limited participation from end users, often resulting in poor experiences when deployed. This is true for both public services as well as those delivered within an enterprise. Governments have found it difficult — or have lacked the motivation — to engage with diverse groups of citizens in a structured and constructive manner when designing public services. Even within an enterprise, hierarchical structures and centralized decision making have often meant that employees have had little influence on services they have to use. Services designed only from the perspective of the provider may ignore key consumer concerns and lead to unwieldy, overly-constrained processes that impose substantial burden on the end user instead of helping them.

Singh articulates the fundamental flaw in the current approaches of service designs and argues for the users and usages of a service to be playing a primary role in the design process [12]. Supporting this argument, service providers are increasingly accepting the necessity and the value of consumer involvement in the service design process. In many cases, governments are leading the way with open government initiatives, that seek to

A. Ghose et al. (Eds.): ICSOC 2012, LNCS 7759, pp. 203–214, 2013.

enhance transparency, accessibility and responsiveness, often through increased citizen participation. This has motivated innovative research such as the COCKPIT project [5] under the EU FP7 program, that encourages citizen participation in the design of public services by offering multiple alternatives to them for their consideration and feedback. At the same time, we are also observing an increasingly young workforce instrumenting a deeper penetration of social computing within the enterprise[1], and rigid business processes are increasingly complemented with unstructured, team-based collaboration, particularly for complex decision making.

These trends suggest that we may be at the tipping point of *participatory service design*, where service providers seek to tap into the collective wisdom and creativity of the "crowd" of consumers, and the design process proceeds through their collective ideation, brainstorming, and refinement. "Crowdsourcing" [6] has emerged as a popular mechanism for fostering community participation, where placing a problem in the public domain along with an open call for responses and appropriate incentives, has sometimes yielded quick or effective solutions. For example, voting can be considered as an extremely simple form of crowdsourcing. The knowledge — the most popular choice — can be extracted trivially. In other crowdsourcing applications involving some form of computation or problem solving, rewards may be determined based on the volume of fine-grained tasks completed (e.g. tagging images), or by the selection of the "best" solution, from amongst the submitted responses, by the crowdsourcer (with a respondent only having visibility into his/her own solution) [8]. However, applying a standard crowdsourcing approach to the task of participatory service design throws up several challenges that we identify next. These challenges have also helped motivate a high-level framework for crowdsourcing service design outlined in this paper.

1.1 Challenges in Crowdsourcing Service Design

The design of a service as well as its evaluation are intellectually challenging tasks. A single design may have many dimensions to it and involve various trade-offs. Hence, the first challenge in crowdsourcing the design of a service is that it is non-trivial (and time consuming) to judge the overall quality or usefulness of any proposed solution.

Second, the scale of responses, e.g., for a public service impacting a large population, or even a business service within a large enterprise - may make it infeasible for the service provider to process and evaluate each response, determine which ones are valid as per the domain constraints, and then evaluate the "goodness" of the valid ones.

Third, we would like the design process to be truly participatory, involving iterations where respondents have visibility into each other's designs and can suggest enhancements to the same. This further exacerbates the problem of scale as new designs emerge across iterations. Also, the "best" design (by whatever evaluation criteria is used) may involve a creative composition of ideas from multiple designs, and it is infeasible for participants to manually generate all possible compositions and determine the best. Note that a "best" design must be adjudged so from the perspective of all the stake holders, including the end users. Hence, choice of what variant to execute cannot

---

[1] http://www.gartner.com/it/page.jsp?id=1470115

be made by end users of a service unilaterally, e.g., citizens in the driver's license case. This is why it is necessary to arrive at the single "best" design.

Finally, richer the collaboration among contributors, the harder it is to define incentives. Crowdsourcing depends on the participation from the crowd. From the perspective of rationality, there must be an incentive for the crowd to participate. If contributors collaborate closely, it is difficult to trace an idea to a contributor and assign credit. But unless credit is attributed to in a fair manner, the crowd may lose interest to participate.

1.2   Contributions

In this paper, we propose a high-level framework to support service design crowdsourcing, motivated by the above challenges. The novelty of the framework lies in its ability to tap into the richness of crowd participation, while suitably tempering it through formal reasoning and analysis to filter out invalid submissions, automatically generate new designs by including "good" aspects from multiple existing submissions, and help focus the attention of the crowd on the most promising design variants. The combination of crowdsourcing and formal reasoning ensures that we can handle scale without sacrificing on the originality of human thinking. It is beyond the scope of this paper to present a concrete realization of the framework - instead, we discuss the various challenges it brings up and possible ways of addressing them, with the goal of fostering further research into the area. We find that the main challenges are in (a) representing the high-level service designs and criteria for comparing alternative detailed designs, (b) generating new detailed designs and assimilating modifications to existing ones such that the new designs include "good" features of all contributed designs, and (c) incentivising contributors eventhough they collaborate closely and have visibility to each others' designs. A case study involving the collaborative design of a driving license issuance service is used to illustrate what the framework is envisioned to achieve without delving into how this can be achieved today.

The rest of the paper is organized as follows. Section 2 presents the case study on the public service of driving licenses. Section 3 describes our framework for crowdsourcing process models. Section 4 applies our framework to the case study of driving licenses and steps through the method for arriving at the *best* model for delivering the driving license service. Section 5 presents the research challenges in realizing our framework and suggests potential approaches. We summarize the related works in Section 6 and conclude in Section 7.

2   Case Study: Driving License Service

The Transport Department of India provides two kinds of services to its citizenry, namely, services related to motor vehicles and those related to individuals. The former includes services such as inspection of vehicles in the incident of an accident, transfer of vehicles from one owner to another, and issuance of fitness certificates to motor vehicles. The individual services include issuance of learner's license, granting of international driving permit and issuance of driver's license. Our case study is based on the Driver's License issuance service. The Motor Vehicle Act of 1988 and its subsequent

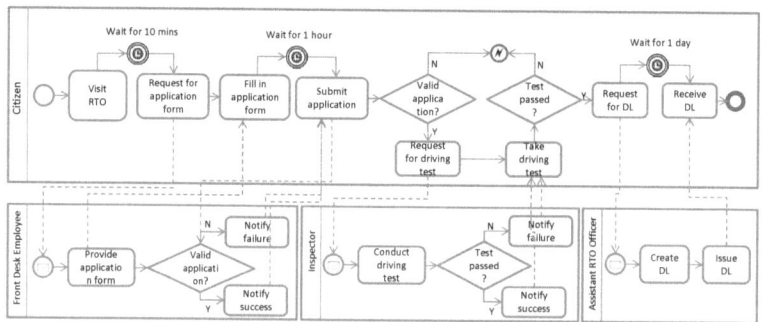

Fig. 1. Case study: Driving license services in India

amendments stipulate the national official licensing process. Individuals must first obtain a temporary license, which grants the right to practice driving under the supervision of a licensed individual.

In this paper, we study the process wherein after 30 days (and within 180 days) of the issuance of the temporary license, the individual may apply for a permanent license. Figure 1 depicts a BPMN process model for this process. Note that BPMN is chosen for illustration and is not a suggested representation for addressing the challenge of crowdsourcing service designs. The applicant must visit the Regional Transport Office (RTO), obtain and fill out an application form and get it validated by the front desk. The application requires supporting documents such as proof of age, proof of residence, a recent passport size photo, and his or her temporary license. If valid, a driving test with an inspector is scheduled and later conducted after a wait. If the test is passed, a driving license may be requested by the applicant and issued by the Assistant RTO. Either invalid application or a test failure results in the rejection of the driving license application. Although this service involves multiple stake holders, we focus on the applicant's perspective in the following discussions. Note that Figure 1 shows simply the current way of achieving the goal of issuing driver's licenses; there can be better ways and the citizens may have ideas for the same. We will revisit this in Section 4.

3   Proposed Framework

Motivated by the challenges identified in Section 1.1, we now propose a high-level framework to support crowdsourcing of service design as shown in Figure 2.

Our approach begins with the service designer (working on behalf of the service provider), who comes up with a abstract specification of a service that may include the goals of the service, some of the key high-level tasks, the constraints that define validity of contributed detailed designs, and criteria for comparing multiple designs. This specification is then published to the "crowd", and design ideas are sought. The crowd may include contributors who submit detailed designs for the entire service or parts thereof, and a potentially larger community of users of the service being designed,

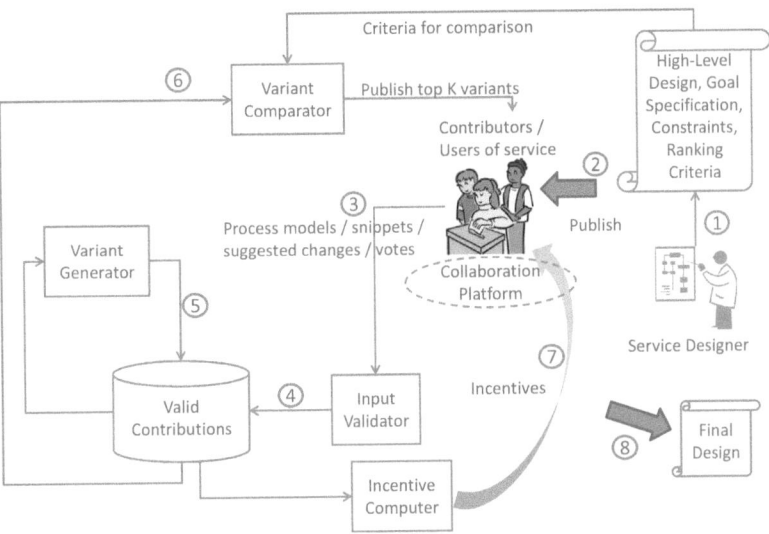

Fig. 2. Framework for crowdsourcing process models

who can review the contributed designs, suggest changes or enhancements, and rate the designs. Our framework includes a collaboration platform through which in-context discussions on service designs may be supported. With a sufficiently large crowd we will encounter the challenge of managing the scale of contributions - ensuring that invalid submissions do not attract undue attention, while good ideas from the many valid submissions are identified and highlighted for further consideration. This is where the formal reasoning and analysis afforded by our framework can play an important role, as we describe next.

The designs submitted by the crowd are passed through an *Input Validator* that automatically checks the validity of contributed designs, based on the formal specification provided by the service designer. Many designs that do not meet the necessary constraints are dropped at this step, and only the valid contributions are persisted with. The next key step is to analyze the existing designs and look for ways in which new variants can be generated by combining useful aspects of these designs. This is handled by the *Variant Generator*. This is a critical step since it involves (a) identifying the useful aspects that can be extracted out, using some notion of value that these aspects may bring (e.g. based on the evaluation criteria defined by the designer) (b) understanding which aspects can be combined and in what order, using a formal semantics for composition that also respects the high-level specification. Finally, the *Variant Comparator* evaluates all the generated variants using the known evaluation criteria and publishes the top K variants back to the crowd for further review and discussions. To ensure systematic progress, we expect alternate time-bound cycles of crowd participation (to review and elicit new ideas) and formal analysis (to filter, compose and prioritize these ideas for the next round of discussion). The process continues till the final design is arrived at, a selection that may be made by the service designer/provider at an appropriate point in time, taking into account the relative merits of the candidate designs (ordered by Variant Comparator), and crowd feedback (e.g. through voting and discussions).

Finally, the participants in service design crowdsourcing need to be rewarded. This will be handled by an *Incentive Computer* that will rank the participants based on the relative strength of their contributions, as determined by it from the value of the designs submitted by or contributed to by each participant, during the crowdsourcing exercise.

4   Applying the Framework to Driver's License Service

This section describes how our framework can be applied to the driver's license case study. Although we do not propose any concrete implementation of the components of our framework, the following discussion should help one understand the overall flow on an actual example, while Section 5 will discuss the key research challenges to be addressed.

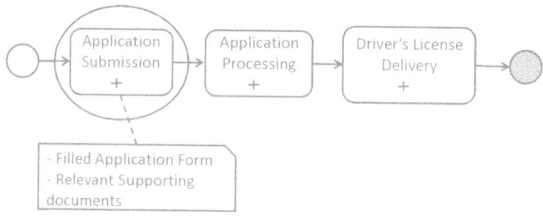

Fig. 3. A high level process published by the service designer

Let us assume that the Transport Department would like to seek ideas from citizens to improve the design of the driver's license issuance service. To align citizen interaction with the core components of the existing design, the designer decomposes it into sub-processes, namely, Application Submission, Application Processing and Driver's License Delivery. Figure 3 shows these subprocesses.

For the purposes of illustration, let us focus on the Application Submission sub-process. As shown in Figure 4, the designer has also provided a high-level subprocess for Application Submission along with the following constraints.

1. The citizen must apply for the Driver's License in person by visiting the RTO office.
2. A set of supporting documents is needed along with the application.
3. If the application and the supporting documents are not valid, the application for license will be rejected.

The contributors create variants of the detailed process from scratch or by modifying variants submitted by others. As shown in Figure 5 the first crowdsourced variant (Variant 1) for the Application Submission sub-process focuses on removing the citizens' pain point of waiting in a long queue before applying for a driver's license. Additional steps are added, without violating the constraints, to take an online appointment before submitting the application in order to avoid the wait.

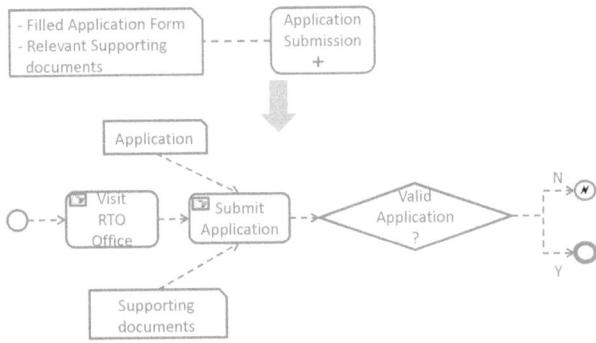

Fig. 4. An elaboration of the the application submission sub-process

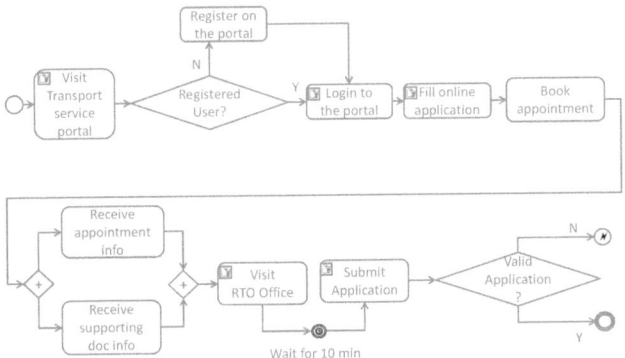

Fig. 5. Variant 1: An online portal is used to make appointments

Next, as shown in Figure 6, a citizen modifies Variant 1 to remove online booking and replaces it with a phone booking. However, just replacing the mode of appointment is not sufficient. With the phone booking, additional tasks are added where citizen receive an SMS reminder for the booked appointment. Also since the application form is no more filled online, the citizen has to fetch the form and fill it manually. The newly created variant (Variant 2) with the phone appointments is shown in Figure 7.

The Variant Generator identifies that the addition of an SMS reminder is compatible with Variant 1, since the prerequisite for receiving an SMS reminder is a booked appointment, which also exists in Variant 1. Hence the Variant Generator creates a new variant (Variant 3) merging Variant 1 and Variant 2, as shown in Figure 8. However, other modifications such as requesting and filling application form in RTO office are not compatible with the Variant 1 and hence does not lead to new variants.

Another citizen prefers to simply visit the RTO office without appointments. Hence, she changes Variant 2 with manual submission of the application as shown in Figure 9. These changes result in the creation of a new variant (Variant 4) as shown in Figure 10.

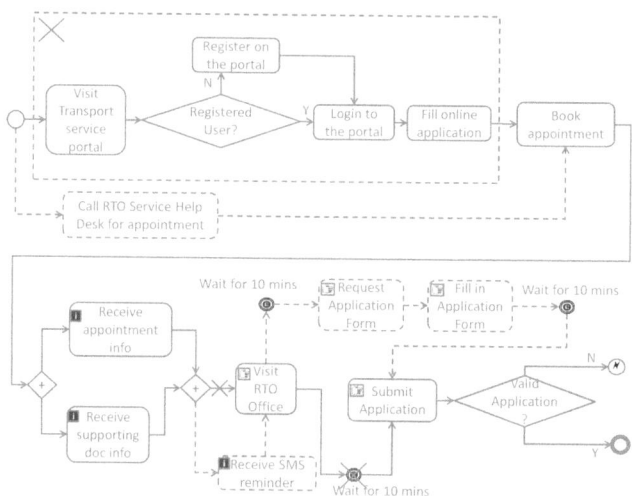

Fig. 6. Changes to Figure 5 to make appointments over phone

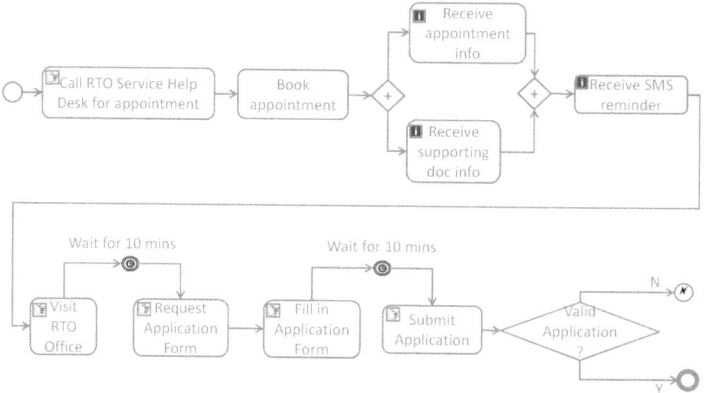

Fig. 7. Variant 2: Service help desk is used to make appointments over phone

Once these four variants are arrived at, the Variant Comparator compares these variants based on certain criteria set by the service designer such as cost, time, convenience, transparency, and susceptibility to corruption. Variants 2 and 3 provide the maximum information back to the citizen and maybe rated higher on transparency than other variants. Variant 3 on the other hand is the least time consuming and Variant 4 is completely manual, hence more prone to corruption. Variant 3 may be perceived as the most suitable one, but the service designer may also choose to retain Variant 2 as an option for citizens who do not have access to the internet for online booking. Additionally the crowd can also vote for their favorite variant. Once the new design is finalized, all the

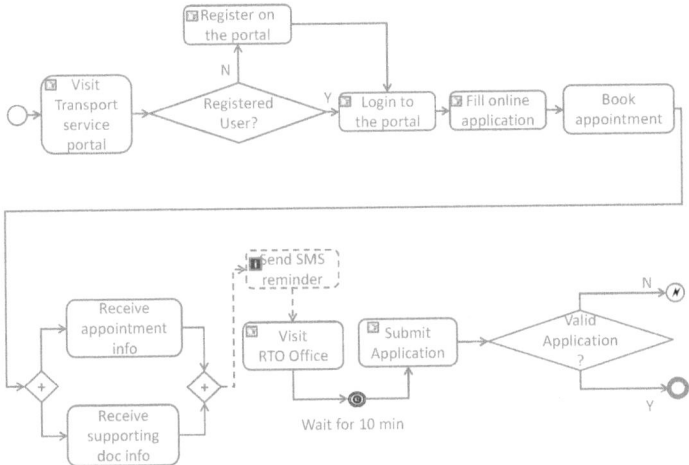

Fig. 8. Variant 3: Variant 2 improved with SMS reminder step suggested in Figure 6

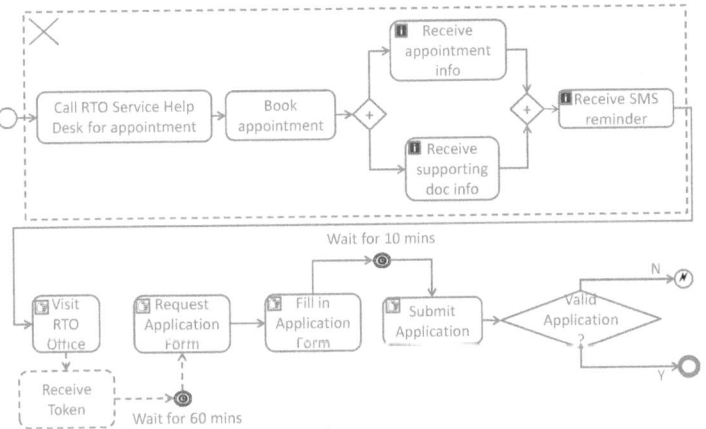

Fig. 9. Changes to Figure 7 to visit without appointments

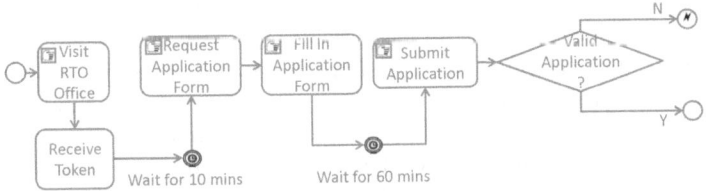

Fig. 10. Variant 4: Visit RTO office without application

contributors to the design are identified and rewarded appropriately, based on the relative merits of their contributions, as determined by the Incentive Computer.

5   Research Challenges

Given the exposition in the previous section, we summarize the broader research challenges that arise as well as hint at the techniques that may help address them.

Representing goals and constraints. The challenge is in capturing what the service designer considers as the high-level purpose of the service. To aid the automatic analysis of the variants, a formal specification of such goals is a necessity. Although the goal-based or commitment-based modeling techniques such as Tropos [3] and Amoeba [4] may come in handy, it is not clear how without a common vocabulary, the crowd and the designer would agree on the semantics of such goals and constraints. Relying on the crowd to manage the vocabulary as the contributions flow in may be a natural solution and needs to be studied.

Representing criteria for evaluation. The challenge here is in defining rules for ranking the variants. This is nontrivial because the criteria may conflict with each other, e.g., cost of the service and the comfort for the citizens. Further, the criteria should be such that the service designs would support evaluation of the chosen criteria, e.g., comfort level afforded by a variant. While multi-objective optimization is not new, some of the important criteria such as satisfaction and comfort are not easy to evaluate. A possible way forward maybe to combine a voting-based evaluation of such "soft" criteria with an automatic evaluation of the machine-friendly criteria such as the average time taken to deliver driver's licenses. Are there generalized rules of thumb that can help us compare variants without dependeing on the crowd for voting?

Representing service designs. Apart from the challenge of having a common vocabulary for a formal representation, we need to enable attribution of the contributed elements of service designs to the contributors. For example, for the single purpose of allowing phone appointments, several changes had to be made in Figure 7. While the newly added elements can be attributed to this contributor, many of the additions are entailed due to the basic purpose and are not novelties in themselves, e.g., having to request an application form now that no application was submitted online. How do we differentiate novel additions from additions required by the novelties?

Generating variants. How shall the variant generator create new variants that combine compatible features from multiple variants? Although service composition has received a lot of attention [9], the challenge here is in the scale of the state space of all possible variants that a typical planner or reasoner would have to deal with. A way forward is to develop a dominance relation between variants so that new variants need to be generated only from the set of variants that is not dominated by any other variant in the set. Such a relation should ideally be based on the criteria of evaluation. However, some of the important criteria are evaluated only by votes from the crowd. Are there other effective ways of pruning the state space?

Incentivizing contributors. How shall we assign credit to the contributors? And what structure of incentives would make this an individually rational mechanism so that participating in it derives a greater utility for the contributors than skipping? Although mechanism design has been an active area with many significant results on mechanisms with individual rationality [10], the core prolem here is in assigning credit for the novelties contributed by a contributor. Naturally, the basis for assigning credit should be the value of the contributed variants. What would be the loss in value had this contributor not participated? Answering this question is nontrivial because the contributors build on top of each others' ideas in an iterative manner and new models of computing long term values may be needed.

6   Related Work

Recent years have seen a spike in interest in collaborative approaches to solving knowledge-oriented problems. Brabhan discusses many case studies of successful crowdsourcing in problem solving [1]. Notable examples include highly technical and scientific problems solved through wisdoms of crowd.

Participatory design is an established approach to design, that actively involves all stakeholders in the design process. Though the term has been used in a variety of fields, it is relatively new in service design [11]. Hartman *et al.* propose an early approach to participatory service designs [5]. However, this work either limits the participation of contributors to specific stages of design or is incapable of scaling when the number of contributors grows large. COCKPIT (Citizens Collaboration and Co-creation in Public Service Delivery) [5] is one such method where governments seek citizens' deliberation in service design and decision making. The methodology limits citizens' participation to voting their preferred design amongst the existing ones identified by the service designer. This technique does not allow citizens to freely specify their preferred way of experiencing the service. Unlike our approach it suffers from lack of true collaboration and co-creation of service value between the government and the citizen.

As demonstrated by Brabhan crowdsourcing is an appropriate model for citizen engagement in public administration, many governments are soliciting citizens' involvement in collectively solving problems at a city, state or national level [2]. With our approach the wisdoms of a crowd can be effectively tapped and utilized. Another more collaborative approach to crowd source workflow designs is displayed by Turkomatic [7,8] Turkomatic is a tool that recruits crowd workers (a.k.a. *turkers*) to aid requesters in planning and solving complex jobs, with the aim of identifying the best split of a complex knowledge task, e.g., writing an essay. The purpose here to ensure that the division of a complex problem into sub-problems aids the workers in solving the sub-problems effectively. Turkomatic's continuous price-divide-solve loop approach that asks workers to recursively divide complex steps into simpler ones, solve them, and later merge them, though is a truly collaborative, unlike our approach is not scalable. This is done with some manual moderation from the task requester to ensure quality of a split and a merge. James Surowiecki examines several cases of crowd wisdom at work, where he states that the wisdom of crowds in not derived from averaging solutions rather from aggregating them [14]. In our approach, we reconfirm the same by showing that the best solution need not necessarily be suggested by one contributor but by smartly aggregating solutions from different contributors in the crowd.

7   Conclusions

In this paper, we have introduced the problem of crowdsourcing service designs, which will enable true participatory design of services taking into account the needs and interests of both providers and consumers of a service. We have identified the challenges involved, and then proposed a high-level framework to address the same. The novelty of the framework lies in combining the richness of crowd participation with the technical rigor afforded by formal reasoning and analysis of service design models. The approach was illustrated through a case study involving a driver's license issuance service. We also discussed the research challenges that need to be addressed to realize the approach. These challenges will also guide our future work on this topic.

References

1. Brabham, D.: Crowdsourcing as a model for problem solving an introduction and cases. Convergence: The International Journal of Research into New Media Technologies 14(1), 75–90 (2008)
2. Brabham, D.: Crowdsourcing the public participation process for planning projects. Planning Theory 8(3), 242–262 (2009)
3. Bresciani, P., Perini, A., Giorgini, P., Guinchiglia, F., Mylopolous, J.: Tropos: An agent-oriented software development methodology. Autonomous Agents and Multi-Agent Systems 8(3), 203–236 (2004)
4. Desai, N., Chopra, A., Singh, M.: Amoeba: A methodology for modeling and evolving cross-organizational business processes. ACM Transactions on Software Engineering and Methodology (TOSEM) 19(2), 1–45 (2009)
5. Hartman, A., Jain, A.N., Ramanathan, J., Ramfos, A., Van der Heuvel, W.-J., Zirpins, C., Tai, S., Charalabidis, Y., Pasic, A., Johannessen, T., Grønsund, T.: Participatory Design of Public Sector Services. In: Andersen, K.N., Francesconi, E., Grönlund, Å., van Engers, T.M. (eds.) EGOVIS 2010. LNCS, vol. 6267, pp. 219–233. Springer, Heidelberg (2010)
6. Howe, J.: The rise of crowdsourcing. Wired Magazine 14(6), 1–4 (2006)
7. Kulkarni, A., Can, M., Hartmann, B., et al.: Collaboratively crowdsourcing workflows with turkomatic. In: Proc. CSCW (2012)
8. Kulkarni, A.P., Can, M., Hartmann, B.: Turkomatic: automatic recursive task and workflow design for mechanical turk. In: Proceedings of the Human Factors in Computing Systems, pp. 2053–2058 (2011)
9. Rao, J., Su, X.: A Survey of Automated Web Service Composition Methods. In: Cardoso, J., Sheth, A.P. (eds.) SWSWPC 2004. LNCS, vol. 3387, pp. 43–54. Springer, Heidelberg (2005)
10. Saijo, T.: Incentive compatibility and individual rationality in public good economies. Journal of Economic Theory 55(1), 203–212 (1991)
11. Sangiorgi, D., Clark, B.: Toward a participatory design approach to service design. In: Participatory Design Conference, pp. 148–151 (2004)
12. Singh, M.: Self-renewing applications. IEEE Internet Computing 15(4), 3–5 (2011)
13. Spohrer, J., Maglio, P., Bailey, J., Gruhl, D.: Steps toward a science of service systems. Computer 40(1), 71–77 (2007)
14. Surowiecki, J.: The wisdom of crowds. Anchor (2005)

Towards an Architectural Framework
for Service-Oriented Enterprises

Nanjangud C. Narendra[1], Lam-Son Lê[2], Aditya K. Ghose[2], and Gandhi Sivakumar[3]

[1] IBM India Software Lab, Bangalore, India
narendra@in.ibm.com
[2] University of Wollongong, Wollongong, Australia
{lelamson,aditya.ghose}@gmail.com
[3] IBM Australia
gandhis@au1.ibm.com

Abstract. Business enterprises today are increasingly being modeled as *service-oriented enterprises (SOEs)*. That is, they are increasingly part of collaborations with other enterprises, with such collaborations being fulfilled by the exchange of business services among the participants. To that end, there is now a felt need for developing formal models of such collaborations, by leveraging past work on Enterprise Architecture (EA) models. In this paper, we present an architectural framework for modeling such collaborations as *virtual enterprises (VEs)*, since these collaborations involve interactions among multiple enterprises. Our framework is modeled by treating the VE as an enterprise itself, but with special characteristics that distinguish it from regular enterprises, viz., nature of collaborations among the participating enterprises, extent of their participation, and conflicts among the participants. The latter characteristic arises due to the autonomy of the participants and the dynamic nature of inter-organizational business interactions, and is especially crucial for VE modeling. Throughout the paper, we illustrate our architectural framework with a realistic running example. We also present and discuss some future challenges regarding modeling dynamic behavior in the VE, in particular, conflict modeling & resolution among the participating enterprises.

Keywords: service-oriented enterprise, enterprise architecture, virtual enterprises, architectural framework.

1 Introduction

Most business enterprises are now being modeled according to the principles of service-oriented computing [1] for the purposes of improving efficiency, agility and response to changing market needs. One of the key aspects of service-oriented computing is the integration of several enterpises into an entity called *virtual enterprise (VE)*. A VE possesses the following characteristics: (i) it is formed for a specific service-oriented process execution (could be short-lived or long term), and may dissolve once that process execution is done; (ii) its models are dependent on the *nature* of the interactions among the participating enterprises; (iii) it is typically formed via a joint alignment of strategies among the participating enterprises; and (iv) since the participating enterprises are autonomous, conflicts could arise among them.

A. Ghose et al. (Eds.): ICSOC 2012, LNCS 7759, pp. 215–227, 2013.

Traditionally, business enterprises have been modeled using enterprise architecture (EA) models. Several EA modeling frameworks have been developed; e.g., CIMOSA [2], TOGAF[1], Zachman [3] in industry; Archimate[2], SEAM[3] in academia; and international standards such as RM-ODP[4]. EA captures the whole vision of an enterprise in various aspects regarding both business and information technology (IT) resources. In EA, the goal is to align the business resources and IT resources in order to improve the competitiveness of the enterprise. EA is a discipline that analyzes the services offered by an enterprise and its partners to the customer, the services offered by the enterprise to its partners and the organization of the enterprise itself and of its IT.

However, most EA frameworks model only single enterprises and do not consider VEs. From our viewpoint, this makes them unsuitable for conceptual modeling of service-oriented enterprises. Hence in this paper we address this lacuna by presenting an architectural framework for VEs. However, as stated above, the behavior of a VE is critically dependent on the *interactions* between its participating enterprises (also referred to interchangeably throughout the rest of this paper as "entities"). Hence our VE model is based on the interaction types, which we refer to in this paper as *collaboration patterns*. We define four types of collaboration patterns, ranging from loosely coupled enterprises that can retain their autonomy, to subcontract-style collaboration where the subcontractor allows itself to be placed under the control of the prime contractor for the duration of the collaboration. To the best of our knowledge, this is the first attempt to develop an integrated model for a VE, with emphasis on modeling the collaboration patterns themselves as first-class objects in the model.

For our model, we adopt the 3-layer approach that consists of the *strategy* layer, the *operational* layer and the *service* layer [4, 5]. The strategy layer models the goals and business rules that define the behavior of the VE and its participants; the operational layer defines the business services [6] that are an abstraction of the actual process and service implementations that form the service layer. The unique feature of our approach is the usage of *(business) artifacts* [7] to model process implementations at the service layer. We use artifacts to model both the actual operation of the VE (collaboration artifacts) and the process executions of each participating entity (entity artifacts). We have incorporated artifact-based modeling in our approach, since this approach provides a convenient abstraction for translating business service models to lower-level IT service implementations. Moreover, since their dynamic behavior can be specified formally via communicating state machines, it is also possible to reason about them and perform formal verification before they are then translated to IT service implementations. Additionally, since IT service implementations are typically too low-level for business managers and analysts to monitor and track progress, artifacts can be used instead. The communicating state machine property of artifacts also renders them amenable to be used to model the collaboration artifact and the associated entity artifacts, and the interactions thereof, in a manner similar to that described in our earlier work [8].

---

[1] http://www.togaf.info/

[2] http://www3.opengroup.org/subjectareas/enterprise/archimate

[3] http://www.seam.ch/

[4] http://www.rm-odp.net/

This paper is organized as follows. Section 2 introduces our running example. Our virtual enterprise architecture models are explained in Section 3. Related work is discussed in Section 4. Finally, we present concluding remarks and suggestions for future work in Section 5.

2   Running Example

We model the VE as per the 3-layered approach as described in [4, 5]. The topmost layer is the Strategy layer, and it represents the following: businesss goals that the VE must fulfill, and policies and business rules of the VE and its participating entities that need to be taken into account while fulfilling the goals. The next lower layer is the Operational layer, which represents the Business Services [6] that each partner offers, and also describes how they are integrated to provide the overall functionality needed to fulfill the business goals specified at the Strategy layer. The actual operations executed and data exchanged are represented at the bottom layer, i.e., Service layer, which is the IT realization of the abstract concepts in the upper two layers.

For our running example we model a car manufacturer $CarMan$ with three partners. $SupSt$ and $SupTy$ are suppliers of steering wheels and tyres, respectively, while $Ship$ is a shipper who transports the completed cars. Together these entities form a (part of a) VE for manufacturing and selling cars. The relationship between $CarMan$ and its partners varies depending on the type of partner.

At the Strategy layer, the common goals of our VE would be "Manufacture Car" and "Ship Manufactured Car", which would also be the goals for $CarMan$. For $SupSt$, its goals could be "Manufacture Steering Wheel" and "Deliver Steering Wheel". For $SupTy$, its goals could be "Manufacture Tyres" and "Deliver Tyres". In order for the VE to be successful, those goals of each participating entity that pertain to the VE should be derivable from the common goals of the VE.

For $CarMan$ one of its business rules could be R1 = "If order amount for any shipment is greater than $1 million, choose lowest cost shipper; else choose $Ship$", whereas a business rule for $SupSt$ could be R2 = "Choose $Ship$ for all shipments". A business rule for $SupTy$ could be R3 = "If order amount between $100,000 and $250,000, choose Ship; else choose the lowest cost shipper". Clearly, these business rules could result in conflicts. For example, for order amounts exceeding $1 million, a conflict between $CarMan$ and $SupSt$ could arise. Whereas, for order amounts between $250,000 and $1 million, a conflict between $CarMan$ and $SupTy$ could arise. This would be handled by specifying consistency rules among the goals of the VE and the participating entities, so as to eliminate conflicts.

The above business goals are then mapped to the appropriate business services at the Operational layer. Some business services for $CarMan$ could be "Car Manufacturing" and "Car Shipment", and would be directly derivable from the common goals. For $SupSt$, some of its business services could be "Steering Wheel Manufacturing", "Steering Wheel Testing" and "Steering Wheel Shipment". While the former two would be directly derivable from the goals of $SupSt$, the third business service would need to be directly linked to "Ship Manufactured Car" goal. This is because delivery of steering wheels is a necessary condition for shipping the finished product, i.e., the car.

It is to be noted that conflicts at the Strategic layer would directly impact the Operational layer also. For example, from the viewpoint of $SupSt$, its "Steering Wheel Shipment" business service would be affected by its policy of choosing $Ship$ for all shipments, and this may need to be redesigned in case of a conflict with $CarMan$. This would also have to be handled via the consistency rules introduced above.

At the Service layer, the (more abstract) business services are mapped onto the (more concrete) IT realizations. We subdivide this layer into two sub-layers, with the top sub-layer being modeled via business artifacts, which are an abstraction of the following: the data exchanged among the participating entities and the operations that they execute in order to fulfill the business goals of the VE. The bottom sub-layer comprises the actual IT services and business processes through which the implementation of the business services takes place. For our running example, some artifacts are `CarAssembly`, `CarShipment`, `SteeringWheelManufacture`.

Our running example raises several interesting research questions. First, we need to investigate what the overall metamodel of the VE and its participating entities should be, with emphasis on the interactions among them. Second, we need to specify the goals, business rules and consistency rules in a manner that enables easy analysis and reasoning. Third, at the Operational and Service layers, we need to investigate how business services [6] should be represented so as to facilitate easy derivation of (collaboration & entity) artifacts and IT service implementations. These research questions will form the focus of the rest of our paper.

3   Models

In this Section we present the key contribution of our paper, i.e., metamodel for VEs. But first we define what we mean by business strategy and business goals. Business strategy is generally regarded as a high-level *plan* specified to achieve an objective. We follow the taxonomy proposed in the KAOS methodology [9] to categorize business goals[5] into: *achieve* (an organization seeks to achieve a condition at some point of time in the future), *cease* (seeks to undo a condition at some point of time in the future), *maintain* (strikes to maintain a condition for a period of time), *avoid* (prevents a condition from becoming true for a period of time) and *optimize* (usually articulated in the form of *maximization* or *minimization*). In our running example, for simplicity, we have restricted business goals to those conditions that are to be *achieve*d, and we will be using the running example to illustrate our metamodel throughout the rest of this section. However, our metamodel would be able to cater to the other goal types also.

Our metamodel definition for VEs will therefore be driven by the overall business strategy of the VE, along with how it impinges on those of the participating enterprises. Also, as already stated earlier in our paper, the VE metamodel will be based on the interactions among the participating enterprises as derived from their business strategies.

---

[5] Goal-oriented modeling in the literature [10] includes both business goals and system goals. As we do business strategy modeling, we address only business goals.

3.1   Collaboration Patterns

We model the interactions among the participating service-oriented enterprises as *collaboration patterns* [11], defined in increasing order of coupling among the enterprises as follows:

- *CP1: Informal Joint Venture*: In this collaboration, a set of enterprises get together on a relatively ad-hoc basis, for a limited period of time, driven by a common business goal. In such a collaboration, each participating entity would have its own business services and derived business processes, but without revealing any internals of their business processes. Hence the entire collaboration would be implemented via exchanges of messages based on a commonly agreed protocol. Conflict resolution in such a collaboration is accomplished primarily via negotiations.

   For example, $CarMan$ could have a short-lived adhoc arrangement with $SupTy$ for the immediate purchase & delivery of a batch of car tyres, and this would be a collaboration of type CP1. The possible conflict in business rules between $CarMan$ and $SupTy$ as described in Section 2 would have to be negotiated among the partners.

- *CP2: Association*: In this collaboration, the participating enterprises agree on a common set of business processes that each enterprise has to comply with. This may necessitate them exposing parts of their internal business processes & operations. Bound as they are together with the common business processes, the participating enterprises' negotiating positions during conflict resolution get constricted. In other words, they would experience a lower degree of freedom as opposed to participation in a CP1-type pattern.

   For example, in the collaboration between $CarMan$ and $SupTy$, if it were of type CP2, then $SupTy$ would be bound by a delivery arrangement, and in any conflict with $CarMan$, such as the one described in Section 2, the onus would be on $SupTy$ to ensure conflict resolution.

- *CP3: Formal Joint Venture*: Moving further onto increased coupling among the participants, this collaboration pattern externalizes all the business rules and constraints on each participant, and makes them part of the overall collaboration. (In the earlier two collaboration types, the rules and constraints governing the actions of each participant are not made public, since many participants may consider them confidential information.) In such a pattern, the VE as a whole dictates conflict resolution.

   For example, in the collaboration between $CarMan$ and $SupTy$, $CarMan$ would dictate how conflict resolution, if any, were to be implemented, since $SupTy$'s business rules would become visible to it.

- *CP4: Subcontract*: This collaboration pattern is the most formal and binding of all; here, one participant - the contractor - controls all the business processes to be executed, as well as the business rules and constraints affecting the participants in the collaboration. Conflicts betwen the contractor and its subcontractors are resolved in favor of the contractor; whereas, conflicts among subcontractors are resolved by the contractor as per preference rankings among the business rules.

   For example, in the collaboration between $CarMan$ and $SupTy$, the latter would become $CarMan$'s subcontractor, hence even its business rules would be under $CarMan$'s control. Similarly, any conflict beween $SupSt$ and $SupTy$, e.g, a scheduling conflict regarding integrated supply of tyres and steering wheels, would also be resolved by $CarMan$.

3.2 Metamodel

Fig. 1 presents our metamodel for VEs. We model the VEs from two different perspectives: collaboration-centric and entity-centric (Subsections 3.3 and 3.4, respectively). In this figure, the metamodel constructs are presented at the three layers, namely the strategy layer, operational layer and service layer (in this order from the top down to the bottom of Fig. 1). A *collaboration* occurs as per a *collaboration pattern*, introduced above. Each collaboration has a *goal*, which is realized by a *plan*, which is a set of steps to achieve the goal. Each plan can be realized via a *schedule*, which is a sequence of *business service* executions in a particular order. Each plan can be realized by more than one schedule. Each business service is defined via its *inputs, outputs, preconditions and postconditions*, which are in turn derived from the attributes of the plan and schedule.

3.3 Service- and Collaboration-Centric Modeling

As depicted in Fig. 1, we model the VE itself – as stated earlier, this model will be based on the nature of the collaborations – and ensuing interactions thereof, that comprise the VE. The entity-centric conceptual model will be presented in Section 3.4.

At the service layer, the business service is finally realized by a *collaboration artifact* [8], which models the business service executions. This artifact represents the execution of the business services involved in the collaboration, and consists of a lifecycle composed of *states*. Each state has *incoming and outgoing transitions*, each of which are implemented by *IT services*. Each IT service is modeled via its own *inputs, outputs, preconditions and postconditions*, which are derived from the conditions governing the incoming and outgoing transitions.

Formally, we represent a collaboration $Coll = \langle\{E_i\}, \{P_j\}, G, \{R_k\}\rangle$, where E_i is a participating enterprise, P_j is a collaboration pattern, G is the goal of the collaboration expressed as a boolean condition to be achieved (as described above), and R_k is a business rule that constrains the dynamic behavior of the collaboration. (Our definition of business rules also includes business compliance requirements [12] that typically apply to all participating entities.) The collaboration pattern P_j is defined as $P_j = \langle\{E_j\}, CP_k\rangle$, where E_j are the participating enterprises in the collaboration pattern and CP_k is the collaboration pattern type as introduced earlier.

We define the goal G of the collaboration as a boolean condition to be achieved. Without loss of generality, we represent G in CNF as $G = G_1 \wedge G_2 \wedge ... \wedge G_n$, where the G_i are sub-goals, typically assigned to the participating enterprises. In other words, the overall goal of the collaboration should be consistent with the goals of the participating enterprises. We express a business rule R_k also as a boolean condition that should be satisfied in addition to the goal. An example of the goal for the VE would be $Car\_Delivered = Car\_Components\_Received \wedge Car\_Manufactured \wedge Car\_Shipped$.

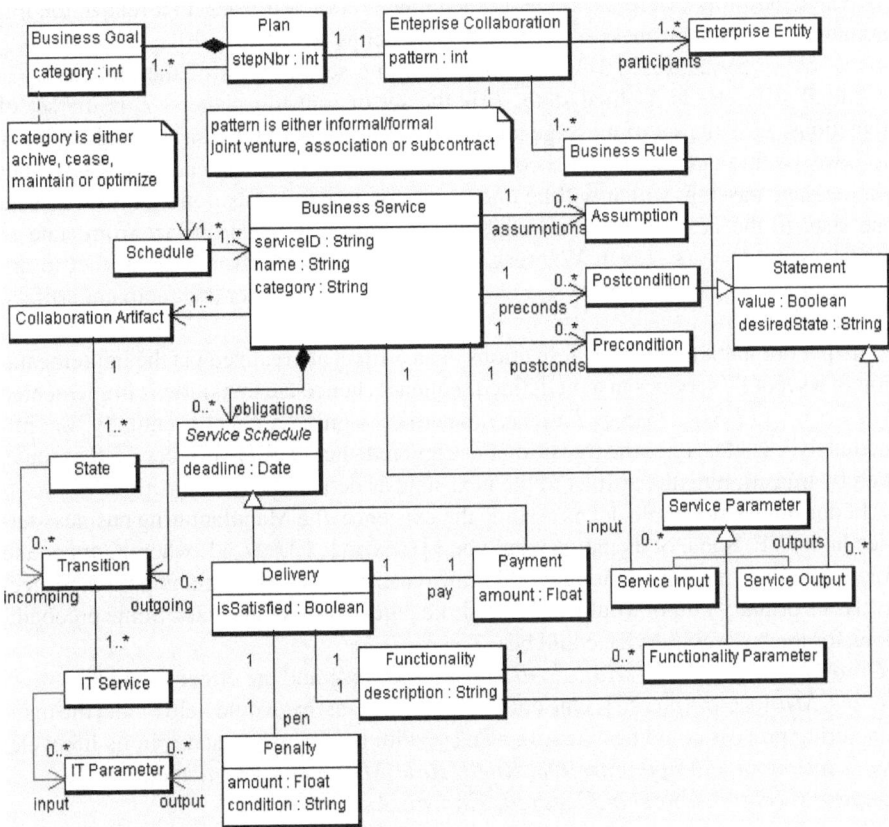

Fig. 1. Virtual Enterprise Architecture Model

Since the Plan is derived from the Goal, we define it as $Plan = \langle G, \{R_k\}, Sch \rangle$, where Sch is the Schedule, defined as $Sch = (\{Pref_j \langle B_i, B_j, rel \rangle\})$. Here, B_i stands for a business service, and rel denotes either "immediately" (IMM) or "eventually" (EVE). That means the schedule defines a set of ordering preferences $Pref_j$ on the execution of the business services to fulfill the Plan. The R_k refer to the business rules that constrain the ordering and execution of the business services while fulfilling the goal.

An example of a business rule for the VE could be the rule R1 described in Section 2; this constrains the VE to select a particular type of shipper to deliver the manufactured cars. This in turn constrains the plan and schedule to be designed; for example, if a Shipping business service were to be invoked, then rule R1 may force the VE to ensure that shipment of all cars occurs at the end of the schedule, instead of shipping the cars as and when they are manufactured.

We define a business service [6] as $B_i = \langle I, O, P, E, \{A_i\} \rangle$, where I is the set of inputs, O is the set of outputs, P is the set of preconditions (expressed as a conjunction of boolean conditions) and E is the set of effects (also expressed as a conjunction of

boolean conditions). Here, A_i refers to the collaboration artifact(s) that realize the implementation of the business service. Hence we define A_i as
$A_i = \langle S, s_0, S_f, L, T, L', M \rangle$ [8], where S is the set of states of the artifact, s_0 is its initial state, S_f is its final state, L is the set of transition labels, T is the set of transitions, L' is the set of message labels, and M is the set of messages. In this definition, we assume that the modeled collaboration artifacts communicate with each other via message passing, which will be one of the triggers for transitioning artifacts from one state to the next. Hence we define a state transition in an artifact from state s_i to state s_j as $t = \langle s_i, l, s_j \rangle$. Whereas, we define a message from one artifact to another as $m = \langle s_i, l', s_j \rangle$, where s_i and s_j are states in the sender and recipient artifact, respectively.

As per our metamodel, state transitions in an artifact are realized via the implementation of a set of IT services in a predefined sequence; hence the transition is implemented by $ITS = \langle \{ITS_i\}, \langle ITS_i, ITS_j, rel \rangle$, where rel signifies either "eventually" or "immediately". That is, once the transition t is triggered, the set of IT services ITS execute, thereby transitioning the artifact to the next state as defined by the transition.

In our running example, let us assume the existence of a Manufacturing business service in the VE. Some of its inputs would be $\{\{Comp_j\}, \{Matl_k\}\}$, where $Comp_j$ and $Matl_k$ are the car components and other raw materials needed for manufacture, respectively. Its primary output would be $\{Car_i\}$, i.e., the manufactured cars. Some preconditions for the business service could be
$\{Components\_received, Raw\_Materials\_received\}$ and the effect would be
$\{Cars\_Manu\_Completed\}$. One collaboration artifact that would help model the manufacturing process could be `CarAssembly`, with the following states in its lifecycle:
$Not\_Activated, Components\_Obtained, Raw\_Materials\_Obtained,$
$Engine\_Created, Chassis\_Created, Engine\_Assembled,$
$Other\_Components\_Assembled, Car\_Tested, Car\_Manufacture\_Completed.$ An example of a transition between states could be $\langle Other\_Components\_Assembled, l_t,$
$Car\_Tested \rangle$, which signifies that `CarAssembly` has transitioned (with the label l_t) from the state where all components have been assembled to the state where the car has been fully tested before it is declared ready for shipment. An illustration of message passing between artifacts is provided in Section 3.4, once the entity metamodel is introduced.

3.4 Entity-Centric Modeling

Each participating enterprise or entity could be part of one or more collaboration patterns with different other entities, even within the same collaboration. This entity also has its own *goal*, realized by a *plan*. Ideally, it is expected that the entity goal should not conflict with that of the collaboration depicted in Fig. 1. This plan is realized by an *entity schedule*. The entity schedule is then realized at the operational layer by the *business services* of the entity. Similar to Fig. 1, each business service is realized by one or more *entity artifacts*, with their respective lifecycles, states, transitions and IT service realizations.

Formally, we define a business enterprise as $E_i = \langle G_i, \{P_j\}, \{R'_k\} \rangle$, where G_i is the goal of E_i, P_j denotes the collaboration patterns of which E_i is a part, and R'_k defines the business rules constraining E_i's behavior. The goal G_i and business rules R'_k are defined in a manner similar to those of the collaboration as already introduced earlier in Section 3.3. The plan for E_i is $Plan_i = \langle G_i, \{R'_k\}, Sch_i \rangle$, where the schedule Sch_i is defined as $Sch_i = (\{< B'_i, B'_j, rel >\})$, where rel is as defined in Section 3.3, and B'_i & B'_j are the business services of the enterprise.

From our running example, for $SupSt$, its goal could be $Deliver\_Steering\_Wheel = Manufacture\_Steering \wedge Deliver\_Steering$. Its business service could be "Steering Wheel Manufacturing", while one of its business rules could be the rule R2 from Section 2. If $SupSt$ were in a CP1-type collaboration with $CarMan$, then the two enterprises would need to negotiate in case business rules R1 and R2 created a conflict. For CP2- and CP3-type collaborations, $SupSt$ would have to modify or remove R2 for conflict resolution. For a CP4-type collaboration, $SupSt$'s business rules may be invalidated by the VE, thereby preventing conflicts from arising in the first place. Again, these business services are as defined in Section 3.3, and their associated enterprise artifacts are also modeled as defined in Section 3.3.

Referring to the illustration in Section 3.3, one possible artifact for $SupSt$ could be SteeringWheelManufacture, with the following states: $Components\_Obtained$, $Raw\_Materials\_Obtained$, $SteeringWheel\_Manufactured$, $SteeringWheel\_Tested$, $SteeringWheel\_Shipped$. An example transition could be $\langle SteeringWheel\_Manufactured, l_v, SteeringWheel\_Tested \rangle$, which signifies that SteeringWheelManufacture has transitioned (with the label l_v) from the state where the steering wheel has been assembled to the state where it has been fully tested, bringing it one step closer to shipment to $CarMan$. The interaction between SteeringWheelManufacture and CarAssembly artifacts can be modeled via message sending from the former to the latter. Once the SteeringWheelManufacture artifact has reached $SteeringWheel\_Shipped$ state, the message can be sent to CarAssembly artifact, which enables the CarAssembly artifact to be instantiated.

Once all components (from other suppliers such as $SupSt$) are obtained, the CarAssembly artifact attains the $Components\_Obtained$ state. One of the triggers for this transition would be a message from SteeringWheelManufacture artifact while in state $SteeringWheel\_Shipped$, to CarAssembly artifact while it is in state $Not\_Activated$.

3.5 Consistency Rules

In order for the VE to work successfully, the dynamic behavior of the collaboration and its participating entities should be consistent. To that end, we define the following consistency rules. At the Strategy layer, the goals and business rules of the collaboration and its participating entities need to be consistent. This can be formally denoted by the following:

- $G \Rightarrow G_i, \forall i$, i.e., the goal of the collaboration should serve as the overall goal for the participating entities
- $R \wedge R'_i \not\models \bot, \forall i$, i.e., the business rules of the collaboration should not conflict with those of any of the participating entities

- *For* $P_j \ni \{E_i, E_j\}, R'_{il} \wedge R'_{kl} \not\models \perp, \forall i, j, k, l$, i.e., no two business rules from each of the participating entities, especially those that are part of a collaboration pattern, should conflict with each other

For example, rules R1 and R2 from Section 2 would be consistent with each other, but this would not be the case for R1 and R3. At the Operational layer, the following consistency rules can be defined:

- The schedules of the collaboration and that of any of the participating enterprises should not conflict. For the collaboration, let the schedule be $Sch_{Coll} = (\{Pref_j = \langle B_i, B_j, rel \rangle\})$ and the schedule of a participating enterprise be $Sch_E = (\{Pref_k = \langle B'_i, B'_j, rel \rangle\})$. Let the combined schedule be the set $Sch' = Sch_{Coll} \cup Sch_E$. Then for any two preference rules $Pref_m$ and $Pref_n$, where $Pref_m \in Sch'$ and $Pref_n \in Sch'$, the following should hold: $Sch' \wedge Sch_i \not\models \perp$.
- Let there be N business services B_i in the collaboration, with the effect of each being Eff_i. Then $Eff_1 \wedge Eff_2 \ldots \wedge Eff_N \models G$, i.e., the business services in the collaboration will entail the goal G of the collaboration.
- For any participating enterprise with goal G_i, let there be M business services B'_i with the effect of each being Eff'_i. Then, in a manner similar to that of the collaboration, $Eff'_1 \wedge Eff'_2 \ldots \wedge Eff'_M \models G_i$, i.e., the business services of the participating enterprise will entail its goal G_i.

For example, one preference rule for our running example from Section 2 could be $\langle Steering\ Wheel\ Manufacturing, Steering\ Wheel\ Shipment, IMM \rangle$ and $\langle Steering\ Wheel\ Shipment, Car\ Manufacturing, EVE \rangle$. The former rule states that steering wheeels should be shipped as soon as their manufacture is completed; the latter rule states that steering wheels are needed in order to complete the manufacture of the cars.

Similarly, at the Service layer, the following consistency rules can be defined:

- The collaboration artifact & enterprise/entity artifacts should not conflict with each other. Since each such artifact is modeled as a state machine, techniques from communicating state machine verification (such as [13]) can be used to verify that the artifacts do not conflict with each other.
- The modeled IT services for the collaboration and the participating enterprises should also be consistent with each other. The verification of this can be accomplished via techniques such as those described in [14].

3.6   Discussion - Conflicts and Conflict Resolution

One of the key advantages of developing a metamodel for VEs, is the ability to use it as a basis for reasoning about dynamic behavior. For our purposes, from the viewpoint of VE modeling, beyond the usual applications of orchestration & choreography for modeling inter-organizational inteactions [15, 16], the crucial question is of modeling conflicts and their resolution. Conflicts can be classified along three orthogonal dimensions - type, origin and impact [17]. The type of conflict would be determined by the highest layer at which they manifest; for example, a conflict in goals or business rules would manifest at the Strategy layer, whereas a conflict among interacting IT services from different participants would manifest at the Service layer. The origin of a conflict would define the participant, or one of its constructs (e.g., business service, IT service, etc.) where the conflict originated; multiple origins could exist for a single conflict. The impact of a conflict would model the side-effects of the conflict on the rest of the participants and the VE itself in general. For example, a minor scheduling conflict among two interacting entities, which can be resolved by the entities themselves, would have local impact. Whereas, a product supply conflict, that could affect the collaboration artifact of a VE, would have global impact.

As part of future work, we will be integrating our earlier work on conflict modeling in B2B applications [17] and formalizing it by incorporating it into our VE metamodel.

4   Related Work

EA Modeling Frameworks: The importance of EA modeling has given rise to several frameworks. One of the earliest was the Zachman framework [3], which provides a formal and highly structured way of viewing and defining an enterprise. It consists of a two dimensional classification matrix based on the intersection of six communication questions (What, Where, When, Why, Who and How) with six rows representing six reification criteria (scope, business, system, technology, component, operations). CIMOSA [2] is a similar EA framework, organized along three dimensions, viz., view (organization, resource, information, function), lifecycle (requirements, design, implementation) & generic (generic, partial, particular). Unlike the Zachman framework, CIMOSA provides a methodology and supporting technology. The other popular framework, TOGAF is modeled at four layers, viz., business, application, data and technology, and provides an integrated approach for designing and implementing an EA. It is to be noted, however, that none of these frameworks attempt to explicitly model VEs.

The VE model described in our paper is inspired in part by our earlier ODP-based work on enterprise modeling [18], and also on the 3-layer service architecture model described in [4, 5]. The latter model also describes how inter-organizational service interactions can be modeled at the strategic, operational and service layers. We have borrowed the layers from [4, 5], but we have redefined them with VEs in mind, i.e., with emphasis on collaboration patterns and consistency rules for conflict handling.

Virtual Enterprise Modeling: The earliest notable work in this realm was about capturing the requirements of a VE using the ODP enterprise language [19]. There exists some recent work focusing on modeling and detailing collaboration pattern types [20, 21, 11]. In those works, the authors have delineated the various ways in which an enterprise and its partners can interact, with emphasis on the various ways in which work can be outsourced from one business to another. Indeed, our idea of collaboration patterns is inspired by those works; however, those works do not consider a layered approach, nor do they model consistency rules for conflict handling. The e³ Value project[6] has also focused on inter-organizational aspects, but primarily from the viewpoint of how B2B interactions can be modeled as value exchanges. Hence we

---

[6] http://e3value.few.vu.nl/

consider e^3 Value to be complementary to our work, and our future work will investigate how it can be integrated into our VE metamodel.

Our work in this paper on conflict handling is based on our earlier work on modeling B2B conflicts in B2B interactions [17], as we have already described in Section 3.6.

Goal & Strategy-Based Business Process Modeling: In the area of goal-based business process modeling [22–26], the citation [22] showed how to model and evaluate business processes at a level of abstraction higher than the business process level. Based on that idea, our earlier work has focused on how to derive business process models from goals [27], which also leveraged the KAOS stepwise refinement approach [9]. We have leveraged this same approach in this paper, by modeling business processes as derivable from goals, via plans and schedules. Our paper also incorporates some of our ongoing work on business service modeling [6], which aims to model business services as an abstraction of IT service implementations. We have further enhanced this abstraction by incorporating our earlier work [8] on artifacts and Web services.

5   Conclusions and Future Work

In this paper, we have addressed the crucial but little-researched area of modeling service-oriented enterprises as virtual enterprises. Since the key constructs in such an enterprise are the types of collaborations among the participating enterprises, we have presented and detailed a metamodel for VEs where these types are modeled upfront as first-class objects. We have also positioned this within a 3-layer framework comprising Strategy, Operational and Service layers, with interactions among the participating enterprises modeled at all these three layers. We have also formally defined consistency rules that are needed in order to ensure that the VE can function without conflicts among the (relatively autonomous) participating enterprises. To the best of our knowledge, this is the first attempt at developing a formal metamodel for VEs.

Future work will include incorporating conflict resolution in our metamodel via techniques such as those presented in [28, 17], and developing a prototype implementation to evaluate and refine our metamodel.

References

1. Huhns, M.N., Singh, M.P.: Service-oriented computing: Key concepts and principles. IEEE Internet Computing 9(1), 75–81 (2005)
2. Cuenca, L., Ortiz, A., Vernadat, F.: From uml or dfd models to cimosa partial models and enterprise components. Int. J. Computer Integrated Manufacturing 19(3), 248–263 (2006)
3. Zachman, J.A.: The information systems management system: A framework for planning. DATA BASE 9(3), 8–13 (1978)
4. Orriens, B., Yang, J., Papazoglou, M.P.: A Rule Driven Approach for Developing Adaptive Service Oriented Business Collaboration. In: Benatallah, B., Casati, F., Traverso, P. (eds.) ICSOC 2005. LNCS, vol. 3826, pp. 61–72. Springer, Heidelberg (2005)
5. Orriens, B., Yang, J.: A rule driven approach for developing adaptive service oriented business collaboration. In: IEEE SCC, pp. 182–189 (2006)
6. Lê, L.-S., Ghose, A., Morrison, E.: Definition of a Description Language for Business Service Decomposition. In: Morin, J.-H., Ralyté, J., Snene, M. (eds.) IESS 2010. LNBIP, vol. 53, pp. 96–110. Springer, Heidelberg (2010)
7. Nigam, A., Caswell, N.S.: Business artifacts: An approach to operational specification. IBM Syst. J. 42, 428–445 (2003)

8. Narendra, N.C., Badr, Y., Thiran, P., Maamar, Z.: Towards a unified approach for business process modeling using context-based artifacts and web services. In: IEEE SCC, pp. 332–339 (2009)

9. Dardenne, A., van Lamsweerde, A., Fickas, S.: Goal-directed requirements acquisition. Journal of Science of Computer Programming 20(1-2), 3–50 (1993)

10. Mylopoulos, J., Chung, L., Yu, E.S.K.: From object-oriented to goal-oriented requirements analysis. Commun. ACM 42(1), 31–37 (1999)

11. Norta, A., Grefen, P.W.P.J.: Discovering patterns for inter-organizational business process collaboration. Int. J. Cooperative Inf. Syst. 16(3/4), 507–544 (2007)

12. Governatori, G., Milosevic, Z., Sadiq, S.W.: Compliance checking between business processes and business contracts. In: EDOC, pp. 221–232 (2006)

13. Peng, W., Purushothaman, S.: Data flow analysis of communicating finite state machines. ACM Trans. Program. Lang. Syst. 13(3), 399–442 (1991)

14. Benatallah, B., Casati, F., Toumani, F.: Representing, analysing and managing web service protocols. Data Knowl. Eng. 58(3), 327–357 (2006)

15. Barros, A., Decker, G., Dumas, M., Weber, F.: Correlation Patterns in Service-Oriented Architectures. In: Dwyer, M.B., Lopes, A. (eds.) FASE 2007. LNCS, vol. 4422, pp. 245–259. Springer, Heidelberg (2007)

16. McIlvenna, S., Dumas, M., Wynn, M.T.: Synthesis of orchestrators from service choreographies. In: APCCM, pp. 129–138 (2009)

17. Maamar, Z., Thiran, P., Narendra, N.C., Subramanian, S.: A framework for modeling b2b applications. In: AINA, pp. 12–19 (2008)

18. Lê, L.-S., Wegmann, A.: Hierarchy-oriented modeling of enterprise architecture using reference-model of open distributed processing. Special Issue on RM-ODP, Computer Standards & Interfaces Journal (February 2012)

19. Oldevik, J., Aagedal, J.: ODP-Modelling of Virtual Enterprises with Supporting Engineering Architecture. In: Proceedings of 3rd EDOC, pp. 172–182. IEEE Computer Society (September 1999)

20. Grefen, P.W.P.J.: Towards dynamic interorganizational business process management. In: WETICE, pp. 13–20 (2006)

21. Norta, A., Grefen, P.W.P.J.: A framework for specifying sourcing collaborations. In: ECIS, pp. 626–638 (2006)

22. Kueng, P., Kawalek, P.: Goal-based business process models: Creation and evaluation. Business Process Management Journal 3, 17–38 (1997)

23. Cardoso, E., Almeida, J., Guizzardi, R.: On the support for the goal domain in enterprise modelling approaches. In: 2010 14th IEEE International Enterprise Distributed Object Computing Conference Workshops (EDOCW), pp. 335–344 (October 2010)

24. Xu, T., Ma, W., Liu, L., Karagiannis, D.: Synthesizing enterprise strategic model and business processes in active-i*. In: 2010 14th IEEE International Enterprise Distributed Object Computing Conference Workshops (EDOCW), pp. 345–354 (October 2010)

25. Neiger, D., Churilov, L.: Goal-Oriented Business Process Modeling with EPCs and Value-Focused Thinking. In: Desel, J., Pernici, B., Weske, M. (eds.) BPM 2004. LNCS, vol. 3080, pp. 98–115. Springer, Heidelberg (2004)

26. De la Vara Gonzalez, J.L., Diaz, J.S.: Business process-driven requirements engineering: a goal-based approach. In: Business Process Management Workshops, http://lams.epfl.ch/conference/bpmds07/program/Gonzalez_23.pdf

27. Ghose, A.K., Narendra, N.C., Ponnalagu, K., Panda, A., Gohad, A.: Goal-Driven Business Process Derivation. In: Kappel, G., Maamar, Z., Motahari-Nezhad, H.R. (eds.) ICSOC 2011. LNCS, vol. 7084, pp. 467–476. Springer, Heidelberg (2011)

28. Bentahar, J., Moulin, B., Bélanger, M.: A taxonomy of argumentation models used for knowledge representation. Artif. Intell. Rev. 33(3), 211–259 (2010)

Monitoring Business Process Interaction

Nico Herzberg, Matthias Kunze, and Mathias Weske

Hasso Plattner Institute at the University of Potsdam
Prof.-Dr.-Helmert-Strasse 2-3, 14482 Potsdam
{nico.herzberg,matthias.kunze,mathias.weske}@hpi.uni-potsdam.de

Abstract. Business process monitoring provides well established means to track the history and state of business processes and to evaluate their performance. However, common techniques and systems lack support of monitoring processes and their interactions with partners, particularly if such processes are not automated or only few events can be detected, rather than a complete log.

In this paper, we present a mechanism to determine the state of business processes with only few events to be detected. Based on this mechanism, we provide a formal framework to monitor processes and their interaction with collaboration partner's processes, as well as to evaluate the processes' performance. The framework has been applied in the context of an industry project, which we used to evaluate our solution.

1 Introduction

Business process management has received considerable interest among modern companies, as it sustains competitiveness in an ever-changing market environment. Organizations capture their operations in business process models for documentation, but also for automation and certification. Evaluating business processes, in particular with respect to execution performance, requires means to monitor the state of a process instance by tracking business relevant events. Business process monitoring is a well-established discipline, and has received considerable support in modern business process management systems [6]. These systems automatically orchestrate a business process, i.e., a workflow engine enacts the technically configured process, and hence knows about the start and end of every activity and decision taken. This information is called a process log and can be used to track the state and history of running and terminated business processes [15].

However, a large share of business processes is enacted in a non-automated manner, i.e., they are not executed by means of a workflow engine but conducted manually by humans following certain guidelines. Consequently, there is no central record of conducted activities comparable to a process log, but only few activities, events, or side effects thereof can be observed in the technical environment of the business process. For instance, the process of creation, review, and iterative update of a document may only be discovered by revision information in a document management system.

Moreover, many processes involve collaboration beyond the boundaries of an organization or department. Such collaboration is typically not controlled centrally, as each organization conducts their own process; interaction is carried out by sending and receiving messages, e.g., requesting and providing feedback on a given document. This

A. Ghose et al. (Eds.): ICSOC 2012, LNCS 7759, pp. 228–240, 2013.
© Springer-Verlag Berlin Heidelberg 2013

makes it difficult to monitor and evaluate the process' execution. However, providing insight into interacting processes to all collaborators increases transparency and suggests to improve collaboration.

In this paper, we address these issues and present a framework to monitor process interaction in absence of a central business process management system. In more detail, we provide a formal framework based on the notion of workflow modules, partner synthesis, and event monitoring points. Even if the log of events is sparse, this allows capturing the state of a process, monitoring process interactions, and detecting whether a partner cannot proceed, because it is waiting for a message from another partner. Based on this framework, we introduce interaction monitoring models, an abstraction of the internal behavior of a process, as a means to monitor the state of a process on a coarsely grained level and to communicate it to collaborators in real time. These models provide instant insight into the current state of a process and allow telling who is currently active, waiting for someone, or responsible for a delay. Additionally, we emphasize how the performance of business processes and process interactions can be evaluated in quantitative terms based on this framework.

The remainder of this paper is structured as follows. We motivate business process interaction monitoring with a case study, to which the proposed framework has been applied, in Section 2. Section 3 provides the formal framework of our approach and explains, how it enables process interaction monitoring and performance evaluation. We then revisit the motivational use case and discuss its implementation in Section 4, before we discuss related work in Section 5, conclude the paper and give a brief outlook on future work, in Section 6.

2 Case Study

In this section, we present the case of a German health insurance company, who carried out mergers of several federal branches, recently. These branches independently carried out similar operations for years. However, after the merger, it turned out that different job specifications existed for the same position in the company across the former branches. Hence, the *organization development* (OD) department became in charge of harmonizing these job specifications.

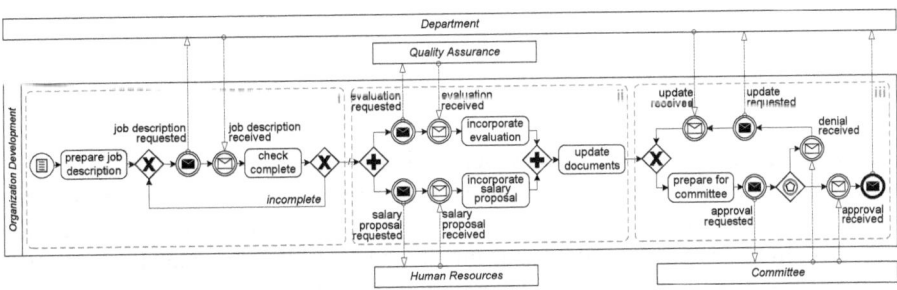

Fig. 1. Job specification harmonization process of a health insurance company (simplified model)

Fig. 1 shows the BPMN process model that has been established to harmonize job specifications. It involves several interaction partners: *Quality Assurance, Human Resources* (HR), a *Department* that embraces the position to be harmonized, e.g., Medical Care, Geriatric Care, IT, and HR, and a *Committee* that eventually approves the harmonized job specifications. It is also possible that one department engages in several roles, e.g., if a position in Human Resources needs to be harmonized.

In the process model, we see that the OD department starts the process and prepares the job description documents. Subsequently, it requests a description of the position from the respective Department and checks it for completeness upon reception. Please note, that interaction between the departments has been modeled as message passing between separate pools in the model. If the job description from the Department is incomplete, the Department must improve it in an iterative fashion. Otherwise, it is handed over to Quality Assurance that ensures that the job description meets the company's requirements. At the same time, Human Resources receive the job description with a request to propose a salary for the position. After both inputs have been incorporated, the OD department updates the job specification documents. Eventually, the job specification is prepared and sent to the Committee whose sole task is to review and approve the specification. In case approval is denied, the respective Department must update it, and it needs to be reviewed again by the Committee.

The OD department strives to harmonize a job specification within three months. However, in a fair amount of cases, one or several of the interaction partners impede progress as they do not respond in a reasonable period of time. Hence, the OD department requires a means (a) to track the status of a process instance, i.e., show the current state, show previous actions, and point out, whether the instance is waiting for a response from one partner, (b) to answer who is responsible for a delay, and (c) to provide time measurements about the duration of the complete process, its activities, and how much time respective interaction partners have spent for their contributions.

Nevertheless, the OD department was reluctant to disclose their internal, detailed process model to interaction partners. Therefore, they identified three phases, *job description* (i), *quality assurance* (ii), and *approval* (iii), grouped by dashed boxes in Fig. 1. The information above should then be projected on a simple model of these phases and be presented to the other departments. By that, the OD department offers process monitoring based solely on their knowledge of the process, i.e., the processes of interaction partners are not known, whilst enabling monitoring and performance evaluation of interactions with its partners.

3   Interaction Monitoring Framework

Based on the requirements and issues mentioned in Section 2, we first introduce workflow modules to formally capture interacting processes in Section 3.1. Subsequently, we show how processes can be monitored, even if only few events can be detected and how this information is used to provide monitoring views that provide insight into the state and history of a process to collaborators (a, b) in Section 3.2, before we explain how to evaluate process performance based on this model (c) in Section 3.3. We briefly discuss basic assumptions and limitations of our approach in Section 3.4.

3.1 Modeling Interactions

To illustrate our approach, we utilize the example process model from Section 2, cf. Fig. 1. Here, we assume that the process along with its interaction partners is captured in a detailed model, whereas the process of the partners is generally unknown. For instance, in BPMN, process interaction is modeled through message events and message flow, and partners can be represented as black box pools.

To formalize the interaction between processes, we resort to workflow modules, which have been introduced in [9]. Workflow modules are essentially Petri nets—a commonly used formalism for execution semantics of business processes [16]—with additional places that represent sent and received messages, referred to as input and output places of a module hereafter.

Definition 1 (Workflow Module). *A* workflow module *is a tuple* $N = (P, T, F, P_i, P_o)$, *where* (P, T, F) *is a Petri net that consists of finite disjoints sets of places* P *and transitions* T, *and a flow relation* $F \subseteq (P \times T) \cup (T \times P)$. *For* $X = P \cup T$, *we refer to* $\bullet x = \{y \in X | (y, x) \in F\}$ *as the preset and* $x\bullet = \{y \in X | (x, y) \in F\}$ *as the postset of a node* $x \in X$, *respectively.*

$P_i \subseteq P$ *denotes the set of of input places of* N, *such that* $\forall p \in P_i : \bullet p = \emptyset$, *and* $P_o \subseteq P$ *the set of output places of* N, *such that* $\forall (p \in P_o) : p\bullet = \emptyset$. *No transition is connected to an input place and an output place at the same time, i.e.,* $\forall p_i \in P_i, p_o \in P_o \nexists t \in T : t \in p_i\bullet \wedge t \in \bullet p_o$. *The state, or* marking, *of* (P, T, F) *is defined by a function* $M : P \to \mathbb{N}$.

For the given process model and each partner, a workflow module needs to be created. Interaction of the respective partners is modeled by fusing input places of one module with output places of another one, i.e., given the set of workflow modules of a process and its interaction partners, $\mathcal{N}$, it holds that $\forall N \in \mathcal{N}$ $P_i^N \subseteq \bigcup_{N' \in \mathcal{N} \setminus \{N\}} P_o^{N'}$, where P_i^N (P_o^N) represents the input (output) places of a module $N \in \mathcal{N}$. Hence, if one module puts a token on one of its output places, this token signals the message transmission, because it is at the same time on the input place of another module.

The process model is translated into a workflow net following common Petri net-based formalizations [8], e.g., activities and events are represented by transitions connected through places, diverging (merging) XOR-gateways by a place that has outgoing (incoming) arcs to (from) several transitions, and forking (joining) AND-gateways by a transition that has outgoing (incoming) arcs to (from) several places. Message exchange (dashed arcs in Fig. 1) between the process and a partner is captured by adding input and output places for each incoming and outgoing message arcs [9].

As the processes of the partners are typically not known, they cannot be translated into workflow modules. However, partners that provide compatible behavior to the process can be synthesized from the internal state and the interaction of the process [18]. A synthesized partner describes the observable behavior at the interface between the partner and the process. By that, we can correlate events observed at the interaction interface of the process.

In the context of process monitoring, internal life cycles for activities have been proposed to be captured, when translating models to Petri nets, e.g., [7], where one activity would be translated into a subnet that becomes enabled, running, and terminated. However, in the present case, we are only interested in the completion of activities or

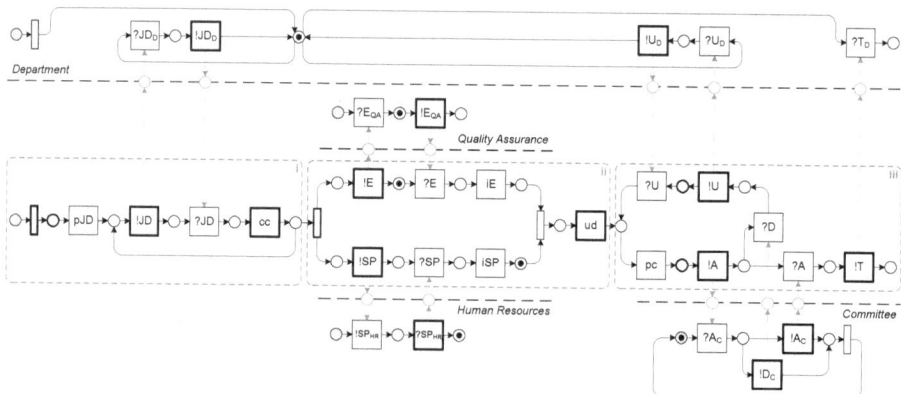

Fig. 2. Workflow modules for the job specification harmonization process, cf. Fig. 1. Shaded places represent start places of the modules. The current marking, i.e., distribution of tokens to places, represents a certain state during the execution of one process instance.

interactions. Hence, an activity or event of the process model can safely be represented as a single transition in the workflow module. Consequently, termination of an activity or event is represented by firing its corresponding transition.

Fig. 2 depicts the fused workflow modules for the job specification harmonization process and its interaction partners. The module in the middle of the figure represents the process, which has been translated into a workflow module as presented above, the partner modules (separated by dashed horizontal lines) of the Department, Quality Assurance, Human Resources and the Committee have been synthesized. For brevity, we used acronyms for activities, e.g., pJD represents activity "process job description" and cc stands for "check complete".

BPMN message events have been translated to transitions, whereas sending a message is marked by a leading "$!$" in the transition label and receiving a message by a leading "$?$". Here, process interaction typically consists of two messages, a request to a partner and the partner's response. For instance, transition $!JD$ stands for requesting a job description. This request is received by the Department, represented through transition $?JD_D$, and responded with $!JD_D$. This response is received by the process through $?JD$. The remaining interactions are analogous.

It is important to understand that the workflow modules of interaction partners may differ from their actual processes as these modules only describe the observable behavior of these partners at the interface of the process. One can understand this as part of the process that is not explicitly modeled.

We captured the process of the Committee as a continuous loop in the corresponding module, rather than as one process instance for each review. This is due to the Committee's sole task to review job specifications, i.e., the Committee may review several job harmonization process instances in the course of one session. Nevertheless, the fused Petri net is free from dead locks.

3.2   Monitoring Interaction

The workflow modules depicted in Fig. 2 are already marked, i.e., some places contain tokens. Based on a marking, we define the state and execution semantics of workflow modules as follows.

Definition 2 (Workflow Module Semantics). *Let* (P, T, F, P_i, P_o) *be a workflow module and M be a marking.*

- *A transition* $t \in T$ *is enabled, iff* $\forall p \in \bullet t : M(p) \geq 1$.
- *A transition* $t \in T$ *is waiting, iff* $\forall p \in \bullet t \backslash P_i : M(p) \geq 1 \wedge \forall p \in \bullet t \cap P_i : M(p) = 0$.
- *The firing of a transition* t *in state* M *where* t *is enabled results in a state* M' *where*
  $\forall p \in \bullet t : M'(p) = M(p) - 1 \wedge \forall p \in t\bullet : M'(p) = M(p) + 1$

In Fig. 2, the process instance is in a state where requests for an evaluation of the job specification and for a salary proposal have been sent to Quality Assurance and Human Resources. While Human Resources has already responded with a proposal that has been incorporated into the job specification, i.e., transition iSP has fired, the process is waiting for a response from Quality Assurance which has not been received—transition $!E_{QA}$ of Quality Assurance has not fired yet. Since only the token from the input place of $?E$ is missing for enablement, transition $?E$ is *waiting*.

To monitor a process instance and interaction with its partners, a set of event monitoring points is required, i.e., information that a state has changed. We represent these by special transitions that do not fire until the corresponding event has been observed. Such events need to be detected in or obtained from the environment of the business process, e.g., by regularly testing, whether the state of a document has changed. Also, for many manually conducted processes, a checklist document, e.g., a spread sheet file, is used to record the accomplishment of an activity with its time and date.

In Section 4 we illustrate the architecture of a system, based on earlier work [7], that obtains events, correlates them with process instances, and provides them to event monitoring points. Here, we assume such events have been detected and correlated, already.

Definition 3 (Event Monitoring Point, Transition Firing). *Let* (P, T, F, P_i, P_o) *be a workflow module. An event monitoring point represents a business event that triggers an observable state change of the net, denoted by the firing of a transition* $t \in T$. *The set of event monitoring points is defined as* $T_e \subseteq T$.

Firing of $t \in T_e$ *is deferred until the event related with* t *has been monitored; all other transitions, i.e.,* $t \in T \backslash T_e$, *fire immediately, when they become enabled.*

In Fig. 2, event monitoring points are visualized by a bold outline. One can see that transition $!E_{QA}$ is enabled. Since a message from Quality Assurance has not been received yet, i.e., the according event has not been detected, $!E_{QA}$ did not fire. As we discussed in Section 1, not every activity may be represented by an event in the process environment, e.g., execution of transitions iSP and iE cannot be detected by an event directly. Nevertheless, to keep the paper concise, we require that each decision can be monitored, i.e., transitions that share an input place must be event monitoring points.

The mechanism above allows obtaining the current state and history of a process, whether it is waiting, which partner it is waiting for, and with which partners it has interacted, by means of workflow modules and a sparse process log, i.e., detected event monitoring points. However, as one may not want to disclose the detailed behavior of a process to external parties, i.e., the interaction partners, we provide a model that hides internal behavior, yet captures interaction of the process with its partners.

Definition 4 (Interaction Monitoring Model, Interaction Semantics). *An interaction monitoring model $I = (V, E)$ is a connected graph of finite sets of interaction activities V and directed edges $E \subseteq V \times V$. The interaction activities provide a partitioning of the transitions of a workflow module (P, T, F, P_i, P_o), i.e., $\pi(T) = \{v_1, v_2, ..., v_n\}$. If transitions of two distinct interaction activities, v_i, v_j, are connected by a place, these interaction activities are connected by an edge, i.e., $t_r \in v_i \wedge t_s \in v_j \wedge v_i \neq v_j \wedge t_r \bullet \cap \bullet t_s \neq \emptyset \Rightarrow (v_i, v_j) \in E$.*

- *An interaction activity $v \in V$ is waiting, if there is no transition $t \in v$ enabled, but at least one of these transitions is waiting.*
- *An interaction activity $v \in V$ is active, if there is at least one transition $t \in v$ that is enabled or waiting.*

Essentially, an interaction model is an abstraction of the process' workflow module. Different techniques for automatic abstraction have been presented, e.g., [12], but they are not in the scope of this paper. We rather assume that abstraction addresses specific requirements of the use case at hand, i.e., to provide partners with a perspective on the state of the interaction, while hiding sensitive information from them.

In Fig. 2, the partitioning of transitions is represented by three dashed rectangles (i–iii) that correspond to the phases of the process that have been identified, cf. Section 2. The resulting interaction monitoring model is illustrated in Fig. 3, which shows the interaction activities that embrace the corresponding transitions, their involved partners, and their state derived from the marking of the workflow module. A legend is provided in Fig. 4.

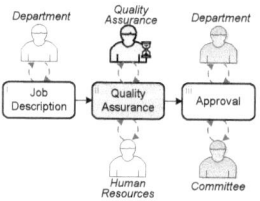
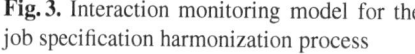
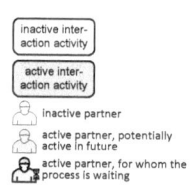

Fig. 3. Interaction monitoring model for the job specification harmonization process

Fig. 4. Interaction monitoring model, notation legend

Based on the marking of transitions $t \in v$, we can deduce the state of an interaction activity. If there is at least one transition that is either enabled or waiting, the interaction activity is considered active, as operations may be carried out. If an interaction activity contains only disabled and at least one waiting transitions, then it cannot proceed until the respective messages are received and the waiting transitions fire. Nevertheless, also a waiting activity is active, because in a future point in time, it can proceed.

From the fused workflow modules we know the partner for every transition that is connected with an input or output place, respectively. Hence, for any marking of the net, we can decide, which of the activities are active and which are waiting, and for which partners an activity is waiting.

The interaction activity "Quality Assurance" (ii) is in state waiting, as no transition in the corresponding partition can fire, but transition $!E_{QA}$ is waiting, cf. Fig. 2. Hence, the whole activity waits for the input from Quality Assurance. This is illustrated in the interaction monitoring model by an active (shaded) partner that is annotated with an hourglass. As Human Resources already provided their input and will no further interact with the process in the current interaction activity, the corresponding participant symbol is not shaded, indicating inactivity. Interaction partners of future activities are also shaded as they may be involved as the process advances.

3.3   Measuring Interaction Performance

In order to accurately derive the state of each activity of an interaction monitoring model and to compute performance measures on the same level of granularity, a minimal set of event monitoring points is required. This incorporates a monitoring point for each sent message, i.e., $\forall p \in P_o : \bullet p \subseteq T_e$, and one monitoring point for every possibility to enter and leave interaction activities, i.e., for all $t_r \in v_i, t_s \in v_j$ such that $(v_i, v_j) \in E \wedge t_r \bullet \cap \bullet t_s \neq \emptyset$ we require that $t_r \in T_e \vee t_s \in T_e$.

From this information, calculation of various performance measures becomes possible. For instance, the duration of an activity is computed by subtracting from the time of the latest detected event monitoring point the time of the earliest detected monitoring point that belongs to this activity. From active and waiting states of transitions, we can compute the amount of time the activity was actually waiting for a collaboration partner.

Consider, for an example, interaction activity "Job Description" represented by the leftmost dashed rectangle in Fig. 2 and the following log entries, i.e., pairs of event monitoring point and point in time. (Here we refer to the first unlabeled transition as τ). $\{(\tau, 0), (!JD, 3), (!JD_D, 7), (cc, 8), (!JD, 9), (!JD_D, 11), (cc, 13)\}$. After one iteration was required to complete the job description, the result provided from the Department was accepted eventually. In this interaction activity instance, the process was active 13 time units, of which it was waiting $(7 - 3) + (11 - 9) = 6$ time units for the Department.

The overall process duration needs to be computed from the first and the last event monitoring point that have been detected. It is not possible to sum the durations of the interaction activities, as they may be active or waiting concurrently. Finally, computation of statistics, e.g., average or median execution durations for process and interaction activities, is carried out by aggregating durations computed from distinct process instances.

3.4   Assumptions and Limitations

Our approach to monitor process interactions is subject to certain assumptions and limitations. First, we assume that, for every partner, we can synthesize a behavior and the combined behavior. That is, fusing input and output places of the process with output and input places of partners yields a model that can be transformed into a workflow net which is weak sound [9]—a correctness property that ensures the absence of deadlocks, while not all transitions of a workflow module need to be executable.

Further, we require that every process instance strictly follows the model, i.e., event monitoring points are only discovered, when the respective transitions are enabled. Violation of the model could be mitigated by relaxed firing semantics of the model, e.g., if there exists a sound firing sequence that leads to a marking that allows firing an event monitoring point transition, we could accept the event monitoring point. Yet, this is not in the focus of this paper and shall be addressed in future work.

In an interaction monitoring model, edges represent only relaxed ordering semantics of interaction activities. An edge indicates that from one activity another may follow, however, two interaction activities that are connected by an edge may be active concurrently. Also, activities may be skipped. More accurate semantics of these edges could be defined by restricting the abstraction provided through the partitioning of transitions. However, the given abstraction proved effective in practice, where often a coarse-grained differentiation in subsequent process phases is desired.

We resorted to a rather simplistic visual representation of the interaction monitoring model, as the focus of this paper is on the framework to track interaction, detect waiting states, and derive performance evaluations. Much more information can be derived from the workflow modules' structure and the record of event monitoring points, e.g., how often have certain messages been sent, how long did each of these interactions take, and whether interaction activities have been active several times and, if so, how often.

4   Implementation

Fig. 5 shows the conceptual architecture of a process monitoring and process performance evaluation system. It comprises an event capturing layer that obtains the event information from various sources. In the aforementioned use case, the events used for monitoring are captured from excel files and business information systems. The event information is correlated with particular process instances, e.g., harmonization of job specification 'clerk for private patients', and a specific activity in the process. Once the event information are correlated to the process instance and its activities and provided to the process monitoring and process performance evaluation components, these can decide which process monitoring points have to be executed, to track the state of the underlying process. Monitoring and evaluation are then provided by means of the mechanisms presented in Section 3.

The health insurance company used the interaction monitoring model to share the state of every process instance with all involved partners. That is, the respective Department can follow the progress of its case, while all involved partners can see, whether the process is stuck due to a missing message. Internally, the OD department uses insights from a more detailed model, i.e., on the same granularity level as the workflow modules, to discover causes for delays and identify cases that violated or are likely to violate the aspired maximum duration of three months to carry out a process instance.

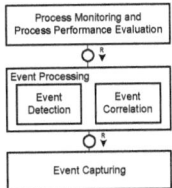

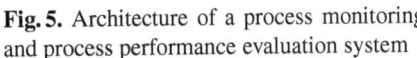

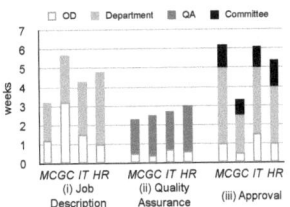

Fig. 5. Architecture of a process monitoring and process performance evaluation system

Fig. 6. Sample report on time spent in different phases of the process

On the executive level, information of this model is used to evaluate the time spent for harmonizing job specifications and to benchmark the performance of different departments in the context of this process, i.e., to compare response times of the departments and investigate potential bottlenecks at their site. Fig. 6 provides a bar chart that shows how much time the respective departments spent within the various phases. The diagram shows average values of time shares among the four departments *Medical Care* (MC), *Geriatric Care* (GC), IT, and HR, i.e., each bar segment shows how much time each interaction partner contributed to a given phase, whereas the height of a bar shows the length of the phase. Since the phases are subsequent to one another, the average process duration can be computed by summing the durations of the respective phases. From the diagram, we can derive that processes involving the MC and GC department have, in average, met the three months (13 weeks) constraint, whereas cases of the IT and HR department took over 13 weeks in average.

5 Related Work

Capabilities to monitor, visualize, and evaluate business process execution are perceived one of the core topics addressed by business process intelligence (BPI) [11], which addresses "managing process execution quality by providing several features, such as analysis, prediction, monitoring, control, and optimization" [6]. Several works discuss the capturing and storing of process execution data for evaluation purposes [6,1,10], but disregard how this information can be used to monitor process interactions.

In [11], the authors argue that process monitoring and analysis are vital to BPI and propose, based on the specific requirements of BPI, a reference architecture, composed of an integration layer, a functional layer, and a visualization layer. The framework presented in this paper targets at the functional and the visualization layer, i.e., provides means to relate event monitoring points with business process state and derive insights. We do not address technical questions, e.g., how actual events are detected in the process environment, and how they are correlated with event monitoring points. A solution toward this is presented in [7].

Dahayanake et al. [4] give an overview of business activity monitoring (BAM) and introduce four classes of BAM systems: pure BAM, discovery-oriented BAM, simulation-oriented BAM, and reporting-oriented BAM. The first is similar to traditional process monitoring, i.e., provides notifications about a certain state, which is already provided by event monitoring points that found the basis of our approach. Reporting-oriented BAM provides a performance context for running processes and is quite similar to the use case we aim for, where the actual state of a process instance is provided as well as information about the performance evaluation at this stage.

With regards to business process evaluation, the concept of process performance indicators (PPI), the process related form of key performance indicators, is introduced in BPM. Del-Río-Ortega et al. [5] introduce an ontology to define PPIs for measuring process execution performance, such as time, costs, and occurrences. These PPIs can be applied directly on top of our framework, as it provides measurements that can be compared to target values. As these measures can already be provided while the process instance is running, violations of tolerance thresholds can be mitigated before the process instance failed a PPI.

As mentioned earlier, none of the above research addressed monitoring of business process interactions. Rinderle-Ma et al. [13] discuss the need of process views to strengthen the understanding of a business process according to the users' needs. In the same vein, the requirements for a process monitoring system for system-spanning business processes are discussed and evaluated in [3]. The requirements drawn in that work lead the authors to a monitoring framework for visualizing the execution of business processes [2], where interaction diagrams are advocated as one of the most suitable forms to show interaction between several parties participating in a business process execution. However, execution information about partner interaction, such as waiting for a partner's input, are not discussed.

In [14] aspects of so-called federated tasks are discussed, where collaboration across companies is encapsulated in one task, rather than conducted through task interaction. The authors also raise the problem of temporal dependencies of tasks between interacting organizations as well, but owe an answer to the reader. [17] presents an approach how collaboration between partners could be simplified by shifting it to the cloud. In this setting, interaction monitoring capabilities are provided, because workflow engines on both partner sites as well as in the cloud are assumed. However, in our setting neither the organization running the process nor the partners that contribute have a workflow engine in place; a cloud with a workflow engine is not applicable in this setting.

The majority of approaches to process monitoring does not target on monitoring and analysis of interaction with partners during process execution. Especially information about partners that are waiting for a message and according performance evaluations are not addressed so far. The presented framework provides the techniques to detect waiting states and derive information about the responsibilities in a certain interaction activity.

6   Conclusion

In this paper we presented a formal framework to capture and express monitoring of business process interactions in non-automated process execution environments. The framework is based on a mechanism to track the state of a process instance even if only few events can be detected and to detect whether certain activities of a running process cannot proceed as they are waiting for a partner. Abstractions of the detailed process can be used to define the context of performance evaluation and to provide monitoring to collaboration partners.

In a case study from an industry project, we showed how the approach has been applied to derive an interaction monitoring model, and how certain performance evaluations are computed by means of the developed framework. The resulting process interaction monitor increased the transparency among interacting processes of collaboration partners, yet keeping partners independent in their actions, and proved effective in reducing process delays.

In future work, we shall address advanced scenarios that arise from the given limitations and assumptions of our approach. Probably, the most challenging assumption is strict execution compliance, i.e., process executions strictly follow the model. While this has proved effective in the aforementioned use case, it does not generally hold. Different techniques to discover violations of the model's prescription, e.g., an event has been detected although the according monitoring point was not enabled, need to be analyzed.

Based on workflow modules, it is possible to detect, when a process model exhibits certain flaws, e.g., a partner might still wait for a message, while the process has already terminated. By means of model checking, such deficiencies can be mitigated and lead to improved process models that reveal partner interaction.

While we argue that process performance indicators can be applied on top of our framework, cf. Section 5, an implementation is currently missing and shall also be addressed in future work.

References

1. Azvine, B., Cui, Z., Nauck, D.D., Majeed, B.: Real Time Business Intelligence for the Adaptive Enterprise. In: IEEE CEC/EEE 2006, p. 29 (2006)
2. Bobrik, R.: Konfigurierbare Visualisierung komplexer Prozessmodelle (2008)
3. Bobrik, R., Reichert, M., Bauer, T.: Requirements for the Visualization of System-Spanning Business Processes. In: BPMPM 2005/DEXA 2005, pp. 948–954. IEEE Computer Society Press (2005)
4. Dahanayake, A., Welke, R.J., Cavalheiro, G.: Improving the understanding of BAM technology for real-time decision support. Int. J. Bus. Inf. Syst. 7, 1–26 (2011)
5. del-Río-Ortega, A., Resinas, M., Ruiz-Cortés, A.: Defining Process Performance Indicators: An Ontological Approach. In: Meersman, R., Dillon, T.S., Herrero, P. (eds.) OTM 2010. LNCS, vol. 6426, pp. 555–572. Springer, Heidelberg (2010)
6. Grigori, D., Casati, F., Castellanos, M., Dayal, U., Sayal, M., Shan, M.C.: Business process intelligence. Computers in Industry 53(3), 321–343 (2004)
7. Herzberg, N., Kunze, M., Rogge-Solti, A.: Towards process evaluation in non-automated process execution environments. In: ZEUS 2012, pp. 96 102. CEUR-WS.org (2012)
8. Lohmann, N., Verbeek, E., Dijkman, R.: Petri Net Transformations for Business Processes – A Survey. In: Jensen, K., van der Aalst, W.M.P. (eds.) ToPNoC II. LNCS, vol. 5460, pp. 46–63. Springer, Heidelberg (2009)
9. Martens, A.: On Compatibility of Web Services. Petri Net Newsletter 65, 12–20 (2003)
10. Melchert, F., Winter, R., Klesse, M., Romano Jr., N.C.: Aligning process automation and business intelligence to support corporate performance management. In: AMCIS 2004, pp. 4053–4063. Association for Information Systems (2004)
11. Mutschler, B., Reichert, M.U.: Aktuelles schlagwort: Business process intelligence. EMISA Forum 26(1), 27–31 (2006)

12. Polyvyanyy, A., Smirnov, S., Weske, M.: The Triconnected Abstraction of Process Models. In: Dayal, U., Eder, J., Koehler, J., Reijers, H.A. (eds.) BPM 2009. LNCS, vol. 5701, pp. 229–244. Springer, Heidelberg (2009)
13. Rinderle, S., Bobrik, R., Reichert, M., Bauer, T.: Business Process Vizualization - Use Cases, Challenges, Solutions, pp. 204–211 (2004)
14. Unger, T., Wagner, S.: Collaboration Aspects of Human Tasks. In: zur Muehlen, M., Su, J. (eds.) BPM 2010 Workshops. LNBIP, vol. 66, pp. 579–590. Springer, Heidelberg (2011)
15. van der Aalst, W., van Hee, K.: Workflow Management: Models, Methods, and Systems. MIT Press, Cambridge (2004)
16. van der Aalst, W.: The Application of Petri Nets to Workflow Management. Journal of Circuits, Systems, and Computers 8(1), 21–66 (1998)
17. Wagner, S., Kopp, O., Leymann, F.: Towards Choreography-based Process Distribution in the Cloud. In: CCIS 2011, pp. 490–494. IEEE Xplore (2011)
18. Wolf, K.: Does My Service Have Partners? In: Jensen, K., van der Aalst, W.M.P. (eds.) ToPNoC II. LNCS, vol. 5460, pp. 152–171. Springer, Heidelberg (2009)

Interactive Product Browsing and Configuration using Remote Augmented Reality Sales Services

Ross Brown[1], Hye-Young Paik[2], and Alistair Barros[1]

[1] Science and Engineering Faculty, Queensland University of Technology
[2] School of Computer Science & Engineering, University of New South Wales
{r.brown,alistair.barros}@qut.edu.au, hpaik@cse.unsw.edu.au

Abstract. Real-time remote sales assistance is an underdeveloped component of online sales services. Solutions involving web page text chat, telephony and video support prove problematic when seeking to remotely guide customers in their sales processes, especially with configurations of physically complex artefacts. Recently, there has been great interest in the application of virtual worlds and augmented reality to create synthetic environments for remote sales of physical artefacts. However, there is a lack of analysis and development of appropriate software services to support these processes. We extend our previous work with the detailed design of configuration context services to support the management of an interactive sales session using augmented reality. We detail the context and configuration services required, presenting a novel data service streaming configuration information to the vendor for business analytics. We expect that a fully implemented configuration management service, based on our design, will improve the remote sales experience for both customers and vendors alike via analysis of the streamed information.

Keywords: sales product configuration, sales context management, augmented reality sales services, virtual world sales services.

1 Introduction

The explosion of online retail Web sites has brought with it much convenience for consumers of goods [1]. However, some items remain problematic to sell remotely, requiring physical interaction in order to be examined effectively.

Typical web collaboration tools, such as audio and video environments [2], do not sufficiently provide an insight into the actual context of actions by the remotely connected sales assistant. The customer may struggle with understanding the actual artefact that is being discussed by the sales assistant, and a lack of relevant gestures and spatial organisation makes the process of service provision by sales staff problematic.

We highlight two main problems with conventional online sales assistance provision, the first is the lack of an inherently spatial representation of the product and services, the second is the lack of ability for remote sales staff to adequately interact with customers in order to provide assistance with the product and other aligned services.

A. Ghose et al. (Eds.): ICSOC 2012, LNCS 7759, pp. 241–252, 2013.

Augmented Reality (AR) represents a view of a physical (real-world) environment whose elements are augmented by computerised sensory input and is often used to enrich user experience and perception of the real world.

Recently, the emergence of cloud computing and its large scale data processing capabilities have contributed to the renewed discussion of AR applications. Using ubiquitous and powerful cloud platforms as a data storage and process backend, users are able to experience fully immersive AR environments, even through mobile and wearable devices with relatively small computing power (e.g., Google's Glass project).

In this work, we aim to create more engaging and realistic virtual shopping environments using AR, in order to allow the customer to experience, interactively, convincing representations of physical products in their own home using a mobile device. In our platform, the products are juxtaposed with their home environment in order to assist goods browsing and selection.

Extending an earlier proposal introduced in [3], we introduce the following new contributions:

- We represent customer interaction actions as various edit actions on the scene representation, and propose a version management mechanism to support navigating the different versions of product configurations to help the customer with the analysis tasks.
- We propose an event streaming model which sends customer interaction events (e.g., touching an object) to the vendor for management purposes.

We present the framework, the key services offered, interactions within a typical session and illustrate with a use case of a large screen television sale using such a framework. We then conclude with discussion of how this preliminary work may be further developed.

2   AR Sales Service Framework Overview

2.1   A Motivating Scenario

Our example customer wants to purchase a large screen TV that will be compatible with his own audio system and the furniture at home - in terms of the size, appearance, technical specifications, etc. The customer is at home and places an augmented reality registration pattern onto the ground, where the actual television is to be installed. A dialog appears requesting customer information to create various contexts - e.g., customer location, size of the room. Then, a sales representative is alerted to the creation of a session, and logs in from the other end to assist with any questions. The user is also able to "load" into the space some of his existing products, such as the audio system and entertainment unit, using our 3D Content Service. The user requests to view large screen televisions from a specified brand. He now can explore the product configuration by performing actions such as placing the TV onto his existing entertainment unit, re-locating the furniture (along with the selected TV) within the room, trying out different colours, probing into technical specifications and compatibility issues with his audio system. The system allows him to "track/navigate" through the history of interactions, enabling him to go back and forth to any point in time and examine the setting. The system also understands the complex contexts within the objects in the interaction space such as 'TV set placed on an entertainment unit' and how to associate transaction and recommendation services with those objects. Figure 1 shows our prototype AR sales service architecture, with a centre image of a large screen television, entertainment unit, stereo and avatar of remotely connected sales assistant demonstrating the entertainment system to the client.

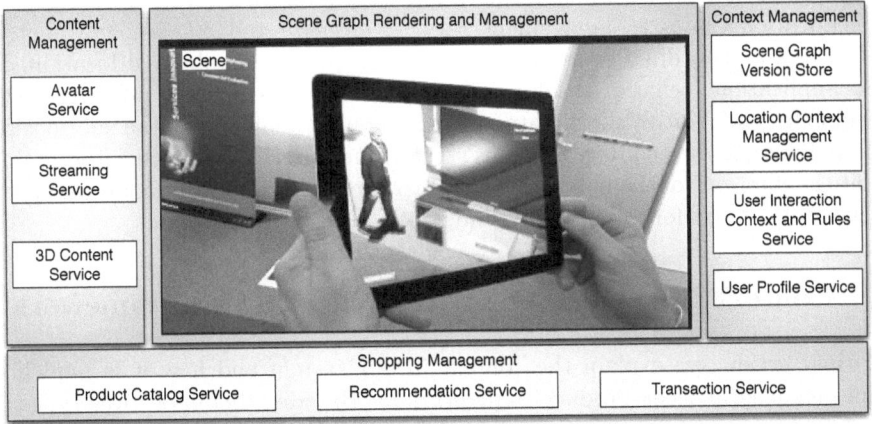

Fig. 1. AR sales prototype service overview, image of running prototype in the middle

2.2   Preliminaries

Services. The AR sales service framework (Figure 1) is supported by four categories of high-level services: Scene Graph Management and Rendering, Content Management, Context Management and Shopping and Service Recommendation Management. The focus of this paper is on the Context Management services. Here we briefly explain some of the other service components the framework relies on.

The Avatar Service (in Content Management) provides a graphical representation of a sales assistant (which can be a chat bot or human controlled avatar). It is also possible that any friends of the customer who are connected through a social network can join to collaborate during the sales sessions. For simplicity, in this paper we assume that the main actors are the customer and sales assistant.

The Product Catalog Service (in Shopping Management) interfaces with the product catalog information available in the system. They provide comprehensive information about a product, including, amongst other things, all configuration options, recommendations, related product suggestions or alternatives and stock level.

The 3D Content Service is responsible for communicating with the product service and 3D rendering engine to send 3D representations of products into running sessions with a customer. The service also understands the compatibility information (in terms of dimensions and weight, for example) with other available or adjacent products.

Representing the Customer Location: Marker-Based Approach. One of the core concepts of our approach is to be able to represent the customers current location and surroundings (in a house) in a virtual environment [3]. Doing so involves two kinds of location-related information which is managed by the Location Context Management Service: *absolute* and *relative* coordinates. The absolute coordinates are derived from the customer's physical location. In our application scenario, absolute coordinates can be the home address of the customer. The relative coordinates are based on an adaptive spatial subdivision of the house, known as Regions. This structuring is derived from the observation that the internals of the home of a customer are divided up into rooms and form a natural context for purchases within a house.

3   Context Management in AR Sales Service Framework

In this section, we explain the context in our system and how it is modelled and managed in scene product configurations. Broadly, there are three types of context in our system, depending on where and how we obtain the data.

- Static and Spatial facts: location of the markers used, dimensions of the room, physical size of the objects, etc.
- Profiled facts: user account details, preferences and profile details (gender, age, job, etc.)
- Derived facts: the information generated by user interactions with the scene. This context can be used also to capture/extract user's interests by events like camera movements, etc.

We have conceptualised the context management of the scene via a versioning tree structure which manages the editing contexts and interacts with the scene graph management system to render the final product configuration to the mobile viewer. Scene graphs are commonly used in graphics applications [4], and are designed to be an efficient data structure for editing and rendering of 3D scene databases in graphics applications. We use the Model-View-Controller pattern to manage the interactions between the user interface and the underlying product representation structure (i.e., the scene graph). With the controller component being a context management service inside the software responding to customer edit actions, contributing to an audit trail of customer interactions with products.

3.1 Customer Actions and Scene Graphs

We identify the following customer interaction actions as the source of generated context in product configurations:

- Interacting with a single object in the scene. These actions trigger editing of product representation node attributes.
  - Addition/Modification/Deletion of object(s) - instantiations of new objects (and combinations thereof) in the scene.
  - Modification of object material(s) - significant changes in object attributes (e.g., material properties)
  - Modification of object relationships - moving an object in the scene, as users only have a translation and maybe a flip function available as objects have a typical orientation
- Aggregated object actions. This type of interaction causes not only editing of scene representation nodes, but also propagation of scengraph changes throughout all nodes according to thematic rules.
  - Application and changes in the themes of the scene (e.g., colour scheme). The change propegates across a number of objects in the scene.
  - Making large changes to the objects, based on relative organisation (e.g., objects that are 'spatially related'). Similar concepts to copying and pasting multiple objects in the scene.
  - Granularity of attribute locking - e.g., one object is fixed as others change.
- User Specified Contexts - explicit creation of contexts led by the user. Representing a parallel list of product configurations, and context change sets, that are assumed to be independent, but can be copied and pasted to different context sets.
- Camera View Changes - context changes when in different viewpoint are sent to the sales person as useful sales and usage information, e.g., how is the object being used in the house, and its physical context.
- Backtracking with locks on previous changes, preventing propagation.

3.2 Context Versioning Fundamentals

Each of the editing operations is stored as contexts within a context versioning structure [5]. This versioning structure is then used to provide configuration management for the user purchases. This is similar to other versioning systems, with the model being based on document structures for the product information. We conjecture that a versioning tree of these atomic commands represents the overall context management for a configuration of products over the time of the sales session. Modifying a tree modelling approach from [5] and [6], we describe the configuration versioning performed in this retail application. The intention is to show that the scene graph can be reconstructed from a versioning tree, to show a purchase configuration at event E_i, and to show that the data structures and interactions are capable of meeting all context management requirements for users as shown above. The structure of the scene graph is controlled by the following commands, which map to user actions on the purchase configuration:

- $C_{INS} = (N_{ID})$ - node ID to insert into the scene graph from a 3D content service site similar to Google Warehouse [7].
- $C_{DEL} = (N_{ID})$ - node ID to remove from the scene graph.
- $C_{MAT} = (N_{ID}, P_{ID})$ - node ID and product info ID to change in the Scene Graph, i.e., modify with new information.
- $C_{TRANS} = (N_{ID}, M)$ - node ID and transformation matrix M (4x4 Homogenous) to load into the scene graph for N_{ID}.
- $C_{ATTACH} = (N_{ID1}, N_{ID2})$ - specifies the two nodes to attach to each other in the scene graph, i.e., the objects are attached to each other, and can have group operations performed.

A *version tree* contains the above commands that may be user or system activated [6]. A traversal of the version tree generates the required product configuration version v as a scene graph for display. The requirements for this tree are the ability to add new versions of the configuration, and to then trace through the versions to generate a scene graph of the present configuration at time t for user u. Each command stored in the version tree creates a new configuration context for representation on the mobile device. The version tree commands derived to maintain these contexts are:

- *Version Refinement* - this is defined as the insertion of a command node C after the present version. Performed at the end of the version traversal trail, forming version v.
- *New Version Branch* - here the insertion is at a version v of less than V_{max} making the insertion form a new branch. This does not insert between nodes.
- *Merge Versions* - the new node is attached, and merges two specified nodes *v1* and *v2* to the new node v.
- *Present Version Return* - the version number is selected, and the tree traversed until that version number is the present node being processed and is returned as v. This is used for returning to specified versions of objects in the tree, to then progress forward with new modifications.
- *Generate Version Configuration* - the version number is selected, and the tree traversed until that version number, to generate the appearance of the configuration for version v as a scene graph.

4   Streaming Consumer Configuration Service for Vendors

In our approach, the above interactions are stored on a database at the user end. We now investigate the streaming of this context management data to a vendor for management purposes. We generate five different streams of information that can be read by the vendor:

1. Versioning - each of the above versioning tree events can be sent to the vendor for analysis, e.g., addition of a new object from a catalogue.
2. Object - features that people touch and operate can be logged and processed as interaction events, e.g., touching the draw on a cabinet to look inside the furniture.

3. Camera - camera movements (i.e., mobile device movements with respect to the fiducial marker) are indicative of consumer interest in components of the device, e.g., user may visually dwell on the controls of a sound system, to understand functionality.

4. Video - the camera stream can be processed, providing information about the setting of the interactions, and the face of the viewer, e.g., the video stream can be processed to obtain the colour of the room, to find context information on user choices.

5. Audio - the audio information from the client can be streamed and processed by the vendor for future analysis, e.g., vocabulary used when analysing a product.

This provides five streams of event data that can be integrated with the configuration histories, and then processed for analysis of user buying habits. An event model has been developed [8] to form a stream of event tags that can then be mined. What should be noted is the rich source of semantic media information proceeding from the AR application during its execution. Not only does the vendor and client have standard editing capabilities, which provide user interface events that are easily defined from elements of executing code, but there is the stream of more continuous real-time data that needs to be processed, including audio and video feeds, along with continuous camera orientation data emerging from the movements of the user. We detail the event groups listed in Table 1.

The first set are *Versioning* events, derived from the user interface interactions we have detailed in the use case: refinement, branch, merge and present. These are readily captured from the versionign system and deposited in the output event stream to the vendor. *Object* interaction events are recorded, which are not related to the versioning system, but involve the user touching objects of interest on the screen. These touches can also be used to highlight objects for discussion by the client and vendor.

AR systems usually use a registered location (marker or marker-less) as the centre of a coordinate system for the objects to be viewed as a 3D camera model, streaming *Camera* events[3]. This movement of the camera can be regarded as a proxy for the visual attention of the viewer [9]. The point of regard is a stream of data proceeding from the movement of the AR viewing device with respect to the registered coordinate system. This data can be streamed to the vendor to identify points of regard on the object via the camera model being used. In addition, fixations can be extracted from the stream using a visual attention algorithm [10]. The zoom, or closeness of the device to the registration point, can be treated in a similar manner, to indicate areas of interest on the objects in question.

The back facing camera on the mobile device contains a video feed of the room in which the transaction is being carried out, and is used to create the augmented view. The camera stream contains *Video* event information regarding the nature of the surrounding environment, including objects and colour schemes of the rooms. Object extraction and recognition algorithms [11] can be utilised in these instances to provide information to the vendor regarding the visual context of the purchase. The front facing camera provides a video feed of the user to the vendor. This can be processed for facial expressions using expression recognition algorithms [12], to be indexed for analysis of the session.

Table 1. Event model derived from Customer-Vendor information stream, with associated data components in the right most column

Stream	Event Type	Components
Versioning	Refinement	Time, VersNum, NewObjID
	Branch	Time, VersNum, NewObjID
	Merge	Time, VersNum, NewObjID
	Present	Time, VersNum
Object	Touch	Time, ObjID, InteractionID
Camera	Orient	Time, CamVec
	Fixation	TimeBegin, TimeInterv, CamVec
	Zoom	TimeBegin, TimeInterv, Scale
Video	Forward Object	Time, ObjectID, RelPos
	Forward ColorPallette	Time, ColorPallette
	Face	TimeBegin, TimeInterv, FaceExpType
Audio	Client Word	Time, KeywordID
	Client Stress	TimeBegin, TimeInterv, StressEventID
	Vendor Word	Time, KeywordID
	Vendor Stress	TimeBegin, TimeInterv, StressEventID

Audio events can be processed in a similar manner. Words can be extracted from the audio stream generating key word events, and can be readily processed with modern audio analysis algorithms [13]. In addition, approaches to audio stress detection, in a similar vein to facial expression recognition, can be applied to detect if the client is unhappy/happy with a passage of interaction with the vendor.

Such rich sales data can be streamed and stored across multiple instances of AR purchasing applications on mobile devices for up to date information to the vendor in real time, and for use later as a business analysis data source. This information can be indexed by the above event model, to identify key queries for business analysis. For example, as per the use case presented, we propose that the gaze points and interaction touches for the objects can uncover new information about how an object is perceived, and what interests people when shopping for these items using the AR system.

5 Version Tree Generation Example

We now illustrate via a brief use case how this information can be extracted from the client vendor interactions to generate a stream of information that is useful to the vendor. As the user starts up the application on their phone, the previous account, street location and region information (within the house, e.g., "lounge room") is extracted, to maintain locational context within the house of the client. We direct the reader to [3] for more details about location context management within our AR sales service framework. As the use case progresses via client interactions with the sales system, a stream of events is generated locally to maintain the sales context structures. As the version tree is created, a path through the version tree from the root to a version v is able to generate a viable product configuration. A sequence of commands from the use case is listed that generate different versions of the configuration, and in turn, different user contexts:

1. Insert Large Screen TV - user selects a large screen TV from the catalogue (Refinement Event).
2. Insert Cabinet - user selects a cabinet from the catalogue (Refinement Event).
3. Insert Amplifier - user selects an amplifier from the catalogue (Refinement Event).
4. Change Brand of Large Screen TV - user selects a new form of TV, thus a branch is formed from the base node with a new TV (Branch Event).
5. Change Colour of Cabinet to Teak - a new node is created for the cabinet location in the version tree (Branch Event).
6. Examine Amplifier - the user moves the mobile device to fixate on the amplifier controls (Camera Fixation Event).
7. Examine Amplifier Controls - the user zooms in on the amplifier by moving forward (Camera Zoom Event).

The first five events generates the following version trees, as shown in Fig. 2. If the user wishes to show, for example, version 4 of the configuration, then the tree is searched for that version number and then rendered to that point.

In addition to this localised retention and management of the information, other event and context information is transmitted to the vendor from the sales scenario. Events six and seven in the above list are drawn from the user camera

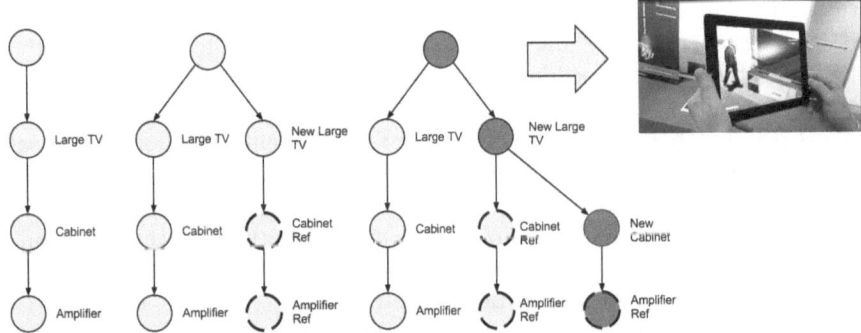

Fig. 2. Shows progression of context changes for TV purchase use case as a version tree from left to right. Note, references to nodes are shown as dashed discs, to reduce memory requirements. Darker discs in the final tree show the path taken to generate the product configuration on the mobile device.

movements via relevant algorithms, and the zoom events are extracted via similar methods.

We model our event stream as an append-only sequence of tuples, where each tuple in a stream has a timestamp (ts), event-type name and event-type specific data fields a_1 ..., a_n. The above use case generates the following stream:

- (14 August 2012 12:34:00 GMT, version_refinement, v1.0, 00987UTV)
- (14 August 2012 12:34:20 GMT, version_refinement, v2.0, 88700UYC)
- (14 August 2012 12:34:40 GMT, v3.0, 000P768UD)
- (14 August 2012 12:34:45 GMT, version_present, v1.0)
- (14 August 2012 12:34:58 GMT, version_branch, v4.0, 009888UTX)
- (14 August 2012 12:35:05 GMT, version_present, v2.0)
- (14 August 2012 12:34:58 GMT, version_branch, v5.0, 889066RR)
- (14 August 2012 12:35:01 GMT, camera_fixation, 3 sec, cam<50,10,89>)
- (14 August 2012 12:35:06 GMT, camera_zoom, 4 sec, 1.2098)

Each event type is accompanied by its own relevant data fields. For instance, version_refinement has version number and object id, whereas camera_fixation has a time interval and coordinates for the position.

6   Related Work

The retail industry is trying to overcome the limitation of conventional online shopping malls and lead innovation in future shopping experiences by adopting augmented reality technology. For example, Tesco [14] introduced a marker-based AR system where, combined with a Web cam, a customer can project a 3D image of a product onto the screen and interact with the image by moving a marker. Furniture companies like IKEA or MyDeco offer browser-based 3D planners for interior decoration [15]. Typically, these systems convert a 2D floor plan to 3D with multiple camera view angles. The backend system is connected with a large database containing product details from the manufacturers. Lu and Zhu's systems [16,17] show an AR-based sales assistant tool where an object (such as a sofa) can be placed in a real scene and the customer can search/switch products in an AR display. Other AR systems have investigated configuration systems [18], but have not incorporated avatar representations for remote sales assistance, and have not defined streaming information to be sent to vendors for each transaction as a business intelligence source. Although these systems aim to achieve similar goals to our system, the interactions with the products are limited and do not support easy navigation of the browsing/configuration history from searching/switching products in a scene.

In terms of representing and managing context in a pervasive computing environment, almost all of the context modelling and management in pervasive computing developed so far has focused on managing various sensor data (GPS, light, temperature, time, movement, etc.) in the physical world and architecting distinct layers to overcome the issues arising from heterogeneous sensor data sources [19]. In our application to the augmented reality environment, the issue of dealing with imperfect or heterogenous data will not be of concern as our context data is not from distributed sensors. However, being able to effectively deal with a timeline (the history of context), effective reasoning and expression of dependencies will be important.

Pitarello [20] presents work on context management for 3D environments, but only in author, and then location based within 3D environments. Cook [21] presents Learning Setting-Generalized Activity Models for Smart Spaces, in which context management is applied in homes for tracking elderly citizens using HMMs. Helal [22] worked on context management for spatial localisation within a family smart home. Thus, the context management is similar, due to the need to provide a mapping between locations and particular services. In summary, space is subdivided in homes, but is not directed by people for retail purposes. In a smart home scenario, the person is already detected by cameras and sensors to provide a spatial location within the environment. We can position this AR ability as a service within a smart house system in general as a digital overlay on the house, for physical service planning etc. - renovations with reference to other data within the environment. Thus, contexts can be maintained automatically within a smart house. For a non-smart house, we default back to explicit context management, using labels assigned to an AR marker or markerless positions.

7   Conclusion and Future Work

In this paper we have developed a data model for the back end of an Augmented Reality sales agent system we have prototyped. We have identified key context manipulation components, and have articulated the events that are generated in a stream sent to the vendor from such a sales application.

Future work involves the incorporation of a cognitive model to better understand the interactions between a human user and the scene environments. We believe that such work can lead us to better model and process the stream events for building a system for analysing the events using already available event-based query systems. Also, to be able to provide a complete augmented reality service information model to vendors, it would be necessary to consider the local and global scope for representing the version graphs, as personalisation and parameterisation of the information stream can be performed at different levels. The scope can also affect the types of data and process mining to be performed on the data set by the vendors.

References

1. Elberse, A.: Should you invest in the long tail? Harvard Business Review 86, 88–97 (2008)
2. Lanubile, F., Ebert, C., Prikladnicki, R.: Collaboration tools for global software engineering. IEEE Software 27, 52–55 (2008)
3. Brown, R.A., Barros, A.P.: Towards a service framework for remote sales support via augmented reality. In: International Workshop on User-Focused Service Engineering, Consumption and Aggregation (USECA 2011) (2011) (in press)

4. Herter, J., Schotte, W., Ovtcharova, J.: Bridging vr and item-based plm systems using an object oriented approach. In: PLM 2008 - 5th International Conference on Product Lifecycle Management, Seoul, South Korea (2008)

5. Koch, C., Firmenich, B.: An approach to distributed building modeling on the basis of versions and changes. Advanced Engineering Informatics 25, 297–310 (2011)

6. Miles, J., Gray, W., Carnduff, T., Santoyridis, I., Faulconbridge, A.: Versioning and configuration management in design using cad and complex wrapped objects. Artificial Intelligence in Engineering 14, 249–260 (2000)

7. Bustos, B., Sipiran, I.: 3D Shape Matching for Retrieval and Recognition. Springer, London (2012)

8. Westermann, U., Jain, R.: Toward a common event model for multimedia applications. IEEE Multimedia 14, 19–29 (2007)

9. Buscher, G., Dumais, S.T., Cutrell, E.: The good, the bad, and the random: an eye-tracking study of ad quality in web search. In: Proceedings of the 33rd International ACM SIGIR Conference on Research and Development in Information Retrieval, SIGIR 2010, pp. 42–49. ACM, New York (2010)

10. Duchowski, A.T., Çöltekin, A.: Foveated gaze-contingent displays for peripheral lod management, 3d visualization, and stereo imaging. ACM Trans. Multimedia Comput. Commun. Appl. 3, 6:1–6:18 (2007)

11. Xu, C., Hanjalic, A., Yan, S., Liu, Q., Smeaton, A.F.: Special section on object and event classification in large-scale video collections. IEEE Transactions on Multimedia 14, 1–2 (2012)

12. Lee, J.-S., Oh, C.-M., Lee, C.-W.: Facial Expression Recognition Using AAMICPF. In: Jacko, J.A. (ed.) Human-Computer Interaction, Part II, HCII 2011. LNCS, vol. 6762, pp. 268–274. Springer, Heidelberg (2011)

13. Keshet, J., Bengio, S.: Automatic Speech and Speaker Recognition: Large Margin and Kernel Methods. Wiley (2009)

14. Barnett, E.: Tesco Trials Augmented Reality (2011), http://www.telegraph.co.uk/technology/news/8895923/Tesco-trials-augmented-reality.html

15. MyDeco: Mydeco 3d planner (2012), http://mydeco.com/3d-planner/

16. Lu, Y., Smith, S.: Augmented Reality E-Commerce Assistant System: Trying While Shopping. In: Jacko, J.A. (ed.) Human-Computer Interaction, Part II, HCII 2007. LNCS, vol. 4551, pp. 643–652. Springer, Heidelberg (2007)

17. Zhu, W., Owen, C.B.: Design of the PromoPad: An Automated Augmented-Reality Shopping Assistant. Journal of Organizational and End User Computing (JOEUC) 20, 41–56 (2008)

18. Andel, M., Petrovski, A., Henrysson, A., Ollila, M.: Interactive Collaborative Scene Assembly Using AR on Mobile Phones. In: Pan, Z., Cheok, D.A.D., Haller, M., Lau, R., Saito, H., Liang, R. (eds.) ICAT 2006. LNCS, vol. 4282, pp. 1008–1017. Springer, Heidelberg (2006)

19. Bettini, C., Brdiczka, O., Henricksen, K., Indulska, J., Nicklas, D., Ranganathan, A., Riboni, D.: A survey of context modelling and reasoning techniques. Pervasive and Mobile Computing 6, 161–180 (2010)

20. Pittarello, F., De Faveri, A.: Semantic description of 3d environments: a proposal based on web standards. In: Proceedings of the Eleventh International Conference on 3D Web Technology, Web3D 2006, pp. 85–95. ACM, New York (2006)

21. Cook, D.: Learning setting-generalized activity models for smart spaces. IEEE Intelligent Systems 27, 32–38 (2012)

22. Helal, S., Mann, W., El-Zabadani, H., King, J., Kaddoura, Y., Jansen, E.: The gator tech smart house: a programmable pervasive space. Computer 38, 50–60 (2005)

The 1st International Workshop on Self-Managing Pervasive Service Systems (SeMaPS 2012)

https://sites.google.com/site/semapsworkshop/

There is a growing trend for the convergence of different computing paradigms, such as cloud computing, pervasive and mobile computing, and service-oriented computing. The applications of Internet of Things (IoT), Internet of Services (IoS), Internet of People (IoP) at a large scale are gaining increasing attention in the converged computing world with unprecedented complexities as a result: the management of applications becomes much more difficult due to large number of involved devices, events and contexts, due to the heterogeneity of networking, hardware and software; the shifting of storage and processing to cloud systems, and security and privacy concerns become more challenging. All in all, applications and systems tend to become more complex than before to manage and operate in the converged world. These challenges call for useful self-managing capabilities to alleviate existing problems. The realization of self-managing pervasive service systems needs cross-discipline research, including pervasive and mobile computing, autonomic computing, artificial intelligence, cloud computing, software engineering, service oriented computing, which are complementary with and often cross-fertilizing each other.

For this year's SeMaPS, we received 11 submissions in total. We accepted 5 full papers (45% acceptance rate) and one short paper. We had two keynote speeches: in the morning session, Professor Yan, Department of Computing, Macquarie University, presented a talk on 'Optimal Social Trust Path Selection in Social Networks'. In the afternoon session, Professor Flavio De Paoli, Università Milano-Bicocca, presented 'The Role of Non-Functional Descriptions in Cloud Systems Management'.

Of the accepted papers, we had two papers on context awareness, e.g. indoor positioning and behavior recognition. To achieve easy integration of self-managing systems, one paper discussed the usage of REST as a communication mechanism to unify interactions. We also had one paper discussing the security aspects of information access protection in pervasive systems. A paper on the supporting system architecture using cloud service, thus making use of the converged computing paradigm, was presented. Finally, a possible research roadmap was presented to discuss challenges and issues for self-managing pervasive service systems in the near future.

A. Ghose et al. (Eds.): ICSOC 2012, LNCS 7759, pp. 253–254, 2013.

Workshop Organisers

Weishan Zhang   Department of Software Engineering, China University of Petroleum, China.
Klaus Marius Hansen   Department of Computer Science, University of Copenhagen, Denmark.
Paolo Bellavista   Department of Computer Science and Engineering (DISI), Università di Bologna, Italy.

Technical Program Committee

Bin Guo   Northwestern Polytechnical University, China
Gang Pan   Zhejiang University, China
Hongyu Zhang   Tsinghua University, China
Jiehan Zhou   Carleton University, Canada
Julian Schütte   Fraunhofer AISEC, Germany
Klaus Marius Hansen   University of Copenhagen, Denmark
Paolo Bellavista   Università di Bologna, Italy
Su Yang, Fudan University, China
Weishan Zhang   China University of Petroleum, China
Yan Liu   Tongji University, China
Yangfan Zhou   Chinese University of Hong Kong, Hong Kong
YouXiang Duan   China University of Petroleum, China
Yue Lv   Eastern China Normal University, China
Zhipeng Xie   Fudan University, China
Zhiwen Yu   Northwestern Polytechnical University, China

A Reformative System Architecture of Cloud Service Based on IEEE 1851

Mingxing Jiang[1], Zhongwen Guo[2], and Chao Liu[2]

[1] Department of Basic Education Center
[2] Department of Information Science and Engineering
Ocean University of China, Qingdao, China
{jamison,guozhw}@ouc.edu.cn, liuchao.ouc@gmail.com

Abstract. A system framework is proposed in IEEE 1851; however it is not organized in cloud computing mode. Actually, since information resource in enterprise can be integrated by web service interfaces in IEEE 1851, architecture of cloud service is preferred for better resource sharing. This paper mainly proposes a reformative architecture of cloud service system based on IEEE 1851, analyzes the mechanism on the cloud, and evaluates the implementation results, etc. Also we discuss the interior in the cloud: a common XML schema is put forward for data interaction; memory scheduling and access control are respectively distributed to gain a high, reliable performance. Analysis with experimental data from the novel architecture shows the applicability of the proposed system architecture.

Keywords: IEEE 1851, home appliance test, cloud computing, web service, memory scheduling.

1   Introduction

Through providing computation, data access, storage, and even platform services, today cloud computing is dynamically revolutionizing information technology and impacting the modern Internet computing and businesses in every aspect [1, 2, 3]. In practice, its impact seems more profound for those large enterprises whose information and software resource are in urgent need of centralization and integration for high efficiency [4, 5, 6].

In IEEE 1851 [7], a system framework oriented SOA is proposed to integrate existing resource (e.g. software and data). However, when a close coupling architecture is implemented or security issue is considered, cloud computing mode is practically preferred as its high resource-centralization and reliable resource-access [8, 9].

The architecture in this paper is proposed in a cloud-computing way: the data source, services on the cloud as system key parts, the clients as the end user and the Internet to tie them together. In this architecture users are more convenient to obtain data from different places. Besides usability and convenience, special mechanisms ensure every client a reliable and timely service.

A. Ghose et al. (Eds.): ICSOC 2012, LNCS 7759, pp. 255–262, 2013.

The rest of this paper is organized as follows. In the next section, we begin with a brief overview of the architecture. Section 3 proposes two practical mechanisms on the cloud. In section 4, we analyze the caching mechanism and illustrate access control issue with a few interface diagrams. The last section summarizes our contribution and lists the limitations of this research.

2   Architecture Overview

The proposed architecture incorporating data sources up to IEEE 1851 can be built using three types of components: user authorization module (UAM), virtual resource manager (VRM), and distributed data access module (DDAM). The design of this architecture is generic enough to integrate data sources in form of IEEE 1851 and put them on the cloud side under multilevel security [10].

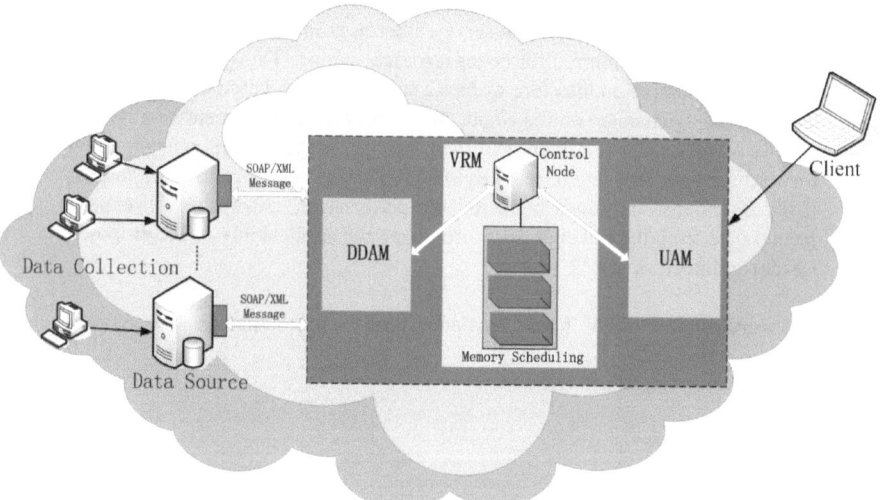

Fig. 1. Cloud Architecture

As Figure 1 shows, in this architecture, VRM is responsible for answering all requests from accredited clients [11]. Once a request comes, firstly UAM will authorize it while expelling invalid ones, then VRM will analyze the request and distribute relevant resource depending on user credentials. Besides, DDAM will take back required data from data source through web service interfaces standardized in IEEE 1851. These data will be loaded into memory for high-speed access.

3   Interior on the Cloud

3.1   Format for Data Interaction

In home appliance test, mass data generates since a large amount of sensors deployed on each test unit are collecting data all the time. We call these data test data, which occupied most of data interaction time from clients to servers in traditional system architecture. Most applications for home appliance test are designed to use a Picture-Box to display these test data and need lots of client-server interactions concerning large volume of data transmission.

Due to this fact, we propose a novel format for data interaction which enables high-efficiency data transmission. Instead of total test data, a result in form of picture will be sent to clients, which markedly reduce volume of data transmission. To be specific, we design a common XML schema for test data interaction. An image that reflects computing result on the cloud is designed to be embedded into an XML document using the Base-64 encoding approach.

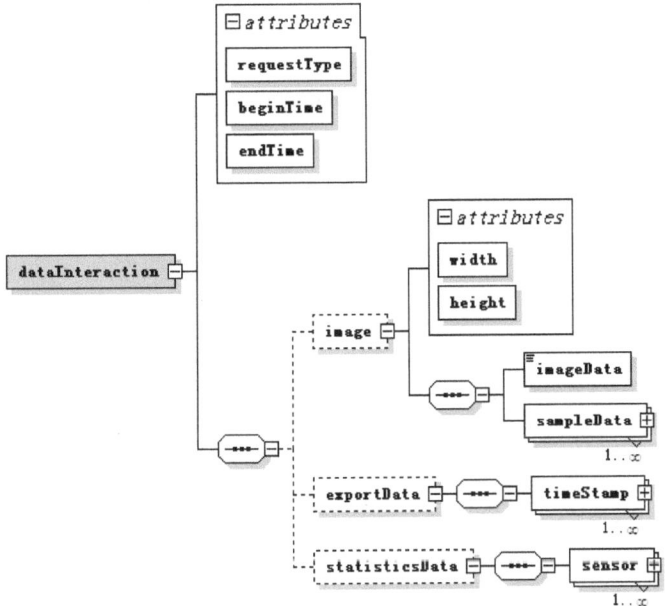

Fig. 2. Structure of dataInteration.xsd

Fig 2 shows the structure of the proposed XML schema. An instance file of the schema will be shared between clients and the cloud. Every request contains 3 basic parameters: beginTime, endTime, and requestType. Since requestType element is an enumeration including Image, Export, Statistics, responses are supposed to fill corresponding element (image, exportData, and statisticsData) with computational results. Three elements are listed below:

• **image:** This element is used to response to the "Image" request. XML instance includes an encoded binary data array about the image. Also is contained is the image size (width and height) and sampleData element.

- **exportData:** This element is used to response to the "Export" request. When user from client side needs test data of a certain period, this type of request will be triggered.
- **statisticsData:** This element is used to response to the "Statistics" request. When users want to view statistics of a certain period, the cloud will fill this element with statistics results.

3.2   Cache Mechanism

Because there are no data available in data center memory at beginning of each client request, required data will be fetched through DDAM by implementing the web service interfaces. Even though those mentioned components are deployed on the cloud, it remains inefficient in data transmission between web service interfaces and DDMA, due to the inherent weakness of web service. Based on this, we proposed a caching mechanism on the cloud to deal with efficiency problem.

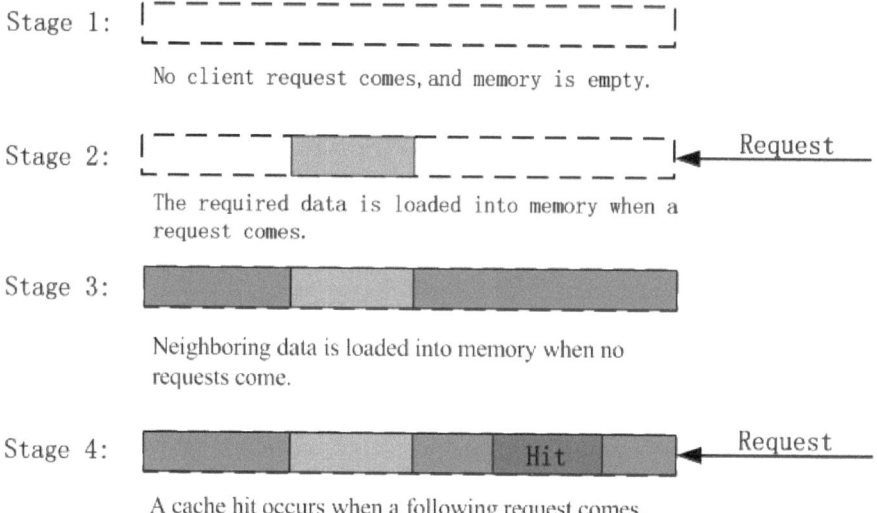

Fig. 3. Sequence diagram of memory scheduling

As Fig. 3 shows, upon receiving request from accredited client, URM will first get the required data from DDAM. After responding the coming request, URM will obtain data related to the latest request and load them into memory. When another request from the same client comes later, the required data will be probably loaded in main memory, because in practice requests from one client usually concentrate on neighboring data.

Based on the above consideration, a cache mechanism is proposed in this paper. The URM will not only allocate storage space for the coming request, but also for probable requests later. Certainly, storage space loaded in main memory is designed to be released when the session between clients and servers ends. In home appliance test, a data set usually contains test data from beginning to end (or till now), so when the proposed mechanism is applied to home appliance test, URM mainly maintains a complete data set of one test in the memory on the cloud.

3.3   Security Mechanism

As is well-known, it is challenging to implement effective security in web service framework. That means exposing web service interfaces on the Internet is a big security flaw. In this proposed architecture, web service interfaces are hidden on the cloud, clients will never be authorized direct access to these interfaces. So, adopting this architecture is part of the security mechanism.

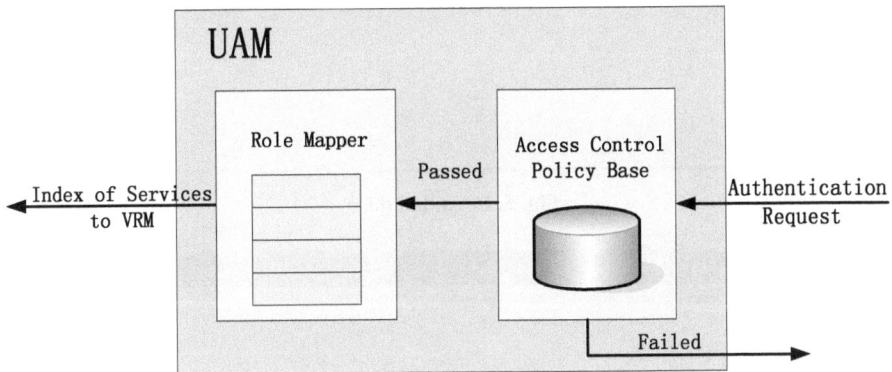

Fig. 4. User Authorization Module (UMA) Architecture

Further, a restrictive user access is adopted to ensure security of this cloud computing architecture. As Fig. 4 illustrates, every request from clients is supposed to turn to UAM for a certification with a pair of username and matched password. What's more, UAM not only responses with a "passed" or "failed" result to client request, but also generates a detailed privilege level if authentication is passed. Then depending on different levels, URM will present different index of services. In this way, we keep web service interfaces only open to certain authenticated users of sufficient authority.

4   Case Study (Implementation Results and Analysis)

In this section, a prototype application was constructed for validating the practicability and security of the proposed architecture. Additionally, we also analyze experimental data and draw some conclusions from it.

Before access to the cloud service, the authentication process is necessary. We use the traditional username and password way to realize this function. The login user interface is shown in Fig.5. After authentication, we could use the service smoothly to display data result in web browser. Fig.6 shows a user interface of household appliance test application. At the top of the frame, several different functions are provided, such as time profile, user profile and so on. The right frame shows the authority information of this user, which is listed in an expandable tree view.

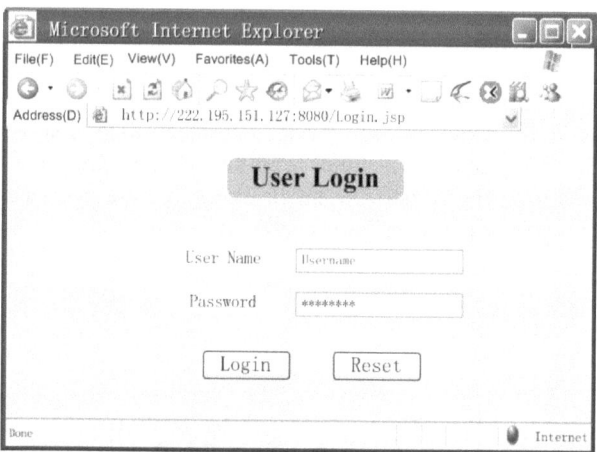

Fig. 5. Login Interface

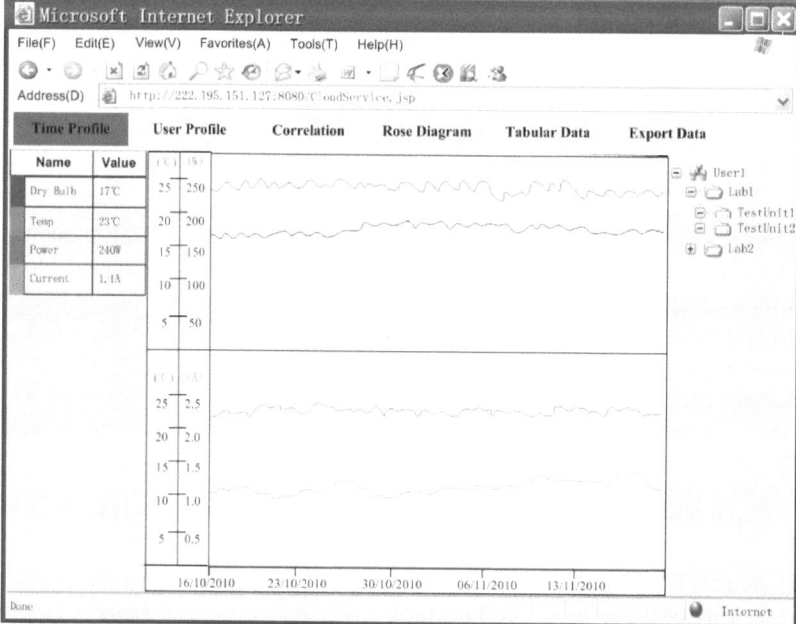

Fig. 6. User Interface

An experiment is done to test and prove that clients can gain a higher efficiency in getting data from server with all request data loaded in memory than from server without it. We define these two methods as cache method and non-cache method. Fig.7 specifies the detailed comparison diagram. Data volume is measured by the amount of time because data generates periodically in home appliance test. Obviously, cache method appears more efficient as its lower time cost. Table 1 indicates the time cost ratio between cache method and non-cache. With the growth of data volume, time cost ratio is stable at nearly 17%. Assume that we would require data covers 1000 hours one time and the cache hit rate is 50%. The system performance would be improved by 55.6%.

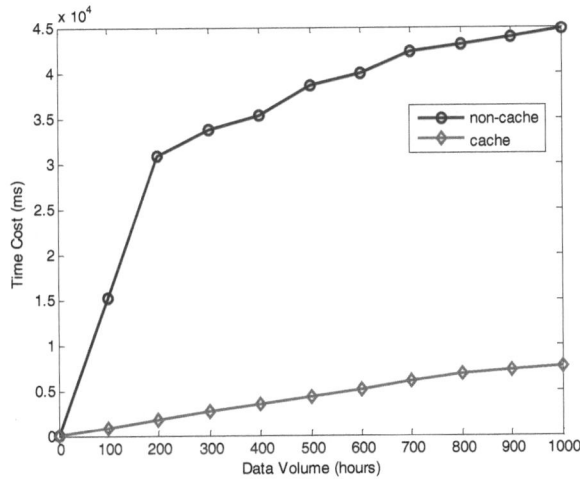

Fig. 7. Performance of cache method and non-cache method

Table 1. Time cost ratio

Data Volume	200	400	600	800	1000
Ratio	5.9%	10.02%	12.74	15.58%	16.9%

5   Conclusion and Future Work

Finally, as the object of study, a reformative architecture based on IEEE 1851 Standard is proposed. Existing resource in an enterprise can be integrated well by adopting this architecture. Furthermore it presents an opportunity for providing service over the Internet to improve resource utilization. We have discussed the challenges and opportunities for maintaining a sustained and stable service in cloud environments. Three important strategies are described to make the proposed architecture more efficient and secure. Implementation result shows practicability of the architecture and effectiveness of these mechanisms.

In this paper, we just implement system security mechanism on a small scale. When the number of users expands，many problems unexpected will have to be dealt with. Besides, according to our cumulative experience, the conclusion that individual user requests usually focus on neighboring data is drawn, and a minimum hit ratio is proposed for reference when a caching mechanism is designed. If more practical data are provided, we can obtain some other instructive results.

References

1. Gerber, C.: Computing in the clouds. Military Information Technology 12(10), 15–17 (2008)
2. Abdulrahman, A., Sarfraz, M.I., Basalamah, S.: A Distributed Access Control Architecture for Cloud Computing. IEEE Software, 36–44 (March/April 2012)
3. Buyya, R., Yeo, C.S., Venugopal, S., Broberg, J., Brandic, I.: Cloud Computing and Emerging IT Platforms: Vision, Hype, and Reality for Delivering Computing as the 5th Utility. Future Generation Computer Systems 25(6), 599–616 (2009)
4. Napper, J., Bientinesi, P.: Can Cloud Computing Reach the Top 500? In: UCHPC-MAW 2009, Ischia, Italy, May 18-20 (2009)
5. Daponte, P., Grimaldi, D., Nigro, L., Pupo, F.: Distributed measurement systems: An object-oriented architecture and a case study. Comput. Stand. Inter. 18(5), 383–395 (1997)
6. Song, E., Lee, K.: Service-oriented Sensor Data Interoperability for IEEE 1451 Smart Transducers. In: Proc. I2MTC, Singapore, May 5-7, pp. 1043–1048 (2009)
7. IEEE 1851, Standard for Design Criteria of Integrated Sensor-based Test Applications for Household Appliances. IEEE Standards Association (2012)
8. Takabi, H., Joshi, J.B.D., Ahn, G.-J.: Security and Privacy Challenges in Cloud Computing Environments. IEEE Security & Privacy 8(6), 24–31 (2010)
9. Amit, G., Heinz, S., David, G.: Formal Models of Virtual Enterprise Architecture: Motivations and Approaches. In: PACIS 2010 Proceeding (2010)
10. Patterson, D.A.: Technical perspective: the Data Center is the Computer. Communications of the ACM 51(1), 105 (2008)
11. Buyya, R., Yeo, C.S., Venugopal, S.: Market-oriented cloud computing: Vision, hype, and reality for delivering IT services as computing utilities. In: Proc. 10th IEEE Int. Conference on High Performance Computing and Communications, HPCC 2008, Dalian, China (September 2008)

Towards RESTful Communications
in Self-managing Pervasive Systems

Meherun Nesa Lucky, Christina Tziviskou, and Flavio De Paoli

Dipartimento di Informatica, Sistemistica e Comunicazione, Università di Milano-Bicocca
Viale Sarca 336/14, 20126, Milan, Italy
{meherun.lucky,christina.tziviskou,depaoli}@disco.unimib.it

Abstract. The presence of heterogeneous communication protocols and interfaces prevents from giving self-managing capabilities to service systems. This paper proposes the exploitation of the widely adopted HTTP protocol to create a shared platform that fosters the definition of services that can be easily integrated and controlled. Such services will be provided with RESTful interface and interaction style to gather data and control behavior of sensors to support the development of sensor services integrated with other services in pervasive systems.

Keywords: RESTful services, Sensors, Web Application, pervasive computing.

1 Introduction

Over the last decade, the Web has grown from a large-scale hypermedia application for publishing and discovering documents (i.e., Web pages) into a programmable medium for sharing data and accessing remote software components delivered as a service. The need of global availability and sharing of huge amount of information through various kinds of heterogeneous devices and services has changed the reference scenario for the development of Web scale applications. The consequent growing complexity and increasing request of adaptive services has made manual management impractical. A possible answer toward self-management is to make services smarter by achieving awareness of the target things' or the applications' physical environment or situations to respond proactively and intelligently. To tackle the problem a first effort should be the definition of a common protocol to foster automated interoperability.

As a matter of facts, the HTTP protocol has been used as a universal mean for tunneling messages in business-to-business scenarios, but quite often to support additional protocols, such as WSDL/SOAP for Web Services or OGC/SOS/SPS for sensors, that are usually not interoperable. In this paper, we investigate the correct and complete use of the HTTP protocol to publish, manage, and operate services on the Web by fully exploiting the REST (REpresentational State Transfer) principles [5]. Today, more and more services published on the Web are claiming to be designed using REST, but actually missing some of the features, like the hypermedia control, which is crucial to automate self-management operations.

A. Ghose et al. (Eds.): ICSOC 2012, LNCS 7759, pp. 263–274, 2013.

The rest of the paper discusses on integrating data from sensors and other services, which will be gathered by invoking different services through standardized interfaces by the Self-manageable Pervasive System to fulfill its task. To investigate the issue, we discuss two scenarios that differentiate between user control activities, where users are asked to invoke different types of services to fulfill a composite task, and self-managing pervasive system, where users invoke a single composite service without further interaction.

2   Motivations

Nowadays, the number and variety of available services on the Web enable for the definition of sophisticated composed services, which can take great advantage from pervasive computing and sensor Web to give users seamless assistance in daily activities. In pervasive computing environments, different devices often use different technologies, which make the communication complex and sometimes even troublesome.   Sensor Web has a central role in addressing new sources of information that need to be dynamically integrated into systems. The Sensor Web Enablement architecture of the Open Geospatial Consortium (OGC)[2] has been developed to enable flexible integration of sensors into any type of software system using standards: the Observations & Measurements and Sensor Model Language specifications define the exchanged sensor data; the Sensor Observation Service (SOS) gives pull-based access to observation data [3]; the Sensor Planning Service (SPS) tasks sensors [15].

We want to point out, through the discussion of a use case, the problems that arise from the diversity of the involved services, and show how the communication burden can be transferred from the user to self-managing pervasive systems. Then, we investigate the advantages of the RESTful approach as a mean for providing a common interface for services communication and control.

2.1   Use Case Scenario

We consider two versions of a scenario in which a user, let's say John, wants to go to watch a movie looks for route directions to available parking spaces close to the cinema hall. In the first version, the user is asked to interact with different Web Services of different types, such as Web Form-based, SOAP, API and RESTful Web services. As we have included sensors in our scenario, different OGC compliant services such as SOS and SPS are invoked. In the second version, a self-managing composite service minimizes the user interaction by transferring the control from the user to the service. Self-management will be achieved by providing sensors and services with RESTful interfaces to make interaction and control similar to the one already in use on the Web and therefore already familiar to both users and developers.

Use Case Scenario with User Control. As depicted in Fig. 1 (a), first John searches for movies by filling up the Web form of the Cinema Portal, and gets the list of movies meeting his search criteria, with the corresponding cinema hall name. Then, John chooses a cinema hall and invokes the Location Service API to get the address. Next, he invokes the Parking System, with RESTful interface, to get information about the available parking spaces close to the selected cinema hall. The Parking System interacts with the SOS and SPS services to get the observations from the video cameras and location sensors installed in the parking lots, and makes decisions about the available parking spaces. Finally, John chooses one parking lot from the list of the available ones, indicates his current position, and invokes the Route Service, through SOAP messages, to get directions on how to reach his destination.

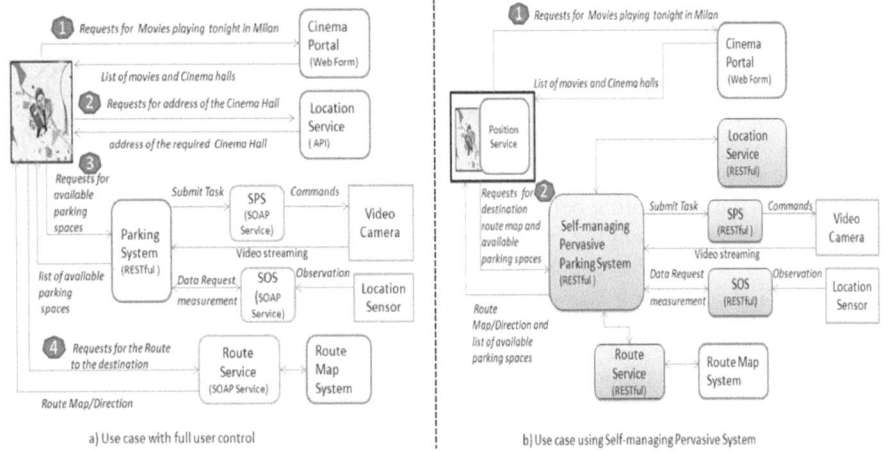

Fig. 1. Use case scenario

Use Case Scenario Based on a Self-managing Approach. In this version, the scenario has been changed to minimize the user control and add self-manageability to the system. The user invokes only two services: the Web Form-based Cinema Portal and the Self-managing Pervasive Parking System. Further, as shown in Fig. 1 (b), the user has the Position Service in his mobile, which is able to get automatically the position of the user and deliver it to other services. At first, John interacts with the Cinema Portal to get the list of movies of his interest, as before. Then, he selects a cinema hall and invokes the Parking System to get all the information needed to reach the destination. The Parking System interacts with different services: (i) invokes the Location Service to get the location of the selected cinema hall, (ii) invokes SOS and SPS to get observations about parking spaces, and decides which are the available parking spaces near to the cinema hall, (iii) gets the route direction for the nearest available parking spaces by interacting with the Position and the Route services, and (iv) delivers the cinema hall route direction to the user with maps.

2.2   Common Interface for Services Interactions: The RESTful Approach

In order to increase the system interoperability, we have designed the Self-managing Pervasive Parking System according to the Resource-Oriented Architecture that is devoted to manage distributed, heterogeneous resources in which client applications interact directly with the resources, by following the REST principles[5]:

1. Resources should be identified properly using URIs, so that each resource is uniquely addressable.
2. Uniform interfaces should be provided through the use of a standard application-level protocol. In this way, the operations to be applied on resources are external and they have well known semantics [12].
3. Resources are manipulated through their representations, since clients and servers exchange self-descriptive messages with each another. A resource can have multiple representations that follow a standardized format or media type and can be negotiated with the Web server. Representations convey the state of the client's interaction within the application and contain hyperlinks that allow clients to discover other resources or change the state of the current resource.
4. Interactions are stateless since servers only record and manage the state of the resources they expose, i.e., client sessions are not maintained on the server. This increases the decoupling between client and server.
5. Hypermedia is the engine of application state, i.e., the application state is build following hyperlinks according to the navigation paradigm. Therefore, the application state is not known a priori, but it is built based on user navigation.

Further, we expose data produced by the services according to the Linked Data paradigm. Linked Data Design defines[1] the following rules for exposing structured data on the Web: (i) use URIs to identify data as names, (ii) use HTTP to look up those names, (iii) provide useful information about URIs using standards, and (iv) include links to other URIs, so that they can discover more things.

Most of the technologies used in the first version of our use case (Fig. 1 (a)) do not follow the REST principles. Consequently, they compromise the interoperability of services and do not facilitate computer-to-computer interactions in the context of self-managing pervasive systems. In particular, the Route, SOS and SPS services communicate through SOAP messages. Thus, the HTTP methods are used as transport protocol while the application protocol is domain specific and the operations invoked by the user lay on the message envelope. Such communication pattern tunnels all the requests to a single URI that identifies an endpoint. HTTP GET and POST are the most-in-use methods but their semantics are not maintained, i.e. GET is used to invoke operations on server side that modify resources state, and therefore, it is not possible to optimize the network traffic by using caching mechanisms. Different is the case of the Web form-based Cinema Portal. The user interacts with different URIs via an html form, using again GET or POST possibly with a different semantics: URIs encapsulate server-side information, like operation names and parameters, revealing implementation details to the user. Such an approach enforces

---

[1] http://www.w3.org/DesignIssues/LinkedData.html

the coupling between the client and the server: if the server implementation changes, then the old URIs become invalid (operation and/or parameter names may change). The Location service publishes an API but interactions with the service are not hypermedia-driven since resources representation does not contain hypermedia controls and the user advances to the next state using some out-of-band information .

The pervasive computing system is expected to be seamlessly adapting, in a fully autonomic way, to different operational conditions to fulfill the user requirements. Autonomous actions need to be performed by enabled devices, sensors and/or services with different levels of capabilities. The Pervasive Parking System needs to access and control services that use different technologies in the communication which make interactions and integrations troublesome. This problem can be addressed by employing a common architectural style for implementing the involved interfaces. We propose to adopt the REST approach because interoperability is fostered by the use of standard technologies, the stateless RESTful interactions support scalability, and hypermedia controls reduce coupling between components by driving clients' interaction. Moreover, REST principles provide the opportunity to reuse and generalize the component interfaces, reduce interaction latency, enforce security, and encapsulate legacy systems by using intermediary components.

3   Related Work

In the domain of SOAP/WSDL services, messages are exchanged between endpoints of published applications by using the Web as a universal transport medium. In this way, the applications interact through the Web but remain "outside" of the Web. In addition, SOAP is the single standardized message format in this approach and messages are exchanged in both directions by using only one HTTP verb (POST). In the literature, there are several papers that compare the SOAP and the REST approaches (e.g., [12]). The major advantage of adopting full semantics of HTTP verbs to expose operations is that applications become part of the Web, making it a universal medium for publishing globally accessible information.

In the domain of sensors, the most relevant works are related to OGC standards. In [8], the authors have given a Linked Data model for sensor data and have implemented a RESTful proxy for SOS in order to improve integration and inter-linkage of observation data for the Digital Earth. We have been inspired from their work regarding the URI scheme for observations data, and the creation of meaningful links between data sets. We do not directly address the publication of sensor data as Linked Data but, according to the view presented in [17], we expose sensor data properly linked following the REST architectural style. Having sensor data properly structured on the Web is fundamental whenever integration needs to take place as in sensor networks. Our proposal extends the work in [8] towards hypermedia-driven interactions with OGC compliant services since we consider the explicit definition of the HTTP idioms used for operations, and the processing of observation groups.

Further approaches have addressed the discovery, selection and use of sensors as a service. An advanced approach in [6] offers search mechanisms of sensors that exploit semantic relationships and harvest sensor metadata into existing catalogues. In

[9], a model-based, service-oriented architecture has been used for composing complex services from elementary ones, on sensor nodes. The selection process evaluates the processing and communication cost of the service. In [1], the authors focus on service composition in pervasive systems. They propose ranking services based on context-related criteria so that the selection is based on the service matching score with the composition features. All the above mechanisms need to address critical aspects like the heterogeneity of interfaces and data models mismatches, and thus, can be used in conjunction to our proposal for the integration of sensor data in sensor networks. In [11], the authors describe the selection of services that match user preferences by collecting and evaluating services' descriptions. RESTful interactions can be integrated into such mechanism to facilitate the descriptions discovery and the services selection, and to enable pervasive systems make use of the selection process. Such solution minimizes the number of services and avoids unsuitable services in pervasive systems since it involves only the services that meet the user requirements.

In [4], an approach similar to ours investigates the use of the REST architectural style for providing the functionality of sensors in pervasive systems. It emphasizes the abstraction of data and services as resources, services interoperation via self-describing data and services orchestration with loosely typed components. We extend the authors effort towards a more structural approach of defining the URI scheme for resources, the HTTP idioms for sensors interactions and the application protocol driven by hypermedia links through standard formats. In [14], the DIGIHOME platform has been developed to deal with the heterogeneity, mobility and adaptation issues in smart homes where devices have advanced computational capabilities to improve the user satisfaction, but the heterogeneity of protocols used constrains the integration of these devices into a larger monitoring system. The platform provides software connectors for devices accessed by a variant of protocols such as ZigBee, SOAP and CAN, while HTTP is the communication protocol for the detection of adaptation situations and the handling of events. In [6], the authors explore REST as a mean to build a "universal" API for web-enabled smart things. They give emphasis on the decoupling of services from their representation and the negotiation mechanisms for the representation format, and they propose AtomPub to enable push interactions with sensors, and gateways that abstract communication with non Web-enabled devices behind a RESTful API. Although [14][6] use HTTP according to the REST principles, they do not make explicit how services with conventional interfaces are mapped to a RESTful API. We complement their research by defining rules for the URL writing, and we explore hypermedia controls for hypermedia driven interactions with the service.

4   Design of a RESTful Interface for OGC Services

In this section, we describe how to design RESTful services that are compliant with the OGC's SOS and SPS standards. We focus on activities that allow data sensor requestors to submit sensor tasks and retrieve the generated observations. These are the SPS operations *GetCapabilities*, *DescribeTasking*, *DescribeResultAccess*, *Submit*,

Update, Cancel and *GetStatus*, and the SOS operations *GetCapabilities*, *DescribeSensor* and *GetObservations*. The proposed paradigm enables computer-to-computer interactions since, in the context of sensor data it is a common need to have automated processes elaborating even raw data to proprietary formats.

The overall goal requires first to identify the structural elements of a RESTful interface because these will become the building blocks for RESTful services. The retrieval and managing of sensor data as resource representations requires the identification of (i) the resources of interest, and (ii) the permitted hypermedia-driven interactions of the consumer with the service offering the sensor data. We explore these two dimensions in terms of the URI scheme used to describe resources, the HTTP idioms (methods, headers, status codes) used to interact with the service, the domain application protocol, and the media type for hypermedia-driven interactions.

4.1   Sensor Data as Resources

In SOS and SPS services, resources result from the computations applied to data describing capabilities of services exposing sensor data, sensors as well as their tasks and their observations. The main data classes of objects retrieved are the following: *SOS Capabilities* provides metadata about a SOS service in terms of (i) parameters that may be used to filter the retrieval of observations, (ii) observation offerings used to further organize observations into sets, and (iii) set of sensors associated with the service; *SPS Capabilities* provides metadata about an SPS service in terms of sensors and phenomena that can be tasked; *Sensor* provides the highest level of detail of sensor metadata; *Task* provides information about the status of the tasking request and the task itself; *Observations* groups a set of observations retrieved using the same criteria; *Observation* associates a retrieved value with the sensor providing it, the offering it belongs to, the time period in which it was taken, etc.

The above classes are not enough to describe all the data objects involved in the interactions with SOS and SPS services, and thus, we introduce: the *FeatureOfInterest* to describe the observed stations; the *Observation Offering* to organize observations; the *ObservedProperty* to describe the phenomenon, i.e. temperature, we want to observe; the *Time* to indicate the time period of observations; and the *Procedure* to describe the method used to observe a phenomenon.

URI Scheme. We assign URIs to the objects of the above classes using the conventions proposed in [13] and used in [8, 16]. The base URI for every class has the form: http://my.host/class. Therefore, the URI http://my.host/observations represents a collection of all the observations published by the service. Further segments following the base URI refer to additional criteria to be used for the retrieval and correspond to parameters to be applied to the GetObservations SOS operation. We have identified the following situations in the parameters:

–   If the operation call requires *multiple parameters*, then two segments are appended to the URI for each parameter: the first segment indicates the data class corresponding to the parameter name, while the second one indicates the parameter value. Although, this is a strict order for the segments of one parameter, the segments of distinct parameters can be appended to the URI in an arbitrary way. The retrieved observations are those that satisfy all the criteria indicated in the URI. The *http://my.host/observations/sensors/urn:ogc:object: Sensor:MyOrg:13/observedProperty/urn:ogc:def:property:MyOrg:AggregateCh emicalPresence* points to the collection of observations about *urn:ogc:def:propertyMyOrg:AggregateChemicalPresence* taken by the sensor *urn:ogc:object:Sensor:MyOrg:13.*

- If a parameter has *multiple values*, then, since order is not relevant, the semicolon is used to separate the values in the corresponding segment. The retrieved observations are those that satisfy the indicated criteria for at least one of the values. The *http://my.host/observations/sensors/urn:ogc:object:Sensor:MyOrg: 13;urn:ogc:object:Sensor:MyOrg:12/observedProperty/urn:ogc:def:property:My Org:AggregateChemicalPresence* points to the collection of observations from the *urn:ogc:object:Sensor:MyOrg:13* or *urn:ogc:object:Sensor:Org:12* sensors.

- If a parameter has *a range of values*, then, since the order is relevant, the comma is used to separate the start value of the range from the end value in the corresponding segment. The *http://my.host/observations/sensors/urn:ogc:object: Sensor:MyOrg:13/eventTime/2011-04-14T17,2012-04-14T17,tm:rel:between/* points to the collection of observations taken from April 14th 2011 at 5pm and April 14th 2012 at 5pm. The time strings are encoded according to ISO 8601.

- If a parameter has *structured values*, then, since the order indicates the meaning of the value and thus, it is relevant, the comma is used to separate the values in the corresponding segment.

The above rules define the meaning of the URI segments and they are applied to all classes for assembling the URIs of the data objects defined by the class. The first segment after the service host indicates the class whose objects are to be retrieved. The successive segments indicate filtering conditions to be applied to the underlying retrieval mechanism. Because of the different computations that may be applied to retrieve the same resource, we have different URIs representing the same resource. This facilitates the resource access, but it could also be troublesome, if clients are not able to distinguish whether different URIs refer to the same resource. We follow the convention stated above and for each resource we keep an URI that serves as a reference for all the other URIs. Then, we explore hypermedia mechanisms to insert this reference URI in the response every time the client requests other URIs.

4.2   Hypermedia-Driven Interactions with Sensor Services

SPS and SOS services are complementary: the former schedules tasks for collecting sensor data, while the latter publishes the collected data. In particular:

- tasking requests are created when the user makes a submission;
- tasks are created by the service when a tasking request has been accepted;
- a user may retrieve tasks as well as tasking requests, to know their status;
- while a task is in execution, it can be updated and/or cancelled;
- during the execution of a task, observations are created and published;
- observations may be retrieved at any time after their publication.

HTTP Idioms. We distinguish the HTTP methods that may be used for the invocation of the above actions. Tasking requests are created with POST, retrieval of resource representations is achieved with GET, and tasks are updated with PATCH and cancelled with DELETE. We use POST instead of PUT for creating tasking requests because the service and not the user will create and associate an URI with the newly created resource. We use PATCH instead of PUT for updating tasks because the service allows incremental and not overall modifications.

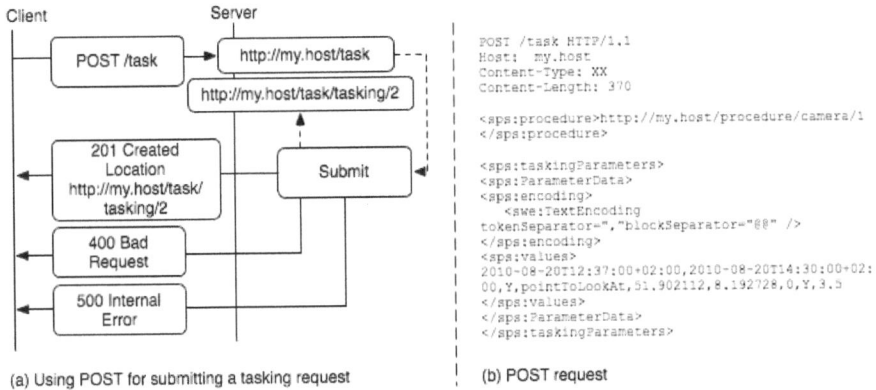

Fig. 2. POSTing a tasking request

In Fig. 2, we exemplify the HTTP request for submitting a tasking request. The request is composed of the POST method, the path that will serve the request at the server and the payload containing the tasking parameters. Upon reception of the request, the control is passed to the Submit operation, but the user remains unaware of this since the operation is inside the server boundaries. The operation creates a tasking request resource and sends the HTTP response to the user. Upon successful creation of the resource, the response status code is 201 Created, and the returned URI identifies its location. In the meanwhile, the system decides whether the requested task will be accepted, rejected or pending. The URI of the tasking request resource identifies also the task to be created and it will be used to GET, PATCH and DELETE the task on the server. Other status codes indicate: (i) a malformed request, and (ii) server failures that prevent the server from fulfilling the request. Similar are the HTTP requests for the remaining actions.

The Domain Application Protocol. Possible interactions a single user may have with both SOS and SPS services constitute an overall protocol for tasking sensors and getting their observations. The partial or complete execution of this protocol changes the state of the resources involved in the communication like tasking request, task and observations. Our method follows the methodology in [16]: resources are the central aspect in the service implementation and the user interactions drive their life cycle.

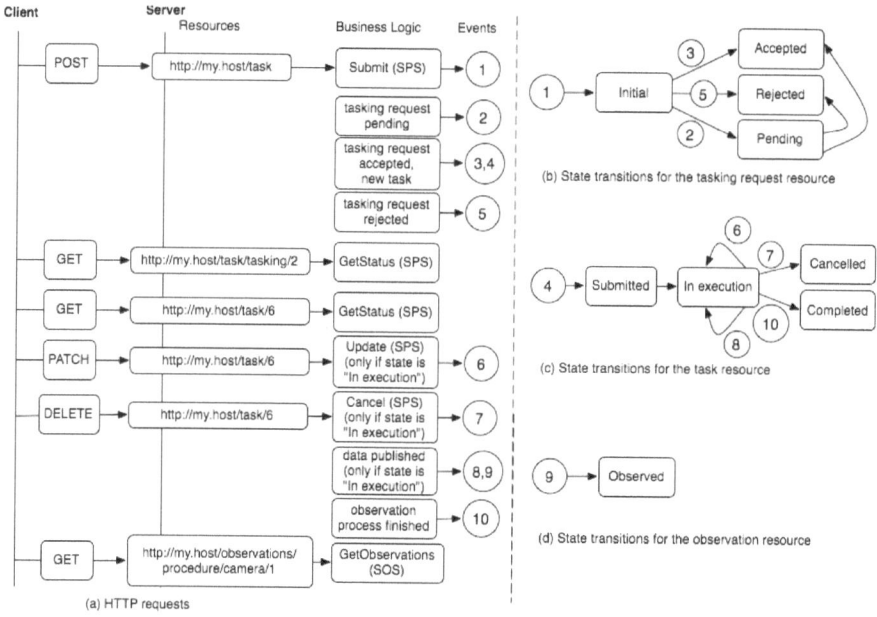

Fig. 3. (a) DAP and (b) resources state transitions

In Fig. 3 (a), we depict the HTTP requests of possible interactions and the events that will fire the state transition for resources. The user POSTs a tasking request, and the SPS Submit operation creates the tasking request resource that enters the *Initial* state (as shown in Fig. 3 (b)). Internal business logic decides whether the tasking resource's state will transition to *Pending*, *Accepted* or *Rejected* state fired by the corresponding events 2, 3 and 5. In case the tasking request is accepted, a new task resource is created, and the event 4 fires the entering of the task resource to the *Submitted* state and then automatically, to *In execution* state (Fig. 3 (c)). After the submission, the user may GET the status of the tasking request and/or task resource. These interactions do not have any server-side effect. As long as the task resource is *In execution* state, the user may PATCH modifications or DELETE the resource firing the events 6 and 7, and the publication of the collected sensor data is enabled. The latter activity fires the newly created observation resource to the *Observed* state (Fig. 3 (b)) and the user may GET its representation. Once the collection process is finished, the task resource transitions to the *Completed* state.

Hypermedia-Aware Media Type. In order to enable the user to create tasking requests and get observations without the need to explore any out-of-band information, we need to provide him with the entry point *http://my.host/task* where he may POST a tasking request, and then insert hypermedia controls in the HTTP responses so that link relations drive the user in the protocol described above. In Fig. 4 (a), we exemplify this mechanism with the HTTP response to the POST tasking request. The response contains both the tasking request resource representation, and links to further steps in the protocol. If the tasking request is pending, then the response provides a link for inquiring again the current tasking request and the task to be generated (it has the same URI as the tasking request). A subsequent user GET request for the tasking request representation, results to a different response since, in the meanwhile, the tasking request has been accepted and the task is in execution.

Fig. 4. Hypermedia-aware resource representation

The representation contains further links for retrieving the task resource, requesting modifications and canceling it, as well as links for getting the observations produced so far. The media type for resource representations must understand the semantics of these links in order to enable their automatic interpretation. We have used XHTML+RDFa in order to enable both human-to-computer and computer-to-computer interactions. RDFa extends XHTML with metadata that have the form of triples: subject-predicate-object. Link elements in Fig. 4 (b), convey the location where the task submitted by the current request maybe (i) retrieved, (ii) updated, and (iii) cancelled, and the location where observations may be retrieved. The *meta* element informs that the current context represents an SPS tasking request with id 2. The XML attribute *property* annotates semantically html elements so that a software agent understanding the SPS definitions can extract the enclosed information.

5   Conclusions

In this paper we have made a step towards the development of Self-managing Pervasive Systems by discussing the definition of RESTful interfaces to existing services, and, in particular to sensor services. The adoption of such a widely used communication standard enables for interoperability, which is the basic requirement to give services the capabilities to adapt their behavior. We have shown how Web services can become smarter and deliver more complex functionality by gathering information from sensors and traditional services with minimal human intervention, using inter-linkage of sensor data with hypermedia controls. A first prototype is under development for demonstrating the applicability of our proposal. In the future, we plan to continue in the effort of extending the adoption of REST and Linked Data paradigms to foster the integration of Internet of Things, Internet of Services, and

Internet of People by developing a common and interoperable platform on the existing Web infrastructure. Furthermore, we intend to adopt REST in the contract-driven selection of services [11] in pervasive systems.

Acknowledgements. The work has been partially supported by RegioneLombardia-IBM-UniMiB research grant n.12A135, and project PON01_00861 SMART-Services and Meta-services for SmART Government.

References

1. Bottaro, A., Gérodolle, A., Lalanda, P.: Pervasive Service Composition in the Home Network: Advanced Information Networking and Applications. In: 21st Int. Conf. on Advanced Networking and Applications, AINA 2007, Canada, pp. 596–603 (2007)
2. Botts, M., Percivall, G., Reed, C., Davidson, J.: OGC® Sensor Web Enablement: Overview and High Level Architecture. In: Nittel, S., Labrinidis, A., Stefanidis, A. (eds.) GSN 2006. LNCS, vol. 4540, pp. 175–190. Springer, Heidelberg (2008)
3. Broring, A., Stasch, C., Echterhoff, J.: OGC Sensor Observation Service Interface Standard. Open Geospatial Consortium (2010)
4. Drytkiewicz, W., Radusch, I., Arbanowski, S., Popescu-Zeletin, R.: pREST: a REST-based protocol for pervasive systems. In: IEEE International Conference on Mobile Ad-hoc and Sensor Systems, Fort Lauderdale, Florida, pp. 340–348. IEEE (2004)
5. Fielding, R.T.: Architectural Styles and the Design of Network-based Software Architectures. Ph.D. thesis, University of California, Irvine (2000)
6. Guinard, D., Trifa, V., Wilde, E.: A Resource Oriented Architecture for the Web of Things. In: Proceedings of the International Conference on Internet of Things 2010, IoT (2010)
7. Ibbotson, J., Gibson, C., Wright, J., Waggett, P., Zerfos, P., Szymanski, B.K., Thornley, D.J.: Sensors as a Service Oriented Architecture: Middleware for Sensor Networks. In: 6th Int. Conf. on Intelligent Environment, Kuala Lumpur, Malaysia, pp. 209–214 (2010)
8. Janowicz, K., Broring, A., Stasch, C., Schade, S., Everding, T., Llaves, A.: A RESTful Proxy and Data Model for Linked Sensor Data. International Journal of Digital Earth, 1–22, doi:10.1080/17538947.2011.614698
9. Jirka, S., Bröring, A., Stasch, C.: Discovery Mechanisms for the Sensor Web. Sensors 9(4), 2661–2681 (2009)
10. Palmonari, M., Comerio, M., De Paoli, F.: Effective and Flexible NFP-Based Ranking of Web Services. In: Baresi, L., Chi, C.-H., Suzuki, J. (eds.) ICSOC-ServiceWave 2009. LNCS, vol. 5900, pp. 546–560. Springer, Heidelberg (2009)
11. Panziera, L., Comerio, M., Palmonari, M., De Paoli, F., Batini, C.: Quality-driven Extraction, Fusion and Matchmaking of Semantic Web API Descriptions. Journal of Web Engineering 11(3), 247–268 (2012)
12. Pautasso, C., Zimmermann, O., Leymann, F.: RESTful Web Services vs. "Big" Web Services: Making the Right Architectural Decision. In: 17th International World Wide Web Conference, Beijing, China. ACM Press (2008)
13. Richardson, L., Ruby, S.: RESTful Web Services. O'Reilly, Sebastopol (2007)
14. Romero, D., Hermosillo, G., Taherkordi, A., Nzekwa, R., Rouvoy, R., Eliassen, F.: RESTful Integration of Heterogeneous Devices in Pervasive Environments. In: Eliassen, F., Kapitza, R. (eds.) DAIS 2010. LNCS, vol. 6115, pp. 1–14. Springer, Heidelberg (2010)
15. Simonis, I., Echterhoff, J.: OGC Sensor Planning Service Implementation Standard (2011)
16. Webber, J., Parastatidis, S., Robinson, I.: REST in Practice. O'Reilly, Sebastopol (2010)
17. Wilde, E.: Linked Data and Service Orientation. In: Maglio, P.P., Weske, M., Yang, J., Fantinato, M. (eds.) ICSOC 2010. LNCS, vol. 6470, pp. 61–76. Springer, Heidelberg (2010)

A Research Roadmap
for Context-Awareness-Based
Self-managed Systems

Weishan Zhang[1], Klaus Marius Hansen[2], and Paolo Bellavista[3]

[1] Department of Software Engineering, China University of Petroleum, No. 66
Changjiang West Road, Qingdao, China, 266580
zhangws@upc.edu.cn
[2] Department of Computer Science (DIKU), University of Copenhagen, Njalsgade
128, 2300 Copenhagen S, Denmark
klausmh@diku.dk
[3] DISI, University of Bologna, V.le Risorgimento, 2 - 40136 Bologna, Italy
paolo.bellavista@unibo.it

Abstract. Cloud computing, autonomic computing, pervasive and mobile computing tends to converge, maximizing the benefits from different
computing paradigms. This convergence makes emerging applications
such as search and rescue applications, smart city and smart planet
applications, e.g., to minimize the power consumption of a full city to
achieve green computing vision, more promising on the one hand, but
more complex to manage on the other hand. Interesting research questions arise due to this convergence. For example, how to efficiently retrieve underlying contexts that are difficult to recognize especially with
resource-limited handheld devices, how to make use of these contexts
for achieving self-management, and how to process large-scale contexts.
These challenges require that researchers from software engineering, artificial intelligence, pattern recognition, high-performance distributed systems, cloud and mobile computing, etc. collaborate in order to make
systems work in an efficiently self-managed manner.

1 Introduction

There is a growing trend for the convergence of different computing paradigms,
such as cloud computing, pervasive and mobile computing, among others due to
the needs of global availability and sharing of information at different scales [5][7].
For example, there are more and more work on mobile cloud computing research
[7] where mobile computing node is enhanced by making use of a cloud computing
infrastructure [6][4], or creating a light weight cloud infrastructure using the
MapReduce architecture [8] [16]. Considering the development of mobile and
pervasive computing, the mobile cloud computing is deemed to evolve to a so
called pervasive cloud computing, where light weight clouds and classical heavy
weight clouds are working harmoniously.

A. Ghose et al. (Eds.): ICSOC 2012, LNCS 7759, pp. 275–283, 2013.

In the converged computing environment, in order to achieve the vision of a smart planet, it is important to obtain meaningful information from various sources at a large scale due to the deployment of the Internet of Things/Services (IoT/IoS). However, it is not always possible to expect stable, reliable, always-available data from surrounding environments, among others due to the uncertainty, fuzziness, unavailability of data from sensors. Most often the processing, retrieval, and reasoning on contexts are to be done (sometimes partially) on small devices, which further calls for a supporting infrastructure, e.g., for dynamic offloading and management of temporarily intermittent connectivity. Therefore, applications and systems tend to become more complex than before to manage and operate in the converged world. This calls for useful self-managing capabilities.

The requirements of self-management capabilities come from different application domains, for example, next-generation e-health applications, smarter cities, up to an envisioned smarter planet where the wide-scale collection of monitoring/sensing data from the whole Earth will enable new forms of mass behavior understanding and powerful predictions (for instance, see the FuturICT Knowledge Accelerator project[1]). But the achievement of self-managing capabilities is hard. Devices/equipment in an application should be able to deal with ever-changing execution environments and information sources while offering their users timely and relevant services. Furthermore, devices should adapt to these changes in a seamless manner by following (often application-specific) quality of service requirements with the support from awareness contexts [22]. Very often the awareness of contexts is hard to achieve also, due to the ambiguity of sensed data, the big scale of the IoT/IoS events, and other factors such as the processing capabilities of handheld devices.

In the following, we will first present the application domains of self-managed pervasive services and discuss of problems that arise in the domain together with some possible solutions and research directions. We then summarize the research challenges of self-management pervasive systems. Finally, we discuss the expected results of our roadmap for near-future research in context-aware self-managed systems.

2   Applications

2.1   E-Health

In many countries, the proportion of people with a high age is increasing, thereby increasing the cost of healthcare. Pervasive health services such as health status monitoring (including for example blood pressure and pulse monitoring) and food recognition and recommendation become essential parts of e-health applications. In these examples, monitoring may be important in treatments for high blood pressure whereas food recognition may be useful for some diseases like Ulcerative Colitis (UC) where food intake may have serious consequences. These

---

[1] http://www.futurict.eu

applications involving small devices require self-managed and optimal running to, e.g., save energy in order to prolong running time.

In these healthcare applications, some contexts are hard to be obtained with resource scarce devices. For example, in a meal, several food items are mixed together maybe with seasoning. In such a case, it is hard to figure out exact food types and calculate the amount of food through hand-held smart phones [10]. Therefore, fast image recognition algorithms running efficiently on mobile phones are needed, as well as a supporting infrastructure like a public computation cloud that can be used for further recognition to improve the results obtained on a mobile phone. For some unknown food that is not in the sample image database, ontological reasoning can be utilized to obtain food type information.

Some interesting research issues that arise are how to make the whole system work in a globally balanced manner to save energy, e.g. through dynamic switching of interaction protocols [23] and which node in the cloud is used to store an ontology knowledge base to get better reasoning performance. Even the mobile phones themselves can be utilized to form a computing cloud in cases the remote cloud is not available, but need processing power in order to handle emergency cases [7]. For such a mobile cloud, self-management to achieve some quality of service requirements is very important, for example having a low response time and saving energy at the same time. Other open issues include how to make decisions on the migration of services/component among cloud nodes at self-managed manner, and which algorithms are used in the migration process.

2.2 Smart Cities

The concept of "smart cities" is emerging as a major innovation driver for better health, environment, life quality and businesses [9]. In a smart city application, the IoT/IoS is typically deployed across a city. For example, traffic jams is a major problem in large cities and here wireless sensor networks can be used to monitor the position and speed of vehicles on road networks in real-time. To handle the incompleteness, complexity and unpredictability of traffic condition information, control strategies like fuzzy sets, case-based reasoning, and genetic algorithms are used to make decisions [19]. Such traffic control systems may also need supporting infrastructures in the form of, e.g., public cloud systems to handle computation intensive tasks like route planning, and store large data sets on vehicles routes. Let us note that also e-health applications, when moving from personal and single-user services towards community-oriented solutions to detect and guide the behaviors of a large set of citizens (e.g., the people under the public health services of an entire region or country), can be seen as a very relevant part of the envisioned smart city applications, sharing with them many technical challenges, as detailed in the following.

Compared to a typical pervasive computing system, a smart city application has some new issues, mainly because the scale of an application is very large, the topology of the networking is unknown due to the uncertainly of the availability of sensors and mobility of some devices, and there is much higher heterogeneity of the inter-connected devices [21]. In such situations, it is hard to realize holistic and comprehensive context-awareness [5] and thus high-level inference is needed to know the actual contexts and make decisions [21]. This could be using a hybrid of different artificial intelligence approaches as in [19]. For large-scale sensing in IoT applications, collaborative sensing can be used to improve context accuracy and reliability [13].

3   Research Challenges

Considering the above applications, we now summarize the technical challenges for context-awareness and self-management research in order to highlight some directions of potential future work.

Context Modeling, Recognition, and Reasoning. More fundamental research is needed to make the currently available modeling languages more capable of expressing and reasoning over probability, fuzziness, and inaccurate situations. We have seen some work towards this, such as [25], but more efforts are needed, e.g., to make the modeling and reasoning work efficiently on resource-scarce devices. To recognize certain contexts, different techniques are under investigation and not yet ready, at least from the industrial application perspective, e.g., we need faster image recognition algorithms to identify food. Also, as noted in [14], hybrid knowledge representation and reasoning is needed to combine benefits from OWL (Web Ontology Language)[2], RDF (Resource Description Framework), text-based information retrieval/extraction, and machine-learning-based probabilistic handling.

Comprehensive Context-Awareness. Critical and highly dynamic contexts are not completely considered in nowadays real-life applications [22], which partially hinder the realization of comprehensive and holistic context-awareness [5]. Also due to the large scale of the IoT/IoS applications, knowing the global dynamic status of systems, efficiently processing large number of events from different resources, and obtaining meaningful contexts from these events are important and open issues. A cloud computing infrastructure can be used to perform computationally intensive tasks, e.g., to extract contexts, and is helpful to realize comprehensive context-awareness [11], which is worth of further investigations.

Quality of Contexts (QoC). Quality of Contexts (QoC) can help to resolve uncertain and conflicting situations involving context information [1]. For instance, context information may not be accurate, such as for identified food items, as discussed above. Other sources of contexts, such as wireless sensors in the field, may be offline at any time. To handle uncertainty and inaccuracy from various context sources, new supporting ontologies are proposed in [21]. QoC may be used in this process and can be parts of context ontologies [18] used to measure raw, derived,

---

[2] http://www.w3.org/TR/owl2-overview/

and inferred contexts. Due to the large number of events and contexts in IoT/IoS applications, QoC can be used to manage such complexity, e.g., by helping to filter out irrelevant context information and keep only the metadata that are expected to be more useful for a specific user/application/execution situation. How and to what extent an application is tolerant enough for such inaccurate and unreliable contexts needs to be investigated.

Unexpected Adaptations. Domain experts can make decisions in unexpected situations on how to bypass problems [21]. How such kind of totally unexpected situations can be handled to make appropriate decisions computationally and automatically is an unsolved technical challenge nowadays [2]. If completely automatic control is not possible, then how can we predict the situation and time when involvement of human experts is necessary? This challenge, central to self-managed context-aware systems, is particularly important and timely for safety-critical applications.

Hybrid Intelligence. Due to the complexity, scale, uncertainty, and fuzziness nature of real-world self-managed systems, a single intelligence mechanism is hardly sufficient to deal with the 'smartness' requirements in, e.g., smart city applications. The current self-management approaches employing mainly single mechanisms cannot always meet the intelligence requirements that challenging smart applications are calling for [3]. How to use hybrid artificial intelligence techniques to get better reasoning capabilities, as shown in [19] and [24] is an interesting issue. Problems need to be resolved on how to make different mechanisms work harmoniously, how to distribute different reasoning capabilities among different nodes in a (partly mobile/pervasive) cloud, and how to make different mechanisms work efficiently on resource-scarce devices by automatically considering the availability of different resources.

Efficient Management of Pervasive Clouds. Pervasive and mobile cloud become promising choices for enhancing the capabilities of pervasie and mobile computing systems. To support the migration of components and services between different nodes in the named pervasive cloud, a comprehensive self-management context knowledge base is needed for pervasive cloud environments, and correspondingly, a context-management framework for pervasive clouds. Also efficient algorithms and mechanisms are needed to support the migration of services following various QoS requirements [15], which may be conflicting with each other. To achieve this, some hybrid intelligence may be needed to support making decisions at different self-management layers.

Tool Support and Testbeds for Development. Tool support for developing context-awareness and self-management applications are critical for their acceptance and adoption. There are some development environments created (for example in the Hydra (LinkSmart) [22] and MUSIC [20] projects), but tool support for self-managed applications are still in their infancy and cannot easily provide testbeds for exploring different self-management features or adding new or removing existing self-management features. In the long run, tools should allow end-users to enable programming by themselves [2] and provide easy-to-use self-management capabilities that can be extended with very limited and rapid efforts by developers.

Unified Architecture and Standards. There has been quite some research on middleware for self-managed pervasive systems, e.g. Hydra (LinkSmart) and the self-adaptive architecture of MUSIC. But there is still no unified solution approach that can be considered as a reference architecture for self-managed systems [3]. We are even not closer to the old question of "What does it mean to program hello world for ubicomp" [2]? The three-layered architecture proposed by Kramer and Magee [12] is abstract and extensible enough to incorporate different self-management strategies, and was adopted in Hydra [22]. This work may have the potential to be used as a high-level reference architecture, but needs to be specialized for different domains and applications. Research work also needs to be expanded on autonomic software components, and formally restricting their adaptiveness to avoid any unexpected violations of architecture constraints at runtime. The lack of a unified and widespread recognized architecture of solution exacerbates the interoperability issues of the systems proposed so far; standardization and interoperability are crucial to reduce development costs and to guarantee long-term value of development efforts/investments in the field.

Security and Privacy. As well as for interoperability, so far there is very little work on enforcing conventional and physical boundaries to improve security mechanisms for context sensing [2]. Location of data thus needs to be investigated, especially in the converged computing environments, for example which node is used for storage and processing of private data in a cloud-based solution for self-managed context-aware systems. As it is hard for users to specify their privacy preferences as used in current approaches, there is a strong need to investigate automated practices and techniques for context-based privacy protection [14].

4   Expected Result

Self-management remains as one of the most important research issues for future Internet applications [17]. The realization of self-management needs cross-discipline research, design, and implementation. For example, software engineering research on autonomic software components, architecture driven self-management, dynamic configuration, and adaptation of autonomic components need to be combined.

Software engineering researchers should develop tools and environments to help the creation of self-management applications. Cloud computing researchers should bring ideas on how to make use of the cloud infrastructure to make the self-management and context-awareness working more efficiently in a more scalable way. At the same time, they will benefit from the ideas of context-awareness on how to optimize the running of cloud systems to provide better services, and expand their services to small, mobile, and embedded devices where to dynamically offload parts of the distributed applications. Artificial intelligence researchers should develop efficient algorithms to run on small devices for conducting efficient reasoning for, e.g., optimizing system configurations and planning how to reach the best configurations. Therefore, collaborations between the different areas of software engineering, context aware computing, system and network engineering, autonomic and self-managed computing, cloud and mobile computing, and artificial intelligence is needed and critical to making the self-managing systems scale in small and resource-scarce devices, with high usability, good performance, and secure services as a result. Given the complexity of the related technical challenges, we claim that cross fertilization among different research areas and strong interdisciplinarity are essential to put together effective solutions for this promising field of context-aware, large-scale, self-managed systems.

Acknowledgments. Weishan Zhang has been supported by "the Fundamental Research Funds for the Central Universities" and also the start up funds for "Academic Top-Notch in China University of Petroleum' professors.

References

1. Bu, Y., Gu, T., Tao, X., Li, J., Chen, S., Lu, J.: Managing quality of context in pervasive computing. In: Sixth International Conference on Quality Software, QSIC 2006, pp. 193–200. IEEE (2006)
2. Cáceres, R., Friday, A.: Ubicomp systems at 20: Progress, opportunities, and challenges. IEEE Pervasive Computing 11(1), 14–21 (2012)
3. Cheng, B.H.C., de Lemos, R., Giese, H., Inverardi, P., Magee, J., Andersson, J., Becker, B., Bencomo, N., Brun, Y., Cukic, B., Di Marzo Serugendo, G., Dustdar, S., Finkelstein, A., Gacek, C., Geihs, K., Grassi, V., Karsai, G., Kienle, H.M., Kramer, J., Litoiu, M., Malek, S., Mirandola, R., Müller, H.A., Park, S., Shaw, M., Tichy, M., Tivoli, M., Weyns, D., Whittle, J.: Software Engineering for Self Adaptive Systems: A Research Roadmap. In: Cheng, B.H.C., de Lemos, R., Giese, H., Inverardi, P., Magee, J. (eds.) Self-Adaptive Systems. LNCS, vol. 5525, pp. 1–26. Springer, Heidelberg (2009)
4. Christensen, J.H.: Using restful web-services and cloud computing to create next generation mobile applications. In: Proceedings of the 24th ACM SIGPLAN Conference Companion on Object Oriented Programming Systems Languages and Applications, pp. 627–634. ACM (2009)
5. Conti, M., Das, S.K., Bisdikian, C., Kumar, M., Ni, L.M., Passarella, A., Roussos, G., Tröster, G., Tsudik, G., Zambonelli, F.: Looking ahead in pervasive computing: challenges and opportunities in the era of cyber-physical convergence. Pervasive and Mobile Computing (2011)
6. Corredor, I., Martínez, J.F., Familiar, M.S.: Bringing pervasive embedded networks to the service cloud: A lightweight middleware approach. Journal of Systems Architecture (2011)
7. Dinh, H.T., Lee, C., Niyato, D., Wang, P.: A survey of mobile cloud computing: architecture, applications, and approaches. In: Wireless Communications and Mobile Computing (2011)

8. Dou, A., Kalogeraki, V., Gunopulos, D., Mielikainen, T., Tuulos, V.H.: Misco: A mapreduce framework for mobile systems. In: Proceedings of the 3rd International Conference on PErvasive Technologies Related to Assistive Environments p. 32. ACM (2010)
9. Komninos, N., Pallot, M., Schaffers, H.: Special issue on smart cities and the future internet in Europe. Journal of the Knowledge Economy, 1–16 (2012)
10. Kong, F., Tan, J.: Dietcam: Automatic dietary assessment with mobile camera phones. Pervasive and Mobile Computing (2011)
11. Kovachev, D., Klamma, R.: Context-aware mobile multimedia services in the cloud. In: Proceedings of the 10th International Workshop of the Multimedia Metadata Community on Semantic Multimedia Database Technologies (2009)
12. Kramer, J., Magee, J.: Self-managed systems: an architectural challenge. In: Future of Software Engineering, FOSE 2007, pp. 259–268. IEEE (2007)
13. Lukowicz, P., Choudhury, T., Gellersen, H.: Beyond context awareness. IEEE Pervasive Computing 10(4), 15–17 (2011)
14. Lukowicz, P., Nanda, S., Narayanan, V., Albelson, H., McGuinness, D.L., Jordan, M.I.: Qualcomm context-awareness symposium sets research agenda for context-aware smartphones. IEEE Pervasive Computing 11(1), 76–79 (2012)
15. Ma, R.K.K., Lam, K.T., Wang, C.L.: excloud: Transparent runtime support for scaling mobile applications in cloud. In: 2011 International Conference on Cloud and Service Computing (CSC), pp. 103–110. IEEE (2011)
16. Marinelli, E.E.: Hyrax: cloud computing on mobile devices using mapreduce. Technical report, DTIC Document (2009)
17. Metzger, A., Cassales Marquezan, C.: Future Internet Apps: The Next Wave of Adaptive Service-Oriented Systems? In: Abramowicz, W., Llorente, I.M., Surridge, M., Zisman, A., Vayssière, J. (eds.) ServiceWave 2011. LNCS, vol. 6994, pp. 230–241. Springer, Heidelberg (2011)
18. Miron, A.D., Satoh, I., Gensel, J., Martin, H., et al.: Modeling and measuring quality of context information in pervasive environments. In: 2010 24th IEEE International Conference on Advanced Information Networking and Applications (AINA), pp. 690–697. IEEE (2010)
19. Nakamiti, G., da Silva, V.E., Ventura, J.H., da Silva, S.A.: Urban Traffic Control and Monitoring – An Approach for the Brazilian Intelligent Cities Project. In: Wang, Y., Li, T. (eds.) Practical Applications of Intelligent Systems. AISC, vol. 124, pp. 543–551. Springer, Heidelberg (2011)
20. Rouvoy, R., Barone, P., Ding, Y., Eliassen, F., Hallsteinsen, S., Lorenzo, J., Mamelli, A., Scholz, U.: MUSIC: Middleware Support for Self-Adaptation in Ubiquitous and Service-Oriented Environments. In: Cheng, B.H.C., de Lemos, R., Giese, H., Inverardi, P., Magee, J. (eds.) Self-Adaptive Systems. LNCS, vol. 5525, pp. 164–182. Springer, Heidelberg (2009)
21. Teixeira, T., Hachem, S., Issarny, V., Georgantas, N.: Service Oriented Middleware for the Internet of Things: A Perspective. In: Abramowicz, W., Llorente, I.M., Surridge, M., Zisman, A., Vayssière, J. (eds.) ServiceWave 2011. LNCS, vol. 6994, pp. 220–229. Springer, Heidelberg (2011)
22. Zhang, W., Hansen, K.M.: Using context awareness for self-management in pervasive service middleware. In: Handbook of Research on Ambient Intelligence and Smart Environments: Trends and Perspectives, vol. 1, p. 248 (2011)

23. Zhang, W., Hansen, K.M., Fernandes, J., Schütte, J., Lardies, F.M.: Qos-aware self-adaptation of communication protocols in a pervasive service middleware. In: 2010 IEEE/ACM Int'l Conference on Green Computing and Communications (Green-Com), & Int'l Conference on Cyber, Physical and Social Computing (CPSCom), pp. 17–26. IEEE (2010)
24. Zhang, W., Hansen, K.M., Kunz, T.: Enhancing intelligence and dependability of a product line enabled pervasive middleware. Pervasive and Mobile Computing 6(2), 198–217 (2010)
25. Zhao, J., Boley, H., Du, W.: A Fuzzy Logic Based Approach to Expressing and Reasoning with Uncertain Knowledge on the Semantic Web. In: Madani, K., Dourado Correia, A., Rosa, A., Filipe, J. (eds.) Computational Intelligence. SCI, vol. 399, pp. 167–181. Springer, Heidelberg (2012)

A 3D Model Based Action Recorder
Using Computer Vision

Yong Li[1], Yuan Rao[2], Youxiang Duan[1], and Weishan Zhang[1]

[1] College of Computer & Communication Engineering, China University of Petroleum
No. 66 Changjiang West Road, Huangdao District, Qingdao, China, 266580
[2] School of Software Engineering, Xi'an Jiaotong University, Xi'an, China, 710049
{evaleao,yxduan,zhangws}@upc.edu.cn, raoyuan@mail.xjtu.edu.cn

Abstract. In healthcare systems, video surveillance, interactive games and many other applications, human action recognition and recording are very important. This paper presents a comprehensive 3D model based action recording system using computer visions. First, a computer captures human motion videos with a network camera and conducts further detection and tracking of the video resources, then a 3D model is created based on the recorded data results. The action recording system includes background capturing, characters capturing, action tracking, 3D modeling and OGRE controlling. OpenCV is used for background and characters capturing where a background image difference algorithm is used to analyze a moving target and extract different elements. For the action tracking, the Camshift (Continuously Adaptive Mean shift Algorithm) tracking algorithm is used to realize continuous tracking and recognition of moving objects and ensure good performance of the action recorder. In our implementation, 3Dmax is used to build a 3D model and skeletal animations, where Ogremax is used to export models, and then to import the skeletal animations into a testing environment. The evaluations show that our motion recognition and recording system has good performance in one aspect, and can obtain accurate result on the other aspect.

Keywords: Target detection and tracking, Background difference, Action recognition.

1   Introduction

Human computer interaction is very active due to computing devices are increasing more and more popular in everyday life. Human movements are usually captured using various kinds of sensors, and then the movement information is recorded to re-produce virtual actions. These sensors include mechanical, acoustic, electromagnetic and optical ones. For example, the SixthSense interactive technology based on OpenCV is a wearable gestural interface device invented by Pranav Mistry at the MIT Media Lab[1], where a pocket projector, a mirror, a camera and a mobile computer are

---

[1] http://www.pranavmistry.com/projects/sixthsense/

A. Ghose et al. (Eds.): ICSOC 2012, LNCS 7759, pp. 284–293, 2013.

involved. Other researchers are working on capturing and keeping track of human action at real time using computer graphics and hardware capabilities, built-in a computer. It transfers human motion parameters to a physical model to reproduce the movements of a target in a virtual scene[2].

Some of the most prominent problems with the current research and prototypes of the motion recognition and recording systems are their high costs due to the usage of expensive sensors and some other high-end equipment, heavy weight computations due to complex recognition algorithms[3]. Some occasions only need to monitor basic actions of the monitored subject, and some cases may only allow to use simple camera to conduct monitoring. Therefore, there need solutions that can make use of cheap and widely available sensors to provide feasible solutions that can be widely adopted for normal every usage.

Considering all these issues, we tried to combine the convenience of SixthSence with some simple algorithms based on computer vision, and to use 3D model action library to present the recorded human actions. Then a comprehensive 3D model based action recording system using computer visions that can work almost anywhere is implemented, where the action recognition and recording is realized using an ordinary network camera and a simple algorithm to reduce costs and resource consumptions. The accuracy of action recognition is enhanced by 3D model actions in a system action library to express new actions.

The rest of the paper is structured as follows: Section 2 presents the design of the action recognition and recording system. Then Section 3, 4, 5 and 6 present how the system works include static background obtaining and updating, characters capturing, action tracking, 3D modeling and OGRE control judgment. Section 7 presents our evaluations in terms of performance and accuracy of recognitions. We compare our work with the related work in Section 8. Conclusions and future work end the paper.

2   Design of an Action Recognition and Recording System

Our action recognition and recording system mainly include the processes of background capturing, characters capturing, action tracking, 3D modeling and OGRE controlling, as shown in Figure 1.

At first in order to obtain a human body that appeared in a scene later, a network camera is used to capture static scene as the basis for moving objects detection. The system background is updated continuously.

Then in the characters capturing step, when a human enters the scene, the system detects the changing area of the image sequences and picks up the motion target from the background image. Usually only the pixel area corresponding to the motion target is considered in the motion tracking process.

After human characters are captured, the system starts to track the extracted detection target using the Camshift algorithm [5][6]. In this step, at first the system considers color information of a tracking target, this color information is used as

---

[2] http://www.pranavmistry.com/projects/sixthsense/

[3] http://en.wikipedia.org/wiki/Motion_capture

features of the tracking target, which is projected to the next frame of images to obtain the target. Then this frame of image is considered as a new source image for its immediate next frame. This process is repeated to achieve continuous tracking.

Finally the information captured from these early steps is expressed using a 3D model. We setup up bones binding where the skeletons are adjusted to the same size of the 3D model. After that, a 3D actions library is built to store different actions of characters. When a human motion is captured in a scene, the 3D model reacted with a corresponding action according to the captured color information. Then the system extracts animations from this 3D model entity and redraws this motion.

OpenCV (Open Source Computer Vision Library) is used for background and characters capturing. A background difference algorithm is used to analyze the moving target and extract different elements. For action tracking, the Camshift tracking algorithm is used to realize continuous tracking and recognition of moving objects and ensure the continuity of the action recorder [1]. 3DMAX is used to build skeletal animations. The skeletal animations are imported into the testing environment using OGRE APIs, which are controlled according to the captured features to realize the recording of body movement. We can see the detailed process as in Figure 1.

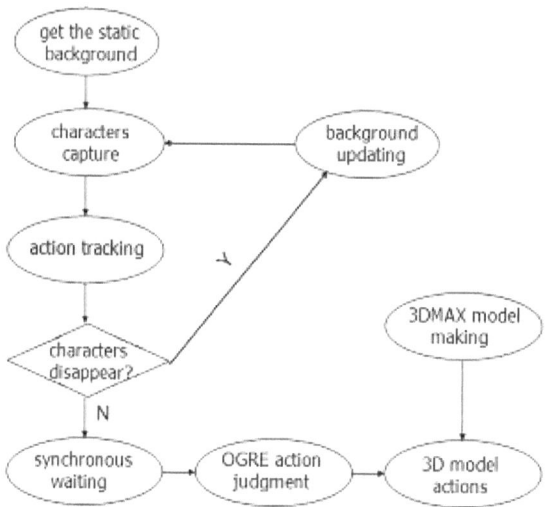

Fig. 1. Work flow of the action recognition and recording system

3   Obtaining Static Background and Background Updating

There are several ways to update background, including multi-frames averaging method, select update method, random update method and so on [2]. The multi-frames averaging method is simple and accurate, but it costs too many resources. The select update method has strong adaptability to light changes, but it is error prone when there is a big light change [2].

Henceforth, in our system, pixels changes are obtained by a series of frame differences calculated from the comparisons of the frames with the background image. In this way, we can avoid the complexities of multi-frames averaging method [3][4], and provide acceptable light adaptability at the same time. If the pixels changes exceed a certain threshold, the original background image should be fused with the current background image to generate an optimized background image. This approach can help to detect whether there are moving objects and whether the background needs to be updated.

4   Characters Capture

There are many target detection methods, including the algorithm of frame difference, optical flow method, background difference method and so on [3]. We choose background difference method to analyze potential targets in a static background. The background difference method [3][4] requires certain differences between the grayscale values of target pixels and the background pixels (the camera should be still), i.e. it compares the target image with the background image to segment the target out, as calculated from Formula (1) and Formula (2).

$$D(x,y) = |C(x,y) - B(x,y)| \tag{1}$$

$$BW(x,y) = \begin{cases} 1, if\,(D(x,y) \geq T) \\ 0, if\,(D(x,y) < T) \end{cases} \tag{2}$$

The B(x, y) stands for the background grayscale image, C(x, y) for the current frame image, D(x, y) for the difference image and BW(x, y) for the binary image. T is the threshold value according to background noise or other factors to make distinctions between changes caused by target and background noise changes.

We can get the binary image and mark its connected area using Formula (2). Then with this connected area, we can make decisions on whether the connected area is a noise zone, or a moving target, based on its pixels number. If this number exceeds a certain threshold, it is a moving target. Or else, the connected area is a noise zone.

In this paper, the system processes the captured images when people enter the static view and detects the human part in which the pixel difference is greater than a threshold set in advance. As shown in the Figure 2, the black part is the background

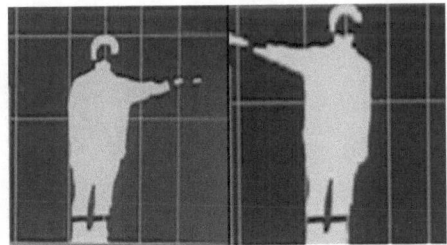

Fig. 2. Background Difference Processing Rendering

after difference, the white part is the human body detected from the initial image, and the background difference method can detect the moving targets correctly. This background difference algorithm only uses brightness values as the detection basis, and if the brightness of the moving target is similar to the brightness of the background, it will be difficult to detect the moving target.

5   Action Tracking

The Camshift algorithm [5][6] has good reliability and can meet real time requirements, which can be used to find a target by color matching, and the color changes are small when the target is moving. Therefore Camshift is used in our project.

At first Camshift method transforms the RGB space to the HSV space and extracts H color component, then it extracts the tracking window and gets the selection zone. After that, the color histogram is used to transform the original image into color probability distribution images. Before processing, each pixel value in the target image describes the color information for that point. After processing, each pixel value means the possibility discretization measurement of the color information in this place. Then after searching from back projection of the target histogram, the system returns a tracking window of next frame. Finally, the system draws the position of the tracking results and loops through this execution.

6   3D Model Actions and OGRE Action Judgment

At first we take the Miku model into 3Dmax, where we set up bones binding and use bone cover technology to control the model. The skeleton is adjusted to the same size to match the Miku model, and all pixel points of the model are embedded into the bone cover, then the bind pose at each index refers to the bone with the same index, as Figure 3 shows.

Then the character model is hidden and only the initial state of the skeleton is left. With the normal playing speed set to the rate of 10 frames per second, the skeleton is adjusted to the optimum time point to make an alteration in order to build the model action. The animation is created when a series of points are operated in such a way, as shown in Figure 4. Then the model can be exported by OGRE.

Fig. 3. Miku Model and Bone Binding

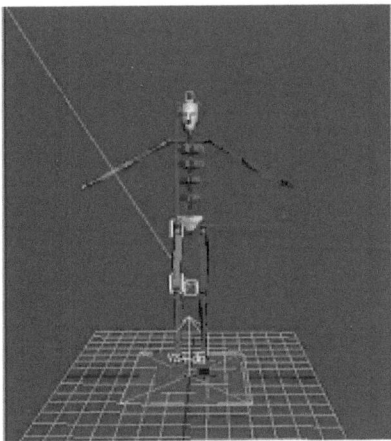

Fig. 4. Character Animation Process

The control part of OGRE is shown in Figure 5. OGRE extracts animations from the model entity after initializing the object model, then the model reacts to the data control with a corresponding action. After that the system uses the variables to record the current action and the animation is redrawn according to the corresponding value under the OGRE redraw mechanism.

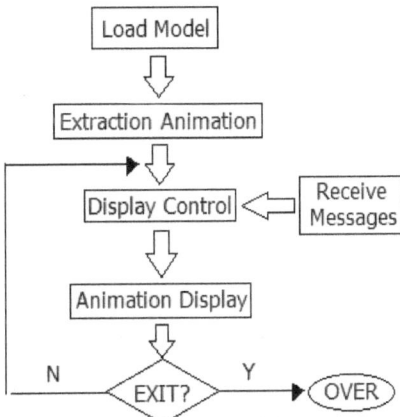

Fig. 5. OGRE Control Part Architecture

7   Testing of the Action Recording System

The system is tested on different platforms, an X86 computer (2GHz processor and 2G memory) and an ARM9 platform (S3c2410X platform, 203.3 MHz processor and 64M sdram). Ten tests were conducted, on average, the system response time is less than 1 second based on an X86 computer, and is less than 2 second based on an ARM9 platform. We show here the tests on an X86 computer.

Table 1. Recognition of Different Actions and the corresponding performance

Test Content	Test Results	Motion Effect	System Delay Average Time (X86 / 10 times)
target turns left	model turns left		target time:0s track time:0.32 s model time:0.43s sum time:0.75s
target turns right	model turns right		target time:0s track time:0.34s model time:0.42s sum time: 0.76s
target squatts down	model squatts down		target time:0s track time:0.29s model time:0.38s sum time:0.67s
target lifts and put down the left hand	model lifts and put down the left hand		target time:0s track time:0.24s model time:0.34s sum time:0.58s
target lifts and puts down the right hand	model lifts and puts down the right hand		target time:0s track time:0.25s model time:0.35s sum time:0.60s

In our tests, the computer captures and tracks the character movement through a network camera, and manipulates the 3D girl [7] to perform corresponding actions as shown in table 1. We can see that all actions can be correctly recognized, and the performance of the recognition process for all the actions is around 0.67s on average.

The system preprocesses the captured image in order to improve performance and recognition accuracy. The preprocessing includes color space transformation, noise reduction and background updates. As shown in table 2, the system requires that the background remains relatively fixed, and also requires certain intensity of illumination, and no motion impurity in the background. The effect of background disturbance, illumination changes and shadows are the problems that must be considered in background difference method, and will be explored in our future work.

Table 2. Testing results

Number	Test Environment	Conclusion	Analysis
1	Indoor, light on and no moving objects	good effects	Under the fixed background and no impurities, light > 200lx, denoising effect is good.
2	Indoor, light on and more than 10 moving objects	modest effects	Under the fixed background and more than 10 impurities, light > 200lx, denoising effect is modest.
3	Indoor, light off and no moving objects	modest effects	Under the fixed background and no impurities, light < 50lx, denoising effect is modest.
4	Indoor, light off and more than 10 moving objects	modest effects	Under the fixed background and more than 10 impurities, light < 50lx, denoising effect is modest.
5	Outdoor, light well and more than 10 moving objects	bad effects	Under the unfixed background and more than 10 impurities, light > 200lx, denoising effect is bad.

8   Related Work

Because human motion capture technology can connect physical world to the electronic world more expediently and effectively, it can be applied to healthcare systems, human-computer interaction, virtual reality systems and many other applications. Due to the availability of cheap sensors such as network camera, there arise needs for useful and simple solutions that have good performance.

Human motion capture technology can be evaluated according to the following criteria: location accuracy, real-time, convenience, cost, anti-jamming and capture range size. In [8][9], although they provided very accurate methods, the capture systems based on sensors are often limited by specialized sensors. For example, in [8] CCD sensors need complex external control circuits to support them, and their speed were not very ideal. In [9] wireless sensors needed a lot of calculation to determine their positions and relationships, and only the skeleton could be extracted in its system. In this paper, we proposed a solution with low requirements and costs for hardware and software, with acceptable performance.

In [11], an improved real-time background update algorithm was proposed. They avoided the influence caused by the variety of background according to the 3σ rule of normal distribution, and proposed a shadow removing algorithm based on the vertical projection. Shadow disappearance is not the best display method, so we used the 3D model and shows the performance is better, where OpenCV effect and 3D model used together for visual display.

Similarly, background difference algorithm was used in [10]. They introduced omnidirectional camera to tracking multiple targets in indoor environments, and built the background model by observing the scene without people first. When the detecting process started, omnidirectional images were changed into the cylindrical panoramic images, and an adaptive background subtraction method was utilized to segment the moving regions and locate the positions of human bodies. The heavy computation would consume more resources. We used very common network camera in our system.

A modified mixture Gaussian model was used in [12]. In their method, foreground objects were segmented based on an improved binary connected component analysis and Kalman filtering was used for object tracking. In [13], a zero Mean normalized cross-correlation method was proposed to achieve the detection of moving targets, and the cumulative histogram method was used to obtain a satisfactory threshold to achieve a precise movement of the extraction of the target under complex background enviroment. Our system requires a certain intensity of illumination and no motion impurity in the background, so the methods in [12] and [13] could be introduced to our system to improve adaptablity to lighting changes, shadows and occlusions.

9   Conclusions and Future Work

In the motion recording system proposed in our paper, we used computer vision (OpenCV library) for human body motion capture. With background difference algorithm and Camshift algorithm, the system captures the human motion video by camera and gets the data results by the detection and tracking of the video resources, then the 3D model is controlled by the captured feature to record the action of human.

The system obtains visual images directly and compares the images with 3D model at real time. The system requires the static scene to build the background model, then the background difference method and the Camshift method are used for detecting and tracking the moving object, so it requires that the environment has enough light (>200lx) and fewer objects. In our system, it is easy to track the bright objects rather than white objects due to low H components in white ones. The tests show that the recording system has good performance and can recognize different actions correctly. The system works well and no lag and jumping frame had detected.

In the future, more cameras will be used to improve its accuracy and anti-jamming capability. With more cameras, multi-angle images information would be obtained to locate the target actions more precisely and to discard impurity elements. In addition, we could improve the accuracy of the 3D model to solve this problem. Then when a new action appeared, the related 3D model action should be edited to join the system action library to express new human motions.

Acknowledgments. Weishan Zhang has been supported by "the Fundamental Research Funds for the Central Universities" and also the start up funds for "Academic Top-Notch in China University of Petroleum" professors.

References

1. Mao, J., Zou, X., Zhu, J.: Improved Plane Template Two-step Camera Calibration. China Journal of Image and Graphics 9(7), 846–852 (2004)
2. Zhang, C., Su, Y.: Digital Image Compression, pp. 20–23. Tsinghua University Press (2006)
3. Park, J.S.: Interactive 3D reconstruction from multiple images: a primitive-based approach. Pattern Recognition Letters 26(16), 2558–2571 (2005)
4. Intel Corporation. Open Source Computer Vision Library Reference Manual (December 2001)
5. de la Torre Frade, F., Marroquín, E.M., Pérez, M.E.S., Moreno, J.A.M.: Moving object detection and tracking system: a real-time implementation (1997)
6. Nascimento, J.C., Marques, J.S.: Performance evaluation of object detection algorithms for video surveillance. IEEE Trans. Multimedia, 761–774 (2006)
7. Wu, F., Li, H., Hu, Z.: A New Camera Self-calibration Method Based on Active Vision System. Chinese Journal of Computers 23(11), 1130–1139 (2000)
8. Feng, L., Wang, R.: Application of CCD Sensors in the Image Detection System of Human Motion. Instrument Technique and Sensor 5, 33–35 (2000)
9. Wang, T., Feng, W., Luo, D.: Application of Wireless Sensor Network for Detection of Human Body Movements. Instrumentation and Measurment 28(8), 83–86 (2009)
10. Pi, W., Liu, H., Cha, H.: Motion Detection for Human Bodies Basing Adaptive Background Subtraction by Using an Omnidirectional Camera. Journal of Peking University 40(3), 458–464 (2004)
11. Cao, D., Zou, W., Wu, Y.: Motion human detection based on difference background image. Opto-Electronic Engineering 34(6), 107–111 (2007)
12. Liu, Y., Ai, H., Xu, G.: Moving object detection and tracking based on background subtraction. Information and Control 31(8), 315–319 (2002)
13. Wei, J., Liu, Z., Zhang, H.: Moving objects detection algorithm under complex background environment. Microcomputer & Its Applications 2, 49–51 (2010)

Protecting Sensitive Attributes
in Attribute Based Access Control

Guoping Zhang, Jing Liu, and Jianbo Liu

School of Computer & Communication Engineering
China University of Petroleum, Qing Dao, China
zhanggp@upc.edu.cn, {liujing415jsj,liuljian2bo3}@163.com

Abstract. Attribute Based Access Control (ABAC) has gradually become a hot research topic in distributed systems. While frequent disclosure of subject attributes, resource attributes or environment attributes may lead to leaks of sensitive information. This article mainly focuses on protecting privacy of resource requester in the process of ABAC, and presents a trust based sensitive attributes protection mechanism which can disclose attributes through comparing resource requester's attribute sensitivity with resource provider's trust level. After experiments comparison with Beth model, we get a conclusion that this mechanism has higher accuracy, without violating resource requester's privacy.

Keywords: Attributes, Sensitivity, Trust Level, Privacy Protection, Malicious Recommendation.

1   Introduction

Most distributed systems are operated in an open and dynamic network environment, across multiple security domains. Because Attribute Based Access Control (ABAC) [1] can offer a fine-grained, dynamic and cross-domain access control mechanism, it has gradually become a hot research topic in distributed systems. There arises an important issue with ABAC model that frequent disclosure of attributes will inevitably lead to leaks of sensitive information.

In order to solve the problem above, this article proposes a trust based sensitive attributes protection mechanism (TSAP). This mechanism includes the concept of trust, and divides trust into direct trust and recommended trust [2]. Meanwhile TSAP can effectively get rid of malicious recommendation. TSAP mechanism decides which attributes to disclose, through comparing resource the requester's attribute sensitivity and the resource provider's trust level.

In this article, we begin with relevant definitions of TSAP mechanism, and basic work flow of TSAP in section 2. In section 3 we describe the concept of trust evaluation about resource provider in detail, and give computational formula of direct trust and recommended trust respectively. Then we verify the validity of TSAP by a simple case study and experiments in section 4 and introduce related work in section 5. At last, we reach the conclusion of this article and point out the future work.

A. Ghose et al. (Eds.): ICSOC 2012, LNCS 7759, pp. 294–305, 2013.
© Springer-Verlag Berlin Heidelberg 2013

2   Trust Based Sensitive Attributes Protection

Generally, an ABAC system is made up of subjects, objects, and access control policies. For simplicity, we replace resource requester (resource provider) with subject (object), and both are uniformly called entities in the following.

2.1   The Relevant Definitions

- *Attribute Sensitivity*: Attribute Sensitivity means the importance level of subject attributes. We represent the attribute sensitivity by $Sens \in [0,1]$.
- *Trust Evaluation*: Trust Evaluation means a trust estimate about an object made by a subject. Here, the trust means the confidence level of the object and we represent object's trust level by T.
- *Direct Trust*: Direct Trust expresses subjective evaluation of a subject to an object, which is gained from history records of direct access from the subject to the object.
- *Recommended Trust*: Recommended Trust is also called indirect trust, which can be gained from a trusted third party or other entities' recommendation
- *Honest Level*: We represent the authentic degree of entities' evaluation about target objects by Honest Level which is called H for short.
- *Attribute Access Policy*: Attribute Access Policy is a kind of access control policy that can protect one's own sensitive attributes, in which an object is supposed to own certain attributes values before it requests for some attributes of the subject.

2.2   TSAP Basic Flow

The whole protection process of TSAP is seen in Fig.1, and it includes division of attribute sensitivities, formulation of attribute access policies, trust evaluations to objects, acquirement of sensitive attributes and access to objects.

2.2.1   Division of Attribute Sensitivity

Generally, different subject attributes reflect different information about a subject, so sensitivities of attributes should also be divided into different values. Attributes of low sensitivity can be published in most network environments. However, attributes of high sensitivity can be published only in a trusted network environment. In addition, a subject defines sensitivities not only for attributes it owns, but also for the attributes it does not own to prevent disclosing information about the subject in case objects learn that the subject does not own certain attributes.

2.2.2   Formulation of Attribute Access Policies

In the process of an access control, a subject may need to disclose some sensitive attributes generally so as to access an object. If a subject distrusts the target object in the beginning, the subject can disclose the corresponding attributes only when the object submits the attributes that formulated in the Attribute Access Policy. For example, an Attribute Access Policy is as follows:

If $ra_1=y_1$ and $ra_2=y_2$; imply disclosure SA_1;

In the description above, ra_1 and ra_2 represents two attribute values of the object, and y_1 and y_2 mean the specific value of corresponding attributes. When this policy is met, the object can receive a response about the attribute SA_1. Otherwise, the attribute request of the object will be refused.

In addition, the subject can also formulate corresponding Attribute Access Policies for attributes of higher sensitivity which are not owned by the subject itself. Only when the object meets these policies, the subject can tell whether it owns those attributes or not.

2.2.3   Trust Evaluation to Objects

In the process of ABAC, an important basis for a subject to disclose attributes is it has trust in objects, which also means trust evaluations to objects. Here, trust evaluations to objects derive from two aspects, one aspect is subjective evaluations from subjects to target objects, namely Direct Trust, and the other aspect is a recommendation from a trusted third party to target object, namely Recommended Trust. Here, we use T to represent trust level from subjects to objects, T_D to direct trust, and T_R to recommended trust.

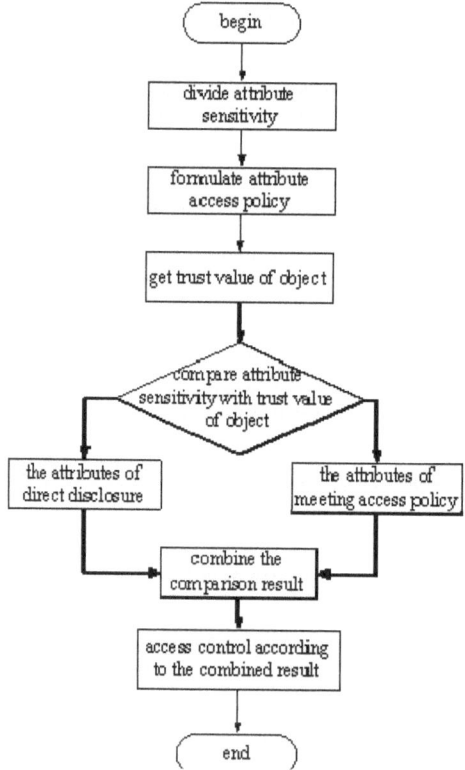

Fig. 1. Work flow of TSAP

2.2.4 Acquirement of Sensitive Attributes

When an object submits its request for subject attributes, the subject will make judgments based on the trust level of the object and the sensitivities of requested attributes. Then the subject will judge which attributes could be directly disclosed to the object, and which attributes can be disclosed to the object only when the following conditions are met:

If the sensitivity of a subject attribute is lower than or equal to the trust level of the target object, the subject will send this attribute to the target object directly or declares that it does not own certain attribute.

If the sensitivity of a subject attribute is larger than or equal to the trust level of the target object, the subject will send out attributes only when the object meets the corresponding Attribute Access Policies.

2.2.5 Access to Objects

After the above comparison judgments by subjects, ordinarily there will be two parts of results. The first part contains attributes that can be disclosed directly, and the other part contains attributes that can be disclosed indirectly after meeting the Attribute Access Policy. Subjects will merge the two parts together and send out the result to PDP (policy decision point) in ABAC. Then PDP will make authorization decisions and decide whether the subject is allowed to access the object or not.

3   Trust evaluation

Currently, there are many trust management models providing trust level calculation methods, such as Beth model, RFSN model and so on. In this section, we will first introduce the Beth model, as we are going to make a comparison between it and TSAP, and then we will describe the TSAP model in detail.

3.1   Beth Model

The Beth model adopts experience to describe and value trust, which mainly comes from history records of interactions between entities. When one interaction is successful, it is called a positive experience; otherwise it is called a negative experience. The experience can also be acquired from other entities' recommendations. Thus trust is divided into direct trust and recommended trust. The direct trust is formulated as follows:

$$V_i(p) = 1 - a^p \tag{1}$$

In Formula 1, p represents the number of successful interactive times, which also is the number of positive experiences, and a represents the expected value of successful interaction times from subjects to objects.

The recommended trust is formulated as follows:

$$V_r(p,n) = \begin{cases} 1 - a^{p-n}, & if\,(p > n) \\ 0, & else \end{cases} \tag{2}$$

In Formula 2, n means the number of failure interactions times while p and a means the same as above.

3.2   TSAP Model

Trust-based Sensitive Attributes Protection mechanism (TSAP) proposed in this paper divides trust into direct trust and recommended trust. TSAP can also exclude malicious recommendations, which is not taken into consideration in the Beth model.

3.2.1   Direct Trust

Direct Trust comes from historical access records of entities. Suppose each entity owns an access list which is composed of successful interactive number of times, and failure times. The list records interactions of one entity with other entities, as is shown in Table 1.

Table 1. Access list of entity m

	Entity1	Entity 2	...	Entity n
Success Times (a)	S_{m1}	S_{m2}	...	S_{mn}
Failure Times (b)	F_{m1}	F_{m2}	...	F_{mn}

S_{mn} means the number of successful interaction times between entity m and entity n, and F_{mn} means the number of failed interaction. Here, notice that S_{mn} is unequal to S_{nm}, and S_{mn} indicates that entity m sends request to entity n. Direct Trust of entity m to entity n can be seen as a subjective expectation for entity m that how entity n is able to fulfill a target task. In other words, it is a guess of probability that whether entity m can access entity n successfully. Each interaction between entity m and entity n can be seen as an independent event, and this event only has two results: success (represented by 1) or failure (represented by 0).

We use θ to represent the predication of next interaction (0 or 1) between entity m and entity n. According to the analysis and models mentioned in paper [10], we find that posterior probability of θ behaves according to Beta distribution (shown in Formula 3). Direct Trust of entity m to entity n can be represented by the expectation of θ (shown in Formula 4).

$$P(\theta) = \frac{Bin(S_{mn}+F_{mn},S_{mn})*Beta(1,1)}{Normalization} = Beta(S_{mn} + 1, F_{mn} + 1) \tag{3}$$

$$T_D = E(P(\theta)) = E(Beta(S_{mn} + 1, F_{mn+1})) \tag{4}$$

3.2.2   Recommended Trust

Trust evaluation of entity m to entity n is not accurate enough only from the subjective evaluation of entity m. It also needs recommendations provided by a trusted third party. Recommended Trust is from historical evaluation records between entities. Suppose that the third party owns a number of evaluation lists which record the evaluative value of target entities after interactions. As is shown in Table 2, where V_{kn} represents the evaluative value of entity k to entity n, and $V_{kn} \in [0,1]$.

Table 2. Evaluation list of entity n

Entity	1	2	...	k
Evaluative Value (V)	V_{1n}	V_{2n}	...	V_{kn}

However, there may be some malicious evaluations from some entities, such as the competitors of homogeneous services, network viruses and so on. Therefore, to get effective recommended trust, we should eliminate entities with malicious recommendations first, and then adopt evaluative values of honest entities.

Here, we use deviation degree of each entity's evaluative value to exclude entities' malicious recommendations. Deviation degree shows the deviation extent of a single entity's evaluative value to a real value. Firstly, we calculate the average value (AV) of all evaluative values about the target entity given by other entities, as is shown in Formula 5. Secondly, certain deviation degree (Δ) is set by the trusted third party. Then we get a D-value of a single entity by comparing its evaluative value with the average value of all entities, and we use DV_k to represent the D-value of entity k, as is shown in Formula 6. Finally, we compare DV_k with Δ. If DV_k is beyond Δ, we exclude the evaluative value of this entity. Otherwise the entity will be included in a set R of entities providing honest evaluation.

$$AV(V_{kn}) = \frac{\Sigma V_{kn}}{N} \text{ , where } k\epsilon\{all \text{ entities that have made evaluation on entity } n\} \quad (5)$$

$$DV_k = |V_{kn} - AV|, \text{ where } k\epsilon\{all \text{ entities that have made evaluation on entity } n\} \quad (6)$$

Meanwhile, in order to avoid malicious evaluations as much as possible, we use honest level to represent the real extent of evaluations about target objects. Here, the honest level of an entity is obtained from the trusted third party who saves an honesty list for all entities that have made their evaluations, as shown in Table 3.

Table 3. Honesty list of entities

	Entity 1	Entity 2	...	Entity n
Real Evaluative Times (HN)	HN_1	HN_2	...	HN_n
Total Evaluative Times (SN)	SN_1	SN_2	...	SN_n

After entity k making evaluation to the object, the total number of evaluation (SN_k) correspondingly adds 1. If this evaluation does not belong to malicious evaluations, the number of real evaluations (HN_k) also needs to add 1. Honest level of entity k (H_k)

is represented by the proportion of the number of real evaluations in the total number of evaluations, as shown in Formula 7.

$$H_k = HN_k/SN_k \tag{7}$$

Through effectively excluding malicious recommendation from entities and getting honest level of various entities, the recommended trust (T_R) can be obtained by the calculation of Formula 8, where V_{kn} represents the evaluative value of entity k to entity n, H_k shows the honest level of entity k, R denotes a set of entities that give honest evaluation of entity n, and N means the number of honest entities.

$$T_R = \frac{\sum H_k * V_{kn}}{N} \tag{8}$$

3.2.3 Comprehensive Trust Evaluation

Trust evaluation of entity m to entity n is composed of direct trust (T_D) and recommended trust (T_R), as shown in Formula 9, where β represents the subjective evaluation's trust extent of entity m, and $\beta \in [0,1]$. If entity m has more faith in its own subjective evaluation, β takes a higher value; otherwise β takes a smaller value.

$$T = \beta T_D + (1 - \beta)T_R \tag{9}$$

4 Case analysis and Experiment Comparison

In this section, we use a simplified recommendation relationship graph as follows to describe the trust relationship between two entities i and j.

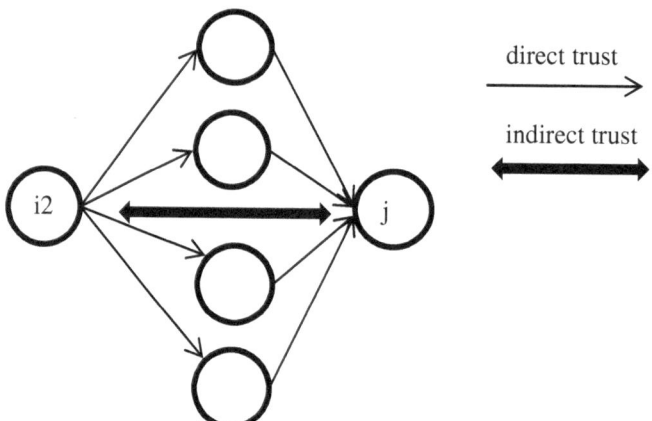

Fig. 2. The trust relationships between entities

As we can see from Fig. 2, entity i trusts entity j indirectly and the other entities directly. The other entities offer one-path recommendations of j.

Suppose that entity i has attributes including {name, age, date of birth, ID number, family address, telephone, marital status, hobbies, work unit, medical history}, and the corresponding sensitivities respectively are {0.25, 0.18, 0.20, 0.80, 0.50, 0.40,

0.20, 0.35, 0.50, 0.90}. Subject formulates the same Attribute Access Policies for ID number, work unit, medical history which have higher sensitivities. For example:

If Security grade= high and Certificate issuer = country institution;
imply disclosure ID number;

In our case, entity i needs to access object j, and entity i gets that the successful interactive number between entity i and entity j is 29 and the failed interactive number is 9 based on the history access record of entity i to entity j, so Direct Trust (T_D) of entity i to entity j is 0.75 according to Formula 2. The evaluation list of entity j provided by the trusted third party is shown in Table 4, and the value range of deviation degree (Δ) is set as[0,0.25]. We can obtain that the average value (AV) of all evaluative values is 0.57 based on the evaluation list of entity j and Formula 3. The D-values (DV) of various entities are shown in Table 5 based on Formula 4. Through comparing DV of every entity with Δ, we exclude evaluative value of entity 5 and entity 8. Honest level (H) of other entities can respectively be calculated to get {0.40, 0.50, 1.0, 0.75, 0.85, 0.73, 0.80, 0.72} via Table 6 provided by the trusted third party. Recommended Trust (T_R) is 0.47 based on Formula 6.

Suppose that entity i has more faith in its own subjective evaluation on entity j. Therefore, when calculating comprehensive trust of entity i on entity j, β takes a higher value, say 0.70. Finally, the comprehensive trust value (T) of entity i on entity j is 0.667 calculated by Formula 7.

Through comparing attribute sensitivities of entity i with comprehensive trust value of entity i on entity j, the attributes which can be disclosed to entity j are {name, age, date of birth, family address, telephone, marital status, hobbies, work unit}. If the attribute values of Security_grade of entity j is high and the attribute values of Certificate_issuer of entity j is country institution, entity j will get the attributes of ID number and medical history of entity i at the same time.

Table 4. Evaluation list of entity j

Entity	1	2	3	4	5	6	7	8	9	10
V	0.70	0.50	0.60	0.80	0.20	0.60	0.70	0.30	0.80	0.50

Table 5. D-value list of entities

Entity	1	2	3	4	5	6	7	8	9	10
DV	0.13	0.07	0.03	0.23	0.37	0.03	0.13	0.27	0.23	0.07

Table 6. Honesty list of entities

Entity	1	2	3	4	6	7	9	10
HN	20	15	20	30	17	44	32	54
SN	50	30	20	40	20	60	40	75

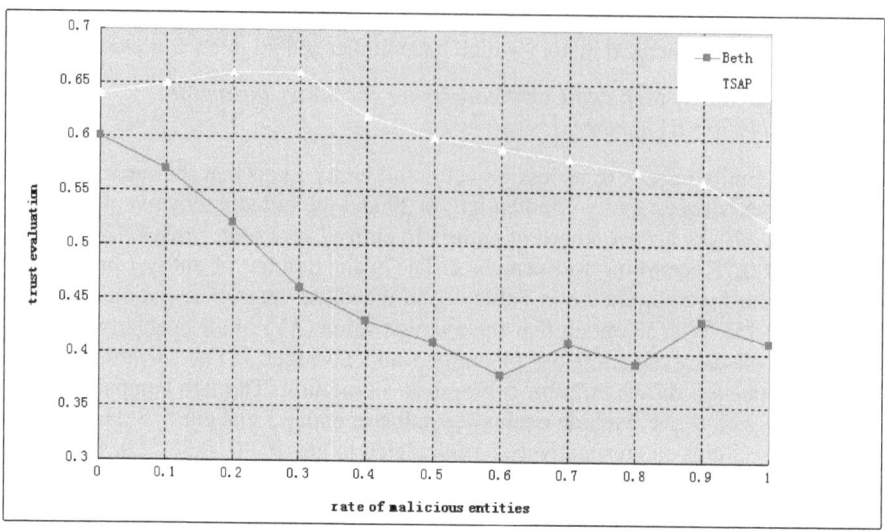

Fig. 3. Result of the first experiment

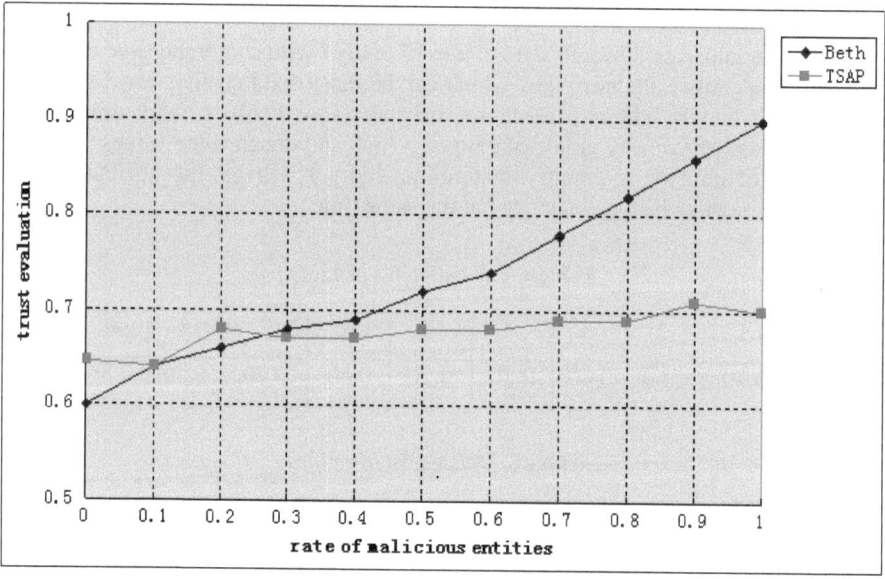

Fig. 4. Result of the second experiment

Here we perform two groups of experiments. In the first group, each malicious ent-ity gives i a much lower trust value than the real value. The result is shown in Fig.3. As we can see from it, the trust valuation of j to i becomes lower as the rate of mali-cious entities increases both in Beth model and our TSAP model. However, the result of trust evaluation in TSAP model is always between 0.5 and 0.7, thus it has less im-pacts on which specific attributes to disclose as we describe in the example in last section while the Beth model makes some attribute with lower sensitivity still cannot be disclosed to entity j.

In the second group, each malicious entity gives i a much higher value. As we can see from Fig.4, the result in Beth model changes a lot as the rate of malicious entities increases. It can even reach the value of 0.9, and this means that there is no sensitive attribute at all, thus j can get all the attributes of i. However, the result of TSAP model does not change much and the attributes to disclose stay the same as in the example in last section.

By comparing the results of the two experiments, we can see that the TSAP model has higher accuracy than the Beth model especially where there are malicious entities offering recommendations. And the TSAP model itself can well bear the changes resulting from the malicious entities which give unusual recommended trust values.

5   Related Work

For the protection of sensitive attributes, Seamons et al. proposed an idea on considering both content-sensitivity of attributes (attribute value) and possession sensitivity of attributes (whether there are certain attribute or not). One can predicate whether the others possess certain attributes by their different behavior with different attributes [3].

Holt et al. proposed hidden credentials based on the principle of elliptic curve encryption, to protect credentials from attacking and prevent leaking sensitive information via setting system parameter [4]. Oblivious signature-based envelope (OSBE) proposed in Paper [6] can avoid the malicious disclosure of attribute information by means of digital signature of attributes. Paper [7] made use of zero knowledge protocol between subjects and objects in which both sides can obtain different information by inputting different attribute value, and both sides cannot know any attribute information about each other. Although plenty of papers presented effective methods to protect sensitive attributes, these methods have fussy encryption or decryption process, which cost a lot of computing time and memory space, and go against some resource limited equipments.

Winsborough et al. proposed an acknowledgement policy (ACK) aiming at possession-sensitivity of attributes [8]. But this method has a problem of abundant workload management and a coarse-grained protection. In paper [9], attribute owners establish the corresponding access control policies for sensitive attributes, and send the access control policies to policy database anonymously. This mechanism effectively protects possession-sensitivity of attribute, while it fails to consider the network environment of system, and may destroy the flexibility of system access. Thus attribute owners may also disclose some sensitive attributes directly in a safe environment.

Through the analysis of existing works, this paper presents a trust based sensitive attributes protection mechanism (TSAP). TSAP mechanism can protect both content-sensitivity and possession-sensitivity of attributes, avoid fussy encryption or decryption process, and flexibly protect sensitive attributes of subjects in different network environments.

6 Conclusions and Future Work

Although the ABAC model can solve the resource sharing and collaboration problems of distributed systems, it can easily cause disclosures of private information. This paper proposes a trust based sensitive attributes protection mechanism. This mechanism discloses sensitive attributes based on attribute sensitivities of a subject and the trust level of an object. It can protect both content-sensitivity and possession-sensitivity of attributes. And an object can independently decide to disclose sensitive attributes, increasing the flexibility of system access.

In the future, we will integrate TSAP mechanism into ABAC access control architecture, in order to provide more secure access control, and will verify the effectiveness of the whole access control architecture at the same time.

References

1. Eric, Y., Jin, T.: Attributed Based Access Control (ABAC) for Web Services. In: Proceedings of the IEEE International Conference on Web Services (ICWS 2005), pp. 560–569 (2005)
2. Beth, T., Borcherding, M., Klein, B.: Valuation of Trust in Open Networks. LNCS, vol. 875, pp. 1–18 (1994)
3. Seamons, K.E., Winslett, M., Yu, T., Yu, L., Jarvis, R.: Protecting Privacy during On-Line Trust Negotiation. In: Dingledine, R., Syverson, P.F. (eds.) PET 2002. LNCS, vol. 2482, pp. 129–143. Springer, Heidelberg (2003)
4. Holt, J.E., Bradshaw, R.W., Seamons, K.E., Orman, H.: Hidden credentials. In: Proceedings of the ACM Workshop on Privacy in the Electronic Society, pp. 1–8 (2003)
5. Bradshaw, R., Holt, J., Seamons, K.E.: Concealing complex policies with hidden credentials. In: Proceedings of the 11th ACM Conference on Computer and Communications Security, pp. 146–157 (2004)
6. Li, N.H., Du, W.L., Boneh, D.: Oblivious signature-based envelope. In: Proceedings of the 22nd ACM Symposium on Principles of Distributed Computing (PODC 2003), pp. 182–189 (2003)
7. Li, J., Li, N.: OACerts: Oblivious Attribute Certificates. In: Ioannidis, J., Keromytis, A.D., Yung, M. (eds.) ACNS 2005. LNCS, vol. 3531, pp. 301–317. Springer, Heidelberg (2005)
8. Winsborough, W.H., Li, N.H.: Protecting sensitive attributes in automated trust negotiation. In: Proceedings of the ACM Workshop on Privacy in the Electronic Society, pp. 41–51 (2002)
9. Irwin, K., Yu, T.: Preventing Attribute Information Leakage in Automated Trust Negotiation. In: Proceedings of the 12th ACM Conference on Computer and Communications Security, pp. 41–51 (2005)
10. Sang, A.: A Subjective Metric of Authentication. In: Proceedings of European Symposium on Research in Security, pp. 329–344 (1998)
11. Yu, T., Winslett, M.: Policy migration for sensitive credentials in trust negotiation. In: Proceedings of the 2003 ACM Workshop on Privacy in the Electronic Society (WPES 2003), pp. 9–20 (2003)
12. Gevers, S., De Decker, B.: Privacy Friendly Information Disclosure. In: Meersman, R., Tari, Z., Herrero, P. (eds.) OTM 2006 Workshops. LNCS, vol. 4277, pp. 636–646. Springer, Heidelberg (2006)

13. Esmaeeli, A., Shahriari, H.R.: Privacy Protection of Grid Service Requesters through Distributed Attribute Based Access Control Model. In: Bellavista, P., Chang, R.-S., Chao, H.-C., Lin, S.-F., Sloot, P.M.A. (eds.) GPC 2010. LNCS, vol. 6104, pp. 573–582. Springer, Heidelberg (2010)
14. Kolter, J., Schillinger, R., Pernul, G.: A Privacy-Enhanced Attribute-Based Access Control System. In: Barker, S., Ahn, G.-J. (eds.) Data and Applications Security 2007. LNCS, vol. 4602, pp. 129–143. Springer, Heidelberg (2007)
15. EI-Khatib, K.: A Privacy Negotiation Protocol for Web Services. In: Workshop on Collaboration Agents: Autonomous Agents for Collaborative Environments Halifax (October 13, 2003)
16. Guajardo, J., Mennink, B., Schoenmakers, B.: Anonymous Credential Schemes with Encrypted Attributes. In: Heng, S.-H., Wright, R.N., Goi, B.-M. (eds.) CANS 2010. LNCS, vol. 6467, pp. 314–333. Springer, Heidelberg (2010)

A Hybrid Indoor Positioning Approach for Supermarkets

Weishan Zhang[1], Yuhao Wang[1], Licheng Chen[1], Yan Liu[1], and Yuan Rao[2]

[1] Department of Software Engineering, China University of Petroleum, No. 66 Changjiang West Road, Qingdao, China, 266580
[2] College of Software Engineering, Xi'an Jiaotong University, Xi'an 710049, China
zhangws@upc.edu.cn, {wangyuhao.upc,lcchen.upc,liuyanup}@gmail.com, raoyuan@mail.xjtu.edu.cn

Abstract. A navigation service that can provide positioning functionalities is benefitial to both customers and supermarkets. Although there are quite a number of indoor positioning algorithms, the accuracy of the existing approaches is not very satisfying. In this paper, we propose a hybrid approach that combines Weighted Centroid Localizatioin Algorithm, Dynamic Position Tracking Model and Location Approximation Algorithm based on Received Signal Strength. The evaluations show that the proposed approach can achieve better accuracy than the existing approaches, with approximately 20% to 40% improvement.

1 Introduction

The majority of us had experiences of having difficulties to locate which aisle the needed goods are stored in a big supermarket. Therefore, a navigation system that shows how and where to reach your targets will be very helpful for customers to save time in a supermarket. On the other hand, such a navigation system will help to improve sales in supermarkets and to reduce man-power costs. Therefore, there arises the requirements for accurately navigate customers to a corresponding location where goods for customers are stored.

From comparisons of various wireless transmission technologies in [?], we can see that ZigBee precisely fill low-rate wireless communication technology vacancies. The complexity of ZigBee system is far less than that of the Bluetooth system, much lower-power comsumption (days versus years) and low-cost are the advantages of ZigBee technology. Although it has a lower data transmission rate, but the transmission rate is still able to meet positioning needs for supermarkets. Generally RFID(Radio Frequency IDentification) technology can be used in indoor positioning, but passive RFID technology is suitable only for close data reading and writing, for a long distance active RFID positioning system as in a medium scale supermarket, the flexibility of the RDFI positoining system is greatly restricted, and the cost of the entire system is no longer cheap compared to Zigbee based systems. Therefore in this paper we will use ZigBee technology to realize indoor positioning.

A. Ghose et al. (Eds.): ICSOC 2012, LNCS 7759, pp. 306–316, 2013.

Currently there are many researches that can provide the capabilities of indoor positioning which may faciliate the customer navigation for supermarkets. For example, using cellular infrastructure of GSM may help to realize indoor positoining [9] but it is found that this GSM based approach is not accurate [10] enough for navigation in a supermarket. Some researches are calculating the distance to the node basing on the time of arrival (TOA) of the signal transmission, where the time differences between transmission and reception are measured [1]. In this process, high accuracy of clocking between nodes should be synchronized in advance, which may not be realistic when there are a lot of nodes.

Received Signal Strength Indicators (RSSIs) are widely used for indoor positioning [13]. RSSI Fingerprinting, RSSI triangulation and trilateration are some of the representative approaches [8]. The RSSI Fingerprinting identifies specific positions with RSSI values [6], which needs a location fingerprint database to compute the current location. This requires a lot of time to build the fingerprint database before running such a navigation system. RSSI triangulation, and trilateration associate RSSI with distance or angular trajectory between a receiver and known transmitter positions [13][8].

Though there is quite some research using the RSSI triangulation and trilateration approaches [10], the accuracy of the existing work is not very satisfying. For example, in [10], using dynamic position tracking model combined with a probability density map, an average error of 1.21m can be achieved for localizing a person. For quite some small supermarkets as in China, the aisle is around 1m. This means that we need an approach that can have better accuracy. Henceforth, in this paper, we present a hybrid approach that helps to achieve this goal, where we combine the Weighted Centroid Localization Algorithm (WCLA) [12], Dynamic Position Tracking Model (DPTM) [10], and Location Approximation Algorithm (LAA) (details are in section 2) based on Received Signal Strength. The evaluations show that we can achieve better accuracy with less than 1m for the average error while positioning.

In the following, we will first present the proposed hybrid indoor positioning approach used for supermarkets navigation. Then we show the design of the navigation system. After that, we will show the evaluations of the proposed approach, where the average localization error, the maximum localization error are measured. Then we will compare our work with the related work. Finally, we discuss the conclusions gained in the project and point out some future work.

2   A Hybrid Positioning Approach

The RSSI (calculated using equation 1) dynamic tracking algorithm takes into account the fact that movement of objects within a certain range is not arbitrary, there is a relationship between the current location and previous location, and then this algorithm uses a speed constant to predict the next location [10]. Using DPTM, we can get the smoothed RSSI. The smoothed RSSI can then be used by the Weighted Centroid Algorithm to calculate an approximate location.

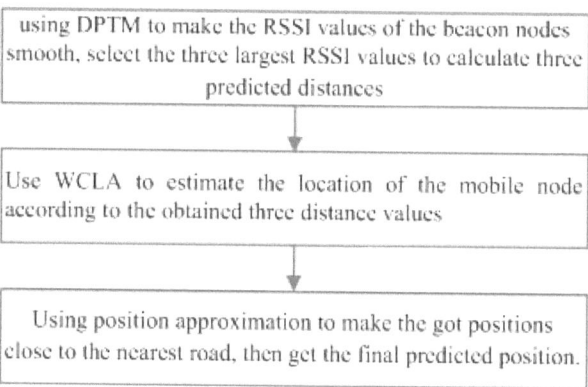

using DPTM to make the RSSI values of the beacon nodes smooth, select the three largest RSSI values to calculate three predicted distances

Use WCLA to estimate the location of the mobile node according to the obtained three distance values

Using position approximation to make the got positions close to the nearest road, then get the final predicted position.

Fig. 1. A hybrid approach for indoor positioning

The Weighted Centroid Localization Algorithm is the improvement of the centroid algorithm by a weighting factor to reflect the beacon node to determine the centroid coordinates, to some extent, it can improve positioning accuracy [12]. Finally, considering the aisle characteristic of a supermarkets which is long and narrow, we make use of the location approximation algorithm to adjust the predicted positions to the nearest road midline to improve positioning accuracy. The whole process using the hybrid positioning approach is shown in Figure 1.

$$RSSI = -(10 \times n \times \lg[d] + A) \tag{1}$$

2.1 Dynamic Position Tracking Model

The dynamic tracking model [10] is based on the fact that the movement of mobile objects within a certain range is not arbitrary, the current location and previous location has relationships where speed between the two locations counts. The equations are as followed [10]:

$$\widehat{R}_{est(i)} = \widehat{R}_{pred(i)} + a\big(\widehat{R}_{prev(i)} - \widehat{R}_{pred(i)}\big) \tag{2}$$

$$\widehat{V}_{est(i)} = \widehat{V}_{pred(i)} + \frac{b}{T_S}\big(\widehat{R}_{prev(i)} - \widehat{R}_{pred(i)}\big) \tag{3}$$

$$\widehat{R}_{pred(i+1)} = \widehat{R}_{est(i)} + \widehat{V}_{est(i)} \cdot T_S \tag{4}$$

$$\widehat{V}_{pred(i)} = \widehat{V}_{est(i)} \tag{5}$$

where $\widehat{R}_{est(i)}$ is the estimated range, $\widehat{R}_{pred(i)}$ is the predicted range, $\widehat{R}_{prev(i)}$ is the measured range, $\widehat{V}_{est(i)}$ is the estimated velocity, $\widehat{V}_{pred(i)}$ is the predicted velocity, a and b are gain constants, and T_S is the time update period.

2.2 Weighted Centroid Localization Algorithm

The basic idea of the WCLA lies in the centroid algorithm. It uses weighting factors to reflect how a reference node (beacon node) determines right values of mass center coordinates, and these weighting factors reflect the degree of influences of the beacon nodes to the position of the mass center [2]. Weighted centroid localization algorithm to some extent, can improve positioning accuracy. But the problems of the WCLA are that the inconsistency of node positions and the random fluctuations of RSSI values, which make WCLA not suitable for accurate positioning [4]. In this paper, we use WCLA based on the smoothed RSSI values from Dynamic Position Tracking Model, to eliminate the randomness of the RSSI for WCLA.

2.3 Location Approximation Algorithm

Considering that usually the width of aisles in a supermarket is around 1m, and these aisles are straight, we can use the midlines of these aisles to represent these aisles. As shown in Figure 2, when an estimated location (say point A) is obtained through some other algorithms (say WCLA), it will be approximated to be on the midline of an aisle where the perpendicular distance is the shortest (A will be approximated to be Ma on midline $M2$).

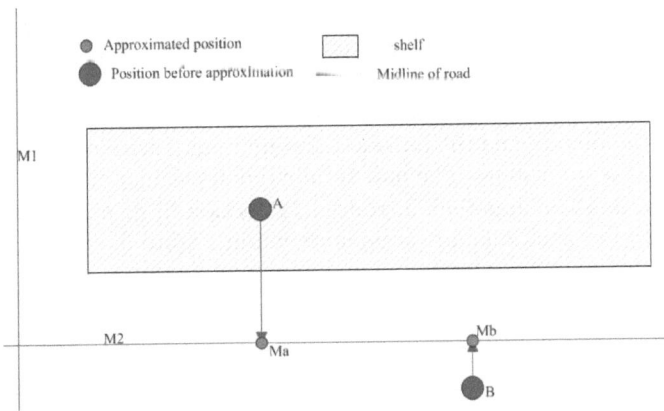

Fig. 2. Location approximation to the midline

The corresponding location approximation algorithm is shown in the following Figure 3:

```
n=the number of roads;
Pxy = location coordinates calculated with WCLA;
loop    i=1 to n
    Calculate vertical distance d between Pxy and the current road function road (i);
    Put d into an array named lenset;
endloop

Sort lenset from small to large;
Find the shortest distance ds, and the corresponding road function road (x);
Get P'xy which is the vertical projection from Pxy to road(x);
```

Fig. 3. Algorithm for location approximation

3   Design and Implementation a Supermarket Navigation System

The network of the positioning system consists of a wireless ad-hoc network and a cable Ethernet network. The front-end uses the ZigBee network for data collection and transmission, the back-end uses the Ethernet network. In order to achieve the best positioning performance, we try to make each node deployed at the same height, and away from the floor, ceiling and walls. A few ZigBee wireless beacons (CC2430) are deployed below the ceiling, which are used as the reference node of the wireless location networks. Some of these wireless beacons are used as ZigBee routing nodes for the collection and transmission of ZigBee wireless signal. CC2431 module is embedded in the navigation system of the supermarket shopping cart and serves as mobile node. Each mobile node has a unique 16-bit segment address to be used to determine location information. Locator transmits 16-bit short address, node location information through a number of router nodes to the coordinator node which has the gateway role, and then the coordinator node transfer data through the wired Ethernet to a system server. Finally the location returned to the user by the system server. The architecture of the positioning system is shown in Figure 4.

Each mobile node (user terminal) has a unique identification address. Every 10 seconds the location information in the user terminal will be refreshed. After the reference node received the terminal information, it will send its signal information to the user terminal. The user terminal will calculate its current position accordingly using the approach introuced in Section 2, display the position on the terminal. The positioning process is shown in Figure 5.

4   Evaluations

To evaluate the effectiveness of the proposed approach, we simulate a running case of supermarket with the deployment of Zigbee devices as shown in Figure 6. Twelve reference nodes are deployed in an area of 40m*40m as shown in Figure 6. Different algorithms are experimentally simulated with Matlab, and the simulation results are shown in Figure 6. In the evaluations, we will compare our work with DPTM + TA (trilateration algorithm), and DPTM + WCLA, which are two popular approaches currently available.

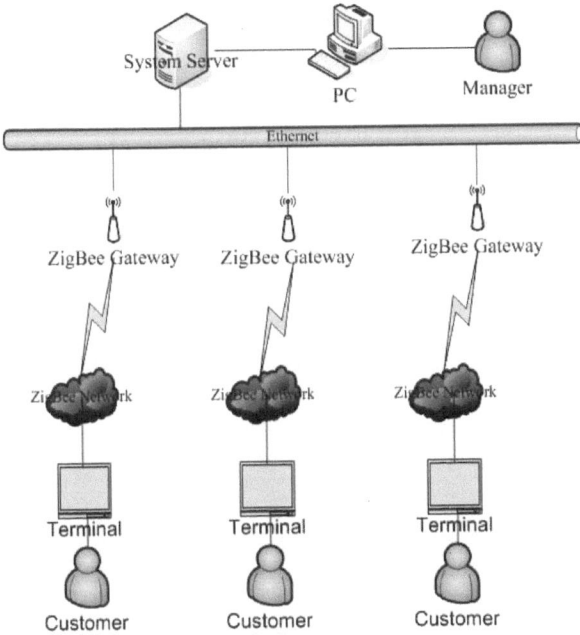

Fig. 4. Architecture of the positioning system

Before simulation using the Matlab, we need to have a clear understanding of aisles in a supermarket, and use linear functions to represent the aisles in order to use the location approximation algorithm. To simulate the RSSI signal, some Gaussian noises are added into the analog RSSI value according to a empirical formula using actual distances from the mobile node to the reference node. Then the dynamic position tracing model is use to smooth these RSSI values, followed by the usage trilateration algorithm or weighted centroid algorithm to estimate the coordinate of the mobile node. For the location approximation algorithm, the distance of a point to a straight line is calculated to make the estimated coordinates approach the nearest aisle.

Figure 7 shows the average error analysis of the three algorithms. It is obvious that the average error of the trilateration algorithm based on DPTM varies greatly, whereas the other two algorithms can get more stable results. However, the average error of our proposed approach is significantly less than that of the weighted centroid algorithm based on DPTM.

We show the detailed measurements in Table 1.

In our simulation, the reference nodes are configured in a reticular way, and at the same time, the nodes are configured to equilateral triangles. Such a configuration can avoid taking three RSSI values in a straight line, and the density of the number of nodes have little effect on the accuracy. This configuration will help to improve the accuracy of localization.

Through these measurements, we can see that the hybrid positioning approach proposed in this paper have a much better accuracy compared to the DPTM +

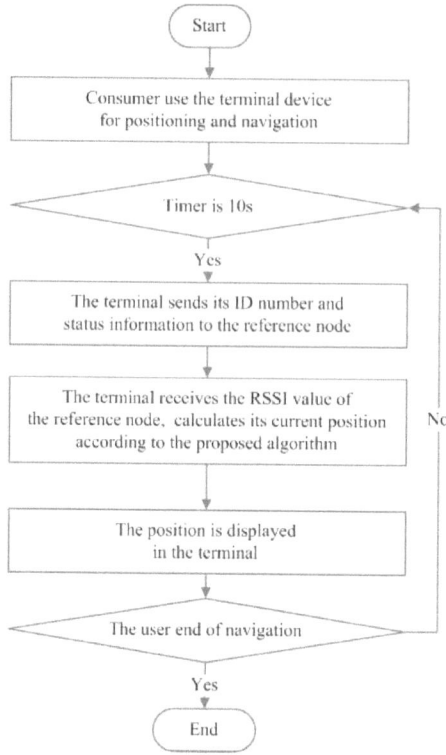

Fig. 5. Working flow the positioning system

TA and DPTM + WCLA approaches. Its accuracy improved 22% compared with DPTM + WCLA, and improved 40% when compared to DPTM + TA. In our approach, the randomly distibuted points are moved to the nearest straight line. This can avoid the possibility of somewhere that are not reachable at all, and makes the positioning more accurate. We may note that our approach has a limitation that it is not accurate for some very wide corridors when a user can move in a large area. But for supermarkets and normal apartments/villa/buildings, the aisle/corridors are usually long and narrow where our approach will work well.

5   Related Work

Reichenbach and Timmermann [3]proposed RSS based localization algorithm with weighted centroid method for indoor wireless senser networks, which offers low communication overhead and low computational complexity. The approach in this paper borrowed these ideas, and we also propose to use the location approximation to enhance the accuracy of positioning. The evaluations show that we achieved better accuracy.

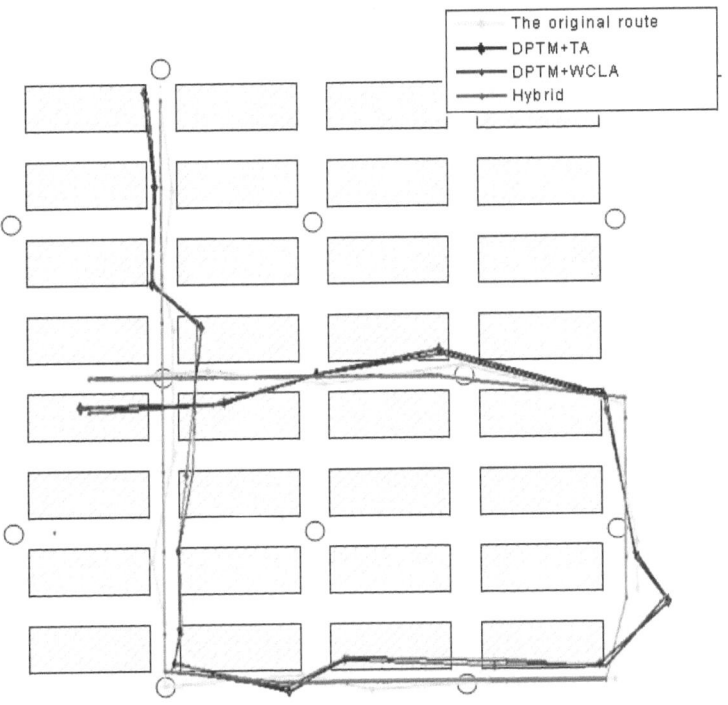

Fig. 6. Simulation result and comparisons of different localization algorithms

Swangmuang and Krishnamurthy [14] propose a new analytical model for estimating the probability distribution of fingerprint selection in an indoor positioning system using WLANs and location fingerprinting. This work needs a lot of efforts to build fingerprint database and we argue that it is more computation-heavy than our approach, as we do not need to compare any fingerpints and analyze these fingerprints, and may not suitable for real time localization, especially when we consider to make the localization work on small devices.

A context-aware tracking system is presented in [10], where power meter nodes are deployed throughout a building. A user carried a mobile node that tracked their current position. A smartphone is used to view the current position for a mobile node , via a cellular or wireless LAN connection. The context-aware tracking system localized a person's position by combining wireless trilateration, a dynamic position tracking model, and a probability density map. Our approach is less complex than that in [10] and we hope that our approach will consume less power. Through evaluations we can also see that our approach can achieve better location accuracy.

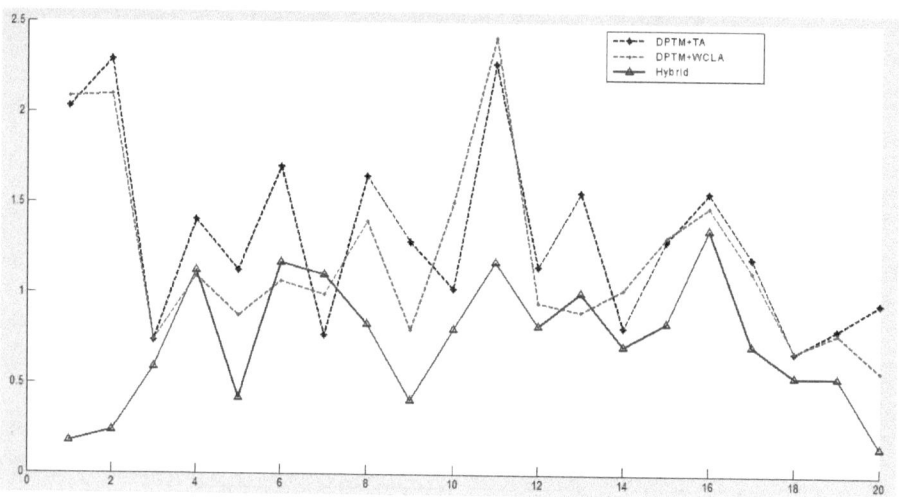

Fig. 7. Average error comparisons of different localization algorithms

Table 1. Detailed measurements for the three approaches

errorm	DPTM + TA	DPTM+ WCLA	Hybrid
Average	1.27	1.04	0.65
Maximum	3.11	1.57	1.28
Average	1.51	1.18	0.9
Maximum	2.9	2.72	2.7
Average	1.66	1.18	0.96
Maximum	4.4	4.02	3.92
Average	1.18	0.81	0.74
Maximum	4.91	2.07	2.29
Average	1.39	1.11	0.83
Maximum	2.7	2.38	2.56
Average	1.22	0.84	0.76
Maximum	2.03	2.24	2.21
Average	1.52	1.28	0.86
Maximum	4.57	3.2	2.6
Average	1.42	1.2	1.01
Maximum	3.05	2.62	3.88
Average	1.11	0.89	0.66

In [7], Kalman filter was applied to the fingerprint based indoor tracking. It was shown that the use of Kalman filter improved the accuracy of the indoor tracking. But for a complex trajectory, the Kalman filter didn't perform well in a corner and could not deal with the nonlinear factors in the tracking. Several filtering methods are compared in [11]. The accuracy of Analytic Moment Calculation (AMC) algorithm is the best among the filters that can achieve the accuracy of 2.5m of average error. Using filtering algorithms alone without considering human behaviors and characteristics of environments, it is hard to achieve high accuracy of positioning. In our work, the average error is in the range of 1m.

6   Conclusions and Future Work

Providing a navigation service in a supermarket is very useful for customers and sellers. Though there are a lot of indoor positioning research, but the problems of the existing approaches are the accuracies are not good enough to be used in a supermarket where the aisle may be long and narrow, and also most of the existing algorithms are too complex. In this paper, we proposed the location approximation algorithm to improve the accuracy of indoor positioning, which can be used together with other algorithms. We explored to use WCLA and DPTM together in this paper, as a hybrid approach to provide supermarket navigation. The evaluations show that our approach can achieve good accuracy compared to the existing approaches.

As the work reported are evaluated only through simulations, we will conduct real tests when we get our Internet of Things testbed which are currently on the way. In the real testing, we will evaluate again the accuracy of positioning and compare the results from simulation. Other important work is that we need to evaluate the power consumption of the mobile nodes and also the reference nodes. Together with the performance testing on how long it takes to obtain the position information. We will also work on viewing the location information on smartphones instead of a terminal screen.

References

1. Balogh, G., Ledeczi, A., Maróti, M., Simon, G.: Time of arrival data fusion for source localization. In: Proceedings of the WICON Workshop on Information Fusion and Dissemination in Wireless Sensor Networks (SensorFusion 2005) (2005)
2. Blumenthal, J., Reichenbach, F., Timmermann, D.: Position estimation in ad hoc wireless sensor networks with low complexity. In: Joint 2nd Workshop on Positioning, Navigation and Communication, pp. 41–49 (2005)
3. Blumenthal, J., Timmermann, D., Buschmann, C., Fischer, S., Koberstein, J., Luttenberger, N.: Minimal transmission power as distance estimation for precise localization in sensor networks. In: Proceedings of the 2006 International Conference on Wireless Communications and Mobile Computing, pp. 1331–1336. ACM (2006)
4. Gao, L., Zhu, M., Yang, D.: Simulation and implement of weighted centroid localization algorithm based on zigbee. Chinese Journal of Sensors and Actuators 1 (2010)
5. Jarzabek, S., Bassett, P., Zhang, H., Zhang, W.: Xvcl: Xml-based variant configuration language. In: Proceedings. 25th International Conference on Software Engineering, pp. 810–811. IEEE (2003)
6. Kuo, W.H., Chen, Y.S., Jen, G.T., Lu, T.W.: An intelligent positioning approach: Rssi-based indoor and outdoor localization scheme in zigbee networks. In: 2010 International Conference on Machine Learning and Cybernetics (ICMLC), vol. 6, pp. 2754–2759. IEEE Computer Society Press, Los Alamitos (2010)

7. Liu, D., Xiong, Y., Ma, J.: Exploit kalman filter to improve fingerprint-based indoor localization. In: 2011 International Conference on Computer Science and Network Technology (ICCSNT), vol. 4, pp. 2290–2293 (December 2011)
8. Liu, H., Darabi, H., Banerjee, P., Liu, J.: Survey of wireless indoor positioning techniques and systems. IEEE Transactions on Systems, Man and Cybernetics, Part C: Applications and Reviews 37(6), 1067–1080 (2007)
9. Otsason, V., Varshavsky, A., LaMarca, A., de Lara, E.: Accurate GSM Indoor Localization. In: Beigl, M., Intille, S.S., Rekimoto, J., Tokuda, H. (eds.) UbiComp 2005. LNCS, vol. 3660, pp. 141–158. Springer, Heidelberg (2005)
10. Ros, M., Boom, J., de Hosson, G.: et al. Indoor localisation using a context-aware dynamic position tracking model. International Journal of Navigation and Observation (2012)
11. Schmid, J., Beutler, F., Noack, B., Hanebeck, U.D., Müller-Glaser, K.D.: An Experimental Evaluation of Position Estimation Methods for Person Localization in Wireless Sensor Networks. In: Marrón, P.J., Whitehouse, K. (eds.) EWSN 2011. LNCS, vol. 6567, pp. 147–162. Springer, Heidelberg (2011)
12. Schuhmann, S., Herrmann, K., Rothermel, K., Blumenthal, J., Timmermann, D.: Improved Weighted Centroid Localization in Smart Ubiquitous Environments. In: Sandnes, F.E., Zhang, Y., Rong, C., Yang, L.T., Ma, J. (eds.) UIC 2008. LNCS, vol. 5061, pp. 20–34. Springer, Heidelberg (2008)
13. Seco, F., Jiménez, A.R., Prieto, C., Roa, J., Koutsou, K.: A survey of mathematical methods for indoor localization. In: IEEE International Symposium on Intelligent Signal Processing, WISP 2009, pp. 9–14 (2009)
14. Swangmuang, N., Krishnamurthy, P.: Location fingerprint analyses toward efficient indoor positioning. In: Sixth Annual IEEE International Conference on Pervasive Computing and Communications, PerCom 2008, pp. 100–109. IEEE (2008)

Introduction to the 8th International Workshop on Engineering Service-Oriented Applications (WESOA'12)

George Feuerlicht[1,2], Winfried Lamersdorf[3], Guadalupe Ortiz[4], and Christian Zirpins[5]

[1] Prague University of Economics
jirif@vse.cz
[2] University of Technology, Sydney
george.feuerlicht@uts.edu.au
[3] University of Hamburg
lamersdorf@informatik.unihamburg.de
[4] University of Cádiz
guadalupe.ortiz@uca.es
[5] SEEBURGER AG
c.zirpins@seeburger.de

The Workshop on Engineering Service Oriented Applications (WESOA) focuses on core service software engineering issues, as well as keeping pace with new developments that include research into methods for engineering of cloud services. Our aim is to facilitate exchange and evolution of ideas in service engineering research across multiple disciplines and to encourage participation of researchers from academia and industry practitioners, avoiding disconnection between these groups. Over the past eight years WESOA has been able to attract high-quality papers across a range of service engineering topics that were published by Springer in its LNCS series and in a special issue of the IJCSSE journal.

The eighth Workshop on Engineering Service Oriented Applications (WESOA'12) was held in Shanghai, China on 12 November 2012. The workshop included a keynote presentation: *Managing Requirements Evolution in Service Oriented System* by Didar Zowghi and six technical papers across a variety of topics. Each paper submitted for the workshop was reviewed by at least four reviewers. The technical session included contributions by Jacky Estublier, et al. *Resource Management for Pervasive Systems*, Muneera Bano Sahibzada, et al. *Service Oriented Requirements Engineering: Practitioner's Perspective*, Daniel Stöhr, et al. *Towards Automated and Correct Composition of Timed Services*, Tri Astoto Kurniawan, et al. *Resolving Violations in Inter-Process Relationships in Business Process Ecosystems*, Inaya Yahya, et al. *An Aspect-oriented Approach to Enforce Security Properties in Business Processes,* and George Feuerlicht, *Evaluation of Quality of Design for Document-centric Software Services.*

Workshop Organizers

George Feuerlicht, University of Technology, Sydney, Australia
Winfried Lamersdorf, University of Hamburg, Germany

A. Ghose et al. (Eds.): ICSOC 2012, LNCS 7759, pp. 317–318, 2013.

Guadalupe Ortiz, University of Cádiz, Spain
Christian Zirpins, SEEBURGER AG, Germany

Program Committee

Marco Aiello, University of Groningen, Netherlands
Vasilios Andrikopoulos, University of Stuttgart, Germany
Sami Bhiri, DERI Galway, Ireland
Alena Buchalcevova, Prague University of Economics, Czech Republic
Anis Charfi, SAP Research CEC Darmstadt, Germany
Jen-Yao Chung, IBM T.J. Watson Research, United States
Daniel Florian, University of Trento, Italy
Valeria de Castro, Universidad Rey Juan Carlos, Spain
Paul Greenfield, CSIRO, Australia
Dimka Karastoyanova, University of Stuttgart, Germany
Rannia Khalaf, IBM T.J. Watson Research, United States
Agnes Koschmieder, Karlsruhe Institute of Technology, Germany
Mark Little, Red Hat, United States
Michael Maximilien, IBM Almaden Research, United States
Massimo Mecella, Univ. Roma LA SAPIENZA, Italy
Daniel Moldt, University of Hamburg, Germany
Rebecca Parsons, ThoughtWorks, United States
Cesare Pautasso, Universitz of Lugano, Switzerland
Pierluigi Plebani, Politecnico di Milano, Italy
Franco Raimondi, Middlesex University, United Kingdom
Wolfgang Reisig, Humboldt-University Berlin, Germany
Norbert Ritter, University of Hamburg, Germany
Nelly Schuster, FZI Forschungszentrum Informatik, Germany
Olaf Zimmermann, ABB, Switzerland

Acknowledgements. Guadalupe Ortiz thanks for the support from Ministerio de Ciencia e Innovación (TIN2011-27242). George Feuerlicht wishes to acknowledge the support of GAČR (Grant Agency, Czech Republic) grant No. P403/11/0574 and the Australian-China Science and Research Fund ACSCRF-01280 from the Australian Department of Innovation, Industry, Science, Research and Tertiary Education (DIISRTE).

The organizers of the WESOA'12 workshop would like to thank all authors for their contributions to this workshop, and members of the program committee whose expert input made this workshop possible. Finally, we thank ICSOC'12 workshop chairs Aditya Ghose and Huibiao Zhu for their direction and guidance.

Towards Automated and Correct Composition of Timed Services

Daniel Stöhr and Sabine Glesner

Technical University of Berlin, Chair Software Engineering for Embedded Systems,
{daniel.stoehr,sabine.glesner}@tu-berlin.de
www.pes.tu-berlin.de

Abstract. The design of programs controlling distributed components in safety-critical domains can be very error-prone and time-consuming. Especially in the presence of real-time requirements the correctness with respect to functional and non-functional properties must be guaranteed. To this end, we develop a technique for the automated and correct composition of timed services based on timed i/o automata, the temporal logic TCTL, and planning algorithms based on model checking. Thus, we can speed up the development of controller programs while assuring correctness.

1 Introduction

The development of controller programs coordinating distributed components in safety and time-critical environments is a very complex task. On the one hand, the correctness with respect to functional and non-functional properties, like timed behaviour, has to be assured. This can be achieved by using verification techniques, e.g., model checking, which automatically proves total correctness but significantly increases the quantity and length of development cycles. On the other hand, development time has to be short to achieve a small time-to-market. In our work, we address the problem of closing the gap between these opposites with development methods assuring correctness by construction.

For this purpose, we lift the problem of creating a controller model to the problem of automated service composition. Our method shall be able to generate controller models for a given set of timed services with respect to functional and non-functional (especially timed) requirements. We describe the behaviour of the services as *timed i/o automata (TIOA)* and the composition requirements in the temporal logic *Timed CTL (TCTL)*. The generated controller, which is an orchestrator in the context of service-oriented computing, is a TIOA handling the input and output actions of the individual automata. To realize our approach, we extend *planning as model checking* which is already able to deal with *untimed* automata-based planning domains and CTL goals. We extend the theory of planning as model checking by introducing time in terms of real-valued clocks. In this paper, we report on our first results with which we can automatically generate plans for a set of timed services and requirements given in a restricted subset of TCTL.

A particularly interesting domain for our approach is the synchronization of medical devices. Here, functional and real-time requirements have to be met in

A. Ghose et al. (Eds.): ICSOC 2012, LNCS 7759, pp. 319–331, 2013.

order to guarantee the patient's safety. We show the applicability of our approach through case study where distinct components of a PCA (patient-controlled analgesia) pump have to be controlled to guarantee functional and time-related requirements. In our case study, we have closed components within a device that can be controlled over a central software. Likewise, other scenarios where distinct devices need synchronization over a network are also possible.

Briefly summarized, the contributions of this paper are:

- We outline an approach realizing the automated composition of timed services by utilizing planning algorithms based on model checking. Timed i/o automata describe the input services, TCTL formulas describe the composition requirements.
- We present our extensions of the existing planning algorithms and we have implemented a prototype realizing planning for a subset of TCTL.
- We provide a case study for our approach that cannot be handled by current composition and planning techniques.

The rest of this paper is structured as follows. In Section 2 we give the background for our work. We present the concept of *timed i/o automata* and *TCTL*, along with a running case example for our approach. Also, we discuss *planning as model checking*. In Section 3 we describe the concept of our overall approach, and present our extensions to the symbolic planning algorithms. Afterwards, in Section 4, we describe our prototype implementation. In Section 5 we discuss related works for automated service composition and temporal planning. Finally, in Section 6, we give a conclusion and outline future work.

2   Preliminaries

In this section, we present the background of our work. In Section 2.1, we describe *timed i/o automata* and in Section 2.2, the temporal logic *TCTL*. In both sections, we introduce the case example for our approach. Finally, in Section 2.3 we describe the concept of *planning as model checking* in detail.

2.1   Timed I/O Automata (TIOA) and Case Example

Timed i/o automata (TIOA), as proposed by David and Larsen [1], enrich the concept of timed automata by adding input and output signals and the concept of parallel composition over signals belonging together.

A TIOA is a tuple $A = (Loc, q_0, Clk, E, Act, Inv)$ where Loc is a finite set of locations, $q_0 \in Loc$ is the initial location, and Clk is a finite set of clocks. $E \subseteq Loc \times Act \times \mathcal{B}(Clk) \times 2^{Clk} \times Loc$ is a set of edges with timed guards ($\mathcal{B}(Clk)$ are all Boolean expressions over Clk) and a set of clocks to be reset. Finally, $Act = Act_i \cup Act_o \cup \{\tau\}$ is a finite set of actions consisting of disjunct sets of input and output actions and the symbol τ for transitions without actions. $Inv : Loc \mapsto \mathcal{B}(Clk)$ is a set of location invariants.

The *parallel composition* $TA_1 \| TA_2$ of TIOA is similar to building up the crossproduct. If an in- and output signal belong together, both transitions are combined as one parallel transition.

It has been shown that web service compositions, e.g. in *WS-BPEL* or *WS-CDL*, can be translated into timed automata and vice versa [2]. Service instances are represented as single automata, messages as synchronized actions, and wait durations or timeouts as guards and invariants. Thus, web services compositions can be analyzed and verified by model checking.

Figure 1 shows the visual representation of a TIOA and gives a use case for our approach. It shows a simplified version of a system controlling a PCA pump [3]. These pumps administer the pain medication for a patient by delivering drug doses at a basal rate. The complete use case contains further requirements. E.g., the pump can raise alarms or the patient can signal the system to give a bolus injection if his pain level is too high. However, the first-mentioned requirement is sufficient for illustrating the benefit our approach, as it cannot be solved by existing tools for automated composition or AI planning (see Section 5).

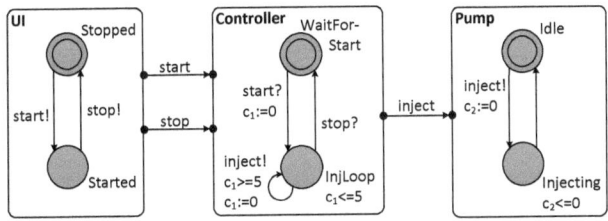

Fig. 1. Composition of TIOA describing the components of a PCA pump and a controller

The system consists of a TIOA `UI` representing the user interface that turns the pump on and off via the output signals `start` and `stop`. The other component is described by `Pump` which just waits for the input signal `inject` triggering an injection dose and resetting the clock c_2. Then, the state `Injecting` is entered and left without letting time progress. This is realized by using an invariant.

The TIOA `Controller` performs the composition according to the above-mentioned requirement. With our approach, we generate such a controller out of a formal requirements specification. In its initial State `WaitForStart`, the controller waits for the signal `start` to turn on the system and to reset the clock c_1. The drug injection has to be triggered in a specific interval (here, 5 time units). The invariant of `InjLoop` and the guard and clock reset on the loop transition ensure that the signal `inject` is emmited every 5 time units. Thus, the controller guarantees the injection rate defined in the composition requirements[1].

---

[1] Our composition requirements leave some flexibility in the controller's design. The controller shown in our example triggers the first injection 5 time units after the system has been started. A controller injecting immediately after the start would also be valid but would have to guarantee that the user cannot bypass the safetey requirement by switching fast between `start` and `stop`. Our extended planning algorithms would generate the latter version. However, to improve the comprehensibility of our example we have chosen the former version.

2.2 Timed CTL (TCTL)

The *Timed Computation Tree Logic* (*TCTL* [4]) is an extension of CTL with clock constraints. TCTL can be used to describe conditions on branching paths in timed i/o automata. The language is defined as follows.

$$\Phi := p \mid (x + c) \le (y + d) \mid \neg \Phi \mid \Phi_1 \wedge \Phi_2 \mid \mathbf{E}(\Phi_1 \mathbf{U} \Phi_2) \mid \mathbf{A}(\Phi_1 \mathbf{U} \Phi_2) \mid x.\Phi$$

where p is an atomic proposition, x and y are clock variables, and $c, d \in \mathbb{N}$.

The semantics of the logical ($\wedge, \neg$) and relational ($\le$) operators are defined as usual. The temporal operator $\mathbf{E}(\Phi_1 \mathbf{U} \Phi_2)$ holds iff there exists a path preserving Φ_1 until Φ_2 holds. $\mathbf{A}(\Phi_1 \mathbf{U} \Phi_2)$ is defined analogously for all paths. $x.\Phi$ is the reset quantifier. Iff clock x is zero, then Φ holds.

Logical ($\vee, \rightarrow, \leftrightarrow$) and relational ($<, \ge, >$) abbreviations are defined as usual, too. The temporal abbreviations $\mathbf{EF}p$ and $\mathbf{EG}p$ hold iff there exists a path where p holds eventually, respectively forever. $\mathbf{AF}p$ and $\mathbf{AG}p$ are defined analogously for all paths. Finally, $\mathbf{EF}_{<c}p$ with $c \in \mathbb{N}$ holds iff there exists a path where eventually p holds in less than c time units.

In the following, we show the requirements of our case study (see Figure 1) expressed as TCTL formulas. In our approach, these formulas are used to automatically generate the controller.

(1) $\mathbf{AG}(\text{Started} \rightarrow (\mathbf{AG}\ \mathbf{AF}\text{Injecting}))$
(2) $\mathbf{AG}(\text{Injecting} \rightarrow \neg \mathbf{EF}_{<5}\text{Injecting})$
(3) $\mathbf{AG}(\text{Injecting} \rightarrow \text{Started})$

Requirement *(1)* describes that whenever the system is started, the drug injection must take place repeatedly. Requirement *(2)* defines the injection rate. Whenever the state Injecting has been entered, it may not be reached again in less than 5 time units. In this scenario, our extended planning tool would solve the goal $\mathbf{AF}\text{Injecting}$ as soon as possible. Hence, these two requirements are sufficient for generating a controller injecting every 5 time units. At last, we need our safety requirement *(3)*, stating that the injection may only be triggered while the system is activated.

2.3 Planning as Model Checking

Methods of AI planning generate plans solving problems in a given domain. In *planning as model checking* [5] the domain is described in an automata-based model and the planning problem consists of sets of initial and goal states. A plan is a list stating which action has to be performed in which state, to reach a goal state from an initial state.

However, the problem of identifying paths leading to the goal is similar to the counter example generation in model checking where a path leading to a violated property is computed. Hence, planning as model checking reduces the planning problem to a model checking problem. As described in Section 3 we extend planning as model checking to cope with time and realize the automated composition approach.

In the following, we give the basic definitions for planning domains, planning problems, and plans. Afterwards, we show how the planning problem can be solved via symbolic model checking.

Basic Definitions. A *planning domain* is a tuple $D = (P, S, A, R)$ where P is a finite set of propositions, $S \subseteq 2^P$ is a finite set of states, A is a finite set of actions, and $R \subseteq S \times A \times S$ is the transition relation.

A *planning problem* is defined as a tuple $P = (D, I, G)$ where D is a planning domain, $I \subseteq S$ is a set of initial states, and $G \subseteq S$ is a set of goal states.

Plans for a given domain $D = (P, S, A, R)$ are expressed as a *state-action table* $\pi \subseteq \{(s, a) | s \in S, a \in A, \exists s' \in S : R(s, a, s')\}$. State-action tables can be *executed* within a domain by starting in an initial state and performing the corresponding action for each state. With regard to non-determinism, the execution may take different *execution paths* through the domain.

Finally, a *strong plan* for a domain $D = (P, S, A, R)$ and problem $P = (D, I, G)$ is a state-action table where each execution path starting in a state of I leads to a state in G. A strong plan is calculated by using the following function:

$Exec(s, a) = \{s' | R(s, a, s')\}$
$StrongPreImage(S) = \{(s, a) | \emptyset \neq Exec(s, a) \subseteq S\}$

StrongPreImage explores all state-action pairs that lead into the set of states S while taking non-determinism into account. The planning algorithm applies that function on the set of goal states, then, on the union of the newly explored and goal states, and so on. The plan generation fails if a fixpoint is reached before all initial states are explored. Otherwise, the set of all collected state-action pairs forming the strong plan, is returned[2].

Planning with CTL formulas as planning goal is also offered [5]. Here, the complex goal is divided into smaller subgoals that are resolved by using functions similar to the preimage function.

Symbolic Planning. Planning as model checking uses techniques of symbolic model checking to solve the planning problem with logical operations. At first, the planning domain is described by Boolean formulas. Then, the preimage function can also be described symbolically by using logical operators.

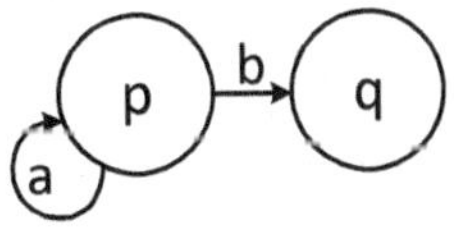

Fig. 2. A planning domain

We give a small example for a planning domain in Figure 2, consisting of two states p and q, a loop transition on p using the action a, and a transition between p and q using action b. The domain is described by the following fomulas:

$T_1 \doteq p \wedge a \wedge p'$ $States \doteq (p \wedge \neg q) \vee (\neg p \wedge q)$
$T_2 \doteq p \wedge b \wedge q'$ $Actions \doteq (a \wedge \neg b) \vee (\neg a \wedge b)$
$T \doteq T_1 \vee T_2$ $D \doteq T \wedge States \wedge Actions$

Every state of the domain is represented by two Booleans p, p', q, and q'. Unprimed state variables describe the source of a transition, the others the destination. The actions are represented by the boolean variables a and b.

---

[2] The complete algorithm uses an additional function ensuring that a state is not explored twice. We have ommited that function due to lack of space.

T_1 describes the loop transition where each conjunct describes an element of the tuple describing the transition in the set-based representation. T_2 describes the other transition. The set of Transitions is described by T. The formulas *States* and *Actions* state that only one state or action may be active at once. Finally, D represents the whole planning domain.

Building on the system's symbolic description, the preimage function is defined symbolically, too. To this end, *quantified Boolean formulas* (QBFs) are used. QBFs extend propositional logics by universal and existential quantifiers. If Φ is a formula and v one of its variables, then $\forall v.\Phi$ is equivalent to $\Phi[v/True] \wedge \Phi[v/False]$. The existential quantification is defined analogously using the logical or.

The symbolic preimage function is defined as follows, where S is the formula describing the set of input states (e.g., $p' \vee q'$ or just p') and D is the formula describing the planning domain.

$$StrongPreImage(S) \doteq \forall p', q'.(D \rightarrow S) \wedge \exists p', q'.D$$

The preimage function is applied in the same way described for the set-based function. Other operations performed in the complete algorithm, are also performed using logical operators. By doing this, very large sets of states can be handled in compact formulas and, hence, the amount of memory usage and computation time can be reduced.

3 Automated Composition of Timed Services

In this section, we describe our approach for the automated and correct composition of timed services. A set of service interfaces, expressed as TIOA, and composition requirements, expressed as TCTL formulas, serve as input. The output is a generated orchestrator, i.e. a central automaton. We do so by using planning algorithms based on model checking where the set of services becomes the planning domain and the composition requirements become planning goals.

Firstly, in Section 3.1 we outline the overall concept of our approach and how we transform the composition problem into a planning problem. Secondly, in Section 3.2, we give a detailed description of our extensions to *planning as model checking*, which realize the composition process. At this moment, we have realized the extensions for a subset of TCTL (formulas in the form of $\mathbf{A}(\neg \phi \mathbf{U} \psi)$ describing unsafe states ϕ and a goal state ψ). However, our results can be extended for full TCTL support.

3.1 Methodology of Our Approach

With our approach, we transform the problem of automatically composing timed services into an AI planning problem. The methodology is visualized in Figure 3. As input we take a set of TIOA $TA_1, ..., TA_n$ describing service interfaces. $TA_{||}$, the parallel composition of these automata, serves as

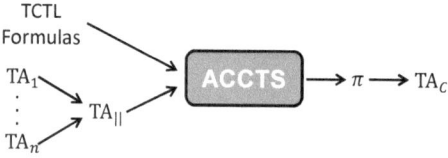

Fig. 3. Our approach for the Automated and Correct Composition of Timed Services (ACCTS)

planning domain. As composition requirements, which describe the properties of the overall composition, we use TCTL formulas reasoning on states and timing constraints. In our example the input automata are UI and Pump, while the composition requirements are a conjunction of the functional and safety requirements.

Afterwards, we use our algorithms for timed planning as model checking to build up a plan π controlling the domain with respect to the composition requirements. The plan is used to build up our controller TA_C, the TIOA that orchestrates the overall composition.

Existing planning techniques cannot deal with timed domains and requirements of that expressiveness (see Section 5.2). Hence, we decided to extend the algorithms of *planning as model checking* that already solves CTL goals in planning domains based on untimed automata. To overcome this restriction, we introduce clocks into the planning theory. In the next section, we describe first extensions we have realized.

3.2   Extending Strong Planning with Time

In the following, we describe how we cope with time by extending the structures and algorithms of planning as model checking (see Section 2.3). Analogously to TIOA (see Section 2.1), we add clock variables, guards, and invariants. For additionally extending the expressiveness of strong goals, we also introduce a possibility to express unsafe states, which a plan has to avoid. Thus, we can plan with TCTL formulas in the form of $\mathbf{A}(\neg\phi\mathbf{U}\psi)$ where ϕ describes the set of unsafe states and ψ describes the set of goal states. Subsequent, we describe how we shifted our extensions to the symbolic representation.

Basic Definitions. A *timed planning domain* is a tuple $D_T = (P, S, Clk, A, R, Inv)$. As before, P is a finite set of propositions, $S \subseteq 2^P$ is a finite set of states, and A is a finite set of actions. Additionally, Clk is the set of clock variables and $R \subseteq S \times A \times B(Clk) \times 2^{Clk} \times S$ is the transition relation enriched with a guard and a set of clocks to be reset. $Inv : S \mapsto B(Clk)$ are the timed invariants of the states.

A *timed planning problem* is defined as a tuple $P_T = (D_T, I, U, G)$ where D_T is a timed planning domain and $I, U, G \subseteq S \times \mathbb{R}_{\geq 0}^{Clk}$ are initial, unsafe, and goal states connected to clock values. Here, $\mathbb{R}_{\geq 0}^{Clk}$ (an abbreviation for the mapping $Clk \mapsto \mathbb{R}_{\geq 0}$) is a *valuation* of the clock variables.

For $(s, v), (s', v') \in S \times \mathbb{R}_{\geq 0}^{Clk}$ (a state and corresponding clock valuation) a discrete transition $(s, v) \xrightarrow{a} (s', v')$ exists, if there exists a tuple $(s, a, g, res, s') \in R$ such that $v' = v[res]$, $v \models g$, and $v' \models Inv(s')$. $v[res]$ denotes the valuation v with all clock in res reset to zero.

We express plans for a given timed domain D_T as a *timed state-action table* $\pi_T \subseteq \{((s, v), a | (s, v) \in S \times \mathbb{R}_{\geq 0}^{Clk}, a \in A, \exists (s', v') \in S \times \mathbb{R}_{\geq 0}^{Clk} : (s, v) \xrightarrow{a} (s', v')\}$. The *execution* of a plan and the resulting *execution paths* do not only consist of performing actions. Also *time progress*, called time transitions, can occur where the clock valuation is increased for all clocks synchronously (within the bounds of the invariants).

Finally, a *strong plan* for a timed domain D_T and timed problem P is a state-action table where each execution path starting in a state of I leads to a state in G. For the calculation of strong plans, we extend the preimage function, as follows:

$$Exec((s,v),a) = \{s'|(s,v) \xrightarrow{a} (s',v')\}$$
$$S \nearrow = \{(s,v-d)|(s,v) \in S \wedge d \in \mathbb{R}_{\geq 0} \wedge v - d \geq 0 \wedge (s, v-d) \models Inv(s)\}$$
$$StrongPreImage(S, U) =$$
$$\{((s,v),a)|\emptyset \neq Exec((s,v),a) \subseteq S \nearrow \wedge v \models Inv(s) \wedge s \notin U\}$$

We extended the *Exec* function which computes all possible results of executing an action in a state and which now considers guards and invariants of s' by using discrete transitions. Also, we define the $\nearrow$ operator which is common in the model checking of timed automata. The argument is a set of states S and the result are all states that can be reached from S by letting time progress backwards. In our extended *StrongPreImage* function, we apply the $\nearrow$ operator to the set of states S (which are the goal states and already discovered states leading to the goal). Thus, we ensure that not only the execution of actions but also time progress is considered. The preimage function now calculates those states that can reach a state in S immediately by executing an action, or by letting time progress and then executing an action. Moreover, we now enforce that the *StrongPreImage* function considers the invariant of the state s and ensure that s is not part of the unsafe states in U.

In the fixpoint algorithm, the *StrongPreImage* function is initially applied to the goal states, then to the states of the resulting state-action pairs, and so on. Thus, we explore the states that can reach the goal states while avoiding unsafe states. The algorithm terminates if the initial states are reached and fails if a fixpoint is reached. Our extended algorithm still terminates, because we have a finite set of states, clock values cannot be lower than 0, and we only use the $\nearrow$ operator. At some point of time, the algorithm will have explored all states and will have counted all clocks to 0 (resp. to the lowest bound enforced by the invariants). Thus we will reach a fixpoint from any given set of states and corresponding clock valuations.

Mapping TIOA into Timed Planning Domains. Our extensions allow us to map the service interfaces, resp. TIOAs, into timed planning domains. As described in Section 3.1, we do so by building the parallel composition of all required services. The resulting single automaton $A_{||} = (Loc, q0, Clk_A, E, Act, Inv_A)$ can easily be mapped into a timed planning domain $D_T = (P, S, Clk_D, A, R, Inv_D)$.

Firstly, we have a property in P for each location in Loc. The set of domain states S ensures that only one property may be true at a time[3]. The sets of clock

---

[3] For higher efficiency it is possible to encode the set of locations as a combination of property values. Another possibility is to allow more than one active property at a time by translating the states of the original parallel automata. However, investigating the efficiency impact of these alternative solutions will be part of future work.

variables Clk_A and Clk_D, as well as the action labels Act and A are identical. Now the transition relation R and the invariants Inv_D can be built up out of E and Inv_A by matching properties and corresponding locations.

Symbolic Planning. For the symbolic planning algorithms, we firstly enrich the system's symbolic representation clock variables and clock constraints. We illustrate this, by using the Pump automaton (see Section 2.1) transformed into a timed planning domain:

$$T_1 \doteq Idle \wedge inject! \wedge c_2' = 0 \wedge Injecting'$$
$$T_2 \doteq Injecting \wedge \neg inject! \wedge c_2' = c_2 \wedge Idle'$$
$$T \doteq T_1 \vee T_2$$
$$States \doteq (Idle \wedge \neg Injecting) \vee (\neg Idle \wedge Injecting \wedge c_2 \leq 0)$$
$$Actions \doteq (inject! \vee \neg inject!)$$
$$D \doteq T \wedge States \wedge Actions$$

As in the untimed version, we still have variables for all propositions and actions. We add the real-valued clock variables c_1, c_1', c_2, and c_2' for describing clock values before or after discrete transitions, and for describing invariants. Formula T_1 describes the left transition of Pump. Source, action, and destination are denoted as before. We add the expression $c_2' = 0$ describing the clock reset. If the transition contained a guard, the correpsonding exepression would refer to c_2.

Also, we need to consider clock variables in the $States$ formula. Here, we add the invariant $c_2 \leq 0$ of $Injecting$. The other formulas, T_2, T, $Actions$, and D are built up as before, since they do not directly refer to clock variables. The expression $\neg inject!$ means that no action is active and stands for τ in the set-based representation.

For the symbolic representation of our extended preimage function, we introduce further quantifications over the clock variables, the $\diagup$ operator, and consider the unsafe states U:

$$StrongPreImage(S, U) \doteq \forall p', q', c_1', c_2'.(D \to S \diagup) \wedge \exists p', q', c_1', c_2'.(D \wedge \neg U)$$

The additional quantifications remove the clock resets from the formula D, leaving only the preimage states, corresponding actions, and guards. The result characterizes the states that can reach S immediately or after time progress.

In summary, our approach provides a methodology for the automated composition of timed services. By transforming the composition problem into a planning problem and by using techniques of model checking, we ensure the correctness of resulting compositions. Within our approach, service interfaces are represented as TIOA and composition requirements as TCTL formulas. So far, we have realized extensions to the existing planning algorithms, that allow us to solve planning goals in the form of $\mathbf{A}(\neg \phi \mathbf{U} \psi)$ where ϕ are the unsafe states and ψ are the goal states. However, our results can be further extended for full TCTL support. In Section 6 we outline how these extensions can be realized.

4 Implementation with MDD+CRDs

For evaluating our first extensions, we have implemented a prototype. To work with logical formulas and operators, we used the open source library $REDLIB$ [6]

which offers *multi-decision- & clock-restriction-diagrams* (*MDD+CRDs*), a data structure representing Boolean formulas with Boolean, discrete, and clock variables. The usual logical operators, variable quantification, and the $\nearrow$ operator are also included. MDD+CRDs were developed for the model checking of timed automata and RED, a model checker based on REDLIB, performs very well in time and space compared to other established model checking tools [7]. Algorithms of model checking generally lead to a high complexity. But by using REDLIB, we hope to improve the scalability of our implementation.

Our prototype takes an xml representation of TIOA and a planning problem, resp. a set of goal and unsafe states, as input. The output is a plan solving the planning problem. Our whole algorithm is executed by performing logical operations.

We tested our prototype by generating a plan for our case study with the simplified, non-cyclic composition requirement **A**(¬Injecting **U** (Started ∧ Injecting))). Also, we generated plans for other small examples. Our evaluation led to promising results where plans have been generated within milliseconds (under Ubuntu 10.04 on an Intel i5, 2,7 Ghz with 2GB RAM). However, for a profound evaluation of the scalability, we will need much larger examples and full TCTL support.

5   Related Work

In this section, we present works related to our approach. In Section 5.1, we discuss approaches for automated service composition. In Section 5.2, we examine techniques for temporal planning.

5.1   Automated Service Composition

The majority of techniques for automated service composition do not consider time as a service property or composition requirement. The *astro* framework [8], e.g., uses planning as model checking to automatically generate a BPEL composition out of a given set of web services and composition requirements. Here, the way how the planning theory was utilized to solve the composition problem is similar to our approach. This work is not able to deal with timed service behaviour or timed requirements. However, timed capabilities are one of the main characteristics of our proposed approach.

Most approaches on the composition of timed services regard time as a measurement for communication latency between world-wide distributed services [9] or telephone servers [10]. They consider time as a *Quality of Service* criterion that serves as parameter for choosing a proper service instance during the composition process. In our work, we see time as a part of the service's behaviour and functionality itself.

To the best of our knowledge, there is only one approach realizing automated service composition with timed composition requirements [11]. In contrast to our approach, this work offers a very low degree of automation because the overall workflow of a BPEL composition has to exist before timed requirements can be woven into the workflow according to specification. In contrast to that, our approach offers a very high degree of automation by generating the workflow of the composition from scratch.

We proposed our approach in an earlyier work [12]. This work only presented the overall concept of the approach. Now, we have refined the concept itself, realized first theoretical foundations, and implemented a prototype.

5.2   Temporal Planning

There are several temporal planning tools of which most only allow planning goals that consist of one or more goal states and deadlines [13,14]. Others create a schedule for a list of atomic actions with regard to specified interaction constraints [15]. These tools are not applicable to our domain because we need to support more complex TCTL goals. In the following, we discuss two temporal planning tools that are interesting with regard to the expressiveness of their goal languages.

The TALPlanner [16] plans over domains and goals expressed in a first order logic, the temporal action logic (TAL). TAL formulas allow the quantification over discrete or clock variables and provide operators that put actions and variable changes in a causal correlation. In contrast to TCTL, TAL specifies linear (opposed to branching) behavior. Moreover, TAL reasons on actions actions, while TCTL reasons on states. Hence, TAL does not cover the expressiveness of TCTL.

Uppaal-TIGA [17] solves game-theoretical problems on timed game automata with respect to reachability or safety properties expressed in a subset of TCTL. These goals do not allow the nesting of TCTL operators or the conjunction of goals using temporal operators. Hence, it is not possible to consider, e.g., the cyclic appearing reachability goal we use in our example (requirement (1) in Section 2.2). The formulas that can be expressed are hard-coded into the algorithms. In constrast to that, the results of our apporach can be continued for full TCTL support.

6   Conclusion and Future Work

In this paper, we have presented first theoretical foundations of our approach for the automated and correct composition of timed services by using timed i/o automata, TCTL, and planning algorithms based on model checking. With our first extensions to the existing untimed planning algorithms, we can generate plans fulfulling composition requirements expressed in a subset of TCTL (formulas in the form of $\mathbf{A}(\neg\phi\mathbf{U}\psi)$). Thus, we already cover those composition requirements where a state has to be reached under occlusion of unsafe states. Moreover, we have implemented a first prototype realizing our extended algorithms. We evaluated our approach by generating the plan for a simplified version of our case study where the composition requirements can be expressed in the above-mentioned subset of TCTL.

In future work, we will realize the support of whole TCTL formulas as planning goals, similar to the extensions for strong planning. Yet, no other automated composition and no planning approach is able to deal with with the expressiveness of full TCTL formulas. The existing algorithms for simple CTL goals [5] divide complex goal formulas into atomic subgoals. According to the corresponding CTL operators, the reachability of subgoals is symbolically calculated by using functions similar to the preimage function. For supporting clock variables, we will extend these functions in a similar way, as we did here.

Furthermore, we introduce TCTL's reset quantifier, $x.\Phi$, as a new subgoal. $x.\Phi$ bounds a new clock variable x to an expression Φ. In the planning context, Φ is a set of subgoals. To solve these goals, we add the new clock variable to the system's symbolic description and assure that x must be zero every time a subgoal of Φ is activated.

Morover, we want to realize the translation of the generated plans into an orchestrator, i.e., a central timed i/o automaton performing the composition. Hence, we will adapt and extend a work translating plans into BPEL compositions without considering time [8]. Moreover, we will perform a larger case study where a PET/CT scanner has to be synchronized with other medical devices over a network. This allows us to investigate the scalability of our approach in the context of real-life applications.

References

1. David, A., Larsen, K.G., Legay, A., Nyman, U.: Timed I/O Automata: A Complete Specification Theory for Real-time Systems. Science (2010)
2. Gregorio, D., Cambronero, M.E., Pardo, J.J., Cuartero, F.: Automatic generation of Correct Web Services Choreographies and Orchestrations with Model Checking Techniques. In: International Conference on Internet and Web Applications and Services, AICT-ICIW 2006 (2006)
3. Arney, D., Jetley, R., Jones, P., Lee, I., Sokolsky, O.: Formal Methods Based Development of a PCA Infusion Pump Reference Model: Generic Infusion Pump (GIP) Project. In: Joint Workshop on High Confidence Medical Devices, Software and Systems and Medical Device Plug-and-Play Interoperability (2007)
4. Alur, R.: Techniques for Automatic Verification of Real-Time Systems. PhD thesis, Stanford University (1991)
5. Pistore, M., Bettin, R., Traverso, P.: Symbolic techniques for planning with extended goals in non-deterministic domains. In: 6th European Conference on Planning (2001)
6. Wang, F.: REDLIB A Library of Integrated BDD-like Diagrams for Dense-Time Model Verification (2012)
7. Wang, F.: Efficient verification of timed automata with BDD-like data structures. International Journal on Software Tools for Technology Transfer 6(1), 77–97 (2004)
8. Pistore, M., Traverso, P., Bertoli, P.: Automated Composition of Web Services by Planning in Asynchronous Domains. Artificial Intelligence 174 (2005)
9. Moussa, H., Gao, T., Yen, I.L., Bastani, F., Jeng, J.J.: Toward effective service composition for real-time SOA-based systems. Service Oriented Computing and Applications 4(1) (2010)

10. Lin, L., Lin, P.: Orchestration in Web Services and Real-Time Communications. IEEE Communications Magazine (July 2007)
11. Kallel, S., Dinkelaker, T., Mezini, M., Charfi, A., Jmaiel, M.: Specifying and Monitoring Temporal Properties in Web services Compositions. In: Seventh IEEE European Conference on Web Services (2009)
12. Stöhr, D., Glesner, S.: Automated Composition of Timed Services by Planning as Model Checking. In: Proceedings of the 4th Central European Workshop on Services and their Composition (2012)
13. Do, M.B., Kambhampati, S.: Sapa: A Domain-Independent Heuristic Metric Temporal Planner. In: Proceedings of European Conference on Planning (2001)
14. Garrido, A., Fox, M., Long, D.: A Temporal Planning System for Durative Actions of PDDL2.1. In: European Conference on AI, vol. 1 (2002)
15. Muscettola, N.: HSTS: Integrating Planning and Scheduling. Intelligent Scheduling (1993)
16. Doherty, P., Kvarnström, J., Heintz, F.: A temporal logic-based planning and execution monitoring framework for unmanned aircraft systems. In: Autonomous Agents and Multi-Agent Systems, vol. 19(3) (2009)
17. Cassez, F., David, A., Fleury, E., Larsen, K.G.: Efficient On-the-fly Algorithms for the Analysis of Timed Games (2005)

Resolving Violations in Inter-process Relationships in Business Process Ecosystems

Tri Astoto Kurniawan*, Aditya K. Ghose, and Lam-Son Lê

Decision Systems Lab., School of Computer Science and Software Engineering,
University of Wollongong, NSW 2522, Australia
{tak976,aditya,lle}@uow.edu.au

Abstract. In service-based environments, each accessible service relies on business process(es) such that changing these services usually requires changing their supporting process(es). Managing process changes is not trivial due to there may exist complex relationships between processes. Changing a process may lead to further changes to related processes to preserve their relationships. We propose resolution patterns, based on semantic effect analysis, to resolve relationship violations between processes.

Keywords: inter-process relationship, semantic effect, resolution patterns, change propagation.

1 Introduction

Service-Oriented Computing (SOC) utilizes services as the constructs to support the development of rapid, low-cost and easy composition of distributed applications [7]. Web Services have emerged as the current most promising technology based on the SOC concept. They provide the basis for the development and execution of business processes, which are normally invisible to the business partners, that are distributed over the network and available via standard interfaces and protocols [7]. As business environments constantly change over time, enterprises are expected to be able to adapt to many changes to their business services to keep their competitiveness. Changes to these services usually require changes to their supporting business processes. Managing process changes challenges the enterprises with the fact that their process repositories have complex features [6], involving hundreds even thousands of models in which they might be related to each other. In this context, changing one single process may lead to further changes made to related processes in order to preserve their relationships. This is, in fact, a process for propagating changes between interrelated processes. In dealing with such complex repositories, it becomes error-prone, costly and labor intensive to propagate, properly, the changes initiated from a process model to its related process(es). As such, identification of changes and development of procedures for preserving the relationships become critical tasks.

---

* On leave from a lecturership at University of Brawijaya, East Java, Indonesia.

A. Ghose et al. (Eds.): ICSOC 2012, LNCS 7759, pp. 332–343, 2013.

Hence, techniques and tools are required to assist process analysts. There has been, however, very little work on supporting change propagation in process model collections [1]. Our proposed framework aims to fill this gap. We view a collection of interrelated process models as an ecosystem [2]. In such ecosystem, process models play a role analogous to that of biological entities in a biological ecosystem. They are created (or discovered, using automated toolkits [3]), constantly changed during their lifetimes, and eventually discarded. Changing a process may cause perturbations (i.e. inconsistencies) in the ecosystem in the form of critical inter-process relationships being violated. In this view, a process ecosystem is considered to be in an (consistency-)equilibrium if its all inter-process relationships are mutually consistent. Change propagation is, therefore, reduced to finding an equilibrium in a process ecosystem.

In this paper, we propose a taxonomy of all possible process changes that can violate relationship constraints between a pair of semantically effect annotated processes. By relying on semantic effect analysis, we also construct a set of resolution patterns to resolve any violation triggered by process changes described in the taxonomy. We develop our framework based upon our previous work in formalizing inter-process relationships [6]. Further, some of these patterns have also been practically used in our previous work in dealing with change propagation in process ecosystems [5]. We, however, illustrate the proposed approach by using a detailed example.

This paper is structured as follows. Sect. 2 briefly describes related foundations. Sect. 3 identifies the taxonomy of process changes. Sect. 4 proposes our resolution patterns. Sect. 5 illustrates the proposed approach. Sect. 6 discusses related work. Sect. 7 concludes and layouts some future work.

2   Foundations

Semantic Effect-Annotated Process Model. An effect annotation relates to a particular result/outcome to an activity in a process [4]. An activity represents the work performed within a process. Activities are either atomic (called a *task*) or compound (called a *sub-process*) [9]. In an annotated BPMN process model, as our approach relies on, we annotate each activity with its (immediate) effects. We define the immediate effects as the immediate results/outcomes of executing an activity in a process. This annotation allows us to determine, at design time, the effects of process execution up to a certain point in the model. These effects are necessarily non-deterministic, since a process might have taken one of many possible alternative paths through a model to get to that point. We define a procedure for *pair-wise effect accumulation*, which, given an ordered pair of activities with their corresponding effect annotations, determines the cumulative effects after both activities have been executed in a contiguous sequence. We, however, only deal with a restricted subset of BPMN framework, i.e. start/end empty events, XOR and AND gateways, task, sub-process and message flow.

Let t_i and t_j be an ordered pair of activities connected by a sequence flow such that t_i precedes t_j. Let $e_i = \{c_{i1}, \ldots, c_{im}\}$ and $e_j = \{c_{j1}, \ldots, c_{jn}\}$ be the effect annotations of t_i and t_j, respectively. If $e_i \cup e_j$ is consistent, then the resulting cumulative effect is $e_i \cup e_j$. Otherwise, we define $e_i' = \{c_k\}$ where $c_k \in e_i$ and $\{c_k\} \cup e_j$ *is consistent*, and the resulting cumulative effect to be $e_i' \cup e_j$. We shall use $ACC\,(e_p, e_q)$ to denote the result of pair-wise effect accumulation of two contiguous activities t_p and t_q with the immediate effects e_p and e_q, respectively. We denote $CE\,(P, t)$ as the cumulative effects of execution of process P at activity t. $CE\,(P, t)$ is defined as a set $\{es_{t1}, \ldots, es_{tm}\}$ of alternative *effect scenarios (ESs)* based on the $1, \ldots, m$ alternative paths reaching t. For a complete process execution, we use $acc\,(P)$ to denote the end cumulative effects. Note that each of $acc\,(P)$ or $CE\,(P, t)$ is a set of ESs. Each ES is represented as a set of clauses and will be viewed, implicitly, as their conjunction. Alternative ESs are introduced by AND-joins or XOR-joins or OR-joins. We accumulate effects through a left-to-right pass of a participant lane, applying the pair-wise effect accumulation procedure on contiguous pairs of activities. Note that we do not consider the possibility of a pair of ESs in AND-joins being inconsistent, since this would only happen in the case of obviously erroneously constructed models.

Inter-process Relationships. We recap definition of three relationship types that commonly occur between processes, i.e. *part-whole, inter-operation* and *generalization-specialization*, described in our previous work [6]. We also extend the definition of the part-whole relationship below.

(a) Part-Whole. A part-whole relationship exists between two processes when one process is required by the other to fulfill some of its functionalities. More specifically, there must be an activity in the 'whole' process representing the functionalities of the 'part' process, which is commonly referred to as a sub-process. Logically, there is an insertion of the functionalities of the 'part' into the 'whole'. We shall use the term 'main process' to refer to the 'whole' process of which the 'part' process represents a sub-process expansion. We define the *insertion point* of a part process $P2$ in a main process $P1$ to be the activity t in $P1$ for which $P2$ is the sub-process expansion. We then define the part-whole relationship as follows: $P2$ is a direct part of $P1$ iff there exists an activity t in $P1$ s.t. $CE\,(P1, t) = CE\,(P1 \uparrow^t P2, t)$. This is a *context-dependent* part-whole relationship definition since it relies on the cumulative effects across all activities preceding t_i. We relax to annotating an activity with multiple ESs due to non-deterministic outcomes of executing such activity, which are independent from the process context. Hence, we define a *context-independent* part-whole relationship as follows: $P2$ is a direct part of $P1$ iff there exists an activity t in $P1$ with multiple immediate ESs $es_{t1}, \ldots, es_{tm}$ such that $\forall es_q \in acc(P2), \exists es_{tp}$ where $es_{tp} \models es_q$ and $\forall es_{tp}, \exists es_q \in acc(P2)$ where $es_q \models es_{tp}$, and $1 \leq p \leq m$.

(b) Inter-operation. An inter-operation relationship exists between two processes when there is at least one message exchanged between them and there is no cumulative effect contradiction between activities involved in exchanging messages. Formally, given processes $P1$ and $P2$, an inter-operation relationship exists between them involving activities t_i and t_j iff the following holds: (i) $\exists t_i$ in $P1$

$\exists t_j$ in $P2$ such that $t_i \rightharpoonup t_j$ denotes that t_i sends a message to t_j, or $t_j \rightharpoonup t_i$, if the message is in the opposite direction; (ii) let $E_i = \{es_{i1}, \ldots, es_{im}\}$ be the cumulative effects of process $P1$ at activity t_i, i.e. $CE(P1, t_i)$, and $E_j = \{es_{j1}, \ldots, es_{jn}\}$ be the cumulative effects of process $P2$ at activity t_j, i.e. $CE(P2, t_j)$. Then, there is no contradiction between E_i and E_j for all $es_{ip} \in E_i$ and $es_{jq} \in E_j$ s.t. $es_{ip} \cup es_{jq} \vdash \bot$ does not hold, where $1 \leq p \leq m$ and $1 \leq q \leq n$. We shall refer to an activity sending a message a *sender* activity, and an activity receiving a message a *receiver* activity. Effect contradiction exists if the expected effects (i.e. computed at the receiver) differ from the given effects (i.e. computed at the sender). If this occurs, we consider that an inter-operation does not exist.

(c) Generalization-Specialization. A generalization-specialization relationship exists between two processes when one process becomes the functional extension of the other. More specifically, the 'specialized' process has the same functionalities as in the 'generalized' one and also extends it with some additional functionalities. Note that the specialized process inherits all functionalities of the generalized process, as formally defined as follows. Given process models $P1$ and $P2$, $P2$ is a specialization of $P1$ iff $\forall es_i \in acc(P1)$, $\exists es_j \in acc(P2)$ s.t. $es_j \models es_i$; and $\forall es_j \in acc(P2)$, $\exists es_i \in acc(P1)$ s.t. $es_i \models es_j$.

3 Taxonomy of Changes Triggering Relationship Violations

In this section, we present a taxonomy of all possible process changes which potentially violate the relationship constraints between a pair of processes $P1$ and $P2$. This taxonomy is useful to construct resolution patterns for such relationship violations. The classification is based upon the relationship types.

Changing a process may also involve the evolution of the capability library (CL) such that it is consistent with any process design within a process repository. Such evolution may be required iff this change introduces a new capability which does not exist in the CL. We argue that a CL is inconsistent with a process repository iff there exist a process design whose activity has immediate effects which are not exactly the same with any activity in the CL. Hence, a CL can be viewed as a repository of all activities used in any process design contained in the process repository, with each activity annotated with immediate effects. This is a critical representation of *enterprise competence* - the intent is that it contains all activities that an enterprise is able to execute, and thus all of the building blocks from which one might build the design of any business process supported by the enterprise. In some cases, this CL needs to be expanded to express the capability extension (potentially affected by process changes) of the enterprise. We can imagine two distinct kinds of changes to it due to any process changes[1]: (i) **Capability repurposing:** In this setting, we take an existing capability T, and use it as the basis for introducing a new capability T' whose effects are (a hopefully small) variant of the effects of T. The resulting CL contains both

---

[1] The establishment and maintenance of the CL is out of scope of this paper.

T and T'. This would allow us to leverage the repurposed version of T, e.g. in resolving a relationship violation, while leaving the definition of T unchanged in the other processes contained in the repository.; (ii) **Capability redefinition:** In this setting, we redefine the semantics (i.e. effects) of an existing capability T in the CL s.t. the change applies to all business processes that leverage T.

Part-Whole

Let $P1$ and $P2$ be the main and the part processes, respectively. In addition, let t_i (with immediate effects e_{t_i}) be an insertion point of $P2$ in $P1$ s.t. the constraints are satisfied: (i) $CE(P1, t_i) = CE(P1 \uparrow^{t_i} P2, t_i)$ for a context-dependent part-whole or (ii) $e_{t_i} = acc(P2)$ for a context-independent part-whole.

(a) **Changes to the Main Process.** Changing $P1$ into $P1'$ may violate its relationship iff it changes t_i that violating the constraints. In fact, this change transforms e_{t_i} into e'_{t_i} with the set of ESs E and E', respectively. We classify this change into three types based on number of ESs $n(E)$ and $n(E')$: (i) they remain; (ii) they are different, where $n(E') \neq 0$ and (iii) they are different, where $n(E') = 0$. These can be achieved by the following basic operations, respectively: (i) **C-W1**: capability repurposing or capability redefinition on t_i s.t. $n(E) = n(E')$; (ii) **C-W2**: capability repurposing or capability redefinition on t_i s.t. $n(E) \neq n(E')$ or (iii) **C-W3**: removing t_i. The capability of t_i can be either expanded (i.e. by adding some new effects) or contracted (i.e. by removing some existing effects) using operations **C-W1** and **C-W2**. The relationship between the processes will no longer exist by applying operation **C-W3**.

(b) **Changes to the Part Process.** Changing $P2$ into $P2'$ may violate the relationship iff $acc(P2) \neq acc(P2')$ with the set of ESs E and E', respectively. We classify this change into two major types based on number of ESs $n(E)$ and $n(E')$: (i) they remain and (ii) they are different. Type (i) can be achieved by performing the following basic operations: (i-a) **C-P1**: adding/removing an activity, whose immediate effects have single effect scenario; (i-b) **C-P2**: capability repurposing on an activity, whose immediate effects have the same number of effect scenarios; (i-c) **C-P3**: capability redefinition on an activity, whose immediate effects have the same number of effect scenarios; (i-d) **C-P4**: replacing an activity with different activity, whose immediate effects have the same number of effect scenarios; (i-e) **C-P5**: swapping activities, whose immediate effects have the same number of effect scenarios, involving XOR gateways and (i-f) **C-P6**: swapping activities, where their immediate effects undo to each other.

Type (ii) can be achieved by performing the following basic operations: (ii-a) **C-P7**: adding/removing an activity, whose immediate effects have multiple effect scenarios; (ii-b) **C-P8**: capability repurposing on an activity, whose immediate effects have different number of effect scenarios; (ii-c) **C-P9**: capability redefinition on an activity, whose immediate effects have different number of effect scenarios; (ii-d) **C-P10**: replacing an activity with different activity, whose immediate effects have different number of effect scenarios; (ii-e) **C-P11**:

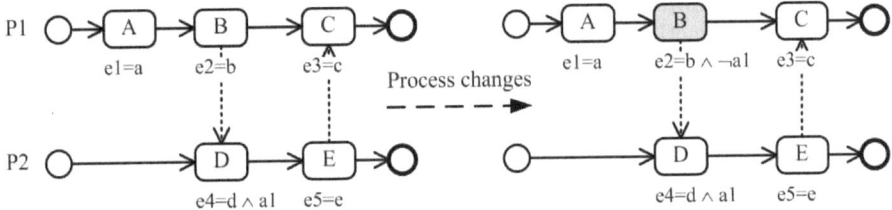

Fig. 1. Inter-operation relationship violation due to process changes (**C-I1**)

adding/removing XOR gateways; (ii-f) **C-P12**: adding/removing branch(es) of the existing XOR gateways and (ii-g) **C-P13**: swapping activities, whose immediate effects have different number of effect scenarios, involving XOR gateways. Note that we would not consider adding/removing AND gateways as operations to change the end cumulative effects of the part process since we do not consider the possibility of ESs between AND branches being inconsistent, as described in Sect. 2. As such, we argue that the sources of these changes stem from the individual activity changes as described above.

Inter-operation

As described in Sect. 2, a relationship violation occurs iff there exist a contradiction between ESs of the cumulative effects at each pair of sender-receiver activities caused by changing a process, as illustrated[2] in Fig. 1. The contradiction can be described as follows. There are two pairs of sender-receiver activities in an inter-operation relationship between processes $P1$ and $P2$, originally shown at the left side, i.e. activities $B - D$ and $E - C$. The computed cumulative effects of each process at these activities are $CE(P1, B) = \{\{a \wedge b\}\}$, $CE(P2, D) = \{\{d \wedge a1\}\}$, $CE(P2, E) = \{\{d \wedge a1 \wedge e\}\}$ and $CE(P1, C) = \{\{a \wedge b \wedge c\}\}$, respectively. Obviously, there is no contradiction between ESs in $CE(P1, B)$ and $CE(P2, D)$, and in $CE(P2, E)$ and $CE(P1, C)$. Now, we would apply capability redefinition on activity B in $P1$, as shown at the right side. This change would get $CE(P1', B) = \{\{a \wedge b \wedge \neg a1\}\}$, which is, in turn, contradicting $CE(P2, D)$ such that $CE(P1', B) \cup CE(P2, D) \vdash \bot$.

Generalization-Specialization

Let $P1$ and $P2$ be the generalized and the specialized processes, respectively, s.t. the constraints are satisfied: $\forall es_i \in acc(P1)$, $\exists es_j \in acc(P2)$ s.t. $es_j \models es_i$; and $\forall es_j \in acc(P2)$, $\exists es_i \in acc(P1)$ s.t. $es_i \models es_j$. Since this relationship is a special case of part-whole relationship, its basic operations will be applicable.

(a) Changes to the Generalized Process. Transforming $P1$ into $P1'$ may violate the relationship iff $acc(P1) \neq acc(P1')$. We can use the aforementioned operations **C-P1** to **C-P13**, i.e. now appled at the generalized process, to describe all possible violations triggered by changing $P1$. However, we argue that

---

[2] Such violations can occur as the result of changing process in many different ways.

changes resulted from removing activity operations (i.e. in operations **C-P1** and **C-P7**) and contracting capability operations (i.e. in operations **C-P2**, **C-P3**, **C-P8** and **C-P9**) will not introduce any violation.

(b) Changes to the Specialized Process. Changing $P2$ into $P2'$ may violate the relationship iff $acc(P2) \neq acc(P2')$. Specifically, the difference must occur at the shared capability with $P1$. This shared capability represents a section in the specialized process that produce outcomes similar to that resulted in the generalized process. We can determine this shared capability through effect accumulation computation. Applying all basic operations **C-P1** to **C-P13** to $P2$, i.e. now viewed as a section in $P2$ that shares capability with $P1$, can introduce any relationship violations. Note that any changes made to $P2$ beyond the shared capability will not violate the relationship.

4   Resolution Patterns

Basically, resolving a relationship violation between two processes is, in fact, the propagation of changes made to one process to the other to preserve their relationship. This also leads to the evolution of the CL. Ideally, an enterprise would prefer to resolve such violation without changing the CL. This might be the case for fixing some violations. But in many other cases, we need to change it. We describe all resolution procedures depending upon the relationship types based upon semantic effect unit of analysis (i.e. immediate effects, ESs and cumulative effects). Given two interrelated processes $P1$ and $P2$, we shall refer to resolution on $P1$ if we need to change $P1$ to resolve any violation stemming from $P2$ changes, and vise versa. The procedures may involve algorithms for searching capabilities in the CL according to the generic formalization of the resolution search problem defined in Definition 1. It guarantees that any capability involved in the resolution is in the capability domain, and permits us to conduct a finite search. Due to space constraint, however, we will not discuss them in this paper.

Definition 1. Resolution search problem. *Given a violated ES es_p (might be an empty set of clauses), a capability library CL and a resolved ES es_r. A resolution function is defined as $R : (es_p \times C) \rightarrow es_q$, where $C \subseteq CL$ is a set of relevant capabilities and es_q is any ES in the ES state space S. This function will search C in CL which are relevant to transform es_p into es_q such that $es_q = es_r$.*

Part-Whole
Let $P1$ and $P2$ be the main and the part processes, respectively. Let t_i (with immediate effects e_{t_i}) be an insertion point of $P2$ in $P1$. Regardless the violation trigger, the resolution procedures will change $P1$ into $P1'$, $P2$ into $P2'$ and e_{t_i} into e'_{t_i} s.t. the constraints are resatisfied: (i) $CE(P1', t_i) = CE(P1' \uparrow^{t_i} P2', t_i)$ for a context-dependent part-whole or (ii) $e'_{t_i} = acc(P2')$ for a context-independent part-whole, where $acc(P2')$ has a set of ESs E'_2.

(a) Resolution on the Main Process. This will transform $P1$ into $P1'$ due to changing $P2$ into $P2'$ using basic operations **C-P1** to **C-P13**. These cause $acc(P2) \neq acc(P2')$, which, in turn, violate the relationship. Based upon the constraints, we consider two corresponding patterns: (i) **(R-PW1: Change at least the insertion point activity)** A set of activities T including t_i and some activities preceding t_i should be changed s.t. the first constraint resatisfied. This can be achieved by many different ways, e.g. capability repurposing and redefinition. This requires analyst involvement, since it is not easy for a tool to deal with such resolution. The difficulties arise due to there might exist various distinct activities being candidates for modifications and many various ways to do such modifications.; (ii) **(R-PW2: Replace the insertion point activity)** The insertion point t_i should be replaced by any activity t_x (with the immediate effects e_{t_x} and a set of ESs E_x) in the CL s.t. the second constraint resatisfied. This can be achieved if the following holds: (a) $n(E_x) = n(E_2')$ and (b) $\forall es_m \in E_2'$, $\exists es_n \in E_x$ s.t. $es_m \models es_n$ and $\forall es_n \in E_x$, $\exists es_m \in E_2'$ s.t. $es_n \models es_m$. Definition 1 is applicable, where each $es_k \in e_{t_i}$, es_n and es_m correspond to es_p, es_q and es_r, respectively. However, if t_x does not exist in the CL, it can be introduced using capability repurposing or capability redefinition approaches.

Furthermore, we can provide a suggestion to the analyst in determining the resolution strategy, as follows: (i) if some ESs in e_{t_i} are violated by any ES in E_2', pattern R-PW2 should be taken and (ii) if all ESs in e_{t_i} are violated by any ES in E_2', patterns R-PW1 and R-PW2 would be the options.

(b) Resolution on the Part Process. This will transform $P2$ into $P2'$ due to changing $P1$ into $P1'$ using **C-W1** and **C-W2**[3]. These cause $e_{t_i} \neq e_{t_i}'$, which, in turn, violate the relationship. We use the second constraint for the resolution. We need to correspond between ESs in e_{t_i}' and $acc(P2)$. $es_m \in e_{t_i}'$ and $es_n \in acc(P2)$ are in correspondence iff there exists no $es_n' \in acc(P2)$ s.t. $(es_m \cap es_n) \subset (es_m \cap es_n')$ ($es_m \cap es_n$ is maximum compared to any $es_n' \in acc(P2)$). We shall refer to all ESs that are in correspondence *bounded ESs (BESs)*. Further, we may have some ESs, either in e_{t_i}' or $acc(P2)$, that are not in correspondence. We shall refer to such ESs *unbounded ESs (UESs)*. We shall refer to all ESs in e_{t_i}' for the resolution. The applicable patterns for all BESs: (i) **(R-PW3: Add activities)** A set of new capabilities C_{add} should be added into es_n iff $C_{add} \subset (es_m \cup es_n) \setminus (es_m \cap es_n)$ and $C_{add} \subset es_m$. Definition 1 is applicable, where es_n and es_m correspond to es_p and es_r, respectively.; (ii) **(R-PW4: Remove activities)** A set of capabilities C_{del} should be removed from es_n iff $C_{del} \subset (es_m \cup es_n) \setminus (es_m \cap es_n)$ and $C_{del} \subset es_n$. All activities whose immediate effects (partially or completely) have capabilities represented in C_{del} must be removed from $P2$. The applicable patterns for all UESs: (i) **(R-PW5: Arrange a group of activities)** A set of activities should be arranged s.t. its end cumulative effects satisfy any $es_j \in E_{add}$, where E_{add} is a set of UESs and $E_{add} \subset e_{t_i}'$. Definition 1 is applicable, where an empty ES es_i and es_j correspond to es_p and es_r, respectively.; (ii) **(R-PW6: Remove a group of activities)** A

---

[3] Applying **C-W3**, no resolution is required since the relationship no longer exists.

set of activities should be removed from $P2$ to transform it into $P2'$ iff the end cumulative effects of the arrangement of such activities satisfy any $es_j \in E_{del}$, where E_{del} is a set of UESs and $E_{del} \subset acc\,(P2)$. This will satisfy $acc\,(P2') = e'_{t_i}$.

Inter-Operation

It will be more complex to resolve violations in an inter-operation relationship triggered by operation **C-I1**. The resolution requires negotiation between roles participating in the relationship in order to determine an appropriate procedure for such resolution. Hence, it needs analyst involvement for negotiating between roles. Once the agreement holds, the analyst could perform some structural changes (e.g. adding, removing, replacing or reordering activities and gateways).

Generalization-Specialization

Let $P1$ and $P2$ be the generalized and the specialized processes, respectively. Regardless the violation trigger, the resolution will change $P1$ into $P1'$ and $P2$ into $P2'$ s.t. the constraints are resatisfied: (a) $\forall es_i \in acc\,(P1')$, $\exists es_j \in acc\,(P'2)$ s.t. $es_j \models es_i$ and (b) $\forall es_j \in acc\,(P'2)$, $\exists es_i \in acc\,(P'1)$ s.t. $es_i \models es_j$.

(a) Resolution on the Generalized Process. This will change $P1$ into $P1'$ due to changing $P2$ into $P2'$ using operations **C-P1** to **C-P13**. These cause $acc\,(P2) \neq acc\,(P2')$, which, in turn, may violate the relationship. We need to correspond between ESs in $acc\,(P1)$ and $acc\,(P2')$. $es_m \in acc\,(P2')$ and $es_n \in acc\,(P1)$ are in correspondence iff there exists no $es'_n \in acc\,(P1)$ s.t. $(es_m \cap es_n) \subset (es_m \cap es'_n)$ $(es_m \cap es_n$ is maximum compared to any $es'_n \in acc\,(P1))$, i.e. BESs. We may also have some ESs which are not in correspondence with any others, i.e. UESs. We refer to all ESs in $acc\,(P2')$ for the resolution. The applicable patterns for all BESs: (i) **(R-GS1: Remove activities)** A set of capabilities C_{del} should be removed from es_n iff $C_{del} \subset (es_m \cup es_n) \setminus (es_m \cap es_n)$ and $C_{del} \subset es_n$. All activities whose immediate effects (partially or completely) have capabilities represented in C_{del} must be removed from $P1$.; (ii) **(R-GS2: Replace activities)** A set of capabilities C_{rep} should be replaced in es_n by capabilities in the CL iff $C_{rep} \subset (es_m \cup es_n) \setminus (es_m \cap es_n)$ and $C_{rep} \subset es_n$. Definition 1 is applicable, where es_n and es_m correspond to es_p and es_r, respectively. The applicable patterns for all UESs: (i) **(R-GS3: Arrange a group of activities)** A set of activities should be arranged s.t. its end cumulative effects satisfy any $es_j \in E_{add}$, where E_{add} is a set of UESs and $E_{add} \subset acc\,(P2')$. Definition 1 is applicable, where an empty ES es_i and es_j correspond to es_p and es_r, respectively.; (ii) **(R-GS4: Remove a group of activities)** A set of activities should be removed from $P1$ to transform it into $P1'$ iff the end cumulative effects of the arrangement of such activities satisfy any $es_j \in E_{del}$, where E_{del} is a set of UESs and $E_{del} \subset acc\,(P1)$. This will satisfy $acc\,(P1') = acc\,(P2')$.

(b) Resolution on the Specialized Process. This will transform $P2$ into $P2'$ due to changing $P1$ into $P1'$ using operations **C-P1** to **C-P13**. These operations cause $acc\,(P1) \neq acc\,(P1')$, which, in turn, always violate the relationship.

Table 1. Resolution patterns summary

Relationship types	Change operations	Resolution patterns
Part-whole	C-W1	R-PW3,R-PW4
	C-W2	R-PW5,R-PW6
	C-W3	No resolution required
	C-P1 to C-P13	R-PW1,R-PW2
Inter-operation	C-I1	Analyst involvement required
Generalization-specialization	C-P1 to C-P6	R-GS1,R-GS2,R-GS5,R-GS6
	C-P7 to C-P13	R-GS3,R-GS4,R-GS7,R-GS8

We need to correspond between ESs in $acc(P2)$ and $acc(P1')$. $es_m \in acc(P1')$ and $es_n \in acc(P2)$ are in correspondence iff there exists no $es'_n \in acc(P2)$ s.t. $(es_m \cap es_n) \subset (es_m \cap es'_n)$ ($es_m \cap es_n$ is maximum compared to any $es'_n \in acc(P2)$), i.e. BESs. We may have some ESs, either in $acc(P1')$ or $acc(P2)$, that are not in correspondence with any other ESs, i.e. UESs. We shall refer to all ESs in $acc(P1')$ for the resolution. The applicable patterns for all BESs: (i) **(R-GS5: Add activities)** A set of new capabilities C_{add} should be added into es_n iff $C_{add} \subset (es_m \cup es_n) \setminus (es_m \cap es_n)$ and $C_{add} \subset es_m$. Definition 1 is applicable, where es_n and es_m correspond to es_p and es_r, respectively.; (ii) **(R-GS6: Replace activities)** A set of capabilities C_{rep} should be replaced in es_n by capabilities in the CL iff $C_{rep} \subset (es_m \cup es_n) \setminus (es_m \cap es_n)$ and $C_{rep} \subset es_m$. Definition 1 is applicable, where es_n and es_m correspond to es_p and es_r, respectively. The applicable patterns for all UESs: (i) **(R-GS7: Arrange a group of activities)** A set of activities should be arranged s.t. its end cumulative effects satisfy any $es_j \in E_{add}$, where E_{add} is a set of UESs and $E_{add} \subset acc(P1')$. Definition 1 is applicable, where an empty ES es_i and es_j correspond to es_p and es_r, respectively.; (ii) **(R-GS8: Remove a group of activities)** A set of activities should be removed from $P2$ to transform it into $P2'$ iff the end cumulative effects of the arrangement of such activities satisfy any $es_j \in E_{del}$, where E_{del} is a set of UESs and $E_{del} \subset acc(P2)$. This will satisfy $acc(P2') = acc(P1')$.

Table 1 summarizes all resolution patterns in correspond to all basic change operations identified in Sect. 3.

5   Detailed Example

Let us use a part-whole relationship between simple processes $P1$ and $P2$ to illustrate our approach, as shown in Fig. 2a. In this scenario, $P2$ is a part of $P1$ such that $P2$ is an expansion of sub-process B in $P1$. This relationship is valid according to its formal definitions given in Sect. 2 for both context-dependent and context-independent constraints. In context-dependent constraint, we compute $CE(P1, B) = \{es_B\}$, where $es_B = a \wedge b1 \wedge b2$. Further, we also compute $CE(P1 \uparrow^B P2, B) = \{es'_B\}$, where $es'_B = a \wedge b1 \wedge b2$. Obviously, we can infer that $P2$ is a part of $P1$ since $CE(P1, B) = CE(P1 \uparrow^B P2, B)$. In a similar

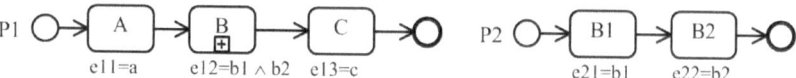

(a) Original processes: process P2 is a part of process P1 at activity B

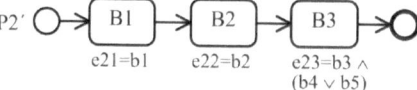

(b) Changing P2 into P2′ by adding activity B3 with multiple effect scenarios (operation **C-P7**): violating the relationship

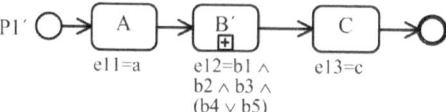

(c) Changing P1 into P1′ by applying pattern **R-PW2**: resolving the violation

Fig. 2. Illustration of applying a resolution pattern in a violated part-whole relationship between processes $P1$ and $P2$

vein, we can also further analyze for the context-independent constraint such that $e_B = acc(P2)$.

Now, we need to change process $P2$ into $P2'$ due to some process change requirements, as shown in Fig. 2b, by using basic operation **C-P7**. This operation introduces multiple effect scenarios into the end cumulative effects of $P2'$ due to the existence of 'OR' symbol ($\vee$) at the immediate effects of the added new activity $B3$, i.e. e_{23}. Further, this change impacts on the end cumulative effects of both processes whereas $acc(P2') \neq acc(P2)$. We compute the end cumulative effects of $P2$ and $P2'$ as $acc(P2) = \{es_{P2}\}$, where $es_{P2} = b1 \wedge b2$ and $acc(P2') = \{es'_{P2}, es''_{P2}\}$, where $es'_{P2} = b1 \wedge b2 \wedge b3 \wedge b4$ and $es''_{P2} = b1 \wedge b2 \wedge b3 \wedge b5$, respectively. Obviously, a violation occurs in the part-whole relationship between, now, $P1$ and $P2'$ since $CE(P1, B) = CE(P1 \uparrow^B P2', B)$ and $e_B \neq acc(P2')$. In order to resolve such violation, we have two options, i.e. using patterns either **R-PW1** or **R-PW2**, since all effect scenarios in e_B are violated. Suppose we prefer to use pattern **R-PW2** for such resolution to transform $P1$ into $P1'$. Hence, we need to replace the insertion point activity B in $P1$ with another activity in the CL such that its immediate effect represents the result of executing $P2'$. In some cases, we may not find such activity in the CL such that we need to introduce capability repurposing based upon the existing activity B. This permits us to create a new activity B' whose immediate effects satisfy the resolution requirement, as illustrated in Fig. 2c.

6   Related Work

Weber *et.al.* [8] propose a number of change patterns and change support features to foster the systematic comparison of existing process management technology in respect to process change support. These support features constitute typical functionalities provided by flexible process-aware information systems (PAISs). Our proposed resolution patterns are inspired by their work to be applied in resolving any inter-process relationship violations between processes. These patterns are directed by a set of basic change operations using semantic effect analysis according to three common relationship types, i.e. part-whole, inter-operation and generalization-specialization. We believe that these patterns become the only one approach in dealing with the resolution of such violations.

7 Conclusion and Future Work

In this paper, we have identified the taxonomy of all possible process changes that can violate relationship constraints between a pair of processes. Further, we also have proposed some patterns in resolving any violation triggered by process changes. These patterns rely on semantic effect unit of analysis, i.e. immediate effects, effect scenarios and cumulative effects. Future work includes developing framework for establishing and maintaining the capability library required in the resolution procedures; machinery tool in constructing a process model from given effect scenarios and cumulative effects.

References

1. Dijkman, R., Rosa, M., Reijers, H.: Managing large collections of business process models-current techniques and challenges. Comp. in Industry 63(2), 91–97 (2012)
2. Ghose, A., Koliadis, G.: Model eco-systems: preliminary work. In: The Fifth Asia-Pacific Conf. on Conceptual Modelling, pp. 19–26. Australian Comp. Society (2008)
3. Ghose, A.K., Koliadis, G., Chueng, A.: Rapid Business Process Discovery (R-BPD). In: Parent, C., Schewe, K.-D., Storey, V.C., Thalheim, B. (eds.) ER 2007. LNCS, vol. 4801, pp. 391–406. Springer, Heidelberg (2007)
4. Koliadis, G., Ghose, A.: Verifying semantic business process models in inter-operation. In: Int. Conf. on Services Computing 2007, pp. 731–738. IEEE (2007)
5. Kurniawan, T.A., Ghose, A.K., Dam, H.K., Lê, L.-S.: Relationship-Preserving Change Propagation in Process Ecosystems. In: Liu, C., Ludwig, H., Toumani, F., Yu, Q. (eds.) ICSOC 2012. LNCS, vol. 7636, pp. 63–78. Springer, Heidelberg (2012)
6. Kurniawan, T.A., Ghose, A.K., Lê, L.-S., Dam, H.K.: On Formalizing Inter-process Relationships. In: Daniel, F., Barkaoui, K., Dustdar, S. (eds.) BPM 2011 Workshops, Part II. LNBIP, vol. 100, pp. 75–86. Springer, Heidelberg (2012)
7. Papazoglou, M., Traverso, P., Dustdar, S., Leymann, F.: Service-oriented computing: a research roadmap. International Journal of Cooperative Information Systems 17(2), 223–255 (2008)
8. Weber, B., Reichert, M., Rinderle-Ma, S.: Change patterns and change support features-enhancing flexibility in process-aware information systems. Data and Knowledge Engineering 66(3), 438–466 (2008)
9. White, S.A., Miers, D.: BPMN: Modeling and Reference Guide. Future Strategies Inc. (2008)

An Aspect-Oriented Approach to Enforce Security Properties in Business Processes

Inaya Yahya[1], Sameh Hbaieb Turki[1], Anis Charfi[2], Slim Kallel[3], and Rafik Bouaziz[1]

[1] MIRACL, University of Sfax, Tunisia
inaya.yahya@gmail.com, turkisameh@yahoo.fr
raf.bouaziz@fsegs.rnu.tn
[2] SAP Research, Darmstadt, Germany
first.lastname@sap.com
[3] ReDCAD, University of Sfax, Tunisia
slim.kallel@fsegs.rnu.tn

Abstract. Security is an essential requirement for business processes. However, we observe that security is mostly addressed at the technical implementation level and not at the design level. In a previous work we motivated the need to address security already in business process modeling. In this paper, we show how one could use Aspect-Oriented Programming (AOP) to enforce security requirements in a modular way. Starting from a business process model where security requirements are expressed using a profile mechanism we generate AspectJ [1] code, which enforces those requirements. This generation is based on a set of Model-to-Text transformation rules. As security is a typical example for crosscutting concerns the usage of aspects allows for a modular implementation, in which the implementation of the business process is separated from the implementation of the security properties.

Keywords: AOP, security, Web services, Separation of concerns, MDA.

1 Introduction

The development of composite web services is a complex task, as it is based on technical and low-level languages such as WS-BPEL or programming languages. It requires a high expertise and can therefore not be done by non-technical users. Further, if a composite web services has to be implemented for different target platforms the implementation has to start from scratch each time due to the lack of reusable design models of the composite service. On the other hand, there are many works that use the model driven architecture (MDA) and model-driven software development to address such problems by raising the level of abstraction and fostering reuse through using design models. In a previous work [2], we presented a model-driven approach to composite web service development, which starts with modeling composite services using business process models defined in the Business Process Modeling Notation (BPMN) [3]. Then, these models are enriched with service related details using BPMN4SOA, which is a service-oriented extension to BPMN that we proposed in [6]. From these models we generate executable service composition code in WS-BPEL or

A. Ghose et al. (Eds.): ICSOC 2012, LNCS 7759, pp. 344–355, 2013.
© Springer-Verlag Berlin Heidelberg 2013

in java using appropriate transformations and code generators. An Eclipse based tool-set was developed to support our approach. In [4] we extended our approach to cover not only the functional side of service composition but also non-functional aspects such as security, quality of service, etc. In that work, we proposed a profile mechanism for BPMN in a similar way to the profile mechanism of UML. Based on this several profiles can be defined to express non-functional properties in BPMN and in BPMN4SOA. In [4] we also presented a security profile for BPMN.

In this paper, we extend the scope of our coverage for non-functional concerns by supporting the transition from modeling to implementation. In particular, we focus on mapping the security properties that can be expressed using the security profile to aspect code in AspectJ [1]. In addition, we present an Xpand [5] based code generation tool which implements that mapping and produces aspect code for enforcing the security properties at runtime. This new generator complements the code generator from BPMN4SOA to Java, which we implemented in a previous work [6]. With both generators we support the functional and non-functional aspects of service composition.

The remainder of this paper is organized as follows. Section 2 gives an overview of our previous work: we start by presenting a generic meta-model to express non-functional concerns in business processes, then we present the security profile which allows expressing security properties in BPMN process models. In Section 3 we present the mapping rules from the security profile to aspect code. In addition, we report on the code generator, which we built based on that mapping. In Section 4 we illustrate our proposal by an example. Section 5 discusses related works and Section 6 concludes this paper.

2   Background

In this section, we introduce the profile mechanism and the security profile, which we proposed in [4]. The non-functional profile that we proposed allows expressing QoS properties in a simple way. The business developer doesn't need to knowledge technical details relied to QoS properties; he just uses some annotations and specifies the value of their attributes. In opposed to some non-functional profiles which are proposed in the literature and expresses more technical concepts. Understanding those concepts is necessary for this paper as the security profile is the source for our mapping and the respective model-to-text transformation. We start by presenting the proposed profile mechanism and the underlying meta-model for expressing non-functional profiles. Then we give an overview of the security profile.

2.1   Meta-model for Non-functional Profiles

In analogy to the profile concept in the Unified Modeling Language (UML) [7] we propose a profile concept for process modeling languages such as BPMN [3]. In Figure 1 we present a meta-model for non-functional profiles and we detail the concepts of this meta-model in the following.

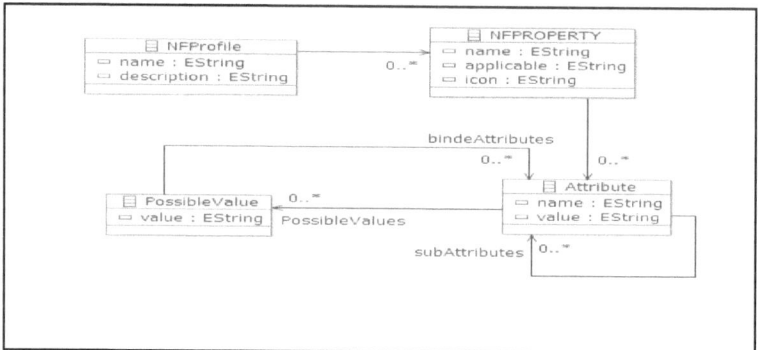

Fig. 1. The meta-model of non-functional profiles

NFProfile: represents a given concern that needs to be expressed in business processes such as security or business performance. It is characterised by two attributes "name" and "description".

NFProperty: represents a property that belongs to a concern. Response time and cost are examples for such properties. It is characterised by three attributes "name", "applicable" i.e. applicability constraints which specify for instance to which process elements a given non-functional property can be applied, and "icon" which specifies the graphical icon for each non-functional property.

Attribute: a property has zero or more attributes and each attribute has a name and a value. For example the property cost may have an attribute called metric and an attribute called amount. One Attribute may define several ***subAttributes*** which at the same time can be bound by one of the predefined available values of the parent meaning that they will only be available when the value that binds them is selected.

For applying our approach to BPMN and defining a BPMN profile for modeling nonfunctional concerns, we use the extension mechanism proposed in BPMN specification [3]. BPMN introduces the artifact concept to add non-standard elements. In our case, we defined two types of artifact: ***NFProfile*** and ***NFProperty*** as shown in Figure 2.

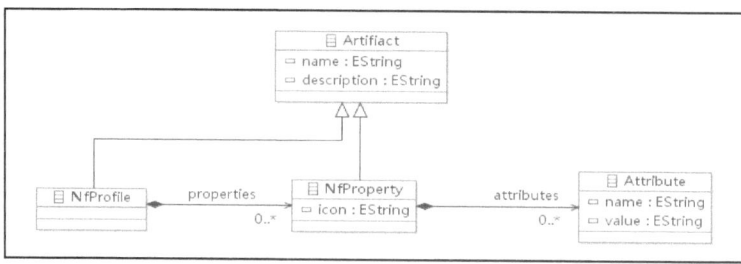

Fig. 2. Definition of the NFProfile and NFProperty artifacts according to BPMN extensibility [3]

2.2 Security Profile

As presented in [4], the security profile has been defined for providing a lightweight extension to BPMN for expressing security properties in business process model. This profile defines a set of annotations and their attributes. We note that we concentrated on the modeling and the implementation of the security aspects only side service composition process and not side partners.

In this paper we will concentrate only on five security properties as shown in the table below. Other properties can be added in this profile and mapped to aspects. To enforce security properties, we adopted a service-oriented approach, which allows invoking a set of web services to realize security aspects. For this reason, we defined for each security property two attributes: "Operation" and "Service" which the developer defines their values.

Table 1. Security properties

Security property	Additional Attributes	Notation
Separation of Duties (SoD): This property expresses that two tasks have to be performed by two different users or user roles to avoid the risk of frauds.	• ***Type***: The possible value are: Static SoD, Simple Dynamic SoD, Object-Based SoD, Operational SoD, Operational Object-Based SoD	
Binding of Duties (BoD): This property expresses that two activities must be performed by the same user or by the same user role.	No one	
Confidentiality: This property expresses that data is confidential and should be only accessible to users with appropriate credentials. Confidentiality is ensured using an encryption algorithm	• ***Key:*** the key used to ensure encryption/decryption operation.	
Integrity: This property expresses that the data must not be modified by a malicious party when transmitted.	• ***Key:*** the key used to ensure integrity operation.	
Authentication: This property expresses that authentication is required for accessing some data object or for performing some activity.	No one	

3 Mapping the Security Profile to Enforcement Aspects in AspectJ

In this section, we first give an overview of AspectJ. Then, we present the mapping rules from security profile to AspectJ aspects.

3.1   Target Language for Enforcing Security Properties: AspectJ

To separate the functional and non-functional parts we use Aspect-Oriented Programming (AOP). The functional part of the composite web service, which is specified using the BPMN process model, is transformed into java code and the non-functional part is transformed into executable aspect code in AspectJ [1], which is an aspect-oriented extension to java. The weaving of these two executable codes is an automatic AspectJ task.

AspectJ provides the possibility to define aspects with their composition rules into the base java code. The main concepts in Aspect-Oriented Programming are join points (which are points in the execution of the program such as method calls), point-cuts (which allow to select one or more join points) and advices (which are behavioral units that contain the crosscutting logic similar to methods). The unit of modularization used by AspectJ is the aspect which is composed of one or more pointcuts and advices. Each pointcut is associated with an advice. AspectJ defines three types of advices: before advice, around advice and after advice. These advice are respectively executed before, instead, and after of the join point matched by their respective point-cuts. We show in the Listing 1 the structure of a logging aspect in AspectJ. The point-cut of this aspect selects all calls to public methods. A before advice is associated with this pointcut, which will print out a message before each matched join point.

```
public Aspect Logging_Aspect {
    pointcut pointcut_Logging(): call(public * *.*(..));
    before():  pointcut_Logging(){
        System.out.println (" call to method " +thisJoinPoint.toLongString());
    }
}
```

Listing.1. The structure of an aspect in AspectJ

With aspects our approach ensures that the security enforcement code is well modularized. The security expert needs to focus only on the security aspect to understand how security policies are enforced. He does not need to look at and understand the code implementing other concerns. Furthermore, when certain non-properties change, for example, an encryption module is upgraded or replaced, only the respective security aspects must be regenerated and redeployed. The core business processes and aspects enforcing other concerns remain unchanged.

3.2   Mapping Rules

In the following, we explain how each property in the security profile is mapped to aspect code in AspectJ and the corresponding java joint point in witch this code will be weaved. We use the following conventions for presenting the following mapping rules:

- Assuming a service activity that calls a given operation. The respective pointcut of the enforcement advice will be named according to this pattern:

PropertyName_OperationName_BPMNelement
- The parameters of the generated pointcut correspond to either the input or the output value of the BPMN element in the business process model.
- We developed a java based library with helper functions which can be used to enforce the security properties and which can be called from the advice. For each security property, we call the respective enforcement function according to this naming pattern: ***PropertyName_Method( )***.

• ***The Confidentiality Property:*** The confidentiality property can be applied to the messages. It is generally mapped to ***before*** advices. Only in the case of end message, it is mapped to an ***after*** advice. Figure 3 illustrates this mapping.

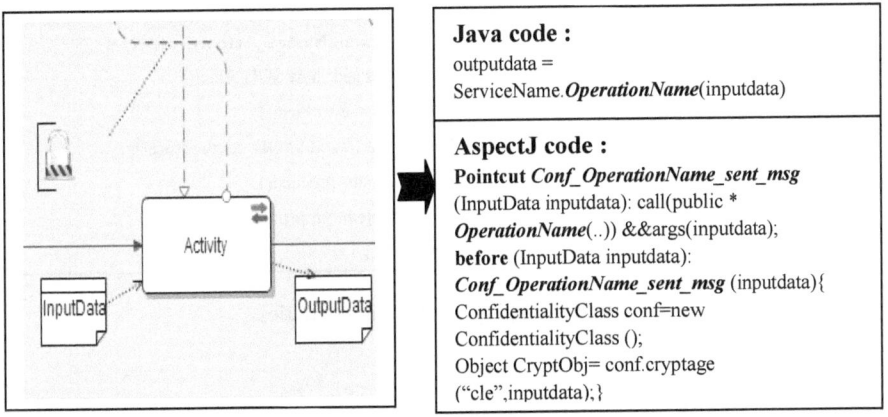

Fig. 3. Mapping of confidentiality

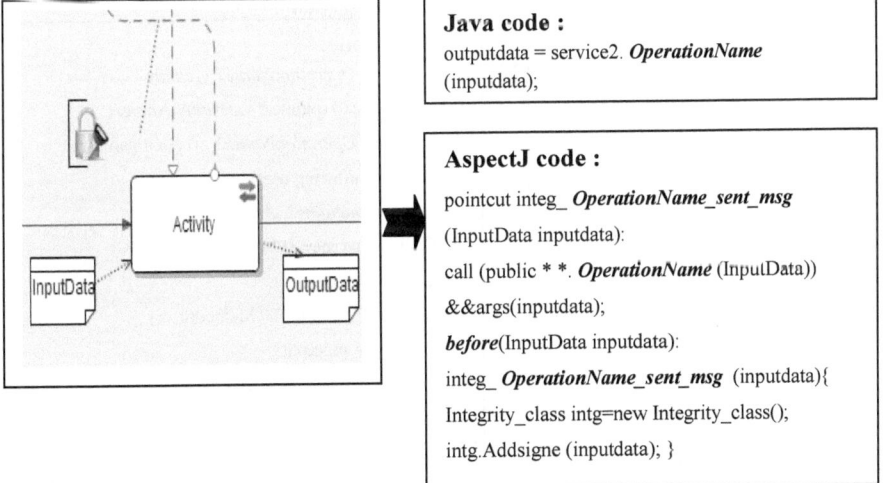

Fig. 4. Mapping of integrity

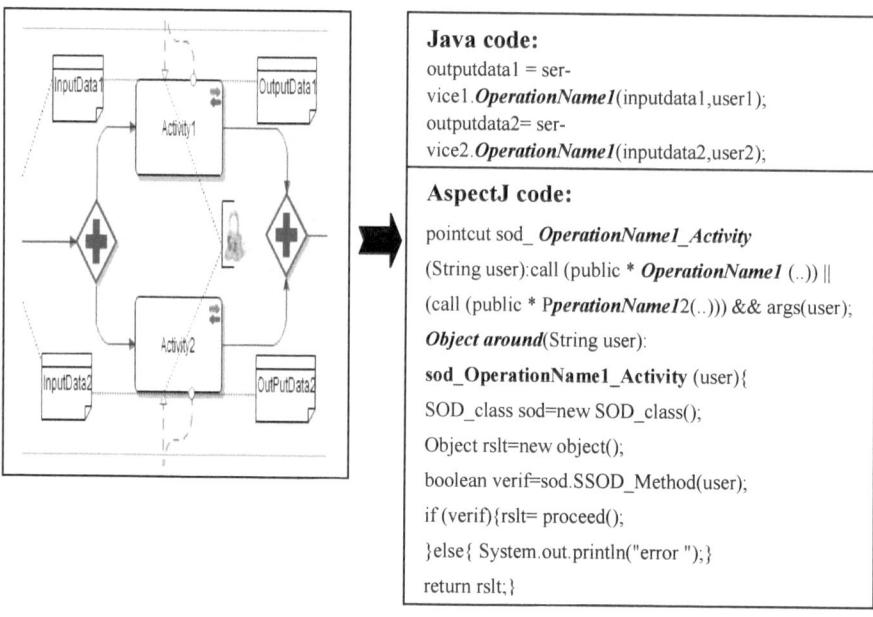

Java code:
outputdata1 = ser-
vice1.*OperationName1*(inputdata1,user1);
outputdata2= ser-
vice2.*OperationName1*(inputdata2,user2);

AspectJ code:

pointcut sod_ *OperationName1_Activity*

(String user):call (public * *OperationName1* (..)) ‖

(call (public * P*perationName1*2(..))) && args(user);

Object around(String user):

sod_OperationName1_Activity (user){

SOD_class sod=new SOD_class();

Object rslt=new object();

boolean verif=sod.SSOD_Method(user);

if (verif){rslt= proceed();

}else{ System.out.println("error ");}

return rslt;}

Fig. 5. Mapping of separation of duties

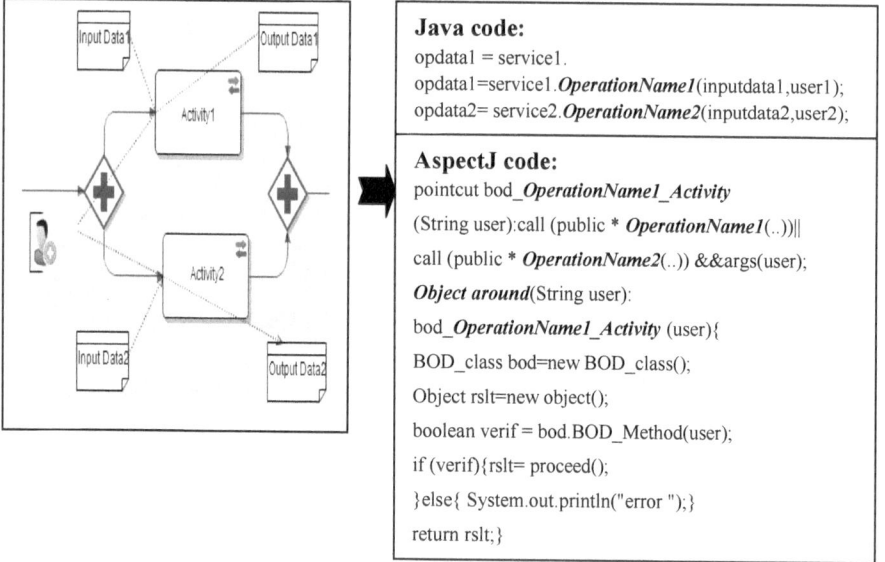

Java code:
opdata1 = service1.
opdata1=service1.*OperationName1*(inputdata1,user1);
opdata2= service2.*OperationName2*(inputdata2,user2);

AspectJ code:
pointcut bod_*OperationName1_Activity*

(String user):call (public * *OperationName1*(..))‖

call (public * *OperationName2*(..)) &&args(user);

Object around(String user):

bod_*OperationName1_Activity* (user){

BOD_class bod=new BOD_class();

Object rslt=new object();

boolean verif = bod.BOD_Method(user);

if (verif){rslt= proceed();

}else{ System.out.println("error ");}

return rslt;}

Fig. 6. Mapping of binding of duties

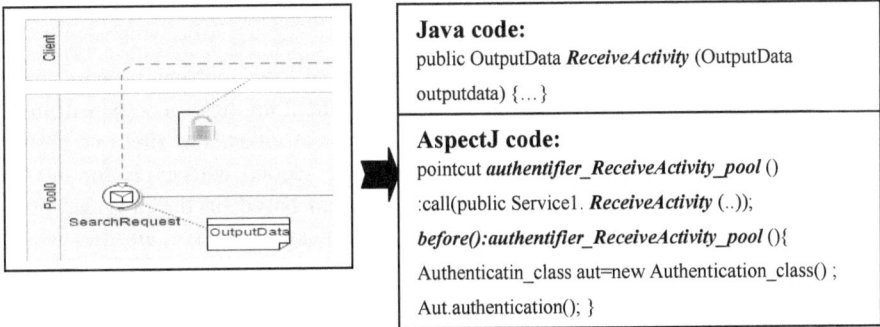

Fig. 7. Mapping of authentication

• **The Authentication property** is mapped to a before advice to guarantee the authentication of the client and the partner before interaction with the service composition pool. Figure 7 shows this mapping.

• **The Integrity Property:** The integrity property can be applied to the messages. It is generally mapped to a **before** advice. Only in the case of end message, it is mapped to an **after** advice, as shown in Figure 4.

• **The Separation of Duties Property** (SOD) is mapped to an **around** advice to guarantee the respect of this property by all activities of the group. Figure 5 shows this transformation.

• **The Binding of Duties Property:** The binding of duties (BOD) property is mapped to an around advice, which guarantees the respect of this property by all activities of the group. Figure 6 illustrates this mapping.

3.3   The AspectJ Code Generator

Based on the mapping presented above, we implemented a code generator from the security profile to AspectJ [1]. This generator is based on the Xpand [5] model-to-text transformation language. Based on an Ecore meta-model of the security profile and templates in Xpand implementing the mapping, the generator takes a business process model annotated by security properties and generates one or more text files with the AspectJ code. The AspectJ generator was developed as Eclipse plugin. For the definition of the source model we used the non-functional editor with annotations as shown in Figure 8. In a previous work [6], we implemented a BPMN to java generator, which is responsible for generating the functional part of the composite service. Both generators can be used together with ours to have both the functional code in java classes and the non-functional code in AspectJ aspects.

4   Case Study

To illustrate our approach we introduce the example of loan approval process (LAP) as shown in Figure 8. This process starts when the client applies for a loan from his bank. The bank will then execute two parallel rating activities. The first one ensures external rating using a credit-reporting agency. The second activity is for internal rating and it verifies the creditworthiness of the client based on the provided documents. If the evaluation of the customer creditworthiness is positive, an offer will be created and subsequently the contract documents will be generated using a contracting web service. Finally the offer and the contract are sent to the customer by email using an appropriate mailing web service.

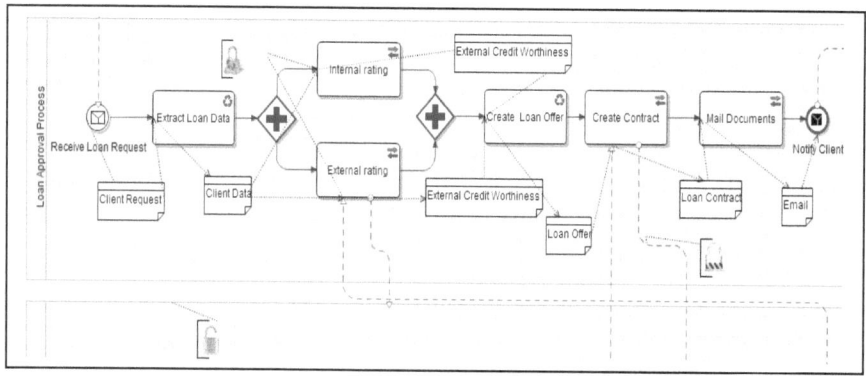

Fig. 8. The Loan Approval Process (LAP) annotated with security properties

In this process we have sensitive data that is transmitted between the different services. Several security requirements arise in this scenario, which can be expressed using the security profile. For example, an authentication property is applied to the partner that will ensure external rating, as we see in Figure 8. That property is associated to the corresponding pool. A separation of duties property is used to express separation of duties between the two parallel rating activities. In fact, these activities should be performed by two different users to avoid the risk of fraud. The message sent to the partner "contracting service" contains confidential information and therefore needs to be encrypted before being sent. To specify this requirement we linked the confidentiality property to that message

Figure 8 shows the LAP process model defined in BPMN and annotated with the properties of the security profile. After modeling the process and annotating it with properties of the security profile we use our AspectJ generator to generate security aspects that enforce the defined security properties. The java generator can be used to generate java classes that implement the modeled composite service.

The generated code is an executable and complete AspectJ code that is organized in three aspects for this example: an aspect for each security property. The first property is authentication, which is enforced using an advice that authenticates the partner before starting the process. As the process is implemented with a generated method called main, the pointcut of the advice matched that method as we see in Listing 2. The second property in this example is separation of duties and the corresponding aspect code is shown in Listing 3. Here, all activities of the group will be captured as join points and we need to guarantee that their respective users are different. The third property in this example is confidentiality and the corresponding aspect is shown in the Listing 4. The advice encrypts the message of the partner invocation before it is sent. This invocation is captured as join point by the pointcut associated with the generated advice. Regarding the advice, we have chosen to implement a java library with methods that enforce each security properties. The advice simply calls those methods. The least step is to combine these aspects with the functional java code to obtain an executable application.

```
public aspect AuthenticationAspect{
        pointcut Authentication_External Rating():execution(public void main(..));
        before():Authentication_External Rating(){
        Authentication_class    authentication_class = new  Authentication_class ();
        authentication_class.AuthenticationMethod();  } }
```

Listing. 2. The Authentication aspect

```
public aspect SOD_Aspect{
 pointcut SOD_Externalrating_Activity(ClientData newClientData , String user):(call(public *
*.getInternalRating(..,String)) || call(public * *.getExternalRating(..,String)))&&
args(newClientData,user)&&!within(LoanApprovalProcessAspect);
 Object around(ClientData newClientData , String user):
SOD_Externalrating_Activity(newClientData,user){
 SOD_class sOD_class  = new  SOD_class ();
boolean exist= sOD_class.SOD_Method("SSOD",newClientData,user);
Object rslt=new Object();
if (exist){c=  proceed(newClientData,user); }else{ System.out.println("error ");}
return c;}}
```

Listing. 3. The Separation of duties aspect

```
public aspect Confidentiality_Aspect{
pointcut Confidentiality_CreateContract_outgoingMessage(LoanOffer newLoanOffer,String user)
:(call(public * *.getLoanContract(..))) &args(newLoanOffer,user)&&!within(Confidentiality_Aspect);
before(LoanOffer newLoanOffer,String  user): Confidentiali-
ty_CreateContract_outgoingMessage(newLoanOffer,user){
newLoanOffer.setIdClient(Confidentiality_class.Encryption(0001,newLoanOffer.getIdClient()));
newLoanOffer.setamount(Confidentiality_class.Encryption(0001,newLoanOffer.getamount()));
newLoanOffer.setdata(Confidentiality_class.Encryption(0001,newLoanOffer.getdata()));}}
```

Listing. 4. The Confidentiality aspect

5   Related Work

The model-driven security in the context of SOA is an emerging research area.

In [8], the authors describe a model-driven architecture that allows the generation of web service security configurations from an UML model. The business process model and security intentions are modeled using standard UML diagrams. According to the MDA approach, the users define the application model enriched by the security intentions, and then detailed security configurations are generated. That work is based on transformations over UML constructs and a security environment model. Unlike our work, the approach presented in [8] does not support composite web services. It also does not support java code generation.

In [9] the authors define an approach, which ensures the generation of security configurations from business process models. In the first step, the business process model is annotated with abstract security intents using different models and notations: like UML'S SOAML profile, UML's QoS profile, and secureUML. The second step consists in composing functional models with access control models or security models. The final step consists in the code generation for specific target platforms. The main limitation of this work is the necessity composing different models, which requires different weaving associations and composition rules. In our work, we defined a common meta-model to support all non-functional properties and we can use different annotations from different profiles for the same business process model.

In [10], the authors propose a model-driven approach that facilitates the transformation of architecture models annotated with simple security intentions to security policies. This transformation is driven by security configuration patterns. The authors propose also a concise domain specific language (DSL) for expressing their security configuration patterns. A pattern engine is provided to execute security intentions and provide corresponding solutions. Comparing with our approach, this work is specific to security aspects and requires the extension of the domain specific language to support others non-functional concerns. Our approach is more generic and support different concerns without requiring any extension. The user can easily define a new non-functional profile and apply this to the business process model.

In [11], the authors propose a methodology for end-to-end security configuration for SOA applications and tools for generating security configurations from the requirements specified in previous phases of their approach. It makes it possible to configure security properly without increasing the workload of the developers.

In [12], the authors propose an extension of BPMN to ensure modeling security requirements into business process models. This extension allow user to incorporate seven security requirements represented by the same symbol (padlock) and for each security requirement a specific capital letter is added on the center of the symbol. The main limitation of this work is that do not provide an approach to generate executable code from the model.

The major advantage of our work over the works mentioned above is that our approach is generic and can be applied to any non-functional concern. It is not specific to security only. A further advantage is the possibility to use multiple non-functional profiles together. We focused in this paper only on security properties mapping, but others mappings can be defined for others QoS properties. In addition, we generate a modular code, which implements non-functional concerns.

6   Conclusion

In this paper, we presented an aspect-oriented approach to mapping the security properties expressed with a profile mechanism for BPMN to modular enforcement code in AspectJ. We implemented also an AspectJ code generator, which is based on the Xpand transformation language.

As future work, we aim to define others mapping rules from others non-functional profiles such as temporal properties to aspects. Another direction is to generate aspects in other AOP languages such as AO4BPEL for enforcing non-functional properties within BPEL process.

References

1. Kiczales, G., Hilsdale, E., Hugunin, J., Kersten, M., Palm, J., Griswold, W.G.: An Overview of AspectJ. In: Lindskov Knudsen, J. (ed.) ECOOP 2001. LNCS, vol. 2072, pp. 327–353. Springer, Heidelberg (2001)
2. Charfi, A., Turki, S.H., Chaâbane, A., Bouaziz, R.: A model-driven approach to developing web service compositions based on BPMN4SOA. J. Reasoning-Based Intelligent Systems 3(3/4) (2011)
3. Object Management Group: Business Process Modeling Notation (BPMN) 2.0, http://www.omg.org/spec/BPMN/2.0
4. Turki, S.H., Bellaaj, F., Charfi, A., Bouaziz, R.: Modeling Security Requirements in Service Based Business Processes. In: Bider, I., Halpin, T., Krogstie, J., Nurcan, S., Proper, E., Schmidt, R., Soffer, P., Wrycza, S. (eds.) BPMDS 2012 and EMMSAD 2012. LNBIP, vol. 113, pp. 76–90. Springer, Heidelberg (2012)
5. Eclipse Xpand Project, http://www.eclipse.org/modeling/m2t/?project=xpand
6. Chaâbane, A., Turki, S.H., Charfi, A., Bouaziz, R.: From Platform Independent Service Composition Models in BPMN4SOA to Executable Service Compositions. In: Proc. of iiWAS, France, pp. 653–656 (2010)
7. OMG.: UML: Superstructure version 2.0 (2005), http://www.omg.org/spec/UML/2.0/
8. Nakamura, Y., Tatsubori, M., Imamura, T., Ono, K.: Model-driven security based on Web services security architecture. In: Proc. of SCC, Florida, USA, pp. 7–15 (2005)
9. Gallino, J.P.S., Miguel, M., Briones, J.F., Alejandro, A.: Domain-Specific Multi-Modeling of Security Concerns in Service-Oriented Architectures. In: Proc. of SCC, Washington, USA, pp. 761–762 (2011)
10. Menzel, M., Warschofsky, R., Meinel, C.: A Pattern-driven Generation of Security Policies for Service-oriented Architectures. In: Proc. of ICWS, Florida, USA, pp. 243–250 (2010)
11. Satoh, F., Nakamura, Y., Mukhi, K.N., Tatsubori, M., Ono, K.: Model-Driven Approach for End-to-End SOA Security Configurations. In: Non-Functional Properties in Service Oriented Architecture: Requirements, Models and Methods, ch. 12, pp. 269–298 (2011)
12. Rodriguez, A., Piattini, E.F.-M.M.: A BPMN Extension for the Modeling of Security Requirements in Business Processes. J. IEICE - Transactions on Information and Systems E90-D(4), 745–752 (2007)

Evaluation of Quality of Design
for Document-Centric Software Services

George Feuerlicht[1,2]

[1] Department of Information Technology,
University of Economics, Prague, W. Churchill Sq. 4, Prague, Czech Republic
[2] Faculty of Engineering and Information Technology,
University of Technology, Sydney,
P.O. Box 123 Broadway, Sydney, NSW 2007, Australia
george.feuerlicht.uts.edu.au

Abstract. As the size and complexity of service oriented applications increases ensuring the quality of design of services that constitute these applications is becoming critical. Poor design of services results in unnecessarily complex and inflexible applications that are difficult to maintain and evolve. Service design has been the subject of intense research interest for almost a decade and there is a wide agreement about the key service design principles that promote maintainability of software services. Recent research efforts include attempts to develop reliable metrics for assessing design quality of service-oriented applications. Most of these metrics were adapted from metrics for object-oriented software and focus on measuring intra-service cohesion and inter-service coupling. In this paper we argue that such metrics are of limited use in assessing the quality of coarse-grained document-centric services used in majority of SOA applications and propose a Message Data Coupling Index (MDCI) - a metric that evaluates orthogonality of a family of XML schemas based on the level of data coupling. We describe the implementation of a prototype tool that computes several variants of the MDCI metric.

Keywords: service design metrics, XML schema evolution, data coupling.

1   Introduction

Service oriented computing has emerged as an active research area more than a decade ago and has now reached high level of maturity with extensive range of technologies available for the construction of complex application systems based on the SOA (Service Oriented Architecture) paradigm. Today, it is not uncommon for such applications to consist of hundreds, and in some cases thousands of individual services that support complex business processes and involve multiple business partners. As the complexity of SOA applications grows it is becoming imperative that software services can be maintained and evolved without costly and time-consuming software modifications often exacerbated by poor design. It is widely accepted that software maintenance accounts for a significant part overall costs and time spent on

A. Ghose et al. (Eds.): ICSOC 2012, LNCS 7759, pp. 356–367, 2013.
© Springer-Verlag Berlin Heidelberg 2013

software projects [1]. Predictions of software maintainability during the design stage of SDLC (Software Development Life Cycle) and early rectification of design defects can lead to a significant reduction of maintenance costs [1]. Maintainability is closely related to software quality as measured by structural properties of software (size, complexity, cohesion and coupling) [2-4]. Design metrics based on measurements of cohesion and coupling have been used extensively in object-oriented software development and were recently adapted for service-oriented software [5]. However, while there are many similarities between object-oriented software and software services, there are also significant differences that make it difficult to apply similar metrics to both approaches. Service-oriented applications typically use coarse-grained document-centric services that lack important characteristics normally associated with software components limiting the potential for reuse and making metrics that measure inter-service coupling inapplicable. Another significant difference is that service interfaces are often based on pre-defined XML (message) schemas developed by various consortia and standards organizations, or internally as organization-wide standards. For example, travel domain web services are based on the OTA (Open Travel Alliance) specification [6] that defines the structure of message payloads that are used to implement travel applications. Changing requirements result in the need to modify message schemas with a corresponding impact on existing services, and related applications and databases. It follows that the problem of maintenance and evolution of SOA applications is closely related to the problem of schema evolution, and that the quality of design of message schemas determines the impact of requirements changes on services. This situation is illustrated in Figure 1 that shows the various layers involved in the implementation of service-oriented applications. The top layer is constituted by the Domain Data Model that represents information requirements for a particular domain of interest and can be expressed as UML class diagram. In practice, the Domain Data Model may need to be retrofitted from the underlying XML schemas and this presents a number of technical challenges as the schemas may overlap and contain inconsistencies [7]. A family of standard XML schemas that define the message structures used for business interactions forms the Message Schemas layer. Services layer represents the services that implement business transactions such as travel booking. For example, OTA airline ticket booking request/response dialog uses the message pair OTA_AirBookRQ/RS to implement flight bookings. This message interchange constitutes a service where the request and response messages form the service interface:

air_booking(OTA_AirBookRQ, OTA_AirBookRS)

The Applications layer consists of SOA applications that are compositions of individual services and implement high-level business functions (e.g. booking a multiple-segment flight). Finally, the Database layer represents databases that store data records generated by business transactions.

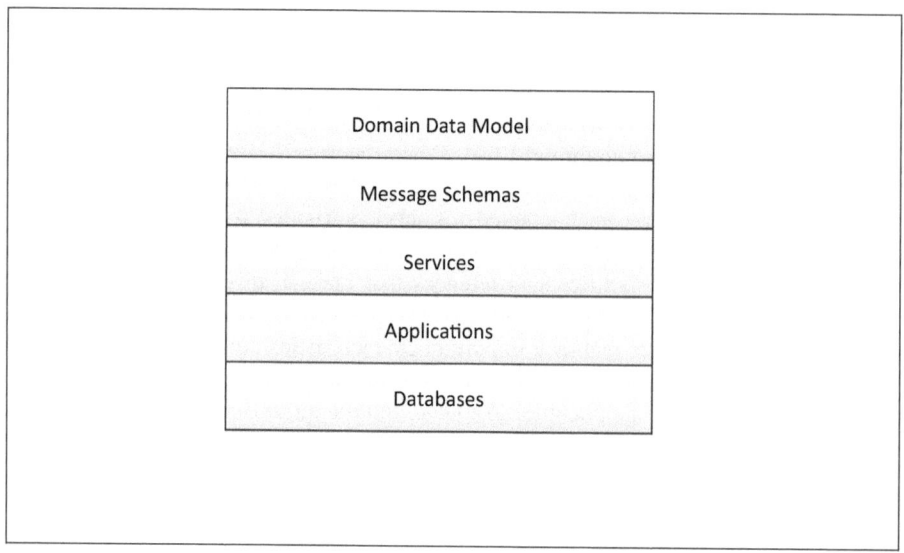

Fig. 1. Layered model of service-oriented applications

As services are implemented on top of pre-existing XML message schemas the design of the schemas determines the structural properties of services and hence their maintainability. Design of XML schemas usually follows document engineering [8-10] or similar methodology that produces XML documents by identifying and aggregating common data elements [11]. For example, OTA message level schemas that represent business transactions are hierarchical collection of XML schemas constructed by aggregation of simple (OpenTravel Simple Types) and complex (OpenTravel Common Types, and Industry Common Types) schema elements [6]. This design approach while ensuring uniform structure and semantics of data elements results in overlapping message schemas and high levels of data coupling reducing maintainability of services [12], [3].

Predicting maintainability of SOA applications has been the subject of recent research interest [1, 5, 13], however the proposed metrics assess structural properties of services at the Service layer and are of limited use in assessing the quality of coarse-grained document-centric services that are used extensively in SOA applications. In this paper we propose a service design metric - MDCI (Message Data Coupling Index) that evaluates orthogonality of a family of XML schemas by estimating the level of data coupling. We describe the implementation of prototype tool that computes the MDCI metric by matching complex schema elements across a family of XML schemas. We first review related literature dealing with service design metrics (section 2.1) and XML schema metrics and change management techniques (section 2.2). In section 3 we describe our proposal for the MDCI metric (section 3.1) and the implementation of a MDCI prototype tool (section 3.2). Section 4 presents our conclusions and outlines further work.

2   Related Work

Metrics for evaluating the quality of service design are essential to allow the comparison of different design strategies and evaluation of their impact on service maintainability. Maintainability of software systems has been the subject of extensive research in the area of object-oriented software and more recently in the context of SOA. Maintainability is closely related to software quality, and a key determinant of software quality is orthogonality of software components. Orthogonality allows individual components to be maintained independently without undesirable side effects (i.e. without impacting on other components) and is achieved by maximizing cohesion and minimizing coupling during the design phase of SDLC [14, 15]. Both coupling and cohesions have been used in traditional software design as indicators of software quality [16], [17, 18]. Maximizing intra-service cohesion and minimizing inter-service coupling improves stability of service-oriented applications by reducing the impact of changes, and at the same time increases potential for reuse [19, 20]. In the following section we review efforts to develop service design metrics that attempt to measure quality of service design (section 2.1), and then discuss XML schema metrics and change management techniques (section 2.2). In the context of the layered model in Figure 1, service design metrics operate at the Services layer and XML metrics operate at the Message Schema layer.

2.1   Service Design Metrics

While the underlying principles of service design are extensively documented in the literature, relatively little work has been done so far on how the adherence to these principles may be quantitatively measured [5]. The original work by Chidamber et al. who proposed the Lack of Cohesion in Methods (LCOM) metric for object-oriented software has been used as the basis for developing metrics for software services. LCOM evaluates similarity of methods for a given class by counting the number of method pairs whose similarity is zero minus the number of method pairs whose similarity is not zero, where similarity of methods is defined as the intersection of the sets of instance variables used by the methods [21]. Several authors have proposed service design metrics based on LCOM. For example, the Service Interface Data Cohesion metric (SIDC) proposed by Perepletchikov et al. [13] measures cohesion by comparing the messages of service operations based on data types. Sindhgatta et al. developed a comprehensive set of metrics to measure service cohesion, coupling, and composability and applied these metrics to case studies in order to evaluate their applicability to practical SOA scenarios [5]. Two variants of the LCOM metric ($LCOS_1$, $LCOS_2$) for use with services were adapted, and several additional metrics have been proposed by the authors in order to evaluate service and message coupling. These metrics include: Service Operational Coupling Index (SOCI) - a measure of dependence of a service on the operations of other services, Inter-Service Coupling Index (ISCI) – based on the number of services invoked by a given service, and Service Message Coupling Index (SMCI) that measures the dependence of a service on the messages derived from the information model of the domain (i.e. messages that service operations receive as inputs, and produce as output via the declared interface). Finally, Sindhgatta et al. propose several metrics dealing directly with service reuse and composability, including Service Reuse Index (SRI), based on the number of existing consumers of a service, Operation Reuse Index (ORI) that counts the number of consumers of a given operation, and Service Composability Index (SCOMP) defined on the basis of the number of compositions in which the service is a (composition) participant and the number of distinct composition participants which succeed or precede the service. Service granularity is closely related to reuse and composability and is evaluated using Service Capability Granularity (SCG) and Service Data Granularity (SDG) metrics, where higher values indicate coarser granularity (i.e. larger functional scope).

As the above design metrics are based on metrics for object-oriented software, the underlying assumption is that the service model consists of a set of services $S = [s_1, s_2...s_S]$ and that each service has a set of operations $O(s) = [o_1, o_2....o_O]$ with interfaces formed by input and output messages $M(o)$ [5]. However, most SOA applications use coarse-grained (document-centric) services that implement the request/response message exchange pattern and do not involve service operations, making such metrics not applicable.

2.2   XML Schema Metrics and Change Management Techniques

Another direction of research of relevance to assessing the quality of service design is work that focuses on evaluating the design of XML schemas [1, 22, 23]. As discussed in section 1 above, pre-existing XML message schemas define the structure of service message payloads, and consequently the structural properties of services. As the message schemas constitute an *interface contract*, poor schema design can affect the overall quality of the software system. Numerous XML schema quality metrics have been proposed primarily with the objective to measure various aspects of schema complexity. McDowell et al. proposed metrics based on counts of complex type declarations, derived complex types, number of global type declarations, etc. [22]. Basci et al. proposed and validated XML schema complexity metric that evaluates the internal structure of XML documents taking into account various sources of complexity that include recursion and complexity arising from importing external schema elements.

An alternative perspective on the problem of maintainability of SOA applications is to focus on change management; i.e. rather than attempting to predict maintainability by assessing the quality of XML schema design, such techniques alleviate the impact of changes in requirements by providing tools for automating change management. The problem of XML schema change management (i.e. schema evolution) has been investigated, but not adequately solved [23]. XML schema evolution in the context of SOA presents a particularly difficult problem as the schemas are often developed in the absence of a Domain Data Model, and are characterized by complex and overlapping data structures [22]. Current work in this area focuses on identifying the impact of changes on XML schemas and developing methods and tools for automating the propagation of these changes. Necasky, et al. proposed a five-level XML evolution architecture with the top level Platform-Independent Model (PIM) that represents the data requirements for a particular domain of interest. PIM model is mapped into a Platform-Specific Model (PSM) that describes how parts of the PIM schema are represented in XML. PSM then maps into Schema, Operational and Extensional level models. Atomic operations (create, update, and remove) for editing schemas are defined on classes, attributes, and associations, and a mechanism for propagating these operations from PIM to PSM schema proposed. Composite operations are constructed from atomic operations to implement complex schema changes [7, 24, 25].

3   Proposed Message Data Coupling Index Metric

In our earlier work we proposed a service design metric that evaluates the quality of service design by estimating the level of data coupling between services (i.e. at the Services layer) [26]. Given a family of XML schemas consisting of pairs of request (RQ) and response (RS) messages $[m_{rq}, m_{rs}]$ that constitute interfaces $[si_1, si_2, si_3, ...si_n]$ for services $[s_1, s_2...s_n]$, DCI (Data Coupling Index) is defined as the average number of (complex) schema elements that are shared between the service interfaces.

In this paper we describe a MDCI (Message Data Coupling Index) metric that evaluates orthogonality of a family of XML schemas that represent a domain of interest (e.g. travel) directly at the Message Schema layer. The rationale for the metric is that maintenance effort required to accommodate new requirements can be estimated based on the level of overlap (lack of orthogonality) of message schemas; i.e. schemas that share a large number of complex data elements are more likely to be impacted as requirements evolve. Conversely, impact of change in requirements on a family of orthogonal schemas is likely to be limited. We rely on data coupling, estimated by counting the number of shared complex elements, as an indirect measure of orthogonality.

Complex elements (composite XML structures with multiple levels of nesting) are used extensively in XML schema specifications. For example, the OTA TravelPreferences complex element type consists of eleven simple elements with two levels of nesting and is embedded in two parent complex element types (AirSearch and OriginDestinationInformation) and three top-level OTA messages (OTA_AirAvailRQ, OTA_AirFareDisplayRQ, and OTA_AirLowFareSearchRQ). Changes in the TravelPreferences element type as the specification evolves will affect all parent data types and messages, with corresponding impact on existing applications and underlying databases.

Coupling through sharing complex schema elements is known in software engineering literature as *stamp coupling* and is regarded as undesirable as it inhibits evolution [17, 27]. Avoiding stamp coupling increases reusability by creating services with simpler interfaces and greater reuse potential [28-30].

3.1   Message Data Coupling Index (MDCI)

Given a family of XML message schemas that represent a domain of interest $[m_1, m_2, m_3, .. m_N]$ MDCI (Message Data Coupling Index) is defined as the sum of the number of shared schema elements for each message pair combination (i.e. cardinality of the intersection of schema elements) divided by the number of message pair combinations r:

$$MDCI = \frac{1}{2r} \sum_{j,k=1}^{N} |M_j \cap M_k| \; ; \text{ where } j \neq k, \text{ and } r = \sum_{i=1}^{N-1} i$$

The calculation of MDCI is based on matching complex schema elements only (i.e. it is a measure of stamp coupling) and gives the average number of shared complex elements evaluated across all message combinations. This is consistent with the approach adopted by McDowell et al. and Visser et al. [22, 23].

3.2   Prototype Tool for Evaluating MDCI

In this section we describe the implementation of a prototype tool for the evaluation of the MDCI metric developed using the Rich Ajax Platform (http://www.eclipse.org/rap/). Given a set of XML messages the MDCI tool reads the message level elements types and the types included in the corresponding libraries. For each message pair combination the tool identifies all complex element types and attempts to match these types producing an average count of matches across all message combinations.

Evaluation of the MDCI metric involves a number of important decisions. Firstly, a decision needs to be made about what constitutes a match between data elements. As noted above we restrict matching to complex element types, i.e. match occurs if two messages that are being compared contain the same complex element type. It is common practice to use extension of complex element types, i.e. complex types derived from other complex types by adding additional elements. For example, as shown in Figure 2 OTA SpecificFlightInfo extends SpecificFlightInfoType by adding elements FlightNo, Airline, and BookingClassPref.

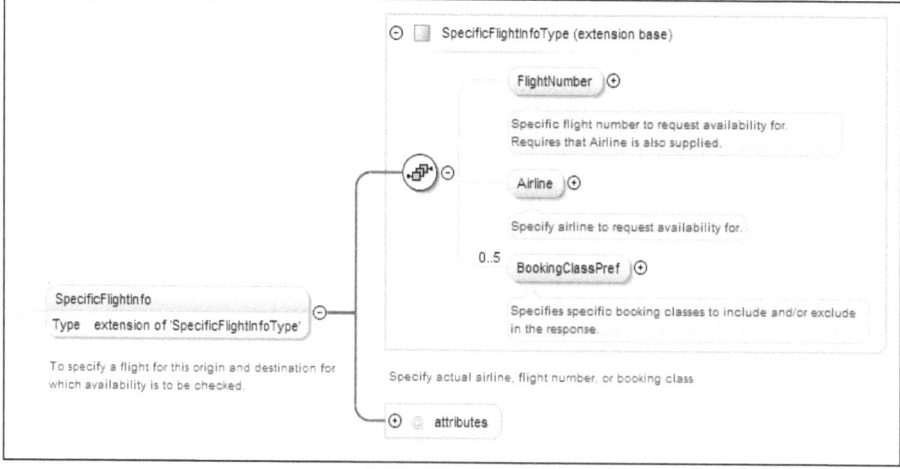

Fig. 2. Extended complex element types

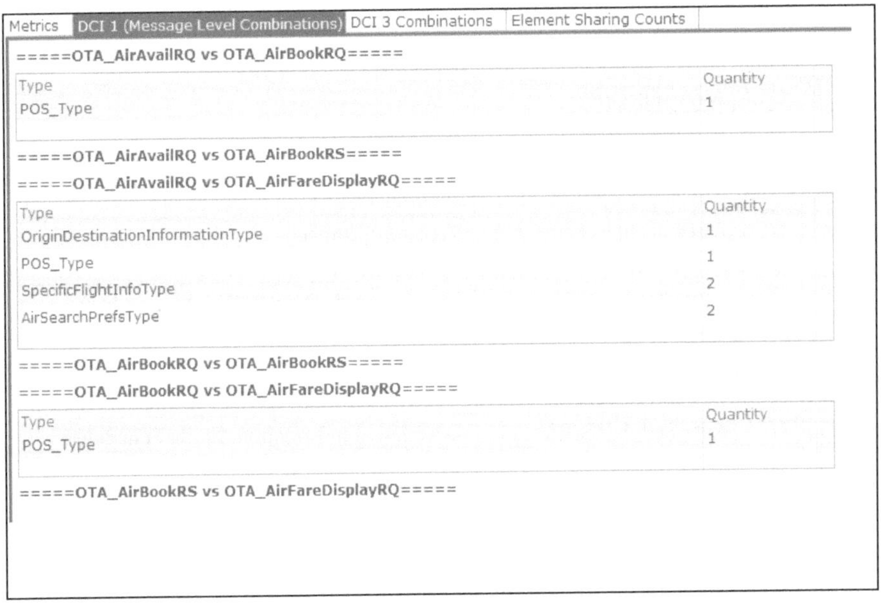

Metrics	DCI 1 (Message Level Combinations)	DCI 3 Combinations	Element Sharing Counts

=====OTA_AirAvailRQ vs OTA_AirBookRQ=====

Type	Quantity
POS_Type	1

=====OTA_AirAvailRQ vs OTA_AirBookRS=====

=====OTA_AirAvailRQ vs OTA_AirFareDisplayRQ=====

Type	Quantity
OriginDestinationInformationType	1
POS_Type	1
SpecificFlightInfoType	2
AirSearchPrefsType	2

=====OTA_AirBookRQ vs OTA_AirBookRS=====

=====OTA_AirBookRQ vs OTA_AirFareDisplayRQ=====

Type	Quantity
POS_Type	1

=====OTA_AirBookRS vs OTA_AirFareDisplayRQ=====

Fig. 3. Multiple element type matches

Computation of MDCI counts the matches between complex elements and their extended versions, as type extensions result in data coupling. As message schemas are constructed by assembling common element types into multi-level hierarchical XML structures, element type matches can occur at different levels of the hierarchy.

We consider two alternatives for the computation of the MDCI index: 1) $MDCI_1$ - counts element matches only at the top-level of the schema, i.e. message level, indicated by the prefix OTA, 2) $MDCI_2$ - counts element matches for all levels of the schema hierarchy. Finally, it is possible for element matches to occur several times for the same message pair as illustrated in Figure 3. The OTA_AirAvailRQ and OTA_AirFareDisplayRQ messages exhibit multiple matches for SpecificFlightInfoType and AirSearchPrefType, indicating that these complex types occur twice in one of the messages. The MDCI tool provides an option to count only unique matches for both $MDCI_1$ and $MDCI_2$ metrics.

3.3   Example Calculations of MDCI

We use a subset of OTA Airline (Air) message schemas (Flattened OTA Schemas version 2011b) shown in Table 1 for the computation of the MDCI index in this paper, but the prototype tool can use message schemas from other sources.

The OTA Air messages implement various business functions related to airline travel, such as checking flight availability, flight booking, etc. For example, the Search and Availability of flights business function is implemented using the Air_AvailabilityRQ/RS request/response message pair [31]. OTA defines common data types (OTA_AirCommonTypes) for the airline messages that form a repository

Table 1. Subset of OpenTravel Air Messages used for calculation of MDCI

Ident.	OpenTravel Message	Business Functionality
AIR01	OTA_AirAvailRQ/RS	Search & Availability
AIR02	OTA_AirBookRQ/RS	Reservation Management: Booking
AIR03	OTA_AirBookModifyRQ	Reservation Management: Modification
AIR04	OTA_AirCheckInRQ/RS	Passenger Check-in & Check-out
AIR05	OTA_AirDemandTicketRQ/RS	Ticket Fulfillment
AIR06	OTA_AirDetailsRQ/RS	Descriptive Information: Flight leg and Codeshare
AIR07	OTA_AirFareDisplayRQ/RS	Fare Search & Display (No Availability)
AIR08	OTA_AirFlifoRQ/RS	Descriptive Information: Flight Operation
AIR09	OTA_AirPriceRQ/RS	Fare Pricing
AIR10	OTA_AirRulesRQ/RS	Fares Rules: Fare Basis & Negotiated Fares
AIR11	OTA_AirScheduleRQ/RS	Descriptive Information: Flight Schedules
AIR12	OTA_AirSeatMapRQ/RS	Seat Availability & Information

of reusable XML Schema components used in the construction OTA Air messages. OTA differentiates between *complex types* (types that contain multiple data elements) and *simple types* (types that contain a single data element).

Using the OTA (Flattened) Air message schemas in Table 1 the value for $MDCI_1 =$ 1.51, and 1.18 for multiple and unique element matches, respectively; i.e. on average the selected OTA Air messages share 1.51 complex elements at the top message schema level, and 1.18 complex elements if only unique matches are counted. Corresponding values for $MDCI_2$ (i.e. counting complex element matches for all levels of the message schema hierarchy) are 77.42 and 6.97 for multiple and unique element matches, respectively.

4   Conclusions and Further Work

Standardized XML schemas that define message structures for domain-specific services form the basis for large-scale SOA applications. Complex hierarchical message schemas with overlapping structures that characterize document-centric services result in applications that are difficult maintain and evolve. Reliable metrics that can identify poor design early during system development can significantly reduce maintenance costs.

We have briefly reviewed existing service design metrics and identified their limitations in the context of coarse-grained document-centric services. Following on from our previous proposal of a service design metric that evaluates data coupling between service interfaces [26] we propose a design metric that estimates orthogonality of a family of message schemas that typically form the basis for the implementation of services for a particular domain of interest (e.g. travel). We argue that the maintenance effort required to accommodate new requirements increases with the extent of overlap (i.e. lack of orthogonality) of message schemas. The proposed MDCI metric relies on evaluating the level of data coupling by counting the number of shared complex schema elements among a set of message schemas. We have described a prototype tool that uses a set of XML schemas as input and provides a number of options for the evaluation of the MDCI metric.

The MDCI metric needs to be empirically validated using different sets of XML schemas and for different design strategies to establish the reliability of MDCI as a measure of design quality. We are currently investigating the of impact service granularity on the orthogonality of the message schemas. We expect that re-designing the schemas to reduce granularity of services will improve the orthogonality of the message schemas and produce a measurable effect on the MDCI index.

Acknowledgments. This research was supported by GAČR (Grant Agency, Czech Republic) grant No. P403/11/0574 and P403/10/0092. Dr George Feuerlicht was supported by the Australian-China Science and Research Fund ACSCRF-01280 from the Australian Department of Innovation, Industry, Science, Research and Tertiary Education (DIISRTE) and the Research Centre for Human Centered Technology Design at the University of Technology, Sydney. We acknowledge the assistance of Enrico Shi with the development of the MDCI prototype tool.

References

1. Basci, D., Misra, S.: Measuring and evaluating a design complexity metric for XML schema documents. Journal of Information Science and Engineering 25(5), 1405–1425 (2009)
2. Bansiya, J., Davis, C.G.: A hierarchical model for object-oriented design quality assessment. IEEE Transactions on Software Engineering 28(1), 4–17 (2002)
3. Etzkorn, L.H., et al.: A comparison of cohesion metrics for object-oriented systems. Information and Software Technology 46(10), 677–687 (2004)
4. Eder, J., Kappel, G., Schrefl, M.: Coupling and cohesion in object-oriented systems. Technical Report, University of Klagenfurt, Austria (1994)
5. Sindhgatta, R., Sengupta, B., Ponnalagu, K.: Measuring the Quality of Service Oriented Design. In: Baresi, L., Chi, C.-H., Suzuki, J. (eds.) ICSOC-ServiceWave 2009. LNCS, vol. 5900, pp. 485–499. Springer, Heidelberg (2009)
6. OTA. OTA Specifications (May 6, 2010), http://www.opentravel.org/Specifications/Default.aspx
7. Necaský, M.: Conceptual Modeling for XML. Dissertations in Database and Information Systems Series. IOS Press/AKA Verlag (2009)
8. Glushko, R., McGrath, T.: Document engineering: analyzing and designing documents for business informatics and Web services. MIT Press Books (January 2008)

9. Glushko, R., McGrath, T.: Patterns and reuse in document engineering. In: XML 2002 Proceedings (2002)
10. Glushko, R.J., McGrath, T.: Document Engineering for e-Business. In: Proceedings of the 2002 ACM Symposium on Document Engineering (DocEng 2002), McLean, Virginia, USA. ACM Press, New York (2002)
11. ebXML. ebXML - Enabling A Global Electronic Market (December 9, 2007), http://www.ebxml.org/
12. Feuerlicht, G., Lozina, J.: Understanding Service Reusability. In: 15th International Conference Systems Integration 2007, Prague, Czech Republic. VSE Prague (2007)
13. Perepletchikov, M., Ryan, C., Frampton, K.: Cohesion metrics for predicting maintainability of service-oriented software, pp. 328–335. qsic (2007)
14. Papazoglou, M.P., Yang, J.: Design Methodology for Web Services and Business Processes. In: Buchmann, A.P., Casati, F., Fiege, L., Hsu, M.-C., Shan, M.-C. (eds.) TES 2002. LNCS, vol. 2444, pp. 54–64. Springer, Heidelberg (2002)
15. Papazoglou, M.P., Heuvel, W.V.D.: Service-oriented design and development methodology. International Journal of Web Engineering and Technology 2(4), 412–442 (2006)
16. Vinoski, S.: Old measures for new services. IEEE Internet Computing 9(6), 72–74 (2005)
17. Pautasso, C., Zimmermann, O., Leymann, F.: Restful web services vs. big'web services: making the right architectural decision. In: 17th International Conference on World Wide Web. ACM, Beijing (2008)
18. Pautasso, C., Wilde, E.: Why is the web loosely coupled?: a multi-faceted metric for service design. In: 18th International Conference on World Wide Web. ACM, Madrid (2009)
19. Stevens, W.P., Myers, G.J., Constantine, L.L.: Structured Design. IBM Systems Journal 38(2 & 3) (1999)
20. Rumbaugh, J., Blaha, M., Premerlani, W., Eddy, F., Lorensen, W.: Object-oriented modeling and design 1991. Prentice Hall, New Jersey (2000)
21. Chidamber, S., Kemerer, C.: A metrics suite for object oriented design. IEEE Transactions on Software Engineering 20(6), 476–493 (2002)
22. McDowell, A., Schmidt, C., Yue, K.B.: Analysis and metrics of XML schema (2004)
23. Visser, J.: Structure metrics for XML Schema. In: Proceedings of XATA (2006)
24. Necaský, M., Mlýnková, I.: A Framework for Efficient Design, Maintaining, and Evolution of a System of XML Applications. In: Proceedings of the Databases, Texts, Specifications and Objects, DATESO, vol. 10, pp. 38–49
25. Necaský, M., Mlýnková, I.: Five-Level Multi-Application Schema Evolution. In: Proceedings of the Databases, Texts, Specifications and Objects, DATESO, vol. 9, pp. 213–217
26. Feuerlicht, G.: Simple Metric for Assessing Quality of Service Design. In: Maximilien, E.M., Rossi, G., Yuan, S.-T., Ludwig, H., Fantinato, M. (eds.) ICSOC 2010. LNCS, vol. 6568, pp. 133–143. Springer, Heidelberg (2011)
27. Page-Jones, M.: The Practical Guide to Structured Systems Design, 2nd edn. Prentice Hall, New Jersey (1988)
28. Feuerlicht, G.: Design of Service Interfaces for e-Business Applications using Data Normalization Techniques. Journal of Information Systems and e-Business Management, 1–14 (2005)

29. Feuerlicht, G.: System Development Life-Cycle Support for Service-Oriented Applications. In: 5th International Conference on Software Methodologies, Tools and Techniques, SoMet 2006, Quebec, Canada. IOS Press, The Netherlands (2006)
30. Schmelzer: Solving the service granularity challenge (December 13, 2007), `http://searchsoa.techtarget.com/tip/` `0,289483,sid26_gci1172330,00.html`
31. Alliance, O.T.: OpenTravel™ Alliance XML Schema Design Best Practices (September 1, 2010), `http://www.opentravel.org/Resources/Uploads/PDF/` `OTA_SchemaDesignBestPracticesV3.06.pdf`

Resource Management for Pervasive Systems

Jacky Estublier, German Vega, and Elmehdi Damou

Grenoble University - LIG, 220 rue de la Chimie 38041 Grenoble BP53 Cedex 9 France
{Jacky.Estublier,German.Vega,Elmehdi.Damou}@imag.fr

Abstract. In pervasive contexts, many different applications, from different providers, will compete for access to resources: physical resources like sensors and actioners, as well as for software resources (services). Sensors provide information about the state of the world, and actioners change the world which can put goods and persons at risk. At least for safety reasons, it is critical to closely control, at any point in time, and in all circumstances, which service(s) are using which resource(s).

Pervasive systems face the difficult challenge of providing some safety, reliability and resilience properties, verified at design and compile time, while executing in many different configurations unknown statically, with dynamic services and devices, competing for resources with unknown applications and facing unpredictable configuration changes. This challenge can be seen from two perspectives: how to design and develop pervasive applications in such a demanding context; how to execute these applications while satisfying the requirements despite the unpredictable context and changes.

This paper discusses the requirements for future pervasive gateways and presents the Apam dynamic service middleware. Apam interprets at run-time a formalism describing the desirable behavior of a system, and enforces this behavior in a very wide range of unplanned configurations while resisting the many changes that may occur.

Keywords: Service Oriented Computing, Service Selection, Service Composition, Composite services, Software engineering environments.

1 Introduction

The wide diffusion of cheap and wireless devices makes it possible for many spaces, public or private, to be populated by communicating devices. Typically, in the house, it is envisioned that the set-top box will play the role of the "universal" residential gateway, supporting many downloaded applications from, for example, the android market place. These applications ignore each other but still compete for the access to the available resources. With respect to "usual" software applications, pervasive applications have at least the three following unusual characteristics:

1. All the applications share the same physical world,
2. Applications must be installed, with zero configuration, in many different contexts,
3. Applications must tolerate unplanned changes that occur during execution.

A. Ghose et al. (Eds.): ICSOC 2012, LNCS 7759, pp. 368–379, 2013.

Although these characteristics, individually, can be found in other domains, their concomitance in pervasive systems constitutes a very serious challenge, so far unresolved. Solving each one of these points requires addressing a number of challenges:

Sharing the Same Physical World. This is probably the most demanding and far reaching issue. For example, in the house, the common world is the house itself, with its equipment and inhabitants. The current state of the world is perceived through many sensors, and it is changing by itself or through actioners. These devices are shared by the different applications running in the house; there is a need to manage the access to these devices, and to avoid conflicts. When applications ignore each other, the global behavior can become inconsistent and unpredictable, which is of critical importance since it is the real world that is changed, and therefore it can put goods and persons at risk. Clearly, an application cannot solve all these issues, because applications are usually designed by different groups of developers that ignore each other, and therefore they can hardly synchronize themselves. This issue requires a high level dynamic middleware that has the capability to control the whole system, made of many applications competing for the same resources and to enforce a "consistent" and "safe" execution of independent applications which can interfere in almost unpredictable ways.

Zero Configuration. These applications are supposed to be bought, installed and run by end users. The market of domestic applications is expected to grow fast, such that the number and variety of applications will rapidly be very large. The challenge, here, is that the whole system must adapt itself, without human intervention, to the different configurations that can be found in the different houses. Since the applications will be developed independently, the challenge falls on the shoulders of the system designers that will have to describe the overall desirable system behavior, without a complete knowledge of the execution context (device, services, and applications).

Unpredictable Changes. Many pervasive applications will run for very long periods of time (e.g. heating control) during which almost any change can occur. These changes are "normal" when it concerns the state of the house (e.g. mobility and actions of their inhabitants) but also, the end user can install or uninstall applications from very large application market place. These changes are unpredictable, both in time and nature. The challenge is that the running system and its running applications must dynamically adapt to these changes. The new devices and applications must be integrated into the current systems without compromising the stability, continuity and consistency of the whole system.

Applications being designed independently, the challenge falls again on the designer's shoulder: he/she has to express which changes are allowed during execution and how they can be integrated such that the new system still satisfies the overall desirable behavior. Addressing these challenges require addressing two different dimensions:

- **The design** point of view, with formalisms capable of describing the "desirable behavior" of the whole system without the complete knowledge of the actual execution context, supporting a large range of unplanned and undefined devices and applications, and adapting to many unplanned dynamic changes.
- **The execution** point of view, interpreting and enforcing the design formalism: enforcing in all circumstances the overall desirable behavior.

Our approach is architecture based. We distinguish the **design architecture** which is an abstract description of the characteristics that all actual architectures should satisfy; and the **execution architecture** which is the actual state of the world, in terms of devices and applications. The design architecture is in terms of abstract services (specifications) and containers (composites) which define scopes and visibility rules. The execution architecture is in terms of service instances (devices are reified as service instances too) and "wires". We have defined a conformity relationship between design and execution architectures such that a large and potentially infinite number of execution architectures can be conforming to the same design, including the dynamic changes.

The paper is illustrated by a scenario in section 3. Section 4 shortly describes the Apam components, section 5 illustrate the dynamic management, and section 6 the protection mechanism: the composites. Section 7 presents the conflict handling strategies; section 8 summarizes and section 9 concludes the paper.

2   State of the Art

The pervasive domain is both in the self-adaptive (autonomic, context aware) and resource management domains. The first one considers a single application in a fluctuant context [1][3], while the second considers multiple applications conflicting on stable resources. We have multiple applications running in a fluctuant context and conflicting on variable resources.

From the design point of view, resource conflict detection and management is an issue in many domains, and has been addressed in many different ways. A static analysis approach, using dedicated languages or model checking, is very powerful, but makes the hypothesis that the applications and at least the devices are statically known. In pervasive computing, each house is potentially different; devices and applications are dynamic, therefore static analysis is not sufficient.

Maybe the oldest way to manage conflicts is using Access Control Lists (ACL) and Role Based Access Control (RBAC) [8] recently adapted to the pervasive context [6] adding a "criticality" status, but as a conceptual model only.

Most propositions in pervasive computing identify a special global attribute (called state [4], mode [5], criticality [6], context [7] ...) and describe the conflict resolution with respect to the value of this attribute. In [7], each application statically defines its actions on the real world and what it considers to be a conflict. Then in each physical space, a conflict manager compares the descriptions and computes if conflicts can happen. This approach moves most of the burden onto the application developer's shoulders, and does not solve the issue of different and incompatible visions of what a conflict is. In [9], it is the user privacy which is the central issue.

It is possible to consider conflict handling as a special case of dependency management, taking also into account the current "state", and priorities. In [10], AOP and "exclusive binding" are used, while [4] propose a DSL in which exclusive actions, ACL, priorities and required resources are defined; from this DSL, conflicts are detected and code is generated. However these approaches are preliminary and ignore many device management issues; dynamic evolution is not really supported since any change requires recompiling, regenerating and redeploying the whole system. A protection based on scope and visibility control, close to our work, can be found in [11], but limited to event based systems and not addressing resources access control.

Our approach can be qualified as architecture based dependency management. In contrast to most approaches, we introduce an architecture in which composite entities encapsulate their content in order to provide a scope for 1) defining the dynamic and conflict management policies and 2) to control the visibility of services. Every level of the architecture has its own "state" and its own policies defined in terms of abstract services that will be mapped to concrete service instances at runtime, allowing a large range of unexpected evolutions, both in terms of devices and new applications.

3   A Scenario

For illustration purpose, suppose that a home gateway supports a number of applications including a security manager which manages fire and intrusion threats. Intrusion itself is based on both movement detection and breaking and entering. The house is supposed to be equipped with many devices, including various smoke detectors, sprinklers, motion and break-in detectors, alarm, and doors that can be locked or unlocked. Alarm and doors require exclusive access. In case of fire, the entrance door must be unlocked (by the Fire application), but at night, the entrance door should be locked (by the Intrusion application). The alarm should be used by the application that needs it. Furthermore, the house owner can install new devices and download new services at any time.

At design time, it would be nice to produce a specification of the system, at the highest possible level of abstraction. Such a specification should contain the design architecture, including the aspects necessary and sufficient to describe the "desirable behavior" of the system. The concepts used in the design architecture should be those established in "house ontology". In our case this design could look as follows, in which rectangles stand for the specification of sub-systems, devices or services.

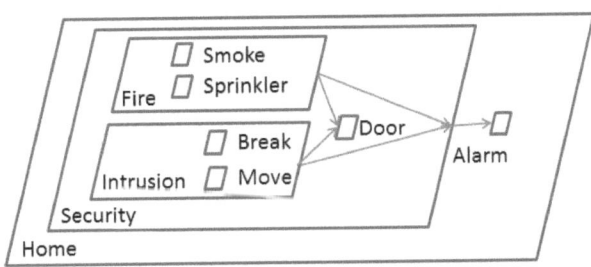

Fig. 1. A possible design architecture

While this figure summarizes roughly our scenario, it is essentially semantic free; the semantics of the specifications is undefined, and it does not give any information about how our challenges are addressed which are to make sure that the different applications (or sub-systems) will perform as expected, despite the fact (1) they ignore each other, (2) they may conflict on some devices (what about a fire at night?) and (3) new devices and applications can appear at any time, with new conflicts.

In substance, our goal is to define a formalism which gives a similar high level vision of the system, but semantically rich enough to include the characteristics expressing how the challenges above are addressed, and allowing to detect, at design and compile time, the inconsistencies and potential conflicts. To that end, the concepts of specification have been made formal, including the resolution process that, at run time, transforms a design architecture into an execution architecture such that the running system behaves in conformity with the design architecture. Let us first introduce the Apam components.

4   Primitive Components: Context Free Behavior

Apam Components are defined at three levels of abstraction: specification, implementation and instances. Specifications mostly define the resources provided and required by the component, and the Java classes containing the provided interfaces. An implementation is a piece of code (Java classes in our system) that implements one specification, (i.e. it provides and requires the resources defined by the specification). An instance is a running Java object in the platform.

Apam relies on the POJO (Plain Old Java Object) approach in which the source code of a component should only be concerned with the application logic. Each component is associated a metadata (in XML currently); at build time that metadata is interpreted and the POJO is transformed into an Apam component (an OSGi bundle). Let us first show how the Fire manager, at the specification and implementation levels, can be described in our system.

```
<specification name="Door" interfaces="home.…Door" exclusive="true"/>
<specification name="Alarm" interfaces="home.…Alarm exclusive="true"/>
<specification name="Sprinkler" ….

<specification name="Fire" interfaces="fr.imag….FireStatus">
   <dependency specification="Alarm"/>
   <dependency specification="Door" id="doors">
   <definition name="hasSprinkler" type="Boolean" default="false" />
</specification>

<implementation name="FireSprinkler" specification="Fire"
classname="fr.imag….FireMng">
   <dependency field="alarm" id="Alarm"/>
   <dependency field="door" id="doors" />
   <property hasSprinker="true" />
   <-- Additional dependencies -->
   <dependency specification="Sprinkler" field="sprinklers"/>
   <dependency specification="Smoke" field="smokeDetectors" />
</implementation>
```

The example above shows the device specifications (Door and Alarm, ..), including the interfaces by which they can be managed and with the property exclusive meaning that such a device can have at most one client. Specification Fire declares the interface it provides FireStatus, and its dependencies towards specifications Alarm and Door. Dependencies have a unique id, by default it is the name of the associated specification; in the example, the dependency toward `Door` is called `doors`, and toward `Alarm` it is called `Alarm`. The line `<definition … hasSprinkler` is the definition of a property that the implementations of `Fire` can instantiate. Specifications are really components; at design and build time they are compiled and packaged as OSGi bundles containing the interfaces and the metadata; they are packaged, stored and deployed exactly as implementations.

The implementation `FireSprinkler` indicates that it implements specification `Fire`, and therefore provides and requires the same resources. It must indicate which class (`FireMng`) implements the interface `FireStatus`, and which (Java) fields in this class are the dependencies `Alarm` and `doors` defined in the specification; the type and cardinality of fields `alarm` and `door` are found in the source code. `FireSprinkler` has additional dependencies toward specifications `Sprinkler` and `Smoke` because this specific fire manager uses smoke detectors and sprinklers to perform its job. To make this clear, that implementation sets the attribute `hasSprinkler`, defined in the specification to `true`. Other implementations could use other ways, (like only using the alarm when the temperature is too high) this is why these dependencies are not in the specification.   This metadata information is stored in files inside the eclipse project in which is developed the associated Java code; it is interpreted transparently during Maven[1] build by a specific Maven plug-in that injects byte code for dependency management and builds the corresponding OSGi bundle.

5   Composites: Context Dependent Behavior

A primitive Apam component (its source code and metadata) does not make any hypothesis about its context of use, the availability and dynamic behavior of resources, or any hypothesis about possible conflicts. Therefore primitive components are easier to program and as reusable as possible. However, Apam requires additional (meta) information to manage the consistency of the system seen as members of an ecosystem (both i.e. actors and subjects of that ecosystem). In Apam, this information is included in the Design Architecture of the system by means of the concept of Composite Component[2]. A Composite component is an actor in the ecosystem defined as a number of connected components (a sub-system, an application). A composite captures the shared knowledge about the ecosystem (expected devices, dynamism) required to express the expected global system behavior in that context; in particular its relationships with the other composites, its protection and conflict management policies.

Usual service platforms have a flat structure, which is very inconvenient because any service can use any other one as soon as it knows its published interface; for example, any service could lock any door at any time: it is scary! A protection mechanism is needed. Apam is based on the concept of composite component, as a

---

[1] `http://maven.apache.org/`
[2] This is a simplified description of the Apam composite concept ; for more detail, see [12].

mechanism for protection applying the concepts of dynamic architecture, scoping and visibility to pervasive systems.

The main protection mechanism is based on visibility control. Suppose that a client instance x, pertaining to composite instance cx, asks for a provider of specification Y. The client instance x pertaining to cx can see y pertaining to composite cy if

- y pertains to cx $(cx = cy)$ or
- cy lends y to its friends, and cx is a friend of cy, or
- cy lends y to the application, and cx and cy pertain to the same application,
- cy lends y to the whole platform.

cx is a friend of cy if a *friend* relationship is established from CY [3] to CX. An instance pertaining to a single composite instance, the instances in a platform are organized as a forest. An application is defined as a tree (i.e., a root composite instance); cx and cy pertain to the same application if they pertain to the same instance tree.

A composite can define which instances can be lent to other composites using the tags *local*, *friend* and *application* The value of these tags is an expression to be applied to instance properties. An instance cannot be lent if it matches the *local Instance* expression; it can be lent to friend composite instances if it matches the *friend Instance* expression; it can be lent to any composite of the same application if it matches the *application Instance* expression; and finally it is lent to the whole platform if it matches none. If it matches more than one expression, the most restrictive one is assumed.

Symmetrically, a composite designer must be able to decide whether or not to borrow the instances lent by other composites. For this purpose, can be specified the tag *borrow Instance=<expression>*. If the requested resource matches the expression, the platform must try to borrow an instance if it exists. If the expression is not matched, an instance must be created. By default, the expression is false, i.e., by default composite should use their own instances. Let us illustrate on our scenario, in which `Fire` is now a specification composite and `FireCompo` is an implementation composite.

```
<Specification name="Fire" interfaces="fr.imag….FireStatus">
    <dependency specification="Alarm"/>
    <dependency specification="Door" id="doors">
    <definition name="hasSprinkler" type="Boolean" default="false" />
    <state type="{normal, onFire}" value="normal" >
</specification>
<composite name="FireCompo" specification="Fire" main="Fire" >
    <dependency specification="Door" id="doors" >
        <constraint filter="(location=entrance)" />
    </dependency >
    <contenMngt>
      <dependency specification="Fire" >
        <preference filter="(hasSprinkler=true)" />
      </dependency>
      <owns specification="{Smoke,Sprinkler}"/>
      <local instance="(exclusive=true)" />           <!-- private. -->
      <borrow instance="false" />                      <!--only use external dep-->
    </contenMngt>
</composite>
```

---

[3] Lower case like cy are instances and upper case like CY are implementations.

The Fire specification composite has a state with two values: `normal` and `onFire`. `FireCompo` first refines dependency `doors` as a door satisfying the constraint `location=entrance`. The `FireCompo` composite, must define its "main implementation", which is any atomic implementation that provides at least the same resources as the composite. Here it must be an implementation of specification `Fire`, that preferably satisfies the constraint `hasSprinkler=true` (`FireSprinkler` is a possible resolution). The `<owns ..>` tag indicates that the services implementing specifications `Smoke` and `Sprinkler` must be owned by the `FireCompo` composite. Apam checks, at compile time and when an application is about to be deployed, that a single composite has a `owns` clause on a given service.

`<local instance="(exclusive=true)"` indicates that the exclusive services it owns, the sprinklers in our example, cannot be lent; they are only to be used by this composite; but the other owned services can be lent freely, for example the smoke detectors. `<borrow instance="false"` indicates that the components inside this composite can only use the components owned by this composite and those explicitly declared in the composite's dependencies (i.e. the alarm and the entrance door). With these declarations, the overall architecture, at instance level is the following:

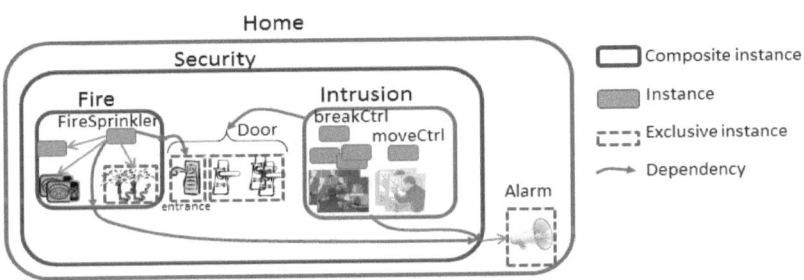

Fig. 2. The instance architecture

Instantiating a composite implementation consists in creating an instance of its main implementation. The main implementation instance will also call its dependencies; by the resolution process Apam will look for a "visible" instance satisfying the constraints. In our example, since the composite declared `borrow instance=false`, are visible only the instances owned by the composite, those that can be deployed from the composite repository, and those visible through the explicit dependencies. For example, `FireSprinkler` can only use the sprinklers own by `FireCompo` (it cannot borrow them). The only way to use a service located outside the composite is through the composite dependencies. When field `doors` is used for the first time, Apam realizes that it is an external dependency, and therefore tries to resolve the dependency from `FireCompo` toward `Door` which turns out to be an entrance door. Once this dependency resolved, Apam resolves the dependency from `FireSprinkler` to `Door` as a subset of `FireCompo` dependencies: `FireSprinkler` will only use the entrance door while it is programmed to manage any door. We say that the `doors` dependency of `FireMain` is promoted as the `FireCompo` doors dependency.

6   Conflict Handling

The ownership control and the fine grained dependency management solve many potential conflicts, but the most serious one remain. In our example, a door can be locked or unlocked, and it is declared `exclusive` which means that a single service can use it at a time. Simultaneously, the `Intrusion` composite declared it requires the door since it has to lock it when the house is empty, while the `Fire` composite declared that it needs to open it in case of fire. Not being explicitly owned, our mechanism would simply give the door to the first one that asks for it, and non-determinism would follow.

In our philosophy, the door control is the responsibility of the composite that owns it; in our case the `Security` composite. To that end, the `Security` composite defines its possible states: `Normal`, `Empty`, `Intrusion`, and `Emergency`.

```
<specification name="Security" interfaces="ccc" main="securitySpec">
    <state type="{Normal, Empty, Intrusion, Emergency}" />
    <owns Specification="Door" />        <!-- all doors.    -->
    <local instance="true"/>             <!-- lends nothing.-->
    <start component="Fire" specification="{Smoke, Sprinkler}" />;
    <start component="Intrusion" specification="Motion" />;
    <start component="Intrusion" specification="Break" />;
    <grant component="Fire" dependencies="{Alarm, doors}"     when="Emergency";
    <grant component="Intrusion" dependencies="{Alarm, Door}"  when="Intrusion";
    <grant component="Intrusion" dependencies="Door"          when="Empty";
</specification>
```

The `Security` composite owns the doors; it is therefore entitled to decide which application can make use of them. In this example, the entrance door is granted to the `Fire` component when the state of the security component is `Emergency`, i.e. when a fire is detected. Granting the entrance door to `Fire` means that the door is pre-empted, i.e. if the door is currently used by another service, that service is turned into the "wait" mode, its connection is removed, and a connection is created between `Fire` and the door. The connection is resumed when the condition (`Emergency`) is no longer satisfied. The when clause only contains values of the current composite state, which allows to check, at compile time, that an exclusive service can only be granted to, at most, one component in each possible state. The capability to automate conflict detection at compile time when assembling large systems, and at execution time when a new application is about to be deployed, is an important property of the system.   In this example the alarm and the entrance door are allocated (granted) to the `Fire` component in case of `emergency`; the door is allocated to the `Intrusion` component when the house is empty, and the doors are available to any service othewise. Only applications inside the security area can ask for a granted access.

7   Designing in a Unpredictable World: Adapting to Changes

A contribution of this work is the definition of a pervasive system at the specification level, i.e. defining a system with partial knowledge, through an architecture containing only the fundamental conditions for a "normal" behavior. Suppose, for example, that the house owner downloads a new and unknown application making use of sprinklers. In our example, it is not the `Fire` specification that owns the sprinklers, but the composite implementation `FireCompo`. If the `Fire` application does not explicitly owns these devices, they can be owned by other application, and the `Fire` application may be denied their use when needed. To avoid this risk, the designer could decide to allocate the management of smoke detectors and sprinklers to `Fire` at the specification level and the break and movement detectors to `Intrusion`. We end up with the picture in Fig. 2 but with precise executable semantics.

With this design, the compiler can check, at specification level, if there is any risk of access conflict and any inconsistent declarations, without any need to indicate the implementations potentially used (and potentially unknown). This design is irrespective of the implementations that will be used, the devices that will be discovered, and the new applications that can be downloaded. For example, downloading, into the Home composite, media applications (sharing the alarms for example), health applications, or different implementations (and vendors) of intrusion or fire managers, adding any kind of device, the fundamental behavior of security, fire and intrusion will be enforced. In the same time, these new applications and devices will be integrated into the system, as long as the `grant` and `owns` primitives are not inconsistent. In our example, the smoke, break and movement detectors, as well as doors and alarms, can be used by these new and unknown applications, without compromising the consistency of the whole system.

8   Implementation

The APAM platform includes a complete design and execution environment. The design environment is an extension of Eclipse [**Error! Reference source not found.**]; components (atomic and composite) are developed and described in XML files. The Apam compiler, which is implemented as a Maven plugin, is transparently executed during the build phase; it checks the architecture validity and builds the bundles.

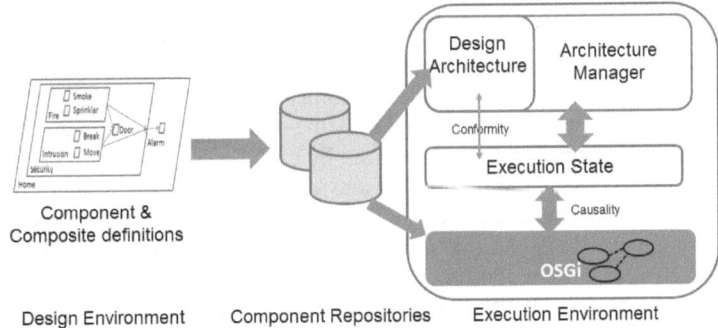

Fig. 3. APAM implementation architecture

Once the application design architecture validated, it is provisioned as bundles into component repositories and it is available for execution. The design architecture is a first class artifact managed at design, deployment and execution time.

The APAM runtime includes iPOJO[2] and a standard OSGi platform in which the services and devices drivers are making up the application. Apam builds an execution state representing the current execution architecture, including specifications and composites. The execution state is a causal model. The architecture layer manages the execution state such that its evolution will be conforming, at all times, to the design architecture [Fig3].

The execution environment is designed to be very efficient; component interactions are implemented as direct object invocations, and the APAM runtime is only triggered when an unresolved dependency is invoked for the first time. Modifications of the architecture are reflected by modifying the injected references of the components. With respect to OSGi, the memory overhead is about 10%, essentially due to the reified state, and the execution efficiency is similar to OSGi. In comparison, component frameworks like JEE or SCA are orders of magnitude slower than APAM.

9   Conclusion

Software engineering's best practices require that each individual application must be developed as if running alone with all the resources it needs; but on the other side, applications in pervasive environments must face an unknown context, unpredictable dynamic changes and must compete for its resources with unknown applications.

Our solution consists in structuring the complete system resources (applications, services and devices) inside composites. The composites being themselves components, the structure can be nested (through the ownership relationship), but also any directed graph (through the dependency and friend relationships). Each composite is in charge of declaring the strategies to be applied to the components it owns and its relationships with the unknown outer world. The strategies discussed in this paper include the dynamic behaviour of resources, the architecture management, and the access conflicts. Composites being components also come at the three levels of abstraction: specification, implementation and instance, corresponding roughly to the design, development and execution phases of a software system life cycle.

We believe that the key point is the capability to design a pervasive system at the specification level in which is described only the management strategies to be applied to the abstract resources owned and required by each service. At that level, there is no need to provide the exact nature, number and availability of the resources that will be used by the system at run-time; because it is not needed, not known or because it may change during execution. The implementation architecture, defined in the composite implementations, can refine the specification architecture.

The second key point is that these strategies are declared in each composite, and the composite architecture is known. The inconsistencies and risks of conflict can be detected, either statically at compile time when assembling large systems, or just before deployment in case of unplanned evolution: strategies are enforced in all cases.

The third key point is that the resolution process transforms at run-time the design architecture (in terms of specifications and dependencies) into execution architecture in terms of instances and wires. The execution state changes only when a resource appears or disappears, or when a wire must be established or deleted. Apam computes the next state of the system such that it is a valid architecture i.e. for a new wire, the selected instance is found in the current state or an implementation is found in an available repository. In all cases, the new state satisfies the dynamic, access control and visibility strategies expressed in the design and implementation architectures.

The design architecture is abstract enough to fit a wide range of execution contexts, and a very large (possibly infinite) number of execution architectures. The lazy nature of Apam resolution makes that the transformation from design architecture to execution is performed "just in time" within the actual context and system state, enforcing both architecture conformity and adaptation to the current context.

We believe that we have met our challenge of checking statically and enforcing dynamically the resource management strategies without the complete knowledge of the available resources and their dynamic behavior; and adapting to the unpredictability of dynamic changes and competing applications.

References

1. Cervantes, H., Hall, R.: Autonomous Adaptation to Dynamic Availability Using a Service-Oriented Component Model. In: Proceedings of the International Conference on Software Engineering, May 1. ICSE Edinburgh, Scotland (2004)
2. Escoffier, C., Hall, R.S., Lalanda, P.: iPOJO: an Extensible Service-Oriented Component Framework. In: IEEE Int. Conference on Services Computing, USA (July 2007)
3. Zhang, W., Hansen, K.: Semantic Web based Self-management for a Pervasive Service Middleware. In: IEEE Int. Conf. on Self-Adaptive and Self-Organizing Systems (2008)
4. Jakob, H., Consel, C., Loriant, N.: Architecturing Conflict Handling of Pervasive Computing Resources. In: Felber, P., Rouvoy, R. (eds.) DAIS 2011. LNCS, vol. 6723, pp. 92–105. Springer, Heidelberg (2011)
5. Mukhija, A., Rosenblum, D.S., Foster, H., Uchitel, S.: Runtime Support for Dynamic and Adaptive Service Composition. In: Wirsing, M., Hölzl, M. (eds.) SENSORIA. LNCS, vol. 6582, pp. 585–603. Springer, Heidelberg (2011)
6. Gupta, S.K.S., Mukherjee, T., Venkatasubramanian, K.: Criticality Aware Access Control Model for Pervasive Applications. In: ICPCC 2006 (2006)
7. Tuttlies, V., Schiele, G., Becker, C.: Comity - conflict avoidance in pervasive computing environments. In: International Workshop on Pervasive Systems (2007)
8. Sandhu, R., Coyne, E.J., Feinstein, H.L., Youman, C.E.: Role Based Access Control. IEEE Computer, 38–47 (1996)
9. Massaguer, D., Hore, B., Diallo, M.H., Mehrotra, S., Venkatasubramanian, N.: Middleware for Pervasive Spaces: Balancing Privacy and Utility. In: Bacon, J.M., Cooper, B.F. (eds.) Middleware 2009. LNCS, vol. 5896, pp. 247–267. Springer, Heidelberg (2009)
10. Retkowitz, D., Kulle, S.: Dependency Management in Smart Homes. In: Senivongse, T., Oliveira, R. (eds.) DAIS 2009. LNCS, vol. 5523, pp. 143–156. Springer, Heidelberg (2009)
11. Fiege, L., Mezini, M., Mühl, G., Buchmann, A.P.: Engineering Event-Based Systems with Scopes. In: Magnusson, B. (ed.) ECOOP 2002. LNCS, vol. 2374, pp. 309–333. Springer, Heidelberg (2002)
12. Moreno-Garcia, D., Estublier, J.: « Model-driven Design, Development, Execution and Management of Service-based Applications. In: SCC, Hawaii, USA (July 2012)
13. Estublier, J., Vega, G.: Managing Multiple Applications in a Service Platform. In: Proceeding PESOS: Workshop on Principles of Engineering Service-Oriented Systems, at ICSE Zurich (June 2012)

Service Oriented Requirements Engineering: Practitioner's Perspective

Muneera Bano Sahibzada and Didar Zowghi

Research Center for Human Centered Technology Design
Faculty of Engineering and Information Technology
University of Technology Sydney, Australia
{Muneera.Bano,Didar.Zowghi}@uts.edu.au

Abstract. Over a decade ago Service Oriented Architecture (SOA) was introduced to provide better alignment between business requirements and IT solutions. During this period a great deal of research interest has emerged from academia and industry alike, to promote this new style of software development. The promise was that SOA based development will improve reusability, agility, platform independence and dynamic discovery, reconfiguration and change management. In spite of all the promises and enhancement in tools and technologies, the service oriented software development continues to face various challenges especially in Requirements Engineering. In this paper we present a qualitative study of Service Oriented Requirements Engineering. Data was collected by conducting interviews with practitioners from IT companies in Sydney, who are experienced in working on SOA based projects. The objective was to explore the issues and challenges faced during requirements analysis in service oriented software development. The results show that Service-Oriented software development has not only inherited existing issues of traditional Requirements Engineering but has also introduced new challenges. The technology has become advanced in SOA but the issues related to the organizational and business aspect of service oriented development need more attention for achieving true benefits of this technology.

Keywords: Service Oriented Software Engineering, Requirements Engineering, issues and challenges.

1 Introduction

The Service Oriented Architecture (SOA) based software development was introduced with promises to bring into reality the true form of reusability along with agility, platform independence and dynamic discovery, reconfiguration and change management. Service Orientation is referred in IT paradigm by various terms such as Service Oriented Architecture (SOA), Software as a Service (SaaS), Service Oriented Computing (SOC), and Service Oriented Software Engineering (SOSE). In current market conditions the development teams are under pressure to meet deadlines while producing quality software within approved budget that would at the same time satisfy the customers. Reusability of

A. Ghose et al. (Eds.): ICSOC 2012, LNCS 7759, pp. 380–392, 2013.
© Springer-Verlag Berlin Heidelberg 2013

software was considered to reduce cost and time for development and various solutions emerged as a result of research on development methodologies. Service-Oriented software development is an evolutionary form of Component based Software Development (CBSD) and Object Oriented (OO) development with the difference that it uses web services instead of objects or packaged components [14]. The use of service requires a contractual agreement between service provider and service consumer. Reusing existing components in form of services in collaborative and distributed environment presented a very interesting perspective for saving time and cost of development. But at the same time it introduces a number of new software engineering challenges [1]. A great deal of research efforts were put into the directions of achieving the true spirit of SOA from academia and industry alike [10] [11].

According to Zave [20], Requirements Engineering (RE) can be defined as: *"the branch of software engineering concerned with the real-world goals for, functions of, and constraints on software systems. It is also concerned with the relationship of these factors to precise specifications of software behavior, and to their evolution over time and across software families."*

RE is considered the most crucial part of software development that establishes the goals and objectives of the system by consulting with all the relevant stakeholders. If these goal and objectives are not articulated correctly at the outset, the end product can not fully satisfy the intended users, no matter how much time and resources are spent for the development. According to Karl Weigner [21], *"If you don't get the requirements right, it doesn't matter how well you do anything else."*

The term Service Oriented Requirements Engineering (SORE) was first used in 2003 by Eck and Wieringa [2], to show that it is different from traditional RE, with two different dimensions as a result of separation of service development and Service-Oriented software development. Service-Oriented solutions have to consider both service provider and service consumer. The service provider needs to understand the functional and non-functional aspects of the service being offered, which has to compete in marketplace with other services. This requires understanding of potential consumers of that service. For service consumers, the challenge is to find the correct solution to the business needs of the organization.

In spite of all the improvements in tools and technologies, the service oriented software development is facing various challenges especially in requirements engineering. Technology is an essential part of providing solutions in form of services, but ignoring the importance of enterprise's business and IT requirements would results in project failure. In SOSE, the developers have software components ready for them in form of services, available over internet or intranet. After requirements elicitation, the ideal situation is to align service to meet business requirements. The organizations require quick solutions and the developers are usually under pressure of tight deadlines. Instead they try to provide solution where requirements are compromised based on available services. This would result in unsatisfied customers and failure of project even though the technology is highly promising.

In this paper, we present findings of interviews conducted from 13 practitioners from different companies in Sydney, who have experience in SOA based software development. The interviews were part of our larger exploratory research project. The objective was to explore the issues and challenges faced by the practitioners in industry in RE phase during Service-Oriented software development.

The rest of the paper is organized as follows; Section 2 outlines our research strategy that we undertook for our investigation. Section 3 gives details of interview design. Section 4 presents analyzed results from interviews. In Section 5, we discuss the various implications of the results. Section 6 presents conclusion and future work.

2   Research Strategy

Our interviews were one part of a larger research plan. The overall aim of our research project is to improve RE in Service-Oriented software development. We divided the task in two phases. The first phase is to understand the problem space and the second is to propose a solution that would bring improvements to the problems of RE in SOSE. Figure 1 depicts all the steps involved in both phases along with their objectives. We have completed Phase 1 and in current study we are presenting the results of industrial interviews, which is the last step of phase 1.

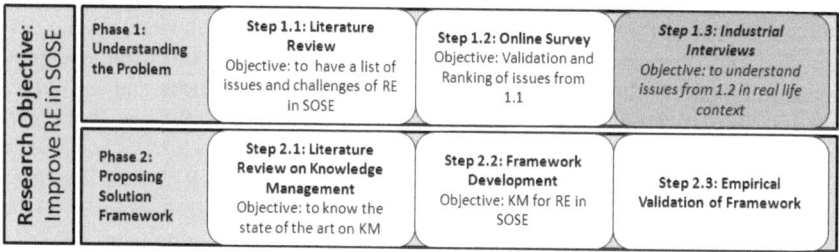

Fig. 1. Complete Research Plan

Our exploration of understanding the problem phase was carried out in three steps. First we performed a comprehensive review of research literature [14], in order to develop a list of issues and challenges reported. As a second step we conducted an online survey [15] [16], and asked the practitioners to confirm and rank the existence of the issues and challenges that we had identified in step 1. Based on the results from survey, we developed a series of questions and approached 13 practitioners working in different IT companies in Sydney for face-to-face interviews. Following is a brief description of the first two steps.

2.1   Literature Review

SOSE had been the subject of research community from different perspectives. Many methods, techniques and tools have been proposed by different mega projects and research teams. These efforts include *"Service Centric System Engineering (SeCSE* [3])*", "Service Oriented Development In a Unified fraMework (SODIUM* [4])*", "Software Engineering for Service Oriented Overlay Computers (SENSORIA* [5])*", "Service Oriented Modeling and Architecture (SOMA)* [6][7]*", "Service Oriented Architecture Framework (SOAF* [8])*", "Service Development Lifecycle Methodology (SDLM* [9])*"*. The real benefits of any research efforts can only be verified when it is applied in a real setting. With the exception of few (e.g. IBM), most of the methods proposed to date are not adapted by industry [11], and hence lack empirical validation of their true value. Only 8 challenges of RE in SOSE have been investigated empirically till 2008 [12]. Failure of the Universal Description Discovery and Integration (UDDI) [13] and the incident of Amazon web service failure last year [21] has put a question mark on the whole idea of service oriented solutions. There is a need for further empirical work in this area with real life projects to provide feedback for improvement in current methods and practices and also to enrich the knowledge in SOA domain and open further research directions [14].

The aim of our literature review was to extract the list of issues and challenges of RE in SOSE that has been reported in published research. We conducted an exhaustive search for publications that were available on online electronic databases. Their inclusion in our review was based on the criteria that they should be pointing out any problem or challenge that is faced during RE for Service-Oriented software development. The challenges identified from the literature were published in [14].

2.2   Online Survey

The purpose of conducting the online survey was to validate the list of issues identified in the research literature, from practitioners working on Service-Oriented system development. The population comprised of the practitioners who have worked on Service-Oriented projects either as technical team member or as a researcher. Due to the fact that it was online web survey, we used convenient and non probabilistic sampling. The instrument for survey was questionnaire based on the identified factors from issues. The items in questionnaire used Likert scale of five levels to measure agreement to the issues. We administered the survey on the web and sent the link through email to invite the practitioners around the world using online special interest groups. A total of 117 responses were received world wide. The survey provided us with verification and ranking of the issues and we were able to refine our list of issues from step 1 so that it includes the important issues on which they all agreed. The results of the analysis of survey data can be summarized in the identification of the following top five important issues [15] [16], *(1) Alignment of business requirements and services (2) Non functional requirements gathering and assessment (3) Iterative service discovery process (4) Integration of Knowledge Management strategy to SOSE life cycle (5) Requirements change management.*

3   Interview Design

Interviews are considered to provide rich qualitative data when a deeper insight of a phenomenon is required. Our survey provided us with surface level of understanding about the issues of RE in SOSE. Interviews were our choice for a deeper and vertical understanding of the issues in their real life context. It was the best choice to get the opinion and reflections of practitioners by talking to them face to face and giving them freedom to express their thoughts on the subject. Based on the refined list from online survey, we designed the interview questions. We presented these issues to the interviewees and asked to them to provide their view on it with reference to the projects on which they have worked.

The criterion for participation was that the interviewee should be a practitioner in industry and should have experience of working as a development team member in Service-Oriented project. The practitioners were contacted using social networking approach followed by snow-ball or referral sampling technique. The interviews were semi structured and open ended. The interviewees were asked to provide their views on the issues with reference to the examples of the SOA based projects they had experienced. The interview questions were focused on the five issues identified (section 2.2) but for further understanding we took advantage of face-to-face interview style to raise follow up questions where ever it was required. Out of these 13 interviews, 2 were conducted online using Skype and rest were conducted face-to-face. Interviews took place during June-August 2012 in Sydney and each lasted between 30 minutes to one hour. They were audio recorded and partly transcribed.The names of the interviewees, the companies and the projects will not be disclosed in this paper as per confidentiality requirement of Human Research Ethics Committee (HREC) at UTS [17] for approval of this research. We will present here the results that we obtained after the qualitative analysis.

The 13 interviewees, who participated in this study, had diverse job experience in various IT based companies. Following are the profiles of their job experience;

1. *Program Manager at a Telecom Company in Sydney; who also owns a small consultancy company where the two Business Analysts are present in Sydney and rest of the development team is in India. The Interviewee had 20 years of working experience in Software industry in Sydney and has managed various Service Oriented Projects.*
2. *Independent ICT consultant in a large organization; also having past experience of working as Project Manager, Senior Business Analyst and Developer.*
3. *Business Architect; having over 10 years of experience working in Software industry as a Programmer, Business Process Analyst, Business Analyst, and IT Consultant. Currently the focus of his work is on integrated context-aware adaptive cloud computing environments (e.g. integrated cloud, social networks, mobile computing) for e-Government and e-Business Solutions.*
4. *SOA integration specialist; who has worked on 4 SOA based projects in Canada.*
5. *Systems Engineering Manager; Director of a Systems Engineering and Safety Management Consulting Company.*
6. *Senior Equity Trading System Development Architect; having experience of building low level mission critical, fault tolerant systems as well as web n-tier based enterprise systems using Service Oriented Architecture based design patterns in finance, telecommunications, retail industries, research organizations.*
7. *Director of IT Consultancy company in Sydney; has over 20 years of experience in the IT industry, in Australia and the UK. The interviewee worked in sales and delivery, focusing specifically on SOA-related activities.*
8. *Business Analyst at IT based company providing solutions to Educational Sector; experience of working on multiple SOA related projects in UK and Australia.*
9. *Knowledge Engineer and Interim CTO (Chief Technology Officer), Coach, consultant and trainer in agile development, IT Leadership, project management, business analysis and business process improvement.*
10. *SOA Service Design Team Lead and Integration Architect/ Lead SOA Service Designer with more than 15 years of experience as Solution Architect, Designer and Developer.*
11. *Product Delivery Manager, Managing development team, ensuring delivery of software product in an agile and lean manner, grow and directing the team to be more efficient and self-running.*
12. *Director of IT Consultancy Company in Sydney, with experience of Enterprise Architect, J2EE Manager and Senior Java Architect.*
13. *Developer in IT based company in Sydney for the last two years; mainly responsible for the detailed designed and implementation of the projects and does not have direct influence on the decisions related to the RE phase but works alongside with business analysts in the team to provide guidance on the technical feasibility of the system requirements.*

4   Findings from Interviews

The results from all 13 interviews were analyzed using qualitative analysis technique such as content analysis. The transcriptions of the interviews were analyzed for the thoughts and concepts presenting for each of the issues. In following we present the aggregated results which emerged after analysis with respect to the challenges of RE in SOSE. Along with the results we present the table for comparison of our findings from all three steps of our exploration.

4.1   Alignment of Business Requirements and Services

One of the differences between SORE and traditional RE is the process of matching and selecting available services against requirements. A service is developed free of context and the environmental details where it would be used. It is up to the business analysts to understand the functionality of existing services, which is context free, and then align them to business requirements which have a specific context attached to them. All the interviewee considered alignment of business requirements to services as most challenging and important due to following reasons:

- The development team pushes the organizations to compromise or modify the requirements according to the available solutions.
- Due to uncertainties or ambiguities in elicited requirements, incorrect services get selected resulting in a system that is useless for the customers.
- The service granularity or abstraction sometimes does not align properly with the requirements, which makes the task more challenging.
- A consistent interpretation of business requirements is required for correct alignment to the service.

Table 1. Alignment of Business Requirements and Services

Findings from Literature Survey	Findings from Online Survey	Findings from Interviews	Conclusion
The main difference of SORE and RE is the alignment of business needs to available service, which is the most challenging part.	The alignment of business requirements and services is challenging due to the fact that they are not at the same level of granularity or abstraction.	The service granularity or abstraction sometimes does not align properly with the requirements, which makes the task more challenging. Sometimes the development team pushes the organizations to compromise or modify the requirements according to the available solutions.	This challenge is the most crucial from RE point of view as it would decide whether the resulting system is what it was suppose to be. According to our analysis each job role in development team has a different perspective on this issue. The Project Managers would deal with this issue with consideration to organizational policy. Business analysts would consider the business needs of the customer and performing gap analysis. The developers would think about the feasibility of the alignment while considering the available technical support.

4.2   Non Functional Requirements Gathering and Assessment

Interviewees stated that non functional requirements in SOSE should be the part of the Service Level Agreement. A service is usually developed for a group of customer without considering a specific context where it will be used. Every organization can have varying criteria for quality and therefore satisfying the non functional aspects (e.g. security, scalability, availability, reliability, performance etc.) for unknown group of customers is another challenging part of RE in SOSE. Usually it is required from the service provider to publish the security and trust related issues along with the functional aspects of the service but in many cases it never happens. Due to variance in the quality level of services, at the time of composition (integration), compatibility among services provided by different providers would be an issue. Customers are mostly not aware of these issues until they actually use the system. This increases the overhead of testing on the part of development team, whereas ideally a service is considered to have been tested for the quality related concerns. For most organization, the matter of trust is crucial when it comes to using services from a third party. The organization may not have an open policy for services from unknown service providers. According to one of the respondent, for safety critical software, the use of loosely coupled services from third party is not even feasible as they have a rigorous process for safety critical requirements evaluation and testing. In case of services, passing this strict evaluation would not be possible as the organizations are not usually provided with the source code.

Table 2. Non Functional Requirements gathering and assessment

Findings from Literature Survey	Findings from Online Survey	Findings from Interviews	Conclusion
NFR can be used as criteria for selection of service against requirements when multiple options are available but gathering and assessing NFR in Service-Oriented development is very challenging.	Service design needs to satisfy the required NFR while considering target consumer group but it is challenging as the users are unknown. If NFR are not satisfied it leads to changes in requirements after the system is deployed which can be very costly.	Services are developed without knowing the context of the environment in which they will be used. Every organization has its own criteria of minimum level of required quality. Testing effort is increased to assess quality for specific context. Some domains are safety critical; the idea of service orientation is not a feasible choice for them.	NFR such as security, scalability and reliability are the most important quality aspects in selecting services in a specific domain against a particular requirement. Organizational policy plays a crucial role in deciding the quality criteria for the system.

4.3   Iterative Service Discovery Process

The idea of iterative discovery process is useful when the development team has to elicit requirements from the stakeholders. The customers are usually not aware of what they actually want and keep changing their mind about their requirements. The requirements provided by them are usually incomplete and do not match the abstraction and granularity of the available service specification. Following an iterative service discovery process gives an opportunity to present available solutions, which are present in form of services, to customers. They can provide their feedback and hence the services can work as prototypes and would help in completing the requirements, or analyze various options like trade-off between requirements and solutions, cost estimation etc. This method is feasible when we have a large central repository across organizations with service description available in structured form. But this process introduces additional concerns. If the development team is using services within organization, then they already know about the solutions they have. In iterative process, service providers try to encourage the customers into accepting the available solutions. From RE perspective, it might not be a good idea to jump to the solution space without fully understanding the problem space. For using third party services from a distributed central repository, this process would be helpful for business analyst in negotiating requirements with users. But the concept of global central repository like UDDI failed around 2006 due to various difficulties faced by developers in using it [13], so this idea might only be useful within organization with huge repository of services available.

Table 3. Iterative Service Discovery Process

Findings from Literature Survey	Findings from Online Survey	Findings from Interviews	Conclusion
As in traditional RE, incomplete requirements are an important challenge but in SOSE, we can start with flexible incomplete requirements and iteratively discover solutions in form of services while we move towards completing our requirements.	Flexible or incomplete requirements can give room to further issues. Some requirements cannot be flexible or compromised. Once requirements are complete discovering services to match those requirements would be more focused thus reducing any duplicate effort. Services are part of the solution space not the problem space, in moving back and forth we are not focusing on the problem properly.	This type of development lifecycle is feasible in large organizations with huge central repository with properly managed information about available services. The problem with this approach is that there is a chance that the development team would use iterative process to manipulate customers in accepting available solutions rather then focusing on what they actually want. The development team would immediately jump to solution rather than understand the problem properly.	Although services can be used as a prototypes to help in the process of elicitation, but the whole point of requirements engineering is to understand the problem space before jumping directly to the solutions. It would be depending largely on the intentions of the development team whether they want to make the process customer-oriented or to develop what is easy for them.

4.4   Integration of Knowledge Management Strategy to SOSE Lifecycle

SOSE requires organizations to take initiative in using IT infrastructure of SOA to bring solutions to their business needs. Knowledge Management (KM) requires organizational strategy for identifying, acquiring, storing, and sharing the knowledge to improve the business and benefit to the organization. According to the interviewees, the benefits of KM are proven for project planning, document management and service versioning control. They pointed out that it is critical for an SOA based organization to take initiatives for implementing a well defined KM strategy to meet demands of dynamic market conditions where there is inevitable change in technology and human resource. In the last 20 years many methods, tools and techniques for KM have been proposed in the research literature. All of the interviewee confirmed the use of various KM Systems, but only large organizations had a proper strategy for implementation of KM. According to the respondents, for small organizations KM brings overhead for the development team in terms of knowledge codification efforts. The respondents referred to it as: *"tedious hard work consuming a whole day for filling up various data forms"*. For the development team, there seems to be a need for great deal of visible effort for invisible benefits. The organizations have to keep track of the Knowledge Base (KB), and specialized personnel are needed for that purpose, whose task is to make sure that the KB is up to date.

Table 4. Integration of Knowledge Management Strategy to SOSE lifecycle

Findings from Literature Survey	Findings from Online Survey	Findings from Interviews	Conclusion
KM would help in improving RE in SOSE as it has been proved to bring improvements in RE for traditional software development and CBSD. But it requires time and efforts to implement a KM strategy in any organization.	KM would not eliminate all the issues completely, but would definitely improve the process and would help in better understanding of requirements and lead to better design and composition. The concepts of KM are already in use in SOSE e.g. service registry. But for a KM strategy resources in terms of cost, management and implementation time are required before actual benefits would be visible. There is also a concern that it might increase complexity of development lifecycle.	KM would help in improving RE in SOSE but organizational initiative is crucial for implementing a KM strategy. Also it increases work overhead on development team for managing knowledge. Specialized human resource is required to properly look after the KM strategy implementation. It is a lot of visible effort for development team for the benefits that are invisible to them.	It is challenging to implement KM as it requires time and budget and also knowledge is a double edged sword; it is very crucial to know how much organizational learning is required and how to make the best use of it. A proper KM strategy encompasses organizational, business and IT aspects of a development environment to assist different roles of development team (i.e. Project managers, Business analysts etc.) in carrying out their respective tasks.

4.5   Requirement Change Management

One of the promises of SOA based solutions was the agility of process where changes in requirements can be easily accommodated where services can be easily replaced according to new requirements. Respondents acknowledge that it is easy to accommodate changes in SOSE but it presents various challenges;

-   Replacing an existing service with new might degrade the whole performance of system after integration.
-   Change of service is very easy in SOSE, but change in requirement may not be that easy especially when requirements and services are not aligned properly in granularity and abstraction.
-   A change within one service requires careful impact analysis as this service can be under the use of multiple clients and the change might not be what everyone would wish for. In this case proper versioning of services is required.

Table 5. Requirement Change Management

Findings from Literature Survey	Findings from Online Survey	Findings from Interviews	Conclusion
In Service-Oriented Paradigm Requirements Change Management should have been easier than traditional software development but it remains to be challenging.	Changes in service requirements are often as a result of end users not being part of the process early in the project.	Changing services is technically easy in SOSE, but change in requirements may not be that easy especially when requirements and services are not aligned properly in granularity and abstraction. Replacing an existing service with a new one might degrade the whole performance of the system after integration. A thorough impact analysis is required as one service can be under the use of multiple clients. A proper versioning system is required for this purpose.	Change is inevitable in current dynamic environment and one of the main objectives of SOA was to enable the development team to easily accommodate change. But it is still challenging for the development team to decide on how to accommodate a particular change request with considerations to system's business requirements and technical details.

4.6 Additional Challenges

Some additional challenges of SORE were identified by the interviewees.
- The research in SOA is focusing too much on giving technological solutions where as the social aspect is not explored properly under this paradigm.
- Lack of real users during RE and testing phase of software development would result in unsatisfied users that could lead to project failure.
- The traditional RE challenge of ambiguities and incomplete requirements is exacerbated due to the distributed and collaborative nature of development style.

5 Discussion

The interviews have not only confirmed most of the issues that were identified as challenging in our online survey, but have also provided more details from real life context. The additional outcome of our interview analysis is that in real life context, the human-factor was found to be more challenging while considering all the issues of RE in SOSE. It is evident that further efforts are required for evaluating the existing practices and providing improved solutions to the social aspect of RE in Service-Oriented paradigm.

With the global marketplace and the focus of IT infrastructure in providing solutions to business needs of organizations, the software industry has adopted the methods that allow distributed, collaborative and dynamic development. SOSE was proposed to deal with a highly dynamic environment for software development by ensuring agility and reusability as central concepts of its philosophy. Over the last ten years improvements have been made as a result of research in technologies and standard protocols for network infrastructure to support distributed development and deployment of services. The technology is important, but how to make best use of that technology by understanding the real objective of the system to build and satisfaction of those who will ultimately use it, is far more crucial. According to all the intervie-wees, agile methodology is frequently used in Service-Oriented software develop-ment. The objective of adopting agile methodology in SOSE was to make it human-centered, but unless the issues of RE are addressed properly, the results would be in form of conflicts between customers, who are not aware of technology, and the devel-opment team, who think only in technical way. This makes the role of RE in SOSE very important. It emphasizes the need for an understanding of the objectives of the system to build, business needs of organizations, full functionality of a service, the context of domain where it will be used and most importantly the group of users who will actually be using that service. Otherwise we might end up with services and ser-vice based systems that are useless though technologically very sound.

6   Conclusion and Future Work

In this paper, we presented the findings from the interviews we conducted as a part of our exploratory study. The focus of research in this field is largely on technological aspect of service orientation. But equally important is the acceptance of the solutions provided to customer developed under this paradigm. Without customer satisfaction and approval the results would be considered a failure no matter how advance the technology would become. From the analysis a pattern emerged, where the issues of SORE could be seen as belonging to one or more of the following categories;

-    *Technical aspect: where the main concerns are related to the tools, techniques, methods and processes that can help in achieving the objectives. Developers take this perspective of requirements during implementation phase.*
-    *Organizational aspect: which focuses on policies and decisions that give directions for achieving objectives. The role of the project manager is to deal with this aspect through-out software development lifecycle.*
-    *Business aspect: which would focus on the customers/clients and the social and psycho-logical factors that would help them understand the business dynamics for achieving their objective. Business/Requirements analysts and consultants are more focused on this aspect in early phases of development.*

All the issues identified from our analysis could belong to more than one of the three categories. Furthermore the relative importance of each of these categories is depen-dant on the role played by the practitioners. According to Mitroff and Linstone [18] technical perspective of any issue would be just a single view of a multifaceted prob-lem and currently is used mostly by organizations to deal with various issues. They suggest multiple perspective concept, with two additional perspectives; organizational and individual. Any solution to the problem would turn out to be useless unless all three perspectives are considered in the process. Following the same concept for the three categories that we have identified in our analysis, the interconnectedness of these three concepts suggest that to improve SORE, it's not just the technology that requires attention but at the same time the social and organizational aspects re-quires equal importance. The highly dynamic IT industry makes continuous learning essential for the organizations to become successful. The knowledge of organization is an important asset to help them improve themselves. According to the results of all three steps of our research, a KM Strategy seems a promising solution in bringing improvements in RE phase of Service-Oriented software development. It can assist in all three aspects described above to overcome the hurdles that currently prevent SOA from achieving its true goals.

Our next step is to evaluate the impact of organizational KM strategy on Service-Oriented software development and to evaluate its effectiveness in addressing some of the important challenges we have identified in our research.

References

[1] Stojanovic, Z., Dahanayake, A.: Service-oriented software system engineering: challenges and practices. Idea Group Publishing (2005)

[2] van Eck, P.A.T., Wieringa, R.J., Gordijn, J., Janssen, M.: Requirements Engineering for Service-Oriented Computing: A Position PaperIn: First International Workshop on e-Services at ICEC 2003, Pittsburgh, Pennsylvania, USA, pp. 23–28 (2003)

[3] Emic, C., Cefriel, E.S.I., Eng, A.: Service Centric System Engineering

[4] Topouzidou, S.: SODIUM, service-oriented development in a unified framework. Final report ISTFP6-004559 (2007), http://www.atc.gr/sodium

[5] Wirsing, M., Hölzl, M. (eds.): SENSORIA. LNCS, vol. 6582. Springer, Heidelberg (2011)

[6] Arsanjani, A.: Service-oriented modeling and architecture. IBM Developer Works (2004)

[7] Arsanjani, A.: Service-oriented modeling and architecture: How to identify, specify and realize services for your SOA (2009), http://www.ibm.com/developerworks

[8] Erradi, A., Anand, S., Kulkarni, N.: SOAF: An architectural framework for service definition and realization. In: IEEE International Conference on Services Computing, SCC 2006, pp. 151–158 (2006)

[9] Papazoglou, M.P., Van Den Heuvel, W.J.: Service-oriented design and development methodology. International Journal of Web Engineering and Technology 2(4), 412–442 (2006)

[10] Kontogogos, A., Avgeriou, P.: An overview of software engineering approaches to service oriented architectures in various fields. In: 18th IEEE International Workshops on Enabling Technologies: Infrastructures for Collaborative Enterprises, WETICE 2009, pp. 254–259 (2009)

[11] Ramollari, E., Dranidis, D., Simons, A.J.H.: A survey of service oriented development methodologies. In: 2nd European Young Researchers Workshop on Service Oriented Computing, Leicester, UK (2007)

[12] Gu, Q., Lago, P.: Exploring service-oriented system engineering challenges: a systematic literature review. In: Service Oriented Computing and Applications, vol. 3(3), pp. 171–188 (2009)

[13] Atkinson, C., Bostan, P., Hummel, O., Stoll, D.: A practical approach to web service discovery and retrieval. In: IEEE International Conference on Web Services, ICWS 2007, pp. 241–248 (2007)

[14] Bano, M., Ikram, N.: Issues and Challenges of Requirement Engineering in Service Oriented Software Development. In: 2010 Fifth International Conference on Software Engineering Advances (ICSEA), pp. 64–69 (2010)

[15] Bano, M., Ikram, N.: KM-SORE: Knowledge Management for Service Oriented Requirements Engineering. In: The Sixth International Conference on Software Engineering Advances, ICSEA 2011, pp. 494–499 (2011)

[16] Bano, M., Ikram, N., Niazi, M.: Knowledge Management in Service Oriented Requirements Engineering (KM – SORE), Keele technical Report (TR/2011-02). School of Computing and Mathematics, Keele University, Keele, UK (2011) ISSN: 1353: 7776

[17] http://www.gsu.uts.edu.au/policies/hrecpolicy.html

[18] Mitroff, I.I., Linstone, H.A.: The unbounded mind: Breaking the chains of traditional business thinking. Oxford University Press, USA (1995)

[19] http://www.computing.co.uk/ctg/news/2189825/amazon-loses-customers-web-services-failure

[20] Zave, P.: Classification of Research Efforts in Requirements Engineering. ACM Computing Surveys 29(4), 315–321 (1997)

[21] Wiegers, K.E.: In search of excellent requirements. The Journal of the Quality Assurance Institute 1 (1995)

Phd Symposium Track: Message from Chairs

Welcome to the PhD Symposium, International Conference on Service Oriented Computing 2012 (ICSOC2012) in Shanghai, China. The ICSOC PhD Symposium 2012 is an international forum for PhD students working in all the areas addressed by the ICSOC conference (http://www.icsoc.org). We particularly encourage students that are still developing their research methodology or are somewhere in the middle of their research program to submit to this symposium.

This year, there are 12 submissions from Australia, Canada, China, France, Germany and Italy respectively. Each submission was reviewed by three program committee members. After rigorous review process, the program committee finally accepted 6 papers for presentation. During the symposium, we were happy to see good attendance and active discussions. This is particularly important to young researchers.

Finally, we would like to thank all authors, their supervisors, and all conference organizers for their support and contribution to this successful event.

PHD Symposium Chairs

Olivier Perrin, Nancy 2 University, France

Jianmin Wang, Tsinghua University, China

Yan Wang, Macquarie University, Australia

A. Ghose et al. (Eds.): ICSOC 2012, LNCS 7759, p. 393–393, 2013.

Data Consistency Enforcement
on Business Process Transactions

Xi Liu*

State Key Laboratory for Novel Software Technology at Nanjing University
Department of Computer Science and Technology, Nanjing University, China
liux@seg.nju.edu.cn

Abstract. Transactions are common in business processes (BPs). Consistency on data, which is defined as satisfaction of a set of data integrity constraints, is one of the basic properties for business process transactions (BPTs). This requires a BPT to bring the BP execution from one consistent state to another consistent state. It is desirable to ensure within BP executions that every BPT preserves data consistency. Besides, the earlier an inconsistency is detected the less recovery is necessary. It is studied in this paper how to detect and recover from potential future inconsistency as early as possible in a BPT execution. We propose a *runtime proactive* mechanism enforcing consistency on BPTs, called "transaction consistency guarding", based on *symbolic execution* of BPEL `scopes` for bounded length and correct design of fault and compensation handlers.

1 Introduction

Data are important assets for any business to make decisions and gain global competitiveness. Transactions are common in business processes (BPs). *Consistency on data* is one of the most desired properties for business process transactions (BPTs). That is, business data must adhere to a set of integrity constraints (ICs) [14] both when the transaction just starts and when the transaction just completes.

In most current business process models, data management is outside BP management, and is carried out by underlying database management systems (DBMSs). Consequently, the vital task of keeping data consistent belongs to the DBMSs. However, this "detached" method is problematic, as argued in [11]. Besides, compared to database transactions [14], BPTs often involve interactions and collaboration with parties and applications outside the BP, and can last for a long duration. Transactional mechanisms in DBMSs, such as roll-back, locking, etc. [14], do not work for BPTs [6,2]. Compensation is used instead for recovery from failure. It is therefore desirable to have BPs responsible for enforcing data consistency on BPTs.

Example 1. Consider an online shopping center BPMart (partially shown in Fig. 1) whose data are managed in an underlying database. Assume IC γ relates the inventory available quantity to the business revenue and product price; defined as $\gamma ::= avail\_qty \geq (revenue/price \times 10\%)$, where *revenue* and *price* are also attributes of relations stored

---

* Supported by the National Grand Fundamental Research 973 Program of China (No.2009CB320702).

A. Ghose et al. (Eds.): ICSOC 2012, LNCS 7759, pp. 394–399, 2013.

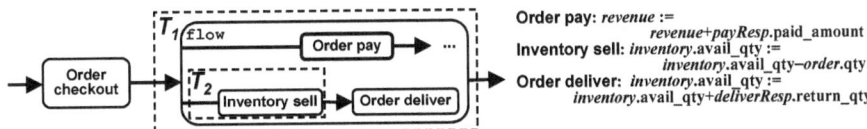

Fig. 1. A segment in BPMart, where round-corner boxes denote actions (details not included), dotted boxed denotes BPEL scopes (fault and compensation handler not included). Updates to the database by the actions correspond to calculations listed on the right.

in the database. The available quantity is updated in "Inventory sell" in BPT T_2: attribute *avail_qty* of the instance of *Inventory* corresponding to *inventory* is updated to *inventory.avail_qty − order.qty*, where *order* and *inventory* are variables denoting the instances of business data classes (stored in database as relations) *Order* and *Inventory*, resp. If "Inventory sell" sets *avail_qty* to a "bad" value not satisfying γ, the database integrity is destroyed when T_2 commits. Since the calculation in "Inventory sell" is deterministic, with the value of *inventory.avail_qty*, *revenue* and *price*, such inconsistency can be detected as soon as T_2 starts. Thus, T_2 aborts immediately and prevents inconsistency caused by the update in "Inventory sell".

Preservation of data consistency by BPs was studied in [11], in which the "guard injection" technique is developed on rule-based workflows. The updates that might violate some ICs are blocked before they are about to execute. No transactional structure is considered in guard injection.

It is preferred to detect potential data inconsistency as early as possible in a BPT execution, so that the BPT aborts immediately and the compensation would be simpler in order to recover the consistency. BPTs are defined using scopes in BPEL. So we look into the Transaction Consistency Problem (TCP): will data inconsistency be detected when a BPEL scope starts? Unfortunately, TCP is generally undecidable.

We developed the *transaction consistency guarding* mechanism to *proactively* enforce consistency of BPEL scopes at runtime. To tackle the undecidability of TCP, only scope executions within bounded length is considered, and strategies like postponed checking and conservativeness are used to check IC satisfaction until all relevant messages are received and assume variables not from messages will cause IC violation.

The proposed transaction consistency guarding mechanism symbolically executes the BPEL scopes for bounded number of steps. When the commitment point of the scope is reached within the bounded length, and inconsistency is detected, the BPEL scope aborts (as if a fault occurs). The scope's fault handler is triggered to recovery consistency, in which sub-scopes are compensated to reverse the committed effect. This mechanism requires correct design of BPTs with fault handling and compensation (such as BPEL scopes). Issues concerning correctness of the proposed mechanism are also discussed: correct design of BPTs as well as soundness and conservative completeness.

The remainder of the paper is organized as follows. Section 2 compares our mechanism with related work. The transaction consistency guarding is introduced in Section 3. Correctness issues are discussed in Section 4. Section 5 concludes the paper.

2   Related Work

Data manipulation and compensable transactions are supported in most BP models. In BPEL, when a variable value does not conform to its definition, faults are thrown and handled. However, current SOA specifications and BP models (e.g., BPEL, BPMN, YAWL, WS-Coordination) put no requirement on effect of transactions. Thus there is no way to ensure data consistency. Besides, web service XML Schemas usually do not constraint inter-related data. Although static analysis on data dependencies in BPEL processes helps the understanding of dataflow [10,16], and verification against data-related temporal logic properties checks the process design [5,4], they offer no guidance for data consistency on BPTs.

In the field of database theory, enforcement of ICs is not new. ICs can be statically verified before short-lived database transactions [1], or checked at runtime [14]. Triggers are a powerful tool to "fix" constraint violations as a reactive means [3]. However, it is often difficult to locate the origin of the constraint violation and fix the error in BPs. It was revealed in [9] the difficulty of IC preservation in distributed databases and investigated the approach to maintain distributed ICs by reducing the necessity to look at remote databases according to specific updates. In our problem, however, concrete updates are unknown. And it is unclear that shared DBMSs would realize protocols to maintain data consistency in loosely coupled databases (e.g., [8]).

Compensation is introduced in Sagas [6]. Although compensation is supported in most BP models, consistency cannot be automatically recovered [7]. In contrast with requiring nothing on the compensation, theoretical work such as cCSP requires the whole world must be restored [2]. This can help to recover consistency. However, due to the open-world assumption of BPTs, such requirement is hardly practical. It is also possible to extend the DBMSs to manage BPTs by adding new intermediate layers, e.g. [15]. But this introduces more complexity and has no feedback to BPs.

The "guard injection" mechanism is developed on rule-based workflows [11] to strengthen the enableness condition of update actions that might violate ICs at design time. However, guard injection is not for runtime detection of violations in future executions of transactions, and therefore do not solve TCP.

3   Transaction Consistency Guarding

Presented in this section is how the guarding is performed at runtime. First the Transaction Consistency Problem is formulated with the undecidable result in general case. The framework for transaction consistency guarding is given next.

3.1   Transaction Consistency Problem

BPEL is a widely used BP modeling language supporting compensable BPT as scopes. Key business data are stored in DBMSs in relational model. For simplicity, we assumed that relational data is supported in BPEL. The semantics of BPEL can be modeled by Petri net [12] or process algebra [13]. The execution of a BPEL process with data access is defined, in this paper, as an sequence of states (s_i, DB_i), denoting the BPEL process state s_i (with variable valuation) together with database snapshot DB_i, and transitions t_i, denoting firing a basic process step (such as a basic activity), where $i \geq 0$.

Transaction Consistency Problem (TCP): *Given a database (snapshot) satisfing a set of ICs* **K**, *a BPEL process* W *with a scope-based transition T, when the execution of T starts in* W, *will it terminates in a state whose database snapshot violates* **K**?

Theorem 1. *Transaction Consistency Problem is undecidable.*

Theorem 1 implies unsolvability to force abortion at the beginning of exactly the set of "bad" BPTs. The undecidability comes from the fact that general BPEL processes (and its scopes) are Turing-complete; and satisfaction problem of first-order formulas, that is the integrity constraints, are undecidable. However, we take strategies like bounding the length of execution for checking and the "conservativeness", and develop a "sound" solution for TCP.

3.2 Transaction Consistency Guarding Framework

The runtime guarding is performed by checking in symbolic execution of the BPEL scopes. When violation is detected, fault handler of the current scope is triggered to restore the IC related data so that the data consistency is recovered.

In the symbolic execution, the actual database should not be updated. A simulation database supporting instances with symbolic values is assumed. Define the database for symbolic execution be the union of the actual database and the symbolic database.

The mechanism is performed by a "process guard" as an extension to BPEL engines. Let a positive integer k be the given bound. The process guard monitors the execution of the target process W and symbolically executes the scope to check violation for the next k steps. The checking starts whenever: (1) a scope starts; (2) a message is received in a scope's execution; or (3) the execution of a scope has continued k steps or more without a checking. Let the scope in question be denoted T. The checking is performed by symbolic execution from current state s to detect inconsistency in the next k steps. If commitment of T is reached within the k-step symbolic execution, and some IC is violated, T is forced to abort at the state s, i.e., the process guard raise a fault on state s. Running sub-scopes are also aborted; then the parent scope's abortion waits until the fault handling of the sub-scopes finishes. Otherwise, the execution continues.

All possible executions (within the bound) must be traversed. When message variable symbols are involved in symbolically checking of some IC, the checking is skipped and execution continues. Because the symbolic checking is called whenever a message comes, the test is actually "postponed" until all necessary messages are received. But if variable symbols are still involved to evaluate the constraint when all relevant messages are received, these symbols denote internal variables (i.e., the variables whose value do not depend on messages). "Conservative" strategy is taken: such scope aborts.

Example 2. Consider the cases as in Example 1. Suppose when T_2 starts, $avail\_qty = 9$ for the *Inventory* instance corresponding to variable *inventory*, $order.qty = 5$ and $(revenue/price \times 10\%) = 5$. If the bound is enough to finish T_2, inconsistency on γ (see Example 1) is detected in the symbolic execution. Then a fault is raised in T_2. Because no actual update is yet made, consistency is preserved.

Consider scope T_1 in Fig. 1, in which business revenue is updated by the actual paid amount in "Order pay"; and, action "Order deliver" replenishes the inventory with returned products. Assume when T_1 starts, $avail\_qty = 9$ for the *Inventory* instance corresponding to variable *inventory* and $order.qty = 5$. Suppose T_2 starts before "Order pay", so that $(revenue/price \times 10\%) = 4$ when T_2 starts. Then T_2 completes successfully. The satisfaction of γ on T_1 depends on both messages *paidResp* and *deliverResp*. The checking is postponed until both messages are received. If then, γ fails to hold, a fault is raised in T_1. Provided that the fault handler of T_1 with compensation of T_2 can reverse the calculation made on *inventory.avail_qty*, *revenue* and *order.qty*, the consistency on γ is recovered.

4 Correctness of Transaction Consistency Guarding

Correctness of BPTs and Compensation

Transaction consistency guarding mechanism relies on the fault and compensation handler to restore data consistency. Because BPEL relies completely on designers to write the code for fault handling and compensation, and ideal recovery (such as [2]) is impractical, correct design of scopes must be investigated.

There are several issues concerning the compensation correctness. First, certain variables must be selected to be critical to scopes. Such variables affect the consistency on ICs and updates to the databases. Second, correctness criteria for scopes must be defined. Such criteria should require the fault and compensation handler of scopes to restore the value of critical variables to the same value as the scope (instance) starts. Note that the fault can also be raised by the process guard when inconsistency is detected in symbolic execution of the scopes. Third, verification techniques need to be studied to ensure that the scope's design conforms to the correctness criteria. Such verification may be done by theorem proving, program analysis and (bounded) model checking.

Correctness and Variants of Transaction Consistency Guarding

The most desired property of the process safe guarding mechanism is *soundness*: no IC violation throughout the execution. However, it is the fact that, when there is no execution at all, no violation can occur. The notion of completeness is therefore necessary. Recall that to gain soundness, conservative strategy is used. The *conservative completeness* requires that, every execution of the original scope without IC violation or assignment to internal variable (variables do not depend on messages) is also an execution of the guarded process. Provided that the fault and compensation handler of every scope can reverse the changes made on IC-related variables in the scope activity, the consistency guarding mechanism is both sound and conservative complete.

Conservativeness may cause scope abortion when no inconsistency occur in actual executions. However, this is necessary to ensure soundness. If restrictions are made so that first order theory is decidable, conservativeness is not necessary. One example is to confine the arithmetic in scopes as: (a) integers or rational numbers with addition; or (b) real numbers with addition and multiplication. Confining the scopes' structure can also help the verification of scopes against desired transactional properties [4].

5   Conclusion

Consistency enforcement in business process transactions is an interesting problem but is hardly solved. To find future inconsistency as early as possible, we first study the generally undecidable Transaction Consistency Problem. Transaction consistency guarding mechanism is suggested with respect to the given bound and strategies of postponed checking and conservativeness, so that after the proactive checking and recovery by the fault handling and compensation, consistency of the transaction is ensured. The correctness of the mechanism depends on correct design of compensable transactions. The transactions may also be restricted to allow relaxed mechanism (e.g., no conservativeness) and to help the verification of compensation design. Future work can be on issues such as: realization and application of the mechanism, validation on real-life BPs, transaction design assurance and more interesting restriction on transaction structures.

References

1. Benedikt, M., Griffin, T., Libkin, L.: Verifiable properties of database transactions. In: Proc. of Symposium on Principles of Database Systems (PODS), pp. 117–127 (1996)
2. Butler, M., Hoare, S.T., Ferreira, C.: A Trace Semantics for Long-Running Transactions. In: Abdallah, A.E., Jones, C.B., Sanders, J.W. (eds.) CSP 25. LNCS, vol. 3525, pp. 133–150. Springer, Heidelberg (2005)
3. Ceri, S., Widom, J.: Deriving production rules for constraint maintainance. In: Proc. Int. Conf. on Very Large Data Bases (VLDB), pp. 566–577 (1990)
4. Deutsch, A., Hull, R., Patrizi, F., Vianu, V.: Automatic verification of data-centric business processes. In: Proc. of Int. Conf. on Database Theory (ICDT), pp. 252–267 (2009)
5. Fu, X., Bultan, T., Su, J.: Model checking XML manipulating software. In: Proc. Int. symposium on Software Testing and Analysis (ISSTA), pp. 252–262 (2004)
6. Garcia-Molina, H., Salem, K.: Sagas. In: Proc. of Int. Conf. on Management of data (SIGMOD), pp. 249–259 (1987)
7. Greenfield, P., Fekete, A., Jang, J., Kuo, D.: Compensation is not enough. In: Proc. of Int. Conf. on Enterprise Distributed Object Computing (EDOC), pp. 232–239 (2003)
8. Grefen, P., Widom, J.: Protocols for integrity constraint checking in federated databases. Distrib. Parallel Databases 5, 327–355 (1997)
9. Gupta, A., Widom, J.: Local verification of global integrity constraints in distributed databases. In: Proc. of Int. Conf. on Management of Data (SIGMOD), pp. 49–58 (1993)
10. Kopp, O., Khalaf, R., Leymann, F.: Deriving explicit data links in WS-BPEL processes. In: Proc. of Int. Conf. on Services Computing (SCC), pp. 367–376 (2008)
11. Liu, X., Su, J., Yang, J.: Preservation of integrity constraints by workflow. In: Proc. of Int. Conf. on Cooperative Information Systems (CoopIS), pp. 64–81 (2011)
12. Lohmann, N.: A Feature Complete Petri Net Semantics for WS-BPEL 2.0. In: Dumas, M., Heckel, R. (eds.) WS-FM 2007. LNCS, vol. 4937, pp. 77–91. Springer, Heidelberg (2008)
13. Qiu, Z., Wang, S., Pu, G., Zhao, X.: Semantics of BPEL4WS-like fault and compensation handling. In: Proc. of Int. Conf. on Formal Methods, pp. 350–365 (2005)
14. Ramakrishnan, R., Gehrke, J.: Database Management Systems, 3rd edn. McGraw-Hill (2002)
15. Wang, R., Salzberg, B., Lomet, D.: Log-based middleware server recovery with transaction support. The VLDB Journal, 1–24 (2010)
16. Amme, W., Martens, A., Moser, S.: Advanced verification of distributed WS-BPEL business processes incorporating CSSA-based data flow analysis. Int. Journal of Business Process Integration and Management 4(1), 47–59 (2009)

An Auction-Based Approach
for Composite Web Service Selection

Mahboobeh Moghaddam[1,2]

[1] School of Information Technologies, University of Sydney, Australia
[2] National ICT Australia (NICTA), Australian Technology Park
Sydney, NSW 1430, Australia
mahboobe@it.usyd.edu.au

Abstract. Web service composition (WSC) offers a range of solutions for rapid creation of complex applications by facilitating the composition of already existing concrete web services. One critical challenge in WSC is the dynamic selection of concrete services to be bound to the abstract composite service. In our research, we identify and elaborate on the challenges involved on developing a market-based mechanism for composite service selection. We propose *a combinatorial procurement auction model* as a useful approach to research service selection, in order to overcome the limitations of the current optimization-based and negotiation-based solutions. The proposed auction model supports dynamic pricing for the offered web services, enables the providers to express their preferences more fully, and creates the incentive for the providers to be truthful about the offered prices.

Keywords: web service composition, service selection, combinatorial procurement auction.

1 Introduction

One of the critical research challenges in realizing the vision of agile and collaborative software development using web services is *Web Service Composition* (WSC) which involves creating a composite service by combining different web services to provide a new value added service. The composite service is usually defined at an abstract level as a high level business process (BP) which comprises a set of tasks, along with the control and data flow among them. Each task has a clear description of the required functionality, and the non-functional properties, aka Quality of Service (QoS) attributes, such as execution time, availability, down time, security, and price.

In WSC, composite web service selection refers to the process of choosing a group of web services which can execute the tasks in a BP. In today's Internet, tens of web services with similar functionality exist online which are offered at different levels of quality and price. The aim of composite service selection is to choose those services that best match service requester's requirements while simultaneously maximizing the user utility in terms of the quality of service and cost. The two current approaches to composite service selection suffer from limitations such as static QoS profile and the

A. Ghose et al. (Eds.): ICSOC 2012, LNCS 7759, pp. 400–405, 2013.

need for a complex decision model. To address these problems, this research aims to develop an auction-based model for service selection. As a market-based mechanism, an auction allows for dynamic pricing which is critical for web services.

The remainder of this paper is as follows: Section 2 discusses the research problem and challenges. Section 3 outlines the proposed approach, a preliminary mathematical model, and related work. Section 4 provides the conclusion and our research plan.

2 Research Problem and Challenges

A natural approach to composite service selection is to map this problem to an optimization model and to solve it using existing optimization methods, e.g. Integer Linear Programming, or Genetic Algorithm. Research in this area includes but not limited to [1-3]. However, optimization-based approaches require the service providers to publish their web services with predetermined values for the QoS attributes. This requirement limits the service requester to have an approach of take-it or leave-it toward the offered services. Moreover, the fixed profile is not very realistic in light of the relatively dynamic environments that characterize the selection and composition of web services. This problem has been referred to as defining the QoS profile in a static non-negotiable, non-configurable manner [4].

To address the static QoS profile, a number of service selection approaches consider a flexible and negotiable quality profile for a service, i.e. negotiation-based service selection [5-7]. In this approach, automated negotiators negotiate on behalf of the service providers and requester. The automated negotiators require a complex decision model which makes their application in real world settings somewhat impractical, at least for the near future. Moreover, the dynamic aspects of negotiation approaches complicate the problem of finding globally optimum solutions.

To address these problems, this research aims to develop a model based on *auction theory* for the *composite web service selection problem*. Auctions are known to be the most widely used mechanism for dynamic pricing [8] which is critical for products such as web services that are characterized by dynamic execution environments (in terms of the provider's available resources), and users with different and changing demands. This is an improvement over totally pre-determined value for the price, as in the optimization-based approaches. In addition auctions can be designed so that complex decision models are not required.

More specifically, this research seeks to answer the following questions: (1) What are the specific requirements for auctions in the WSC domain and how do these differ from other domains such as transportation, communication networks, and resource scheduling? (2) How can we compare different auctions to elicit these requirements? What are the dimensions of this comparison? (3) What are the necessary elements for developing an auction model to solve composite service selection? (4) What are the desirable auction properties for the context of our research? e.g. incentive compatibility, Pareto efficiency, economic efficiency, or maximizing auctioneer revenue.

In our research, we face a number of interesting challenges. First, as auction theory is rather a broad area with extensive research from different communities, one challenge is to integrate and adapt models and methods based on an inter-disciplinary approach drawing on economics, game theory and theoretical CS. Second, we do not have an existing baseline to validate our answers to the research questions. The challenge is to develop the validation criteria alongside the answer to each question. Finally, since the current literature is quite limited, our proposed solution must be evaluated using innovative approaches. The challenge is to define the comparison criteria. We can draw on other areas, such as negotiation-based service selection, and develop similar evaluation metrics, e.g. utility of the service requester.

3   Combinatorial Procurement Auction

In a reverse or procurement auction model for composite service selection, the service requester is the auctioneer and the service providers bid for offering services for the tasks in the BP. Our interest is in a specific type of the auction, called *combinatorial auction*. In this auction, multiple distinct items are auctioned simultaneously and the bidders can bid over a combination of items, or *bundles*. Bundling enables the bidders to express their preferences over the items more fully, which leads to economic efficiency and greater auction revenue [9]. Bundling is particularly important when bidders have preferences not just for specific items but for item bundles due to the complementarities or substitutability effects that exist among the items [10].

In WSC domain, services that are bound to a BP are inter-dependent on factors such as execution time, recourses consumed, and data. These dependencies make it attractive for service providers to provide services for dependent tasks as a bundle. Offering services in bundles helps them internalize some of the service execution cost, and consequently leads to offering a lower price for the bundle. From the requester's point of view, this enables requesters to exploit the modular structure that may exist when decomposing the abstract BP.

The design of an auction includes two key, inter-dependent elements. The first element, Winner Determination Problem (WDP), decides which bidder gets what items. The second element, pricing schema, determines the price the bidders should pay (general auctions), or will receive (a procurement auction). When designing these elements, the primary design objective is to achieve a mechanism with desirable properties [11]. One of the most important of these properties is *incentive-compatibility* or *truthfulness*. In a truthful auction, the dominant strategy for bidders is to bid truthfully since this gives them the highest utility [12]. The incentive for truthful bidding is provided through the design of appropriate pricing schema.

To model composite service selection as a combinatorial procurement auction, we have designed the two elements so that the achieved mechanism is incentive-compatible. In the WDP part, we mapped the composite service selection to an Integer Linear Programming problem. The objective function is to minimize the cost for the service requester, subject to quality constraints. For the pricing schema, we draw on the Vickrey-Clarke-Groves (VCG) model [13]. VCG is the best known auction for multiple items that is incentive-compatible. Its objective function is to maximize the economic efficiency which we have mapped to minimizing the cost for the auctioneer, following [8, 10]. In VCG, the pricing schema for each winning bidder defines a price which is independent of the winning bidder's bid.

3.1 Combinatorial Procurement Auction Model

Let B be the set of all received bids from all providers, with an arbitrary member denoted as b_i where $i \in I$ (set of bid indices), $I = \{1,..,N\}$ and N is the total number of all received bids. Let $Task$ be denoted as the set of all tasks in the business process, with an arbitrary member defined as $task_j$ where $j \in J$ (set of task indices), $J = \{1,..,M\}$ and M is the total number of tasks in the BP. Each bid b_i is defined as $b_i = (T_i, c_i, \vec{q}_i)$, where c_i is the cost of providing service(s) for the task(s) in the set T_i ($T_i \subseteq Task$) with the offered quality vector of $\vec{q}_i$ for the service(s). For the current model, we consider two quality attributes in the quality vector; availability and response time denoted as v_i and r_i respectively; i.e. $\vec{q}_i = (v_i, r_i)$.

The objective is to minimize the cost for the service requester, equation (1), subject to quality constraints. Equation (2) ensures that each task is assigned to no more than one provider. To get the unique assignment, we defined matrix A_{I*J} with an arbitrary element of a_{ij} which is 1 if T_i (in b_i) includes $task_j$ and 0 otherwise.

$$\text{min.} \quad \sum_{i \in I} c_i * z_i \tag{1}$$

$$\text{s.t.} \quad \sum_{i \in I} a_{ij} * z_i \; = 1 \quad \forall j \in J \tag{2}$$

$$\sum_{i \in I} \ln(v_i) * z_i \geq \ln(V) \tag{3}$$

$$\sum_{i \in I} r_i * z_i \; \leq R \tag{4}$$

Inequalities (3) and (4) define the quality constraints for availability and response time, where V and R are the service requester's acceptable minimum availability and maximum response time levels for the composite service (the availability's aggregation function is linearized using a logarithm function [2]). The decision variable is denoted as z_i to be 1 if b_i is a winning bid and 0 otherwise.

The VCG pricing schema is defined as follows [8]:

$$p_k = \sum_{j \in B \setminus B_k} c_i z_i^{*\neg k} - \sum_{j \in B \setminus B_k} c_i z_i^* \tag{5}$$

In the equation (5), z_i^* are the decision variable values for the optimal solution (z_i^* is 1 for the winning bid, and 0 for others), and $z_i^{*\urcorner k}$ are the variable values of the optimal assignment, if we remove the bids of provider k from the set of bids. Let $B_k = \{b_i \in B | b_i \ is \ a \ bid \ from \ bidder \ k\}$. We define $B \backslash B_k$ as the set of indices of all bids without the bids of provider k. The price p_k to be paid to the winning bidder k is the result of subtracting the cost of all other bids in z_i^* from the sum of the cost of bids in $z_i^{*\urcorner k}$.

3.2   Related Work in Auction-Based Service Selection

There is limited research on the application of dynamic market mechanisms such as auctions for service selection. The combinatorial procurement auction discussed in [14, 15] is in fact another optimization-based approach with the objective function as maximizing the composite service's quality, subject to a budget constraint [14], or minimizing the cost subject to quality and interface matching constraints [15]. The main innovation is that, in the IP formulation proposed in the papers, the service provider is able to offer services for more than one task in the BP. However, the proposed technique does not discuss two critical aspects of a typical auction, namely pricing schema and design objectives such as incentive-compatibility property.

A multidimensional procurement auction is proposed in [16] for trading composite services. The objective is to maximize the joint utility of the service requester and providers and the mechanism is incentive compatible with respect to all the dimensions of a bid (quality and price). However, the proposed auction is not combinatorial and the service requester cannot define any constraint for the composite service required quality or budget. In addition, every service provider needs to prepare a bid for each combination of her service with possible precedent services from other providers. This is not trivial especially in the domain of web services and Internet, where it is difficult for a provider to obtain enough information about others.

4   Conclusion and Research Plan

In this research, we elaborate on the challenges involved in developing an auction-based solution for composite service selection. As the first step, we proposed a combinatorial procurement auction-based model and discussed it in terms of the WDP element, and the pricing schema. Our design ensures that the achieved mechanism is truthful, which prevents the bidders from spending resources learning about other bidders' values or strategies [13].

Our future work includes extending the current model along two directions. The first direction is extending the model to include requirements that are specific to the WSC domain. For example, considering the multi-attribute nature of web services offer, one possibility is to extend the current model to include other service's quality attributes as part of the objective function, which will affect the VCG pricing schema. Second, we will study the relation between an auction design objective and different environmental settings that characterize a WSC problem. These environmental settings include factors such as how severe the QoS requirements are, or the BP popularity (how many providers are willing to offer service for its tasks). We plan to design and carry out a number of simulation and laboratory experiments with human participants as service providers who bid for bundles of services, and a prototype system as an independent auctioneer that implements different auction models. The outcome of the experiments will be a set of recommendations and strategies that will specify the appropriate auction models for web service selection under different conditions.

References

1. Ardagna, D., Pernici, B.: Adaptive Service Composition in Flexible Processes. IEEE Trans. on Software Eng. 33(6), 369–384 (2007)
2. Zeng, L., et al.: QoS-Aware Middleware for Web Services Composition. IEEE Trans. Softw. Eng. 30(5), 311–327 (2004)
3. Canfora, G., et al.: An approach for QoS-aware service composition based on genetic algorithms. In: Proceedings of the 2005 Conference on Genetic and Evolutionary Computation, pp. 1069–1075. ACM, Washington DC (2005)
4. Comuzzi, M., Pernici, B.: A framework for QoS-based Web service contracting. ACM Trans. Web 3(3), 1–52 (2009)
5. Yan, J., et al.: Autonomous service level agreement negotiation for service composition provision. Future Generation Computer Systems 23(6), 748–759 (2007)
6. Chhetri, M.B., et al.: A coordinated architecture for the agent-based service level agreement negotiation of Web service composition. In: Australian Software Engineering Conference (ASWEC), pp. 90–99 (2006)
7. Richter, J., et al.: Establishing composite SLAs through concurrent QoS negotiation with surplus redistribution. Concurrency and Computation: Practice and Experience (2011)
8. Bichler, M.: The future of eMarkets: multi-dimensional market mechanisms. Cambridge University Press (2001)
9. Cramton, P.C., Shoham, Y., Steinberg, R.: Combinatorial Auctions. MIT Press, Cambridge (2006)
10. de Vries, S., Vohra, R.V.: Combinatorial Auctions:A Survey. INFORMS Journal on Computing 15(3), 284 (2003)
11. Schnizler, B., et al.: Trading grid services – a multi-attribute combinatorial approach. European Journal of Operational Research 187(3), 943–961 (2008)
12. Nisan, N.: Introduction to Mechanism Design. In: Algorithmic Game Theory, pp. 209–241. Cambridge University Press (2007)
13. Ausubel, L.M., Milgrom, P.: The Lovely but Lonely Vickrey Auction. In: Cramton, P.C., Shoham, Y., Steinberg, R. (eds.) Combinatorial Auctions. MIT Press, Cambridge (2006)
14. Mohabey, M., et al.: A Combinatorial Procurement Auction for QoS-Aware Web Services Composition. In: IEEE International Conference on Automation Science and Engineering, CASE 2007, pp. 716–721 (2007)
15. Mohabey, M., et al.: An Intelligent Procurement Marketplace forWeb Services Composition. In: IEEE/WIC/ACM International Conference on Web Intelligence, pp. 551–554 (2007)
16. Blau, B., Conte, T., van Dinther, C.: A multidimensional procurement auction for trading composite services. Electron. Commer. Rec. Appl. 9(5), 460–472 (2010)

Data-Centric Probabilistic Process: A PhD. Symposium Paper for ICSOC

Haizhou Li

Universit Blaise Pascal Laboratoire LIMOS - UMR 6158 Complexe Scientifique des Czeaux, 63177 AUBIERE cedex, France
li@isima.fr

Abstract. The theory of business process management system actively plays a principle role in the domain of semantic web service and business process management. This paper briefly described my current Ph.D work result and the perspective about specification and verification of data-centric probabilistic business process system which integrating traditional probabilistic business process and probabilistic database. The probabilistic business process system is described by probabilistic automaton which is an abstracted framework for the transition system. By integrating probabilistic database, probabilistic automaton would be provided greater expressive power to handle the probabilistic event and high volume probabilistic data.

Keywords: Data-centric probabilistic process system, probabilistic automata, probabilistic database.

1 Introduction

This paper is a description of my Ph.D. work. My work focus on data-centric business process management system which integrates the theory of business process management described by transition system methodology (ex. probabilistic business process modelled by probabilistic automata)and extending class of incomplete database(incomplete database,probabilistic database and uncertain database). My current research focus on a specification and verification of data-centric probabilistic business process system which are capable to represent probabilistic transition system and uncertain data with the help of probabilistic automata and probabilistic database. This paper organized as follows. Section 2 states the problem and the main challenge of my research. Section 3 provides a coarse model of data-centric business process system depicted by probabilistic automata integrating probabilistic database. In Section 5, I tries to compare the envisioned research outcome with current literature. Last section is a conclusion.

2 Problem Statement

The research of business process management methodology is blooming and researched by numerous researchers in disparate way. Number of techniques and

A. Ghose et al. (Eds.): ICSOC 2012, LNCS 7759, pp. 406–411, 2013.

models are integrated in the domain of business process management. My work mainly focus on the process system and uncertain data. Due to the main task of business process management, the model and the methodology are served to improve the business efficiency and aid the business people to manage their business. So we would like to propose updated framework to enhance the expressive power of existing models. Supply chain management is always a suitable entry point as an experimental field for a novel method of business process management. In the traditional supply chain management system, researchers are fond of process system or called transition system to describe the work flows of supply chain system. Theoretically, a transition system could be interpreted as a finite automaton (In this paper, we focus on finite transition system. Moreover in reality, there would be infinite process occurred due to errors, deadlocks, design problem,etc.). Normally, an automaton consists of four components as follows:

- A set of finite states $\{s_0, s_1, ..., s_n\}$ which stand for the current state of the system, denoted as S.
- A non-empty start states s_0.
- A set of actions $\{a_0, a_1..., a_n\}$ denoted as Act.
- Transition relations(or called steps) denoted as $\rightarrow \subseteq S \times Act \times S$ present the transition from one state to another assigned by actions

The behaviours of automata are described by traces denoted as $trace(S)$ or execution fragments which are a sequence of alternating states and actions starting with a state. A trace would be exampled as follows: $trace(S)_i = \{s_0 a_0 s_1 a_1 ... s_n a_n\}$. Figure 1 shows a common work flow (described in finite state automaton). We would like to know if we selected different product, how the process would be. Imaging if we would like to query data from high volume dataset such as database and also show this data in the automata. There are several ways to introduce data into the process, converting the actions of the transitions is a kind of expressive method and we could find out clearly how the data flow and how the data influence the transitions in the automata at the same time. So we expand the notion of actions to guarding formulas which could query or update the database to return a boolean value $true$ of $false$ such that we capture a kind of notion of data-centric process model which could be described by finite state automata ([6] discussed a similar web service model).

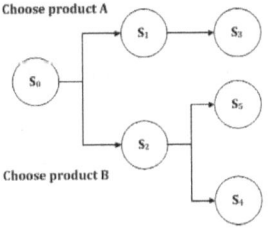

Fig. 1. An example work flow

2.1 Probabilistic Database Centric

After introducing the notion of data-centric service, integrating deterministic database is not a innovative domain. Nowadays, in the wake of information explosion, the system is facing to the problem of selecting duplicate data from the different sources, managing uncertain data etc. Probabilistic database is a ideal tool to manage the uncertain data.

A probabilistic database (in [2], [3]) is a set of finite possible complete database which distributed by probabilities denoted as $P - DB : \{W, Pr\}$, $W = \{D_1, D_2, ...Dn\}$, Pr is a function $Pr : W \rightarrow [0,1]$ such that $\sum_{D \in W} Pr(D) = 1$. Formally, a probabilistic instance consists of a collection of tuples which are distributed by probabilities and relation between tuples are disjoint (or called mutually exclusive) or independent. Table 1 shows an example of a probabilistic instance in which t_1 and t_2 are disjoint (capable to be considered as a cluster) and t_2 and t_3 are independent, as well as the possible world of this probabilistic instance.

Table 1. Example of probabilistic database and its possible world

ID	pr		PW	tuples	Pr
t_1	A	70%	W_1	$\{t_1\}$	35%
t_2	B	30%	W_2	$\{t_2\}$	15%
t_3	c	50%	W_3	$\{t_1, t_3\}$	35%
			W_4	$\{t_2, t_3\}$	15%

As a result, we would like to integrate probabilistic database as the data source in the data-centric process model described above. Figure 2 shows a data-centric probabilistic process model by reusing the example in figure 1 and formal definition of data-centric probabilistic process will be provided in section 3. In the state of art of investigating the probability and processes, the methodology of probabilistic process is a critical field. It is valuable to review the methodology of probabilistic process.

2.2 Probabilistic Process

The methodology of automata has been widely utilized to illustrate the structure and the behaviours of a system but researchers found that it was not adequate for more complicated utilizations. In order to increase the expressive power of the automata, researches considered the probability of the events and the branches in the automata. Probabilistic business process model (introduced in [4], [8])which described by probabilistic automata (depicted in [5]) is an attractive innovation to the theory of process system. As its name described, probabilistic automata reuse the main components of the traditional automata in additional to provide probability on the transitions. The transitions of probabilistic automata are assigned not only actions but also probability distributions $\{\mu_0, \mu_1, ..., \mu_n\}$ denoted as $Distri(S)$ such that the transition relation of probabilistic automata is denoted as $\rightarrow \subseteq S \times Act \times Distri(S) \times S$.

2.3   Research Problems and Challenge

Our approach attempts to integrate probabilistic process and probabilistic database in the form of data-centric probabilistic automata. It would be a combination of two asynchronous semantics of probability methodology. In the theory of probabilistic process, the probability distribution from different branches in one step are mutually exclusive but in contrast, due to the guarding formulas querying independent tuples from probabilistic database, the transition relation by considering guarding formulas would be independent transitions. So the research problems and challenge of my work are as follows:

- Modelling data-centric probabilistic business process especially finding a proper way to present these two asynchronous semantics of probability as above described.
- Verifying if the data-centric probabilistic process model could be reduced to the model of probabilistic process and reuse some algorithms which have been proposed in the probabilistic process.
- Verifying the simulation relation between two data-centric probabilistic processes if their guarding formulas queried one certain probabilistic instance, one uncertain probabilistic instance or two different probabilistic instances and compare with probabilistic process if the simulation relation algorithm of probabilistic process could be reused.
- Programming a prototype system to make this model into reality.

3   Proposed Solution

In this section, I would like to introduce this data-centric process model which captures the stochastic transitions and probabilistic data. Data-centric probabilistic process system has a collection of probabilistic distributions on the transitions and data. This system could provide an ability to manage uncertain data and support probability branching choices in the domain of business process management.

In the model of data-centric probabilistic process system, there are five principle components as follows.

- A set of finite states $\{s_0, s_1, ..., s_n\}$ which stand for the current state of the system, denoted as S.
- A nonempty start states s_0.
- The real world is modelled by probabilistic database which denoted as p-D.
- A set of actions $\{a_0, a_1 ..., a_n\}$ denoted as Act. An action a_n may be a guarding formula f_n. A guarding formula queries probabilistic database p-D returning a boolean value *true* or *false* or update the database (insertion, deletion or modification) returning a boolean value *true* or *false*..
- Transition relations which are signed by actions and accompany with probabilistic distributions $\{\mu_0, \mu_1, ..., \mu_n\}$ which denoted as $Distri(S)$. Transition relations denoted as $\rightarrow \subseteq S \times Act \times Distri(S) \times S$

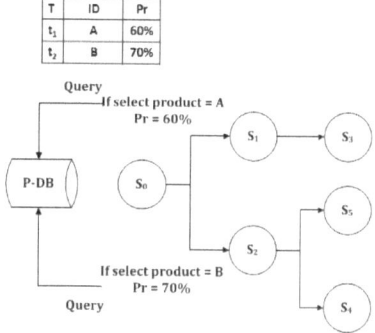

Fig. 2. An example of data-centric probabilistic business process

The behaviour of this model is described by traces. For a given set of state S, there are several traces $\{trace(S)_0, trace(S)_1, ..., trace(S)_n\}$ denoted as $Trace(S)$ corresponding to the transition relations $Tr(S)$. A possible trace includes principle components of the model and depict the execution order of the states inside. A trace is just like the follows $trace(S)_0 = \{s_0 a_0 \mu_0 s_1 a_1 \mu_1 s_3 a_3 \mu 3 ... s_n a_n \mu_n\}$. In the context of finite process model, we just consider complete trace which is definitely finite. Figure 2 shows a data-centric probabilistic process and its possible world modelled by an instance of probabilistic database.

4   Comparison between the Envisioned Research Outcome and Current Literature

The data-centric probabilistic process model integrated probabilistic process and probabilistic database ([2] and [3] described the semantic of probabilistic database and the query method of probabilistic database in details). [4] provided a specification model of probabilistic business process and [9] described a mathematical methodology about probabilistic process. [8] discussed the method of testing probabilistic pre-order which could be a infrastructure if we discussed the simulation relation of data-centric probabilistic business model. Comparing with traditional probabilistic business process model, data-centric probabilistic process model introduced the accessing ability to probabilistic database and accommodated massive data manipulation. The theory of probabilistic database extends from incomplete database (Specifically presented in [1] and [7]) and provide a tool to manage and store enormous stochastic data. The idea of atomic process accessing database is inspired by [6] which was introduced "Colombo" model. "Colombo" model is a data-centric process model without considering probabilistic transitions or probabilistic data and it is specific in composition of web service. Our data-centric probabilistic process model introduced probabilistic business process and utilized probabilistic database to focus on stochastic data management and random event occurrence in the field of process system.

Meanwhile, our model described a framework of data-centric probabilistic process system and it could be utilized not only in web service but also other business process management system by adding specification features.

5   Conclusion

This paper coarsely stated the principle problem of my Ph.D work and introduced a model of data-centric probabilistic process system which integrate probabilistic process and probabilistic database. In future, we would like to improve this model and discuss the verification of this model. Following the theoretical work, the prototype of this model would be designed to attempt to handle the realistic applications.

References

1. Imielinkski, T., Lipski Jr., W.: Incomplete information and dependencies in relational databases. In: Proc. ACM-SIGMOD International Conference on Management of Data, pp. 178–184 (1983)
2. Dalvi, N., Suciu, D.: Efficient query evaluation on probabilistic databases. University of Washington Technical Report (TR 04-03-04) (2004)
3. Dalvi, N., Re, C., Suciu, D.: Query evaluation on probabilistic database. IEEE Data Engineering Bulletin 29(1), 25–31 (2006)
4. Deutch, D., Milo, T.: On models and query languages for probabilistic processes. SIGMOD Record 39(2), 27–38 (2010)
5. Stoelinga, M.: An introduction to probabilistic automata. Alea jacta est: verification of probabilistic, real-time and parametric systems. PhD thesis, University of Nijmegen, the Netherlands, ch. 2 (2002)
6. Berardi, D., Calvanese, D., De Giacomo, G., Hull, R., Mecella, M.: Automatic composition of transition-based semantic web services with messaging. In: Proceedings of the 31st VLDB Conference, pp. 613–624 (2005)
7. Grahne, G.: The problem of incomplete information in relational database. University of Helsinki (1991)
8. Jonsson, B., Wang, Y.: Testing pre-orders for probabilistic processes can be characterized by simulations. Theoretical Computer Science 282, 33–51 (2002)
9. Lustig, Y., Nain, S., Vardi, M.Y.: Synthesis from probabilistic components. In: Proc. CSL 2011. LIPICS, vol. 12, pp. 412–427 (2011)

Detection of SOA Antipatterns

Francis Palma[1,2]

[1] Ptidej Team, DGIGL, École Polytechnique de Montréal, Canada
[2] Département d'informatique, Université du Québec à Montréal, Canada
francis.palma@polymtl.ca

Abstract. Like any other large and complex systems, user requirements may change for Service Based Systems (SBSs), as well as their execution contexts, in the form of evolution and maintenance. Consequently, these changes may cause degradation of design, and Quality of Service (QoS), resulting to the bad practiced solutions, commonly known as *Antipatterns*. Therefore, detecting SOA (Service Oriented Architecture) antipatterns deserves an extra importance for assessing the design and QoS of SBSs. Also, this detection may facilitate the future evolution and maintenance. Despite of its importance, there are no methods and techniques for detecting SOA antipatterns within SBSs. The subject of my PhD thesis is to propose a novel and innovative approach, supported by a framework for specifying and detecting SOA antipatterns. My contributions are: (1) an approach for SOA antipatterns detection, (2) a framework supporting analysis and detection for SOA antipatterns in SBSs, and finally (3) a concrete empirical evidence to show the effectiveness of the proposed approach and framework.

Keywords: SOA Antipatterns, Service Based Systems, Detection, Quality of Service, Design, Software Evolution and Maintenance.

1 Introduction

The wide acceptance of SOA [2] is mainly due to its flexibility, scalability and inexpensive development efforts. SBSs developed with such architectural style, are composed of loosely-coupled and platform independent reusable units, i.e., *service* easily accessible over Internet. Amazon and eBay are two examples of SBSs. In fact, the emergence of SBSs is unable to avoid some common software engineering challenges, e.g., evolution, to fit new user requirements or changes in execution contexts. All these changes may degrade the quality of design and QoS of SBSs, thus may cause the presence of common bad practiced solutions, i.e., *antipatterns* - oppose to *design patterns*, that are good solutions to recurring problems. *Multi Service* and *Tiny Service* are two common and recurring antipatterns in SBSs, and it is shown, in particular, *Tiny Service* is the root cause of many SOA failures [5]. *Multi Service* is an SOA antipatterns that corresponds to a service implementing a multitude of methods related to different business and technical abstractions. Such a service has low reusability and is often unavailable to the end-users [1]. Conversely, *Tiny Service* is a small service with just a few methods, which only implements part of an abstraction. Such

A. Ghose et al. (Eds.): ICSOC 2012, LNCS 7759, pp. 412–418, 2013.
© Springer-Verlag Berlin Heidelberg 2013

service often requires several coupled services to be used together, resulting in higher development complexity and reduced usability [1].

The remainder of this paper is organized as follows. The next few Sections discuss more details on the problem. Section 2 summarizes the related work. Section 3 introduces the proposed approach and the framework, in short. Section 4 identifies key research assumptions and presents some preliminary results. Finally, Section 5 concludes and sketches the future work.

Context: Assessment of Design and QoS, Maintenance and Evolution of SBSs - The 'bad' solutions to the recurring problems, i.e., *antipatterns* are the cause of low maintainability and may hinder the evolution of the system (Klimas et al., 1996). Like Object Oriented (OO) systems, SBSs also faces challenges with low maintainability and evolvability due to *antipatterns*. Thus, it becomes difficult for engineers to make changes, i.e., adding new or modifying existing functionalities.

Problem: No Approach and Framework for the Detection of SOA Antipatterns - Promoting the adoption of SOA refers to more usage of SBSs. SBSs operate in Internet-based dynamic environment and its smooth operations depend on many factors including quality design and good QoS. These made the detection of SOA antipatterns challenging but still an open problem. There are a number of contributions in the literature for the detection and correction of OO antipatterns. However, there is no concrete methods and techniques for such detection in SBSs and to assess the QoS. Specification of SOA antipatterns is the primary step for this purpose, and another open problem.

Motivation: Solving the problem of detection of SOA antipatterns, and assessing design and QoS in SBSs, help to ease maintenance and evolution of SBSs. Software maintenance is one of the longest and important activity, it requires more expenses and resources with time [3]. In 1980, Lientz and Swanson showed that software maintenance requires 60% to 80% of total budget in its whole lifespan. The detection of the SOA antipatterns within SBSs is also a part of maintenance. Detection of such antipatterns may also help improving QoS. In summary, by proposing an approach for detecting SOA antipatterns, we can contribute to better maintenance and evolution of SBSs.

Therefore, with the above context, problem definition and motivation, my PhD thesis will mainly focus on proposing a novel and innovative approach, named as SODA (Service Oriented Detection for Antipatterns), for specifying and detecting SOA antipatterns. SODA is supported by a underlying framework, named as SOFA (Service Oriented Framework for Antipatterns). I also intend to provide a concrete empirical evidence supporting my research hypotheses.

Research Challenges: Key research challenges are:

(a) *Specifying SOA Antipatterns*: The current literature for SOA antipatterns is not matured enough and there are limited number of journals, proceedings and books on SOA antipatterns. Researchers and practitioners mostly depend on online resources, i.e, open forums, blogs, shared resources. Therefore, available references for specifying SOA antipatterns are not adequate.

(b) *Repository of SBSs*: The research on the detection of SOA antipatterns still did not gain much attention despite of its importance. And, there is no repository of SBSs to perform experiments, as the community did not make the effort to provide it. We can find some Web Service search engines, i.e., *Seekda*[1], *Woogle*[2] but no complete systems. Researchers are still in the lack of freely available SBSs as testbed.

(c) *Handling Dynamic Environment of SOA*: SBSs are developed adopting SOA design principles, and the execution environment of SBSs is dynamic involving many operating factors, e.g., implementation technologies, inter-operability, QoS, critical design criteria. Thus, handling dynamic environment of SOA for analyzing SBSs is another major research challenge.

Major Impacts: The major impact of this research work is threefold: (a) Industrial practitioners will find a way to handle SOA antipatterns. Many applications are now Web-based and there exists no accepted approach within the industrial community. Successful familiarization of a novel approach will encourage them to develop advanced tools, for the detection of SOA antipatterns, (b) Academic researchers will commence new research directions and analysis paths towards the detection of SOA antipatterns, till now which is not considered with a greater importance, and finally, (c) A fruitful collaboration between industrial practitioners and academic fellows will ensure SBSs with good QoS, cheaper maintenance and easier evolution, with the increased adoption of SOA.

2 Related Work

Much analysis with service orientation and commercial aspect of SOA exist in the literature, but the architectural-design aspect is still not highlighted properly [9]. Design quality is essential for building well maintainable and evolvable SBSs. Design patterns and antipatterns are two major ways for expressing design issues and related solutions. Nonetheless, unlike OO antipatterns, there is no detection methods and techniques for SOA antipatterns in SBSs.

For SOA, a few number of books and papers dealt with antipatterns, and most of the references are Web sites, forums and blogs where practitioners share their experiences in SOA design and development. The book by Dudney *et al.* [1] is the first book to introduce a number of architectural, design and implementation antipatterns for the systems based on J2EE technologies. But, most of them cannot be detected automatically. Also, Král *et al.* [4] specified briefly seven SOA antipatterns, but did not discuss their detection. Several methods and tools exist for the detection [7] of antipatterns in OO systems. But, all these OO detection methods and tools are not applicable to SOA, because of its granularity difference in their building blocks. Moreover, the more dynamic nature of SOA-based SBSs

---

[1] http://webservices.seekda.com/
[2] http://db.cs.washington.edu/woogle.html

brings in several issues to confront, that do not exist in OO systems. There are a couple of works that deal with the detection of antipatterns: Wong *et al.* [10] used a genetic algorithm for detecting software faults and anomalous behavior; and, Parsons *et al.* [8] performed the detection of performance antipatterns in component-based enterprise systems, using a rule-based approach with static and dynamic analysis. Though there is no significant contributions in the literature to support the detection of SOA antipatterns, all the above OO methods and techniques can form a baseline to formulate a generic approach for detecting SOA antipatterns.

3   Proposed Methodology

The Approach: SODA - Figure 1 shows the proposed approach, SODA, for detecting SOA antipatterns in SBSs. The steps include:

Step 1: Specification - Includes performing a domain analysis by studying definitions and specifications from the literature to identify relevant static and dynamic properties (a.k.a. *metrics*), to specify SOA antipatterns. Then, using these properties as the basis for the vocabulary to define domain specific language (DSL), and finally formalizing the rule cards. A rule card is the representation of a SOA antipattern at a high-level of abstraction. Figure 2 shows an example of rule cards for *Multi Service* and *Tiny Service*.

Step 2: Generation - With the rule cards of SOA antipatterns, I generate detection algorithms automatically using a simple *template*-based technique.

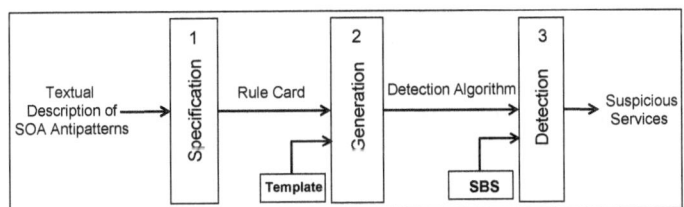

Fig. 1. Proposed SODA Approach

```
1 RULE_CARD: MultiService {                    1 RULE_CARD: TinyService {
2 RULE: MultiService {INTER MultiMethod        2 RULE: TinyService {INTER FewMethod
3 HighResponse LowAvailability LowCohesion};   3                    HighCoupling};
4 RULE: MultiMethod {NMD VERY_HIGH};           4 RULE: FewMethod {NMD VERY_LOW};
5 RULE: HighResponse {RT VERY_HIGH};           5 RULE: HighCoupling {CPL HIGH};
6 RULE: LowAvailability {A LOW};               6 };
7 RULE: LowCohesion {COH LOW};
8 };
            (a) Multi Service                              (b) Tiny Service
```

Fig. 2. Example Rule Cards for Multi Service and Tiny Service

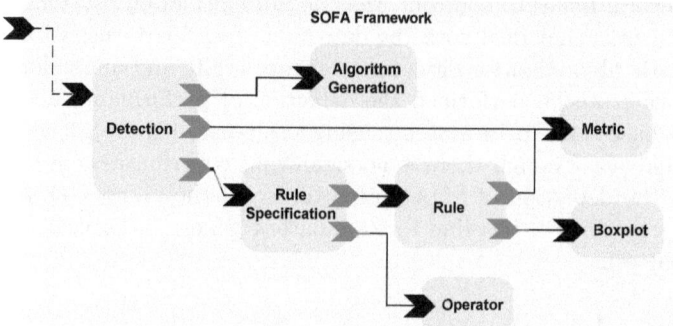

Fig. 3. SOFA: Underlying Framework for the SODA Approach (black arrows represent service provided by the component, grey arrows dependency on referenced component)

Step 3: Detection - For the detection of SOA antipatterns, an underlying framework, SOFA is introduced. All the computations of static and dynamic metrics, i.e., identified relevant properties, and related analysis are performed in SOFA.

The Framework: SOFA - Figure 3 shows the underlying framework, SOFA, that supports the specification and detection of SOA antipatterns in SBSs. SOFA has seven modules, programmatically each of which represents a component providing a stand-alone service. The components include: (1) *Detection Component*, representing the main detection engine that initiates and controls the overall detection process, (2) *Metric Component* that provides the computation of all metrics from the metric suite, both static and dynamic ones, (3) *Rule Specification Component* is responsible for specifying rule cards using the *Rule Component* and *Operator Component*, (4) *Algorithm Generation Component* generates the detection algorithms automatically from the specified rules, (5) *Rule Component* represents all the singleton rules that are composed of metrics, and depends on *Metric Component* to get required metrics, (6) *Operator Component* provides all the boolean and comparison operators, and finally, (7) *Boxplot Component* provides the means for computing boundary values and setting threshold values. The SOFA itself is a *service*-based framework.

4   Preliminary Experiments and Results

4.1   Key Research Hypotheses

Here, I define key research assumptions for the experimental purpose. The initial set of assumptions includes:

Table 1. Primary Results for the Detection of the Four SOA Antipatterns in the Original and Evolved Version of the *Home-Automation* System *(S: Static, D: Dynamic)*

ANTIPATTERN NAME	SUSPICIOUS SERVICES	VERSION	ANALYSIS	METRICS	DETECTION TIME
Tiny Service	[MediatorDelegate]	evolved	S	NOR: 4 CPL: 0.440 NMD: 1	0.194s
Multi Service	[IMediator]	original	S, D	COH: 0.027 NMD: 13 RT: 132ms	0.462s
Duplicated Service	[Communication-Service] [IMediator]	original	S	ANIM: 25%	0.215s
Bottleneck Service	[IMediator] [PatientDAO]	original	S, D	NIR: 7 NOR: 7 CPL: 1.0 RT: 40ms	0.246s

A1. Generality: The DSL allows the specification of many different SOA antipatterns, from simple to more complex ones.

A2. Accuracy: The generated detection algorithms have a recall of 100%, i.e., all existing antipatterns are detected, and a precision greater than 75%, i.e., more than three-quarters of detected antipatterns are true positive.

A3. Extensibility: The DSL and the proposed framework, SOFA is extensible for adding new SOA metrics and SOA antipatterns to detect.

A4. Performance: The computation time required for the detection of antipatterns using the generated algorithms is reasonably very low, i.e., in the order of few seconds.

A5. Technology: The proposed approach, SODA supports any technologies, i.e., capable of handling any SBSs implemented with diverse technologies, i.e., SOAP-RPC, SCA, REST, Web services, WCF etc.

Preliminary Results: With the aim of supporting previous hypotheses, I conducted some preliminary experiments, showing the results in Table 4.1. Column 1 shows the SOA antipatterns to detect, Column 2 shows the identified suspicious service(s), Column 3 and 4 show the version of the system and analyses methods I applied. Column 5 shows all the metric values for the service(s), and finally, Column 6 shows the required detection times in Table 4.1. The detection were performed on an SBS, *Home-Automation*. Here, I briefly discuss the detection result for *Multi Service*. In Table 4.1, `IMediator` is detected as *Multi Service* because of its very high number of methods (*i.e.,* NMD equal 13) and its low cohesion (*i.e.,* COH equal 0.027). These values are evaluated by the *Box-Plot* service as high and low in comparison with the values of other services of *Home-Automation*.

More details on the detection results are available in our ICSOC '12 paper [6]. Textual descriptions of these four antipatterns with their corresponding rule cards, an elaborative presentation on *Home-Automation*, and more materials are available on http://sofa.uqam.ca.

5   Conclusion and Future Work

Due to the importance of the detection of SOA antipatterns in SBSs, I proposed a novel and innovative approach, SODA, supported by an underlying framework, SOFA. The framework supports the specification and detection of SOA antipatterns using a DSL and generated detection algorithms. In a preliminary experiment, I detected four common SOA antipatterns in *Home-Automation* and I reported suspicious service(s). As future work, I intend to support all the research hypotheses, stated in Section 4.1. In particular, I intend to perform thorough experiments with larger and more complex SBSs using different experimental and control groups. The rectification of the detected SOA antipatterns is also in the future plan.

References

1. Dudney, B., Asbury, S., Krozak, J.K., Wittkopf, K.: J2EE AntiPatterns. John Wiley & Sons Inc. (2003)
2. Erl, T.: Service Oriented Architecture: Concepts, Technology and Design (2005)
3. Hanna, M.: Maintenance Burden Begging for a Remedy. Datamation, 53–63 (1993)
4. Král, J., Žemlička, M.: Crucial Service-Oriented Antipatterns, vol. 2, pp. 160–171. International Academy, Research and Industry Association, IARIA (2008)
5. Kral, J., Zemlicka, M.: Popular SOA Antipatterns. In: Future Computing, Service Computation, Cognitive, Adaptive, Content, Patterns, Computation World, pp. 271–276 (2009)
6. Moha, N., Palma, F., Nayrolles, M., Conseil, B.J., Guéhéneuc, Y.-G., Baudry, B., Jézéquel, J.-M.: Specification and Detection of SOA Antipatterns. In: Liu, C., Ludwig, H., Toumani, F., Yu, Q. (eds.) ICSOC 2012. LNCS, vol. 7636, pp. 1–16. Springer, Heidelberg (2012)
7. Munro, M.J.: Product Metrics for Automatic Identification of "Bad Smell" Design Problems in Java Source-Code. In: Proceedings of the 11th International Software Metrics Symposium. IEEE Computer Society Press (September 2005)
8. Parsons, T., Murphy, J.: Detecting Performance Antipatterns in Component Based Enterprise Systems. Journal of Object Technology 7(3), 55–90 (2008)
9. Rotem-Gal-Oz, A., Bruno, E., Dahan, U.: SOA Patterns. Manning Publications Co. (2012) (to be published in Summer 2012)
10. Wong, S., Aaron, M., Segall, J., Lynch, K., Mancoridis, S.: Reverse Engineering Utility Functions Using Genetic Programming to Detect Anomalous Behavior in Software. In: Proceedings of the 2010 17th Working Conference on Reverse Engineering, pp. 41–149. IEEE Computer Society, Washington, DC (2010)

Requirements-Driven Software Service Evolution

Feng-Lin Li[1,2]

[1] Dept of Information Engineering and Computer Science, University of Trento, Trento, Italy
[2] School of Software, Tsinghua University, Beijing, China

Abstract. Evolution is of key importance for software services as they need to satisfy ever-changing customer requirements under open and dynamic operating environment. The majority of current research on service evolution is focused on maintaining the compatibility between evolved service and existing clients, while few works look into its root cause. This paper proposes to study service evolution from a requirements' perspective. The key research problems - change propagation and traceability - in requirements-driven service evolution are discussed and the concept of "*feature*" is used to bridge the gap between requirements model and services model. A feature-oriented approach is presented, which includes model transformation & refinement (from goal model to feature model), and specification derivation (from feature model to service design space), to effectively address these challenges.

1   Introduction

For many years, scientists have been wondering how the turtle shell comes into being. Until recently, the unearthed fossils of Odontochelys (toothed turtle with half-shell, the oldest known tortoise) in China may help to answer this evolutionary enigma. The discovery provides interesting evidence stating that turtle shell formed from the bottom - plastron first - and grew bony extensions of ribs and bone formation above backbones that eventually joined to form the carapace that the modern turtles have.

In this example, certain existing features (*rib* and *backbone*) evolve and find a new use. As time unfolds, new features (*back shell*) develop. In a similar spirit, in software /service engineering, we can view services as a set of functional and non-functional features, which can evolve, to adapt to ever-changing requirements and environment.

We treat feature as evolution unit because of its two-fold interpretation: feature as atomic requirement, and feature as atomic functionality/quality of software service[1]. Moreover, in the days of *on-demand* use and *pay-as-you-go* consumption, it is sensible to think of service as a bundle of features that users choose from and subscribe to.

With the promotion of Service Orientation, software services are receiving increasing attention because they offer a loosely coupled architecture for enterprise application integration. Meanwhile, services reside in an open and constantly changing internet environment, and need to cope with ever-changing user requirements. Accordingly, services need to change continuously, which would give rise to evolution.

This thesis aims to study the mechanisms of requirements-driven service evolution. Our proposal is inspired by biological evolution and uses a feature-oriented approach to propagate requirements change to service evolution.

A. Ghose et al. (Eds.): ICSOC 2012, LNCS 7759, pp. 419–425, 2013.
© Springer-Verlag Berlin Heidelberg 2013

2   Problem Statement

According to Jackson and Zave's definition [2], the requirements problem is stated as: Given a set of requirements R, and a set of domain assumptions D, find a specification S such that $D, S \vDash R$. In our proposal, we assume that a specification is a set of services, and each service has a set of features.

We use an *Airline Ticket Booking* service to illustrate the research problems under discussion. In Fig 1, the functional and non-functional requirements are represented as hard-goals (ovals) and soft-goal (clouds); domain assumptions and specifications are represented as resources (rectangles) and tasks (hexagons) respectively. A case of the requirements problem is: to satisfy the goal *"Ticket be Paid Online"*(R), the service need to support task *"Processing Credit Card Payment"*(S) under the domain assumption *"Customer owns a Credit Card with Available Credits"*(D).

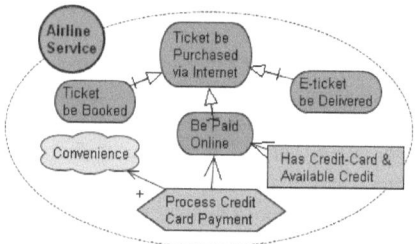

Fig. 1. The Partial Goal Model the Airline Ticket Booking Service

In this example, several changes are possible. For instance, since credit card information could be stolen and misused, customers may require the payment to be authorized. To fulfill this new requirement R_1, a new functionality *"Validate Customer Identity"* may be added into the existing specification S. Such requirement change leads to a propagation problem: **given $D, S \vDash R$ holds, if requirement R changes into R', how to evolve specification S to S' so that $D, S' \vDash R'$ still holds?** [1]

Similarly, the change of domain assumption would also result in specification evolution. E.g., if a customer who has only debit card also wants to buy ticket online (the assumption *"Customer owns a Credit Card with Available Credits"* is violated), then a new feature *"Processing Debit Card Payment"* would be in need. In this case, the problem can be stated as: **given $D, S \vDash R$ holds, if domain assumption D changes into D', how to find a new specification S' so that $D', S' \vDash R$ still holds?**

Meanwhile, service providers themselves will sometimes update existing services because of economic cost or technical progress. The unilateral evolution would raise the question of whether the changed specification could still satisfy the original requirements. This traceability problem can be noted as: **given $D, S \vDash R$ holds, if the specification S changes to S', would the entailment $D, S' \vDash R$ still be true?**

With the problem settings as our basis, we aim to solve the following principal research problems in requirements-driven service evolution: How to project the changes

---

[1] Keep in mind that changes could occur in both functional and non-functional requirements.

in user requirements to service design space (propagation)? How to evaluate whether existing (evolved) services still satisfy changed (original) requirements (traceability)?

3   The Proposed Solution

This work proposes a systematic approach to address the above presented problems. Basically, we specify requirements using goal model, and then identify features from the fully refined requirement model. At the same time, we associate each operational goal with a service, and compose services when their goals are closely related. Thus a service will have a set of cohesive features and is able to satisfy relevant goal(s). The change of requirements will be first manifested in goal model, and then be propagated to services through features.

3.1   Conceptual Model

The relation between goal, feature and service is shown in the conceptual model of Fig. 2. As it shows, a goal could be either hard-goal or soft-goal, both of which can be decomposed into sub-goals; a goal is usually achieved by more than one service, and a service is able to support more than one goal; generally, a goal would imply the corresponding features of a service: a functional feature is able to support more than one hard-goal and contribute to several soft-goals; also, non-functional feature would reflect the soft-goals of customers.

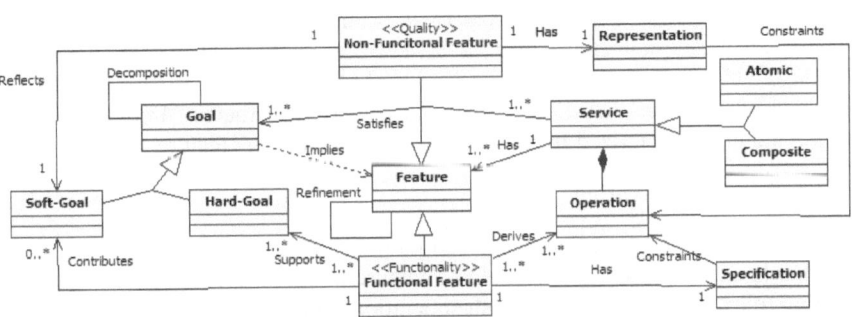

Fig. 2. The Conceptual Model of Goal, Feature and Service

On the other hand, service has two types: *atomic* and *composite*; structurally, a service is a set of operations with input, output, pre-condition and effect (IOPE); meanwhile, a service could be characterized as a set of functional and non-functional features, which could be further refined. Through refinement to functional features, we are able to derive service operations and capture its behavior. Also, non-functional features will be described properly to support evolving services.

3.2   Methodology

In accordance with the conceptual model, we propose a feature-oriented approach to deal with the change propagation from goals to services, and its reverse process. The approach includes two phrases: *model transformation & refinement* and *specification derivation*. The former focuses on identifying and refining features; the later would derive service operations from refined feature model and build service behavior model based on its operations.

— Model Transformation and Refinement

In our approach, we first need to have a refined goal model available, in which each operationalized goal will be assigned to an atomic or composite service. It is possible for more than one operational goal to be associated with the same service. Also, services could be composed according to the structure of goal graph. E.g., if a goal g is AND-decomposed into operational goal g_1 and g_2, which are associated with service s_1 and s_2, then s_1 and s_2 could be composed if g_1 and g_2 are closely related.

Next, we need to identify feature from the refined goal model, which includes tasks, domain assumptions and quality constraints (the concretization of soft-goal). Regarding the refinement of an operational goal g_o, there are some general guidelines for identifying candidate features: a) each OR-decomposed task of g_o; b) each/a combination of AND-decomposed tasks of g_o; c) each (or several cohesive) quality constraint(s). As for the domain assumptions, since they are usually attached to tasks, whether it should be considered as feature candidates needs further exploration.

After the coarse-grained features are identified, we need to further refine them to derive specification. The refinement includes [3]: *decomposition* (refine a feature into its constituent features), *specialization* (make it more detailed), and *characterization* (identify attributes of feature). E.g., a "*Check-out*" feature can be decomposed into "*Pricing*" and "*Taxation*"; then "*Taxation*" could be specialized to "*Fixed-Rate Taxation*" and "*Rule-Based Taxation*"; finally, at least two attributes "*Amount*" and "*Tax-rate*" could be characterized from the "*Fixed-Rate Taxation*" feature.

— Specification Derivation

Through model transformation, we get to know what features a service will have; on the other hand, based on the fully refined feature model, together with a set of proper enacting rules, we are able to derive the operations that a service needs.

Briefly, the enacting rules are as follows: in the refinement process of a feature f, *a)* if f is decomposed into several constituent features $f_{1...m}$, then f will be mapped to an operation and be viewed as the virtual root of the sub-diagram that starts from it; *b)* if f is specialized into sub-features $f_{1...m}$, then each f_i $(1 \leq i \leq m)$ will be a concrete value of one specific parameter of service operation. The parameter stands for the feature specialization and the operation is the lowest virtual root along the backward path from f; *c)* if f is characterized as a set of attributes $a_{1...n}$, each attribute a_i $(1 \leq i \leq n)$ will be mapped to a parameter of the specific operation.

It is expected progress when moving from feature model to service design space. However, it is insufficient without specifying its behavior because service is composite by nature for better fulfilling extensive functionalities.

In this proposal, we model service as hierarchical state machine and specify transitions using an *event-condition-action* (ECA) language on the basis of service operations. The syntax of the ECA language could be briefly noted as:

$$t_i : event\ [guard]\ /\ action\ [effect]$$

in which t_i is the label of transition, *event* is external world-change phenomena (e.g. sending or receiving a message), *guard* is the condition upon which corresponding *action* (usually referrers to service operations) will be performed, and finally the *effect* (e.g. service state change) will be brought about.

As an example, *?bookTicket[HasTicket]/reserveTicket()* [*tickets-1*] describes when a "*bookTicket*" message is received, if the guard ("*HasTicket*") holds, the service will make a reservation and preserve a seat (action: *reserveTicket*). Consequently, the number of available tickets will be decreased (effect).

On the other hand, we model non-functional features as quality constraints. For each non-functional feature, we at first identify its soft-goal and key performance indicator (KPI), and then model the KPI's contribution to the soft-goal as its value varies. Similar to soft-goal contribution, the support a KPI provides could be sufficient/partial positive or negative (++/+/--/-).

> **NonFunctional Feature**: *Comfort Level*
> **SoftGoal** : *Travel Comfort*
> **KPI**: *Leg Room Space*
> **Contribution** : *Leg Room Space* $\geq X$: ++ ; ...

Take the non-functional feature "*Comfort Level*" in airline service as an example: its soft-goal and KPI are "*Travel Comfort*" and "*Leg Room Space*" respectively. We model the contribution of "*Leg Room Space*" to "*Travel Comfort*" as "++" if it is $\geq X$. To better satisfy the soft-goal, one way is to offer a "*Priority Boarding*" feature, which enable customers who board first to place carry-on luggage in overhead bins and thus gain more "*Travel Comfort*" by enhancing the KPI - "*Leg Room Space*". Afterwards, following the aforementioned method, the "*Priority Boarding*" feature will derive new service operation(s) and evolve service behavior model.

3.3   Evaluation

To evaluate the approach, we will develop a tool that extends classical feature model with refinement relationship, transforms refined feature to service operation automatically, enacts service behavior model on the basis of its operations systematically, and demos how clients should evolve synchronously when service changes. In brief, we will validate our approach in a semi-automatic experiment setting.

4   Related Work

Much interesting work has been done on mapping goal model to feature model. For example, Yu et al. [4] discuss the generation of feature model from goal model automatically through one-to-one mapping between goal and feature. Similarly, K. Uno et al. [5] present a systematic approach to derive feature model from an integrated goal model (which is obtained by merging multiple goal graphs) through identifying common and variable features. Their work is valuable for establishing traceability between requirements and features; however, it is insufficient in supporting of evolutionary changes at either goal- or feature- model level.

Also, feature has recently been applied to model diversified functionalities of services and enabling service customization. T. Nguyen et al. [6] propose a template-based approach to build the mapping between feature and service operations. Their approach customizes service interfaces according to selected features, but could not support service evolution due to the lacking of feature semantics.

In software service evolution, the well-known challenge is to keep the compatibility between evolved service and existing client applications at either structural [7] or behavior level [8][9]. Through our extensive survey [10], we found that starting from the definition of service evolution given by M. Papazoglou [9], many efforts have committed themselves to solve the problem by using kinds of tactics, such as versioning, design pattern/adaptor, model and theory [7], but few of them paid enough attention to the change propagation from requirements to services, one of the fundamental problem of evolution.

5   Conclusion

In this paper, a feature-oriented approach is proposed to address the problems in requirements-driven service evolution. The methodology is designed for propagating changes from requirements to services as well as tracing influence back from services to requirements. It is able to identify how service structure should evolve and how service behavior should adapt when requirements change. Being different from the majority of work that merely concentrate on the incompatibility (i.e. the influence of evolution), we are able to answer the more fundamental problems in service evolution: what needs to evolve and how should it evolve.

References

1. Reid Turner, C., Fuggetta, A., Lavazza, L., Wolf, A.L.: A conceptual basis for feature engineering. Journal of Systems and Software 49(1), 3–15 (1999)
2. Jackson, M., Zave, P.: Deriving specifications from requirements: an example. In: 17th International Conference on Software Engineering, ICSE 1995, pp. 15–15 (1995)
3. Kang, K.C., Cohen, S.G., Hess, J.A., Novak, W.E., Peterson, A.S.: Feature-oriented domain analysis (FODA) feasibility study. DTIC Document (1990)
4. Yu, Y., do Prado Leite, J.C., Lapouchnian, A., Mylopoulos, J.: Configuring features with stakeholder goals. In: Proceedings of the 2008 ACM Symposium on Applied Computing, pp. 645–649 (2008)
5. Uno, K., Hayashi, S., Saeki, M.: Constructing feature models using goal-oriented analysis. In: 9th International Conference on Quality Software, QSIC 2009, pp. 412–417 (2009)
6. Nguyen, T., Colman, A.: A Feature-Oriented Approach for Web Service Customization. In: 2010 IEEE International Conference on Web Services (ICWS), pp. 393–400 (2010)
7. Andrikopoulos, V.: A Theory and Model for the Evolution of Software Services. Open Access publications from Tilburg University (2010)

8. Ryu, S.H., Casati, F., Skogsrud, H., Benatallah, B., Saint-Paul, R.: Supporting the dynamic evolution of web service protocols in service-oriented architectures. ACM Transactions on the Web (TWEB) 2(2), 13 (2008)
9. Papazoglou, M.P.: The Challenges of Service Evolution. In: Bellahsène, Z., Léonard, M. (eds.) CAiSE 2008. LNCS, vol. 5074, pp. 1–15. Springer, Heidelberg (2008)
10. Li, F.L., Liu, L., Mylopoulos, J.: Software Service Evolution: A Requirements Perspective. In: Proceedings of the 2012 IEEE International Conference on Computer Software and Applications Conference (COMPSAC), Izmir, Turkey, July 16-20, pp. 353–358 (2012)

Detecting Runtime Business Process Compliance with Artifact Lifecycles

Qi He[1,2]

[1] School of Computer Science, Fudan University, China
[2] College of Information Technology, Shanghai Ocean University, China
061021059@fudan.edu.cn

Abstract. Detecting business process compliance in runtime is the complementary to static compliance checking in the stage of process design, and allows checking whether an execution of a business process satisfies a given constraint. In this paper, runtime compliance checking is used for artifact-centric business process and artifact lifecycles are treated as business constraints. Previous methods for runtime compliance checking mainly put focus on activities in business process and lose the attention for data. In this work we concentrate on both the evolution of artifacts (data) and services (activities) to identify the frontier between decidability and undecidability of the runtime compliance problem. We also provide decidable results and the implement method under regular and context-free artifact lifecycles.

Keywords: BPM, artifact, compliance, decidability.

1 Introduction

As the technique to ensure business processes conforming to rules and regulations, compliance checking occurs in almost full stages of BPM (business processes management) lifecycle. More and more enterprises and organizations are focusing on employing this technique into their BPM systems to improve business efficiency.

Traditionally, the BPM systems are organized in control-centric business process models in which activities are focused on and data just serve as inputs and outputs of some services. In recent years, as a data-centric approach, the artifact-centric methodology[1] has emerged as a new paradigm to support business process management. In the future, most business processes will be implemented based on the artifact-centric idea and this methodology will become the major tendency of BPM.

Currently, researches on compliance of artifact-centric business processes have been carried out by guaranteeing business process models complying with business constraints in the process design phase [2,3,4]. But, it is not comprehensive to only consider compliance during the process of design. For example, in many business processes, non-compliant behaviors can most likely emerge during business process executions for human errors. So, how to detect runtime business process compliance is a crucial challenge of business process management.

A. Ghose et al. (Eds.): ICSOC 2012, LNCS 7759, pp. 426–432, 2013.
© Springer-Verlag Berlin Heidelberg 2013

As key information records in business process, artifacts include both the business-relevant data and their own lifecycles which constrain how they can evolve over time from being created to being achieved as the result of services being applied to them. In general, artifact lifecycles reflect rules that constrain business process. Therefore artifact lifecycles can be regarded as business constraints.

In this paper, our goal is thus to discuss the problem of detecting runtime compliance between artifact-centric business processes executions and business constraints (artifact lifecycles). We propose the formal definition of artifact lifecycles which are languages over special alphabets. Based on this definition, we define the problem of runtime compliance as the acceptance problem for languages. Then we identify the frontier between decidability and undecidability of this problem. To obtain various decidability results, we focus on two kinds of business constraints, regular and context-free artifact lifecycles, and provide the result of decidability. To our knowledge, the present work is the first to study the runtime compliance problem by considering both data (artifacts) and activities (services) formally.

The paper is organized as follows. In Section 2 we survey related works. In Section 3 we formulate the problem of runtime compliance checking with artifact lifecycles. In Section 4 we study the decidability of runtime compliance checking, provide decidable results and the implement method under regular and context-free artifact lifecycles. Section 5 concludes the paper.

2   Related Work

Compliance checking for artifact-centric business processes can be executed both in the stage of process design and the stage of process implementation.

In the stages of process design, compliance checking is developed to verify if business process models is complied with business constraints. [2,3] puts attentions on static analyzing the properties of artifact-centric business processes, such as general temporal constraints. [4] discusses static checking problem, based on the conditions that business processes are represented in artifact systems and the rules are expressed in linear-time temporal logic.

In the stages of process implementation, the runtime compliance checking usually utilizes the results of business process executions to judge if the operations do not violate business rules. In [5, 6], the problem of conformance checking is discussed, which is to check whether the business process executions recorded in logs is consistent with the business process models. [7] presents a novel runtime verification framework based on linear temporal logic, and translates constraint model into colored automata to monitor the business process execution. But, these techniques for runtime compliance checking only consider the activities of business and omit the evolution of data entities.

In this paper, we propose a novel approach to implement runtime compliance checking. And in our works, the changes of data and activities are all considered.

3   Problem Statement

For formulating the problem of runtime compliance for artifact-centric business processes, we provide the definitions of artifact schema, artifact instance, and artifact. We assume the existence of the infinite set $D = \{D_1, D_2, \ldots, D_i, \ldots\}$, where D_i is a finite domain.

Definition 1. An *artifact schema* Γ (simply schema) is a tuple of (U, τ), where (1) U is a finite set of attributes, a special attribute $ID \in U$ is identifier attribute, and (2) $\tau:U \to D$ is a total mapping.

Definition 2. An *artifact instance* a_Γ of schema Γ is a tuple of (id, μ), where (1) μ is a partial mapping that assigns each attribute X in U a value x, $x \in \tau(X)$, and (2) $id \in \tau(ID)$ is an identifier.

Definition 3 [8]. An *artifact* A_Γ of schema Γ is a tuple of (id, T, AI, λ), where (1) id is the identifier of artifact, (2) $T=\{t_1, t_2,\ldots, t_n\}$ is the domain of time, (3) AI is the set of artifact instances of Γ, the identifiers of which are id, (4) $\lambda: T \to AI$ is a total mapping.

Example 1. We briefly describe an example of a business process for equipment sale in shops to illustrate concepts as we introduce them. In this application, only one artifact schema *Order*, shown in Table 1, is included. Table 2 and Table 3 show some artifact instances and artifacts of *Order*.

Table 1. Artifact Schema *Order*

U	$\tau(X), X \in U$
ID	{ 01, 02 }
equipName	{printer, displayer }
Customer	{ Tom, Jack}
checkAvail	{yes, no}
checkPaied	{yes, no}

Table 2. Artifact Instances of *Order*

Artifact Instances Name	id	equipName	Customer	checkAvail	checkPaid
a_{11}	01	printer	Tom	null	null
a_{12}	01	printer	Tom	yes	null
a_{13}	01	printer	Tom	yes	yes
a_{21}	02	displayer	Jack	null	null
a_{22}	02	displayer	Jack	no	null
a_{23}	02	displayer	Jack	yes	null
a_{24}	02	displayer	Jack	yes	yes

Table 3. Artifacts of Order

Artifact Name	id	equipName	Customer	checkAvail	checkPaid	TimeStamp
A_1	01	printer	Tom	null	null	20-10,09:12
	01	printer	Tom	yes	null	21-10,10:11
	01	printer	Tom	yes	yes	21-10,15:09
A_2	02	displayer	Jack	null	null	20-10,19:05
	02	displayer	Jack	no	null	21-10,10:30
	02	displayer	Jack	yes	null	23-10,10:05
	02	displayer	Jack	yes	yes	23-10,13:15

Services are used to modify the values of artifact attributes. The evolutions of artifacts are recorded in execution logs in form of sequences made up of alternate services and artifact instances. In this paper, we define the sequence as a string over an alphabet.

Definition 4. A *service artifact-instance string* ω (simply s-a string) of Γ is a string over the alphabet Σ, where $\Sigma \subseteq S \times AI$, AI is a set of artifact instances of Γ, S is a set of services acting on artifacts of Γ and artifact instances occurring in the string have the same identifier.

Example 2. For the artifact schema *Order* in Example 1, there exist the set of services S_{Order} and the set of artifact instances AI_{Order}, where $S_{Order} = \{s_{o1}, s_{o2}, s_{o3}\}$,

s_{o1}: Create artifacts of *Order*; s_{o2}: Check whether equipments are available,

s_{o3}: Check whether the order is paid,

and $AI_{Order} = \{a_{11}, a_{12}, a_{13}, a_{21}, a_{22}, a_{23}, a_{24}\}$. Let alphabet $\Sigma_{Order} \subseteq S_{Order} \times AI_{Order}$, and $\Sigma_{Order} = \{(s_{o1}, a_{11}), (s_{o1}, a_{21}), (s_{o2}, a_{12}), (s_{o2}, a_{22}), (s_{o2}, a_{23}), (s_{o3}, a_{13}), (s_{o3}, a_{24})\}$. ω_1, ω_2, ω_3 are three s-a strings of *Order*, where

$\omega_1 = (s_{o1}, a_{11})(s_{o2}, a_{12})(s_{o3}, a_{13})$, $\omega_2 = (s_{o1}, a_{21})(s_{o2}, a_{22})(s_{o2}, a_{23})(s_{o3}, a_{24})$,

$\omega_3 = (s_{o1}, a_{21})(s_{o2}, a_{22})(s_{o2}, a_{22})(s_{o2}, a_{23})(s_{o3}, a_{24})$.

Next, we introduce two operations which are provided to get artifact instance sequences (simply AISs) from an artifact and from an s-a string respectively.

Definition 5. Given an artifact $A_\Gamma = (id, T, AI, \lambda)$ of schema Γ and a set of AISs Q in which a AIS is sequence of artifact instances in AI, we provide *the operation α*, $\alpha: \{A_\Gamma\} \to Q$, where $\alpha(A_\Gamma)$ is a AIS $a_1 a_2 \ldots a_i \ldots a_n$ and $a_i = \lambda(t_i)$, $0 \le i \le n$.

Definition 6. Let $\omega = (s_1, a_1)(s_2, a_2) \ldots (s_i, a_i) \ldots (s_n, a_n)$ be a s-a string over $\Sigma \subseteq S \times AI$ and Q be a set of AISs in which a AIS is sequence of artifact instances in AI. We provide *the operation β*, $\beta: \{\omega\} \to Q$, where $\beta(\omega)$ is the AIS $a_1 a_2 \ldots a_i \ldots a_n$.

Example 3. We apply the operation α to A_1, A_2 in Example 1 and apply β to ω_1, ω_2, ω_3 in Example 3. The results are following.

$\alpha(A_1) = a_{11} a_{12} a_{13}$, $\alpha(A_2) = a_{21} a_{22} a_{23} a_{24}$,

$\beta(\omega_1) = a_{11} a_{12} a_{13}$, $\beta(\omega_2) = a_{21} a_{22} a_{23} a_{24}$, $\beta(\omega_3) = a_{21} a_{22} a_{22} a_{23} a_{24}$

Definition 7. Given an artifact A_Γ of schema Γ and a s-a string ω of Γ, ω is the *evolution* of A_Γ if $\alpha(A_\Gamma) = \beta(\omega)$.

Now, we can say that ω_1 is the evolution of artifact A_1, and ω_2 is the evolution of artifact A_2.

Definition 8. Let AI be a set of artifact instances of schema Γ and S is a set of services acting on artifacts of Γ. An *artifact lifecycle* L of Γ is a language over alphabet Σ, $\Sigma \subseteq S \times AI$, i.e., $L = \{\omega \mid \omega \text{ is a s-a string of } \Gamma\}$.

Example 4. Suppose that $L_{Order} = \{\omega_1, \omega_2, \omega_3\}$, and ω_1, ω_2, ω_3 are s-a strings of Γ shown in Example 3. Then L_{Order} is an artifact lifecycle of Γ.

According to the above definitions, we can know that the execution of an artifact-centric business process can be recorded in form of the evolutions of artifacts, and that the problem of runtime compliance is equivalent to the membership problem for an artifact lifecycle L. Formally, we state the problem as follows:

Runtime Compliance Problem: Suppose that Γ is an artifact schema, A_Γ is an artifact of Γ. Given an artifact lifecycle L of Γ and the evolution ω of A_Γ, we say that the execution of business process on artifact A_Γ is in accordance with artifact lifecycle, if $\omega \in L$ is hold.

4   Detecting Runtime Business Process Compliance

Firstly, we address the decision problem of Runtime Compliance Problem. As illustrated in Section 3, an artifact lifecycle is an arbitrary language over alphabet $\Sigma \subseteq S \times AI$, then we show that some artifact lifecycles are not Turing-recognizable.

Theorem 1. Let Γ be an artifact schema, AI be a set of artifact instances of schema Γ and S be a set of services acting on artifacts of Γ. Some artifact lifecycles of Γ are not Turing-recognizable.

Clearly, if an artifact lifecycle is an arbitrary language over alphabet Σ, Runtime Compliance Problem is probable not Turing-recognizable for the reason that the artifact lifecycle is not Turing-recognizable. Therefore we consider the case that the artifact lifecycle is described in a Turing machine. The artifact lifecycle described in a Turing machine is called TM artifact lifecycle in this paper.

Theorem 2. Let Γ be an artifact schema, A_Γ be an artifact of Γ, L_M be a TM artifact lifecycle of Γ and L_M be described in a Turing machine M. Given L_M and the evolution ω of A_Γ, Runtime Compliance Problem is undecidable.

Proof Idea. This proof is obvious, because L_M described in a Turing machine M and the acceptance problem for Turing machine is undecidable. $\square$

Theorem 1 shows that there are artifacts whose lifecycles are not Turing-recognizable, and Theorem 2 implies that Runtime Compliance Problem is undecidable under the condition that an artifact lifecycle is described in Turing machine. To obtain various decidability results, we focus on artifact lifecycles that are described in regular expressions and pushdown automatons.

Definition 9. Let L_1 and L_2 be artifact lifecycles. We define the regular operations *union, concatenation,* and *star* as follows:

1. Union. $L_1 \cup L_2 = \{x \mid x \in L_1 \text{ or } x \in L_2, \}$.
2. Concatenation. $L_1 \circ L_2 = \{xy \mid x \in L_1, y \in L_2, \text{ and the artifact instances occurring in } x \text{ and } y \text{ have the same identifier}\}$.
3. Star. $L_1^* = \{x_1 x_2 \dots x_k \mid k \geq 0, \text{ each } x_i \in L_1, \text{ and the artifact instances occurring in } x_1, x_2, \dots, x_k \text{ have the same identifier}\}$.

Definition 10. Let Γ be an artifact schema, AI be a set of artifact instances of schema Γ and S is a set of services acting on artifacts of Γ. For an alphabet $\Sigma \subseteq S \times AI$, say that

R is a *regular artifact lifecycle expression* of Γ (simply regular ALE) over Σ if R is any form listed below.

1. (s, a) for some (s, a) in the alphabet Σ,
2. ε,
3. $\varnothing$,
4. $(R_1 \cup R_2)$, where R_1 and R_2 are regular ALEs,
5. $(R_1 {\circ} R_2)$, where R_1 and R_2 are regular ALEs,
6. (R_1^*), where R_1 is a regular ALE.

An artifact lifecycle described in a regular ALE is a regular artifact lifecycle.

Theorem 3. Let Γ be an artifact schema, A_Γ be an artifact of Γ, L_R be a regular artifact lifecycle of Γ and be described in a regular ALE R. Given L_R and the evolution ω of A_Γ, Runtime Compliance Problem is decidable.

The regular ALE provides us a powerful tool to describe artifact lifecycles. But the fact still exists that some artifact lifecycles cannot be described in this way. So, we present pushdown automata (PDA) as more powerful tools to describe artifact lifecycles, and call artifact lifecycles described in pushdown automata context-free artifact lifecycles.

Definition 11. Let Γ be an artifact schema, AI be a set of artifact instances of schema Γ and S be a set of services acting on artifacts of Γ. A *pushdown automata* N of Γ is a 6-tuple$(Q, \Sigma, Z, \delta, q_0, F)$, where

1. Q is the set of finite states,
2. Σ is the finite input alphabet, $\Sigma \subseteq S {\times} AI$,
3. Z is the finite stack alphabet,
4. δ: $Q {\times} \Sigma_\varepsilon {\times} Z_\varepsilon {\rightarrow} P(Q \times Z_\varepsilon)$, where $\Sigma_\varepsilon = \Sigma \cup \{\varepsilon\}$, $Z_\varepsilon = Z \cup \{\varepsilon\}$, and $P(Q \times Z_\varepsilon)$ is the power set of $Q \times Z_\varepsilon$,
5. $q_0 \in$ is the start state, and
6. $F \subseteq Q$ is the set of accept states.

The language recognized by PDA N is a context-free artifact lifecycles L_N of Γ.

Theorem 4. Let Γ be an artifact schema, A_Γ be an artifact of Γ, L_N be a context-free artifact lifecycle of Γ and be described in a PDA N. Given L_N and the evolution ω of A_Γ, Runtime Compliance Problem is decidable.

We applied our approach to detecting business process compliance with artifact lifecycles without considering state explosion problems. Here, we provide the framework of this method below:

1. Describe business constraints in regular artifact lifecycles or context-free artifact lifecycles;
2. Generate the corresponding language accepters from the business constraints;
3. Abstract the service artifact-instance string ω (s-a string) from business process execution logs, and ensure ω is the evolution of A_Γ;

4. Provide ω to accepters. If ω is accepted, we can return the result that the execution of business process on artifact A_{Γ} is in accordance with artifact lifecycles.

5   Summary and Future Work

This paper studies the runtime compliance checking for artifact-centric business process. Based on the approach in this paper, we can effectively check whether business processes are compliant with artifact lifecycles in runtime. In future, we are going to build up a comprehensive compliance checking environment for BPM.

References

1. Nigam, A., Caswell, N.S.: Business artifacts: An approach to operational specification. IBM Systems Journal 42(3), 428–445 (2003)
2. Bhattacharya, K., Gerede, C.E., Hull, R., Liu, R., Su, J.: Towards Formal Analysis of Artifact-Centric Business Process Models. In: Alonso, G., Dadam, P., Rosemann, M. (eds.) BPM 2007. LNCS, vol. 4714, pp. 288–304. Springer, Heidelberg (2007)
3. Gerede, C.E., Su, J.: Specification and Verification of Artifact Behaviors in Business Process Models. In: Krämer, B.J., Lin, K.-J., Narasimhan, P. (eds.) ICSOC 2007. LNCS, vol. 4749, pp. 181–192. Springer, Heidelberg (2007)
4. Deutsch, A., Hull, R., Patrizi, F., Vianu, V.: Automatic verification of data-centric business processes. In: International Conference on Database Theory (ICDT 2009), pp. 252–267. ACM Press (2009)
5. Rozinat, A., Jong, I., Gunther, C., Aalst, W.: Conformance Analysis of ASML's Test Process. In: GRCIS 2009, vol. 459, pp. 1–15. CEUR-WS.org (2009)
6. Fahland, D., de Leoni, M., van Dongen, B.F., van der Aalst, W.M.P.: Conformance Checking of Interacting Processes with Overlapping Instances. In: Rinderle-Ma, S., Toumani, F., Wolf, K. (eds.) BPM 2011. LNCS, vol. 6896, pp. 345–361. Springer, Heidelberg (2011)
7. Maggi, F.M., Montali, M., Westergaard, M., van der Aalst, W.M.P.: Monitoring Business Constraints with Linear Temporal Logic: An Approach Based on Colored Automata. In: Rinderle-Ma, S., Toumani, F., Wolf, K. (eds.) BPM 2011. LNCS, vol. 6896, pp. 132–147. Springer, Heidelberg (2011)
8. Ying, W., Guohua, L., Zhen, H., et al.: The Research on Validity of Artifact in BPM. In: International Conference on Business Management and Electronic Information, pp. 15–18. IEEE, Piscataway (2011)

Introduction to the Demo Track

Service oriented computing (SOC) has rapidly transformed from a vision, in the beginning of the century, to reality with technologies such as Web services, Cloud services, and the Internet of Things. While this has provided the industry and practitioners with the opportunities for a new generation of products and services, it has also raised many fundamental research challenges and open issues. The International Conference on Service Oriented Computing (ICSOC) is a premier annual event for researchers, practitioners and industry leaders to discuss and share the success and achievements in this vibrant and rapidly expanding area.

The ICSOC Demonstration Track offers an exciting and highly interactive way to show research prototypes/work in SOC and related areas. Proposals for research prototype demonstrations focus on developments and innovation in the areas of service engineering, operations and management, cloud services, implementation of services as well as development and adoption of services in specific organizations, businesses and the society at large.

This year we received 13 submissions from 10 countries. Each demo proposal has been reviewed by at least three members of the Program Committee. The submissions were evaluated based on originality (novelty), problem significance, technical/scientific quality, and research contributions of the demonstration system. The Program Committee eventually selected seven papers for the Demonstration Track. The selected papers cover a wide range of topics in SOC from service engineering, quality of service, privacy and trust to service modelling, service composition, as well as emerging areas such as Cloud computing.

We thank all authors for their submissions and their active participation and the Program Committee members for their excellent work. We also would like to thank Dr Mike Ma and Dr Jian Yu who chaired the two demonstration sessions.

December 2012

Alex Delis
Quan Z. Sheng

Program Committee
Marco Aiello, University of Groningen, The Netherlands
Claudio Bartolini, HP Labs, USA
Ivona Brandic, Vienna University of Technology, Austria
Sonia Ben Mokhtar, LIRIS, CNRS, France
Djamal Benslimane, University of Lyon, France
Athman Bouguettaya, RMIT University, Australia
Zhong Chen, Peking University, China
Vincenzo D'Andrea, University of Trento, Italy
Dragan Gasevic, Athabasca University, Canada

A. Ghose et al. (Eds.): ICSOC 2012, LNCS 7759, pp. 433–434, 2013.

A Dynamic SCA-Based System
for Smart Homes and Offices

Thomas Calmant[1,2], João Claudio Américo[1], Didier Donsez[1] and Olivier Gattaz[2]

[1] Grenoble University, LIG ERODS Team, Grenoble, France
[2] IsandlaTech, Grenoble, France
{Joao.Americo,Didier.Donsez}@imag.fr,
{Thomas.Calmant,Olivier.Gattaz}@isandlatech.com

Abstract. We demonstrate in this paper the interoperability and the dynamism capabilities in SCA-based systems in the context of smart habitats. These capabilities are due to three developed tools: a Python-based OSGi runtime and service-oriented component model (Pelix and iPOPO, respectively); a tool to publish SCA services as OSGi services (NaSCAr) ; and a tool to publish UPnP devices as SCA services (UPnPServiceFactory). By this, we have developed a service robot and robot pilot agent, which can dynamically add and remove sensors and widgets. This use case follows and responds to the ubiquitous computing trend and the runtime adaptivity needed in such systems.

Keywords: SCA, Service-Oriented Architectures, Component-Based Design, Dynamic Adaptability, Smart Habitats.

1   Introduction

One of the biggest concerns in smart habitats is the integration of the often heterogeneous networked systems and devices that compose them. One of the principal solutions used in the industry nowadays to ease developers' burden concerning integration issues is the use of service-oriented architectures. Thus, service platforms, like UPnP [1], IGRS [2], Echonet [3] and DPWS [4], are very often used, despite their lack of support to ease software development, such as component models. Meanwhile, the Service Component Architecture (SCA) [5] is a technology-agnostic standard for developing service-oriented components. SCA has several runtime implementations, such as OW2 Frascati[6], Apache Tuscany[7], Oracle Tuxedo[8] and IBM WebSphere Application Server Feature Pack for SCA[9]. Nevertheless, these platforms (and the SCA specification itself) do not take into account another problem inherent to networked systems and devices: dynamism. In these highly dynamic scenarios, components (i.e. devices) have dynamic availability, and may appear and disappear several times during the execution time. In this demonstration, we present system infrastructure which enables both the dynamism and the interoperability between two service-oriented component models (SOCMs), one targeting Java/OSGi applications, and the other Python applications. This infrastructure consists of a robot whose devices can be dynamically added and removed. These devices' information collectors are implemented as components in Python and Java-based service-oriented component models.

A. Ghose et al. (Eds.): ICSOC 2012, LNCS 7759, pp. 435–438, 2013.

2   Used Tools

This demonstration software stack is based on four frameworks, the last three being developed by the authors.

The OSGi Service Platform[10] is the basis for most existing SOCMs, such as iPOJO [11] and Declarative Services [12], and it is considered as the standard *de facto* for modularity in Java. It also offers life-cycle management for its modules and enables them to interact by means of its service registry. SOCMs ease components development, by automatically managing SOA mechanisms, such as publication and discovery.

IPOPO is a Python-based service-oriented component model inspired of the iPOJO component model. As iPOJO turns on the top of an OSGi Service platform, iPOPO is executed on an Python-based OSGi container called Pelix.

NaSCAr[14] is a tool which transforms SCA composites into OSGi bundles and deploys them on an OSGi Service Platform. NaSCAr is also based on the iPOJO component model and includes a SCA binding extension that enables dynamic service publication, discovery and binding for SCA composites.

UPnPServiceFactory is a tool which exposes UPnP services in an OSGi Registry.

We intend to present in this demonstration the interoperability between service-oriented component models enabling software development with Java (OSGi) and Python, by composing iPOPO and NaSCAr/iPOJO components dynamically. The components in the system correspond to sensors (robots) and widgets, which are installed as plug-ins and used to display data [15].

3   RobAIR, a Telepresence Robot for Smart Habitats

The use of robotics for personal assistance (named *service robotics*) is growing. It differs from *industrial robotics* in that the service robot coexists and cooperates with humans. In Europe, this area is at the heart of very important societal issues, due to its aging population. A telepresence robot is a mobile service that allows persons to attend meetings, visit factories, warehouses, hospital rooms, museums and so forth. It can be used by technical experts as well as by elderly persons wishing to travel without leaving their houses. A basic implementation would be a video conferencing system mounted on a mobile robotic platform, with or without self-motion control.

In this demonstration, we present RobAIR (Robot for Ambient Intelligence Rooms, depicted in Figure 1), a telepresence robot which can be deployed in smart habitats.

Pilots can remotely control the robot by using an user-agent running on a PC or a tablet. The hardware platform of RobAIR is based on a Wifibot [16]. We have added sensors for piloting (*e.g.* lidar and pan-tilt webcam) and collecting environmental data (*e.g.* geiger counter). New sensors can be dynamically plugged to adapt RobAIR to a specific domain usage (*e.g.* safety inspection for monitoring elderly people or museum visits). Their corresponding components can be dynamically installed as well, without the need to restart the robot. While connected to the robot, the user agent queries the robots components in order to list the current sensors and then dynamically deploys and starts the widgets for the visualization of the sensors data (in this case, radiation level).

The software components inside RobAIR were developed using a SOA approach. They were modeled as SCA components. These components were deployed on an OSGi

Fig. 1. RobAIR - platform and sensors (geiger, toxic gaz)

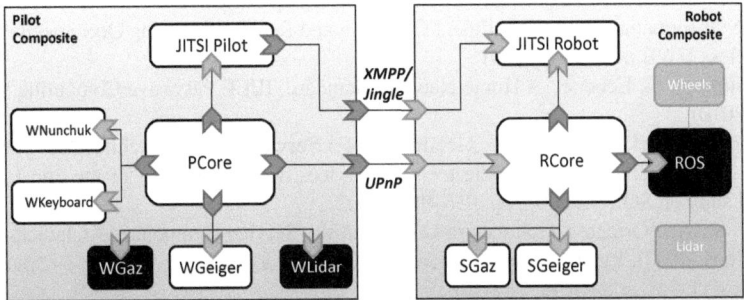

Fig. 2. SCA Modelisation of RobAIR's Robot and Pilot components

platform in both pilot and robot, thanks to NaSCAr and UPnPServiceFactory capabilities. The complete architecture (containing the robot and the pilot's user-agent) is represented by the Figure 2. Black boxes represent Python components, whereas white boxes correspond to Java components.

The robot and the pilot's user agent composites are bound to each other at runtime. The robot composite publishes its services using the UPnP protocols. Pilot's user agent can discover this service and get its description inside a network, like Small-office/Home-Office (SOHO). We have implemented a set of UPnP Device Control Protocols containing three distinct services: a *RobotPilot* service, for piloting the robot; a *SensorCollect* service, to collect the robot sensors; and a *XMPPSession* service, to allow a XMPP audio/video session between the robot and pilot agents.

The two main components are implemented in Java. Inside the *Robot composite*, the sensor components (*i.e. SGaz, SGeiger* and *SLidar*) collect the data from their corresponding sensors. They are instantiated and bound to the component *RCore* when the sensor is plugged to the robot's main board USB connectors, by the means of the UPnPServiceFactory tool. The component *RCore* is also connected to the *JITSI* component in order to exchange audio/video between the robot and the pilot. In turn, inside the *Pilot composite*, the widget components (*i.e. WGaz, WGeiger* and *WLidar*) display collected sensors data. They are instantiated and bound to the component *PCore* when *RCore* notifies changes in the robot's sensors configuration. In addition, controllers (such as Nintendo Wii's Nunchuk and keyboards) can be dynamically bound to *PCore* for piloting the robot.

4   Conclusions

This demonstration paper presents the dynamic and opportunistic composition of heterogeneous services in the highly-variable context of smart habitats. Most of the implemented components aimed to dynamically integrate heterogeneous legacy and off-the-shelfs components, like ROS[17] (250 KLoC in C++) and JITSI[18] (750 KLoC in Java). More information about RobAIR can be found at `http://air.imag.fr/mediawiki/index.php/RobAIR-Wifibot`.

References

1. UPnP: Universal Plug and Play, `http://www.upnp.org/`
2. IGRS: Information Device Intelligent Grouping and Resource Sharing QoS Specification for Wireless UWB networks (2008)
3. Matsumoto, S.: Echonet: A Home Network Standard. IEEE Pervasive Computing 9(3), 88–92 (2010)
4. Zeeb, E., Bobek, A., Bohn, H., Golatowski, F.: Service-oriented architectures for embedded systems using devices profile for web services. In: Proceedings of the 2nd Int'l IEEE Workshop on SOCNE 2007, pp. 956–963 (2007)
5. Open Service-Oriented Architecture Collaboration: Service Component Architecture Specifications (2007), `http://www.osoa.org/display/Main/Service+Component+Architecture+Specifications`
6. Seinturier, L., et al.: Recongurable SCA Applications with the FraSCAti Platform. In: Proceedings of the 6th IEEE Int'l Conference on Service Computing, pp. 268–275 (2009)
7. Apache Foundation: Apache TuSCAny, `http://tuscany.apache.org`
8. Oracle Corporation: Oracle Tuxedo, `http://www.oracle.com/technetwork/middleware/tuxedo/overview/index.html`
9. International Business Machines Corporation: IBM WebSphere Application Server Feature Pack for SCA, `http://www-01.ibm.com/software/webservers/appserv/was/featurepacks/sca`
10. The OSGi Alliance: OSGi service platform core specification, release 4.3 (2011), `http://www.osgi.org/Specifications`
11. Escoffier, C., Hall, R., Lalanda, P.: iPOJO: An Extensible Service-Oriented Component Framework. In: Proc. IEEE Int'l Conf. Services Computing (SCC 2007), pp. 474–481 (2007)
12. Cervantes, H., Hall, R.: Autonomous Adaptation to Dynamic Availability Using a Service-Oriented Component Model. In: ICSE 2004, pp. 614–623 (2004)
13. Calmant, T., Américo, J.C., Gattaz, O., Donsez, D., Gama, K.: A dynamic and service-oriented component model for Python long-lived applications. In: Proceedings of the 15th ACM SIGSOFT Symposium on Component-Based Software Engineering, pp. 35–40 (2012)
14. Américo, J.C., Donsez, D.: Service Component Architecture Extensions for Dynamic Systems. In: Liu, C., Ludwig, H., Toumani, F., Yu, Q. (eds.) ICSOC 2012. LNCS, vol. 7636, pp. 32–47. Springer, Heidelberg (2012)
15. Gama, K., Pedraza, G., Lévêque, T., Donsez, D.: Application management plugin-ins through dynamically pluggable probes. In: Proceedings of the 1st Workshop on Developing Tools as Plug-ins (ICSE Workshop), pp. 32–35 (2011)
16. Wifibot EURL: Wifibot, `http://www.wifibot.com/`
17. Robot Operating System, `http://www.ros.org/`
18. JITSI Community, `https://www.jitsi.org/`

Realizing Elastic Processes with ViePEP

Stefan Schulte[1], Philipp Hoenisch[1], Srikumar Venugopal[2],
and Schahram Dustdar[1]

[1] Distributed Systems Group, Vienna University of Technology, Austria
{s.schulte,dustdar}@infosys.tuwien.ac.at
[2] School of Computer Science and Engineering,
The University of New South Wales, Sydney, Australia

Abstract. Online business processes are faced with varying workloads
that require agile deployment of computing resources. Elastic processes
leverage the on-demand provisioning ability of Cloud Computing to allocate and de-allocate resources as required to deal with shifting demand.
To realize elastic processes, it is necessary to track the current and future
system landscape, monitor the process execution, reason about how to
utilize resources in an optimal way, and carry out the necessary actions
(e.g., start/stop servers, move services).

Traditional Business Process Management Systems (BPMS) do not
consider such needs of elastic process. Within this demo, we present
ViePEP, a research BPMS able to execute and monitor resource-, cost-
and QoS-elastic, service-based workflows and optimize the overall system
landscape based on a reasoning of the non-functional requirements of
current and forthcoming elastic processes.

1 Significance to the Field

Resource-intensive tasks are nowadays not only common within scientific workflows, but are also getting more and more common in business processes.[1]. For
example, compute- and data-intensive analytical processes are found in the finance industry and in managing smart grids in the energy industry. In the latter
case, data from a very large number of sensors needs to be gathered, processed
and stored in real-time in order to offer consumers consumption reports or even
guarantee grid stability [5]. As the number of active sensors differs during a day,
the amount of data also fluctuates to a very large extent. Furthermore, certain
processes or process steps are permitted to be postponed to the future, while
others need to be carried out immediately.

In such a scenario, the permanent provisioning of IT capacity able to handle
peak system loads is obviously not the best solution, as the capacities will not be
utilized most of the time. With the advent of Cloud Computing, organizations
nowadays have got a much more cost-savvy alternative which allows them to
make use of computing resources in an on-demand, utility-like fashion [1].

---

[1] In the following, we will also make use of the term "workflows" to name the automated parts of business processes.

A. Ghose et al. (Eds.): ICSOC 2012, LNCS 7759, pp. 439–442, 2013.
© Springer-Verlag Berlin Heidelberg 2013

To the best of our knowledge, so far, little effort has been put into the investigation of methods and tools to integrate automated process execution and Cloud Computing in order to realize so-called *elastic processes* [2].

Nevertheless, scalability and cost-effective allocation of single tasks and applications have been observed by many researchers, e.g., [4]. So far, applications are mostly regarded in isolation, i.e., a process perspective across utilized resources (software, hardware, humans) is typically not applied. While Cloud resources have been used for executing scientific workflows [3], Service Level Agreements (SLAs) are typically not as much a concern in this domain as they are for business processes. In our experience, there is a lack of a BPMS able to carry out many service-based workflows in parallel, estimate their current *and* future resource demand under given Quality of Service (QoS) constraints, and allocate resources dynamically to meet their individual SLAs. This needs analysing the process to discover which of its steps determine the performance of its execution and prioritising them, allocating resources to services to address demand and balancing load on the resources by moving services between them.

Within this demo paper, we will present our *Vienna Platform for Elastic Processes (ViePEP)* [6], which is a research-driven, prototypical BPMS capable to execute elastic processes, monitor the current utilization of invoked resources as well as reason about future resource demands, and carry out necessary actions.

2   System Overview

In this section, we present the overall system architecture of ViePEP as depicted in Figure 1. Within ViePEP, processes are modeled making use of a XML-based description format, which also defines non-functional constraints and preferences for each process step. Each process step is mapped to a particular service which is able to fulfill it. The execution of processes is constantly monitored and the results are fed to a centralised manager. Based on the monitoring data, and knowledge about current and future process instances and their individual non-functional requirements, it is possible to reason about the best allocation of services to Virtual Machines (VMs) as well as more general actions, e.g., starting and terminating servers.

Figure 1 shows an overview of ViePEP using an FMC Block Diagram. Both the BPMS and Backends are running inside dedicated VMs. For the sake of simplicity, only one Backend VM is depicted; however, an arbitrary number of Backend VMs may be invoked. The BPMS consists out of the following main components:

- The **Workflow Manager** controls the workflow executions. It invokes the services step by step. Before each invocation, it queries the Load Balancer for the best fitting service instance for the next step. In addition, the Workflow Manager measures service-specific QoS data like response time.
- The **Load Balancer** retrieves the actual VM states from the shared memory and is responsible to balance the service invocations, so that the system load of all Backend VMs does not exceed a predefined threshold.

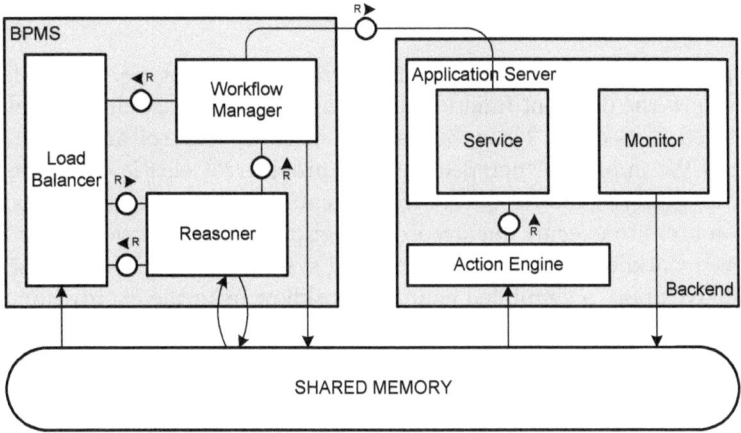

Fig. 1. Framework Architecture

– Reasoning is performed in order to estimate the future resource demand and optimize the overall process landscape, e.g., by choosing between different actions like duplicating, or moving Web services from one VM to another or starting and terminating servers [4]. For this, dynamic resource and cost information must be taken into account in order to decide how to utilize resources in a cost-efficient way while guaranteeing the non-functional constraints of each process step or overall process, respectively.

In ViePEP, the **Reasoner** is responsible for reasoning and optimization of the process landscape. It requests information about future workflow instantiations and service invocations from the Workflow Manager. Furthermore, it retrieves the status of all Backend VMs from the shared memory and communicates with the Load Balancer in order to decide whether a particular Backend VM is sufficient to carry out a service, if another VM hosting that service needs to be started, or if a VM can be stopped due to low load.

The ViePEP-enabled Backend VMs contain the following components:

– An **Application Server** (here: Apache Tomcat) hosting a Web service.
– A **Monitor** is part of the Application Server. After an elastic process has been modeled and the corresponding workflow executed, it is necessary to monitor the current resource workload as well as the non-functional behavior of the single invocation services. Therefore, ViePEP allows to monitor the CPU and RAM utilization of all Cloud servers within a system. Monitoring data is stored in a shared memory based on Tuple Spaces, allowing the ViePEP BPMS to access the status of all running VMs.
– The **Action Engine** is responsible to execute commands to the Application Server. It gets according commands from the Reasoner through the shared memory data structure. It can copy the whole system state and start a new VM or shut itself down if necessary.

3 Demonstration

At this point, ViePEP is a fully functional research prototype. In the demo, we will show how the different functionalities (monitoring, reasoning, optimization) as presented in Section 2 can be used in order to control an elastic process landscape. We apply the perspective of a provider of elastic processes, i.e., a broker who gets workflow requests from clients and automatically provides the Cloud resources to execute the according workflow steps (services). For this, we show how a workflow is added to an existing system landscape and consequently executed. We apply a simplified example workflow from the energy domain. For reasons of simplicity, we are applying only one workflow model; however, the model is instantiated several times in parallel in order to show how changing loads on a VM leads to the start and termination of VMs.

We will show how the monitoring data is visualized and consequently exploited in order to assess current resource demands. Furthermore, we will compute future workflow instantiations and service invocations. Based on this, it is possible to derive the future resource demand and consequently carry out actions as explained above. The according screencast can be found at `http://www.infosys.tuwien.ac.at/prototypes/ViePEP/ViePEP_index.html`

Acknowledgements. This work is partially supported by the Commission of the European Union within the SIMPLI-CITY FP7-ICT project (Grant agreement no. 318201) and the Austrian Science Fund (FWF): P23313-N23.

Part of the implementation has been done during Philipp's stay at the University of New South Wales, which was supported by a scholarship from Vienna University of Technology's International Office. We'd like to thank Han Li for his help with the implementation.

References

1. Buyya, R., Yeo, C.S., Venugopal, S., Broberg, J., Brandic, I.: Cloud computing and emerging IT platforms: Vision, hype, and reality for delivering computing as the 5th utility. Future Generation Computing Systems 25(6), 599–616 (2009)
2. Dustdar, S., Guo, Y., Satzger, B., Truong, H.L.: Principles of Elastic Processes. IEEE Internet Computing 15(5), 66–71 (2011)
3. Juve, G., Deelman, E.: Scientific Workflows and Clouds. ACM Crossroads 16(3), 14–18 (2010)
4. Li, H., Venugopal, S.: Using reinforcement learning for controlling an elastic web application hosting platform. In: 8th International Conference on Autonomic Computing (ICAC 2011), pp. 205–208 (2011)
5. Rusitschka, S., Eger, K., Gerdes, C.: Smart Grid Data Cloud: A Model for Utilizing Cloud Computing in the Smart Grid Domain. In: 1st IEEE International Conference on Smart Grid Communications (SmartGridComm), pp. 483–488 (2010)
6. Schulte, S., Hoenisch, P., Venugopal, S., Dustdar, S.: Introducing the Vienna Platform for Elastic Processes. In: Zhu, H., Ghose, A., Yu, Q., Perrin, O., Wang, J., Wang, Y., Delis, A., Sheng, Q.Z. (eds.) ICSOC 2012. LNCS, vol. 7759, pp. 179–190. Springer, Heidelberg (2013)

A Social Network Based Collaborative Video Story Composition Platform

Chen Wang, Meng Meng, Xiangmin Zhou, and Rajiv Ranjan

Information Engineering Lab, CSIRO ICT Centre, Australia
{chen.wang,mendy.meng,xiangmin.zhou,raj.ranjan}@csiro.au

1   Introduction

There is a large number of videos produced and stored in data repositories on a daily basis. Story-telling is a common use-case for using these videos where a user composes a set of videos together to tell a story, either for learning purposes or sharing experiences. For example, a news editor may search and compose story based on video collected from multiple private and public repositories; an instructor may produce teaching materials using a set of publicly available video clips. Existing search engines have limitation on identifying useful video contents for users with different needs [2]. For a user who attempts to compile a story using a variety of videos, there are a few challenges with existing technologies. A search engine often returns a long list of videos that are relevant to the keywords the user enters into the search engine. How the videos in the list are suitable for the story line requires the user's further investigation and the amount of work involved often overwhelms the user considering the number of videos returned by a search engine. It is often the case that the highly ranked videos are not the most appropriate ones for a story line under composing. In addition, videos are not organized in a structured manner based on the content, which makes identifying videos that match the story topic difficult and time consuming.

Many existing work tackle this problem by integrating textual and visual concepts to group videos [3]. Our method treats story-telling as a collaborative process. It is different to other methods mainly in that we integrate collaborators' contributions via social networking services to help story-telling. These contributions include adding comments, recommending relevant videos etc. With certain automated information processing, the method can effectively reduce the workload of an individual when composing a story out of a large number of videos from various sources.

We assume that the story composer has a number of friends or collaborators who have knowledge on the story and are willing to contribute to the story. It is common in the real world that these people participate in a same event or have mutual interests on the topics of the story. As stories are diverse and the group of people who may be interested in contributing them are dynamic, managing these users with different interests is a challenging problem. We address this problem by leveraging the power of social networks to organize a dynamic group of people for contributing to a story.

A. Ghose et al. (Eds.): ICSOC 2012, LNCS 7759, pp. 443–446, 2013.
© Springer-Verlag Berlin Heidelberg 2013

The proposed story composition platform has the following novelties:

1. The platform makes story-telling a collaborative process and supports the main author of a story to interactively integrate collaborators' input including comments and recommendations;
2. The collaboration is dynamically organized by leveraging the services provided by social networks, in our case, Facebook services;
3. The platform aggregates collaborators' recommendations and comments. It is capable of processing certain information in an automatic manner, e.g., it can organize information based on topics and timeline to further help story composition.

2   System Overview

The platform mainly consists of the following two components:

1. A Web user interface as a working bench for a story author to compose stories. The user interface requires the story author to login using her Facebook account. The authentication is done using *OAuth 2.0 protocol* [1]. The access of user information is through Facebook Open Graph API.
2. A social information aggregator that does the following tasks:
    (a) publishes the story author's activities to a social networking site. The activities include the metadata of the story under authoring as well as ongoing editing activities;
    (b) retrieves relevant information contributed by collaborators, including a collaborator's comments to the story and recommended relevant videos by the collaborator;
    (c) processes the information and discovers certain topics as well as timelines to present to the story author.

Fig. 1 gives an example that shows the basic information flow in the platform. In this scenario, an author creates a story about Sam Stosur, an Australian tennis player. Firstly, the author, e.g., a sports news editor, signs in the platform using her Facebook account. Secondly, she submits a query with keyword "Sam Stosur" to search for videos to start a story. The platform passes the query to the search services of video repositories. Each video repository returns a list of relevant videos. The author may select one and add it to the storyboard. Thirdly, the platform automatically publish the action to Facebook. Fourthly, a collaborator who is in the author's friend list in Facebook may add comments or recommend videos that are related to the story. In the next step, the recommender subsystem processes these comments and recommendations. It then presents recommendations to the story author who may take the recommendation and make changes on the storyboard.

Apparently, an active collaborator is likely to recommend videos that are more relevant to the story line or add comments that can help the author to improve the story line. However, when there are a number of collaborators, reviewing recommendations and comments may become a time consuming process. In our platform, we provide a recommendation service for easing the task.

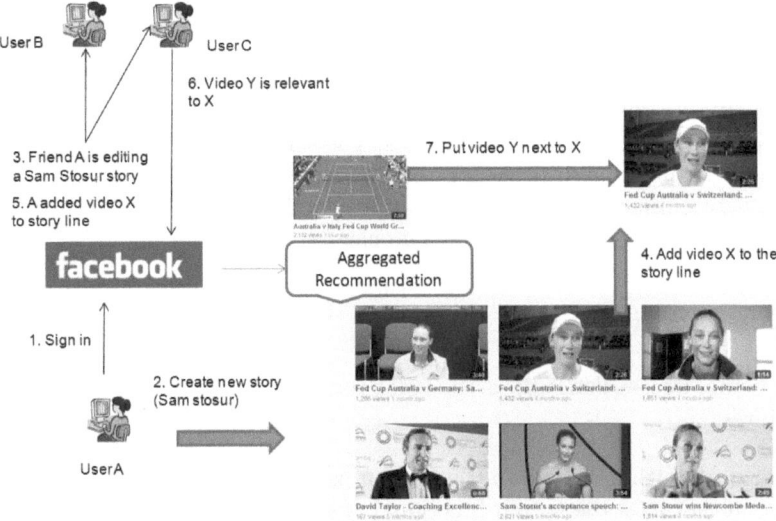

Fig. 1. An example of the basic information flow in the platform (the blue arrow represents the activities of the story author)

2.1   Recommender

The recommendation service fits into the system as shown in Fig. 2. The recommender refines both video and text data from video sources and the social information aggregator. A video data source can be a private data repository or a public data repository. The social information aggregator maintains information such as the author's story creating activities, the collaborator list and manages the input from collaborators. The recommendation service produces the following three types of recommendations to the story author:

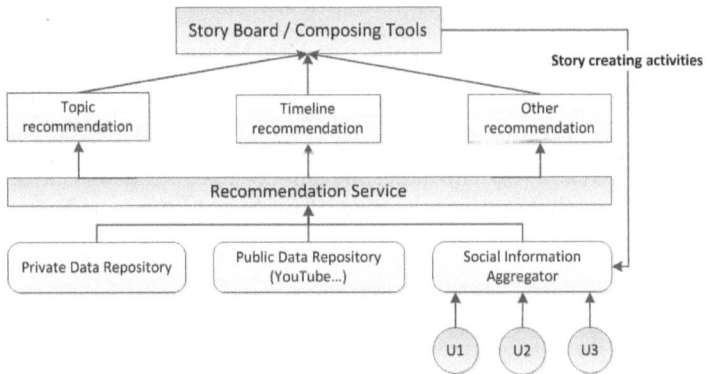

Fig. 2. The recommender architecture

1. Relevant topics: a list of videos categorized by topics that can be derived from the story line under composition. A collaborator is capable of identifying topics among a set of videos and recommending these videos to the author.
2. Timeline recommendation: a group of collaborators may annotate videos based on the event time in the videos. The service can present related videos along the time line to help story composition.
3. Other recommendation: mainly contains comments collected from the social information aggregator that have no clear structures.

3   Demo Script

In this demo, we use YouTube as the video repository and will show the following procedures:

1. The story author signs into the system using her Facebook account;
2. The author uses the search functionality to find videos. This will show how the search results are presented and how a story is initiated;
3. The collaborators sign in to their Facebook account and see the actions of the story author;
4. A collaborator recommends related videos and comments on the story;
5. The storyboard organizes collaborators' input based on different topics. We will show how the story author uses the recommendations to further develop the story.

The video for the demo is accessible at `http://www.youtube.com/watch?v=XvgwL6n9ZZI` (A high resolution version can be found at `http://www.ict.csiro.au/staff/chen.wang/demo/icsoc12-demo.mp4`).

References

1. Hammer-Lahav, E., Recordon, D., Hardt, D.: The oauth 2.0 authorization protocol. Network Working Group Internet-Drafts,
   `http://tools.ietf.org/pdf/draft-ietf-oauth-v2-12.pdf`
2. Hong, R., Tang, J., Tan, H.-K., Ngo, C.-W., Yan, S., Chua, T.-S.: Beyond search: Event-driven summarization for web videos. ACM Trans. Multimedia Comput. Commun. Appl. 7(4), 35:1–35:18 (2011)
3. Wu, X., Ngo, C.-W., Li, Q.: Threading and autodocumenting news videos: a promising solution to rapidly browse news topics. IEEE Signal Processing Magazine 23(2), 59–68 (2006)

BPMashup: Dynamic Execution of RESTful Processes

Xiwei Xu[1], Ingo Weber[1,2], Liming Zhu[1,2], Yan Liu[3,2], Paul Rimba[1,2],
and Qinghua Lu[1,2]

[1] Software System Research Group, NICTA, Australia
[2] School of Computer Science and Engineering, UNSW, Australia
[3] Pacific Northwest National Laboratory, USA
{first.last}@nicta.com.au, Yan.Liu@pnnl.gov

1   Introduction

While WS*-based Service-Oriented Architecture (SOA) is employed heavily in the
enterprise application & integration space, end-user-oriented organizations such as
Facebook, Google or Yahoo! adopted the REST paradigm. Web service ecosystems
[1] have been established around web service offerings like social networking, where
open platforms enable third-party developers to easily leverage the infrastructure
provided by the social networks, to build web applications and plugged-in services for
a massive user base. Such a web service ecosystem typically comprises a service provider opening up their product public service platform, a set of external value-added-
resellers, and a community of users building and sharing customizations [2]. The
lower layers of the traditional SOA-based WS* standards stack provide a loosely
coupled infrastructure for Web service ecosystems. However, process layers on top of
the standards stack introduce a comparatively tight coupling between the process
logic and the WSDL interface definition [3], which tends to be brittle.

Composition of RESTful web services is usually achieved as light-weight Mashups
– focusing on combining data from various sources, or handling events – or by using
textual documentation to allow developers to understand processes involved. Traditional process-centric composition methods hardly fit the new paradigm.

REST and Resource-Oriented Architecture principles [4] are well established, and
have been applied to web-based cross-enterprise business processes [5, 6] as an alternative way of implementing Web services. However, most existing approaches focus
on building a RESTful facade to traditional service technologies without fundamen-
tally using the REST principles. In traditional SOA, many approaches have been
proposed to extend BPEL, e.g., with adaptation mechanisms using aspect-oriented
programming [7] or rules [8]. These approaches still introduce tight coupling between
process definition and Web service description. Some approaches [9] use WSDL-like
descriptions for RESTful services, which arguably means losing most of the benefits.

In contrast, we present *BPMashup* in this demonstration: a framework that tailors
REST principles towards process-aware information systems. BPMashup consists of
the previously published server component, *RESTfulBP* [10], as well as a novel
client-side JavaScript library – the Localized Process Execution Engine, *LPEE* – for
executing processes and rendering UI widgets referring to individual service invocations. It has previously been shown that RESTfulBP can improve the adaptability and

A. Ghose et al. (Eds.): ICSOC 2012, LNCS 7759, pp. 447–450, 2013.

interoperability of process-aware systems [10]. Through the comprehensive framework of BPMashup, these benefits are applied also to processes combining services from more than one source. This is achieved by splitting business processes into distributed process fragments that are transferred dynamically at runtime.

A demonstration video and a technical report are available[1]. The report gives in-depth details on related work and technology, such as built-in security and encryption mechanisms and the coverage of workflow patterns.

2   BPMashup Overview

BPMashup provides a RESTful infrastructure for mashing up processes in web service ecosystems, using process fragments and dynamic next-step pointers that link to other services. A client-side process execution engine allows the processes to be executed at the edge of the system, to enable local decision making and improve adaptability of the business processes. While this demonstration focuses on the process execution phase, a BPMN-based modeling tool has been implemented[2], including a translation from BPMN to the artifacts required for process execution in BPMashup. Fig. 1 provides an overview of the system.

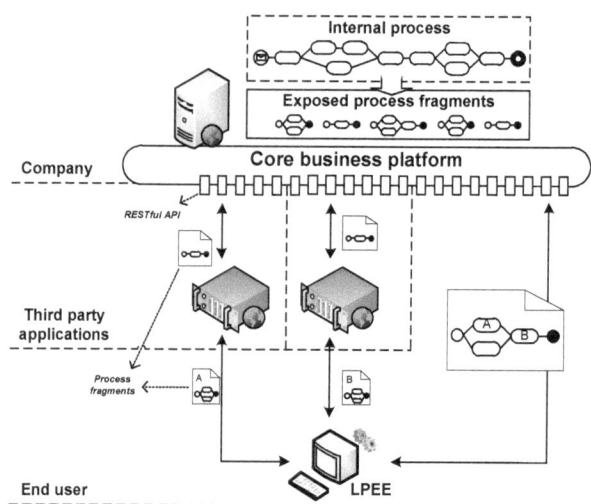

Fig. 1. BPMashup architecture

The **business platform** exposes parts of the internal business processes of a company, as far as this is needed for partners and customers of the company to interact with a given process. The process coordination mechanism of BPMashup defines the exposed parts of processes as a set of loosely connected process fragments that can be transferred among participants to enable localized process execution.

---

[1] http://nicta.info/bpmashup

Third-party applications in a web service ecosystem based on BPMashup allow the external development of applications, faster co-creation and execution of cross-enterprise processes. The extensions are available as fragments as well.

BPMashup supports **end-users** through client-side process execution and localized decision making by providing LPEE (Localized Process Execution Engine). The end-users can thus drive the process execution, by selecting the most suitable process fragment from a group of candidate fragments in the current execution state.

Most notably, LPEE executes an overall composition (shown on the right in Fig. 1), which can include **sub-processes** that are provided by third-party applications (examples *A* and *B* in Fig. 1). A sub-process can be an atomic service invocation or a **process fragment**, which, in turn, may refer to other sub-processes. Furthermore, the messages exchanged with a service include both payload information and a process fragment's control flow. As such, sub-process implementations can be modified at any point in time, without breaking the overall composition. Process fragments from third-party applications can be included in the overall composition (e.g., fragments *A* and *B* in Fig. 1). However, due to the same-origin policy implemented in most browsers, all traffic of the JavaScript-based LPEE has to go through the platform.

3   Example Scenario

For illustration purposes, we demonstrate BPMashup via the Virtual Travel Agent (VTA) example, as shown in Fig. 2. In BPMashup's VTA solution, all participating providers platformize their business as process fragments. For existing services, this means implementing a BPMashup wrapper. The hotel and airline partners are the third-party application providers, offering availability/price checking and booking in process fragments. The travel agent provides the platform's composition of these fragments, along with an integrated payment system. Messages from BPMashup include payload data, process fragments, and visualization information for steps. LPEE renders the process fragments according to the visualization instructions, as shown in Fig. 3, where the areas highlighted in red correspond to the enumerated fragments in Fig. 2.

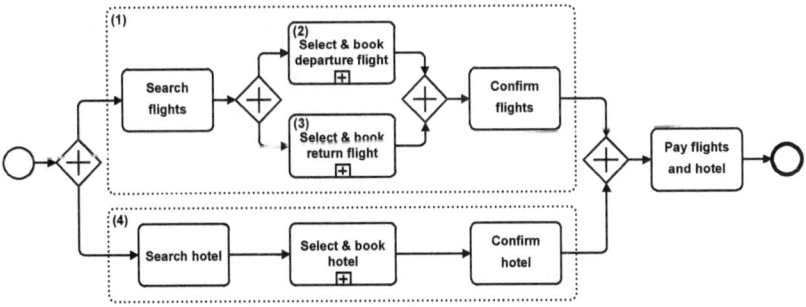

Fig. 2. Process model of travel agent, with enumeration of some areas

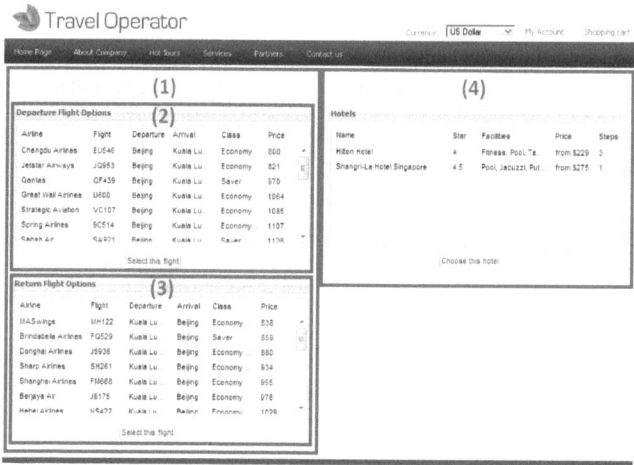

Fig. 3. Snapshot of hotel and flight selection page, where red boxes highlight certain snippets

4   Conclusion

The BPMashup framework enables executing process-centric compositions of RESTful web services. Following REST principles, BPMashup decouples the relationships between the process participants, while allowing to hide internal business logic behind exposed process fragments. The process fragments are executed on the client side, allowing flexible process definitions which can be adapted dynamically: fragments can be changed at runtime, as long as the overall composition remains intact.

References

1. Veryard, R.: Ecosystem SOA. In: Richard Veryard on Architecture (2009)
2. Jansen, S., et al.: A Sense of Community: A Research Agenda for Software Ecosystems. In: 31st International Conference on Software Engineering, ICSE 2009 (2009)
3. Pautasso, C., Wilde, E.: Why is the web loosely coupled? A multi-faceted metric for service design. In: 18th International Conference on World Wide Web (WWW 2009) (2009)
4. Richardson, L., Ruby, S.: RESTful Web Services. O'Reilly Media (2007)
5. Overdick, H.: Towards Resource-Oriented BPEL. In: The 2nd ECOWS Workshop on Emerging Web Services Technology (WEWST 2007) (2007)
6. Pautasso, C.: BPEL for REST. In: Dumas, M., Reichert, M., Shan, M.-C. (eds.) BPM 2008. LNCS, vol. 5240, pp. 278–293. Springer, Heidelberg (2008)
7. Charfi, A., Mezini, M.: AO4BPEL: An Aspect-oriented Extension to BPEL. Journal of World Wide Web 10(3), 309–344 (2007)
8. Baresi, L., Guinea, S.: Self-Supervising BPEL Processes. IEEE Transactions on Software Engineering 37(2), 247–263 (2011)
9. WADL, http://www.w3.org/Submission/wadl/ (accessed October 06, 2010)
10. Xu, X., Zhu, L., Kannengiesser, U., Liu, Y.: An Architectural Style for Process-Intensive Web Information Systems. In: Chen, L., Triantafillou, P., Suel, T. (eds.) WISE 2010. LNCS, vol. 6488, pp. 534–547. Springer, Heidelberg (2010)

SODA: A Tool Support for the Detection of SOA Antipatterns

Mathieu Nayrolles[1,2], Francis Palma[2,3],
Naouel Moha[2], and Yann-Gaël Guéhéneuc[3]

[1] CESI.eXia, École Supérieur d'Informatique, France
mathieu.nayrolles@viacesi.fr
[2] Département d'Informatique, Université du Québec à Montréal, Canada
moha.naouel@uqam.ca
[3] Ptidej Team, DGIGL, École Polytechnique de Montréal, Canada
{francis.palma,yann-gael.gueheneuc}@polymtl.ca

Abstract. During their evolution, Service Based Systems (SBSs) need to fit new user requirements and execution contexts. The resulting changes from the evolution of SBSs may degrade their design and Quality of Service (QoS), and thus may cause the appearance of common poor solutions, called *Antipatterns*. Like other complex systems, antipatterns in SBSs may hinder the future maintenance and evolution. Therefore, the automatic detection of such antipatterns is an important task for assessing the design and QoS of SBSs, to facilitate their maintenance and evolution. However, despite of their importance, no tool support exists for the detection of antipatterns in SBSs. In this paper, we introduce a prototype tool, called SODA, for detecting SOA (Service Oriented Architecture) antipatterns in SBSs.

Keywords: Antipatterns, Service Based Systems, Detection, Specification, Quality of Service.

1 Introduction

Service Based Systems (SBSs) evolve to fit new user requirements, e.g., additional functionalities or better Quality of Service (QoS). These technical and functional changes may degrade the design and QoS of SBSs and often introduce poor solutions, called *Antipatterns*, by opposition to *patterns* which are good solutions to recurring problems. *Multi Service* and *Tiny Service* are two common and recurring antipatterns in SBSs, and it is revealed, in particular, that *Tiny Service* is the root cause of many SOA failures [4]. *Multi Service* is an SOA antipattern that corresponds to a service that implements a multitude of methods related to different business and technical abstractions. Such a service is not easily reusable because of the low cohesion of its methods and is often unavailable to end-users [1]. Conversely, *Tiny Service* is a small service with just a few methods, which only implements part of an abstraction. Such service often requires several coupled services to be used together, resulting in

A. Ghose et al. (Eds.): ICSOC 2012, LNCS 7759, pp. 451–455, 2013.

higher development complexity and reduced usability [1]. While degrading the design and QoS of SBSs, antipatterns may make it harder for engineers to perform maintenance and evolution tasks. SOA antipatterns are more dynamic in nature, thus more challenging to detect. Therefore, the automatic detection of such SOA antipatterns is an important activity to assess the design and QoS of SBSs, and thus ease the maintenance and evolution tasks of the engineers. However, a number of works have been devoted for the development of detection tools within Object Oriented (OO) systems [2,5,6]. Yet, for the detection of SOA antipatterns in SBSs, there is no tool support. In this paper, we present a SOA antipatterns detection tool, SODA (Service Oriented Detection for Antipatterns) to help engineers, for detecting SOA antipatterns automatically in SBSs. SODA provides the means for both static and dynamic analysis of SBSs.

The remainder of this paper is organized as follows. Section 2 surveys related work on tool support for the detection of OO code and design issues. Section 3 presents our detection tool, SODA, along with the underlying approach and some results. Finally, we conclude and sketch future work in Section 4.

2   Related Work

With the goal of detecting OO code and design related issues, a number of tools have been introduced in the literature [2,5,6]. Nevertheless, researchers and developers have rarely considered tools to perform detection for SOA antipatterns, i.e., in SBSs. Král et al. [3] specified briefly seven SOA antipatterns, but did not discuss their detection. SOA antipatterns are not well documented and empirically validated in the literature. To this end, we contribute to the progress in this area by proposing a tool, called SODA, as support for detecting SOA antipatterns.

3   Overview of SODA Approach

We developed the tool SODA being inspired from our approach of the same name, SODA, proposed in [7]. Figure 1 represents the three main steps of SODA: (1) Specifying SOA antipatterns in the form of rule cards from their textual descriptions, (2) Generating detection algorithms conformed to the antipattern specifications, and (3) Detecting automatically SOA antipatterns and involved suspicious service(s) in the analyzed SBS.

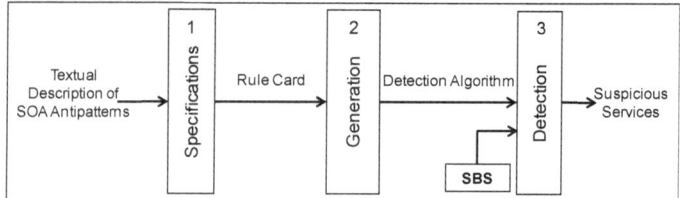

Fig. 1. SODA Approach for the Detection of SOA Antipattern

In [7], we perform a domain analysis to specify SOA antipatterns by studying their definitions and specifications from the literature to pinpoint significant
static and dynamic properties (represented as *metrics*). We then use these properties as the basis for the vocabulary to define our own domain specific language
(DSL), and formalize rule cards. A rule card is the specification of a certain
SOA antipattern at a high-level of abstraction using a combination of multiple
singleton rules. Starting from the specifications of SOA antipatterns described
with rule cards, we generate detection algorithms automatically from rule cards,
by applying a simple *template*-based technique. We also develop a framework,
called SOFA (Service Oriented Framework for Antipatterns) [7], that supports
metric-based detection of SOA antipatterns in SBSs. SOFA assists the tool SODA,
and provides all services needed for the detection of SOA antipatterns, such as,
static and dynamic analyses, essentially in the form of *metrics*.

3.1   Description of SODA Tool

Figure 2 presents the snap-shot of our SODA tool. We mark different sections of
the tool from 1 to 7. Section 1 enlists the SOA antipatterns that can be detected.
For the selected antipattern, Section 2 provides textual description, while Section
3 shows the corresponding rule card; Section 4 presents the results, i.e., suspicious
service(s); Section 5 provides values for all metrics (from the associated rule
card), for each service; Section 6 exposes the generated association rules. Finally,
Section 7 helps to visualize the suspicious service(s) within the analyzed SBS.

Most of the dynamic and static metrics calculated by SOFA use only the
service interfaces that are freely available. An extension of our tool, called SO-
DAAR (Service Oriented Detection for Antipatterns based on Association Rules)
enables SODA to identify suspicious service(s) by mining association rules [8]
to discover interesting relations between services, i.e., patterns, using execution
traces. Association rules are implications of the form $A \rightarrow B$ (i.e., if-then statement), where A and B may be a single service or a subset of services. In SODAAR,
each execution trace is considered as a *transaction* and invoked methods identified within traces as *items*. Based on these association rules, we can classify
suspicious services. Considering the metric-based framework, i.e., SOFA and our
extended SODAAR, we developed a complete tool, SODA.

Principal Features of SODA

1. SODA does direct import of an SBS as a JAR package.
2. SODA has a straight forward detection interface for the users, which is handy
   both for beginners and experts.
3. SODA shows all the detection details, i.e., metric values, corresponding rule
   cards, textual descriptions of antipatterns etc.
4. For the detection, SODA supports both well-known metric based and execution trace based analysis of SBSs.
5. Also, SODA exposes all the execution traces, association rules generated from
   those traces, and relations among them, that is also useful to the users to
   better understand the SBS analyzed.

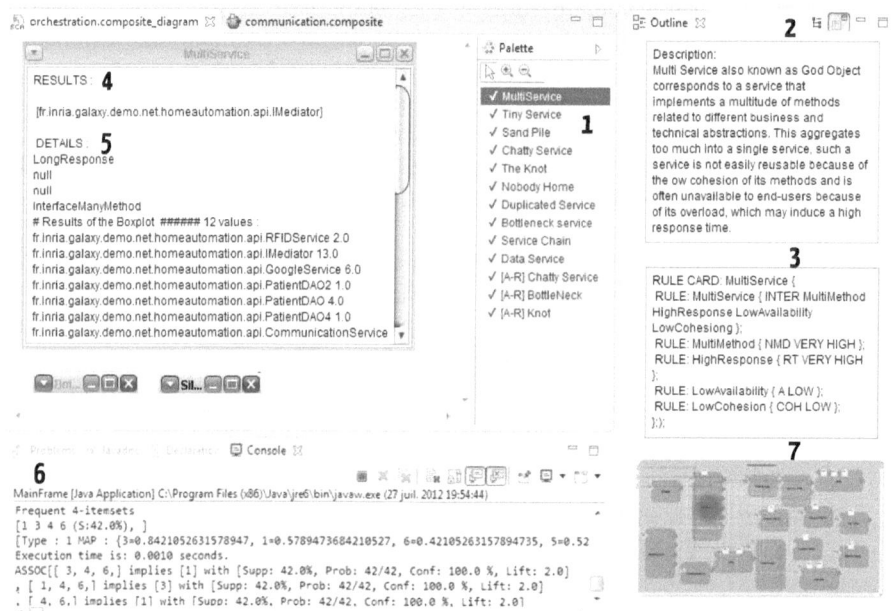

Fig. 2. Detection of SOA Antipatterns with SODA

Figure 2 shows the detection results for *Multi Service* antipattern. An elaborative presentation about the SODA tool, more detection results and further materials are available at http://sofa.uqam.ca/tool.html. We also show the precision and recall of the detection algorithms used by SODA tool in [7]. Currently SODA can detect 10 SOA antipatterns, and users can extend this number by adding new metrics and thus new rule cards for new antipatterns.

4   Conclusion and Future Work

In this paper, we presented SODA that incorporates the framework, SOFA, i.e., metrics based analysis. SODAAR, an extension of SODA, is based on execution trace analysis. As the future work, we intend to develop SODA as an Eclipse plug-in and provide a graphical interface to visualize the detected antipatterns easily by the engineers. At present, SODA performs detection for services with simple interfaces, i.e., WSDL-based SBSs. We intend to extend SODA for other SOA technologies including RESTful, Web Services, SCA and EJB. Also, employing rule mining or heuristic approach can improve detection performance.

References

1. Dudney, B., Asbury, S., Krozak, J., Wittkopf, K.: J2EE AntiPatterns. John Wiley & Sons Inc. (2003)
2. Fokaefs, M., Tsantalis, N., Chatzigeorgiou, A.: JDeodorant: Identification and Removal of Feature Envy Bad Smells. In: IEEE International Conference on Software Maintenance, ICSM 2007, pp. 519–520 (October 2007)
3. Král, J., Žemlička, M.: Crucial Service-Oriented Antipatterns, vol. 2, pp. 160–171. International Academy, Research and Industry Association, IARIA (2008)
4. Kral, J., Zemlicka, M.: Popular SOA Antipatterns. In: Future Computing, Service Computation, Cognitive, Adaptive, Content, Patterns, Computation World (2009)
5. Marinescu, R.: Detection Strategies: Metrics-based Rules for Detecting Design Flaws. In: Proc. IEEE International Conference on Software Maintenance (2004)
6. Moha, N., Guéhéneuc, Y.G., Duchien, L., Meur, A.F.L.: DECOR: A Method for the Specification and Detection of Code and Design Smells. IEEE Trans. Softw. Eng. 36(1), 20–36 (2010), http://dx.doi.org/10.1109/TSE.2009.50
7. Moha, N., Palma, F., Nayrolles, M., Conseil, B.J., Guéhéneuc, Y.-G., Baudry, B., Jézéquel, J.-M.: Specification and Detection of SOA Antipatterns. In: Liu, C., Ludwig, H., Toumani, F., Yu, Q. (eds.) ICSOC 2012. LNCS, vol. 7636, pp. 1–16. Springer, Heidelberg (2012)
8. Oracle: Data Mining Concepts 11g Release 1 (11.1) Part Number B28129-04, http://docs.oracle.com

Method and System for In-Place Modeling of Business Process Extensions as First-Class Entities

Heiko Witteborg, Anis Charfi, Wei Wei, and Ta'id Holmes

SAP Research Darmstadt
Bleichstr. 8, Darmstadt, Germany
`firstname.lastname@sap.com`

Abstract. The adaptation of business applications and their underlying business processes is key to meeting the specific needs of a certain customer or domain. The core objective of an extender is to modify the (process) artifacts provided by a base software vendor – yet, existing approaches do not support this directly but force the developer to explicitly use complex extensibility constructs and tools. Based on generic extensibility concepts, this demonstration proposal introduces a novel method and system for business process extensions that supports the intuitive in-place modification of processes. The extensions are extracted automatically and stored as first-class entities, ready to be recomposed or reused in other contexts.

Keywords: process extensions, extensibility, business process modeling, model-driven.

1 Introduction

Modern business software systems realize the typical business services of organizations. However, in several cases these services and the underlying business processes have to be adapted to the particular needs of the customer organization or those of its domain. This is typically done via extensions, either built by the customer or by a third party such as an independent software vendor (ISV). In fact, there is an ecosystem of ISVs and consulting organizations around leading business software providers, which specialize in configuring base software and building extensions to it. In some cases reusable extensions are made available to customers through an appropriate marketplace. Yet, extending business applications is a complex task for both the base application provider and the extender. There is a need to raise the abstraction level to other layers such as the process and the service layer in order to ease understanding, developing, and managing extensions and systems that result from base software and extensions.

This demonstration proposal describes a novel method and system for defining business process extensions in an intuitive way. We illustrate our approach by a real-life scenario of extending a sales quotation creation process with a customer rating service (Figure 3). The extension is shown as the blue activity which consults an external credit reporting agency upon receiving a customer request. The obtained customer rating can then be used to better judge customer credibility, such as to lower the risk of fraudulent payments and encourage customers of high credibility with discounts and rewards. Without this extended business process as an abstract level, it would be difficult to

A. Ghose et al. (Eds.): ICSOC 2012, LNCS 7759, pp. 456–459, 2013.

realize the extension solely at the code level because (1) it requires a thorough understanding of the base software code; (2) it is hard to estimate the impact of the extension on the original business process; and (3) it is hard to assure its compatibility with the base software as well as with other extensions.

2   Approach for In-Place Modeling of Process Extensions

Based on the process extension meta-model that is introduced in [1], this approach allows the intuitive definition of business process extensions as first-class entities. The generic idea of the method is to give the extender artifacts (i.e., in this instantiation, business processes) of the software applications and to provide a system, in which the extender gets the impression of modifying directly the contained elements (referred to as "in-place extension definition"). Once an extension is saved these tools extract the modification (the delta) in a separate extension module and the original artifacts of the software provided are kept unmodified. Figure 1 depicts a development process for (and the realized features of) the in-place definition of extensions. It comprises four phases:

Definition of extensibility views and base artifacts. In this phase the base software provider decides which business processes he wants to expose to extenders.

Target artifact selection. In the second phase, an extender (e.g., an ISV that develops extensions) selects a business process of the software application as base process for his extension. He may reapply existing extensions to create an extended base process.

In-place extension definition. The extender defines the modifications by apparently directly adapting the base process, although this process is owned by the base software provider and is generally provided as a read-only artifact. This is achieved by annotating the original model in the background, and through appropriate tooling that adapts the visualization accordingly.

Extraction and storage of extensions. In the fourth phase, the modifications defined using the in-place extension technique are automatically extracted into first-class extension modules. They can be later reapplied to the respective base process, restoring the extended process, or they can be reused in a new context.

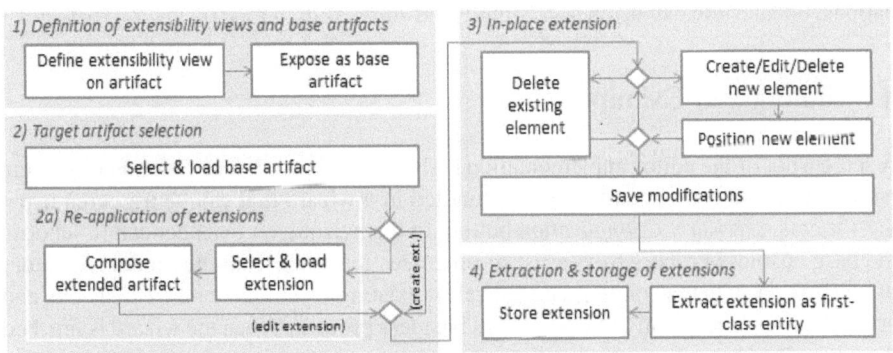

Fig. 1. Development Process and Realized Features of In-Place Extensibility

3   System Overview

To support this development process, an instantiation of this approach should provide
the repositories and components depicted in Figure 2. With the *Base Artifact Explorer*,
an extender can select and load base processes from the *Base Artifact Repository*. He
can initiate a new extension for the selected process, or he can retrieve and edit an existing extension from the *Extension Repository* using the *Extension Explorer*. This extension is automatically reapplied to the selected process (*Composer*) by adding and/or
annotating the involved elements. In case that the extension of extended base process is
supported, a *Conflict Resolution* component may help detecting and resolving potential
conflicts.

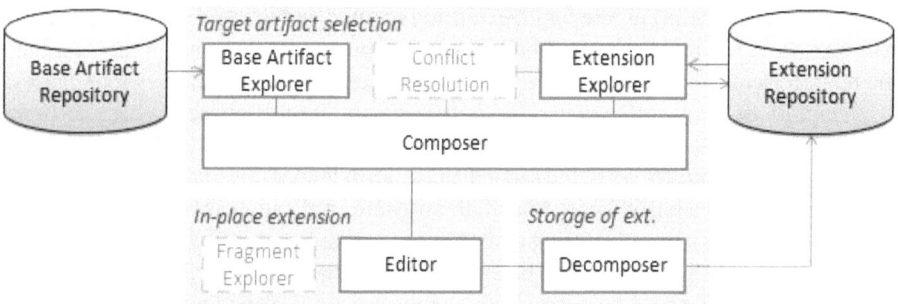

Fig. 2. System Overview of the In-Place Extension Tooling

   The *Editor* shows the result of the artifact selection, the target process, and provides
functionality to modify this process, similar to other editors of the underlying process
language, yet, in accordance with the modification restrictions defined by the base software owner. Optionally, a *Fragment Explorer* component can help to reuse extension
parts in different contexts. Finally, the *Decomposer* automatically identifies the modifications, updates the extension accordingly and stores it in the *Extension Repository*.

4   Tooling and Example

A screenshot of the editor implementation is shown in Figure 3. The functionality of the
target artifact selection components is bundled in a wizard that can be triggered using
the *Process Extension Configuration* button. In this wizard, an extender can (a) choose
the base business process from a list of processes retrieved from the model repository
of an SAP on-demand solution and (b) select existing or initialize new extensions and
apply them to the currently selected target business process. When the wizard is finished
the editor is triggered to show the target business process.
   The business process editor allows the extender to model modifications, similar to
editing the process in a standard editor. Nonetheless, the editor ensures that the deleted
or newly added elements are annotated accordingly, in the background. Based on these

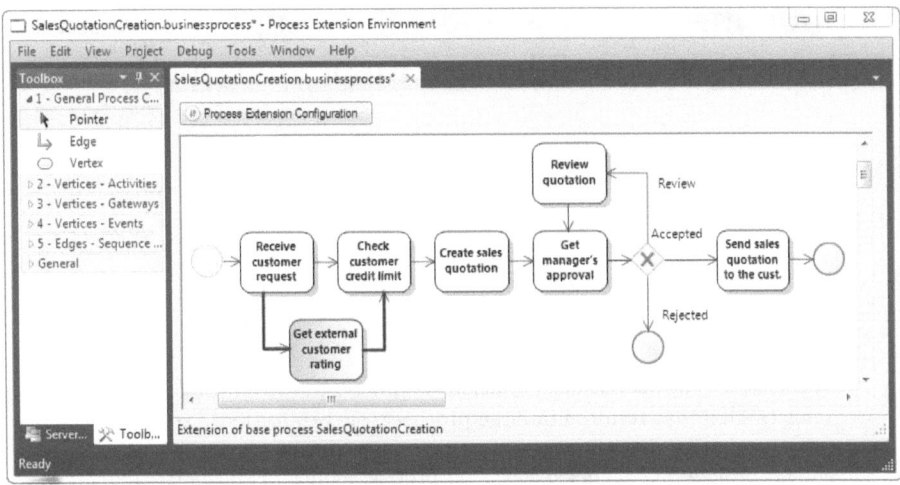

Fig. 3. Business Process Extension Editor

annotations, the new elements are slightly highlighted or shown as grayed out. In the example scenario, the extender can add and weave in a new *Get external customer rating* task into the *Sales Quotation Creation* process. The extender can save his work using the established ways, e.g., via menu entry or keyboard shortcut. However, the editor overrides the standard behavior of saving the complete artifact. Instead, it calls the *Business Process Decomposer* component to extract and store the extension.

5 Conclusion

Extensibility is a key requirement of a modern business application and its underlying business processes, to be able to adapt it to the specific use case and to increase the attractiveness of the application, e.g., by establishing an ecosystem of extenders. However, extensions are typically only supported on code layer, or extenders have to cope with complex extensibility concepts. Based on a generic approach, this demonstration proposal presented a method and system for business process extensibility that supports the intuitive in-place definition of extensions, the extraction of the modifications into first-class entities, and the composition of extended processes.

Acknowledgments. The authors would like to thank Mohamed Aly for his contributions to the extensibility concept. The work presented was performed in the context of the Software-Cluster project Emergent. It was partially funded by the German Federal Ministry of Education and Research under grant no. 01IC10S01.

Reference

1. Witteborg, H., Charfi, A., Aly, M., Holmes, T.: Business Process Extensions as First-Class Entities — A Model-Driven and Aspect-Oriented Approach. In: Liu, C., Ludwig, H., Toumani, F., Yu, Q. (eds.) ICSOC 2012. LNCS, vol. 7636, pp. 763–770. Springer, Heidelberg (2012)

Supporting Business and IT through Updatable Process Views: The *proView* Demonstrator

Jens Kolb and Manfred Reichert

Ulm University, Germany
{jens.kolb,manfred.reichert}@uni-ulm.de
http://www.uni-ulm.de/dbis

Abstract. The increasing adoption of process-aware information systems (PAISs) has resulted in large process model collections. To support business and IT users having different perspectives on processes, a PAIS should provide personalized views on process models. Especially, changing process models is frequent use case due to evolving processes or unplanned situations. This demonstration presents the *proView* framework for changing large process models through updating process views, while ensuring up-to-dateness and consistency of all related process views. More precisely, update operations can be applied to a process view and are correctly propagated to the underlying process model. Further, all views related to this process model are then correctly migrated to its new version. Overall, the *proView* framework enables users to evolve process models over time based on appropriate model abstractions.

1   Introduction

Process-aware information systems (PAISs) separate process logic from application code relying on explicit *process models* [1]. This separation of concerns increases maintainability and reduces costs of change. The increasing adoption of PAISs has resulted in large process model collections. In turn, each process model may refer to different domains and user roles as well as dozens or even hundreds of activities. Usually, the different user roles (e.g., business or IT) need customized views on process models, enabling personalized process abstraction and visualization [2]. For example, managers rather prefer an abstract overview, whereas the IT department needs a detailed view of process parts implemented by a PAIS [3]. Hence, providing personalized process views is a much needed feature. Existing approaches for creating process abstractions, however, do not consider *change* and *evolution*, which are fundamental for PAISs [4]. In addition to view-based process abstractions, users should be allowed to change large process models through updating respective process views. However, this must not be accomplished in an uncontrolled manner to avoid inconsistencies or errors.

The *proView*[1] framework provides powerful view-creation operations [5]. The operations allow abstracting process models through *reduction* and *aggregation* of process elements. In addition, update operations allow adapting process views

---

[1] http://www.dbis.info/proView

A. Ghose et al. (Eds.): ICSOC 2012, LNCS 7759, pp. 460–464, 2013.

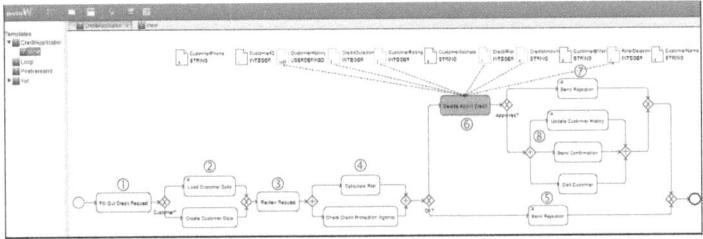

Fig. 1. Credit Application Process

and propagating the changes to the underlying process model as well as to other related process views [6]. We will demonstrate these aspects of the *proView* framework in an integrated way.

Section 2 introduces a scenario. Section 3 sketches the *proView* framework and the view operations it supports. Section 4 describes how the scenario can be supported by using the *proView* framework. Section 5 concludes the paper.

2 Application Scenario

Figure 1 shows a credit request process modeled in terms of BPMN. The process involves human activities referring to three user roles (i.e., *customer*, *clerk*, and *manager*) as well as automated activities (i.e., services) executed by the PAIS. Assume that the process is started by the customer filling out a credit request form (Step ①). Afterwards, the PAIS checks whether for this customer an entry in the CRM exists (Step ②). In this case, customer data is retrieved. Then, the clerk reviews the credit request (Step ③), calculates the risk, and checks creditworthiness (Step ④). After completing these tasks, he decides whether to reject the request (Step ⑤) or to forward it to his manager who decides about the request (Step ⑥). If the manager rejects, an email is sent (Step ⑦). Otherwise, a confirmation email is sent, the CRM is updated, the clerk calls the customer (Step ⑧), and the process completes. Assume that a process change is required: Before filling out the credit form, the customer shall select the desired credit type. For this purpose, the clerk adds an activity to the process model. Obviously, this change is relevant for all participants.

The *proView* framework addresses such a user-centered visualization and adaptation of large process models. Hence, it enables personalized views of the credit request process for each user role, i.e., customer, clerk, and manager. The following requirements must be met in order to properly support such a scenario:

R1: For each user role, it should be possible to provide specific process views on a process model as well as flexibly defining those views.

R2: Based on personalized process views and visualizations, elementary model adaptations shall become possible, e.g., to insert or delete activities in a user-centered process model (i.e., process view).

R3: If an authorized user changes his process view other process views may have to be updated to ensure up-to-dateness of all process participants.

R4: Since domain experts hardly have technical process knowledge, high-level operations for creating and adapting user-centered process views are required.

3   proView Framework

Figure 2 gives an overview of the implemented *proView* framework, which consists of two major components: *proViewServer* and *proViewClient*. The *proViewClient* is instantiated for each user and handles the interactions with the user as well as the visualization of his process models and views. In turn, the proViewClient is based on the *vaadin* web-framework and interacts with the proViewServer using a RESTful protocol. The *proViewServer* implements the logic of the *proView* framework and provides engines for *visualization, change,* and *execution & monitoring* [7]. It captures a *business process* through a *Central Process Model (CPM)*; additionally, so-called *creation sets (CS)* are defined, with, each CS specifiying the schema and appearance of a process view [6].

The *visualization engine* generates a specific process view based on a given CPM and creation set CS, i.e., the CPM is transformed to the view by applying the *view-creation operations* specified in CS (Step ⑤). Afterwards, the obtained view is *simplified* by applying well-defined *refactoring operations* (Step ⑥). Finally, Step ⑦ customizes the visual appearance of the view; e.g., by creating a tree-, form-, or flow-based visualization).

When a user updates a view, the *change engine* is triggered (Step ①). First, the view-based model change is propagated to the CPM using well-defined propagation algorithms (Step ②). Next, the CPM is simplified (Step ③), i.e., behaviour-preserving refactorings are applied to foster model comprehensibility (e.g., by removing gateways not needed anymore). Afterwards, the creation sets of all views associated with the CPM are migrated to the new CPM version (Step ④). This becomes necessary since a creation set may be contradicting with the changed CPM. Finally, all views are recreated (Steps ⑤-⑦).

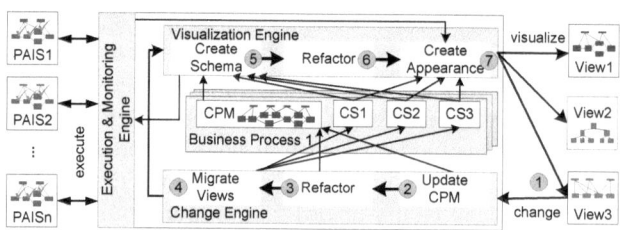

Fig. 2. The proView Framework

4   proView Demonstration

We revisit our scenario from Section 2 and show how the described requirements can be addressed by the *proView* framework.

Requirement R1: The proViewServer allows creating an arbitrary number of process views by applying aggregation and reduction operations specified in a creation set; e.g., a *reduction* removes an activity from the respective view, while an *aggregation* combines a set of connected activities to one node.

Requirement R2: The proViewServer provides *view-update* operations which allow inserting and deleting activities as well as AND/XOR branchings [6]. These operations can be applied by an end-user to his process view. Furthermore, *parametrization* allows for automatically resolving ambiguities when propagating view changes; i.e., change propagation behaviour can be customized.

Requirement R3: Updates triggered by users are applied to the CPM as well as to associated process views. Their view creation sets are then migrated to the new version of the CPM. Hence, all affected views will be re-created.

Requirement R4: The proViewServer supports high-level operations to create process views. For example, one may create a view can showing all technical activities or activities of a specific user role.

All these aspects are illustrated in a screencast: www.dbis.info/proView.

5   Conclusion

In our demonstration, we present the *proView* framework and its operations; *proView* supports the creation of personalized process views as well as the view-based change of business processes, i.e., process abstractions not only serve visualization purpose, but also lift process changes up to a higher semantical level. A set of change operations enables users to update their view. The respective change is then propagated to the CPM representing the overall business process and other process views are migrated to the CPM.

The *proView* framework is implemented as a client-server application to concurrently edit a process model based on views. The implementation of the proView framework has proven the applicability of our approach. Further, the *proView* demonstrator shall be extended to also execute process views in a PAIS. Overall, we believe that the *proView* framework offers promising perspectives to users for evolving their business processes.

References

1. Reichert, M., Weber, B.: Enabling Flexibility in Process-aware Information Systems - Challenges, Methods, Technologies. Springer (2012)
2. Rinderle, S., Bobrik, R., Reichert, M., Bauer, T.: Businesss Process Visualization - Use Cases, Challenges, Solutions. In: Proc. ICEIS 2006, pp. 204–211 (2006)
3. Bobrik, R., Reichert, M., Bauer, T.: Requirements for the Visualization of System-Spanning Business Processes. In: Proc. DEXA 2005 Workshops, pp. 948–954 (2005)
4. Weber, B., Reichert, M., Rinderle, S.: Change Patterns and Change Support Features - Enhancing Flexibility in Process-Aware Information Systems. Data & Knowledge Engineering 66(3), 438–466 (2008)

5. Reichert, M., Kolb, J., Bobrik, R., Bauer, T.: Enabling Personalized Visualization of Large Business Processes through Parameterizable Views. In: Proc. 26th Symposium on Applied Computing (SAC 2012), Riva del Garda (Trento), Italy (2012)

6. Kolb, J., Kammerer, K., Reichert, M.: Updatable Process Views for User-Centered Adaption of Large Process Models. In: Liu, C., Ludwig, H., Toumani, F., Yu, Q. (eds.) ICSOC 2012. LNCS, vol. 7636, pp. 484–498. Springer, Heidelberg (2012)

7. Kolb, J., Hübner, P., Reichert, M.: Automatically Generating and Updating User Interface Components in Process-Aware Information Systems. In: Proc. 10th Int'l Conf. on Cooperative Information Systems (CoopIS 2012), pp. 444–454 (2012)

Author Index